500CHRISTMAS
RECIPES

500 CHRISTMAS RECIPES

Make Christmas special with this comprehensive collection of classic festive recipes, shown in more than 500 inspirational photographs

EDITED BY EMMA HOLLEY

LORENZ BOOKS

This edition is published by Lorenz Books,
an imprint of Anness Publishing Ltd, Blaby Road, Wigston,
Leicestershire LE18 4SE; info@anness.com

www.lorenzbooks.com; www.annesspublishing.com

If you like the images in this book and would like to investigate
using them for publishing, promotions or advertising, please visit
our website www.practicalpictures.com for more information.

Publisher: Joanna Lorenz
Project Editor: Anne Hildyard
Recipes: Catherine Atkinson, Jane Bamforth, Alex Barker,
Valerie Barrett, Judy Bastyra, Jacqueline Clark, Carole Clements,
Joaana Farrow, Christine France, Brian Glover, Nicola Graimes,
Juliet Harbutt, Christine Ingram, Becky Johnson, Lucy Knox,
Christine McFadden, Marlene Spieler, Kate Whiteman,
Rosemary Wilkinson, Elizabeth Wolf-Cohen and Jeni Wright
Photography: Karl Adamson, Edward Allwright, Steve Baxter,
Nicki Dowey, James Duncan, Ian Garlick, Michelle Garrett,
Amanda Heywood, Janine Hosegood, David Jordan, Dave King,
Don Last, William Lingwood, Patrick McLeavey, Thomas Odulate,
Craig Robertson, Bridget Sargeson and Sam Stowell
Jacket Design: Nigel Partridge
Copy Editor: Jay Thundercliffe
Proofreading Manager: Lindsay Zamponi
Desk Editor: Barbara Toft
Production Controller: Mai-Ling Collyer

Notes

Bracketed terms are intended for American readers.
For all recipes, quantities are given in both metric and imperial measures and, where appropriate,
in standard cups and spoons. Follow one set of measures, but not a mixture, because they are not interchangeable.
Standard spoon and cup measures are level. 1 tsp = 5ml, 1 tbsp = 15ml, 1 cup = 250ml/8fl oz.
Australian standard tablespoons are 20ml. Australian readers should use 3 tsp in place of 1 tbsp for measuring small quantities.
American pints are 16fl oz/2 cups. American readers should use 20fl oz/2.5 cups in place of 1 pint when measuring liquids.
Electric oven temperatures in this book are for conventional ovens. When using a fan oven, the temperature will probably need to
be reduced by about 10–20°C/20–40°F. Since ovens vary, you should check with your manufacturer's instruction book for guidance.
The nutritional analysis given for each recipe is calculated per portion (i.e. serving or item), unless otherwise stated. If the recipe
gives a range, such as Serves 4–6, then the nutritional analysis will be for the smaller portion size, i.e. 6 servings.
The analysis does not include optional ingredients, such as salt added to taste.
Medium (US large) eggs are used unless otherwise stated.

Main front cover image shows Moist and Rich Christmas Cake – for recipe, see page 223

Contents

Introduction

Christmas is the main festival of the year for those in the West and has been celebrated in the Christian world for centuries. Many of the traditions coincide with even earlier pagan rituals and festivals. However, Christmas is also regarded as a secular holiday since so many people join in the relatively modern traditions of card and gift giving; decorating the festive tree

and the home; and, probably most importantly, eating and drinking a range of fine celebration foods. Many of these traditions are no older than 200 years yet they are now regarded as an essential part of the holiday season.

Food and drink play an important role in the Christmas and New Year celebrations, and this compilation of Christmas recipes will help you to cope with entertaining during the festive season while still having plenty of time to relax with your family and friends. In this volume you will find all the recipes associated with a Christmas feast and plenty more tempting delights to try. There is a choice of recipes for traditional meals, whether it is to be a turkey, chicken, goose or another meat such as beef or lamb. The accompaniments to the main centrepiece are vital and they are all included here, from the stuffing and roast potatoes to the cranberry sauce. There are recipes to add a sparkle to vegetables, such as Stir-fried Brussels Sprouts, Sweet and Sour Red Cabbage or Peas with Baby Onions and Cream. Vegetarians are not forgotten, and Festive Lentil and Nut Roast or Chestnut and Mushroom Loaf, with all the trimmings, each make a delightful main course. Of course, the Christmas feast would be not be complete without a range of hot and cold desserts to enjoy, as well as a variety of classic cakes and innovative cup cakes with Christmassy motifs. This book has them all, from Christmas Pudding

with Brandy Butter and mince pies with a twist, to spicy rich fruitcakes and stollen. The book also contains a range of sweets, treats and confections, such as Champagne Truffles, Sugar Mice, Turkish Delight, Peppermint Chocolate Sticks and Creamy Fudge that will make delightful gifts. Sweet and spicy cookies in all shapes and sizes include Christmas Star Cookies, Festive Holly Cookies and Christmas Tree Angels – all delicious at teatime, or perfect for last-minute gifts. In addition to all the well-known favourites there is a multitude of recipes that will take you through all the days of the holiday, whether you need a light, tasty lunch, an exotic Christmas Day brunch or ideas for nibbles and party treats.

Many recipes in this collection can be made in advance, which is a bonus at Christmas time when parties, feasts, celebratory meals and buffets tend to follow one after another. Also, since it is an opportunity to spend time with friends and family, careful planning and preparation can ensure that the person cooking can socialize with their guests, without thinking about what is happening in the kitchen.

The 500 deliciously tempting festive recipes in this compilation are clearly explained in step-by-step instructions and feature a shot of the finished dish so you can see exactly what you are aiming to create, and ensure that your Yuletide catering is a success. The book is organized so that you can quickly find the recipes you want, when you need them. Welcome your guests with a warming Mulled Claret or, for children, a fruity Cranberry Frost. There is a choice of soups or appetizers to get your meal off to a good start: try Watercress Soup, Salmon Soup with Salsa and Rouille or Scallops with Black Bean Sauce for a light opening. Patés, terrines and mousses are always popular as appetizers. You can choose from a selection of fish, duck or pork to make Smoked Haddock and Avocado Mousse or Duck Liver Paté and Redcurrant Sauce. For the main event, the recipes include Classic Roast Turkey, Roast Goose with Black Pudding and Duck with Orange Sauce. And don't forget seasonal side dishes, such as Bread Sauce, Cranberry Sauce and Chestnut Stuffing. Packed full of fantastic recipes and ideas, you'll find this book will become an indispensable source when celebrating this wonderful festival every year.

Potato and Leek Soup

Smooth and creamy, this simple soup can be served warm as an appealing appetizer for a Christmas feast or as a light meal. It is also delicious served cold, as vichyssoise.

Serves 4–6

25g/1oz/2 tbsp unsalted butter
1 onion, thinly sliced
2–3 leeks (white and pale green parts only), thinly sliced
3 garlic cloves, roughly chopped
120ml/4fl oz/½ cup dry white vermouth or white wine (optional)
3 medium waxy potatoes, peeled and chopped small
1.5 litres/2½ pints/6¼ cups chicken or vegetable stock
3 sprigs fresh parsley
3 sprigs fresh thyme
1 bay leaf
200ml/7fl oz/scant 1 cup single (light) cream or milk (optional)
salt and ground white pepper
30ml/2 tbsp chopped fresh chives or chopped parsley, to garnish

1 Heat the butter in a large, heavy pan over medium heat. Add the onion, leeks and garlic to the pan and sauté gently for about 12 minutes, stirring occasionally, until the onions and leeks have softened but not browned.

2 Increase the heat to high and pour in the vermouth or wine, if using. Boil vigorously for about 4 minutes, or until the mixture is almost dry. Add the potatoes and stock.

3 Tie the fresh parsley, thyme and bay leaf into a bouquet garni with a piece of kitchen string (twine). Add to the soup.

4 Bring to the boil, lower the heat and cover the pan, leaving the lid slightly ajar to let the excess steam escape. Simmer for 20 minutes, until the potatoes are very tender.

5 Lift out and discard the bouquet garni. With a hand-held blender or in a food processor, purée the soup until the desired consistency is reached.

6 If using the milk or cream, whisk it into the soup. Season and heat through. Divide among warm soup bowls, garnish with chives or parsley and serve immediately.

Creamy Corn and Red Chilli Chowder

Corn and chillies are traditional buddies, and here the cool combination of creamed corn and milk is the perfect foil for the raging heat of the chillies.

Serves 6

2 tomatoes, skinned
1 onion, roughly chopped
375g/13oz can creamed corn
2 red (bell) peppers, halved and seeded
15ml/1 tbsp olive oil, plus extra for brushing
3 fresh red chillies, seeded and chopped
2 garlic cloves, chopped
5ml/1 tsp ground cumin
5ml/1 tsp ground coriander
600ml/1 pint/2½ cups milk
350ml/12fl oz/1½ cups vegetable stock
3 cobs of corn, kernels removed
450g/1lb potatoes, finely diced
60ml/4 tbsp double (heavy) cream
60ml/4 tbsp chopped fresh parsley
salt and ground black pepper

1 Process the tomatoes and onion in a food processor or blender to a smooth purée. Add the creamed corn and process again, then set aside. Preheat the grill (broiler) to high.

2 Put the peppers, skin sides up, on a grill rack and brush with oil. Cook for 8 minutes, until the skins blacken and blister. Transfer to a bowl, cover and leave to cool. Peel and dice the peppers.

3 Heat the oil in a large pan and add the chopped chillies and garlic. Cook, stirring, for 2–3 minutes, until softened.

4 Add the ground cumin and coriander, and cook for 1 minute. Add the corn purée and cook for 8 minutes, stirring occasionally.

5 Pour in the milk and stock, then stir in the corn kernels, potatoes, red pepper and seasoning to taste. Cook for 15–20 minutes, until the corn and potatoes are tender.

6 Pour the soup into deep bowls and add the cream, pouring it slowly into the middle of the bowls. Sprinkle with the chopped parsley and serve immediately.

Potato and Leek Soup Energy 127kcal/534kJ; Protein 3.4g; Carbohydrate 19.6g, of which sugars 3.9g; Fat 4.4g, of which saturates 2.4g; Cholesterol 9mg; Calcium 40mg; Fibre 3.2g; Sodium 180mg.
Corn Chowder Energy 294kcal/1241kJ; Protein 8.9g; Carbohydrate 47.8g, of which sugars 20.8g; Fat 8.9g, of which saturates 4.8g; Cholesterol 20mg; Calcium 168mg; Fibre 4.2g; Sodium 299mg.

Roasted Garlic and Butternut Squash Soup with Tomato Salsa

Hot and spicy tomato salsa gives bite to this warming winter soup.

Serves 4–5
2 garlic bulbs, outer skin removed
a few fresh thyme sprigs
75ml/5 tbsp olive oil
1 large butternut squash, halved and seeded
2 onions, chopped
5ml/1 tsp ground coriander
1.2 litres/2 pints/5 cups vegetable stock

30–45ml/2–3 tbsp chopped fresh oregano or marjoram
salt and ground black pepper

For the salsa
4 large ripe tomatoes, halved and seeded
1 red (bell) pepper, seeded
1 large fresh red chilli, halved and seeded
30ml/2 tbsp extra virgin olive oil
15ml/1 tbsp balsamic vinegar
pinch of caster (superfine) sugar

1 Preheat the oven to 220°C/425°F/Gas 7. Wrap the garlic and thyme, drizzled with half the oil, in foil. Place on a baking sheet. Add the squash, brushing with 15ml/1 tbsp of the remaining oil. Add the tomatoes, pepper and chilli for the salsa. Roast the vegetables for 25 minutes. Remove the tomatoes, pepper and chilli. Reduce the setting to 190°C/375°F/Gas 5 and cook the squash and garlic for 20–25 minutes more.

2 Heat the remaining oil gently in a pan. Cook the onions and coriander for 10 minutes, until soft and beginning to brown. Squeeze the roasted garlic out into the onions and scoop the squash out of its skin into the pan. Add the stock, salt and pepper. Bring to the boil, then simmer for 10 minutes.

3 Skin the pepper and chilli, then process them in a food processor or blender with the tomatoes and the oil for the salsa. Stir in the vinegar, seasoning and sugar.

4 Stir half the fresh oregano or marjoram into the soup and purée until smooth. Reheat without boiling, then season and ladle into bowls. Top with salsa, sprinkle with the remaining oregano or marjoram, and serve.

Sweet-and-Sour Vegetable Borscht

There are many variations of this classic Eastern European soup: this one includes cabbage, tomatoes and potatoes, and will add festive colour to the table.

Serves 6
1 onion, chopped
1 carrot, chopped
4–6 raw or cooked beetroot (beets), 3–4 diced and 1–2 coarsely grated
400g/14oz can tomatoes

4–6 new potatoes, cut into bitesize pieces
1 small white cabbage, thinly sliced
1 litre/1¾ pints/4 cups vegetable stock
45ml/3 tbsp sugar
30–45ml/2–3 tbsp white wine or cider (apple) vinegar
45ml/3 tbsp chopped fresh dill, plus extra to garnish
salt and ground black pepper
sour cream, to garnish
buttered rye bread, to serve

1 Put the onion, carrot, diced beetroot, tomatoes, potatoes and cabbage in a large pan. Pour in the stock and bring to the boil.

2 Reduce the heat and cover the pan. Simmer the soup for about 30 minutes, or until the potatoes are tender.

3 Add the grated beetroot, sugar, wine or vinegar to the soup and continue to cook for 10 minutes.

4 Taste for a good sweet-sour balance and add more sugar and/or vinegar if necessary. Season to taste.

5 To serve, stir in the chopped dill and ladle the soup into bowls. Garnish each portion with sour cream and more dill. Serve immediately, accompanied by the rye bread.

Variation
To make meat borscht, place 1kg/2¼lb chopped beef in a large pan. Pour over water to cover and crumble in 1 beef stock (bouillon) cube. Bring to the boil, then reduce the heat and simmer until tender. Skim any fat from the surface, then add the vegetables and proceed as above.

Roasted Garlic Soup Energy 238kcal/986kJ; Protein 2.9g; Carbohydrate 11.9g, of which sugars 10.3g; Fat 20.2g, of which saturates 3.1g; Cholesterol 0mg; Calcium 79mg; Fibre 4.1g; Sodium 11mg.
Sweet-and-Sour Borscht Energy 46kcal/196kJ; Protein 1.6g; Carbohydrate 9.8g, of which sugars 6.4g; Fat 0.4g, of which saturates 0.1g; Cholesterol 0mg; Calcium 22mg; Fibre 1.9g; Sodium 29mg.

Mushroom Soup with Tarragon

This is a light mushroom soup that is subtly flavoured with tarragon.

Serves 6
15g/¹⁄₂oz/1 tbsp butter
4 shallots, finely chopped
450g/1lb brown cap (cremini) mushrooms, finely chopped
300ml/¹⁄₂ pint/1¹⁄₄ cups vegetable stock
300ml/¹⁄₂ pint/1¹⁄₄ cups milk
15–30ml/1–2 tbsp chopped fresh tarragon
30ml/2 tbsp dry sherry (optional)
salt and ground black pepper
sprigs of fresh tarragon, to garnish

1 Melt the butter in a large pan, add the shallots and cook gently for 5 minutes, stirring occasionally. Add the mushrooms and continue to cook gently for 3 minutes, stirring.

2 Pour in the stock and milk, stirring. Bring to the boil, then reduce the heat and cover the pan. Simmer the soup gently for about 20 minutes or until the vegetables are soft.

3 Stir in the tarragon and season to taste with salt and pepper. Allow the soup to cool slightly, then purée it in a food processor or blender, in batches if necessary, until smooth. Return the soup to the rinsed-out pan and reheat gently.

4 Stir in the sherry, if using, then ladle the soup into warmed bowls and serve garnished with sprigs of tarragon.

Variations
• Use a mild onion instead of the shallots. Add a bay leaf, a pinch of ground mace and a tiny pinch of ground cloves. Omit the milk but add single (light) cream when reheating.
• For a stronger flavour, use a mixture of wild and brown cap (cremini) mushrooms, or try adding a few dried cultivated mushrooms.
• For a delicate soup, use pale button (white) mushrooms instead of the stronger brown cap (cremini) variety. Use a little chopped fresh parsley and chopped fresh dill instead of the tarragon.

Creamy Mushroom Soup with Savoury Croûtes

This classic soup will brighten up a festive meal, especially with the addition of delicious cheese and mushroom croûtes.

Serves 6
1 onion, chopped
1 garlic clove, chopped
25g/1oz/2 tbsp butter
450g/1lb/6 cups chestnut or brown cap (cremini) mushrooms, roughly chopped
15ml/1 tbsp plain (all-purpose) flour
45ml/3 tbsp dry sherry
900ml/1¹⁄₂ pints/3³⁄₄ cups vegetable stock
150ml/¹⁄₄ pint/²⁄₃ cup double (heavy) cream
salt and ground black pepper
sprigs of fresh chervil, to garnish

For the croûtes
15ml/1 tbsp olive oil, plus extra for brushing
1 shallot, chopped
115g/4oz/1¹⁄₂ cups button (white) mushrooms, finely chopped
15ml/1 tbsp chopped fresh parsley
6 brown cap (cremini) mushrooms
6 slices baguette
1 small garlic clove
115g/4oz/1 cup soft goat's cheese

1 Cook the onion and garlic in the butter for 5 minutes. Add the mushrooms, cover and cook for 10 minutes, stirring often. Stir in the flour and cook for 1 minute. Stir in the sherry and stock and bring to the boil, then simmer for 15 minutes. Cool slightly, then purée it in a food processor or blender.

2 For the croûtes, heat the oil in a small pan. Add the shallot and button mushrooms, and cook for 8–10 minutes, until softened. Drain well and transfer to a food processor. Add the parsley and process until finely chopped.

3 Preheat the grill (broiler). Brush the mushrooms with oil and grill (broil) for 5–6 minutes. Toast the baguette, rub with the garlic and top with goat's cheese. Add the grilled mushrooms and fill these with the chopped mushroom mixture.

4 Return the soup to the pan and stir in the cream. Season, then reheat gently. Ladle the soup into six bowls. Float a croûte in the centre of each and garnish with chervil.

Mushroom Soup Energy 55kcal/230kJ; Protein 3.2g; Carbohydrate 3.5g, of which sugars 3.1g; Fat 3.3g, of which saturates 1.9g; Cholesterol 8mg; Calcium 68mg; Fibre 1g; Sodium 41mg.
Creamy Mushroom Soup Energy 368kcal/1533kJ; Protein 10.3g; Carbohydrate 25.1g, of which sugars 3.1g; Fat 25g, of which saturates 14.5g; Cholesterol 61mg; Calcium 99mg; Fibre 2.4g; Sodium 399mg.

Cream of Wild Mushroom Soup

Dried mushrooms can be used for this soup if you are making it at Christmas time when fresh wild mushrooms may be hard to find.

Serves 4
10g/¼oz/1 tbsp dried mushrooms, such as ceps, if wild are unavailable
400g/14oz mushrooms, preferably wild, sliced
1.25 litres/2¼ pints/5½ cups vegetable or chicken stock
50g/2oz/4 tbsp butter
30–45ml/2–3 tbsp plain (all-purpose) flour
60ml/4 tbsp double (heavy) cream, plus extra to garnish
a squeeze of fresh lemon juice
15–30ml/1–2 tbsp medium sherry (optional)
salt and ground black pepper
chopped fresh parsley, to garnish

1 If using dried mushrooms, put in a small bowl and pour over plenty of boiling water. Leave to soak for 20 minutes, until soft. Using a slotted spoon, remove the mushrooms, then strain the liquid and reserve. Chop the soaked mushrooms.

2 Put the sliced mushrooms in a pan, cover with the stock and simmer for 10 minutes. Strain the stock and reserve.

3 Melt the butter in a large pan, add the sliced mushrooms and the soaked mushrooms and fry gently for 2–3 minutes. Stir in seasoning and the flour and cook gently for 1–2 minutes, without colouring. Remove from the heat and add the reserved stock and soaking liquid to form a smooth sauce. Bring to the boil, stirring. Lower the heat and simmer for 5–10 minutes.

4 Add the cream, lemon juice to taste and sherry, if using. Pour into bowls and top with a little cream and chopped parsley.

Cook's Tips
• *Wild mushrooms have an intense flavour that makes this soup rich and satisfying.*
• *Choose a single type of wild mushroom or combine varieties, adding some cultivated mushrooms, if you like, according to whatever is available and personal preference.*

Mushroom, Leek and Shallot Soup

Dried wild porcini mushrooms are quite expensive, but they have an intense flavour, so only a small amount is needed for this recipe. Beef stock may seem unusual for a vegetable soup, but it helps strengthen the earthy flavour of the mushrooms.

Serves 4
25g/1oz/½ cup dried porcini mushrooms
30ml/2 tbsp olive oil
15g/½oz/1 tbsp butter
2 leeks, thinly sliced
2 shallots, roughly chopped
1 garlic clove, roughly chopped
225g/8oz/3 cups fresh wild mushrooms, such as ceps or chanterelles
about 1.2 litres/2 pints/5 cups beef stock
2.5ml/½ tsp dried thyme
150ml/¼ pint/⅔ cup double (heavy) cream
salt and ground black pepper
fresh thyme sprigs, to garnish

1 Put the dried porcini in a bowl, add 250ml/8fl oz/1 cup warm water and leave to soak for 20–30 minutes. Lift out of the water and squeeze over the bowl to remove the soaking liquid. Strain the liquid and reserve. Finely chop the porcini.

2 Heat the oil and butter in a large pan until foaming. Add the leeks, shallots and garlic and cook gently for about 5 minutes, stirring frequently, until softened but not coloured.

3 Chop or slice the fresh mushrooms and add to the pan. Stir over medium heat for a few minutes until the mushrooms begin to soften. Add the stock and bring to the boil.

4 Add the porcini, soaking liquid, thyme and salt and pepper. Lower the heat, half-cover the pan and simmer gently for 30 minutes, stirring occasionally.

5 Pour about three-quarters of the soup into a blender or food processor and process until smooth. Return to the soup remaining in the pan, stir in the cream and heat through. Check the consistency and add more stock if the soup is too thick. Taste for seasoning, adding more if needed. Serve hot, garnished with thyme sprigs.

Wild Mushroom Soup Energy 154kcal/638kJ; Protein 3.2g; Carbohydrate 9.3g, of which sugars 0.5g; Fat 11.8g, of which saturates 7.2g; Cholesterol 29mg; Calcium 26mg; Fibre 1.6g; Sodium 82mg.
Mushroom and Leek Soup Energy 287kcal/1184kJ; Protein 2.8g; Carbohydrate 3.1g, of which sugars 2.4g; Fat 29.4g, of which saturates 15.4g; Cholesterol 59mg; Calcium 41mg; Fibre 2.3g; Sodium 35mg.

French Onion Soup with Croûtes

This is perhaps the most famous of all onion soups.

Serves 6
50g/2oz/¼ cup butter
15ml/1 tbsp olive or groundnut
   (peanut) oil
2kg/4½lb onions, sliced
5ml/1 tsp chopped fresh thyme
5ml/1 tsp caster (superfine) sugar
15ml/1 tbsp sherry vinegar
1.5 litres/2½ pints/6¼ cups good
   vegetable stock
25ml/1½ tbsp plain
   (all-purpose) flour
150ml/¼ pint/⅔ cup dry
   white wine
45ml/3 tbsp brandy
salt and ground black pepper

For the croûtes
6–12 thick slices day-old French
   bread, about 2.5cm/1in thick
1 garlic clove, halved
15ml/1 tbsp French mustard
115g/4oz Gruyère cheese, grated

1 Heat the butter and oil in a large pan. Add the onions and stir. Cook over medium heat for 5–8 minutes, stirring once or twice, until the onions begin to soften. Stir in the thyme. Reduce the heat to very low, cover and cook the onions for 20–30 minutes, stirring frequently, until very soft and golden.

2 Uncover the pan and increase the heat slightly. Stir in the sugar and cook for 5–10 minutes, until the onions start to brown. Add the sherry vinegar and increase the heat again, then continue cooking, stirring frequently, until the onions turn a deep, golden brown – this could take up to 20 minutes.

3 Bring the stock to the boil in another pan. Stir the flour into the onions and cook for 2 minutes, then gradually stir in the stock, wine, brandy and seasoning to taste. Bring to the boil, stirring, reduce the heat and simmer for 10–15 minutes.

4 For the croûtes, preheat the oven to 150°C/300°F/Gas 2. Place the bread on a greased baking tray and bake for 15–20 minutes, until lightly browned. Rub with the garlic and spread with mustard, then sprinkle with the cheese.

5 Preheat the grill (broiler) on the hottest setting. Ladle the soup into six flameproof bowls. Add the croûtes and grill (broil) until the cheese melts, bubbles and browns. Serve immediately.

Onion, Almond and Saffron Soup

The Spanish combination of onions, sherry and saffron is delicious in this golden soup thickened with almonds. It is also good chilled, so is ideal for serving during the busy Christmas period.

Serves 4
40g/1½oz/3 tbsp butter
2 large onions, thinly sliced
1 small garlic clove, finely chopped
pinch of saffron threads
50g/2oz blanched almonds,
   toasted and finely ground
750ml/1¼ pints/3 cups
   vegetable stock
45ml/3 tbsp fino sherry
2.5ml/½ tsp paprika
salt and ground black pepper

For the garnish
30ml/2 tbsp flaked (sliced) or
   slivered almonds, toasted
chopped fresh parsley

1 Melt the butter in a heavy pan over low heat. Add the onions and garlic, and stir for about a minute to ensure that they are thoroughly coated in the melted butter.

2 Cover the pan with a tight-fitting lid and cook the onions over very low heat, stirring frequently, for about 15–20 minutes, until they have turned soft and golden.

3 Add the saffron threads to the pan and cook, uncovered, for 3–4 minutes. Add the almonds to the pan and cook, stirring constantly, for a further 2–3 minutes.

4 Pour in the stock and sherry with 5ml/1 tsp salt and the paprika. Season with plenty of ground black pepper. Bring to the boil, stirring, then lower the heat, cover the pan and simmer gently for about 10 minutes.

5 Pour the soup into a food processor or blender and process until smooth, then return it to the rinsed-out pan. Reheat gently, without allowing the soup to boil, stirring occasionally. Taste for seasoning, adding more salt and pepper if required.

6 Ladle the soup into warmed serving bowls. Garnish with the toasted flaked or slivered almonds and add a little chopped fresh parsley, then serve immediately.

French Onion Soup Energy 415kcal/1745kJ; Protein 13g; Carbohydrate 61.6g, of which sugars 12.6g; Fat 14.1g, of which saturates 6.7g; Cholesterol 25mg; Calcium 240mg; Fibre 4.1g; Sodium 1022mg.
Onion and Almond Soup Energy 255kcal/1054kJ; Protein 5.8g; Carbohydrate 11.5g, of which sugars 8.1g; Fat 19.6g, of which saturates 6.1g; Cholesterol 21mg; Calcium 82mg; Fibre 3.2g; Sodium 68mg.

Fresh Cabbage Soup

Soups play an important part in most cuisines and this vegetarian soup is one of the most popular everyday soups. Variations are numerous and it can be adapted to suit the festive period with seasonal winter produce.

Serves 4

40g/1¹/₂oz/3 tbsp butter
1 onion, sliced
1 head white cabbage, total
   weight 750g/1lb 10oz,
   shredded

1 carrot, shredded or grated
1 piece celeriac, total weight
   50g/2oz, shredded and grated
2 bay leaves
5 black peppercorns
1.5 litres/2¹/₂ pints/6¹/₄ cups
   vegetable stock
5 new potatoes, diced
15ml/1 tbsp sunflower oil
1 (bell) pepper, cored and sliced
2 tomatoes, chopped
salt and ground black pepper
45ml/3 tbsp chopped fresh dill,
   to garnish
sour cream or crème fraîche and
   rye bread, to serve

1 Melt the butter in a large pan over medium heat. Add the onion to the pan and cook, stirring frequently, for 3 minutes, until softened but not browned. Add the cabbage, carrot and celeriac and cook for 3 minutes.

2 Add the bay leaves, peppercorns and 200ml/7fl oz/scant 1 cup of stock. Bring to the boil, then reduce the heat, cover and simmer for 15 minutes, stirring occasionally

3 Add the remaining stock and the potatoes and simmer for further 10 minutes until the potatoes are soft.

4 Meanwhile, heat the oil in a small frying pan over medium heat. Add the pepper and tomatoes and fry for 2–3 minutes, until softened, stirring occasionally. Transfer the pepper and tomatoes to the soup and simmer for 5 minutes. Season with salt and ground black pepper to taste.

5 Spoon the soup into warmed bowls, and sprinkle with the chopped fresh dill. Top each serving with a little sour cream or crème fraîche and serve immediately while piping hot, accompanied by slices of rye bread.

Egg and Lemon Soup with Rice

This soup is a great favourite in Greece. It can be eked out with extra rice if you have unexpected guests during the festive season.

Serves 4

900ml/1¹/₂ pints/3³/₄ cups chicken
   stock, preferably home-made

50g/2oz/generous ¹/₃ cup long
   grain rice
3 egg yolks
30–60ml/2–4 tbsp lemon juice
30ml/2 tbsp finely chopped
   fresh parsley
salt and ground black pepper
lemon slices and parsley sprigs,
   to garnish

1 Pour the chicken stock into a large, heavy pan and bring to simmering point. Rinse the rice under cold running water and drain, then add to the pan with the hot stock.

2 Half-cover the pan and cook for about 10–12 minutes until the rice is just tender. Season with plenty of salt and ground black pepper to taste.

3 Whisk the egg yolks in a bowl, then add about 30ml/2 tbsp of the lemon juice, whisking constantly until the mixture is smooth and bubbly. Add a ladleful of soup and whisk again.

4 Remove the soup from the heat and slowly add the egg mixture, whisking all the time. The soup will turn a pretty lemon colour and will thicken slightly.

5 Taste and add more lemon juice if necessary. Stir in the parsley. Serve immediately, without reheating, garnished with lemon slices and fresh parsley sprigs.

> **Cook's Tip**
> The key to a successful egg and lemon soup is to add the egg mixture to the hot liquid without it curdling. Avoid whisking the mixture into boiling liquid. It is safest to remove the soup from the heat entirely and then whisk in the mixture in a slow but steady stream. Do not reheat the soup as curdling would be almost inevitable.

Fresh Cabbage Soup Energy 273kcal/1141kJ; Protein 6g; Carbohydrate 36.7g, of which sugars 17.4g; Fat 12.2g, of which saturates 5.8g; Cholesterol 21mg; Calcium 122mg; Fibre 7.2g; Sodium 106mg.
Egg and Lemon Soup Energy 96kcal/404kJ; Protein 3.3g; Carbohydrate 10.9g, of which sugars 0.2g; Fat 4.7g, of which saturates 1.2g; Cholesterol 151mg; Calcium 39mg; Fibre 0.4g; Sodium 10mg.

Courgette, Carrot and Noodle Soup

If you have the time during the festivities, it is worth the effort making your own stock for this recipe, whether vegetable, meat or chicken. The cut-out shapes of the vegetables floating in the soup give this dish a wonderful festive feel.

Serves 4
1 yellow (bell) pepper
2 large courgettes (zucchini)
2 large carrots
1 kohlrabi
900ml/1½ pints/3¾ cups well-
  flavoured vegetable stock
50g/2oz rice vermicelli
salt and ground black pepper

1 Cut the pepper into quarters, removing the seeds and core. Cut the courgettes and carrots lengthways into 5mm/¼in thick slices and slice the kohlrabi into 5mm/¼in rounds.

2 Using tiny pastry (cookie) cutters, stamp out shapes from the vegetables or use a very sharp knife to cut the sliced vegetables into stars and other decorative festive shapes.

3 Place the vegetables and stock in a pan and simmer for 10 minutes, until the vegetables are tender. Season to taste with salt and ground black pepper.

4 Meanwhile, place the vermicelli in a bowl, cover with boiling water and set aside for 4 minutes. Drain, then divide among four warmed soup bowls. Ladle over the soup and serve.

Cook's Tips
• *This is a great soup for children and a good way of getting them to eat vegetables. Try adding potatoes and swede (rutabaga), cut into shapes. Any left-over Christmas ham can also be cut into shapes and added to the soup. Soup pasta shapes can be used instead of the vermicelli.*
• *Make little crunchy cheese toasts to go with the soup by cutting festive bread shapes, toasting one side, topping the untoasted side with cheese and toasting until golden.*
• *Sauté the left-over vegetable pieces in a little oil and mix with cooked brown rice to make a tasty risotto.*

Carrot and Coriander Soup

Root vegetables, such as carrots, are great for slow-cooker soups. Their earthy flavour becomes rich and sweet when cooked slowly, making this soup a lovely winter warmer during the festive period.

Serves 4
450g/1lb carrots, preferably
  young and tender

15ml/1 tbsp sunflower oil
40g/1½oz/3 tbsp butter
1 onion, chopped
1 stick celery, plus 2–3 leafy tops
2 small potatoes, peeled
900ml/1½ pints/3¾ cups boiling
  vegetable stock
10ml/2 tsp ground coriander
15ml/1 tbsp chopped fresh
  coriander (cilantro)
150ml/¼ pint/⅔ cup milk
salt and ground black pepper

1 Trim and peel the carrots and cut into chunks. Heat the oil and 25g/1oz/2 tbsp of the butter in a pan and fry the onion over low heat for 3–4 minutes until slightly softened.

2 Slice the celery and chop the potatoes, and add them to the onion in the pan. Cook for 2 minutes, then add the carrots and cook for a further 1 minute. Transfer the fried vegetables to the ceramic cooking pot of the slow cooker.

3 Pour the hot stock over the vegetables, then season with salt and ground black pepper. Cover the pot with the lid and cook on low for 4–5 hours until the vegetables are tender.

4 Reserve six to eight tiny celery leaves from the leafy tops for the garnish, then finely chop the remaining celery tops. Melt the remaining butter in a large pan and add the ground coriander. Fry for 1 minute, stirring constantly, until the aromas are released.

5 Reduce the heat and add the chopped celery tops and fresh coriander. Fry for about 30 seconds, then remove from the heat.

6 Ladle the soup into a food processor or blender and process until smooth, then pour into the pan with the celery tops and coriander. Stir in the milk and heat gently until piping hot. Check the seasoning, adding more if necessary, then serve garnished with the reserved celery leaves.

Courgette and Noodle Soup Energy 120kcal/501kJ; Protein 4.1g; Carbohydrate 24.3g, of which sugars 13.6g; Fat 1g, of which saturates 0.3g; Cholesterol 0mg; Calcium 63mg; Fibre 4.6g; Sodium 526mg.
Carrot and Coriander Soup Energy 168Kcal/697kJ; Protein 3g; Carbohydrate 11.9g, of which sugars 9.2g; Fat 12.4g, of which saturates 6g; Cholesterol 24mg; Calcium 94mg; Fibre 3.1g; Sodium 758mg.

Broccoli and Stilton Soup

This is a really easy, but rich, soup and is a classic winter dish that will make an ideal warming appetizer. Choose something simple to follow, such as plainly roasted or grilled meat, poultry or fish.

Serves 4
350g/12oz broccoli
25g/1oz/2 tbsp butter
1 onion, chopped
1 leek, white part only, chopped
1 small potato, cut into chunks
600ml/1 pint/2½ cups hot chicken stock
300ml/½ pint/1¼ cups milk
45ml/3 tbsp double (heavy) cream
115g/4oz Stilton cheese, rind removed, crumbled
salt and ground black pepper

1 Break the broccoli into florets, discarding the tough stems. Set aside two small florets for the garnish.

2 Melt the butter in a large pan and cook the onion and leek until soft but not coloured. Add the broccoli and potato, then pour in the stock. Cover and simmer for about 15–20 minutes, until the vegetables are tender.

3 Cool slightly, then purée in a blender or food processor. Strain back into the pan through a sieve (strainer).

4 Add the milk, cream and seasoning to the pan and reheat gently. At the last minute add the cheese, stirring until it just melts. Do not allow it to boil.

5 Meanwhile, blanch the reserved broccoli florets and cut them vertically into thin slices. Ladle the soup into warmed bowls and garnish with the broccoli florets and a generous grinding of black pepper.

> **Variation**
> If you like, you can make this into a more substantial meal by frying or grilling (broiling) some bacon rashers (strips) until crisp, then chop them and use to garnish the soup.

Watercress Soup

In Roman times, eating watercress was thought to prevent baldness. Later on it became the food of the working classes and was often eaten in a sandwich. As a soup, it makes a sophisticated appetizer for a festive dinner party. Both stalks and leaves are used for a lovely peppery flavour.

Serves 6
2 bunches of watercress, about 175g/6oz in total
25g/1oz/2 tbsp butter
1 onion, finely chopped
1 potato
900ml/1½ pints/3¾ cups vegetable stock
300ml/½ pint/1¼ cups milk
salt and ground black pepper
single (light) cream, to serve

1 Roughly chop the watercress, reserving a few small sprigs to add as a garnish at the end.

2 Melt the butter in a large pan and add the onion. Cook over medium heat for about 5 minutes, stirring occasionally, until the onion is soft and just beginning to brown.

3 Stir in the potato and the chopped watercress, then add the stock. Bring to the boil, reduce the heat and cover the pan. Simmer gently for 15–20 minutes, until the potato is very soft.

4 Remove from the heat, leave to cool slightly and then stir in the milk. Process or blend the soup until it is completely smooth. Return the soup to the rinsed-out pan and adjust the seasoning to taste, if necessary.

5 Reheat gently and ladle the soup into warmed bowls. Top each serving with a spoonful of cream and a few watercress leaves. Serve immediately.

> **Variations**
> • Try adding a little finely grated orange rind and the juice of an orange in step 4.
> • If you have a glut of Stilton over the Christmas period, you can sprinkle a little over the soup as a garnish.

Broccoli Soup Energy 316kcal/1314kJ; Protein 14.7g; Carbohydrate 11.8g, of which sugars 7.2g; Fat 23.4g, of which saturates 14.7g; Cholesterol 60mg; Calcium 255mg; Fibre 3.7g; Sodium 310mg.
Watercress Soup Energy 68kcal/280kJ; Protein 1.5g; Carbohydrate 1.4g, of which sugars 1g; Fat 6.3g, of which saturates 2.4g; Cholesterol 8mg; Calcium 79mg; Fibre 0.9g; Sodium 45mg.

Classic Tomato Soup

This creamy soup owes its good flavour to a mix of fresh and canned tomatoes – in summer you could, of course, use all fresh, but do make sure they are really ripe and full of flavour. When making this soup at Christmas it is best to stick to the mix of fresh and canned varieties.

Serves 4–6
25g/1oz/2 tbsp butter
1 onion, finely chopped
1 small carrot, finely chopped
1 celery stick, finely chopped
1 garlic clove, crushed
450g/1lb ripe tomatoes,
    roughly chopped
400g/14oz can chopped tomatoes
30ml/2 tbsp tomato
    purée (paste)
30ml/2 tbsp sugar
15ml/1 tbsp chopped fresh thyme
    or oregano leaves
600ml/1 pint/2½ cups
    chicken or vegetable stock
600ml/1 pint/2½ cups milk
salt and ground black pepper

1 Melt the butter in a large pan. Add the onion, carrot, celery and garlic. Cook over medium heat for about 5 minutes, stirring occasionally, until soft and just beginning to brown.

2 Add the tomatoes, purée, sugar, stock and herbs, retaining some to garnish. Bring to the boil, then cover and simmer gently for 20 minutes or until all the vegetables are very soft.

3 Process or blend the mixture until smooth, then press it through a sieve (strainer) to remove the skins and seeds.

4 Return the strained soup to the cleaned pan and stir in the milk. Reheat the soup gently.

5 Stir, without allowing it to boil. Season to taste with salt and ground black pepper. To serve, ladle the soup into bowls and garnish with the remaining herbs.

Cook's Tip
If using canned tomatoes, buy the best quality you can find. This will ensure that the soup is packed with flavour.

Chunky Roasted Tomato Soup

Slow roasting tomatoes gives a rich, full flavour. The costeno amarillo chilli is fresh and light, making it perfect with rich tomatoes.

Serves 6
500g/1¼lb tomatoes
4 small onions, peeled but
    left whole
5 garlic cloves
sea salt
1 fresh rosemary sprig, chopped
2 costeno amarillo chillies
grated rind and juice of ½
    small lemon
30ml/2 tbsp extra virgin
    olive oil
300ml/½ pint/1¼ cups
    tomato juice
1.5ml/¼ tsp soft dark
    brown sugar

1 Preheat the oven to 160°C/325°F/Gas 3. Cut the tomatoes in half and place them in a roasting pan. Peel the onions and garlic and add them to the pan. Sprinkle with sea salt. Roast for 1¼ hours or until the tomatoes are beginning to dry. Do not let them burn or blacken or they will have a bitter taste.

2 Peel the tomatoes and place them in a food processor with the onions and garlic. Process until coarsely chopped and transfer to a large pan. Add 350ml/12fl oz/1 cup water to the roasting pan and bring it to the boil, stirring to scrape all the residue off the bottom of the pan. Boil for a minute, then pour the liquid into the pan with the other ingredients.

3 Soak the chillies in hot water for about 10 minutes until soft. Drain, remove the stalks, slit them and scrape out the seeds. Chop the flesh finely and add it to the tomato mixture.

4 Stir in the lemon rind and juice, the olive oil, tomato juice and sugar. Bring to the boil, stirring, then reduce the heat, cover and simmer gently for 5 minutes. Taste for seasoning before serving, sprinkled with the remaining rosemary.

Cook's Tip
Use plum tomatoes or vine tomatoes, which tend to have more flavour than tomatoes grown for their keeping properties.

Classic Tomato Soup Energy 107kcal/447kJ; Protein 2.3g; Carbohydrate 11.4g, of which sugars 10.9g; Fat 6.1g, of which saturates 3.5g; Cholesterol 13mg; Calcium 50mg; Fibre 3.9g; Sodium 71mg.
Chunky Tomato Soup Energy 74kcal/310kJ; Protein 1.8g; Carbohydrate 8.6g, of which sugars 6.1g; Fat 3.9g, of which saturates 0.6g; Cholesterol 0mg; Calcium 24mg; Fibre 1.7g; Sodium 119mg.

Curried Parsnip Soup

The mild sweetness of parsnips and mango chutney is given an exciting lift with a blend of spices in this simple and festive soup.

Serves 4
30ml/2 tbsp olive oil
1 onion, chopped
1 garlic clove, crushed
1 small green chilli, seeded and finely chopped
15ml/1 tbsp grated fresh root ginger
5 large parsnips, diced
5ml/1 tsp cumin seeds

5ml/1 tsp ground coriander
2.5ml/½ tsp ground turmeric
30ml/2 tbsp mango chutney
1.2 litres/2 pints/5 cups water
juice of 1 lime
salt and ground black pepper
60ml/4 tbsp natural (plain) yogurt and mango chutney, to serve
chopped fresh coriander (cilantro), to garnish (optional)

For the sesame naan croûtons
45ml/3 tbsp olive oil
1 large naan, cut into small dice
15ml/1 tbsp sesame seeds

1 Heat the oil in a large pan and add the onion, garlic, chilli and ginger. Cook for 4–5 minutes, until the onion has softened. Add the parsnips and cook for 2–3 minutes. Sprinkle in the cumin seeds, coriander and turmeric, and cook for 1 minute, stirring.

2 Add the chutney and the water. Season well and bring to the boil. Reduce the heat, cover and simmer for 15 minutes, until the parsnips are soft and tender.

3 Cool the soup slightly, then purée it in a food processor or blender and return it to the pan. Stir in the lime juice.

4 To make the naan croûtons, heat the oil in a large frying pan and cook the diced naan for 3–4 minutes, stirring, until golden all over. Remove from the heat and drain off any excess oil. Add the sesame seeds and return the pan to the heat for no more than 30 seconds, until the seeds are pale golden.

5 Ladle the soup into bowls. Spoon a little yogurt into each portion, then top with a little mango chutney and some of the sesame naan croûton mixture. Garnish with the chopped fresh coriander, if you like.

Sweet Potato and Parsnip Soup

The sweetness of two of the most popular winter root vegetables – which are used in both the main part of the dish and the garnish – comes through beautifully in this delicious soup.

Serves 6
15ml/1 tbsp sunflower oil
1 large leek, sliced
2 celery sticks, chopped

450g/1lb sweet potatoes, diced
225g/8oz parsnips, diced
900ml/1½ pints/3¾ cups vegetable stock
salt and ground black pepper

For the garnish
15ml/1 tbsp chopped fresh parsley
roasted strips of sweet potatoes and parsnips

1 Heat the oil in a large pan and add the leek, celery, sweet potatoes and parsnips. Cook gently for about 5 minutes, stirring to prevent them browning or sticking to the pan.

2 Stir in the vegetable stock and bring to the boil, then cover and simmer gently for about 25 minutes, or until the vegetables are tender, stirring occasionally. Season to taste. Remove the pan from the heat and allow the soup to cool slightly.

3 Purée the soup in a food processor or blender until smooth, then return the soup to the pan and reheat gently.

4 Ladle the soup into warmed soup bowls to serve and sprinkle over the chopped fresh parsley and the roasted strips of sweet potatoes and parsnips.

> **Cook's Tip**
> Making and freezing soup is a practical way of preserving a glut of root vegetables that are unlikely to keep well. Not only can excess vegetables be used this way, but left-over boiled, mashed or roasted root vegetables can all be added to soup when puréed, cooled or frozen. This is great way of using up the seemingly endless amount of left-over food that is inevitable over the Christmas period.

Curried Parsnip Soup Energy 150kcal/623kJ; Protein 4.7g; Carbohydrate 7.8g, of which sugars 6.8g; Fat 11.4g, of which saturates 7g; Cholesterol 32mg; Calcium 170mg; Fibre 0.8g; Sodium 112mg.
Sweet Potato Soup Energy 113kcal/479kJ; Protein 2.1g; Carbohydrate 21.6g, of which sugars 7.2g; Fat 2.6g, of which saturates 0.4g; Cholesterol 0mg; Calcium 45mg; Fibre 4.3g; Sodium 40mg.

Roasted Pumpkin Soup

The pumpkin is roasted whole, then split open and scooped out to make this real treat of a soup. It makes a lovely festive appetizer for Christmas guests.

Serves 6–8
1.5kg/3–3½lb pumpkin
90ml/6 tbsp olive oil
2 onions, chopped
3 garlic cloves, chopped
7.5cm/3in piece fresh root
   ginger, grated

5ml/1 tsp ground coriander
2.5ml/½ tsp ground turmeric
pinch of cayenne pepper
1 litre/1¾ pints/4 cups
   vegetable stock
salt and ground black pepper
15ml/1 tbsp sesame seeds and
   fresh coriander leaves (cilantro)
   to garnish

For the pumpkin crisps
wedge of fresh pumpkin,
   seeds removed
120ml/4fl oz/½ cup olive oil

1 Preheat the oven to 200°C/400°F/Gas 6. Prick the pumpkin on top several times. Brush with plenty of the oil and bake for 45 minutes or until tender. Leave until cool enough to handle.

2 Taking care as there may be hot steam inside, split and scoop out the pumpkin, discarding the seeds. Chop the flesh.

3 Heat 60ml/4 tbsp of the remaining oil in a large pan. Add the onions, garlic and ginger. Cook for 4–5 minutes, then stir in the coriander, turmeric and cayenne, and cook for 2 minutes. Stir in the pumpkin and stock. Bring to the boil, reduce the heat and simmer gently for 20 minutes.

4 Cool the soup slightly, then purée it in a food processor or blender until smooth. Return the soup to the rinsed-out pan and season well with salt and pepper.

5 Meanwhile, prepare the pumpkin crisps. Using a vegetable peeler, pare long thin strips off the wedge of pumpkin. Heat the oil in a small pan and fry the pumpkin strips in batches for 2–3 minutes, until crisp. Drain on kitchen paper.

6 Reheat the soup and ladle it into bowls. Serve, topped with the pumpkin crisps and garnish with sesame seeds and coriander.

Pumpkin and Parsnip Soup

The textures of carrot, parsnip and pumpkin go so very well together, making a soup that is wonderfully rich in texture and packed with festive flavours.

Serves 4
15ml/1 tbsp olive oil or
   sunflower oil
15g/½oz/1 tbsp butter
1 onion, chopped
225g/8oz carrots, chopped
225g/8oz parsnips, chopped

225g/8oz pumpkin
about 900ml/1½ pints/3¾ cups
   vegetable stock
lemon juice, to taste
salt and ground black pepper

For the garnish
7.5ml/1½ tsp olive oil
½ garlic clove, finely chopped
45ml/3 tbsp chopped fresh
   parsley and coriander
   (cilantro), mixed
a good pinch of paprika

1 Heat the oil and butter in a large pan and fry the onion for about 3 minutes until softened, stirring occasionally. Add the carrots and parsnips, stir well, cover and cook over a gentle heat for a further 5 minutes.

2 Cut the pumpkin into chunks, discarding the skin and pith, and stir into the pan. Cover and cook for a further 5 minutes, then add the stock and seasoning, and slowly bring to the boil. Reduce the heat if necessary. Cover the pan and simmer the soup for 35–40 minutes until the vegetables are tender.

3 Allow the soup to cool slightly, then pour it into a food processor or blender and purée until smooth. Add a little extra stock or water if the soup seems too thick. Pour the soup back into the rinsed-out pan and reheat gently.

4 To make the garnish, heat the oil in a small pan and fry the garlic and herbs for 1–2 minutes. Add the paprika and stir well.

5 Taste the soup and adjust the seasoning, then stir in lemon juice to taste. Pour the soup into bowls and spoon a little of the prepared garnish on each portion. Carefully swirl the garnish through the soup using a skewer or cocktail stick (toothpick), or the point of a knife. Serve immediately.

Roasted Pumpkin Soup Energy 203kcal/639kJ; Protein 2.3g; Carbohydrate 8.3g, of which sugars 6.2g; Fat 18.1g, of which saturates 2.7g; Cholesterol 0mg; Calcium 82mg; Fibre 2.8g; Sodium 2mg.
Pumpkin and Parsnip Soup Energy 137kcal/568kJ; Protein 2.3g; Carbohydrate 14.3g, of which sugars 9.5g; Fat 8.2g, of which saturates 2.7g; Cholesterol 8mg; Calcium 83mg; Fibre 5.3g; Sodium 47mg.

Pumpkin and Coconut Soup

This simple, yet punchy, festive soup is rich with coconut balanced by an intriguing hint of sugar and spice. Just firm, but still fluffy, white rice provides an unusual garnish, but it is the perfect contrast for the silken texture of this soup. Following the amount given here, you should have just enough left over to serve as an accompaniment.

Serves 4
about 1kg/2¼lb pumpkin
750ml/1¼ pints/3 cups
  vegetable stock
750ml/1¼ pints/3 cups
  coconut milk
10–15ml/2–3 tsp sugar
115g/4oz/1 cup white rice
salt and ground black pepper
5ml/1 tsp ground cinnamon,
  to garnish

1 Remove any seeds or strands of fibre from the pumpkin, cut off the peel and chop the flesh. Put the prepared pumpkin in a pan and add the stock, coconut milk, sugar and seasoning.

2 Bring to the boil, reduce the heat and cover. Simmer for about 20 minutes, until the pumpkin is tender. Purée the soup in a food processor or blender. Return it to the rinsed-out pan.

3 Place the rice in a pan and rinse it in several changes of cold water, then drain in a sieve (strainer) and return it to the pan. Add plenty of fresh cold water to cover and bring to the boil. Stir once, reduce the heat and simmer for 15 minutes, until the grains are tender. Drain in a sieve.

4 Reheat the soup and taste it for seasoning, then ladle into bowls. Spoon a little rice into each portion and dust with cinnamon. Serve immediately, offering more rice at the table.

> **Variation**
> *You can use butternut squash in place of pumpkin, and brown rice in place of white rice, if you prefer. Much will depend on what is in the stores over the Christmas period. You could make this soup at Halloween and freeze it until December.*

Curried Pumpkin and Leek Soup

Ginger and cumin give this pumpkin soup a terrifically warm and spicy festive flavour. It makes a hearty, full-flavoured meal.

Serves 4
900g/2lb pumpkin, peeled and
  seeds removed
30ml/2 tbsp extra virgin
  olive oil
2 leeks, sliced
1 garlic clove, crushed
5ml/1 tsp ground ginger
5ml/1 tsp ground cumin
900ml/1½ pints/3¾ cups
  vegetable stock
salt and ground black pepper
coriander (cilantro) leaves,
  to garnish
60ml/4 tbsp Greek (US strained
  plain) yogurt, to serve

1 Cut the pumpkin flesh into even chunks. Heat the oil in a large pan and add the leeks and garlic. Cover the pan with a lid and cook gently, stirring occasionally, for about 15 minutes, until the vegetables are softened.

2 Add the ground ginger and cumin and cook, stirring, for a further 1 minute. Add the pumpkin chunks and the vegetable stock and season with salt and pepper. Bring the mixture to the boil, reduce the heat and cover the pan. Simmer for 30 minutes, or until the pumpkin is tender.

3 Process the soup, in batches if necessary, in a food processor or blender until smooth. Then return it to the rinsed-out pan.

4 Reheat the soup gently, and ladle out into four warmed individual bowls. Add a spoonful of Greek yogurt on the top of each and swirl it through the top layer of soup. Garnish with chopped fresh coriander leaves.

> **Variations**
> *• Use marrow (large zucchini) instead of pumpkin and replace half the stock with coconut milk.*
> *• For a spicy twist, add 1 seeded and chopped fresh green chilli to the yogurt before swirling it into the soup.*
> *• Use double the ginger and omit the cumin, if you like.*

Curried Pumpkin Soup Energy 98kcal/409kJ; Protein 3g; Carbohydrate 7.5g, of which sugars 5.8g; Fat 6.4g, of which saturates 1.1g; Cholesterol 0mg; Calcium 86mg; Fibre 4.2g; Sodium 2mg.
Pumpkin Soup Energy 148kcal/627kJ; Protein 8.8g; Carbohydrate 20.7g, of which sugars 13.5g; Fat 4g, of which saturates 2.3g; Cholesterol 11mg; Calcium 308mg; Fibre 2.8g; Sodium 81mg.

Cream of Pea and Spinach Soup

Although best made with peas, spinach and mint picked fresh from the garden, these are out of season at Christmas time. Frozen peas are a perfectly good substitute for fresh, and the soup will not suffer as a result.

Serves 6

25g/1oz/2 tbsp butter
1 onion, finely chopped

675g/1½lb frozen peas
1.5ml/¼ tsp sugar
1.2 litres/2 pints/5 cups chicken
    or vegetable stock
handful of fresh mint leaves
450g/1lb young spinach leaves
150ml/¼ pint/⅔ cup double
    (heavy) cream
salt and ground black pepper
15ml/1 tbsp chopped fresh
    chives, to garnish

1 Melt the butter in a large pan and add the onion. Cook over low heat for about 8–10 minutes, stirring occasionally, until they are soft and just turning brown.

2 Add the peas, sugar, stock and half the mint. Cover the pan and simmer gently for 10 minutes, until the peas are almost tender.

3 Stir the spinach into the peas and simmer gently for a further 5 minutes, until the spinach leaves have just wilted.

4 Leave to cool slightly. Add the remaining mint and process or blend until smooth. Return the soup to the rinsed-out pan and season to taste with salt and pepper.

5 Stir in the cream and reheat gently without boiling. Serve immediately, garnished with chopped chives.

> **Variation**
> Tender broccoli is also delicious with peas and spinach in this soup, if it is in season. Add the chopped stems for about 10 minutes and the tops of the chopped florets for 5 minutes when adding the spinach.

Chestnut and White Bean Soup

This substantial soup is a great dish to make at Christmas, when chestnuts are plentiful and at their best. Chestnuts have a long history of cultivation in Europe, and were eaten long before potatoes. You can freeze chestnuts if you buy too many – so long as you remember to peel them first.

Serves 4

100g/3¾oz/½ cup dried white
    beans, soaked overnight in cold
    water and drained
90g/3½oz peeled chestnuts,
    thawed if frozen
1 bay leaf
50ml/2fl oz/¼ cup olive oil
1 onion, chopped
salt

1 Put the beans, chestnuts and bay leaf in a large pan. Pour in 1 litre/3¾ pints/4 cups water and bring to the boil. Lower the heat, cover the pan with a lid and simmer the beans for about 1½ hours, until they are tender.

2 Heat the oil in a frying pan. Add the onion and cook over low heat, stirring occasionally, for 5 minutes, until softened. Do not allow the oil to overheat.

3 Add the onion and its cooking oil to the soup. Stir well, seasoning to taste with salt. Remove and discard the bay leaf. Mash the beans and chestnuts with a fork or vegetable masher, so they are crushed into the soup but not smooth.

4 Ladle the soup into four warmed soup bowls and serve immediately, while it is piping hot and freshly laced with the olive oil and chopped onion.

> **Cook's Tip**
> If using fresh chestnuts, do not store them for more than a week. The easiest way to shell them and remove their inner skins is to make a small cut in each one and par-boil or roast in the oven at 180°C/350°F/Gas 4 for about 5 minutes. Remove the shells and rub off the skins with a dish towel. Peeled frozen chestnuts are a simpler option.

Cream of Pea Soup Energy 121kcal/506kJ; Protein 6.1g; Carbohydrate 9.2g, of which sugars 5.2g; Fat 7g, of which saturates 4.2g; Cholesterol 18mg; Calcium 113mg; Fibre 3g; Sodium 123mg.
Chestnut and Bean Soup Energy 184kcal/773kJ; Protein 6.2g; Carbohydrate 20.5g, of which sugars 3.1g; Fat 9.2g, of which saturates 1.4g; Cholesterol 0mg; Calcium 39mg; Fibre 5.1g; Sodium 8mg.

Chicken and Leek Soup

This is a simple variation of an old French recipe.

Serves 4

1 boiling fowl (stewing chicken)
7.5ml/1 1/2 tsp salt
1 small leek
1 bouquet garni
1 mace blade
1.5 litres/2 1/2 pint/6 1/4 cups water
65g/2 1/2oz/1/3 cup rice
1 egg yolk
50ml/2fl oz/1/4 cup
  whipping cream

1 Put the fowl, salt, leek, bouquet garni, mace and water in a large pan. Boil, cover and simmer for 2 hours. Remove the fowl and cool. Strain the stock into a clean pan. Add the rice, bring to the boil and cook for 30 minutes. Purée the soup.

2 Dice the meat from the fowl. Add it to the soup and boil again. Remove from the heat. Beat the egg yolk with a ladleful of the soup, then stir it into the pan with the cream. Warm through, but do not boil. Season to taste and serve.

Split Pea and Bacon Soup

This popular soup is great on really cold days.

Serves 4–6

350g/12oz/1 1/2 cups dried split
  yellow or green peas
25g/1oz/2 tbsp butter
6 rashers (strips) rindless streaky
  (fatty) bacon, finely chopped
1 onion, finely chopped
1 carrot, thinly sliced
1 celery stick, thinly sliced
1.75 litres/3 pints/7 1/2 cups ham
  or chicken stock
60ml/4 tbsp double
  (heavy) cream
salt and ground black pepper
croûtons and fried bacon, to serve

1 Soak the split peas in boiling water to cover. Melt the butter in a large pan. Add the bacon, onion, carrot and celery and cook for 10–15 minutes, stirring until soft and browning.

2 Drain and add the peas and stock. Bring to the boil, cover and simmer gently for 1 hour or until the peas are very soft. Process or blend until smooth. Season, add the cream and reheat. Serve with croûtons and pieces of crisp bacon on top.

Cauliflower Soup with Broccoli

Creamy cauliflower soup is a classic winter dish and is given real bite by adding chunky cauliflower and broccoli florets. Crusty bread piled high with bacon and melting Cheddar cheese transforms this dish into a real festive treat.

Serves 4

1 onion, chopped
1 garlic clove, chopped
50g/2oz/1/4 cup butter
2 cauliflowers, broken into florets
1 large potato, cut into chunks
900ml/1 1/2 pints/3 3/4 cups
  chicken stock
225g/8oz broccoli, broken
  into florets
150ml/1/4 pint/2/3 cup single
  (light) cream
6 rindless streaky (fatty) bacon
  rashers (strips)
1 small baguette, cut in 4 pieces
225g/8oz/2 cups medium-mature
  (sharp) Cheddar cheese, grated
salt and ground black pepper
roughly chopped fresh parsley,
  to garnish

1 Cook the onion and garlic in the butter for 4–5 minutes. Add half the cauliflower, all the potato and the stock. Bring to the boil, reduce the heat and simmer for 20 minutes.

2 Boil the remaining cauliflower for about 6 minutes, or until just tender. Use a draining spoon to remove the florets and refresh under cold running water, then drain well. Cook the broccoli in the water for 3–4 minutes, until just tender. Drain, refresh under cold water, then drain. Add to the cauliflower.

3 Cool the soup slightly, then purée it until smooth and return it to the rinsed pan. Add the cream and seasoning, then heat gently. Add the cauliflower and broccoli and heat through.

4 Preheat the grill (broiler) to high. Grill (broil) the bacon until crisp, then cool slightly. Ladle the soup into flameproof bowls.

5 Place a piece of baguette in each bowl. Sprinkle grated cheese over the top and grill for 2–3 minutes, until the cheese is melted and bubbling. Take care when serving the hot bowls.

6 Crumble the bacon and sprinkle it over the melted cheese, then sprinkle the parsley over the top and serve immediately.

Chicken and Leek Soup Energy 194kcal/811kJ; Protein 13g; Carbohydrate 20.1g, of which sugars 1.8g; Fat 6.8g, of which saturates 3.6g; Cholesterol 66mg; Calcium 45mg; Fibre 0.8g; Sodium 320mg.
Split Pea and Bacon Soup Energy 378kcal/1584kJ; Protein 20.2g; Carbohydrate 34.9g, of which sugars 3.1g; Fat 18.5g, of which saturates 8.7g; Cholesterol 47mg; Calcium 45mg; Fibre 3.4g; Sodium 527mg.
Cauliflower Soup Energy 737kcal/3071kJ; Protein 34.8g; Carbohydrate 45.5g, of which sugars 9.2g; Fat 46.2g, of which saturates 26.4g; Cholesterol 121mg; Calcium 589mg; Fibre 6.6g; Sodium 1206mg.

Lobster Bisque

Bisque is a luxurious, velvety soup, which can be made with any crustaceans. A lobster version, laced with brandy, will go down a treat at a Christmas dinner party.

Serves 6
500g/1¼lb cooked lobster
75g/3oz/6 tbsp butter
1 onion, chopped
1 carrot, diced
1 celery stick, diced
45ml/3 tbsp brandy, plus extra for serving (optional)
250ml/8fl oz/1 cup dry white wine
1 litre/1¾ pints/4 cups fish stock
15ml/1 tbsp tomato purée (paste)
75g/3oz/scant ½ cup long grain rice
1 fresh bouquet garni
150ml/¼ pint/⅔ cup double (heavy) cream, plus extra to garnish
salt, ground white pepper and cayenne pepper

1 Cut the lobster into pieces. Melt half the butter in a large pan, add the vegetables and cook over low heat until soft. Add the lobster and stir for 30–60 seconds.

2 Pour over the brandy and set it alight. When the flames die down, add the wine and boil until reduced by half. Pour in the fish stock and simmer for 2–3 minutes. Remove the lobster.

3 Stir in the tomato purée and rice, add the bouquet garni and cook until the rice is tender. Meanwhile, remove the lobster meat from the shell and return the shells to the pan. Dice the lobster meat and set it aside.

4 When the rice is cooked, discard all the larger pieces of lobster shell. Transfer the mixture into a blender or food processor and process to a purée.

5 Press the purée through a sieve (strainer) placed over a clean pan. Stir, then heat until almost boiling. Season with salt, pepper and cayenne, then lower the heat and stir in the cream.

6 Dice the remaining butter and whisk it into the bisque. Add the diced lobster meat and serve immediately. If you like, pour a small spoonful of brandy into each soup bowl and swirl in a little extra double cream to garnish.

Spicy Pumpkin and Prawn Soup

The natural sweetness of the pumpkin is balanced by chillies, shrimp paste and dried shrimp in this colourful soup. The cooked shellfish adds further colour and a decent amount of bite, making this dish a real delight to the senses. This tasty warming soup would be ideal for serving as part of a festive feast.

Serves 4–6
2 garlic cloves, crushed
4 shallots, finely chopped
2.5ml/½ tsp shrimp paste
1 lemon grass stalk, chopped
2 fresh green chillies, seeded and chopped
15ml/1 tbsp dried shrimp, soaked for 10 minutes in warm water
600ml/1 pint/2½ cups chicken stock
450g/1lb pumpkin, peeled, seeded and cut into 2cm/¾in chunks
600ml/1 pint/2½ cups coconut cream
30ml/2 tbsp fish sauce
5ml/1 tsp sugar
115g/4oz peeled cooked prawns (shrimp)
salt and ground black pepper

To garnish
2 fresh red chillies, seeded and

1 Put the garlic, shallots, shrimp paste, lemon grass, green chillies and salt to taste in a mortar. Drain the dried shrimp, discarding the soaking liquid, and add them to the mortar, then use a pestle to grind the mixture into a paste. Alternatively, place all the ingredients in a food processor or blender and process until you have a paste.

2 Bring the chicken stock to the boil in a large pan. Add the ground paste and stir well to dissolve. Add the pumpkin chunks and simmer for 10–15 minutes, or until tender.

3 Stir in the coconut cream, then bring the soup back to simmering point. Do not let it boil. Add the fish sauce, sugar and ground black pepper to taste.

4 Add the prawns and cook for a further 2–3 minutes, until they are heated through. Serve in warm soup bowls, garnished with chillies and basil leaves.

Lobster Bisque Energy 406kcal/1684kJ; Protein 20.3g; Carbohydrate 13.7g, of which sugars 3.1g; Fat 25.2g, of which saturates 15g; Cholesterol 153mg; Calcium 84mg; Fibre 0.7g; Sodium 365mg.
Spicy Prawn Soup: Energy 73kcal/310kJ; Protein 6.5g; Carbohydrate 10.4g, of which sugars 9.8g; Fat 0.9g, of which saturates 0.4g; Cholesterol 56mg; Calcium 102mg; Fibre 1.3g; Sodium 399mg.

Salmon Soup with Salsa and Rouille

This elegant seafood soup is perfect for serving at a Christmas gathering.

Serves 4

90ml/6 tbsp olive oil
1 onion, chopped
1 leek, chopped
1 celery stick, chopped
1 fennel bulb, roughly chopped
1 red (bell) pepper, seeded
   and sliced
3 garlic cloves, chopped
grated rind and juice of 2 oranges
1 bay leaf
400g/14oz can chopped tomatoes
1.2 litres/2 pints/5 cups fish stock
pinch of cayenne pepper

800g/1¾lb salmon fillet, skinned
300ml/½ pint/1¼ cups double
   (heavy) cream
salt and ground black pepper
4 thin slices baguette, to serve

For the ruby salsa

2 tomatoes, peeled, seeded
   and diced
½ small red onion, very
   finely chopped
15ml/1 tbsp cod's roe
15ml/1 tbsp chopped fresh sorrel

For the rouille

120ml/4fl oz/½ cup mayonnaise
1 garlic clove, crushed
5ml/1 tsp sun-dried tomato paste

1 Heat the oil in a large pan. Add the onion, leek, celery, fennel, pepper and garlic. Cover and cook gently for 20 minutes.

2 Add the orange rind and juice, bay leaf and tomatoes to the pan. Cover with a lid and cook for 4–5 minutes, stirring occasionally. Add the stock and cayenne, cover the pan again and simmer gently for about 30 minutes.

3 Add the salmon and poach it for 8–10 minutes, until just cooked. Lift out the fish and flake it coarsely, discarding bones.

4 Mix all the salsa ingredients and set aside. For the rouille, mix the mayonnaise with the garlic and the sun-dried tomato paste. Toast the baguette slices on both sides and set aside.

5 Purée the soup and strain it back into the rinsed pan. Stir in the cream, seasoning and salmon. Heat gently but do not boil.

6 To serve, ladle the soup into bowls. Top the baguette slices with rouille, float on the soup and spoon over the salsa.

Seafood Chowder

Like most chowders, this is a substantial slow-cooker dish, and could be served with crusty bread for a tasty lunch or supper.

Serves 4

25g/1oz/2 tbsp butter
1 small leek, sliced
1 small garlic clove, crushed
1 celery stalk, chopped
2 smoked streaky (fatty) bacon
   rashers (strips), finely chopped
200g/7oz/generous 1 cup
   drained, canned corn kernels

450ml/¾ pint/scant 2 cups milk
5ml/1 tsp plain (all-purpose) flour
450ml/¾ pint/scant 2 cups hot
   chicken or vegetable stock
115g/4oz/generous ½ cup easy-
   cook (converted) rice
4 large scallops, with corals
115g/4oz white fish fillet,
   such as monkfish
15ml/1 tbsp chopped fresh
   parsley, plus extra to garnish
pinch of cayenne pepper
45ml/3 tbsp single (light)
   cream (optional)
salt and ground black pepper

1 Melt the butter in a frying pan, add the leek, garlic, celery and bacon and cook, stirring frequently, for 10 minutes, until soft but not browned. Transfer the mixture to the ceramic cooking pot and switch the slow cooker on to high.

2 Place half the corn kernels in a food processor or blender. Add about 75ml/2½fl oz/⅓ cup of the milk and process until the mixture is well blended and fairly thick and creamy.

3 Sprinkle the flour over the leek mixture and stir in. Gradually add the remaining milk, stirring after each addition. Stir in the stock, followed by the corn mixture. Cover the slow cooker with the lid and cook for 2 hours.

4 Add the rice to the pot and cook for 30 minutes. Meanwhile, pull the corals away from the scallops and slice the white flesh into 5mm/¼in slices. Cut the fish into bitesize chunks. Add the scallops and fish to the chowder and gently stir to combine. Cover and cook for 15 minutes.

5 Add the corals, parsley and cayenne pepper and cook for 5–10 minutes, or until the vegetables, rice and fish are tender. Add the cream, if using. Serve hot, garnished with fresh parsley.

Salmon Soup Energy 1153kcal/4772kJ; Protein 44.9g; Carbohydrate 13.7g, of which sugars 12.5g; Fat 102.5g, of which saturates 34.9g; Cholesterol 225mg; Calcium 127mg; Fibre 4.7g; Sodium 268mg.
Seafood Chowder Energy 355Kcal/1497kJ; Protein 18.5g; Carbohydrate 45.9g, of which sugars 10.8g; Fat 12.1g, of which saturates 5.8g; Cholesterol 49mg; Calcium 179mg; Fibre 1.5g; Sodium 655mg.

Chicken, Leek and Celery Soup

This makes a substantial main course soup with fresh crusty bread.

Serves 4–6
1.3kg/3lb chicken
1 small head of celery, trimmed
1 onion, coarsely chopped
1 bouquet garni
3 large leeks

65g/2½oz/5 tbsp butter
2 potatoes, cut into chunks
150ml/¼ pint/⅔ cup dry
  white wine
30–45ml/2–3 tbsp single (light)
  cream (optional)
salt and ground black pepper
90g/3½oz pancetta, grilled until
  crisp, to garnish

1 Cut the breasts from the chicken and set aside. Chop the rest of the chicken carcass into eight to ten pieces and place in a pan. Chop four or five of the celery sticks and add them to the pan with the onion and bouquet garni. Pour in 2.4 litres/ 4 pints/10 cups water to cover the ingredients and bring to the boil. Reduce the heat, cover the pan, then simmer for 1½ hours.

2 Remove the chicken and cut off and reserve the meat. Strain the stock, then return it to the pan and boil rapidly until it has reduced to about 1.5 litres/2½ pints/6¼ cups.

3 Set about 150g/5oz leeks aside. Slice the remaining leeks and the remaining celery, reserving any celery leaves. Melt half the butter in a pan. Add the sliced leeks and celery, cover and cook over low heat for 10 minutes, until soft but not brown. Add the potatoes, wine and 1.2 litres/2 pints/5 cups of the stock. Season, bring to the boil and reduce the heat. Part-cover and simmer for 15–20 minutes, or until the potatoes are cooked.

4 Dice the reserved uncooked chicken. Melt the remaining butter in a pan and fry the chicken for 5–7 minutes, until cooked. Slice the remaining leeks, add to the chicken and fry, stirring occasionally, for a further 3–4 minutes, until just cooked.

5 Purée the soup and diced chicken from the stock. Season and add more stock if the soup is thick. Stir in the cream and chicken and leek mixture. Reheat gently and serve, topped with pancetta and the chopped reserved celery leaves.

Celeriac and Bacon Soup

Versatile, yet often overlooked, celeriac is a winter vegetable that makes excellent soup.

Serves 4
50g/2oz/¼ cup butter
2 onions, chopped
675g/1½lb celeriac, roughly diced
450g/1lb potatoes, roughly diced
1.2 litres/2 pints/5 cups
  vegetable stock
150ml/¼ pint/⅔ cup single
  (light) cream

salt and ground black pepper
sprigs of fresh thyme,
  to garnish

For the topping
1 small Savoy cabbage
50g/2oz/¼ cup butter
175g/6oz rindless streaky (fatty)
  bacon, roughly chopped
15ml/1 tbsp roughly chopped
  fresh thyme
15ml/1 tbsp roughly chopped
  fresh rosemary

1 Melt the butter in a pan. Add the onions and cook for 4–5 minutes, until softened. Add the celeriac. Put a lid on sthe pan and cook gently for 10 minutes.

2 Stir in the potatoes and stock. Bring to the boil, reduce the heat and simmer for 20 minutes or until the vegetables are very tender. Leave to cool slightly. Using a slotted spoon, remove about half the celeriac and potatoes from the soup and set them aside.

3 Purée the soup in a food processor or blender. Return it to the rinsed-out pan with the reserved celeriac and potatoes.

4 Prepare the topping. Discard the tough outer leaves from the cabbage. Roughly tear the remaining leaves, discarding any hard stalks, and blanch them in boiling salted water for 2–3 minutes. Refresh under cold running water and drain.

5 Melt the butter in a large frying pan and cook the bacon for 3–4 minutes. Add the cabbage, thyme and rosemary, and stir-fry for 5–6 minutes, until tender. Season well.

6 Add the cream to the soup and season it well, then reheat gently. Ladle the soup into bowls and pile the cabbage mixture in the middle. Garnish with sprigs of fresh thyme.

Chicken Soup Energy 294kcal/1246kJ; Protein 40.5g; Carbohydrate 22.1g, of which sugars 5.9g; Fat 2.8g, of which saturates 0.7g; Cholesterol 105mg; Calcium 69mg; Fibre 4.8g; Sodium 124mg.
Celeriac Soup Energy 462kcal/1919kJ; Protein 12.3g; Carbohydrate 24.3g, of which sugars 7.3g; Fat 35.8g, of which saturates 20.4g; Cholesterol 97mg; Calcium 144mg; Fibre 4.3g; Sodium 954mg.

Duck Broth with Spiced Dumplings

Handle the dumplings gently for a light texture to match their delicious flavour.

Serves 4
1 duckling, about 1.8kg/4lb,
  with liver
1 large onion, halved
2 carrots, thickly sliced
1/2 garlic bulb
1 bouquet garni
3 cloves
bunch of chives, in short lengths

For the spiced dumplings
2 thick slices white bread
60ml/4 tbsp milk
2 rashers (strips) rindless streaky
  (fatty) bacon
1 shallot, finely chopped
1 garlic clove, crushed
1 egg yolk, beaten
grated rind of 1 orange
2.5ml/1/2 tsp paprika
50g/2oz/1/2 cup plain
  (all-purpose) flour
salt and ground black pepper

1 Set the duck liver aside. Cut off the breasts and set them aside. Put the carcass into a pan and pour in enough water to cover. Bring to the boil and skim the scum off the surface.

2 Add the onion, carrots, garlic, bouquet garni and cloves to the pan. Reduce the heat, cover, then simmer for 2 hours, skimming off any scum occasionally.

3 Lift the carcass from the broth. Remove all meat from the carcass and shred it finely, then set it aside. Strain the broth and skim off any fat. Return the broth to the pan and then simmer, uncovered, until reduced to 1.2 litres/2 pints/5 cups.

4 For the dumplings, soak the bread in the milk for 5 minutes. Remove the skin and fat from the duck breasts. Mince (grind) the meat with the duck liver and bacon. Squeeze the milk from the bread, then mix the bread into the meat with the shallot, garlic, egg yolk, orange rind, paprika, flour and seasoning.

5 Shape the mixture into balls, a little smaller than walnuts to make 20 small dumplings. Bring a pan of lightly salted water to the boil. Poach the dumplings for 4–5 minutes, until just tender.

6 Boil the broth. Add the dumplings. Divide the shredded duck among bowls and ladle in the broth. Sprinkle with chives.

Cream of Duck Soup

This rich soup is ideal to begin a festive meal.

Serves 4
2 duck breast fillets
4 rindless streaky (fatty) bacon
  rashers (strips), chopped
1 onion, chopped
1 garlic clove, chopped
2 carrots, diced
2 celery sticks, chopped
4 large mushrooms, chopped
15ml/1 tbsp tomato purée (paste)
2 duck legs, chopped into pieces
15ml/1 tbsp plain
  (all-purpose) flour
45ml/3 tbsp brandy
150ml/1/4 pint/2/3 cup port

300ml/1/2 pint/1 1/4 cups red wine
900ml/1 1/2 pints/ 3 3/4 cups
  chicken stock
1 bay leaf
2 sprigs fresh thyme
15ml/1 tbsp redcurrant jelly
150ml/1/4 pint/2/3 cup double
  (heavy) cream
salt and ground black pepper

For the blueberry relish
150g/5oz/1 1/4 cups blueberries
15ml/1 tbsp caster
  (superfine) sugar
grated rind and juice of 2 limes
15ml/1 tbsp chopped
  fresh parsley
15ml/1 tbsp balsamic vinegar

1 Score the skin and fat on the duck breast fillets. Brown in a hot heavy pan, skin down, for 8–10 minutes. Turn and cook for 5–6 minutes, until tender. Remove the duck. Drain off some of the duck fat, leaving about 45ml/3 tbsp in the pan.

2 Add the bacon, onion, garlic, carrots, celery and mushrooms and cook for 10 minutes, stirring. Stir in the tomato purée and cook for 2 minutes. Remove the skin and bones from the duck legs and chop the flesh. Add to the pan and cook for 5 minutes.

3 Stir in the flour, then the brandy, port, wine and stock. Boil, stirring. Stir in the bay, thyme and jelly. Reduce the heat and simmer for 1 hour. Strain the soup and simmer for 10 minutes.

4 Mix all the ingredients for the blueberry relish in a mixing bowl, crushing some berries as you mix.

5 Discard the skin and fat from the duck breast fillets. Cut the meat into strips and add to the soup with the cream. Season and reheat, then ladle into bowls and serve, topped with relish.

Cream of Duck Soup Energy 642kcal/2673kJ; Protein 39.2g; Carbohydrate 14.2g, of which sugars 13.6g; Fat 35g, of which saturates 17.2g; Cholesterol 252mg; Calcium 83mg; Fibre 2.8g; Sodium 384mg.
Duck Broth Energy 289kcal/1214kJ; Protein 29.9g; Carbohydrate 19g, of which sugars 2.8g; Fat 13g, of which saturates 3.1g; Cholesterol 196mg; Calcium 63mg; Fibre 1.3g; Sodium 373mg.

Broccoli Timbales

To avoid last-minute fuss over the hectic Christmas period, make these timbales a few hours ahead.

Serves 4
350g/12oz broccoli florets
45ml/3 tbsp crème fraîche or whipping cream
1 egg, plus 1 egg yolk
15ml/1 tbsp chopped spring onion (scallion)
pinch of freshly grated nutmeg
salt and ground black pepper
white wine butter sauce, to serve (optional)
fresh chives, to garnish

1 Preheat the oven to 190°C/375°F/Gas 5. Lightly butter four 175ml/6fl oz ramekins. Line the bases of the ramekins with baking parchment and butter the parchment.

2 Steam the broccoli in the top of a covered steamer over boiling water for 8–10 minutes until very tender.

3 Put the cooked broccoli in a food processor or blender fitted with the metal blade and process with the cream, egg and egg yolk until smooth.

4 Add the spring onion and season with salt, pepper and nutmeg. Process again to mix.

5 Spoon the purée into the ramekins and place them in a baking dish. Add boiling water to come halfway up the sides, then bake for 25 minutes, until just set. Invert on to warmed plates and peel off the paper. Pour a little white wine butter sauce around each timbale, if using, and garnish with chives.

Cook's Tip
To make white wine sauce: melt 50g/2oz butter in a pan, add ¼ sliced onion and fry for 4–5 minutes. Pour in 150ml/¼ pint/ ⅔ cup white wine, turn up the heat and boil for 5 minutes, or until the liquid has reduced by half. Stir in 100ml/3½fl oz/scant ½ cup double (heavy) cream, season, then reduce the heat and simmer for 3–4 minutes, until the sauce has thickened slightly.

Blinis with Mushroom Caviar

These little Russian pancakes are ideal for serving at a Christmas party or as part of a festive buffet.

Serves 4
115g/4oz/1 cup strong white bread flour
40g/1½oz/⅓ cup buckwheat flour
2.5ml/½ tsp salt
300ml/½ pint/1¼ cups milk
5ml/1 tsp active dried yeast
2 eggs, separated

For the caviar
350g/12oz/4½ cups mixed assorted mushrooms such as field (portabello) mushrooms, brown cap (cremini), porcini and oyster mushrooms
5ml/1 tsp celery salt
30ml/2 tbsp walnut oil
15ml/1 tbsp lemon juice
45ml/3 tbsp chopped fresh parsley
ground black pepper
200ml/7fl oz/scant 1 cup sour cream or crème fraîche

1 To make the caviar, trim and chop the mushrooms, then place them in a glass bowl, toss with the celery salt and cover with a weighted plate.

2 Let the mushrooms stand for 2 hours until the juices have run out into the bottom of the bowl. Rinse the mushrooms thoroughly to remove the salt, drain and press out as much liquid as you can with the back of a spoon. Return them to the bowl and toss with walnut oil, lemon juice, parsley and a twist of ground black pepper. Chill in the refrigerator.

3 Sift the two flours together with the salt in a large mixing bowl. Heat the milk to approximately body temperature. Add the yeast, stirring until dissolved, then pour into the flour, add the egg yolks and stir to make a smooth batter. Cover with a damp cloth and leave in a warm place.

4 Whisk the egg whites in a clean bowl until stiff, then gently fold them into the risen batter.

5 Heat a cast-iron pan or griddle to a moderate temperature. Moisten with oil, then drop spoonfuls of the batter on to the pan. When bubbles rise to the surface, turn them over and cook briefly on the other side. Spoon on the sour cream, top with the mushroom caviar and serve.

Broccoli Timbales Energy 106kcal/438kJ; Protein 6.4g; Carbohydrate 1.9g, of which sugars 1.6g; Fat 8.1g, of which saturates 4g; Cholesterol 111mg; Calcium 70mg; Fibre 2.3g; Sodium 30mg.
Buckwheat Blinis Energy 380kcal/1586kJ; Protein 12.5g; Carbohydrate 38.8g, of which sugars 6.2g; Fat 20.6g, of which saturates 8.5g; Cholesterol 130mg; Calcium 205mg; Fibre 2.3g; Sodium 94mg.

Roquefort Tartlets

These festive treats can be made in shallow tartlet tins to serve hot as a first course. You could also make them in tiny cocktail tins to serve warm as bitesize snacks with a Christmas drink before a meal.

Serves 12
175g/6oz/1½ cups plain
  (all-purpose) flour
large pinch of salt
115g/4oz/½ cup butter
1 egg yolk
30ml/2 tbsp cold water

For the filling
15g/½oz/1 tbsp butter
15g/½oz/1 tbsp flour
150ml/¼ pint/⅔ cup milk
115g/4oz Roquefort
  cheese, crumbled
150ml/¼ pint/⅔ cup double
  (heavy) cream
2.5ml/½ tsp dried mixed herbs
3 egg yolks
salt and ground black pepper

1 To make the pastry, sift the flour and salt into a bowl and rub the butter into the flour until it resembles breadcrumbs. Mix the egg yolk with the water and stir into the flour to make a soft dough. Knead until smooth, wrap in clear film (plastic wrap) and chill for 30 minutes. (You can also make the dough in a food processor, if you prefer.)

2 Melt the butter in a pan, stir in the flour and then the milk. Boil to thicken slightly, stirring constantly. Off the heat, beat in the cheese and season with salt and pepper. Set aside.

3 In a separate pan, bring the cream and mixed herbs to the boil. Reduce the liquid to about 30ml/2 tbsp. Beat the herby cream into the sauce with the egg yolks.

4 Preheat the oven to 190°C/375°F/Gas 5. On a lightly floured work surface, roll out the pastry 3mm/⅛in thick. Stamp out rounds with a fluted pastry (cookie) cutter and use to line your chosen tartlet tins (muffin pans).

5 Divide the filling between the tartlets; they should be filled only two-thirds full. Stamp out smaller fluted rounds or star shapes for the tops and lay on top of each tartlet. Bake for 20–25 minutes, or until puffed and golden brown.

Red Onion and Goat's Cheese Pastries

Fresh thyme adds a tasty edge to the mellow red onion in these scrumptious pastries, which are topped with luscious goat's cheese. The puff pastry rises around the festive-coloured filling to create attractive tartlets.

Serves 4
15ml/1 tbsp olive oil
450g/1lb red onions, sliced
30ml/2 tbsp fresh thyme or
  10ml/2 tsp dried thyme
15ml/1 tbsp balsamic vinegar
425g/15oz packet ready-rolled
  puff pastry, thawed if frozen
115g/4oz goat's cheese, cubed
1 egg, beaten
salt and ground black pepper
fresh oregano sprigs, to
  garnish (optional)
mixed green salad leaves,
  to serve

1 Heat the oil in a large frying pan, add the onions and fry over low heat for 10 minutes, or until soft, stirring occasionally.

2 Add the thyme and balsamic vinegar to the pan, and season with salt and ground black pepper. Cook for another 5 minutes. Remove the pan from the heat and leave the onions to cool.

3 Preheat the oven to 220°C/425°F/Gas 7. Unroll the puff pastry and, using a 15cm/6in plate as a guide, cut four rounds. Place the pastry rounds on a dampened baking sheet and, using the point of a knife, score a border, 2cm/¾in inside the edge of each round. (Do not cut through the pastry.)

4 Divide the cooked onions among the pastry rounds and top with the cubes of goat's cheese. Brush the edge of each pastry round with a little beaten egg.

5 Bake the pastries in the oven for 25–30 minutes, or until they are golden. Garnish with fresh oregano sprigs, if you like, before serving with mixed salad leaves.

> **Variation**
> *Ring the changes by spreading the pastry base with pesto or tapenade before you add the filling.*

Roquefort Tartlets Energy 252kcal/1045kJ; Protein 5.1g; Carbohydrate 13.2g, of which sugars 1.2g; Fat 20.9g, of which saturates 12.2g; Cholesterol 117mg; Calcium 100mg; Fibre 0.5g; Sodium 217mg.
Red Onion Pastries Energy 595kcal/2482kJ; Protein 15.4g; Carbohydrate 50.8g, of which sugars 8.1g; Fat 39.4g, of which saturates 5.9g; Cholesterol 74mg; Calcium 139mg; Fibre 1.6g; Sodium 543mg.

Wild Mushroom and Fontina Tartlets

Fontina cheese gives these tarts a creamy, nutty flavour.

Serves 4
25g/1oz/½ cup dried wild
  mushrooms
30ml/2 tbsp olive oil
1 red onion, chopped
2 garlic cloves, chopped
30ml/2 tbsp medium-dry sherry
1 egg
120ml/4fl oz/½ cup single
  (light) cream

25g/1oz fontina cheese,
  thinly sliced
salt and ground black pepper
rocket (arugula) leaves,
  to serve

For the pastry
115g/4oz/1 cup wholemeal
  (whole-wheat) flour
50g/2oz/4 tbsp unsalted butter
25g/1oz/¼ cup walnuts, roasted
  and ground
1 egg, lightly beaten

1 To make the pastry, rub the flour and butter together until the mixture resembles fine breadcrumbs. Add the nuts, then the egg and mix to a soft dough. Wrap, then chill for 30 minutes.

2 Meanwhile, soak the mushrooms in 300ml/½ pint/1¼ cups boiling water for 30 minutes. Drain and reserve the liquid. Cook the onion in the oil over a low heat for 5 minutes, then add the garlic and cook for about 2 minutes, stirring frequently.

3 Add the soaked mushrooms and cook for 7 minutes over a high heat until the edges become crisp. Add the sherry and the reserved soaking liquid. Cook over a high heat for 10 minutes, until the liquid evaporates. Season to taste and set aside to cool.

4 Preheat the oven to 200°C/400°F/Gas 6. Lightly grease four 10cm/4in tartlet tins (muffin pans). Roll out the pastry on a lightly floured work surface and use to line the tartlet tins.

5 Prick the pastry, line with baking parchment and baking beans and bake blind for 10 minutes. Remove the paper and beans.

6 Whisk the egg and cream to mix, add to the mushroom mixture, then season. Spoon into the pastry cases (pie shells), top with cheese slices and bake for 20 minutes, until the filling is set. Serve warm with rocket leaves.

Tomato and Tapenade Tarts

These delicious individual tarts look and taste fantastically Christmassy, despite the fact that they demand very little time or effort. The mascarpone cheese topping melts as it cooks to make a smooth, creamy sauce.

Serves 4
500g/1¼lb puff pastry, thawed
  if frozen
60ml/4 tbsp black or green
  olive tapenade
500g/1¼lb cherry tomatoes
90g/3½oz/scant ½ cup
  mascarpone cheese

1 Preheat the oven to 220°C/425°F/Gas 7. Lightly grease a large baking sheet and sprinkle it with water.

2 Roll out the puff pastry on a lightly floured surface and cut out four 16cm/6½in rounds, using a bowl or small plate as a guide for cutting out the rounds.

3 Transfer the pastry rounds to the prepared baking sheet. Using the tip of a sharp knife, mark a shallow cut 1cm/½in in from the edge of each round to form a rim.

4 Reserve half the tapenade and spread the rest over the pastry rounds, keeping the paste inside the marked rim.

5 Cut half the tomatoes in half. Pile all the tomatoes, whole and halved, on the pastry, again keeping them inside the rim. Season lightly with salt and pepper.

6 Place the baking sheet in the oven and bake the tarts for 20 minutes, until the pastry is well risen and golden.

7 Dot the tarts with the remaining tapenade. Spoon a little of the mascarpone cheese on the centre of the tomatoes and season with ground black pepper.

8 Bake the tarts in the oven for a further 10 minutes, until the mascarpone cheese has melted to make a sauce over the cherry tomatoes. Serve the tarts warm, accompanied by a mixed green side salad, if you like.

Mushroom Tartlets Energy 409kcal/1701kJ; Protein 10.2g; Carbohydrate 21.9g, of which sugars 2.3g; Fat 31g, of which saturates 13.4g; Cholesterol 143mg; Calcium 121mg; Fibre 2.3g; Sodium 199mg.
Tomato Tarts Energy 543kcal/2269kJ; Protein 10.2g; Carbohydrate 50.8g, of which sugars 6.2g; Fat 35.9g, of which saturates 2.4g; Cholesterol 9mg; Calcium 91mg; Fibre 1.7g; Sodium 736mg.

Vegetable Tempura

These deep-fried fritters are perfect for serving to guests at a festive party or to make a tasty start to a meal.

Serves 4
2 medium courgettes (zucchini)
$^1/_2$ medium aubergine (eggplant)
1 large carrot
$^1/_2$ small Spanish (Bermuda) onion

1 egg
120ml/4fl oz/$^1/_2$ cup iced water
115g/4oz/1 cup plain
  (all-purpose) flour
salt and ground black pepper
vegetable oil, for deep-frying
sea salt flakes, lemon slices and
  Japanese soy sauce (shoyu),
  to serve

1 Using a vegetable peeler, pare strips of peel from the courgettes and aubergine to give a decorative striped effect.

2 Cut the courgettes, aubergine and carrot into strips about 7.5–10cm/3–4in long and 3mm/$^1/_8$in wide.

3 Put the courgettes, aubergine and carrot into a colander and sprinkle liberally with salt. Leave for about 30 minutes, then rinse thoroughly under cold running water. Drain well.

4 Thinly slice the onion from top to base, discarding the plump pieces in the middle. Separate the layers so that there are lots of fine, long strips. Mix all the vegetables together and season with salt and pepper.

5 Make the batter immediately before frying. Mix the egg and iced water in a bowl, then sift in the flour. Mix briefly with a fork or chopsticks. Do not overmix; the batter should remain lumpy. Add the vegetables to the batter and mix to combine.

6 Half-fill a wok with oil and heat to 180°C/350°F. Scoop up one heaped tablespoon of the mixture at a time and carefully lower it into the oil. Deep-fry in batches for approximately 3 minutes, until golden brown and crisp.

7 Drain the cooked tempura on kitchen paper. Serve each portion with salt, slices of lemon and a tiny bowl of Japanese soy sauce for dipping.

Spicy Peanut Balls

Tasty rice balls, rolled in chopped peanuts and deep-fried, make a delicious festive appetizer. Serve them simply as they are, or with a chilli sauce for dipping.

Serves 4
1 garlic clove, crushed
1cm/$^1/_2$in piece fresh root ginger,
  peeled and finely chopped
1.5ml/$^1/_4$ tsp turmeric
5ml/1 tsp sugar

2.5ml/$^1/_2$ tsp salt
5ml/1 tsp chilli sauce
10ml/2 tsp fish sauce or
  soy sauce
30ml/2 tbsp chopped fresh
  coriander (cilantro)
juice of $^1/_2$ lime
225g/8oz/2 cups cooked white
  long grain rice
115g/4oz/1 cup peanuts, chopped
vegetable oil, for deep-frying
lime wedges and chilli dipping
  sauce, to serve (optional)

1 Process the garlic, ginger and turmeric in a food processor or blender until the mixture forms a paste.

2 Add the sugar, salt, chilli sauce and fish sauce or soy sauce, with the chopped coriander and lime juice. Process briefly to mix together the ingredients.

3 Add three-quarters of the cooked rice to the paste and process until smooth and sticky. Scrape into a mixing bowl and stir in the remainder of the rice.

4 Divide the rice mixture into 16 pieces. Wet your hands and shape each piece into a ball.

5 Place the chopped peanuts on a plate. Roll the rice balls in the peanuts, making sure they are evenly coated.

6 Heat the oil in a deep-fryer or wok to 190°C/375°F. Check the oil is hot enough by dropping in a piece of bread; it should sizzle and brown within about 40 seconds. Deep-fry the peanut balls, in batches if necessary, until crisp.

7 Drain the cooked balls on kitchen paper and then pile on to a serving platter. Serve the balls while hot with lime wedges and a chilli dipping sauce, if you like.

Vegetable Tempura Energy 313kcal/1305kJ; Protein 7.1g; Carbohydrate 30.6g, of which sugars 7.3g; Fat 18.9g, of which saturates 2.5g; Cholesterol 48mg; Calcium 94mg; Fibre 3.6g; Sodium 28mg.
Spicy Peanut Balls Energy 123kcal/512kJ; Protein 2.9g; Carbohydrate 12.4g, of which sugars 0.8g; Fat 6.8g, of which saturates 1g; Cholesterol 0mg; Calcium 7mg; Fibre 0.4g; Sodium 45mg.

Potato Skewers with Mustard Dip

These potatoes are best cooked on the barbecue, but have a great flavour and a lovely crisp skin even when cooked under the grill when the weather over the festive period is inclement.

Serves 4
For the dip
4 garlic cloves, crushed
2 egg yolks
30ml/2 tbsp lemon juice
300ml/½ pint/1¼ cups extra
 virgin olive oil
10ml/2 tsp wholegrain mustard
salt and ground black pepper

For the skewers
1kg/2¼lb small new potatoes
200g/7oz shallots, halved
30ml/2 tbsp olive oil
15ml/1 tbsp sea salt

1 If cooking on a barbecue, prepare it for cooking before you begin. To make the dip, place the garlic, egg yolks and lemon juice in a blender or a food processor fitted with the metal blade and process for a few seconds until the mixture is thoroughly combined and smooth.

2 Keep the blender motor running and add the oil very gradually, pouring it in a thin stream, until the mixture forms a thick, glossy cream. Add the mustard and stir the ingredients together, then season with salt and pepper. Chill until needed.

3 Par-boil the potatoes in their skins in boiling water for about 5 minutes. Drain well and then thread them on to metal skewers, alternating with the shallots.

4 Brush the skewers with oil and sprinkle with salt. Cook over a barbecue or under the grill (broiler) for 10–12 minutes, turning occasionally. Serve immediately, accompanied by the dip.

Cook's Tip
New potatoes and salad potatoes have the firmness necessary to help them stay on the skewer. Don't be tempted to use other types of small potato, they will probably split or fall off the skewers during cooking.

Thai Potato Samosas

Most samosas are deep-fried, but these are baked, making them a healthier option. They are also ideal for festive parties as no deep-frying is needed.

Serves 25
1 large potato, about
 250g/9oz, diced
15ml/1 tbsp groundnut
 (peanut) oil
2 shallots, finely chopped
1 garlic clove, finely chopped
60ml/4 tbsp coconut milk
5ml/1 tsp Thai red or green
 curry paste
75g/3oz/¾ cup peas
juice of ½ lime
25 samosa wrappers or
 10cm/4in × 5cm/2in strips
 of filo pastry
salt and ground black pepper
oil, for brushing

1 Preheat the oven to 220°C/425°F/Gas 7. Bring a small pan of water to the boil, add the diced potato, cover and cook for 10–15 minutes, until tender. Drain and set aside.

2 Meanwhile, heat the groundnut oil in a large frying pan and cook the shallots and garlic over medium heat, stirring occasionally, for 4–5 minutes, until softened and golden.

3 Add the drained potato, coconut milk, red or green curry paste, peas and lime juice to the frying pan. Mash coarsely with a wooden spoon. Season to taste with salt and pepper and cook over a low heat for 2–3 minutes, then remove the pan from the heat and set aside until the mixture has cooled a little.

4 Lay a samosa wrapper or filo strip flat on the work surface. Brush with a little oil, then place a generous teaspoonful of the mixture in the middle of one end. Turn one corner diagonally over the filling to meet the long edge.

5 Continue folding over the filling, keeping the triangular shape as you work down the strip. Brush with a little more oil if necessary and place on a baking sheet. Prepare all the other samosas in the same way.

6 Bake for 15 minutes, or until the pastry is golden and crisp. Leave to cool slightly before serving.

Potato Skewers Energy 488kcal/2024kJ; Protein 4.3g; Carbohydrate 29.5g, of which sugars 4.1g; Fat 40g, of which saturates 6.1g; Cholesterol 65mg; Calcium 28mg; Fibre 2.2g; Sodium 49mg.
Thai Potato Samosas Energy 42kcal/178kJ; Protein 1.2g; Carbohydrate 8.5g, of which sugars 0.6g; Fat 0.6g, of which saturates 0.1g; Cholesterol 0mg; Calcium 14mg; Fibre 0.5g; Sodium 4mg.

Rosemary Potato Wedges with Salmon Dip

This creamy dip with spiced herby potato wedges can be served as an appetizer or as part of a festive buffet lunch. Smoked salmon is an essential ingredient at Christmas time and it is delicious in this creamy dip with the potato wedges.

Serves 4
115g/4oz smoked salmon
250g/9oz/generous 1 cup
  mascarpone cheese
60ml/4 tbsp chopped fresh chives

grated rind and juice of 1 lemon
1 red (bell) pepper, seeded and
  cut into strips
1 yellow (bell) pepper, seeded and
  cut into strips
sea salt and ground
  black pepper

For the potato wedges
675g/1½lb large potatoes
60ml/4 tbsp olive oil
30ml/2 tbsp chopped
  fresh rosemary
1 fresh red chilli, seeded and
  finely chopped

1 Preheat the oven to 200°C/400°F/Gas 6. To make the wedges, cut the potatoes into thick pieces. Pour the oil into a roasting pan and heat it in the oven for 10 minutes. Toss the wedges in the pan, then sprinkle over the rosemary and the chilli. Shake the pan to coat the potatoes in the oil, rosemary and chilli. Season and bake for 50–60 minutes until tender, turning occasionally.

2 Cut the smoked salmon into small pieces, using kitchen scissors or a sharp filleting knife. Put the mascarpone cheese, chives and lemon rind in a large bowl and mix with a fork until thoroughly blended.

3 Add the lemon juice, a little at a time, to the dip. Mix it constantly, so that the mixture is thinned and is given a lemony tang, but does not curdle.

4 Add the salmon to the cheese mixture and season with pepper. Place in a serving bowl, cover and chill until required.

5 To serve, arrange the pepper strips and wedges around the edge of a serving platter and place the dip in the centre.

Cheese and Leek Sausages

These tasty sausages, which are flavoured with herbs and mustard, are the ideal appetizer for vegetarian guests at Christmas time, since they are made from cheese and leeks rather than the usual meat.

Makes 8
150g/5oz/2½ cups fresh
  breadcrumbs
150g/5oz generous cup grated
  Caerphilly cheese
1 small leek, very finely chopped

15ml/1 tbsp chopped
  fresh parsley
leaves from 1 thyme
  sprig, chopped
2 eggs
7.5ml/1½ tsp English (hot)
  mustard powder
about 45ml/3 tbsp milk
plain (all-purpose) flour,
  for coating
15ml/1 tbsp oil
15g/½oz/1 tbsp butter, melted
salt and ground black pepper
salad leaves and tomato halves,
  to serve

1 Mix together the breadcrumbs, cheese, leek and herbs in a large bowl. Season with salt and ground black pepper.

2 In another bowl, whisk the two eggs together with the English mustard and reserve about 30ml/2 tbsp. Stir the rest into the bowl with the cheese mixture. Pour in enough milk to bind the mixture together.

3 Divide the cheese mixture into eight portions and then form them into sausage shapes with your hands. Wet your hands slightly if the mixture is sticky.

4 Dip the sausages in the reserved egg to coat. Season the flour, then roll the sausages in it to give a light, even coating. Chill for about 30 minutes until they are firm.

5 Preheat the grill (broiler) and oil the rack. Mix the oil and melted butter together and use to brush over the sausages.

6 Cook the sausages under the grill for 5–10 minutes, turning them carefully every now and then, until golden brown all over. Serve the sausages hot or cold, accompanied by some mixed salad leaves and tomato halves.

Potato Wedges Energy 487kcal/2030kJ; Protein 16.9g; Carbohydrate 33.2g, of which sugars 7.9g; Fat 32.7g, of which saturates 14.2g; Cholesterol 71mg; Calcium 124mg; Fibre 3.9g; Sodium 774mg.
Cheese and Leek Sausages Energy 193kcal/809kJ; Protein 8.8g; Carbohydrate 15.1g, of which sugars 0.9g; Fat 10.9g, of which saturates 5.7g; Cholesterol 70mg; Calcium 179mg; Fibre 0.8g; Sodium 309mg.

Grilled Goat's Cheese with Baby Beetroot

Beetroot are at their best around the festive period and this recipe is an ideal way to make the most of them. The goat's cheese marries well with the earthy sweetness of the beetroot.

Serves 4
6 small raw beetroot (beets)
6 slices French bread
6 slices (about 250g/9oz)
   goat's cheese
30ml/2 tbsp walnut oil
salt and ground black pepper

1 Cook the beetroot in a pan of boiling salted water for about 40 minutes until tender. Set aside to cool slightly.

2 Wearing disposable rubber gloves, remove and discard the skin and slice the beetroot.

3 Toast the French bread slices on both sides under a medium-hot grill (broiler). Arrange the beetroot slices in a fan on the toasted bread then place a slice of the goat's cheese on top of the beetroot.

4 Place the slices on a grill pan and grill (broil) until the goat's cheese has melted and is golden brown. Serve immediately, drizzled with a little of the walnut oil and with plenty of black pepper ground over the top.

> **Cook's Tip**
> Handle the beetroot carefully because it is important to ensure that the skin isn't pierced before or during the cooking process. If this happens, the nutrients and some of the vibrant colour of the vegetables will be lost in the cooking water.

> **Variation**
> To save time, you can make this dish with ready-cooked whole beetroot, but avoid the ones that have been soaked in vinegar.

Stilton with Herb Spread and Melba Toast

Christmas wouldn't be the same without a large chunk of Stilton, and this appetizer is an elegant way of making the most of this fine cheese.

Serves 8
225g/8oz Stilton or other
   blue cheese
115g/4oz cream cheese
15ml/1 tbsp port

15ml/1 tbsp chopped
   fresh parsley
15ml/1 tbsp chopped fresh
   chives, plus extra to garnish
50g/2oz/½ cup finely
   chopped walnuts
salt and ground black pepper

For the Melba toast
12 thin slices white bread

1 Place the Stilton, cream cheese and port in a bowl or food processor and beat until smooth.

2 Stir in the remaining ingredients and season with salt and ground black pepper to taste.

3 Spoon the mixture into individual ramekin dishes and level the tops. Cover with clear film (plastic wrap) and chill until firm. Sprinkle with chopped chives before serving.

4 Preheat the oven to 180°C/350°F/Gas 4. To make the Melba toast, grill (broil) the bread on both sides. While the toast is hot, cut off the crusts, and cut each slice horizontally in two.

5 While the bread is still warm, place it in a single layer on baking trays and bake for 10–15 minutes, until golden brown and crisp. Continue with the remaining slices in the same way. Serve warm with the potted Stilton.

> **Cook's Tip**
> This can be made the day before serving, helping to take the strain off a busy festive schedule. The Melba toast will keep in an airtight container for a day or two.

Grilled Goat's Cheese Energy 290kcal/1215kJ; Protein 13.3g; Carbohydrate 26.7g, of which sugars 5g; Fat 15.2g, of which saturates 7.9g; Cholesterol 39mg; Calcium 114mg; Fibre 1.9g; Sodium 530mg.
Stilton with Herbs Energy 363kcal/1512kJ; Protein 14.3g; Carbohydrate 21g, of which sugars 0.9g; Fat 24.6g, of which saturates 15.4g; Cholesterol 70mg; Calcium 339mg; Fibre 0.6g; Sodium 576mg.

Lacy Potato Pancakes

These pretty, lacy pancakes can be served as canapés with Christmas drinks. They're also good served as an appetizer, topped with smoked salmon, crème fraîche or sour cream, and chopped red onion.

Serves 6
6 large potatoes
1 leek, finely sliced
1 carrot, grated (optional)
15g/½oz/1 tbsp butter
15ml/1 tbsp vegetable oil
salt and ground black pepper

1 Peel and grate the potatoes. Put in a bowl, add the leek and carrot, if using, and mix them all together.

2 Heat the butter and oil in a frying pan and when smoking, add spoonfuls of the potato mixture to make 7.5cm/3in pancakes. Fry the pancakes, turning once, until golden brown on both sides. Season with salt and pepper and serve hot.

Prawn Cocktail

This 1960s dinner-party appetizer is a delight, as long as it includes really crisp lettuce and is assembled at the last minute. It makes a frequent appearance on Christmas Day menus.

Serves 6
60ml/4 tbsp double (heavy) cream, lightly whipped

60ml/4 tbsp mayonnaise
60ml/4 tbsp tomato ketchup
10ml/2 tsp Worcestershire sauce
juice of 1 lemon
450g/1lb cooked peeled prawns (shrimp)
½ crisp lettuce, finely shredded
salt, ground black pepper and paprika
thinly sliced brown bread, butter and lemon wedges, to serve

1 Mix the cream, mayonnaise, ketchup, Worcestershire sauce and lemon juice in a bowl. Stir in the prawns and season.

2 Part-fill six glasses with lettuce. Spoon the prawns over and sprinkle with paprika. Serve immediately.

Potted Shrimp

Tiny brown shrimp found in the seas around England (most famously those from Morecambe Bay) have been potted in spiced butter since about 1800. Serve them as an appetizer for a festive feast or as part of a Christmas buffet.

Serves 4
225g/8oz cooked, shelled shrimp
225g/8oz/1 cup butter
pinch of ground mace
salt
cayenne pepper
dill sprigs, to garnish
lemon wedges and thin slices of brown bread and butter, to serve

1 Chop about a quarter of the shrimp. In a pan, melt 115g/4oz/½ cup of the butter over very low heat.

2 Skim off any foam that rises to the surface of the butter. Stir in all the shrimp, the mace, salt and cayenne and heat gently without boiling. Pour the mixture into four individual dishes and leave to cool.

3 Melt the remaining butter in a small pan, then spoon the clear butter over the shrimp, leaving the sediment behind. When the butter is almost set, place a dill sprig in the centre of each dish. Cover and chill.

4 Remove the potted shrimp from the refrigerator about 30 minutes before serving. Lemon wedges and brown bread and butter are ideal accompaniments.

Cook's Tip
This is a great appetizer to prepare ahead of a festive feast, but ensure that you remove it from the refrigerator and allow to come to room temperature before serving.

Variation
Brown bread is the traditional accompaniment with this dish but you can serve it with slices of Melba toast, if you prefer.

Lacy Potatoes Pancakes Energy 182kcal/767kJ; Protein 3.9g; Carbohydrate 33.1g, of which sugars 3.3g; Fat 4.6g, of which saturates 1.8g; Cholesterol 5mg; Calcium 20mg; Fibre 2.7g; Sodium 38mg.
Prawn Cocktail Energy 193kcal/802kJ; Protein 13.9g; Carbohydrate 4g, of which sugars 3.9g; Fat 13.6g, of which saturates 4.6g; Cholesterol 167mg; Calcium 79mg; Fibre 0.4g; Sodium 374mg.
Potted Shrimp Energy 460kcal/1895kJ; Protein 9.6g; Carbohydrate 0.4g, of which sugars 0.4g; Fat 46.7g, of which saturates 29.4g; Cholesterol 193mg; Calcium 83mg; Fibre 0g; Sodium 555mg.

Crab Salad with Coriander

Crab is delicious when it is simply dressed and served in a mixed salad, as with this festive treat. The crab's richness is blended with cream, which contrasts with the apples and spring onions.

Serves 6
1 romaine lettuce
2 eating apples
juice of 1 lemon
1 bunch spring onions (scallions), chopped
150ml/¼ pint/⅔ cup whipping cream
135ml/4½fl oz crème fraîche
30ml/2 tbsp chopped fresh coriander (cilantro), plus extra to garnish
brown and white meat of 2 crabs
salt

1 Shred the lettuce and arrange in a shallow serving bowl, reserving four bowl-shaped leaves. Peel, quarter and core the apples, then cut into small dice. Put in a bowl, add the lemon juice and toss together. Add the spring onions and mix together.

2 Whisk the cream in a large bowl until it stands in soft peaks, then fold in the crème fraîche. Add the apple mixture and chopped coriander to the bowl and mix in.

3 Mix together the brown and white crab meat and season with salt to taste. Fold the meat into the cream mixture. Check the seasoning and place in the centre of the reserved lettuce leaves. Serve garnished with chopped coriander.

> **Cook's Tip**
> This dish makes a great appetizer before a Christmas meal as it can be prepared a few hours ahead. Let the salad come to room temperature before serving.

> **Variation**
> For a more substantial dish, which can be served as a light lunch or supper, simply accompany the crab salad with chopped hard-boiled eggs.

Hot Crab Soufflés

These delicious little soufflés must be served as soon as they are ready, so ensure your Christmas guests are at the table before taking the soufflés out of the oven.

Serves 6
50g/2oz/¼ cup butter
45ml/3 tbsp fine wholemeal (whole-wheat) breadcrumbs
4 spring onions (scallions), finely chopped
15ml/1 tbsp Malayan or mild Madras curry powder
25g/1oz/¼ cup plain (all-purpose) flour
105ml/7 tbsp coconut milk or milk
150ml/¼ pint/⅔ cup whipping cream
4 egg yolks
225g/8oz white crab meat
mild green Tabasco sauce
6 egg whites
salt and ground black pepper

1 Use some of the butter to grease six ramekin dishes or a 1.75 litre/3 pint/7½ cup soufflé dish.

2 Sprinkle the fine wholemeal breadcrumbs into the ramekins or soufflé dish. Roll the dishes or dish around to coat the base and sides completely, then tip out the excess breadcrumbs. Preheat the oven to 200°C/400°F/Gas 6.

3 Melt the remaining butter in a pan, add the spring onions and Malayan or mild Madras curry powder and cook over low heat for about 1 minute, until softened. Stir in the flour and cook for a further 1 minute.

4 Gradually add the coconut milk or milk and the cream, stirring constantly. Cook until smooth and thick. Off the heat, stir in the egg yolks, then the crab. Season with salt, ground black pepper and Tabasco sauce.

5 In a grease-free bowl, beat the egg whites stiffly with a pinch of salt. With a metal spoon stir one-third into the crab mixture then fold in the rest. Spoon into the dishes or dish.

6 Bake until well risen, golden brown and just firm to the touch. Individual soufflés will take 8 minutes; a large soufflé will take 15–20 minutes. Serve immediately.

Hot Crab Soufflés Energy 270kcal/1122kJ; Protein 14g; Carbohydrate 11.6g, of which sugars 2.2g; Fat 18.9g, of which saturates 12.1g; Cholesterol 181mg; Calcium 123mg; Fibre 1g; Sodium 426mg.
Crab Salad Energy 382kcal/1585kJ; Protein 20.6g; Carbohydrate 6.4g, of which sugars 6.2g; Fat 30.6g, of which saturates 19.3g; Cholesterol 151mg; Calcium 188mg; Fibre 1.4g; Sodium 571mg.

Scallops with Black Bean Sauce

When scallops are fresh, they taste exquisite when simply steamed in their shells. Here they are served with a little flavoursome sauce made from Chinese wine, black bean sauce and fresh ginger, which perfectly complements the sweet, tender flesh of the scallops.

Serves 4

8 scallops, preferably in the shell
30ml/2 tbsp Chinese wine
15ml/1 tbsp fermented
    black beans
15ml/1 tbsp chopped fresh
    root ginger
2.5ml/½ tsp sugar
15ml/1 tbsp sliced spring onions
    (scallions), to garnish

1 Preheat the oven to 160°C/325°F/Gas 3. Spread the scallop shells in a single layer on a baking sheet. Heat them for a few moments until they gape, then remove them from the oven.

2 Hold a scallop in a clean dish towel, flat side up. Using a long, flexible knife, run the blade along the inner surface of the flat shell to cut through the muscle that holds the shells together. Ease the shells apart completely.

3 Lift off the top shell. Pull out and discard the black intestinal sac and the yellowish frilly membrane. Cut the white scallop and orange coral from the bottom shell and rinse briefly under cold water. Remove and discard the white ligament attached to the scallop flesh.

4 Mix the wine, black beans, ginger and sugar in a shallow dish. Add the scallops and marinate for 30 minutes.

5 Return the scallops and marinade to the half shells and place them in a steamer. If you have bought shelled scallops, divide them – and the marinade – among four ramekins. Steam for 10 minutes. Serve immediately, garnished with spring onions.

> **Cook's Tip**
> Scallops are at their best in the autumn and early winter so are ideal for serving over the festive season.

Toast Skagen

This luxurious dish makes an ideal opener to a festive dinner party. It is quick and easy to prepare so you can spend more time with your guests.

Serves 6–8

1kg/2¼lb shell-on cooked
    prawns (shrimp)
250ml/8fl oz/1 cup sour cream
250ml/8fl oz/1 cup thick
    mayonnaise
30ml/2 tbsp chopped fresh dill,
    plus fronds to garnish
30ml/2 tbsp chopped fresh chives
a squeeze of lemon juice
25–50g/1–2oz/2–4 tbsp butter
8 slices bread, halved
salt and ground black pepper
5ml/1 tsp red lumpfish roe,
    to garnish

1 Carefully remove the shells from the prawns, keeping them intact. Put the sour cream, mayonnaise, chopped dill, chives and lemon juice in a large bowl.

2 Season the mixture with salt and ground black pepper to taste, then stir in the prawns.

3 Melt the butter in a large frying pan, add the bread slices and fry until golden brown on both sides.

4 Serve the prawn mixture piled on top of the fried bread slices and garnish each serving with a small amount of the lumpfish roe and a frond of fresh dill.

> **Cook's Tip**
> You can use peeled prawns (shrimp) for this dish, but those with their shell on taste and look better.

> **Variation**
> If you can't find lumpfish roe then salmon roe is ideal as a substitute to use as a garnish, as its beautiful orange colour and large eggs make the dish look rather special and festive. Grated horseradish is another good accompaniment.

Scallops Energy 75kcal/319kJ; Protein 12.3g; Carbohydrate 3.9g, of which sugars 0.9g; Fat 0.8g, of which saturates 0.2g; Cholesterol 24mg; Calcium 19mg; Fibre 0.3g; Sodium 91mg.
Toast Skagen Energy 415kcal/1726kJ; Protein 14.5g; Carbohydrate 15.2g, of which sugars 2.5g; Fat 33.4g, of which saturates 9.2g; Cholesterol 180mg; Calcium 128mg; Fibre 0.7g; Sodium 1065mg.

Prawn Salad with Spicy Marinade

This warm salad is a real treat on a cold wintry day. Serve with garlic and herb bread for a more substantial meal for your festive guests.

Serves 8
225g/8oz large, cooked, shelled
    prawns (shrimp)
225g/8oz smoked streaky (fatty)
    bacon rashers (strips), chopped
mixed lettuce leaves

30ml/2 tbsp chopped fresh
    chives, to garnish

For the spicy marinade
1 garlic clove, crushed
finely grated rind of 1 lemon
15ml/1 tbsp lemon juice
60ml/4 tbsp olive oil
1.5ml/¼ tsp chilli paste, or a
    large pinch dried ground chilli
15ml/1 tbsp light soy sauce
salt and ground black pepper

1 In a glass bowl, mix the prawns with the garlic, lemon rind and juice, 45ml/3 tbsp of oil, the chilli paste and soy sauce. Season with salt and black pepper. Cover the bowl with a piece of clear film (plastic wrap) and leave to marinate in a cool place for at least one hour.

2 Gently cook the bacon in the remaining oil in the pan until crisp. Drain well on kitchen paper and set aside.

3 Wash and dry the lettuce, tear the leaves into bitesize pieces and arrange them in individual bowls or on plates.

4 Just before serving, put the prawns with their marinade into a large frying pan. Bring the mixture to the boil.

5 Add the bacon to the pan with the prawns and cook for one minute. Spoon the prawns and bacon over the salad and sprinkle with chives. Serve immediately.

> **Cook's Tip**
> *This dish is handy to make over the festive season as the ingredients can be prepared in advance. If you do this, cook the marinated prawns (shrimp) and bacon just before serving, spoon them over the salad and serve immediately.*

Seafood Salad

This crustacean salad is delicious served with a glass of cold beer when enjoying a festive drink with friends.

Serves 6–8
200g/7oz fresh asparagus spears
1kg/2¼lb shell-on cooked
    prawns (shrimp)
200g/7oz can mussels in brine
100g/3½oz can crab meat in
    brine or the meat from 2 large
    cooked crabs
200g/7oz small mushrooms, sliced
1 cos or romaine lettuce

For the dressing
105ml/7 tbsp mayonnaise
5ml/1 tsp tomato purée (paste)
pinch of salt
1 garlic clove, crushed
15ml/1 tbsp chopped fresh dill

For the garnish
1 potato
vegetable oil, for deep-frying
4 baby tomatoes or cherry
    tomatoes, quartered
2 lemons, cut into wedges
1 bunch fresh dill

1 Stand the asparagus spears upright in a deep pan, pour in enough boiling water to come three-quarters of the way up the stalks and simmer for about 10 minutes until tender. Drain and, when cool enough to handle, cut into 5cm/2in lengths.

2 Remove the shells from the prawns, keeping them intact. If using canned mussels and crab, drain the brine. Mix the prawns with the mussels, crab, asparagus and mushrooms.

3 To make the potato garnish, finely grate the potato and rinse under cold running water. Pat dry the potato on a dish towel. Heat the oil in a deep-fryer or pan to 180–190°C/350–375°F or until a cube of bread browns in 30 seconds. Add the potato and fry until golden brown, then remove with a slotted spoon. Drain on kitchen paper and leave to cool.

4 For the dressing, mix together the mayonnaise, tomato purée, salt, garlic and dill. Add the dressing to the fish mixture and mix carefully, keeping the prawns and mussels whole.

5 To serve, chop the lettuce finely and place on individual plates. Place the salad on the lettuce and garnish with the fried potato, tomatoes, lemon wedges and dill.

Prawn Salad Energy 298kcal/1240kJ; Protein 18.8g; Carbohydrate 28.1g, of which sugars 1.6g; Fat 12.1g, of which saturates 2g; Cholesterol 146mg; Calcium 102mg; Fibre 1.4g; Sodium 586mg.
Seafood Salad Energy 594kcal/2531kJ; Protein 113.3g; Carbohydrate 2.8g, of which sugars 1.2g; Fat 14.6g, of which saturates 2.9g; Cholesterol 1337mg; Calcium 565mg; Fibre 0.9g; Sodium 7723mg.

Gravlax with Mustard and Dill Sauce

Gravlax may be widely available commercially but, for a festive treat, the home-made version really has no comparison. The key to making successful gravlax is in the mustard and dill sauce with which the fish is served.

Serves 6–8
1kg/2¼lb fresh salmon, filleted
 and boned, with skin on
50g/2oz/½ cup sea salt
50g/2oz/½ cup caster
 (superfine) sugar
10ml/2 tsp crushed
 white peppercorns
200g/7oz/2 cups chopped fresh
 dill with stalks
fresh dill fronds, to garnish

For the mustard and dill sauce
115g/4oz Dijon mustard
115g/4oz/generous ½ cup sugar
15ml/1 tbsp vinegar
5ml/1 tsp salt
ground black pepper
300ml/½ pint/1¼ cups
 vegetable oil
115g/4oz/2 cups chopped fresh
 dill fronds

1 Using tweezers, remove any pinbones from the salmon. Then mix the salt and sugar together. Sprinkle a little on to the centre of a sheet of foil and place half the salmon fillet, skin side down, on top. Sprinkle the salmon with a little more salt mixture.

2 Sprinkle the white pepper on the flesh side of both salmon fillets and then add the chopped dill to both fillets. Place the second salmon fillet, skin side up, on top of the first fillet and finally sprinkle over the remaining salt mixture.

3 Wrap the foil around the salmon fillets and leave in the refrigerator for 48 hours, turning the salmon every 12 hours.

4 To make the sauce, put the mustard, sugar, vinegar and salt and pepper into a bowl and mix them all together. Then very slowly drizzle the oil into the mixture, whisking it all the time until you end up with a thick, shiny sauce. Finally add the chopped fresh dill to the mixture.

5 When the salmon has marinated slice it thinly, from one end, at an angle of 45 degrees. Serve on individual serving plates or on one large dish with the sauce. Garnish with dill fronds.

Salmon and Scallop Brochettes

With their delicate colours, really superb flavour and attractive lemon grass skewers, these brochettes make the perfect opener for a sophisticated dinner party at Christmas time.

Serves 4
8 lemon grass stalks
225g/8oz salmon fillet, skinned
8 shucked queen scallops, with
 their corals if possible
8 baby (pearl) onions, peeled
 and blanched
½ yellow (bell) pepper, cut into
 8 squares
25g/1oz/2 tbsp butter
juice of ½ lemon
salt, ground white pepper
 and paprika

For the sauce
30ml/2 tbsp dry vermouth
50g/2oz/¼ cup butter
5ml/1 tsp chopped fresh tarragon

1 Preheat the grill (broiler) to medium-high. Cut off the top 7.5–10cm/3–4in of each lemon grass stalk. Reserve the bulb ends to use in another dish.

2 Cut the salmon fillet into twelve 2cm/¾in cubes. Thread the salmon, scallops, corals if available, onions and pepper squares on to the lemon grass and arrange the brochettes in a grill pan.

3 Melt the butter in a small pan, add the lemon juice and a pinch of paprika and stir well to combine. Brush the mixture all over the brochettes.

4 Grill (broil) the skewers for about 2–3 minutes on each side, turning and basting the brochettes every minute, until the fish and scallops are just cooked through, but are still very juicy and succulent. Transfer to a platter and keep hot while you make the tarragon butter sauce.

5 Pour the dry vermouth and the leftover cooking juices from the brochettes into a small pan. Bring to the boil and continue to boil fiercely to reduce the liquid by half.

6 Add the butter and melt, then stir in the chopped fresh tarragon and salt and ground white pepper to taste. Pour the butter sauce over the brochettes and serve.

Gravlax Energy 543kcal/2258kJ; Protein 26.4g; Carbohydrate 21g, of which sugars 20.7g; Fat 39.8g, of which saturates 5.4g; Cholesterol 63mg; Calcium 58mg; Fibre 0.3g; Sodium 428mg.
Salmon Brochettes Energy 321kcal/1336kJ; Protein 23.5g; Carbohydrate 4.8g, of which sugars 2.7g; Fat 22.4g, of which saturates 11.1g; Cholesterol 92mg; Calcium 36mg; Fibre 0.6g; Sodium 231mg.

Melon and Prosciutto Salad

Cool fragrant melon wrapped with air-dried ham makes a delicious appetizer. If making this dish outside the festive period, when strawberries are in season, serve with a fruity salsa.

Serves 4
1 large cantaloupe, Charentais or Galia melon
175g/6oz prosciutto or Serrano ham, thinly sliced

For the salsa
225g/8oz/2 cups strawberries
5ml/1 tsp caster (superfine) sugar
30ml/2 tbsp groundnut (peanut) or sunflower oil
15ml/1 tbsp orange juice
2.5ml/½ tsp finely grated orange rind
2.5ml/½ tsp finely grated fresh root ginger
salt and ground black pepper

1 Halve the melon and scoop the seeds out with a spoon. Cut the rind away with a paring knife, then slice the melon thickly. Chill until ready to serve.

2 To make the salsa, hull the strawberries and cut them into large dice. Place in a small mixing bowl with the sugar and crush lightly to release the juices.

3 Add the oil, orange juice, rind and ginger and mix until all the ingredients are combined. Season to taste with salt and pepper.

4 Arrange the sliced melon on a serving plate, lay the ham over the top and serve with a bowl of salsa, handed round separately for diners to help themselves.

> **Cook's Tip**
> Prosciutto means 'ham' in Italian, and is a term generally used to describe seasoned, salt-cured and air-dried hams. Parma ham is the most famed prosciutto. Italian prosciuttos are designated prosciutto cotto, or cooked, and prosciutto crudo, or raw – although edible due to curing. They are labelled according to the place of origin, such as prosciutto di Parma and prosciutto di San Daniele. Buy it in supermarkets and Italian delicatessens.

Figs with Prosciutto and Roquefort

In this easy, stylish dish, figs and honey balance the richness of the ham and cheese. Serve with warm bread for a simple light appetizer before any rich festive meal.

Serves 4
8 fresh figs
75g/3oz prosciutto
45ml/3 tbsp clear honey
75g/3oz Roquefort cheese
ground black pepper

1 Preheat the grill (broiler). Quarter the figs and place on a foil-lined grill rack. Tear each slice of prosciutto into two or three pieces. Crumple the pieces of prosciutto and place them on the foil beside the figs. Brush the figs all over with about 15ml/1 tbsp of the clear honey and cook under the grill until lightly browned all over.

2 Crumble the Roquefort cheese and divide among four plates, setting it to one side. Add the honey-grilled figs and ham and pour over any cooking juices caught on the foil. Drizzle the remaining honey over the figs, ham and cheese, and serve seasoned with plenty of ground black pepper.

> **Cook's Tip**
> Fresh figs are a delicious treat, whether you choose dark purple, yellowy green or green-skinned varieties. When they are ripe, you can split them open with your fingers to reveal the soft, sweet flesh full of edible seeds.

> **Variations**
> • Any thinly sliced cured ham can be used instead of prosciutto: Westphalian, Bayonne, Culatello or Serrano.
> • The figs could be replaced with fresh pears. Slice two ripe but firm dessert pears in quarters and remove the cores. Toss in olive oil and cook on a hot ridged grill or griddle pan for 2 minutes on each side. Drizzle balsamic vinegar over and cook for 1 minute more until nicely coloured.

Melon Salad Energy 147kcal/614kJ; Protein 9.2g; Carbohydrate 12.2g, of which sugars 12.2g; Fat 7.1g, of which saturates 1.2g; Cholesterol 25mg; Calcium 29mg; Fibre 1.1g; Sodium 568mg.
Figs with Prosciutto Energy 326kcal/1378kJ; Protein 10.7g; Carbohydrate 57.4g, of which sugars 57.4g; Fat 7.5g, of which saturates 3.8g; Cholesterol 25mg; Calcium 324mg; Fibre 6.9g; Sodium 512mg.

Carpaccio with Rocket

Invented in Venice, carpaccio is named in honour of the Renaissance painter. In this sophisticated Italian dish, raw beef is lightly dressed with lemon juice and olive oil, and it is traditionally served with shavings of Parmesan cheese. Use very fresh meat of the best quality and ask the butcher to slice it very thinly.

Serves 4

I garlic clove, peeled and
    cut in half
1½ lemons
50ml/2fl oz/¼ cup extra virgin
    olive oil
2 bunches rocket (arugula)
4 very thin slices of beef fillet
115g/4oz Parmesan
    cheese, shaved
salt and ground black pepper

1 Rub the cut side of the garlic over the inside of a bowl. Squeeze the lemons into the bowl, then whisk in the olive oil. Season with salt and ground black pepper, then leave to stand for at least 15 minutes.

2 Carefully wash the bunches of rocket and tear off any thick stalks. Spin dry or pat dry with kitchen paper. Arrange the rocket around the edge of a large serving platter or divide it among four individual plates.

3 Place the sliced beef in the centre of the platter and pour the dressing over, ensuring that the meat gets an even covering.

4 Arrange the Parmesan shavings on top of the meat slices and serve immediately.

Variation
You can also serve meaty fish, such as tuna, in the same way if you have festive guests who eat fish but not meat. Place a fresh tuna steak between sheets of clear film (plastic wrap) and pound with a rolling pin to flatten. Roll it up tightly and wrap in clear film. Place in the freezer for 4 hours until firm. Unwrap the fish and cut the fish crossways into slices as thin as possible. Serve in the same way as the beef carpaccio.

Steak Tartare on Toast

Steak tartare is delicious used to top toast or spread on a baguette for a festive appetizer. The key to a successful and, above all, safe steak tartare is to use only ultra-fresh beef of superior quality, and to chop it only at the very last minute.

Serves 4

2 fresh egg yolks
15ml/1 tbsp Dijon mustard
15ml/1 tbsp tomato ketchup
10ml/2 tsp Worcestershire sauce
Tabasco sauce, to taste
75ml/5 tbsp vegetable oil
2 shallots, finely chopped

30ml/2 tbsp capers, rinsed
6 cornichons (small pickled
    gherkins), finely chopped
30ml/2 tbsp finely chopped parsley
500g/1¼lb fresh sirloin steak,
    finely minced (ground) or
    finely chopped
4 slices good quality white bread,
    toasted, crusts removed
15g/½oz/1 tbsp
    unsalted butter
salt and ground black pepper

For the garnish

4 lettuce leaves
16 tomato slices
4 cornichons
4 fresh parsley sprigs

1 Place the egg yolks in a large stainless steel bowl. Add the mustard. With a wire whisk, mix in the ketchup, Worcestershire sauce and Tabasco, with a little salt and pepper. Slowly whisk in the oil until the mixture is smooth. Fold in the shallots, capers, cornichons and the chopped parsley.

2 Add the chopped or minced (ground) raw meat to the bowl and mix well, using a spoon or clean hands. Shape into four patties by hand or use a small round mould.

3 Spread the toasted bread with the butter. Place a patty of the steak tartare on each slice of toast and press it down to cover the surface of the toast evenly.

4 Using a paring knife, score diamond shapes into the meat. Garnish four plates with lettuce leaves and top with the toast. Place four tomato slices alongside. Slice each cornichon lengthways, keeping one end intact, then fan the slices out. Place one fan on each slice of toast and garnish with a fresh parsley sprig. Serve immediately.

Carpaccio Energy 244kcal/1013kJ; Protein 17.3g; Carbohydrate 0.1g, of which sugars 0.1g; Fat 19.4g, of which saturates 7.9g; Cholesterol 44mg; Calcium 384mg; Fibre 0.4g; Sodium 336mg.
Steak Tartare Energy 538kcal/2237kJ; Protein 29.7g; Carbohydrate 20.4g, of which sugars 5.5g; Fat 38.3g, of which saturates 12.7g; Cholesterol 184mg; Calcium 84mg; Fibre 1.5g; Sodium 318mg.

Guacamole

Serve this classic Mexican dip at a festive party. Nachos or tortilla chips are the perfect accompaniment.

Serves 4

2 ripe avocados
2 fresh red chillies, seeded
1 garlic clove
1 shallot
30ml/2 tbsp olive oil, plus
    extra to serve
juice of 1 lemon
salt
5ml/1 tsp flat leaf parsley leaves,
    to garnish

1 Halve the avocados, remove their stones (pits) and, using a spoon, scoop out their flesh into a bowl.

2 Mash the flesh well with a potato masher or a large fork until it is slightly coarse.

3 Finely chop the fresh red chillies, garlic and shallot, then stir into the mashed avocado. Drizzle in the olive oil and lemon juice and mix well. Add salt to taste.

4 Spoon the mixture into a small serving bowl. Drizzle over a little olive oil and sprinkle with a few flat leaf parsley leaves. Serve immediately with tortilla chips for dipping.

Cook's Tip
• Avocado flesh will discolour quickly when exposed to the air. If preparing this in advance for a Christmas party, ensure that it is tightly covered with clear film (plastic wrap).
• Ripe avocados will yield slightly when squeezed on the ends. To speed up the ripening process, place avocados in a paper bag and set them aside at room temperature.

Variation
Make a completely smooth guacamole by whizzing the ingredients in a blender or food processor. For a chunkier version, add a diced tomato or red (bell) pepper.

Tsatziki

Cool, creamy and refreshing, tzatziki is wonderfully easy to make and even easier to eat. Serve this classic Greek dip with slices of toasted pitta bread as part of a festive buffet spread, as a healthy appetizer or with a selection of chargrilled vegetables.

Serves 4

1 mini cucumber
4 spring onions (scallions)
1 garlic clove
200ml/7fl oz/scant 1 cup Greek
    (US strained plain) yogurt
45ml/3 tbsp chopped fresh mint
fresh mint sprig, to garnish
    (optional)
salt and ground black pepper

1 Trim the ends from the mini cucumber, then cut the flesh into dice about 5mm/¼in in size.

2 Cut the ends from the spring onions, keeping plenty of the green parts, and the garlic, then chop both very finely.

3 Beat the yogurt until smooth, if necessary, then gently stir in the cucumber, onions, garlic and mint.

4 Transfer the mixture to a serving bowl and add salt and plenty of ground black pepper to taste. Chill until ready to serve and then garnish with a small mint sprig, if you like.

Cook's Tip
Choose Greek (US strained plain) yogurt for this dip – it has a higher fat content than most yogurts, which gives the tsatziki a deliciously rich, creamy texture.

Variation
A similar, but smoother, dip can be made in the food processor. Peel one mini cucumber and process with two garlic cloves and 75g/3oz/3 cups mixed fresh herbs to a purée. Stir the purée into 200ml/7fl oz/scant 1 cup sour cream, and season to taste with salt and ground black pepper.

Guacamole Energy 156kcal/645kJ; Protein 2.1g; Carbohydrate 3.7g, of which sugars 2.5g; Fat 14.7g, of which saturates 3.1g; Cholesterol 0mg; Calcium 26mg; Fibre 3.5g; Sodium 11mg.
Tsatziki Energy 67kcal/279kJ; Protein 4g; Carbohydrate 2.3g, of which sugars 1.6g; Fat 5.3g, of which saturates 2.6g; Cholesterol 0mg; Calcium 107mg; Fibre 0.3g; Sodium 39mg.

Hummus

This nutritious dip is great served as a dip with crudités at a festive party or spread over hot toast.

Serves 4
400g/14oz can chickpeas, drained
2 garlic cloves

30ml/2 tbsp tahini or smooth
   peanut butter
60ml/4 tbsp olive oil
juice of 1 lemon
2.5ml/½ tsp cayenne pepper
15ml/1 tbsp sesame seeds
sea salt

1 Rinse the chickpeas well and place in a food processor or blender with the garlic and a good pinch of sea salt. Process until very finely chopped.

2 Add the tahini or smooth peanut butter and process until fairly smooth. With the motor still running, slowly pour in the olive oil and the lemon juice.

3 Stir in the cayenne pepper and add more salt, to taste, if necessary. If the mixture is too thick, stir in a little cold water. Transfer the purée to a serving bowl.

4 Heat a small non-stick pan and add the sesame seeds. Cook for 2–3 minutes, shaking the pan, until the seeds are golden. Allow to cool, then sprinkle over the purée. Serve immediately on toasted bread or with crudités.

Cook's Tip
Tahini is a classic ingredient in this Middle Eastern dip. It is a thick, smooth and oily paste, which is made from sesame seeds. It is usually available from health food stores and large supermarkets, in light and dark varieties.

Variation
The peanut butter would not be used in a traditional recipe but it is a useful substitute if tahini is not available.

Saucy Tomato Dip

This versatile dip is delicious and can be made up to a day in advance, so is ideal for serving at a Christmas drinks party.

Serves 4
1 shallot
2 garlic cloves

handful of fresh basil leaves,
   plus extra to garnish
500g/1¼lb ripe tomatoes
30ml/2 tbsp olive oil
2 fresh green chillies, halved and
   seeds removed
salt and ground black pepper

1 Peel and halve the shallot and garlic cloves. Place in a blender or food processor with the basil leaves, then process the ingredients until they are very finely chopped.

2 Halve the tomatoes and add to the shallot mixture. Pulse the power until the mixture is well blended and all the tomatoes are finely chopped.

3 With the motor still running, slowly pour in the olive oil. Add salt and black pepper to taste.

4 Finely slice the fresh green chillies into tiny strips and stir them into the tomato mixture. Serve at room temperature. Garnish with a few torn basil leaves.

Cook's Tip
You may need to wear a pair of kitchen gloves while preparing chillies or cut them up with a knife and fork if you find that they irritate your skin. Wash your hands in warm, soapy water after preparing the chillies.

Variation
This dip is best made with full-flavoured, sun-ripened tomatoes. Over the festive period, when tomatoes are out of season, you can use a drained 400g/14oz can of plum tomatoes instead.

Hummus Energy 210kcal/880kj; Protein 10.3g; Carbohydrate 16.9g; of which sugars 0.6g; Fat 11.8g; of which saturates 1.6g; Cholesterol 0mg; Calcium 146mg; Fibre 5.5g; Sodium 223mg.
Saucy Tomato Dip Energy 81kcal/336kJ; Protein 2.3g; Carbohydrate 4.2g, of which sugars 4.2g; Fat 6.2g, of which saturates 0.9g; Cholesterol 0mg; Calcium 24mg; Fibre 1.3g; Sodium 15mg.

Taramasalata

This delicious speciality makes an excellent start to any meal, or to serve at a festive party, accompanied by fruity black olives and slices of warm pitta bread. This dip is a central part of any Greek meze table, and home-made taramasalata is incomparably better than the ready-made versions sold in supermarkets.

Serves 4
115g/4oz smoked mullet roe
2 garlic cloves, crushed
30ml/2 tbsp grated onion
60ml/4 tbsp olive oil
4 slices white bread,
    crusts removed
juice of 2 lemons
30ml/2 tbsp milk or water
ground black pepper
warm pitta bread, to serve

1 Place the smoked fish roe, crushed garlic, grated onion, oil, bread and lemon juice in a blender or food processor and process until the mixture is smooth.

2 Scrape down the edges of the food processor or blender to ensure that all the ingredients are properly incorporated. Blend the mixture quickly once more.

3 Add the milk or water and process again for a few seconds. (This will give the taramasalata a creamier texture.)

4 Pour the taramasalata into a serving bowl, cover with clear film (plastic wrap) and chill in the refrigerator for 1–2 hours before serving. Sprinkle the dip with ground black pepper and serve with warm pitta bread.

> **Cook's Tip**
> The smoked roe of grey mullet is traditionally used for taramasalata, but it is expensive and can be difficult to obtain. Smoked cod's roe is often used instead to make this dish. It varies in colour and may be paler than the burnt-orange colour of mullet roe, but is still very good. When buying smoked cod's roe, make sure that it is not overcooked as this makes it hard and prevents it blending well.

Blue Cheese Dip

This dip can be mixed up in next to no time and is delicious served with pears. Add more yogurt to make a great dressing. It is a great way to make use of the traditional block of Stilton that appears in many kitchens at Christmas time.

Serves 4
150g/5oz blue cheese, such
    as Stilton, Roquefort or
    Danish Blue
150g/5oz/⅔ cup soft white
    (farmer's) cheese
75ml/5 tbsp Greek (US strained
    plain) yogurt
salt and ground black pepper

1 Crumble the blue cheese into a bowl. Using a wooden spoon, beat the cheese to soften it.

2 Add the soft cheese to the bowl and beat well to blend the two cheeses together.

3 Gradually beat in the Greek-style yogurt, adding enough to give you the consistency you prefer.

4 Season the dip with lots of ground black pepper and a little salt. Chill until ready to serve, taking it out of the refrigerator about 15 minutes before serving.

> **Cook's Tip**
> The thinner salad-dressing version of this dip is made by adding a little more yogurt, and is the classic accompaniment to Buffalo wings. These deep-fried chicken wings are named after the city of Buffalo in the state of New York in the USA. There they will invariably come with a bowl of blue cheese dressing on the side for dipping the wings.

> **Variation**
> This is a very thick dip to which you can add a little more Greek-style yogurt, or you can stir in a little milk, for a softer consistency, if you prefer.

Blue Cheese Dip Energy 267kcal/1106kJ; Protein 12.1g; Carbohydrate 0.4g, of which sugars 0.4g; Fat 24.4g, of which saturates 15.4g; Cholesterol 62mg; Calcium 253mg; Fibre 0g; Sodium 595mg.
Taramasalata Energy 185kcal/770kJ; Protein 8.4g; Carbohydrate 11.4g, of which sugars 1.7g; Fat 12.1g, of which saturates 1.8g; Cholesterol 95mg; Calcium 38mg; Fibre 0.5g; Sodium 139mg.

Butternut Squash and Parmesan Dip

Butternut squash has a rich, nutty flavour and tastes especially good when roasted, as in this recipe. Serve this dip accompanied by Melba toast or cheese straws alongside drinks at a Christmas cocktail party or family gathering.

Serves 4
1 butternut squash
15g/½oz/1 tbsp butter
4 garlic cloves, unpeeled
30ml/2 tbsp freshly grated
   Parmesan cheese
45–75ml/3–5 tbsp double
   (heavy) cream
salt and ground black pepper

1 Preheat the oven to 200°C/400°F/Gas 6. Halve the squash lengthways, then scoop out and discard the seeds.

2 Use a small, sharp knife to deeply score the flesh in a criss-cross pattern: cut as close to the skin as possible, but take care not to cut all the way through it.

3 Arrange both halves in a small roasting pan and dot with the butter. Sprinkle with salt and pepper and roast for 20 minutes.

4 Tuck the unpeeled garlic cloves around the squash in the roasting pan and continue baking in the oven for 20 minutes, until the pumpkin squash is tender and softened.

5 Scoop the flesh out of the squash shells and place it in a blender or food processor. Slip the garlic cloves out of their skins and add to the squash. Process until smooth.

6 With the motor running, add all but 15ml/1 tsp of the Parmesan cheese and then the cream. Check the seasoning and spoon the dip into a serving bowl: it is at its best served warm. Sprinkle the reserved cheese over the dip.

> **Cook's Tip**
> If you don't have a blender or food processor, simply mash the squash in a bowl using a potato masher, then beat in the grated cheese and cream using a wooden spoon.

Red Onion Raita

Raita is a traditional Indian accompaniment for hot curries. It is also delicious served with poppadums or crudités as a dip.

Serves 4
5ml/1 tsp cumin seeds
1 small garlic clove

1 large red onion
1 small green chilli
150ml/¼ pint/⅔ cup natural
   (plain) yogurt
30ml/2 tbsp chopped fresh
   coriander (cilantro), plus extra,
   to garnish
2.5ml/½ tsp sugar
salt

1 Heat a small pan and dry-fry the cumin seeds for about 1–2 minutes, until they release their aroma and begin to pop.

2 Lightly crush the seeds in a mortar and pestle or flatten them with the heel of a heavy-bladed knife.

3 Finely chop the garlic and red onion and add to the yogurt. Halve the green chilli, remove the seeds, then finely chop the flesh. Stir into the yogurt with the cumin seeds and coriander.

4 Add sugar and salt to taste to the raita. Spoon it into a small serving bowl and chill in the refrigerator until ready to serve. Garnish with extra coriander before serving.

> **Cook's Tip**
> For an extra tangy raita, stir in 15ml/1 tbsp lemon juice.
> To make a pretty garnish, reserve a few thin wedges of onion, before chopping the rest.

> **Variations**
> • Instead of using red onion in this raita, use two skinned, seeded and chopped tomatoes and about 15ml/1 tbsp of chopped fresh coriander (cilantro).
> • If you prefer, the red onion can be grated, rather than chopped, before adding to the yogurt.

Butternut Squash Energy 145kcal/602kJ; Protein 4.7g; Carbohydrate 4.9g, of which sugars 3.8g; Fat 12g, of which saturates 7.5g; Cholesterol 31mg; Calcium 158mg; Fibre 2.1g; Sodium 107mg.
Red Onion Raita Energy 32kcal/134kJ; Protein 2.6g; Carbohydrate 4.6g, of which sugars 4g; Fat 0.6g, of which saturates 0.2g; Cholesterol 1mg; Calcium 100mg; Fibre 0.9g; Sodium 36mg.

Mellow Garlic Dip

Two whole heads of garlic may seem like a lot but, once cooked, it becomes sweet and mellow. Serve with crunchy bread sticks and crudités as part of a festive buffet spread or with drinks at a party.

Serves 4

2 whole garlic heads
15ml/1 tbsp olive oil
60ml/4 tbsp mayonnaise
75ml/5 tbsp Greek (US strained plain) yogurt
5ml/1 tsp wholegrain mustard
salt and ground black pepper

1 Preheat the oven to 200°C/400°F/Gas 6. Separate the garlic cloves and place them in a small roasting pan.

2 Pour the olive oil over the garlic cloves and turn them with a spoon to coat them evenly. Roast for 20–30 minutes, until the garlic is tender and softened. Leave to cool for 5 minutes.

3 Trim off the root end of each roasted garlic clove. Peel the cloves and discard the skins.

4 Place the roasted garlic on a chopping board and sprinkle with salt. Mash with a fork until puréed.

5 Place the garlic in a small bowl and stir in the mayonnaise, yogurt and wholegrain mustard. Check and adjust the seasoning, then spoon the dip into a bowl. Cover the bowl and chill until ready to serve.

> **Cook's Tip**
> *Outside of the festive period, you can cook the garlic on a barbecue. Leave the garlic heads whole and cook them on the hot barbecue until tender, then peel and mash.*

> **Variation**
> *For a low fat version of this dip, use reduced-fat mayonnaise and low-fat natural (plain) yogurt.*

Spiced Carrot Dip

This is a delicious low-fat dip with a sweet and spicy flavour. Serve it over the festive period as a healthy snack if you are suffering from over-indulgence.

Serves 4
1 onion
3 carrots, plus extra, to garnish

grated rind and juice of 2 oranges
15ml/1 tbsp hot curry paste
150ml/1/4 pint/2/3 cup low-fat natural (plain) yogurt
handful of fresh basil leaves
15–30ml/1–2 tbsp fresh lemon juice, to taste
red Tabasco sauce or hot chilli sauce, to taste
salt and ground black pepper

1 Finely chop the onion. Peel and grate the carrots. Place the onion, carrots, orange rind and juice and curry paste in a small pan. Bring the mixture to the boil, cover and simmer for about 10 minutes, until tender.

2 Process the mixture in a blender or food processor until smooth. Leave to cool completely.

3 Stir in the yogurt, then tear the basil leaves into small pieces and stir them into the carrot mixture.

4 Add the lemon juice, Tabasco, salt and pepper to taste. Serve within a few hours at room temperature. Garnish with grated carrot and serve with your favourite accompaniments.

> **Cook's Tip**
> *Serve this versatile dip as an appetizer on its own with wheat crackers or fiery tortilla chips, or with a variety of raw vegetables for a healthy snack.*

> **Variation**
> *Greek (US strained plain) yogurt or sour cream may be used in place of the natural (plain) yogurt to make a richer, creamier dip, if you prefer.*

Mellow Garlic Dip Energy 179kcal/741kJ; Protein 3.6g; Carbohydrate 4.9g, of which sugars 1.1g; Fat 16.5g, of which saturates 3.1g; Cholesterol 11mg; Calcium 38mg; Fibre 1.2g; Sodium 139mg.
Spiced Carrot Dip Energy 70kcal/294kJ; Protein 3.1g; Carbohydrate 11.1g, of which sugars 9.4g; Fat 1.9g, of which saturates 0.4g; Cholesterol 1mg; Calcium 130mg; Fibre 3.2g; Sodium 69mg.

Hoisin Dip

This dip needs no cooking and can be made in a few minutes – it is great served with spring rolls or prawn crackers for festive nibbles.

Serves 4

4 spring onions (scallions)
4cm/1½in piece fresh root ginger
2 fresh red chillies
2 garlic cloves
60ml/4 tbsp hoisin sauce
120ml/4fl oz/½ cup passata
   (bottled strained tomatoes)
5ml/1 tsp sesame or
   groundnut (peanut)
   oil (optional)

1 Trim off and discard the green ends of the spring onions. Slice the remainder very thinly.

2 Peel the fresh root ginger with a vegetable peeler, then chop it finely.

3 Halve the chillies lengthways, remove their seeds and discard. Finely slice the flesh widthways into tiny strips. Finely chop the garlic.

4 In a mixing bowl, stir together the hoisin sauce, passata, spring onions, ginger, chilli, garlic and sesame or groundnut oil, if using, and serve within 1 hour.

Cook's Tips
• Hoisin sauce makes an excellent base for full-flavour dips and sauces, especially when combining crunchy vegetables and other Chinese seasonings.
• Chillies can irritate the skin so ensure you wash your hands in hot soapy water after handling, and be careful not to touch sensitive parts of the body such as the eyes.

Variation
If you don't have any fresh chillies to hand, you can add heat to the dip with hot chilli sauce or Tabasco sauce.

Fat-free Saffron Dip

Serve this mild dip with fresh vegetable crudités. It is particularly good with florets of cauliflower.

Serves 4

15ml/1 tbsp boiling water
small pinch of saffron strands
200g/7oz/scant 1 cup fat-free
   fromage frais or fat-free
   cream cheese
10 fresh chives
10 fresh basil leaves
salt and ground black pepper

1 Pour the boiling water into a small container and add the saffron strands. Leave to infuse (steep) for 3 minutes.

2 Place the fromage frais or cream cheese in a mixing bowl. Beat the mixture until smooth, then add the infused saffron liquid and stir well to combine.

3 Use a pair of scissors to chop the chives into the dip. Tear the basil leaves into small pieces and stir them in.

4 Add salt and ground black pepper to taste. Serve the dip immediately, or cover tightly with clear film (plastic wrap) and chill in the refrigerator until needed.

Cook's Tip
Saffron is the yellow-orange stigmas from a small purple crocus. It is the most expensive spice in the world because each flower provides only three stigmas, which have to be hand-picked and then dried. It takes a great deal of intensive labour and over 14,000 of these tiny stigmas for each 25g/1oz of saffron. Thankfully, only a small amount is needed in this recipe – but what better way to luxuriate over the festive

---

Variation
Omit the saffron and add a squeeze of lemon or lime juice instead, if you prefer.

Oriental Hoisin Dip Energy 29kcal/123kJ; Protein 1.3g; Carbohydrate 6g, of which sugars 5.4g; Fat 0.2g, of which saturates 0g; Cholesterol 0mg; Calcium 13mg; Fibre 0.6g; Sodium 315mg.
Fat-free Saffron Dip Energy 29kcal/124kJ; Protein 3.8g; Carbohydrate 3.2g, of which sugars 2.7g; Fat 0.3g, of which saturates 0.1g; Cholesterol 1mg; Calcium 69mg; Fibre 0.8g; Sodium 21mg.

Corn Tostaditas with Salsa

This is just the right snack to keep hungry guests from feeling the effects of too many Christmas drinks. It is best if you make the tostaditas using a griddle either on the barbecue – weather permitting – or on the stovetop.

Serves 6
30ml/2 tbsp chilli oil
15ml/1 tbsp sunflower oil
8 yellow corn tortillas, total weight about 300g/11oz

For the salsa
4 tomatoes, seeded and diced
30ml/2 tbsp chopped fresh basil
juice of ½ lime
20ml/4 tsp good-quality sweet chilli sauce
1 small red onion, finely chopped (optional)
salt and ground black pepper

For the guacamole
4 avocados
juice of ½ lime
1 fresh fat mild chilli, seeded and finely chopped

1 Make the salsa one or two hours ahead if possible, to allow the flavours to blend. Mix the diced tomatoes with the chopped basil, lime juice and sweet chilli sauce. Stir in the onion, if using, then add salt and pepper to taste.

2 Make the guacamole. Cut the avocados in half, prise out the stones (pits), then scoop the flesh into a bowl. Add the lime juice, chilli and seasoning. Mash to a fairly rough texture.

3 Prepare the barbecue. Mix the oils together. Brush the tortillas lightly with the oil mixture on both sides. Repeat with the remaining tortillas, to make a stack. Slice the whole stack diagonally into six fat pointed triangles.

4 When the barbecue is ready, heat a griddle on the grill rack (or on the stovetop) until a few drops of water sprinkled on to the surface evaporate instantly. Cook a few tostaditas at a time for 30 seconds each side, pressing down for good contact with the surface of the griddle.

5 Transfer them to a bowl, so that they are supported by its sides. As they cool, they will shape themselves to the curve of the bowl. Serve with the salsa and guacamole.

Pepitas

These crunchy, spicy and slightly sweet pumpkin seeds are absolutely irresistible, especially if you use hot and tasty chipotle chillies to spice them up. Serve bowls of pepitas with Christmas drinks as an alternative to nuts.

Serves 4–6
250g/9oz/2 cups pumpkin seeds
8 garlic cloves, crushed
2.5ml/½ tsp salt
20ml/4 tsp dried chillies, finely crushed
10ml/2 tsp caster (superfine) sugar
2 wedges of lime (optional)

1 Heat a small, heavy frying pan, add the pumpkin seeds and dry-fry for a few minutes, stirring constantly as they swell.

2 When all the seeds have swollen, add the garlic and cook for a few minutes more, stirring constantly. Add the salt and the crushed chillies and stir to mix. Turn off the heat, but keep the pan on the stove. Sprinkle the sugar over the seeds and shake the pan to make sure that they are all coated.

3 Transfer the pepitas into a bowl and serve with the wedges of lime for squeezing over the seeds. If the lime is omitted, the seeds can be set aside to cool and stored in an airtight container for serving cold or reheating later, but they are best served while still fresh and warm.

> **Cook's Tips**
> • It is important to keep the pumpkin seeds moving as they cook. Watch them carefully and do not allow them to burn, otherwise they will taste bitter.
> • Chipotle chillies are smoke-dried jalapeño chillies.

> **Variation**
> If you are serving the pepitas cold, they can be mixed with cashew nuts and dried cranberries to make a spicy and fruity bowl of festive nibbles.

Pepitas Energy 299kcal/1242kJ; Protein 10.3g; Carbohydrate 11.2g, of which sugars 2g; Fat 23.8g, of which saturates 2.3g; Cholesterol 0mg; Calcium 57mg; Fibre 3.2g; Sodium 2mg.
Corn Tostaditas Energy 334kcal/1396kJ; Protein 5.6g; Carbohydrate 36.8g, of which sugars 6.3g; Fat 19.1g, of which saturates 3.6g; Cholesterol 0mg; Calcium 71mg; Fibre 4.4g; Sodium 313mg.

Tapas of Almonds, Olives and Cheese

Serving a few choice nibbles with drinks is the perfect way to get a Christmas evening off to a good start, and when you can get everything ready ahead, life's a lot easier.

Serves 6–8

For the marinated olives
2.5ml/½ tsp coriander seeds
2.5ml/½ tsp fennel seeds
2 garlic cloves, crushed
5ml/1 tsp chopped fresh rosemary
10ml/2 tsp chopped fresh parsley
15ml/1 tbsp sherry vinegar
30ml/2 tbsp olive oil
115g/4oz/⅔ cup black olives
115g/4oz/⅔ cup green olives

For the marinated cheese
150g/5oz goat's cheese
90ml/6 tbsp olive oil
15ml/1 tbsp white wine vinegar
5ml/1 tsp black peppercorns
1 garlic clove, sliced
3 fresh tarragon or thyme sprigs
tarragon sprigs, to garnish

For the salted almonds
1.5ml/¼ tsp cayenne pepper
30ml/2 tbsp sea salt
25g/1oz/2 tbsp butter
60ml/4 tbsp olive oil
200g/7oz/1¾ cups
    blanched almonds
extra sea salt for sprinkling
    (optional)

1 To make the marinated olives, crush the coriander and fennel seeds in a mortar with a pestle. Work in the garlic, then add the rosemary, parsley, vinegar and olive oil. Mix well. Put the olives in a small bowl and pour over the marinade. Cover with clear film (plastic wrap) and chill for up to 1 week.

2 To make the marinated cheese, cut the goat's cheese into bitesize pieces, removing any rind, and place the pieces in a small bowl. Combine the oil, vinegar, peppercorns, garlic, tarragon or thyme and pour over the cheese. Cover with clear film and chill for up to 3 days.

3 To make the salted almonds, combine the cayenne pepper and salt in a bowl. Melt the butter with the oil in a frying pan. Add the almonds and fry them, stirring, for 5 minutes. Transfer the almonds into the salt mixture in the bowl and toss until they are evenly coated. Leave to cool, then store in an airtight container for up to 1 week. Serve the almonds, olives and cheese in separate dishes.

Mini Cocktail Savouries

Tiny savoury crackers always make lovely party snacks. Try making them in a range of festive shapes for Christmas, and flavour them with various cheeses.

Makes 80
350g/12oz/3 cups plain
    (all-purpose) flour, plus
    extra for dusting
pinch of salt

2.5ml/½ tsp ground black pepper
5ml/1 tsp wholegrain mustard
175g/6oz/¾ cup unsalted
    butter, diced
115g/4oz/1 cup grated
    Cheddar cheese
1 egg, beaten
5ml/1 tsp chopped nuts
10ml/2 tsp dill seeds
10ml/2 tsp curry paste
10ml/2 tsp chilli sauce

1 Line several large baking trays with sheets of baking parchment and set them aside.

2 Sift the flour into a large mixing bowl and add the salt, pepper and wholegrain mustard. Mix well.

3 Add the butter and rub it in with your fingertips until the mixture resembles fine breadcrumbs. Stir in the cheese with a fork until it is thoroughly incorporated. Add the egg and mix together to form a soft dough.

4 Turn out the dough on to a floured surface, knead lightly until smooth, then divide it into four equal pieces.

5 Knead chopped nuts into one piece, dill seeds into another, and curry paste and chilli sauce into the remaining pieces. Wrap each piece in clear film (plastic wrap) and chill for 1 hour.

6 Preheat the oven to 200°C/400°F/Gas 6. Roll out each piece of dough in turn. Use a floured pastry (cookie) cutter to stamp out about 20 shapes from the curry-flavoured dough. Use a different cutter to cut out the chilli-flavoured dough. Repeat with the remaining dough.

7 Arrange the shapes on the baking sheets and bake for about 6–8 minutes, until pale gold. Cool on wire racks.

Tapas Energy 432kcal/1784kJ; Protein 10.3g; Carbohydrate 1.8g, of which sugars 1.1g; Fat 42.3g, of which saturates 9.7g; Cholesterol 25mg; Calcium 217mg; Fibre 2.7g; Sodium 805mg.
Cocktail Savouries Energy 39kcal/162kJ; Protein 0.9g; Carbohydrate 3.5g, of which sugars 0.1g; Fat 2.4g, of which saturates 1.5g; Cholesterol 8mg; Calcium 18mg; Fibre 0.1g; Sodium 25mg.

Cheeselets

These crispy cheese biscuits are irresistible, and will disappear in moments if you serve them with Christmas drinks. They also make a lovely festive gift to take to a party.

Makes 80

115g/4oz/1 cup plain (all-purpose) flour

2.5ml/½ tsp salt
2.5ml/½ tsp cayenne pepper
2.5ml/1½ tsp dry mustard
115g/4oz/½ cup butter
50g/2oz/½ cup grated
    Cheddar cheese
50g/2oz/½ cup grated
    Gruyère cheese
1 egg white, beaten
15g/1 tbsp sesame seeds

1 Preheat the oven to 220°C/425°F/Gas 7. Line several baking sheets with baking parchment. Sift the flour, salt, cayenne pepper and mustard into a mixing bowl. Cut the butter into pieces and rub into the flour mixture.

2 Divide the mixture in half, add the Cheddar cheese to one half and the Gruyère cheese to the other. Using a fork or your fingertips, work each mixture into a soft dough and knead on a floured surface until smooth.

3 Roll out both pieces of dough very thinly and cut it into 2.5cm/1in squares. Transfer the squares to the lined baking sheets. Brush them with the beaten egg white, sprinkle with sesame seeds and bake for about 5–6 minutes or until slightly puffed up and pale gold in colour.

4 Cool the cheeselets on the baking sheets, then carefully remove with a metal spatula. Repeat the process until you have used up all the dough. Pack the cheeselets in airtight tins or present as a gift, packed in attractive gift boxes and tied with colourful festive ribbon and bows.

> **Variation**
> *Try using different cheeses sprinkled with a variety of seeds to give alternative flavours to these cheese bites.*

Olive and Anchovy Bites

These little melt-in-the-mouth morsels are very moreish, and make perfect accompaniments for festive drinks. They are made from two ingredients that feature in many recipes for party nibbles – olives and anchovies. The reason for this association is that both ingredients contain plenty of salt, which helps to stimulate thirst and so causes more drinking.

Makes 40–45

115g/4oz/1 cup plain (all-purpose) flour
115g/4oz/½ cup chilled butter, diced
115g/4oz/1 cup finely grated mature (sharp) Cheddar or Gruyère cheese
50g/2oz can anchovy fillets in oil, drained and roughly chopped
50g/2oz/½ cup pitted black olives, roughly chopped
2.5ml/½ tsp cayenne pepper
sea salt, to serve

1 Place the flour, butter, cheese, anchovies, olives and cayenne pepper in a food processor and process to a firm dough.

2 Wrap the dough loosely in a piece of clear film (plastic wrap). Chill for 20 minutes.

3 Preheat the oven to 200°C/400°F/Gas 6. Roll out the dough thinly on a lightly floured surface.

4 Cut the dough into 5cm/2in wide strips, then cut across each strip in alternate directions, to make triangles. Transfer to baking sheets and bake for 8–10 minutes until golden. Cool on a wire rack. Sprinkle with sea salt before serving.

> **Variations**
> *• To add a little extra spice, dust the olive and anchovy bites lightly with cayenne pepper before baking.*
> *• Crisp little nibbles set off most drinks. Serve these bites alongside little bowls of seeds and nuts, such as sunflower seeds and pistachios. These come in the shell, the opening of which provides a diversion while chatting and gossiping. Toasted chickpeas are another popular party snack.*

Cheeselets Energy 22kcal/93kJ; Protein 0.6g; Carbohydrate 1.2g, of which sugars 0g; Fat 1.7g, of which saturates 1g; Cholesterol 4mg; Calcium 13mg; Fibre 0.1g; Sodium 19mg.
Olive Bites Energy 145Kcal/602kJ; Protein 4.7g; Carbohydrate 6.3g, of which sugars 0.6g; Fat 11.4g, of which saturates 7.4g; Cholesterol 33mg; Calcium 108mg; Fibre 0.4g; Sodium 407mg.

Poppy Seed and Sea Salt Crackers

These little crackers are ideal as the base for Christmas party canapés, or they can be served plain as tasty festive snacks in their own right.

Makes 20
115g/4oz/1 cup plain
    (all-purpose) flour, plus
    extra for dusting
pinch of salt
5ml/1 tsp caster
    (superfine) sugar
15g/½oz/1 tbsp butter
15ml/1 tbsp poppy seeds
about 90ml/6 tbsp single
    (light) cream
sea salt, for sprinkling

1 Preheat the oven to 150°C/300°F/Gas Mark 2. In a large mixing bowl, sift together the flour, salt and sugar. Add the butter and rub in with your fingertips until the mixture resembles fine breadcrumbs.

2 Stir the poppy seeds into the mixture. Add just enough single cream to form a stiff dough.

3 Turn the dough on to a lightly floured surface and roll out to a 20 × 25cm/8 × 10in rectangle. Cut the dough into 20 squares with a sharp knife.

4 Put the crackers on to one or two ungreased baking sheets and brush the tops lightly with milk. Sprinkle a few flakes of the sea salt over each cracker.

5 Bake for about 30 minutes, or until crisp but still quite pale. Using a metal spatula, carefully transfer the crackers to a wire rack and leave to cool completely.

> **Variations**
> • You can substitute white poppy seeds for the black ones used here or use a mixture of the two.
> • Vary the flavour of these crackers by using other small seeds: for example, celery seeds for sharpness, caraway for piquancy or sesame for a slight sweetness.

Festive Cheese Nibbles

You can shape these spicy cheese snacks into festive designs if you wish. Serve them with drinks, from ice-cold cocktails to hot and spicy mulled wines.

Makes 60
115g/4oz/1 cup plain (all-purpose)
    flour, plus extra for dusting
5ml/1 tsp mustard powder
pinch of salt
115g/4oz/½ cup butter
75g/3oz/¾ cup Cheddar
    cheese, grated
pinch of cayenne pepper
30ml/2 tbsp water
1 egg, beaten
poppy seeds, sunflower seeds or
    sesame seeds, to decorate

1 Preheat the oven to 200°C/400°F/Gas 6. Lightly grease two baking sheets with oil.

2 Sift the flour, mustard powder and salt into a bowl and rub in the butter until the mixture resembles fine breadcrumbs.

3 Stir in the Cheddar cheese and cayenne pepper and sprinkle on the water. Add half the beaten egg, mix to a firm dough and knead lightly until smooth.

4 Roll out the dough on a lightly floured surface and cut out a variety of shapes. Re-roll the trimmings and cut more shapes until all the dough has been used up.

5 Place the shapes on the prepared baking sheets and brush with the remaining egg. Sprinkle on the seeds.

6 Bake in the oven for about 8–10 minutes, or until puffed up and evenly golden. Leave to cool on the baking tray for a few minutes before carefully removing to a wire rack with a metal spatula. Leave to cool completely before serving.

> **Cook's Tip**
> Serve these festive nibbles as they are with Christmas drinks, or you can add them to the cheeseboard at the end of the Christmas Day meal, if you prefer.

Poppy Seed Crackers Energy 39kcal/164kJ; Protein 0.8g; Carbohydrate 4.8g, of which sugars 0.4g; Fat 2g, of which saturates 1g; Cholesterol 4mg; Calcium 17mg; Fibre 0.2g; Sodium 6mg.
Festive Cheese Nibbles Energy 27kcal/113kJ; Protein 0.6g; Carbohydrate 1.5g, of which sugars 0g; Fat 2.1g, of which saturates 1.3g; Cholesterol 8mg; Calcium 13mg; Fibre 0.1g; Sodium 22mg.

Herby Seeded Oatcakes

These oatcakes are the ideal
accompaniment to cheese –
try them spread with goat's
cheese or with festive Stilton.

Makes 32
rolled oats, for sprinkling
175g/6oz/1½ cups wholemeal
(whole-wheat) flour, plus extra
for dusting

175g/6oz/1½ cups fine oatmeal
pinch of salt
1.5ml/¼ tsp bicarbonate of soda
(baking soda)
75g/3oz/6 tbsp white vegetable
fat (shortening)
15ml/1 tbsp fresh thyme
leaves, chopped
30ml/2 tbsp sunflower seeds

1 Preheat the oven to 150°C/300°F/Gas 2. Sprinkle two
ungreased, non-stick baking sheets with rolled oats. Set aside.

2 Put the flour, oatmeal, salt and bicarbonate of soda in a large
bowl and rub in the fat until the mixture resembles fine
breadcrumbs. Stir in the chopped fresh thyme.

3 Add just enough cold water (about 90–105ml/6–7 tbsp) to
the dry ingredients to mix to a stiff, but not sticky dough.

4 Gently knead the dough on a lightly floured surface until
smooth, then cut roughly in half and roll out one piece on a
lightly floured surface to make a 23–25cm/9–10in round.

5 Sprinkle sunflower seeds over the dough and press them in
with the rolling pin. Cut into triangles and arrange on one of the
baking sheets. Repeat with the remaining dough.

6 Bake in the preheated oven for 45–60 minutes, or until crisp
but not brown. Leave on the sheets for a minute to cool slightly,
then transfer to wire racks with a metal spatula. Leave them
to cool completely before serving.

Variation
These oatcakes are also great sprinkled with sesame seeds
or poppy seeds, if you prefer.

Rye and Caraway Seed Sticks

These crisp sticks are
wonderful with Christmas
cocktails at a party or with
pre-dinner drinks, and they
are a great addition to the
festive cheeseboard. They
are made with rye flour
and have deliciously
crunchy caraway seeds
inside and out.

Makes 18–20
90g/3½oz/generous ¾ cup plain
(all-purpose) flour
75g/3oz/¾ cup rye flour
pinch of salt
2.5ml/½ tsp baking powder
90g/3½oz/7 tbsp unsalted
(sweet) butter, diced
10ml/2 tsp caraway seeds
60ml/4 tbsp boiling water

1 Preheat the oven to 180°C/350°F/Gas 4. Put the flours, salt
and baking powder in a bowl and mix together. Add the butter
and rub it in gently with your fingertips until the mixture
resembles fine breadcrumbs.

2 Stir in 5ml/1 tsp of the caraway seeds. Add the water and
mix well to form a soft dough.

3 Divide the dough into about 18 even pieces and, using your
fingers, gently roll each one out to a long thin stick about
25cm/10in long. Do not use any flour when rolling out the
sticks unless the mixture is a little too moist. Try to make
the sticks as uniform as possible.

4 Place the sticks on a non-stick baking sheet. Sprinkle over the
remaining caraway seeds, rolling the sticks in any spilled seeds.

5 Bake the sticks in the oven for about 20 minutes, until crisp.
Remove from the oven and transfer carefully to a wire rack.
Leave to cool completely before serving.

Cook's Tip
Rye flour has a rich and distinctive flavour that complements
smoked fish. Try serving these sticks with a dip, such as
taramasalata or smoked fish pâté, as part of a festive buffet
table. They are also delicious served with a seafood soup.

Herby Seeded Oatcakes Energy 62kcal/259kJ; Protein 1.6g; Carbohydrate 7.7g, of which sugars 0.2g; Fat 3g, of which saturates 0.9g; Cholesterol 0mg; Calcium 6mg; Fibre 0.9g; Sodium 21mg.
Rye Sticks Energy 64kcal/269kJ; Protein 0.9g; Carbohydrate 6.4g, of which sugars 0.1g; Fat 4.1g, of which saturates 2.4g; Cholesterol 10mg; Calcium 12mg; Fibre 0.6g; Sodium 77mg.

Fennel and Chilli Ring Crackers

Based on an Italian recipe, these cookies are made with yeast and are dry and crumbly. Try them with festive drinks, dips or with a selection of antipasti.

Makes 30
500g/1lb 2oz/4½ cups type 00 flour, plus extra for dusting

115g/4oz/½ cup white vegetable fat (shortening)
5ml/1 tsp easy-blend (rapid-rise) dried yeast
15ml/1 tbsp fennel seeds
10ml/2 tsp crushed chilli flakes
15ml/1 tbsp olive oil
400–550ml/14–18fl oz/1⅔–2½ cups lukewarm water
olive oil, for brushing

1 Put the flour in a bowl and rub in the fat until the mixture resembles fine breadcrumbs.

2 Add the yeast, fennel and chilli and mix well. Add the oil and enough water to make a soft but not sticky dough. Turn out on to a floured surface and knead lightly.

3 Take small pieces of dough and shape into sausages about 15cm/6in long. Shape into rings and pinch the ends together.

4 Place the rings on a non-stick baking sheet and brush lightly with olive oil. Cover with a dish towel and set aside at room temperature for 1 hour to rise slightly.

5 Meanwhile, preheat the oven to 150°C/300°F/Gas 2.

6 Bake the cookies for 1 hour, until they are dry and only slightly browned. Leave on the baking sheet to cool completely.

> **Cook's Tip**
> *Type 00 is an Italian grade of flour used for pasta. It is milled from the centre part of the endosperm so that the resulting flour is much whiter than plain (all-purpose) flour. It contains 70 per cent of the wheat grain. It is available from Italian delicatessens and some large supermarkets. If you cannot find it, try using strong white bread flour instead.*

Polenta Dippers

These tasty Parmesan-flavoured batons are best served warm with guacamole or a spicy, tangy dip such as chilli dipping sauce.

Makes 80
1.5 litres/2½ pints/6¼ cups water
10ml/2 tsp salt

375g/13oz/3¼ cups instant polenta
150g/5oz/1½ cups freshly grated Parmesan cheese
90g/3½oz/7 tbsp butter
10ml/2 tsp cracked black pepper
olive oil, for brushing

1 Put the water in a large heavy pan and bring to the boil over high heat. Reduce the heat, add the salt and pour the polenta in a steady stream into the pan, stirring constantly with a wooden spoon. Cook the mixture over low heat, stirring constantly, until the mixture thickens and comes away from the sides of the pan – about 5 minutes.

2 Remove the pan from the heat and add the cheese, butter and cracked black pepper and salt to taste. Stir until the butter melts and the mixture is smooth.

3 Pour on to a smooth surface, such as a baking sheet. Spread the polenta to a thickness of about 2cm/¾in and shape into a rectangle. Leave for at least 30 minutes to become quite cold.

4 Preheat the oven to 200°C/400°F/Gas 6. Lightly oil two or three baking sheets with some olive oil.

5 Cut the polenta slab in half, then cut into even strips. Bake for about 40–50 minutes, until dark golden brown and crunchy. Turn the strips over from time to time during cooking. Serve immediately while still warm.

> **Cook's Tip**
> *This is a very handy Christmas recipe because the dough can be made a day ahead, then wrapped in clear film (plastic wrap) and kept chilled until ready to bake.*

Polenta Dippers Energy 34kcal/142kJ; Protein 1.2g; Carbohydrate 3.4g, of which sugars 0g; Fat 1.7g, of which saturates 1g; Cholesterol 4mg; Calcium 23mg; Fibre 0.1g; Sodium 27mg.
Fennel Crackers Energy 92kcal/385kJ; Protein 1.6g; Carbohydrate 13g, of which sugars 0.3g; Fat 4.1g, of which saturates 1.5g; Cholesterol 1mg; Calcium 24mg; Fibre 0.5g; Sodium 31mg.

Herb and Garlic Twists

These twists are very crumbly, made with garlic-flavoured dough layered with fresh herbs and some chilli flakes for an extra kick. They are a very popular festive nibble.

Makes 20

90g/3¹/₂oz/scant ¹/₂ cup butter, at room temperature, diced
2 large garlic cloves, crushed

1 egg
1 egg yolk
175g/6oz/1¹/₂ cups self-raising (self-rising) flour
large pinch of salt
30ml/2 tbsp chopped fresh mixed herbs, such as basil, thyme, marjoram and flat leaf parsley
2.5–5ml/¹/₂–1 tsp dried chilli flakes
paprika or cayenne pepper, for sprinkling

1 Preheat the oven to 200°C/400°F/Gas 6. Put the butter and garlic into a mixing bowl and beat well. Add the egg and yolk and beat in thoroughly. Stir in the flour and the salt and mix to a soft but not sticky dough.

2 Roll the dough out on a sheet of baking parchment to a 28cm/11in square. Using a sharp knife, cut the dough in half to make two equal rectangles.

3 Sprinkle the herbs and chilli flakes over one of the rectangles, then place the other rectangle on top. Gently roll the rolling pin over the herbs and chilli flakes to press them into the dough.

4 Cut the dough into 1cm/¹/₂in sticks. Make two twists in the centre of each one and place on a non-stick baking sheet.

5 Bake the twists for 15 minutes, or until crisp and golden brown. Leave on the baking sheet to cool slightly, then carefully transfer to a wire rack to cool completely. To serve, sprinkle with a little paprika or cayenne pepper, according to taste.

> **Cook's Tip**
> If the dough is too soft to handle, wrap it in clear film (plastic wrap) and chill to firm up. It will be much easier to roll it out.

Bitesize Cheese Brioches

These mouthfuls of golden, buttery dough have melting cheese in the middle, so are best enjoyed warm.

Makes 40

450g/1lb/4 cups plain (all-purpose) or strong white bread flour, plus extra for kneading
5ml/1 tsp salt
5ml/1 tsp ground turmeric

1 sachet easy-blend (rapid-rise) dried yeast
150ml/¹/₄ pint/²/₃ cup warm milk
2 eggs, plus 2 egg yolks
75g/3oz/6 tbsp butter, melted and slightly cooled
50g/2oz mature (sharp) Cheddar cheese, grated
50g/2oz cheese, such as Gouda, Cheshire, or Port Salut, cut into cubes

1 Sift the dry ingredients with the yeast and make a hollow. Mix the milk, eggs and 1 yolk with the butter and Cheddar.

2 Pour the liquid into the dry ingredients and blend with a fork. Continue blending until it is evenly mixed. Turn out the mixture on to a lightly floured surface and knead, working in as little flour as possible, until the surface is smooth and dry.

3 Place the dough in a lightly greased mixing bowl. Lightly grease the top of the dough, cover with a cloth and leave in a warm place for at least 1 hour, until the dough doubles in size.

4 Turn out on to a floured surface and knead the dough until it becomes firm and elastic again. Divide the dough into four batches, then divide each batch into eight to ten pieces. Knead each piece until smooth.

5 Press a cube of cheese into the middle of each piece of dough, shape into a round and place in a paper sweet case. Place the cases in mini muffin trays, or put the dough in doubled paper cases. Set aside in a warm place until they are well risen and have almost doubled in size.

6 Preheat the oven to 200°C/400°F/Gas 6. Mix the remaining yolk with 15ml/1 tbsp water and glaze the brioches with the mixture, using a pastry brush. Bake for about 15 minutes until golden brown, well risen and firm underneath if tapped.

Herb and Garlic Twists Energy 71kcal/295kJ; Protein 1.4g; Carbohydrate 6.9g, of which sugars 0.2g; Fat 4.4g, of which saturates 2.5g; Cholesterol 29mg; Calcium 19mg; Fibre 0.3g; Sodium 32mg.
Bitesize Brioches Energy 64kcal/270kJ; Protein 2.1g; Carbohydrate 9g, of which sugars 0.4g; Fat 2.5g, of which saturates 1.3g; Cholesterol 25mg; Calcium 27mg; Fibre 0.4g; Sodium 75mg.

Curry Crackers

Crisp curry-flavoured crackers are very good with creamy cheese or yogurt dips and make an unusual nibble with festive drinks. Add a pinch of cayenne pepper for an extra kick.

Makes 30

175g/6oz/1½ cups self-raising (self-rising) flour, plus extra for dusting
pinch of salt
10ml/2 tsp garam masala
75g/3oz/6 tbsp butter, diced
5ml/1 tsp finely chopped fresh coriander (cilantro)
1 egg, beaten

For the topping
beaten egg
black onion seeds
garam masala

1 Preheat the oven to 200°C/400°F/Gas 6. Put the flour, salt and garam masala into a bowl. Rub in the butter until the mixture resembles fine breadcrumbs. Stir in the coriander, add the egg and mix to a soft dough.

2 Turn out on to a lightly floured surface and knead gently until smooth. Roll out to a thickness of about 3mm/⅛in.

3 Cut the dough into neat rectangles measuring about 7.5 × 2.5cm/3 × 1in. Brush with a little beaten egg and sprinkle each cracker with a few black onion seeds.

4 Place the crackers on non-stick baking sheets and bake for 12 minutes, until the crackers are light golden brown all over.

5 Remove from the oven and transfer to a wire rack using a metal spatula. Put a little garam masala in a saucer and, using a dry pastry brush, dust each cracker with a little of the spice mixture. Leave to cool before serving.

> **Cook's Tip**
> Garam masala is a mixture of Indian spices that usually contains a blend of cinnamon, cloves, peppercorns, cardamom seeds and cumin seeds. You can buy it ready-made or make your own.

Cheese Aigrettes

These delicious choux buns, flavoured with mature Gruyère cheese and dusted with grated Parmesan, are a bit fiddly to make over the busy festive season, but the dough can be prepared ahead and then deep-fried, and the taste is well worth the effort.

Makes 30

100g/3¾oz/scant 1 cup plain (all-purpose) flour
2.5ml/½ tsp paprika
2.5ml/½ tsp salt
75g/3oz/6 tbsp cold butter, diced
200ml/7fl oz/scant 1 cup water
3 eggs, beaten
75g/3oz/¾ cup coarsely grated mature (sharp) Gruyère cheese
corn or vegetable oil, for deep-frying
50g/2oz piece of Parmesan cheese, finely grated
ground black pepper
sprigs of flat leaf parsley, to garnish

1 Sift the flour, paprika and salt on to a large sheet of foil or baking parchment. Add a generous grinding of black pepper.

2 Put the butter and water into a medium pan and heat gently. As soon as the butter has melted and the liquid starts to boil, add in all the seasoned flour at once and beat hard with a wooden spoon until the dough forms a ball and comes away from the sides of the pan.

3 Remove the pan from the heat and cool the paste for about 5 minutes. This step is important if the aigrettes are to rise well. Gradually beat in enough of the beaten egg to give a stiff dropping consistency that still holds a shape on the spoon. Mix in the Gruyère cheese.

4 Heat the oil for deep-frying to 180°C/350°F or until a cube of bread, added to the hot oil, browns in about 1 minute. Take a teaspoonful of the choux paste and use a second spoon to slide it into the oil. Make more aigrettes in the same way. Fry for 3–4 minutes until golden brown. Drain on kitchen paper and keep warm while cooking successive batches.

5 To serve, pile the aigrettes on a warmed serving dish, sprinkle with Parmesan and garnish with sprigs of parsley.

Curry Crackers Energy 39kcal/164kJ; Protein 0.6g; Carbohydrate 4.6g, of which sugars 0.1g; Fat 2.2g, of which saturates 1.3g; Cholesterol 5mg; Calcium 11mg; Fibre 0.3g; Sodium 17mg.
Cheese Aigrettes Energy 84kcal/348kJ; Protein 2.2g; Carbohydrate 2.4g, of which sugars 0.1g; Fat 7.3g, of which saturates 2.7g; Cholesterol 28mg; Calcium 46mg; Fibre 0.1g; Sodium 58mg.

Sausage Rolls

Small sausage rolls rank high in the league of popular Christmas party foods. They are delicious when home-made, particularly if quality butcher's sausage meat is used to fill them. Serve them hot or cold. They also make an ideal addition to a picnic or packed lunch.

Makes 16

175g/6oz/1½ cups plain (all-purpose) flour
pinch of salt
40g/1½oz/3 tbsp lard or white cooking fat, diced
40g/1½oz/3 tbsp butter, diced
250g/9oz pork sausage meat (bulk sausage)
beaten egg, to glaze
salt and ground black pepper

1 To make the pastry, sift the flour and salt into a large mixing bowl and add the lard or white cooking fat and the butter. Rub the fats into the flour with your fingertips until the mixture resembles fine crumbs.

2 Stir in about 45ml/3 tbsp cold water until the mixture can be gathered into a smooth ball of dough. Wrap in clear film (plastic wrap) and chill for 30 minutes.

3 Preheat the oven to 190°C/375°F/Gas 5. Roll out the pastry on a lightly floured surface to make a rectangle about 30cm/12in long. Cut lengthways into two long strips.

4 Season the sausage meat and divide into two pieces and, on a lightly floured surface, shape each into a long roll the same length as the pastry. Lay a roll on each strip of pastry.

5 Brush the pastry edges with water and fold them over the meat, pressing the edges together to seal them well.

6 Turn the rolls over and, with the seam side down, brush the top with beaten egg. Cut each roll into eight and place on a baking sheet, evenly spaced.

7 Bake in the hot oven for 30 minutes until crisp and golden brown. Transfer to a wire rack and leave to cool.

Cheese Straws

Cheese-flavoured pastries became popular when it was customary (for gentlemen, particularly) to eat a small savoury at the end of a long, sophisticated meal. Now we are more likely to eat cheese straws as an appetizer with pre-dinner drinks or as nibbles at a festive party.

Makes 10

75g/3oz/²⁄₃ cup plain (all-purpose) flour
40g/1½oz/3 tbsp butter, diced
40g/1½oz mature (sharp) hard cheese, such as Cheddar, finely grated
1 egg
5ml/1 tsp mustard
salt and ground black pepper

1 Preheat the oven to 180°C/350°F/Gas 4. Line a large baking sheet with baking parchment.

2 Sift the flour and seasoning and add the butter. Rub the butter into the flour until the mixture resembles fine crumbs. Stir in the grated cheese.

3 Beat the egg and mustard. Add half to the flour, stirring until the mixture can be gathered into a smooth ball of dough.

4 Roll the dough out to make a square measuring about 15cm/6in. Cut into ten lengths. Place on the baking sheet and brush with the remaining egg. Bake in the oven for 12 minutes or until golden brown. Transfer to a wire rack and serve warm.

Stilton Croquettes

These are perfect little festive bites, which you can make in advance and reheat when needed.

Serves 4–6

350g/12oz floury potatoes, peeled and cut into chunks
75g/3oz creamy Stilton, crumbled
3 eggs, hard-boiled, peeled and chopped
few drops of Worcestershire sauce
a little plain (all-purpose) flour
1 egg, beaten
60ml/4 tbsp fine breadcrumbs
vegetable oil, for deep-frying
salt and ground black pepper
dipping sauce, to serve

1 Boil the potatoes for about 15 minutes, or until they are tender, but not too soft. Drain thoroughly and leave to cool.

2 Mash the potatoes until smooth. Add the Stilton cheese, chopped egg and Worcestershire sauce. Add seasoning to taste.

3 Divide the potato and cheese mixture into approximately 20 pieces and shape into small sausage or cork shapes, no longer than about 2.5cm/1in.

4 Coat in flour, then dip into the beaten egg and coat evenly in breadcrumbs. Reshape, if necessary. Chill for about 30 minutes.

5 Deep-fry, seven or eight croquettes at a time, in hot oil, turning frequently until they are golden brown all over.

6 Drain on kitchen paper, transfer to a serving dish and keep warm for up to 30 minutes. Serve with a dipping sauce.

Sausage Rolls Energy 125kcal/521kJ; Protein 2.5g; Carbohydrate 10.3g, of which sugars 0.5g; Fat 8.4g, of which saturates 3.9g; Cholesterol 14mg; Calcium 23mg; Fibre 0.4g; Sodium 142mg.
Cheese Straws Energy 174kcal/735kJ; Protein 6.8g; Carbohydrate 29.2g, of which sugars 3.3g; Fat 4.2g, of which saturates 1.1g; Cholesterol 5mg; Calcium 92mg; Fibre 1g; Sodium 307mg.
Stilton Croquettes Energy 264kcal/1095kJ; Protein 7.4g; Carbohydrate 12.7g, of which sugars 0.8g; Fat 20.6g, of which saturates 4.7g; Cholesterol 117mg; Calcium 60mg; Fibre 0.6g; Sodium 189mg.

Angels on Horseback

This recipe dates back to the 19th century, when oysters were plentiful and cheap. It became fashionable in England to serve a savoury at the end of a meal, mainly to revive the palates of the gentlemen after dessert and before the arrival of the port. Nowadays, this little dish makes a delicious appetizer to serve at Christmas.

Serves 4
16 oysters, removed from shells
fresh lemon juice
8 rindless rashers (strips) of
*   streaky (fatty) bacon*
8 small slices of bread
butter, for spreading
paprika (optional)

1 Preheat the oven to 200°C/400°F/Gas 6. Sprinkle the oysters with a little of the lemon juice.

2 Lay the streaky bacon rashers on a chopping board, slide the back of a knife along each one to stretch it out a little and then cut each in half crossways.

3 Wrap a piece of bacon around each oyster and secure with a wooden cocktail stick (toothpick). Arrange on a baking sheet.

4 Place the oysters and bacon into the hot oven for about 8–10 minutes until the bacon is just cooked through.

5 Meanwhile, toast the bread. When the bacon is cooked, butter the hot toast and serve the bacon-wrapped oysters on top. Sprinkle with a little paprika, if using.

Cook's Tip
To shell an oyster, wrap a dish towel around your hand, then grip the oyster in the same hand, with the cupped shell down in the palm and the hinge pointing towards you. Insert a shucking knife (or a short, sharp knife) into the gap in the hinge and twist it from side to side until the hinge breaks. Lever open the top shell, then run the knife along the edges to free the oyster, then cut it away from the muscle that binds it to the bottom shell.

Devils on Horseback

This is another popular savoury, designed to be served at the end of a lavish dinner, that makes a good appetizer. These tasty bites will be welcome at any festive gathering. They can be served on crisp, fried bread instead of toast.

Serves 4
16 pitted prunes
fruit chutney, such as mango
8 rindless rashers (strips) of
*   streaky (fatty) bacon*
8 small slices of bread
butter, for spreading

1 Preheat the oven to 200°C/400°F/Gas 6. Ease open the prunes and carefully spoon a small amount of the fruit chutney into each prune cavity.

2 Lay the streaky bacon rashers on a chopping board, slide the back of a knife along each one to stretch it out and then cut each in half crossways.

3 Wrap a piece of bacon around each prune, secure with a cocktail stick (toothpick) and place on a baking sheet. (Alternatively, omit the cocktail sticks and lay them close together on the baking sheet so that they won't unroll in the oven.)

4 Place the wrapped prunes into the hot oven for about 8–10 minutes until the bacon is just cooked through.

5 Meanwhile, toast the bread. When the bacon is cooked, butter the hot toast and top each piece with a bacon-wrapped prune. Serve immediately.

Variations
• *Instead of filling the prunes with fruit chutney, why not try some variations. If you prefer, the prunes can be stuffed with pâté, olives, whole almonds or nuggets of cured meat.*
• *For an adult version at Christmas time, soak the prunes in a glass of red wine for about 3–4 hours before stuffing and wrapping with the bacon.*

Angels on Horseback Energy 326kcal/1365kJ; Protein 20.3g; Carbohydrate 26.4g, of which sugars 1.4g; Fat 16.2g, of which saturates 6.9g; Cholesterol 79mg; Calcium 147mg; Fibre 0.8g; Sodium 1483mg.
Devils on Horseback Energy 309kcal/1303kJ; Protein 14.7g; Carbohydrate 41.7g, of which sugars 18.3g; Fat 10.4g, of which saturates 3.5g; Cholesterol 30mg; Calcium 75mg; Fibre 3.6g; Sodium 1132mg.

Smoked Salmon with Warm Potato Cakes

Although the ingredients are timeless, this combination makes an excellent modern dish, which is deservedly popular as an appetizer or as a substantial canapé to serve with festive drinks. It also makes a perfect brunch dish to serve on Christmas Day, accompanied by lightly scrambled eggs and freshly squeezed orange juice. Choose wild fish if possible.

Serves 6
450g/1lb potatoes, cooked and mashed
75g/3oz/²/₃ cup plain (all-purpose) flour
2 eggs, beaten
2 spring onions (scallions), chopped
a little freshly grated nutmeg
50g/2oz/¼ cup butter, melted
150ml/¼ pint/²/₃ cup sour cream
12 slices of smoked salmon
salt and ground black pepper
chopped fresh chives, to garnish

1 Put the potatoes, flour, eggs and spring onions into a large mixing bowl. Season with salt, ground black pepper and a little nutmeg, and add half the butter.

2 Mix thoroughly until the mixture is well combined and shape into 12 small potato cakes.

3 Heat the remaining butter in a non-stick frying pan and cook the potato cakes until browned on both sides.

4 To serve, mix the sour cream with some salt and pepper. Fold a piece of smoked salmon and place on top of each potato cake. Top the salmon with the cream and then the chives and serve immediately.

> **Cook's Tip**
> *If it is more convenient, you can make the potato cakes in advance and keep them overnight in the refrigerator. When required, warm them through in a hot oven about 15 minutes before assembling and serving.*

Russian Pancakes with Mixed Toppings

These mini pancakes make delicious festive canapés. They can be made with caviar or smoked salmon, or with crème fraîche, soused herring and onion.

Makes 20
25g/1oz fresh yeast
5ml/1 tsp caster (superfine) sugar
50ml/2fl oz/¼ cup warm water
2 egg yolks
250ml/8fl oz/1 cup warm milk
2.5ml/½ tsp salt

175g/6oz/1½ cups plain white (all-purpose) flour
3 egg whites
150ml/¼ pint/²/₃ cup rapeseed (canola) oil

For the toppings
slices of smoked salmon
pickled herring, chopped
chopped onion
crème fraîche
caviar
lemon wedges and dill, to garnish

1 Put the yeast, sugar and warm water in a bowl and blend until smooth. Leave in a warm place for 20 minutes until frothy.

2 Mix the egg yolks, 200ml/6fl oz/¾ cup of the warm milk and the salt in a bowl. Stir in the yeast mixture and the flour, a little at a time, to form a smooth batter. Leave to rise in a warm place for 4–5 hours, stirring three or four times.

3 Stir the remaining 50ml/2fl oz/¼ cup of the milk into the batter. Whisk the egg whites in a dry bowl until they form soft peaks. Fold into the batter and set aside for 30 minutes.

4 Heat the oil in a frying pan and add 25–30ml/1½–2 tbsp of batter for each pancake. Fry over medium heat until set and risen, then cook the other side. Cook the remaining batter to make 20 pancakes. Let your guests choose their own toppings.

> **Cook's Tip**
> *Start the batter a minimum of 3 hours before frying for the yeast to rise fully. Stir the batter 3–4 times while rising.*

Salmon with Cakes Energy 326kcal/1365kJ; Protein 21.9g; Carbohydrate 22.9g, of which sugars 2.3g; Fat 17g, of which saturates 8.6g; Cholesterol 119mg; Calcium 70mg; Fibre 1.2g; Sodium 1315mg.
Russian Pancakes Energy 89kcal/372kJ; Protein 2g; Carbohydrate 7.6g, of which sugars 0.7g; Fat 5.9g, of which saturates 0.9g; Cholesterol 21mg; Calcium 30mg; Fibre 0.3g; Sodium 16mg.

Butterfly Prawn Skewers with Chilli and Raspberry Dip

The success of this dish depends upon the quality of the prawns, so it is worthwhile getting really good ones, which have a fine flavour and firm texture.

Serves 4–6
*30 raw king prawns
(jumbo shrimp), peeled*

*15ml/1 tbsp sunflower oil
sea salt*

*For the chilli
and raspberry dip*
*30ml/2 tbsp raspberry vinegar
15ml/1 tbsp sugar
115g/4oz/²⁄₃ cup raspberries
1 large fresh red chilli, seeded
and finely chopped*

1 If using wooden skewers, soak 30 of them in cold water for 30 minutes so that they don't burn during cooking.

2 Make the dip by mixing the vinegar and sugar in a small pan. Heat gently until the sugar has dissolved, stirring constantly, then add the raspberries.

3 When the raspberry juices start to flow, transfer the mixture into a sieve (strainer) set over a bowl. Push the raspberries through the sieve using the back of a ladle or wooden spoon. Discard the seeds left in the sieve.

4 Stir the chilli into the purée and leave to cool. When the dip is cold, cover and place in a cool place until it is needed.

5 Preheat the grill (broiler). Remove the dark spinal vein from the prawns using a small, sharp knife. Make an incision down the curved back and butterfly each prawn.

6 Mix the sunflower oil with a little sea salt in a bowl. Add the prawns and toss to coat them completely. Thread the prawns on to the drained skewers, spearing them head first.

7 Grill (broil) the prawns for about 5 minutes, depending on their size, turning them over once. Serve immediately while hot, with the chilli and raspberry dip.

Breaded Tiger Prawn Skewers with Parsley

Fresh parsley and lemon are all that is required to create a lovely tiger prawn dish. They are quick and easy to make so will be ideal for a festive buffet.

Serves 4
*900g/2lb raw tiger prawns (jumbo
shrimp), peeled*

*60ml/4 tbsp olive oil
45ml/3 tbsp vegetable oil
75g/3oz/1¼ cups very fine
dry breadcrumbs
1 garlic clove, crushed
15ml/1 tbsp chopped
fresh parsley
salt and ground black pepper
lemon wedges, to serve*

1 Slit the tiger prawns down their backs and, using the point of a sharp knife, remove the dark vein. Rinse the prawns under cold running water and dry them thoroughly between sheets of kitchen paper.

2 Put the olive and vegetable oils in a large bowl and add the prawns. Stir to ensure the oils are well combined and the prawns are evenly coated.

3 Add the fine breadcrumbs, crushed garlic and chopped parsley to the bowl of prawns. Season with salt and plenty of ground black pepper. Using your hands, or a wooden spoon, toss the prawns thoroughly to give them an even coating of the breadcrumb mixture.

4 Cover the bowl with clear film (plastic wrap) and leave to marinate for 1 hour in a cool place.

5 Carefully thread the breaded tiger prawns on to four metal or wooden skewers, curling them up as you work, so that the tails of the prawns are skewered neatly in the middle.

6 Preheat the grill (broiler) to a moderate heat. Place the prawn skewers in the grill pan and cook for about 2–3 minutes on each side until they are golden and cooked through. Serve immediately with the lemon wedges.

Prawns Skewers Energy 156kcal/635kJ; Protein 12.5g; Carbohydrate 7.3g, of which sugars 0.5g; Fat 8g, of which saturates 1.3g; Cholesterol 157mg; Calcium 64mg; Fibre 0.3g; Sodium 316mg.
Tiger Prawn Skewers Energy 415kcal/1734kJ; Protein 42.2g; Carbohydrate 14.9g, of which sugars 0.8g; Fat 21.1g, of which saturates 2.8g; Cholesterol 439mg; Calcium 227mg; Fibre 1.1g; Sodium 574mg.

Grilled Chicken Balls on Skewers with Yakitori Sauce

These tasty morsels make a great low-fat appetizer or snack to serve at a Christmas drinks party.

Serves 4
300g/11oz skinless chicken, minced (ground)
2 eggs
2.5ml/½ tsp salt
10ml/2 tsp plain (all-purpose) flour
10ml/2 tsp cornflour (cornstarch)
90ml/6 tbsp dried breadcrumbs
2.5cm/1in piece fresh root ginger, grated

For the yakitori sauce
60ml/4 tbsp sake
75ml/5 tbsp Japanese soy sauce
15ml/1 tbsp mirin (rice wine)
15ml/1 tbsp sugar
2.5ml/½ tsp cornflour (cornstarch) blended with 5ml/1 tsp water

1 Soak eight bamboo skewers for about 30 minutes in water. Put all the ingredients for the chicken balls, except the ginger, in a food processor and process to blend well.

2 Shape the mixture into a small ball about half the size of a golf ball. Make a further 30–32 balls in the same way.

3 Squeeze the juice from the grated ginger into a small mixing bowl. Discard the pulp. Preheat the grill (broiler).

4 Add the ginger juice to a small pan of boiling water. Add the chicken balls, and boil for about 7 minutes, or until the colour of the meat changes and the balls float to the surface. Scoop the balls out using a slotted spoon and drain on kitchen paper.

5 In a small pan, mix all the ingredients for the yakitori sauce, except the cornflour liquid. Bring to the boil, then simmer until the sauce has reduced slightly. Add the cornflour liquid and stir until thickened. Transfer to a small bowl.

6 Drain the skewers and thread three to four balls on each. Grill (broil) for a few minutes, turning frequently until they brown. Brush with sauce and return to the heat. Repeat twice, then serve immediately.

Fragrant Spiced Lamb on Mini Poppadums

Crisp, melt-in-the-mouth mini poppadums make a great base for these divine little bites. Top them with a drizzle of yogurt and a spoonful of mango chutney, then serve immediately. To make an equally tasty variation, you can use chicken or pork in place of the lamb.

Makes 25
30ml/2 tbsp sunflower oil
4 shallots, finely chopped
30ml/2 tbsp medium curry paste
300g/11oz minced (ground) lamb
90ml/6 tbsp tomato purée (paste)
5ml/1 tsp caster (superfine) sugar
200ml/7fl oz/scant 1 cup coconut cream
juice of 1 lime
60ml/4 tbsp chopped fresh mint leaves
25 mini poppadums
vegetable oil, for frying
salt and ground black pepper
natural (plain) yogurt and mango chutney, to drizzle
red chilli slivers and mint leaves, to garnish

1 Heat the oil in a wok over medium heat and add the shallots. Stir fry for 4–5 minutes, until softened, then add the curry paste. Stir-fry for 1–2 minutes.

2 Add the lamb and stir-fry over high heat for 4–5 minutes, then stir in the tomato purée, sugar and coconut cream.

3 Cook the lamb over a gentle heat for 25–30 minutes, or until the meat is tender and all the liquid has been absorbed. Season with salt and pepper and stir in the lime juice and mint leaves. Remove from the heat and keep warm.

4 Fill a separate wok one-third full of oil and deep-fry the mini poppadums for about 30–40 seconds, or until puffed up and crisp. Drain on kitchen paper.

5 Place the poppadums on a large serving platter. Put a spoonful of spiced lamb on each one, then top with a little yogurt and mango chutney. Serve immediately, garnished with slivers of red chilli and mint leaves.

Grilled Chicken Balls Energy 332kcal/1398kJ; Protein 30.4g; Carbohydrate 29g, of which sugars 7.4g; Fat 9.7g, of which saturates 2.6g; Cholesterol 339mg; Calcium 84mg; Fibre 0.6g; Sodium 325mg.
Fragrant Spiced Lamb Energy 63kcal/260kJ; Protein 2.7g; Carbohydrate 2.7g, of which sugars 1.3g; Fat 4.7g, of which saturates 1.4g; Cholesterol 9mg; Calcium 7mg; Fibre 0.3g; Sodium 45mg.

Skewered Lamb with Onion Salsa

This tasty appetizer is ideal for festive entertaining. The refreshing salsa is quick and easy to make and is the ideal accompaniment to the lamb. They are also great cooked on a barbecue, if making them in summer.

Serves 4
225g/8oz lean lamb, cubed
2.5ml/½ tsp ground cumin
5ml/1 tsp paprika
15ml/1 tbsp olive oil
salt and ground black pepper

For the salsa
1 red onion, very thinly sliced
1 large tomato, seeded and chopped
15ml/1 tbsp red wine vinegar
3–4 fresh basil or mint leaves, coarsely torn
small fresh mint leaves, to garnish

1 Place the lamb in a bowl with the cumin, paprika, oil and seasoning. Toss well until the lamb is coated with spices.

2 Cover the bowl with clear film (plastic wrap). Set aside in a cool place for a few hours, or in the refrigerator overnight, so that the lamb absorbs the flavours.

3 Spear the marinated lamb cubes on to four small skewers. Ensure that the cubes are not to tightly packed together.

4 To make the salsa, put the sliced onion, tomato, red wine vinegar and basil or mint leaves in a small bowl and stir together until thoroughly blended. Season to taste with salt, garnish with mint, then set aside while you cook the lamb.

5 Cook the skewers under a preheated grill (broiler) for 5–10 minutes, turning frequently, until the lamb is well browned. Serve while hot, with the salsa.

Cook's Tip
If using wooden or bamboo skewers, soak them first in cold water for at least 30 minutes to prevent them from burning under the grill (broiler) during cooking.

Bacon-wrapped Beef on Skewers

These tasty little skewers are packed with Asian flavours thanks to the tangy marinade. Serve as part of a festive buffet spread or as nibbles for Christmas guests.

Serves 4
225g/8oz beef fillet (tenderloin) or rump (round) steak, cut across the grain into 12 strips
12 thin rashers (strips) of streaky (fatty) bacon
ground black pepper
chilli sambal, for dipping

For the marinade
15ml/1 tbsp groundnut (peanut) oil
30ml/2 tbsp fish sauce
30ml/2 tbsp soy sauce
4–6 garlic cloves, crushed
10ml/2 tsp sugar

1 To make the marinade, mix all the ingredients in a large bowl until the sugar dissolves. Season generously with black pepper.

2 Add the beef strips to the marinade, stir to coat them thoroughly, and set aside for about an hour.

3 Preheat a griddle pan over high heat until very hot. Remove the beef strips from the marinade and roll up each strip, then wrap it in a slice of bacon. Thread the rolls on to the skewers, so that you have three rolls on each one.

4 Cook the bacon-wrapped rolls on the hot griddle for about 4–5 minutes, turning once during the cooking process, until the bacon is golden and crispy. Serve immediately, with a bowl of chilli sambal on the side for dipping.

Cook's Tip
These tasty skewers can also be cooked under a preheated grill (broiler), or over hot coals on the barbecue. Simply cook for 6–8 minutes, turning every couple of minutes so that the bacon is browned but not burned. Serve them as an appetizer ahead of the main course – they will whet the appetite without being too filling.

Skewered Lamb Energy 135kcal/563kJ; Protein 11.4g; Carbohydrate 2g, of which sugars 1.6g; Fat 9.2g, of which saturates 3.4g; Cholesterol 43mg; Calcium 10mg; Fibre 0.5g; Sodium 51mg.
Bacon-wrapped Beef Energy 282kcal/1172kJ; Protein 21.7g; Carbohydrate 1.1g, of which sugars 1.1g; Fat 21.3g, of which saturates 7.1g; Cholesterol 69mg; Calcium 7mg; Fibre 0g; Sodium 745mg.

Parmesan Tuiles

These lacy tuiles look very impressive, but they couldn't be easier to make. Believe it or not, they use only a single ingredient – grated Parmesan cheese.

Serves 8–10
115g/4oz Parmesan cheese

1 Preheat the oven to 200°C/400°F/Gas 6. Line two baking sheets with baking parchment.

2 Grate the cheese using a fine grater, pulling it down the grater slowly to make long strands.

3 Spread the grated cheese out in 7.5–9cm/3–3½in rounds. Do not spread the cheese too thickly; it should only just cover the baking parchment. Bake in the oven for 5–7 minutes, until bubbling and golden brown.

4 Leave the tuiles on the baking sheet for about 30 seconds, and then carefully transfer them, using a metal spatula, to a wire rack to cool and set. Alternatively, drape them over a rolling pin while they are still warm so that they set in a curved shape.

Cook's Tip
Parmesan cheese will keep for months if stored properly. Wrap it in foil and store in a plastic box in the least cold part of the refrigerator, such as the salad drawer or one of the compartments in the door.

Variation
Tuiles can be made into little cup shapes by draping over an upturned egg cup. These little tuiles can be filled to make tasty treats to serve with drinks. Try a little cream cheese flavoured with herbs as a filling.

Filo Cigars with Feta and Herbs

These classic cigar-shaped pastries are a popular snack and appetizer, and they are also good as nibbles with Christmas pre-dinner drinks. They are filled with cheese and herbs, but can be made with aromatic minced meat, baked aubergine, or mashed pumpkin, cheese and dill.

Serves 3–4
225g/8oz feta cheese
1 large (US extra large) egg, lightly beaten
1 small bunch each of fresh flat leaf parsley, mint and dill, finely chopped
4–5 sheets of filo pastry
sunflower oil, for deep-frying
dill fronds, to garnish (optional)

1 In a bowl, mash the feta with a fork. Beat in the egg and fold in the herbs. Working with one sheet at a time, cut the filo into strips about 10–13cm/4–5in wide, and pile them on top of each other. Keep the strips covered with a damp dish towel.

2 Place a heaped teaspoon of the cheese filling along one of the short ends of a strip. Roll the end over the filling, quite tightly to keep it in place, then tuck in the sides to seal in the filling and continue to roll until you get to the other end.

3 Brush the tip with a little water to help seal the roll. Place the filled cigar, join side down, on a plate and cover with another damp dish towel to keep it moist. Continue with the remaining sheets of filo and filling.

4 Heat enough oil for deep-frying in a wok or other heavy, deep-sided pan, and deep-fry the filo cigars in batches for about 5–6 minutes until crisp and golden brown. Lift out of the oil with a slotted spoon and drain on kitchen paper. Serve immediately, garnished with dill fronds if you like.

Cook's Tips
• The filo pastry can be folded into triangles, if you prefer.
• The cigars can be prepared in advance and kept under a damp dish towel in the refrigerator until you are ready to fry them, at the last minute before serving.

Parmesan Tuiles Energy 52kcal/216kJ; Protein 4.5g; Carbohydrate 0g, of which sugars 0g; Fat 3.8g, of which saturates 2.4g; Cholesterol 12mg; Calcium 138mg; Fibre 0g; Sodium 125mg.
Filo Cigars Energy 311Kcal/1291kJ; Protein 12.4g; Carbohydrate 11.2g, of which sugars 1.6g; Fat 24.4g, of which saturates 9.5g; Cholesterol 92mg; Calcium 278mg; Fibre 1.6g; Sodium 838mg.

Corn Muffins with Ham

These delicious little muffins are simple to make and make a delicious festive breakfast on Christmas Day morning. If you like, serve them unfilled with a pot of herb butter.

Makes 24

50g/2oz/scant ½ cup yellow cornmeal
65g/2½ oz/9 tbsp plain (all-purpose) flour
30ml/2 tbsp sugar
7.5ml/1½ tsp baking powder
pinch of salt
50g/2oz/4 tbsp butter, melted
120ml/4fl oz/½ cup whipping cream
1 egg, beaten
1–2 jalapeño or other medium-hot chillies, seeded and finely chopped (optional)
pinch of cayenne pepper
butter, for spreading
grainy mustard or mustard with honey, for spreading
50g/2oz oak-smoked ham

1 Preheat the oven to 200°C/400°F/Gas 6. Lightly grease a muffin tin (pan) with 24 4cm/1½in cups.

2 In a large bowl, combine the cornmeal, flour, sugar, baking powder and salt. In another bowl, whisk together the melted butter, cream, beaten egg, chopped fresh chillies, if using, and the cayenne pepper.

3 Make a well in the cornmeal mixture, pour in the egg mixture and gently stir in just enough to blend (do not over-beat – the batter does not have to be smooth).

4 Drop 15ml/1 tbsp batter into each muffin cup. Bake for 12–15 minutes, until golden. Leave to cool completely.

5 Split the muffins, spread each bottom half with a little butter and mustard and top with ham.

> **Cook's Tip**
> The muffins can be made in advance and stored in airtight containers. Bring them to room temperature or warm slightly before filling and serving.

Cheese and Mustard Scones

Depending on their size, these cheese scones can be served as little canapé bases, festive supper treats or even as a quick pie topping.

Serves 12

250g/9oz/2¼ cups self-raising (self-rising) flour, plus extra for dusting
5ml/1 tsp baking powder
pinch of salt
40g/1½oz/3 tbsp butter
175g/6oz/1½ cups grated mature (sharp) Cheddar cheese, plus extra for sprinkling
10ml/2 tsp wholegrain mustard
about 150ml/¼ pint/⅔ cup milk, buttermilk or natural (plain) yogurt
1 egg yolk beaten with 5ml/1 tsp water, to glaze (optional)
ground black pepper
garlic-flavoured cream cheese, chopped fresh chives and sliced radishes, to serve (optional)

1 Preheat the oven to 220°C/425°F/Gas 7.

2 Sift the flour, baking powder and salt into a bowl, then rub in the butter until the mixture resembles fine breadcrumbs. Season with pepper and stir in the cheese.

3 Mix the mustard with the milk, buttermilk or yogurt. Add to the dry ingredients and mix quickly until the mixture just comes together. Do not over-mix or the scones will be tough.

4 Knead the dough lightly on a lightly floured surface, then pat it out with your hands to a depth of 2cm/¾in. Cut into squares, or use a 5cm/2in cutter to stamp out rounds, re-rolling the dough as necessary.

5 Place the squares or rounds on a non-stick baking sheet. Brush the tops with the egg glaze, if using, and sprinkle with extra grated cheese.

6 Bake for about 10 minutes, until risen and golden. You can test scones by pressing the sides, which should spring back. Transfer to a wire rack to cool.

7 Serve spread with garlic-flavoured cream cheese. Top with chopped chives and sliced radishes, if using.

Corn Muffins Energy 54kcal/227kJ; Protein 1.5g; Carbohydrate 6.8g, of which sugars 1.6g; Fat 2.5g, of which saturates 1.4g; Cholesterol 14mg; Calcium 13mg; Fibre 0.2g; Sodium 43mg.
Cheese Scones Energy 169kcal/706kJ; Protein 6.4g; Carbohydrate 16.8g, of which sugars 1g; Fat 8.5g, of which saturates 5.2g; Cholesterol 39mg; Calcium 156mg; Fibre 0.7g; Sodium 146mg.

Mushroom and Bean Pâté

Making pâté in the slow cooker results in this light and tasty version. It is delicious served on triangles of wholemeal toast for vegetarian guests at Christmas, or with crusty French bread as a light lunch served with salad.

Serves 8
450g/1lb/6 cups mushrooms, sliced
1 onion, finely chopped
2 garlic cloves, crushed

1 red (bell) pepper, seeded
  and diced
30ml/2 tbsp vegetable stock
30ml/2 tbsp dry white wine
400g/14oz can red kidney beans,
  rinsed and drained
1 egg, beaten
50g/2oz/1 cup fresh wholemeal
  (whole-wheat) breadcrumbs
10ml/2 tsp chopped fresh thyme
10ml/2 tsp chopped fresh rosemary
salt and ground black pepper
salad leaves, fresh herbs and
  tomato wedges, to garnish

1 Put the mushrooms, onion, garlic, red pepper, stock and wine in the ceramic cooking pot. Cover and cook on high for 2 hours, then set aside for about 10 minutes to cool.

2 Transfer the mixture to a food processor or blender and add the beans. Process to make a smooth purée, stopping the machine once or twice to scrape down the sides.

3 Lightly grease and line a 900g/2lb loaf tin (pan). Put an inverted saucer or metal pastry ring in the bottom of the ceramic cooking pot. Pour in 2.5cm/1in of hot water, and set to high.

4 Transfer the vegetable mixture to a bowl. Add the egg, breadcrumbs and herbs, and season. Mix thoroughly, then spoon into the loaf tin and cover with cling film (plastic wrap) or foil.

5 Put the tin in the slow cooker and pour in enough boiling water to come just over halfway up the sides of the tin. Cover with the lid and cook on high for 4 hours, or until lightly set.

6 Remove the tin and place on a wire rack until cool. Chill for several hours, or overnight. Turn the pâté out of the tin, remove the lining paper and serve garnished with salad leaves, fresh herbs and tomato wedges.

Broccoli and Chestnut Terrine

Chestnuts are a classic ingredient at Christmas time and feature in this versatile terrine, which is delicious served hot or cold. It is ideal for a festive dinner party or, if making in the summer, taking on a picnic.

Serves 4–6
450g/1lb broccoli, cut into
  small florets

225g/8oz cooked chestnuts,
  roughly chopped
50g/2oz/1 cup fresh wholemeal
  (whole-wheat) breadcrumbs
60ml/4 tbsp low-fat natural
  (plain) yogurt
30ml/2 tbsp Parmesan cheese,
  finely grated
pinch of grated nutmeg
salt and ground black pepper
2 eggs, beaten

1 Preheat the oven to 180°C/350°F/Gas 4. Line a 900g/2lb loaf tin (pan) with baking parchment.

2 Blanch or steam the broccoli for 3–4 minutes until just tender. Drain well. Reserve one-quarter of the smallest florets and chop the remainder finely.

3 Place the chestnuts, breadcrumbs, yogurt and Parmesan in a mixing bowl and mix gently until well combined, then season with nutmeg, salt and ground black pepper.

4 Add the beaten eggs to the mixture, followed by the chopped broccoli and the reserved florets. Gently stir the mixture until all the ingredients are combined.

5 Spoon the mixture into the prepared tin, ensuring that the mixture is evenly distributed.

6 Place the loaf tin in a roasting pan and pour in boiling water to come halfway up the sides of the loaf tin.

7 Bake in the preheated oven for about 20–25 minutes, or until the eggs are completely set.

8 Remove from the oven and carefully transfer to a plate or tray. Serve, cut into even slices.

Mushroom Pâté Energy 85kcal/358kJ; Protein 5.5g; Carbohydrate 12.3g, of which sugars 3.8g; Fat 1.6g, of which saturates 0.4g; Cholesterol 28mg; Calcium 47mg; Fibre 3.7g; Sodium 187mg.
Broccoli Terrine Energy 169kcal/711kJ; Protein 9.4g; Carbohydrate 22g, of which sugars 4.5g; Fat 5.4g, of which saturates 1.9g; Cholesterol 69mg; Calcium 152mg; Fibre 3.7g; Sodium 157mg.

Garden Vegetable Terrine

Perfect for a Christmas buffet menu or as an appetizer for a dinner party, this is a softly set, creamy terrine of colourful vegetables wrapped in glossy spinach leaves.

Serves 6
225g/8oz fresh leaf spinach
3 carrots, cut in sticks
3–4 long, thin leeks
about 115g/4oz long green
   beans, topped and tailed
1 red (bell) pepper, cut in strips
2 courgettes (zucchini),
   cut into sticks
115g/4oz broccoli florets

For the sauce
1 egg and 2 yolks
300ml/½ pint/1¼ cups single
   (light) cream
fresh nutmeg, grated
5ml/1 tsp salt
50g/2oz/½ cup grated
   Cheddar cheese
oil, for greasing
ground black pepper

1 Preheat the oven to 180°C/350°F/Gas 4. Blanch the spinach quickly in boiling water, then drain and carefully pat dry.

2 Grease a 900g/2lb loaf tin (pan) and line the base with a sheet of baking parchment. Line with the spinach leaves, allowing them to overhang the tin.

3 Blanch the rest of the vegetables in boiling, salted water until just tender. Drain and refresh in cold water then, when cool, pat dry with pieces of kitchen paper.

4 Place the vegetables into the loaf tin in a colourful mixture, making sure the sticks of vegetables lie lengthways.

5 Beat the sauce ingredients together and slowly add to the vegetables. Tap the tin to distribute the sauce. Fold over the spinach leaves at the top of the terrine to make a neat surface.

6 Cover the terrine with a sheet of greased foil, then bake in a roasting pan half full of boiling water for 1–1¼ hours until set.

7 Cool the terrine in the tin, then chill. To serve, loosen the sides and shake out gently. Serve cut in thick slices.

Cannellini Bean Pâté

Serve this simple bean pâté with slices of Melba toast or toasted wholegrain bread as an appetizer or snack at Christmas time. It makes a great alternative to other meat-based pâtés, and any vegetarian guests at a festive party will love it.

Serves 4
2 × 400g/14oz cans cannellini
   beans, drained and rinsed
45ml/3 tbsp olive oil
50g/2oz mature (sharp) Cheddar
   cheese, finely grated
30ml/2 tbsp chopped
   fresh parsley
salt and ground black pepper

1 Put the cannellini beans in a food processor or blender with the olive oil, and process to a chunky paste.

2 Transfer the paste to a mixing bowl and stir in the grated cheese and the chopped fresh parsley. Season to taste with salt and ground black pepper.

3 Spoon the pâté into a serving dish and sprinkle a little paprika on top, if you like.

Cook's Tips
• Canned beans are usually in a sugar, salt and water solution so always drain and rinse them thoroughly before use – otherwise the finished pâté may be rather too salty.
• Dried beans can be used instead of canned, if you have the time to prepare them during the festivities. Soak them overnight in plenty of water before boiling in a large pan of fresh water for about 10 minutes, skimming off any scum that rises to the surface. Reduce the heat and then simmer the beans until tender – about 1 to 2 hours.

Variations
• A liberal dusting of paprika will give the pâté an extra kick.
• You can also use other types of canned beans, if you like, such as kidney beans.

Garden Terrine Energy 205kcal/854kJ; Protein 8.3g; Carbohydrate 19.2g, of which sugars 7.7g; Fat 10.6g, of which saturates 6.6g; Cholesterol 27mg; Calcium 196mg; Fibre 3g; Sodium 203mg.
Cannellini Bean Pâté Energy 155kcal/650kJ; Protein 7.4g; Carbohydrate 18.4g, of which sugars 3.9g; Fat 6.3g, of which saturates 0.9g; Cholesterol 0mg; Calcium 96mg; Fibre 6.9g; Sodium 394mg.

Grilled Vegetable Terrine

A colourful, layered terrine, this appetizer uses a variety of Mediterranean vegetables.

Serves 6

2 large red (bell) peppers, quartered, cored, seeded
2 large yellow (bell) peppers, quartered, cored, seeded
1 large aubergine (eggplant), sliced lengthways
2 courgettes (zucchini), sliced lengthways
90ml/6 tbsp olive oil
1 large red onion, thinly sliced
75g/3oz/1/2 cup raisins
15ml/1 tbsp tomato purée (paste)
15ml/1 tbsp red wine vinegar
400ml/14fl oz/1 2/3 cups tomato juice
15g/1/2oz/2 tbsp powdered gelatine
fresh basil leaves, to garnish

For the dressing

90ml/6 tbsp extra virgin olive oil
30ml/2 tbsp red wine vinegar
salt and ground black pepper

1 Place the peppers skin side up under a hot grill (broiler) and cook until the skins are blackened. Transfer to a bowl and cover. Leave to cool. Arrange the aubergine and courgette slices on separate baking sheets. Brush them with oil and cook under the grill, turning occasionally, until they are tender and golden.

2 Heat the remaining olive oil in a frying pan, and add the onion, raisins, tomato purée and red wine vinegar. Cook gently until the mixture is syrupy. Set aside and leave to cool.

3 Lightly oil a 1.75 litre/3 pint/7 1/2 cup terrine, then line it with clear film (plastic wrap), leaving a little hanging over the sides. Pour half the tomato juice into a pan, and sprinkle with the gelatine. Dissolve over low heat, stirring frequently.

4 Place a layer of red peppers in the base of the terrine, and pour in enough tomato juice with gelatine to cover. Continue layering the vegetables, pouring tomato juice over each layer. Finish with a layer of red peppers. Pour the remaining tomato juice into the terrine. Cover and chill until set.

5 To make the dressing, whisk together the oil and vinegar, and season. Turn out the terrine and remove the clear film. Serve in slices, drizzled with dressing and garnished with basil leaves.

Asparagus and Egg Terrine

For festive entertaining, this terrine is a delicious choice.

Serves 8

150ml/1/4 pint/2/3 cup milk
150ml/1/4 pint/2/3 cup double (heavy) cream
40g/1 1/2oz/3 tbsp butter
40g/1 1/2oz/3 tbsp plain (all-purpose) flour
75g/3oz herbed or garlic cream cheese
675g/1 1/2lb asparagus, cooked
vegetable oil, for brushing
2 eggs, separated
15ml/1 tbsp chopped fresh chives
30ml/2 tbsp chopped fresh dill
salt and ground black pepper
fresh dill sprigs, to garnish

For the hollandaise sauce

15ml/1 tbsp white wine vinegar
15ml/1 tbsp fresh orange juice
4 black peppercorns
1 bay leaf
2 egg yolks
115g/4oz/1/2 cup butter, melted and cooled slightly

1 Heat the milk and cream in a small pan to just below boiling point. Melt the butter in a medium pan, stir in the flour and cook over low heat, stirring constantly, to a thick paste. Gradually stir in the milk, whisking as it thickens. Stir in the cream cheese, season to taste and leave to cool slightly.

2 Trim the asparagus to fit the width of a 1.2 litre/2 pint/5 cup loaf tin (pan) or terrine. Lightly oil the tin and then base line with baking parchment. Preheat the oven to 180°C/350°F/Gas 4.

3 Beat the egg yolks into the sauce. Whisk the whites until stiff. Fold in with the chives, dill and seasoning. Layer the asparagus and egg mixture in the tin, starting and finishing with the asparagus. Cover with foil, place in a roasting pan and half fill with hot water. Cook for 45–55 minutes, until firm. Cool, then chill.

4 To make the sauce, put the vinegar, orange juice, peppercorns and bay leaf in a pan and heat gently until reduced by half. Cool the sauce slightly, then whisk in the egg yolks, then the butter, over a very gentle heat. Season to taste and continue whisking until thick. Keep the sauce warm over a pan of hot water.

5 Invert the terrine on to a serving dish, remove the paper and garnish with the dill. Serve in slices with the warmed sauce.

Vegetable Terrine Energy 296kcal/1229kJ; Protein 3.5g; Carbohydrate 20.2g, of which sugars 19.7g; Fat 22.9g, of which saturates 3.4g; Cholesterol 0mg; Calcium 42mg; Fibre 3.8g; Sodium 169mg.
Asparagus Terrine Energy 359kcal/1483kJ; Protein 6.6g; Carbohydrate 7.1g, of which sugars 3.2g; Fat 34.1g, of which saturates 20.2g; Cholesterol 175mg; Calcium 87mg; Fibre 1.6g; Sodium 179mg.

Shrimp, Egg and Avocado Mousses

A light creamy mousse, with lots of texture and a great mix of flavours, will go down a treat at Christmas time.

Serves 6
a little olive oil
20ml/4 tsp powdered gelatine
juice and rind of 1 lemon
60ml/4 tbsp mayonnaise
60ml/4 tbsp chopped fresh dill
5ml/1 tsp anchovy essence (paste)
5ml/1 tsp Worcestershire sauce
1 large avocado, ripe but just firm
4 hard-boiled eggs, peeled and chopped
175g/6oz/1 cup cooked peeled prawns (shrimp), coarsely chopped if large
250ml/8fl oz/1 cup double (heavy) or whipping cream, lightly whipped
2 egg whites, whisked
salt and ground black pepper
fresh dill or parsley sprigs, to garnish
warmed multigrain bread or toast, to serve

1 Prepare six small ramekins. Lightly grease the dishes with olive oil, then wrap a baking parchment collar around the top of each and secure with tape. This makes sure that you can fill the dishes as high as you like and that the extra mixture will be supported while it is setting. The mousses will, therefore, look really dramatic when you remove the paper. Alternatively, prepare just one small soufflé dish.

2 Dissolve the gelatine in the lemon juice with 15ml/1 tbsp hot water in a small bowl set over hot water, until clear, stirring occasionally. Allow to cool slightly, then blend in the lemon rind, mayonnaise, dill, anchovy essence and Worcestershire sauce.

3 In a medium bowl, mash the avocado flesh. Add the eggs and prawns. Stir in the gelatine mixture and then fold in the cream, egg whites and seasoning to taste. When evenly blended, spoon into the ramekins or soufflé dish and chill for 3–4 hours. Garnish with the herbs and serve with bread.

> **Cook's Tip**
> *Other seafood can be a good alternative to prawns (shrimp). Use the same quantity of smoked trout, or cooked crab meat.*

Smoked Salmon Pâté

This pâté is in individual ramekins lined with smoked salmon so that it looks really special. It is the ideal appetizer for an elaborate dinner party or special feast over the festive season. Taste as you are making it; add more lemon juice and seasoning if necessary.

Serves 4
350g/12oz thinly sliced smoked salmon (wild if possible)
150ml/¼ pint/⅔ cup double (heavy) cream
finely grated rind and juice of 1 lemon
salt and ground black pepper
Melba toast, to serve

1 Line four small ramekin dishes with clear film (plastic wrap), then line the dishes with 115g/4oz of the smoked salmon cut into strips long enough to flop over the edges.

2 In a food processor fitted with a metal blade, process the rest of the salmon with the double cream, lemon rind and juice, salt and plenty of ground black pepper.

3 Pack the lined ramekins with the smoked salmon pâté, pressing it down gently. Wrap the loose strips of smoked salmon over the top of the pâté.

4 Cover the ramekins with clear film and chill for at least 30 minutes in the refrigerator.

5 To serve the pâtés, invert the ramekins on to plates. Serve, accompanied by slices of Melba toast.

> **Cook's Tip**
> *Melba toast was created by the celebrated chef Auguste Escoffier for opera singer Dame Nellie Melba. It is sold packaged in most supermarkets but is easy to make at home. Simply toast a slice of bread under a grill (broiler), cut off the crusts and then carefully cut it in half to make two slices of half the thickness. Return the halved slices of bread to the grill to brown the untoasted sides.*

Shrimp Mousses Energy 384kcal/1589kJ; Protein 12g; Carbohydrate 2.1g, of which sugars 1.7g; Fat 38.9g, of which saturates 15.7g; Cholesterol 245mg; Calcium 88mg; Fibre 1.3g; Sodium 230mg.
Smoked Salmon Pâté Energy 311kcal/1293kJ; Protein 22.9g; Carbohydrate 0.8g, of which sugars 0.8g; Fat 24.1g, of which saturates 13.2g; Cholesterol 82mg; Calcium 36mg; Fibre 0g; Sodium 1654mg.

Smoked Salmon Terrine

This salmon terrine makes a spectacular first course for a Christmas dinner.

Serves 6
4 sheets leaf gelatine
60ml/4 tbsp water
400g/14oz smoked salmon, sliced

300g/11oz/scant 1½ cups
    cream cheese
120ml/4fl oz/½ cup
    crème fraîche
30ml/2 tbsp dill mustard
juice of 1 lime
lemon leaves, to
    garnish, optional

1 Soak the gelatine in the water in a small bowl until softened. Meanwhile, line a 450g/1lb loaf tin (pan) with clear film (plastic wrap). Use some of the salmon to line the pan, laying the slices widthways across the base and up the sides, leaving enough hanging over the edge to fold over the top.

2 Set aside enough of the remaining salmon to make a middle layer the length of the pan. Chop the rest finely.

3 In a bowl, beat the cream cheese, crème fraîche and dill mustard until well combined. Mix in the chopped salmon.

4 Squeeze out the gelatine and put the sheets in a small, heavy pan. Add the lime juice. Place over low heat until the gelatine has melted, cool slightly, then stir into the salmon mixture.

5 Spoon half the mixture into the lined tin. Lay the reserved smoked salmon slices on the mixture along the length of the pan, then spoon on the rest of the filling and smooth the top.

6 Fold over the overhanging salmon slices to cover the top. Cover the pan with clear film and place in the refrigerator to chill for at least 4 hours, preferably 6–8 hours. Turn out the terrine and slice. Serve, garnished with lemon leaves, if using.

> **Variation**
> For a special lemon garnish, cut a 'V' from the side of a lemon. Repeat at 5mm/¼in intervals. Separate to form 'leaves'.

Smoked Haddock Pâté

Arbroath smokies are salted and hot-smoked, creating a fantastic flavour, which is perfect for this festive dish.

Serves 6
butter, for greasing
3 large Arbroath smokies, about
    225g/8oz each

275g/10oz/1¼ cups soft white
    (farmer's) cheese
3 eggs, beaten
30–45ml/2–3 tbsp lemon juice
ground black pepper
chervil sprigs, to garnish
lemon wedges and lettuce leaves,
    to serve

1 Preheat the oven to 160°C/325°F/Gas 3. Carefully butter six ramekin dishes. Lay the smokies in an ovenproof dish and heat through in the oven for 10 minutes.

2 Carefully remove the skin and bones from the smokies, then flake the flesh into a bowl.

3 Mash the fish with a fork and work in the cheese, then the eggs. Add lemon juice and pepper.

4 Divide the fish mixture equally among the ramekins and place in a roasting pan. Pour enough hot water into the roasting pan to come halfway up the side of the dishes. Bake for about 30 minutes, until just set.

5 Allow to cool for 2–3 minutes, then run a knife point around the edge of each dish to loosen and then invert on to a warmed plate. Garnish with chervil sprigs and serve with the lemon wedges and lettuce leaves.

> **Cook's Tip**
> The traditional Arbroath method of smoking haddock has earned it the Protected Geographical Indication status, granted by the European Commission. As with other items, such as Parma ham and Champagne, the name 'Arbroath smokie' can only be used to describe the genuine article, made within an 8-km/5-mile radius of Arbroath in Scotland.

Salmon Terrine Energy 187kcal/785kJ; Protein 27.5g; Carbohydrate 0.3g, of which sugars 0.2g; Fat 8.5g, of which saturates 3.7g; Cholesterol 95mg; Calcium 31mg; Fibre 0g; Sodium 735mg.
Smoked Haddock Pâté Energy 307kcal/1274kJ; Protein 22.2g; Carbohydrate 1.5g, of which sugars 1.5g; Fat 23.7g, of which saturates 7.3g; Cholesterol 166mg; Calcium 59mg; Fibre 0g; Sodium 723mg.

Salmon and Pike Mousse

When sliced, this light-textured mousse loaf reveals a pretty layer of pink salmon. For a festive occasion, serve topped with red salmon roe.

Serves 8
10ml/2 tsp oil
225g/8oz salmon fillet, skinned
600ml/1 pint/2½ cups fish stock
finely grated rind and juice of ½ lemon
900g/2lb pike fillets, skinned
4 egg whites
475ml/16fl oz/2 cups double (heavy) cream
30ml/2 tbsp chopped fresh dill
salt and ground black pepper
red salmon roe or a fresh dill sprig, to garnish (optional)

1 Preheat the oven to 180°C/350°F/Gas 4. Brush a 900g/2lb loaf tin (pan) with oil and line with baking parchment.

2 Cut the salmon into 5cm/2in strips. Pour the stock and lemon juice into a pan and bring to the boil, then turn off the heat. Add the salmon strips, cover and leave for 2 minutes. Remove with a slotted spoon.

3 Cut the pike into cubes and process in a food processor or blender until smooth. Lightly whisk the egg whites with a fork. With the motor of the food processor or blender running, slowly pour in the egg whites, then the cream through the feeder tube or lid. Finally, add the lemon rind and dill. Taste the mixture and add a little salt and ground black pepper if you think more seasoning is needed.

4 Spoon half of the pike mixture into the prepared loaf tin. Arrange the poached salmon strips on top, then carefully spoon in the remaining pike mixture.

5 Cover the loaf tin with foil and put in a roasting pan. Add enough boiling water to come halfway up the sides of the loaf tin. Bake for 45–50 minutes, or until firm.

6 Leave the tin on a wire rack to cool, then chill for at least 3 hours. Invert on to a serving plate and remove the lining paper. Serve the mousse in slices. Garnish with red salmon roe or a sprig of fresh dill, if you like.

Smoked Haddock and Avocado Mousse

The fresh-tasting salsa complements the smooth creaminess of the mousse.

Serves 6
225g/8oz undyed smoked haddock fillets, skinned
½ onion, cut into thick rings
25g/1oz/2 tbsp butter
1 bay leaf
150ml/¼ pint/⅔ cup milk
1 ripe avocado, peeled and diced
2 gelatine leaves
30ml/2 tbsp dry white wine
105ml/7 tbsp double (heavy) cream
1 egg white, beaten until stiff
salt, ground white pepper and grated nutmeg

For the salsa
3 tomatoes, peeled, seeded and diced
1 avocado, peeled and diced
1 small red onion, finely chopped
1–2 garlic cloves, finely chopped
1 large fresh green chilli, seeded and finely chopped
45ml/3 tbsp extra virgin olive oil
juice of 1 lime
12 lime slices, to garnish

1 Arrange the fish in a layer in a large pan and top with the onion rings. Dot with butter, season with pepper, add the bay leaf and pour over the milk. Poach over low heat for 5 minutes, until cooked through. Remove the fish and set aside.

2 Remove the bay leaf and onion. Boil the milk until reduced by two-thirds. Flake the fish into a food processor and strain over the milk. Process until smooth. Place in a bowl with the avocado.

3 Soak the gelatine leaves in a little cold water until soft. Add the wine and heat until dissolved. Mix into the fish mixture.

4 Whip the cream in a bowl. Fold the cream, then the beaten egg white into the fish mixture. Season and add a little nutmeg. Pour the mixture into six ramekins or moulds, cover with clear film (plastic wrap) and chill for about 1 hour.

5 To make the salsa, mix the tomatoes with the avocado, onion, garlic and chilli. Pour in the oil and lime juice, and season. Chill.

6 Dip the moulds in hot water, invert on to plates and tap to release. Put a little salsa on the plates and on the top of each mousse. Serve with a couple of lime twists.

Smoked Haddock Mousse Energy 248kcal/1029kJ; Protein 9.2g; Carbohydrate 4g, of which sugars 3g; Fat 21.4g, of which saturates 9.8g; Cholesterol 46mg; Calcium 31mg; Fibre 2.1g; Sodium 331mg.
Salmon Mousse Energy 477kcal/1977kJ; Protein 27.8g; Carbohydrate 1g, of which sugars 1g; Fat 40.3g, of which saturates 21.4g; Cholesterol 171mg; Calcium 89mg; Fibre 0g; Sodium 105mg.

Sea Trout Mousse

This deliciously creamy mousse makes a little sea trout go a long way.

Serves 6
250g/9oz sea trout fillet
120ml/4fl oz/½ cup fish stock
2 gelatine leaves, or 15ml/1 tbsp
    powdered gelatine
juice of ½ lemon
30ml/2 tbsp dry sherry or
    dry vermouth

30ml/2 tbsp freshly grated
    Parmesan
300ml/½ pint/1¼ cups
    whipping cream
2 egg whites
15ml/1 tbsp sunflower oil
salt and ground white pepper

For the garnish
5cm/2in piece of cucumber, with
    peel, thinly sliced and halved
fresh dill or chervil

1 Put the sea trout in a shallow pan. Pour in the fish stock and heat to simmering point. Poach the fish for about 3–4 minutes, until it is lightly cooked. Strain the stock into a jug (pitcher) and leave the trout to cool. Add the gelatine to the hot stock and stir until it has dissolved completely. Set aside until required.

2 When the trout is cool enough to handle, remove the skin and flake the flesh. Pour the stock into a food processor or blender. Process briefly, then gradually add the flaked trout, lemon juice, sherry or vermouth and Parmesan through the feeder tube, continuing to process the mixture until it is smooth. Scrape into a large bowl and leave to cool.

3 Lightly whip the cream in a bowl; fold it into the cold trout mixture. Season to taste, then cover with clear film (plastic wrap) and chill until the mousse is just beginning to set. It should have the consistency of mayonnaise.

4 In a grease-free bowl, beat the egg whites with a pinch of salt until softly peaking. Using a large metal spoon, stir one-third into the trout mixture to slacken it, then fold in the rest.

5 Lightly grease six ramekins with the oil. Divide the mousse among the ramekins and level the surface. Chill for 2–3 hours, until set. To serve, arrange a few slices of cucumber and a small herb sprig on each mousse and add a little dill or chervil.

Anchovy Terrine

This dish is based on a traditional Swedish recipe and uses anchovies as the main ingredient – in this case the Swedish variety, flavoured with cinnamon, cloves and allspice.

Serves 6–8
5 hard-boiled eggs
100g/3½oz can Swedish or
    matjes anchovies
2 gelatine leaves

200ml/7fl oz/scant 1 cup
    sour cream
½ red onion, chopped
1 bunch fresh dill, chopped
15ml/1 tbsp Swedish or
    German mustard
salt and ground black pepper
peeled prawns (shrimp) or
    lumpfish roe and dill fronds,
    to garnish
Melba toast or rye bread,
    to serve

1 Line a 20cm/8in terrine with clear film (plastic wrap). Mash the hard-boiled eggs in a bowl. Drain the juice from the anchovy can and add to the mashed eggs. In a large, separate bowl, mash the anchovies.

2 Melt the gelatine leaves as directed on the packet and add to the mashed eggs with the sour cream, mashed anchovies, chopped onion, dill and mustard. Season with salt and ground black pepper to taste and stir thoroughly together until all the ingredients are well combined.

3 Pour the mixture into the prepared terrine and chill in the refrigerator for about 2 hours.

4 To serve, carefully turn out the terrine and garnish with freshly peeled prawns or lumpfish roe and dill fronds. Serve with Melba toast or rye bread.

Cook's Tip
If you have neither Swedish nor matjes anchovies, you can soak normal, salted canned anchovies in milk for about 2–3 hours before you use them, adding a final sprinkling of ground cinnamon and cloves.

Sea Trout Mousse Energy 241kcal/999kJ; Protein 12.3g; Carbohydrate 1.8g, of which sugars 1.8g; Fat 20g, of which saturates 14.5g; Cholesterol 9mg; Calcium 104mg; Fibre 0.1g; Sodium 127mg.
Anchovy Terrine Energy 127kcal/529kJ; Protein 8.1g; Carbohydrate 1.8g, of which sugars 1.6g; Fat 9.9g, of which saturates 4.3g; Cholesterol 142mg; Calcium 88mg; Fibre 0.3g; Sodium 602mg.

Fish Terrine

This layered terrine makes a spectacular presentation for a special festive occasion.

Serves 6
450g/1lb skinless white fish fillets
225–275g/8–10oz thinly sliced
    smoked salmon

2 cold egg whites
1.5ml/¼ tsp each salt and
    white pepper
pinch of freshly grated nutmeg
250ml/8fl oz/1 cup
    whipping cream
50g/2oz/2 cups spinach leaves
lemon mayonnaise, to serve

1 Cut the fish fillets into 2.5cm/1in pieces, removing any bones as you work. Spread out the fish pieces on a plate, cover with clear film (plastic wrap). Place in the freezer for 15 minutes.

2 Lightly grease a 1.2 litre/2 pint/5 cup terrine or loaf tin (pan) and line with baking parchment. Line the base and sides of the tin with salmon slices, letting them overhang the edge. Preheat the oven to 180°C/350°F/Gas 4.

3 Process the fish in a food processor until it is a very smooth purée. Add the egg whites, one at a time, then add the salt, pepper and nutmeg. With the machine running, pour in the cream and stop as soon as it is blended.

4 Transfer the fish mixture to a bowl. Put the spinach leaves into the food processor and purée. Add one-third of the fish mixture to the spinach and process until just combined.

5 Spread half the plain fish mixture in the base of the tin and smooth it level. Spoon the spinach/fish mixture over the top and smooth, then cover with the remaining plain mixture and smooth again. Fold the overhanging salmon pieces over the top to enclose. Tap the tin and cover with a double layer of foil.

6 Put the terrine in a roasting pan and pour in enough boiling water to come halfway up the sides of the terrine. Bake for about 1 hour. Allow to cool, wrap and chill until firm.

7 To serve, turn out on to a board and slice. Arrange slices on individual plates and serve with lemon mayonnaise.

Haddock and Smoked Salmon Terrine

This substantial terrine makes a superb appetizer for a Christmas buffet.

Serves 10–12
15ml/1 tbsp sunflower oil,
    for greasing
350g/12oz oak-smoked salmon
900g/2lb haddock fillets, skinned

2 eggs, lightly beaten
105ml/7 tbsp crème fraîche
30ml/2 tbsp drained capers
30ml/2 tbsp drained soft green
    or pink peppercorns
salt and ground white pepper
crème fraîche, peppercorns, fresh
    dill and rocket (arugula),
    to garnish

1 Preheat the oven to 200°C/400°F/Gas 6. Grease a 1 litre/1¾ pint/4 cup loaf tin (pan) or terrine with the oil. Use half of the salmon to line the tin or terrine, letting some of the ends overhang the mould. Reserve the remaining smoked salmon.

2 Cut two long slices of haddock the length of the tin or terrine and set aside. Cut the rest of the haddock into small pieces. Season all the haddock.

3 Combine the eggs, crème fraîche, capers and peppercorns in a bowl. Season, then stir in the small pieces of haddock. Spoon into the tin or terrine until one-third full. Smooth the surface. Wrap the reserved long haddock fillets in the reserved salmon. Lay them on top of the fish mixture in the tin or terrine.

4 Fill the tin or terrine with the rest of the fish mixture, smooth the surface and fold over the overhanging pieces of salmon. Cover with a double thickness of foil. Stand the terrine in a roasting pan and pour in boiling water to come halfway up the sides. Place in the oven and cook for 45 minutes to 1 hour.

5 Take the terrine out of the roasting pan, but do not remove the foil cover. Place two or three large heavy cans on the foil to weight it and leave until cold. Chill in the refrigerator for 24 hours.

6 About 1 hour before serving, lift off the weights and remove the foil. Carefully invert the terrine on to a serving plate and lift off the terrine. Serve the terrine in thick slices with crème fraîche, peppercorns, fronds of dill and rocket leaves.

Fish Terrine Energy 248kcal/1030kJ; Protein 24g; Carbohydrate 2.2g, of which sugars 0.6g; Fat 15.9g, of which saturates 5.7g; Cholesterol 74mg; Calcium 51mg; Fibre 0.7g; Sodium 108mg.
Haddock Terrine Energy 187kcal/785kJ; Protein 27.5g; Carbohydrate 0.3g, of which sugars 0.2g; Fat 8.5g, of which saturates 3.7g; Cholesterol 95mg; Calcium 31mg; Fibre 0g; Sodium 735mg.

Cardamom Chicken Mousselines

These mousselines are made in the slow cooker and make an elegant appetizer. They should be served warm, not hot, so when they are cooked, turn off the slow cooker and leave to cool for half an hour before eating.

Serves 6
350g/12oz skinless chicken
  breast fillets
1 shallot, finely chopped

115g/4oz/1 cup full-fat soft white
  (farmer's) cheese
1 egg, lightly beaten
2 egg whites
crushed seeds of 2 cardamom pods
60ml/4 tbsp white wine
150ml/¼ pint/⅔ cup double
  (heavy) cream
oregano sprigs, to serve

For the tomato vinaigrette
350g/12oz ripe tomatoes
10ml/2 tsp balsamic vinegar
30ml/2 tbsp olive oil

1 Chop the chicken and put in a food processor with the shallot. Process until fairly smooth. Add the cheese, beaten egg, egg whites, cardamom seeds and wine and season with salt and pepper. Process again until the ingredients are blended.

2 Gradually add the cream, using the pulsing action, until the mixture has a smooth and creamy texture. Transfer to a bowl, cover with clear film (plastic wrap) and chill for 30 minutes.

3 Meanwhile, prepare six 150ml/¼ pint/⅔ cup ramekins or dariole moulds that will all fit in the slow cooker. Lightly grease the base of each one, then line. Pour about 2cm/¾ in hot water into the ceramic cooking pot and switch the cooker to high.

4 Divide the mixture among the dishes. Cover with foil and put in the ceramic cooking pot. Add more hot water to come halfway up the dishes. Cover and cook for 2½–3 hours until firm.

5 Meanwhile, peel, quarter, seed and dice the tomatoes. Place in a bowl and sprinkle with the vinegar and salt. Stir well.

6 To serve, unmould the mousselines on to warmed plates. Place tomato vinaigrette around each, then drizzle over a little olive oil and add black pepper. Garnish with sprigs of oregano.

Chicken and Pistachio Pâté

This simplified pâté can be made using either chicken pieces or left-over turkey meat. Serve it as part of a festive buffet accompanied by a herb mayonnaise.

Serves 10–12
900g/2lb boneless chicken meat
1 skinless chicken breast fillet
  (about 175g/6oz)
25g/1oz/⅔ cup fresh
  white breadcrumbs
120ml/4fl oz/½ cup
  whipping cream

1 egg white
4 spring onions (scallions),
  finely chopped
1 garlic clove, finely chopped
75g/3oz cooked ham, cut into
  1cm/½in cubes
50g/2oz/⅓ cup shelled
  pistachio nuts
45ml/3 tbsp chopped
  fresh tarragon
pinch of grated nutmeg
5ml/1 tsp salt
7.5ml/1½ tsp pepper
green salad, to serve

1 Trim all the fat, tendons and connective tissue from the 900g/2lb chicken meat and cut into 5cm/2in cubes. Put in a food processor fitted with the metal blade and pulse to chop the meat to a smooth purée, in two or three batches if necessary.

2 Preheat the oven to 180°C/350°F/Gas 4. Cut the chicken breast fillet into 1cm/⅜in cubes.

3 In a large mixing bowl, soak the breadcrumbs in the cream. Add the puréed chicken, egg white, spring onions, garlic, ham, pistachio nuts, tarragon, nutmeg and salt and pepper. Using a wooden spoon or your fingers, mix until very well combined.

4 Lay out a piece of extra-wide strong foil about 45cm/18in long on a work surface and lightly brush oil on a 30cm/12in square in the centre. Spoon the chicken mixture on to the foil to form a log shape about 30cm/12in long and about 9cm/3½in thick across the width of the foil. Bring together the long sides and fold over to enclose. Twist the ends and tie with string.

5 Transfer to a baking dish and bake for 1½ hours. Leave to cool in the dish and chill until cold, preferably overnight. Serve the pâté sliced, with a green salad.

Cardamon Mousselines Energy 191kcal/795kJ; Protein 18.1g; Carbohydrate 2g, of which sugars 2g; Fat 11.6g, of which saturates 5g; Cholesterol 96mg; Calcium 30mg; Fibre 0.7g; Sodium 130mg.
Chicken Pâté Energy 189kcal/790kJ; Protein 22.5g; Carbohydrate 2.8g, of which sugars 0.8g; Fat 9.8g, of which saturates 3.9g; Cholesterol 54mg; Calcium 26mg; Fibre 0.4g; Sodium 203mg.

Chicken and Pork Terrine

Serve this delicate pâté with warm, crusty bread as an elegant appetizer before the main Christmas Day meal.

Serves 6–8
225g/8oz rindless, streaky
  (fatty) bacon rashers (strips)
375g/13oz chicken breast
  fillet, skinned
15ml/1 tbsp lemon juice

225g/8oz lean minced
  (ground) pork
½ small onion, finely chopped
2 eggs, beaten
30ml/2 tbsp chopped
  fresh parsley
5ml/1 tsp salt
5ml/1 tsp green peppercorns,
  lightly crushed
fresh green salad, radishes and
  lemon wedges, to serve

1 Preheat the oven to 160°C/325°F/Gas 3. Put the bacon rashers on a board and stretch them using the back of a knife so that they can be arranged in over-lapping slices over the base and sides of a 900g/2lb loaf tin (pan).

2 Cut 115g/4oz of the chicken into strips about 10cm/4in long. Sprinkle with lemon juice and set aside.

3 Place the rest of the chicken in a food processor or blender with the minced pork and the chopped onion. Process briefly until the mixture is fairly smooth.

4 Add the eggs, parsley, salt and peppercorns to the meat mixture and process again briefly. Spoon half the mixture into the loaf tin and then level the surface.

5 Arrange the chicken strips on top, then spoon in the remaining meat mixture and smooth the top. Give the tin a couple of sharp taps to knock out any pockets of air.

6 Cover with a piece of oiled foil and put in a roasting pan. Pour in enough hot water to come halfway up the sides of the loaf tin. Bake for about 45–50 minutes, until firm.

7 Allow the terrine to cool in the tin before turning out and chilling. Serve sliced, with a fresh green salad, radishes and wedges of lemon to squeeze over.

Duck Liver Pâté and Redcurrant Sauce

This tasty pâté is easy to prepare and will keep for about a week in the refrigerator if the butter seal is not broken.

Serves 4–6
1 onion, finely chopped
1 large garlic clove, crushed
115g/4oz/½ cup butter
225g/8oz duck livers
10–15ml/2–3 tsp chopped fresh
  mixed herbs, such as parsley,
  thyme or rosemary
15–30ml/1–2 tbsp brandy

50–115g/2–4oz/¼ –½ cup
  clarified butter, or melted
  unsalted butter
salt and ground black pepper
a sprig of flat leaf parsley,
  to garnish

For the redcurrant sauce
30ml/2 tbsp redcurrant jelly
15–30ml/1–2 tbsp port
30ml/2 tbsp redcurrants

For the Melba toast
8 slices white bread,
  crusts removed

1 Cook the onion and garlic in 25g/1oz/2 tbsp of the butter in a pan over gentle heat, until just turning colour.

2 Add the duck livers to the pan with the herbs and cook together for about 3 minutes, or until the livers have browned on the outside but are still pink in the centre. Allow to cool.

3 Dice the remaining butter, then process the liver mixture in a food processor, gradually working in the cubes of butter by dropping them down the chute, to make a smooth purée.

4 Add the brandy, then check the seasoning and transfer to a 450–600ml/¾–1 pint dish. Seal the pâté with clarified or unsalted butter. Cool, and then chill until required.

5 For the sauce, put the jelly, port and redcurrants into a pan. Bring to the boil, then simmer to reduce a little. Leave to cool.

6 To make the Melba toast, toast the bread on both sides, then slice vertically to make 16 very thin slices. Place the untoasted side face up on a grill (broiler) rack and grill (broil) until browned. Serve the chilled pâté garnished with parsley and accompanied by Melba toast and the redcurrant sauce.

Chicken Terrine Energy 191kcal/798kJ; Protein 22g; Carbohydrate 0.6g, of which sugars 0.4g; Fat 11.3g, of which saturates 3.8g; Cholesterol 115mg; Calcium 15mg; Fibre 0.1g; Sodium 417mg.
Duck Liver Pâté Energy 794kcal/3312kJ; Protein 101.3g; Carbohydrate 11.3g, of which sugars 9.9g; Fat 36.8g, of which saturates 19g; Cholesterol 2213mg; Calcium 73mg; Fibre 1.3g; Sodium 608mg.

Chicken Liver and Brandy Pâté

This rich pâté is quick and easy to make and tastes so much better than anything you can buy in the supermarkets. Serve as an appetizer with Melba toast or crackers.

Serves 4

350g/12oz chicken livers
50g/2oz/¼ cup butter
30ml/2 tbsp brandy
30ml/2 tbsp double
  (heavy) cream
salt and ground black pepper

1 Trim any fat from the chicken livers and discard. Chop the livers roughly. Heat the butter in a large frying pan.

2 Add the chicken livers to the pan and cook over medium heat for 3–4 minutes, stirring occasionally, until evenly browned all over and cooked through.

3 Pour the brandy into the pan with the chicken livers and allow to bubble for a few minutes. Remove the pan from the heat and set aside to cool slightly.

4 Place the livers and brandy in a food processor or blender. Pour in the double cream and season with salt and plenty of ground black pepper.

5 Process the mixture until smooth and then spoon it into ramekin dishes. Level the surface of each dish and chill overnight in the refrigerator to set. Serve garnished with sprigs of fresh parsley to add a little colour.

Cook's Tips
• If you can't find any fresh chicken livers, look out for them in the freezer section of large supermarkets. Ensure that they are fully defrosted before using.
• This is a useful dish for serving on Christmas Day as it can be made a few days in advance, which helps to take some of the strain off the busy festive period. If you are making the pâté more than 1 day ahead, seal the surface of each portion in the ramekin dish with a layer of melted butter.

Game Terrine

Any game can be used to make this country terrine – hare, rabbit, pheasant or pigeon – so choose the best meat your butcher has to offer.

Serves 8

225g/8oz rindless, unsmoked
  streaky (fatty) bacon
  rashers (strips)
225g/8oz lamb's or pig's liver,
  minced (ground)

450g/1lb minced (ground) pork
1 small onion, finely chopped
2 garlic cloves, crushed
10ml/2 tsp mixed dried herbs
225g/8oz game of your choice
60ml/4 tbsp port or sherry
1 bay leaf
50g/2oz/½ cup plain
  (all-purpose) flour
300ml/½ pint/1¼ cups aspic jelly,
  made up as packet instructions
salt and ground black pepper

1 Stretch each rasher with the back of a knife, then use to line a 1 litre/1¾ pint/4 cup terrine. The terrine must have a lid to help seal in the flavours during cooking.

2 Mix the minced meats with the onion, garlic and mixed dried herbs. Season well with plenty of salt and ground black pepper.

3 Cut the game into thin strips, and place in a large mixing bowl with the port or sherry. Season with salt and pepper.

4 Put one-third of the minced mixture into the terrine. Press the mixture well into the corners. Cover with half the strips of the game and repeat these layers, ending with a minced layer. Level the surface and lay the bay leaf on top.

5 Preheat the oven to 160°C/325°F/Gas 3. Put the flour into a small bowl and mix it to a firm dough with 30–45ml/2–3 tbsp cold water. Cover the terrine with a lid and seal it with the flour paste. Place the terrine in a roasting pan and pour in hot water to come halfway up the sides of the tin. Bake for 2 hours.

6 Remove the lid and weigh the terrine down with a 2kg/4½lb weight. Leave to cool. Remove any fat from the surface and cover with warmed aspic jelly. Leave overnight before turning out on to a serving plate. Serve in thin slices with a mixed salad.

Chicken Liver Pâté Energy 227kcal/942kJ; Protein 15.7g; Carbohydrate 0.2g, of which sugars 0.2g; Fat 16.3g, of which saturates 9.6g; Cholesterol 369mg; Calcium 13mg; Fibre 0g; Sodium 144mg.
Game Terrine Energy 266kcal/1112kJ; Protein 27.1g; Carbohydrate 6.4g, of which sugars 1.4g; Fat 14g, of which saturates 5g; Cholesterol 182mg; Calcium 25mg; Fibre 0.3g; Sodium 432mg.

Spiced Pork Pâté

This pâté has an Asian twist: it is steamed in banana leaves, which are available in African and Asian markets. However, if you cannot find them you can use large spring green leaves or several Savoy cabbage leaves instead.

Serves 6

45ml/3 tbsp Thai fish sauce
30ml/2 tbsp sesame oil
15ml/1 tbsp sugar
10ml/2 tsp five-spice powder
2 shallots, peeled and
    finely chopped
2 garlic cloves, crushed
750g/1lb 10oz/3¼ cups minced
    (ground) pork
25g/1oz/¼ cup potato starch
7.5ml/1½ tsp baking powder
1 banana leaf, trimmed into a
    strip 25cm/10in wide
vegetable oil, for brushing
salt and ground black pepper
Thai dipping sauce and a
    baguette or salad, to serve

1 In a bowl, beat the fish sauce and oil with the sugar and five-spice powder. Once the sugar has dissolved, stir in the shallots and garlic. Add the pork and seasoning, and knead well until thoroughly combined. Cover and chill for 2–3 hours.

2 Knead the mixture again, thumping it down into the bowl to remove any air. Add the potato starch and baking powder and knead until smooth and pasty. Mould the pork mixture into a fat sausage, about 18cm/7in long, and place it on an oiled dish.

3 Lay the banana leaf on a flat surface, brush it with a little vegetable oil, and place the pork sausage across it. Lift up the edge of the banana leaf nearest to you and fold it over the sausage mixture, tuck in the sides, and roll it up into a firm, tight bundle. Secure the bundle with a piece of string, so that it doesn't unravel during cooking.

4 Fill a wok one-third full with water. Balance a bamboo steamer, with its lid on, above the level of the water. Bring to the boil, lift the lid and place the banana leaf bundle on the rack, being careful not to burn yourself. Re-cover and steam for about 45 minutes. Leave the pâté to cool in the leaf, then open it up and cut it into slices. Drizzle with the sauce, and serve accompanied by a baguette or salad.

Herbed Liver Pâté Pie

Serve this highly flavoured pâté with a glass of Pilsner beer and some spicy dill pickles to complement the strong tastes.

Serves 10

675g/1½lb minced (ground) pork
350g/12oz pork liver
350g/12oz/2 cups diced
    cooked ham
1 small onion, finely chopped
30ml/2 tbsp chopped
    fresh parsley
5ml/1 tsp German mustard
30ml/2 tbsp Kirsch
5ml/1 tsp salt
beaten egg, for sealing and glazing
25g/1oz sachet aspic jelly
250ml/8fl oz/1 cup boiling water
ground black pepper
mustard, bread and dill pickles,
    to serve

For the pastry
450g/1lb/4 cups plain
    (all-purpose) flour
275g/10oz/1¼ cups butter
2 eggs plus 1 egg yolk
30ml/2 tbsp water

1 Preheat the oven to 200°C/400°F/Gas 6. For the pastry, sift the flour and salt and rub in the butter. Beat the eggs, egg yolk and water, and mix into the flour. Knead the pastry dough until it becomes smooth. Roll out two-thirds on a lightly floured surface and use to line a 10 × 25cm/4 × 10in hinged loaf tin (pan). Trim any excess pastry.

2 Process half the pork and all of the liver until fairly smooth. Stir in the remaining pork, ham, onion, parsley, mustard, Kirsch, salt and black pepper. Spoon into the tin and level the surface.

3 Roll out the remaining pastry and use it to top the pie. Seal the edges with egg. Decorate with pastry trimmings and glaze with egg. Make four holes in the top.

4 Bake for 40 minutes, then reduce the oven temperature down to 180°C/350°F/Gas 4 and cook for another hour. Cover with foil and leave to cool in the tin.

5 Dissolve the aspic jelly in the boiling water, then leave to cool slightly. Make a small hole near the pie edge and pour in the aspic. Chill for 2 hours. Serve the pie in slices, accompanied by mustard, bread and dill pickles.

Spiced Pork Pâté Energy 234kcal/978kJ; Protein 28g; Carbohydrate 8g, of which sugars 3g; Fat 10g, of which saturates 2g; Cholesterol 79mg; Calcium 46mg; Fibre 0.4g; Sodium 700mg.
Liver Pâté Pie Energy 576kcal/2407kJ; Protein 32.9g; Carbohydrate 36g, of which sugars 1.6g; Fat 33.7g, of which saturates 18.1g; Cholesterol 273mg; Calcium 87mg; Fibre 1.5g; Sodium 888mg.

Seared Scallops with Chive Sauce

Scallops are partnered with a chive sauce and a pilaff of wild and white rice with leeks and carrots.

Serves 4
12–16 shelled scallops
45ml/3 tbsp olive oil
50g/2oz/⅓ cup wild rice
65g/2½oz/5 tbsp butter
4 carrots, cut into long thin strips
2 leeks, cut into diagonal slices

I small onion, finely chopped
115g/4oz/⅔ cup long grain rice
I fresh bay leaf
200ml/7fl oz/scant I cup
   white wine
450ml/¾ pint/scant 2 cups
   fish stock
60ml/4 tbsp double (heavy) cream
a little lemon juice
25ml/5 tsp chopped fresh chives
30ml/2 tbsp chervil sprigs
salt and ground black pepper

I Lightly season the scallops, brush with 15ml/1 tbsp of the olive oil and set aside. Cook the wild rice in plenty of boiling water for about 30 minutes, until tender, then drain.

2 Melt half the butter in a frying pan and cook the carrots for 5 minutes. Add the leeks and fry for 2 minutes. Season and add 30–45ml/2–3 tbsp water, then cover and cook for a few minutes more. Uncover and cook until the liquid has reduced.

3 Melt half the rest of the butter with 15ml/1 tbsp of the remaining oil in a pan. Fry the onion for 3–4 minutes. Add the long grain rice and bay leaf and stir-fry for 3–4 minutes.

4 Pour in half the wine and half the stock. Season with salt and bring to the boil. Stir, then cover and simmer for 15 minutes, or until the liquid is absorbed and the rice is cooked and tender. Stir the carrots, leeks and wild rice into the long grain rice. Boil the remaining wine and stock in a pan until reduced by half.

5 Heat a frying pan over high heat. Add the remaining butter and oil. Sear the scallops for 1–2 minutes each side, then set aside. Pour the reduced stock and cream into the pan and boil until thick. Season and stir in the lemon juice, chives and scallops.

6 Stir the chervil into the rice and pile it on to plates. Arrange the scallops on top and spoon the sauce over the rice.

Spicy Squid

This aromatically spiced squid dish is simple yet delicious. Squid can be bought ready-cleaned from fish stores, market stalls and the fish counters of large supermarkets, making this dish quick to prepare over the busy festive season.

Serves 3–4
675g/1½lb squid, cleaned
45ml/3 tbsp groundnut
   (peanut) oil

I onion, finely chopped
2 garlic cloves, crushed
I beefsteak tomato, peeled
   and chopped
15ml/1 tbsp dark soy sauce
2.5ml/½ tsp grated nutmeg
6 cloves
150ml/¼ pint/⅔ cup water
juice of ½ lemon or lime
salt and ground black pepper
fresh coriander (cilantro) leaves
   and shredded spring onions
   (scallions), to garnish

I Rinse and drain the squid, then slice lengthways along one side and open it out flat. Score the inside of the squid in a lattice pattern, using the blunt side of a knife blade, then cut it crossways into long thin strips.

2 Heat a wok and add 15ml/1 tbsp of the oil. When hot, toss in the squid strips and stir-fry for 2–3 minutes, by which time the squid will have curled into attractive shapes or into firm rings. Lift out and set aside.

3 Wipe out the wok, add the remaining oil and heat it. Stir-fry the onion and garlic until soft and beginning to brown.

4 Stir in the tomato, soy sauce, nutmeg, cloves, water and lemon or lime juice. Bring to the boil, lower the heat and add the squid with salt and black pepper to taste.

5 Cook the mixture gently for a further 3–5 minutes, stirring occasionally to prevent it from sticking to the base of the pan. Take care not to overcook the squid.

6 Spoon the spicy squid on to warm plates. Garnish with fresh coriander leaves and shredded spring onions and serve. Boiled rice is an ideal accompaniment.

Spicy Squid Energy 310kcal/1301kJ; Protein 35.8g; Carbohydrate 8.6g, of which sugars 4.7g; Fat 15.1g, of which saturates 3g; Cholesterol 506mg; Calcium 46mg; Fibre 1.2g; Sodium 610mg.
Seared Scallops Energy 598kcal/2489kJ; Protein 30.8g; Carbohydrate 38.9g, of which sugars 6.3g; Fat 32g, of which saturates 15.3g; Cholesterol 108mg; Calcium 88mg; Fibre 3.1g; Sodium 321mg.

Lobster Noodles

This dish is in the luxury league so it is ideal for impressing your guests when entertaining over the festive season. Restaurants present this dish with great fanfare, with the lobster sitting in all its pink-shelled glory on top of the plate of cooked noodles, so why not follow their example?

Serves 4
1 large live or freshly cooked
  lobster, about 1kg/2¼lb
400g/14oz dried egg noodles
30ml/2 tbsp vegetable oil
15ml/1 tbsp crushed garlic
115g/4oz/½ cup beansprouts
200ml/7fl oz/scant 1 cup water
30ml/2 tbsp oyster sauce
5ml/1 tsp ground black pepper
30ml/2 tbsp sesame oil

1 If the lobster is live, place it in a plastic bag and put it in the freezer for 5–7 hours. Bring a large pan of water to the boil, add the comatose lobster and cook for 10 minutes or until the shell has turned scarlet. Remove and set aside to cool.

2 Heat a separate pan of water and cook the noodles according to the instructions on the packet. Drain and set aside.

3 When the lobster is cool enough to handle, use a sharp knife to cut off the head and the tip of the tail. Rinse and set aside for the garnish. Twist off the claws and set aside.

4 Using a sharp pair of poultry shears or strong scissors, cut down the shell from the top to the tail. Remove the lobster meat, and slice it into rounds. Remove the meat from the claws and legs. Set all the lobster meat aside.

5 Heat the oil in a wok or large frying pan, and fry the garlic for about 40 seconds. Add the beansprouts and cook over the heat for 2 minutes, stirring constantly.

6 Add the noodles, water, oyster sauce, black pepper and sesame oil to the pan and cook, stirring, for 2 minutes.

7 Add the lobster slices and toss lightly. Arrange on a large oval plate, making sure that the lobster pieces are fairly prominent. Decorate with the lobster head and tail.

Lobster and Crab Steamed in Beer

This recipe is very easy to make and, although it may be expensive, it is a wonderful dish for a festive occasion.

Serves 4
4 uncooked lobsters, about
  450g/1lb each
4 uncooked crabs, about
  225g/8oz each
600ml/1 pint/2½ cups beer
4 spring onions (scallions),
  trimmed and chopped into
  long pieces
4cm/1½in fresh root ginger,
  peeled and finely sliced
2 green or red Thai chillies,
  seeded and finely sliced
3 lemon grass stalks, finely sliced
1 bunch fresh dill,
  fronds chopped
1 bunch each fresh basil and
  coriander (cilantro), stalks
  removed, leaves chopped
about 30ml/2 tbsp Thai fish
  sauce, plus extra for serving
juice of 1 lemon
salt and ground black pepper

1 Clean the lobsters and crabs thoroughly and rub them with salt and ground black pepper. Place them in a large steamer and pour the beer into the base.

2 Sprinkle half the spring onions, ginger, chillies, lemon grass and herbs over the lobsters and crabs, and steam for about 10 minutes, or until the lobsters turn red. Lift them on to a warmed serving dish.

3 Add the remaining flavouring ingredients to the beer with the fish sauce and lemon juice. Pour into a dipping bowl and serve immediately with the hot lobsters and crabs, with extra splashes of fish sauce, if you like.

Cook's Tip
Whether you cook the lobsters and crabs at the same time depends on the number of people you are cooking for and the size of your steamer. However, they don't take long to cook so it is easy to steam them in batches. You can make this recipe for as many people as you like because the quantities are simple to adjust, so even if you are having a lot of guests over for a Christmas dinner party, this recipe can be made to suit.

Lobster and Crab Energy 264kcal/1112kJ; Protein 48g; Carbohydrate 4g, of which sugars 1g; Fat 7g, of which saturates 1g; Cholesterol 210mg; Calcium 185mg; Fibre 0.5g; Sodium 130mg.
Lobster Noodles Energy 501kcal/2110kJ; Protein 29.9g; Carbohydrate 56.9g, of which sugars 4g; Fat 18.8g, of which saturates 3.5g; Cholesterol 123mg; Calcium 83mg; Fibre 2.6g; Sodium 559mg.

Dublin Bay Prawns in Garlic Butter

Although they are caught in the Irish Sea, Dublin Bay prawns are in fact the ubiquitous 'scampi'. This home-made, all-time favourite is sure to be popular at Christmas, whether as a first or main course. Try it with lemon wedges, rice and a salad.

Serves 4

32–36 large Dublin Bay prawns (jumbo shrimp)
225g/8oz/1 cup butter
15ml/1 tbsp olive oil
4 or 5 garlic cloves, crushed
15ml/1 tbsp lemon juice
sea salt and ground black pepper

1 If the prawns are still in their shells, twist off the heads and the long claws, then peel the shell off the tails and remove the meat. If the claws are big it is worthwhile extracting any meat you can from them with a lobster pick.

2 Make a shallow cut along the back of each prawn. Remove the trail (the dark vein) that runs along the back.

3 Heat a large heavy pan over medium heat, add the butter and oil and the garlic. When the butter is foaming, sprinkle the prawns with a little salt and pepper, and add them to the pan. Cook for 2 minutes until the prawns are heated through.

4 Add lemon juice to taste, and adjust the seasoning if necessary, and then turn the prawns and their buttery juices on to warmed plates and serve immediately.

Cook's Tips
• *Dublin Bay prawns (jumbo shrimp), or langoustines, can weigh up to 225g/8oz each, although the average weight is 45g/1¾oz. You'll need 8–9 per person for a main course, or 3–4 per person for an appetizer.*
• *When fresh, Dublin Bay prawns have a slightly sweet flavour that is often lost when they have been frozen.*
• *Take care not to ovecook Dublin Bay prawns or they will become tough.*

Crumb-coated Prawns

These delicious prawns have a fiery kick and will add some spice to any festive dinner party.

Serves 4

90g/3½oz/¾ cup polenta
about 5–10ml/1–2 tsp cayenne pepper, to taste
2.5ml/½ tsp ground cumin
5ml/1 tsp salt
30ml/2 tbsp chopped fresh coriander (cilantro) or parsley
1kg/2¼lb large raw prawns (shrimp), peeled and deveined
plain (all-purpose) flour, for dredging
50ml/2fl oz/¼ cup vegetable oil
115g/4oz/1 cup coarsely grated Cheddar cheese
lime wedges and tomato salsa, to serve

1 Put the polenta, cayenne pepper, cumin, salt and chopped coriander or parsley in a bowl and mix well until combined.

2 Coat the prawns lightly in a little of the plain flour, then dip them in cold water and roll in the polenta mixture until they are evenly coated.

3 Heat the oil in a large, heavy frying pan. When hot, add the prawns, in batches if necessary. Cook over medium heat, stirring and tossing well, for 2–3 minutes on each side, until they are cooked through. Drain on kitchen paper.

4 Preheat the grill (broiler). Place the prawns in a flameproof dish, or in four individual ones. Sprinkle over the grated cheese.

5 Grill (broil) the prawns for about 2–3 minutes until the cheese is bubbling and golden brown. Serve immediately with lime wedges and tomato salsa.

Cook's Tip
To make a tomato salsa, mix 3 diced tomatoes with 1 finely chopped red onion, 1 finely chopped garlic clove and 1 seeded and chopped fresh green chilli. Pour in 45ml/3 tbsp extra virgin olive oil and the juice of 1 lime, and season with salt and black pepper. Mix well and chill until needed.

Dublin Bay Prawns Energy 498kcal/2054kJ; Protein 13g; Carbohydrate 0.4g, of which sugars 0.4g; Fat 49.4g, of which saturates 29.8g; Cholesterol 260mg; Calcium 67mg; Fibre 0g; Sodium 478mg.
Coated Prawns Energy 467kcal/1950kJ; Protein 53.4g; Carbohydrate 16.5g, of which sugars 0g; Fat 19.9g, of which saturates 7.4g; Cholesterol 515mg; Calcium 411mg; Fibre 0.5g; Sodium 683mg.

Steamed Lettuce-wrapped Sole with Mussels

Lemon sole, trout, plaice, flounder and brill are all excellent cooked this way, but for festive entertaining, you won't better the taste and texture of Dover sole.

Serves 4
2 large sole fillets, skinned
15ml/1 tbsp sesame seeds
15ml/1 tbsp sunflower or
  groundnut (peanut) oil
10ml/2 tsp sesame oil
2.5cm/1in piece fresh root ginger,
  peeled and grated
3 garlic cloves, finely chopped
15ml/1 tbsp soy sauce or Thai
  fish sauce
juice of 1 lemon
2 spring onions (scallions),
  thinly sliced
8 large soft lettuce leaves
12 large fresh mussels, scrubbed
  and bearded

1 Cut the sole fillets in half lengthways. Season with salt and pepper, and set aside. Prepare a steamer.

2 Heat a heavy frying pan until hot. Toast the sesame seeds lightly but do not allow them to burn. Set aside in a bowl until required.

3 Heat the oils in the frying pan over medium heat. Add the ginger and garlic and cook until lightly coloured; stir in the soy sauce or fish sauce, lemon juice and spring onions. Remove from the heat; stir in the toasted sesame seeds.

4 Lay the pieces of fish on baking parchment, skinned side up; spread each evenly with the ginger mixture. Roll up each piece, starting at the tail end. Place on a baking sheet.

5 Plunge the lettuce leaves into the boiling water for the steamer and lift them out. Gently pat them dry. Wrap each sole parcel in two lettuce leaves, making sure the filling is well covered.

6 Arrange the fish parcels in a steamer basket, cover and steam over simmering water for 8 minutes. Add the mussels and steam for 2–4 minutes, until opened. Discard any that remain closed. Put the parcels on individual plates, halve and garnish with mussels. Serve immediately.

Fried Flat Fish with Lemon and Capers

Several species of flat fish can be simply fried and served with lemon wedges to squeeze over the top. Intensely flavoured capers make a pleasant tangy addition to the very simple and quick-to-make sauce in this recipe. For a festive dinner party, try to find whole flat fish that are small enough to serve one per diner.

Serves 2
30–45ml/2–3 tbsp plain
  (all-purpose) flour
4 sole, plaice or flounder fillets,
  or 2 whole small flat fish
45ml/3 tbsp olive oil
25g/1oz/2 tbsp butter
60ml/4 tbsp lemon juice
30ml/2 tbsp pickled
  capers, drained
salt and ground black pepper
fresh flat leaf parsley, to garnish
lemon wedges, to serve

1 Sift the flour on to a plate and season well with salt and ground black pepper. Dip the fish fillets into the flour, coating evenly on both sides.

2 Heat the oil and butter in a large shallow pan until foaming. Add the fish fillets and fry them over medium heat for about 2–3 minutes on each side.

3 Lift out the fillets carefully with a metal spatula and place them on a warmed serving platter. Season with salt and ground black pepper.

4 Add the lemon juice and capers to the pan, heat through and pour over the fish. Garnish with parsley and serve immediately with lemon wedges.

Cook's Tip
This is a tasty and very quick and easy way to prepare any small flat fish, or fillets of any white fish. The delicate flavour of the fish is enhanced by the lemon juice and the capers without being overwhelmed.

Steamed Sole Energy 118kcal/492kJ; Protein 15.3g; Carbohydrate 0.9g, of which sugars 0.9g; Fat 5.9g, of which saturates 0.7g; Cholesterol 41mg; Calcium 46mg; Fibre 0.3g; Sodium 359mg.
Fried Flat Fish Energy 425kcal/1773kJ; Protein 34.2g; Carbohydrate 5.9g, of which sugars 0.2g; Fat 29.7g, of which saturates 9.3g; Cholesterol 111mg; Calcium 103mg; Fibre 0.3g; Sodium 316mg.

Sole with Vodka Sauce and Caviar

Christmas time is the ideal excuse to treat yourself to a little caviar.

Serves 4
500–600g/1¼lb–1lb 6oz sole, flounder or plaice fillets
200ml/7fl oz/scant 1 cup fish stock
60ml/4 tbsp caviar
salt
4 lemon wedges and fresh dill, to garnish
hot boiled potatoes, to serve

For the vodka sauce
25–40g/1–1½oz/2–3 tbsp butter
5–6 shallots, finely diced
5ml/1 tsp plain (all-purpose) flour
200ml/7fl oz/scant 1 cup double (heavy) cream
200ml/7fl oz/scant 1 cup fish stock
100ml/3½fl oz/scant ½ cup dry white wine
30ml/2 tbsp vodka
salt and ground black pepper

1 Season the fish fillets with salt. Roll up and secure each fillet with a cocktail stick (toothpick).

2 Heat the stock in a small pan. Place the fish rolls in the pan, cover and simmer for 5–8 minutes, until the fish is tender. Remove from the pan and keep warm.

3 Meanwhile, make the sauce. Melt the butter in a pan, add the shallots and fry gently for 3–5 minutes, until softened but not browned. Add the flour and stir until well mixed.

4 Gradually add the double cream and fish stock to the flour mixture. Stir well until the mixture is smooth. Slowly bring to the boil, stirring frequently, until the sauce bubbles. Reduce the heat and simmer over low heat for about 3–5 minutes, until the sauce has thickened.

5 Remove the shallots from the pan with a slotted spoon. Add the white wine and vodka and bring to the boil. Season with salt and ground black pepper to taste.

6 Pour the sauce over the base of four warmed plates. Place the fish rolls on top and add a spoonful of the caviar to each. Garnish with lemon wedges and fresh dill, and serve immediately with hot boiled potatoes.

Fried Fish with Tartare Sauce

Deep-fried fish served with a tartare sauce is a favourite with the whole family. You can serve this dish as an appetizer or with fries and salad as a main meal. Home-made tartare sauce is vastly superior to the store-bought variety.

Serves 4
700g/1lb 10oz perch fillet, skinned and boned
5ml/1 tsp salt
15ml/1 tbsp fresh lemon juice
115g/4oz/1 cup plain (all-purpose) flour
150ml/¼ pint/⅔ cup light beer
1 egg white
about 1 litre/1¾ pints/4 cups rapeseed (canola) oil
lemon wedges, to garnish
green salad, to serve

For the tartare sauce
3 large pickled gherkins
200g/7fl oz/scant 1 cup mayonnaise
15ml/1 tbsp capers
5ml–10ml/1–2 tsp finely chopped fresh dill
15ml/1 tbsp finely chopped fresh parsley
2.5ml/½ tsp mustard
1.5ml/¼ tsp salt
1.5ml/¼ tsp ground black pepper

1 To make the tartare sauce, peel and finely chop the gherkins. Put in a bowl with the mayonnaise, capers, dill, parsley and mustard. Mix together. Add salt and black pepper to taste, and transfer to a serving bowl.

2 Cut the fish fillets into bitesize pieces measuring about 3cm/1¼in and put on a plate. Sprinkle the fish pieces with plenty of salt and lemon juice.

3 Put the flour and beer in a bowl and whisk together until it forms a smooth batter. In a separate bowl, whisk the egg white until it stands in soft peaks, then fold into the batter.

4 Heat the oil in a deep fryer to 180°C/350°F or until a cube of bread browns in 1 minute. Dip and turn the fish pieces in the batter and then drop them into the hot oil. Fry for about 1–2 minutes, or until golden. Using a slotted spoon, remove from the pan and drain on kitchen paper.

5 Serve the fish hot with lemon wedges and the tartare sauce.

Sole with Vodka Energy 470kcal/1952kJ; Protein 27.9g; Carbohydrate 3.2g, of which sugars 1.9g; Fat 35g, of which saturates 20.4g; Cholesterol 188mg; Calcium 103mg; Fibre 0.3g; Sodium 548mg.
Fried Fish Energy 719kcal/2986kJ; Protein 36.7g; Carbohydrate 24.3g, of which sugars 2.1g; Fat 53.4g, of which saturates 7.6g; Cholesterol 118mg; Calcium 95mg; Fibre 1.8g; Sodium 352mg.

Skate Wings with Capers

This sophisticated way of serving skate wings is perfect for a festive dinner party.

Serves 6
50g/2oz/¼ cup butter
6 small skate wings
grated rind and juice of
  2 limes
30ml/2 tbsp salted capers,
  rinsed and drained
salt and ground black pepper
handful of rocket (arugula),
  to garnish

1 Heat the butter in a large frying pan and add one of the skate wings. Fry for about 4–5 minutes on each side, until golden and cooked through.

2 Using a metal spatula, carefully transfer the cooked skate wing to a warmed serving plate and keep warm while you cook each of the remaining skate wings in the same way.

3 Return the pan to the heat and add the lime rind and juice, and capers. Season with salt and ground black pepper to taste and allow to bubble for 1–2 minutes.

4 Place the skate wings on warmed serving plates. Spoon a little of the juices and the capers over each skate wing and serve immediately, garnished with rocket.

Cook's Tips
• Skate can occasionally omit a faint smell of ammonia. If you notice this odour, don't be put off because it will completely vanish when the fish is cooked.
• Skate wings can vary greatly in size. If all you can find is large wings, then simply serve half a wing per diner.

Variation
If fresh limes are not available, then fresh lemons can be used instead.

Grilled Hake with Lemon and Chilli

Choose firm hake fillets, as thick as possible for this recipe. This is an excellent low-fat dish to help you recover from any over-indulgence during the festive celebrations. Try it served with fresh green vegetables and boiled potatoes.

Serves 4
4 hake fillets, each weighing
  about 150g/5oz
25ml/1½ tbsp olive oil
finely grated rind and juice of
  1 unwaxed lemon
15ml/1 tbsp crushed dried
  chilli flakes
salt and ground black pepper

1 Preheat the grill (broiler) to high. Brush the hake fillets all over with the olive oil and place them all, skin side up and well spaced, on a baking sheet.

2 Grill (broil) the fish for 4–5 minutes, until the skin is crispy, then carefully turn them over using a fish slice or metal spatula.

3 Sprinkle the fillets with the lemon rind and chilli flakes and season with salt and black pepper.

4 Grill the fillets for a further 2–3 minutes, or until the hake is cooked through. (Test by using the point of a sharp knife; the flesh should flake easily.) Squeeze over the lemon juice just before serving the fish.

Cook's Tip
The rind or zest is the outermost part of citrus fruits such as lemons and limes. For the purest flavour, the rind must be removed from the fruit without a trace of the bitter white pith underneath. Use a zester or a stainless steel vegetable peeler, or rub the fruit carefully against the finest cutter on a grater to achieve finely grated rind.

Variation
This dish is just as delicious if made with cod, haddock or pollock fillets, if you prefer.

Skate Wings Energy 300kcal/1256kJ; Protein 26.4g; Carbohydrate 7g, of which sugars 6.7g; Fat 14.3g, of which saturates 8.8g; Cholesterol 36mg; Calcium 114mg; Fibre 1.2g; Sodium 272mg.
Grilled Hake Energy 176kcal/738kJ; Protein 27g; Carbohydrate 0g, of which sugars 0g; Fat 7.6g, of which saturates 1.1g; Cholesterol 35mg; Calcium 21mg; Fibre 0g; Sodium 150mg.

Hake au Poivre with Pepper Relish

This version of the classic steak au poivre can be made with monkfish or cod. It has a festive appearance thanks to the red pepper relish, green basil leaves and white fish.

Serves 4

30–45ml/2–3 tbsp mixed
    peppercorns (black, white,
    pink and green)
4 hake steaks, 175g/6oz each
30ml/2 tbsp olive oil

For the (bell) pepper relish

2 red (bell) peppers, halved, cored
    and seeded
15ml/1 tbsp olive oil
2 garlic cloves, chopped
4 ripe tomatoes, peeled, seeded
    and quartered
4 drained canned anchovy
    fillets, chopped
5ml/1 tsp capers
15ml/1 tbsp balsamic vinegar,
    plus extra for drizzling
12 fresh basil leaves, shredded,
    plus a few extra to garnish
salt and ground black pepper

1 Put the peppercorns in a mortar and crush them coarsely with a pestle. Season the hake fillets lightly with salt, then coat them on both sides with the crushed peppercorns. Set aside.

2 Make the relish. Cut the peppers into 1cm/½in-wide strips. Heat the oil in a frying pan that has a lid. Add the peppers and stir them for about 5 minutes, until they are slightly softened. Stir in the chopped garlic, tomatoes and the anchovies, then cover the pan and simmer the mixture very gently for about 20 minutes, until the peppers are very soft.

3 Transfer the contents of the pan into a food processor and process to a coarse purée. Transfer to a bowl and season to taste with salt and pepper. Stir in the capers, balsamic vinegar and basil. Keep the relish hot.

4 Heat the olive oil in a shallow pan, add the hake steaks and cook them, in batches if necessary, for 5 minutes on each side, turning them once or twice, until they are just cooked through.

5 Place the fish steaks on warmed plates and spoon some relish on to the side of each plate. Garnish with basil leaves and a little balsamic vinegar. Serve the rest of the relish separately.

Roast Cod Wrapped in Prosciutto

Wrapping chunky fillets of cod in wafer-thin slices of prosciutto keeps the fish succulent and moist, at the same time adding flavour and visual impact. Serve with baby new potatoes and a herb salad for a stylish supper at Christmas time.

Serves 4

2 thick skinless cod fillets, each
    weighing about 375g/13oz
75ml/5 tbsp extra virgin
    olive oil
75g/3oz prosciutto,
    thinly sliced
400g/14oz vine tomatoes
salt and ground black pepper

1 Preheat the oven to 220°C/425°F/Gas 7. Pat the fish dry on kitchen paper and remove any stray bones. Season lightly on both sides with salt and pepper.

2 Place one fillet in an ovenproof dish and drizzle 15ml/1 tbsp of the oil over it. Cover with the second fillet, laying the thick end on top of the thin end of the lower fillet.

3 Lay the ham over the fish, overlapping the slices to cover the fish in an even layer. Tuck the ends of the ham under the fish and tie it in place at intervals with fine string.

4 Using kitchen scissors, snip the tomato vines into four portions and add to the dish. Drizzle the tomatoes and ham with the remaining oil and season lightly.

5 Roast for 35 minutes, until the tomatoes are tender and the fish is cooked through. Test the fish by piercing one end of the parcel with the tip of a sharp knife to check that it flakes easily.

6 Slice the fish and transfer the portions to warm plates, adding the tomatoes. Spoon over the cooking juices from the dish and serve immediately.

> **Variation**
> You can use Serrano ham, or other air-dried ham, in place of the prosciutto, if you prefer.

Hake au Poivre Energy 283kcal/1186kJ; Protein 33.7g; Carbohydrate 8.2g, of which sugars 8g; Fat 13g, of which saturates 1.9g; Cholesterol 42mg; Calcium 47mg; Fibre 2.3g; Sodium 304mg.
Roast Cod Energy 281kcal/1172kJ; Protein 32.8g; Carbohydrate 3.1g, of which sugars 3.1g; Fat 15.3g, of which saturates 2.3g; Cholesterol 81mg; Calcium 23mg; Fibre 1g; Sodium 116mg.

Fish Fillets in a Creamy Mustard Sauce

You can use any kind of fish that is good for pan-frying for this dish. The mustard sauce is made with grainy mustard to add texture to the dish. Fried potatoes with bacon and onions are a good accompaniment.

Serves 4
300ml/½ pint/1¼ cups fish stock
100ml/3½fl oz/scant ½ cup
  single (light) cream
10ml/2 tsp grainy mustard
1kg/2¼lb boiled potatoes,
  thinly sliced
150g/5oz bacon, diced into cubes
1 onion, finely chopped
small bunch chives, chopped
800g/1¾lb fish fillets (cod,
  salmon, trout, pike or perch)
juice of 1 lemon
oil, for frying
salt and ground white pepper
fresh dill, to garnish

1 Heat the fish stock in a pan and season it, if necessary, with salt and pepper. Add the cream and mustard and simmer over low heat for 5 minutes to make the sauce.

2 Heat some oil in a frying pan over high heat and fry the potato slices and the bacon until browned and crisp.

3 Add the onion to the pan and fry for another 5 minutes. Season with salt and pepper and stir in the chives.

4 Meanwhile, season the fish with lemon juice, salt and pepper. Heat some oil in another pan and fry the fillets, turning once, until golden on both sides.

5 Arrange the fried potatoes in the middle of a warmed serving plate with the fish round them, and pour the sauce around. Garnish with fresh dill and serve.

> **Cook's Tip**
> If the sauce seems too thin, thicken it with about 5ml/1 tsp cornflour (cornstarch) slaked in a little cold water.

Baked Cod Steaks with Herby Cream Sauce

Always versatile, cod is enjoyed throughout the year, but baked or poached whole fresh cod is a supreme dish to serve for dinner on New Year's Eve. The simple preparation shows off the lean, firm texture of the flavoursome white fish. Serve the fish with boiled potatoes, remoulade or mustard sauce and peas.

Serves 4–6
1.3kg/3lb cod steaks
15ml/1 tbsp salt
1 egg, beaten
50g/2oz/½ cup fine white
  breadcrumbs
40g/1½oz/3 tbsp butter, cut into
  small pieces
300ml/½ pint/1¼ cups single
  (light) cream
45ml/3 tbsp chopped fresh
  parsley, to garnish
8 lemon wedges, to garnish

1 Preheat the oven to 190°C/375°F/Gas 5. Pat the fish steaks dry and rub the salt over the skin.

2 Place in a lightly greased baking dish, brush with the egg, sprinkle with breadcrumbs and dot with butter. Pour the cream around the steaks.

3 Bake the fish for 15–20 minutes, depending on thickness, until the topping is browned and the flesh flakes easily with a fork. Serve garnished with the parsley and lemon wedges.

> **Cook's Tip**
> If you can find a whole cod, bake it in the oven for around 1 hour, adding the single (light) cream about 20 minutes before the end of the cooking time.

> **Variation**
> Haddock, hake or monkfish steaks are just as delicious as cod when cooked in this way.

Fish Fillets Energy 570kcal/2387kJ; Protein 47.9g; Carbohydrate 42.5g, of which sugars 5.1g; Fat 24.1g, of which saturates 6.9g; Cholesterol 126mg; Calcium 62mg; Fibre 2.7g; Sodium 738mg.
Baked Cod Energy 355kcal/1484kJ; Protein 42.5g; Carbohydrate 8.9g, of which sugars 1.4g; Fat 16.7g, of which saturates 9.8g; Cholesterol 141mg; Calcium 78mg; Fibre 0.2g; Sodium 261mg.

Halibut Fillets in Parsley Sauce

This traditional dish features the highly prized halibut and is often served with steamed cauliflower and buttered new potatoes, but shredded green cabbage or braised leeks would also work well.

Serves 4
900g/2lb halibut fillet
2 eggs, beaten
10ml/2 tsp water
75g/3oz/1½ cup fine breadcrumbs
10ml/2 tsp salt
2.5ml/½ tsp white pepper
50g/2oz/4 tbsp butter
4 lemon wedges, to garnish

For the parsley sauce
50g/2oz/4 tbsp butter
60ml/4 tbsp plain
 (all-purpose) flour
350ml/12fl oz/1½ cups milk
45ml/3 tbsp chopped parsley
salt

1 Cut the halibut fillet into four even pieces. Whisk the eggs and water together in a shallow dish. Place the breadcrumbs in a second shallow dish.

2 Dip the fish into the egg mixture, then into the breadcrumbs, to coat both sides evenly. Sprinkle with salt and pepper. Allow the fish to rest at least 10 minutes before cooking.

3 To make the parsley sauce, melt the butter in a pan over medium heat, and whisk in the flour. Reduce the heat and cook the roux for 3–5 minutes until pale beige.

4 Slowly add the milk into the roux; cook, whisking constantly, for about 5 minutes, until the sauce comes to the boil and becomes smooth and thick.

5 Season the sauce with salt and pepper, add the parsley and simmer for 2 minutes. Cover and keep warm.

6 Melt the butter in a large pan over medium-high heat. Place the halibut fillets in the pan and cook for about 4 minutes on each side, turning once, until the coating is golden brown and the fish flakes easily when tested with a fork. Serve the halibut fillets immediately with the sauce spooned over, accompanied by freshly cooked vegetables.

Halibut with Coconut Milk

This aromatic dish is traditionally cooked and served in an earthenware dish. It is delicious when served with plenty of white rice and flavoured cassava flour to soak up all the delicious sauce.

Serves 6
6 halibut, cod, haddock or
 monkfish fillets, each about
 115g/4oz
juice of 2 limes
8 fresh coriander (cilantro) sprigs
2 red chillies, seeded and chopped
3 tomatoes, sliced into thin rounds
1 red (bell) pepper, seeded and
 sliced into thin rounds
1 green (bell) pepper, seeded and
 sliced into thin rounds
1 small onion, sliced into
 thin rounds
200ml/7fl oz/scant 1 cup
 coconut milk
60ml/4 tbsp palm oil
salt
cooked white rice, to serve

**For the flavoured
cassava flour**
30ml/2 tbsp palm oil
1 medium onion, thinly sliced
250g/9oz/2¼ cups cassava flour

1 Place the fish in a large, shallow dish and pour over water to cover. Pour in the lime juice and set aside for 30 minutes. Drain the fish and pat dry with kitchen paper. Arrange the fish in a single layer in a heavy pan that has a tight-fitting lid.

2 Sprinkle the coriander and chillies over the fish, then top with a layer each of tomatoes, peppers and onion. Pour the coconut milk over, cover and leave to stand for 15 minutes.

3 Season with salt, then place the pan over high heat and cook until the coconut milk comes to the boil. Lower the heat and simmer for 5 minutes. Remove the lid, pour in the palm oil, cover again and simmer for 10 minutes.

4 Meanwhile, make the flavoured cassava flour. Heat the oil in a large frying pan. Add the onion and cook for 8–10 minutes until soft. Stir in the cassava flour and cook, stirring, for 1–2 minutes until toasted and evenly coloured by the oil. Season with salt.

5 Serve the fish immediately, accompanied by the white rice and flavoured cassava flour.

Halibut Fillets Energy 594kcal/2493kJ; Protein 58.2g; Carbohydrate 30.4g, of which sugars 5g; Fat 27.6g, of which saturates 14.1g; Cholesterol 227mg; Calcium 234mg; Fibre 0.9g; Sodium 487mg.
Halibut with Coconut Energy 336kcal/1410kJ; Protein 41.9g; Carbohydrate 8.4g, of which sugars 8.1g; Fat 15.2g, of which saturates 2.1g; Cholesterol 66mg; Calcium 73mg; Fibre 2.2g; Sodium 622mg.

Sea Bass with Citrus Fruit

Try this recipe for friends or family who would appreciate an alternative to meat or poultry at Christmas time; it would be an ideal choice for a New Year's Eve dinner.

Serves 6
1 small grapefruit
1 orange
1 lemon
1 sea bass, about 1.3kg/3lb, cleaned and scaled
6 fresh basil sprigs
plain (all-purpose) flour, for dusting
45ml/3 tbsp olive oil
4–6 shallots, peeled and halved
60ml/4 tbsp dry white wine
15g/½oz/1 tbsp butter
salt and ground black pepper
fresh dill, to garnish

1 Remove the rind from the grapefruit, orange and lemon. Cut into julienne strips, cover and set aside. Peel off the white pith from the fruits and, working over a bowl to catch the juices, cut out the segments from the grapefruit and orange and set them aside for the garnish. Slice the lemon.

2 Preheat the oven to 190°C/375°F/Gas 5. Wipe the fish dry inside and out and season. Make three slashes on each side. Reserve a few basil sprigs for the garnish and fill the cavity with the remaining basil, the lemon and half the strips of citrus rind.

3 Dust the fish with flour. In a large roasting pan or flameproof casserole, heat 30ml/2tbsp of the olive oil over a medium-high heat and cook the fish for about 1 minute until the skin just crisps and browns on one side. Add the shallots to the pan.

4 Bake for about 15 minutes, then carefully turn the fish over and stir the shallots. Drizzle with the remaining oil and bake for a further 10–15 minutes until the flesh is opaque throughout.

5 Transfer the fish to a serving dish and remove and discard the cavity stuffing. Pour off any excess oil and add the wine and 30–45ml/2–3 tbsp of the fruit juices to the pan. Bring to the boil over high heat, stirring. Stir in the remaining strips of citrus rind and boil for 2–3 minutes, then whisk in the butter. Spoon the shallots and sauce around the fish, and garnish with fresh dill and the reserved basil and grapefruit and orange segments.

Sea Bass in a Salt Crust

Baking a whole fish in a crust of sea salt enhances the flavour. Any firm fish, such as grey mullet and striped bass, can be cooked this way. Break open the crust at the table to release the glorious aroma and create an impressive centrepiece for a festive dinner party.

Serves 4
1 sea bass, about 1kg/2¼lb, gutted and scaled
1 sprig each fresh fennel, rosemary and thyme
mixed peppercorns
2kg/4½lb coarse sea salt
seaweed or samphire, to garnish
lemon slices, to serve

1 Preheat the oven to 240°C/475°F/Gas 9. Fill the cavity of the sea bass with the fennel, rosemary and thyme sprigs and grind over some of the mixed peppercorns.

2 Spread half the coarse sea salt in a shallow baking tray and lay the stuffed sea bass on it.

3 Cover the fish all over with a 1cm/½in layer of salt, pressing it down firmly. Bake in the oven for 30 minutes, or until the salt coagulates and is beginning to colour.

4 Leave the fish on the baking tray; garnish it with seaweed or samphire. Bring the fish to the table in its salt crust and use a sharp knife to break open the crust to release the aromas. Serve the fish immediately.

Cook's Tips
• Whole fish encased in salt are traditionally baked whole and ungutted. Supermarkets always sell them gutted, so use the opportunity to add flavourings inside.
• Once baked, the salt sticks to the fish skin, and brings it off as it is peeled away. Scrape back the layer of salt and lift out the top fillet in sections. Snip the backbone with scissors and lift out. Discard the herbs and remove the bottom fillet pieces. Add a lemon slice to each plate.

Sea Bass in a Crust Energy 150kcal/632kJ; Protein 29g; Carbohydrate 0g, of which sugars 0g; Fat 3.8g, of which saturates 0.6g; Cholesterol 120mg; Calcium 196mg; Fibre 0g; Sodium 2069mg.
Bass with Citrus Energy 258kcal/1081kJ; Protein 32.7g; Carbohydrate 3.9g, of which sugars 3.9g; Fat 11.8g, of which saturates 2.8g; Cholesterol 139mg; Calcium 241mg; Fibre 0.7g; Sodium 133mg.

Fried Carp in Breadcrumbs

This farmhouse dish is perfect for a Christmas Eve feast, but it also makes a delicious meal at any time of the year. Chunks of carp are coated in breadcrumbs and fried in oil, and served simply with lemon wedges.

Serves 4

1 carp, about 900g/2lb, cleaned
   and filleted
2.5ml/½ tsp salt
50g/2oz/½ cup plain
   (all-purpose) flour
pinch of ground black pepper
1–2 eggs, lightly beaten
115g/4oz/2 cups dry white
   breadcrumbs
90ml/6 tbsp vegetable oil,
   for frying
lemon wedges, to serve

1 First scald the carp by putting it into a large heatproof dish or roasting pan and pouring boiling water over it. Turn and repeat on the other side. Drain.

2 Cut the cleaned and scalded carp into even portions and sprinkle lightly with salt. Leave to stand for about 30 minutes. Remove the skin, if you like.

3 Mix together the flour and pepper in a medium bowl. Put the beaten egg in another, and the breadcrumbs in a third.

4 Dip the fish pieces first into the flour, then into the egg, then into the breadcrumbs, coating them evenly at each stage.

5 Heat the oil in a large, heavy pan, until very hot. Carefully add the coated fish pieces and cook for about 5 minutes on each side, until golden brown all over.

6 Remove the fish pieces using a slotted spoon and drain on kitchen paper. Serve with lemon wedges.

Cook's Tip
Ask your fishmonger to clean and fillet the whole carp if you are unsure about how to do it.

Poached Carp with Caraway Seeds

Carp makes a delicious alternative to meat or poultry at Christmas time.

Serves 4

4 carp fillets, about 175–200g/
   6–7oz each
15ml/1 tbsp caraway seeds,
   roughly crushed
40g/1½oz/3 tbsp butter
30ml/2 tbsp chopped
   fresh chives
1 onion, finely sliced
juice of 1 lemon
175ml/6fl oz/¾ cup dry
   white wine
salt and ground black pepper
fresh dill and mint, to garnish
polenta and green beans,
   to serve

1 Wipe the fish fillets and pat dry with kitchen paper. Season well with salt and pepper and press the roughly crushed caraway seeds into the flesh.

2 Heat half the butter in a large frying pan and stir in half the fresh chives, the onion, lemon juice and dry white wine. Bring the mixture to the boil, reduce the heat and gently simmer for about 10–12 minutes.

3 Add the fish fillets to the pan and poach gently for about 10 minutes. Carefully remove the fillets with a fish slice and keep them warm on a serving plate.

4 Continue cooking the stock over a medium-high heat to reduce it a little, then whisk in the remaining butter. Adjust the seasoning if necessary.

5 Pour the sauce over the fish and top with the remaining fresh chives. Garnish with the fresh herbs and serve with polenta and green beans.

Cook's Tips
• The caraway seeds give the dish a very distinctive and delicious flavour, so be liberal with them.
• Polenta is a mash made from cornmeal. It can be eaten hot with butter or cooled and cut into squares and fried.

Fried Carp Energy 479kcal/2008kJ; Protein 32.3g; Carbohydrate 32g, of which sugars 0.9g; Fat 25.6g, of which saturates 4.1g; Cholesterol 148mg; Calcium 133mg; Fibre 1g; Sodium 301mg.
Poached Carp Energy 333kcal/1391kJ; Protein 35.3g; Carbohydrate 1.5g, of which sugars 1.2g; Fat 17.7g, of which saturates 7g; Cholesterol 155mg; Calcium 104mg; Fibre 0.2g; Sodium 149mg.

Baked Salmon with Watercress Sauce

This is a great festive dish as the whole fish looks very impressive at the table.

Serves 6–8

2–3kg/4½–6¾lb salmon, cleaned, with head and tail left on
3–5 spring onions (scallions), thinly sliced
1 lemon, thinly sliced
1 cucumber, thinly sliced
fresh dill sprigs, to garnish
lemon wedges, to serve

For the watercress sauce

3 garlic cloves, chopped
200g/7oz watercress leaves, finely chopped
40g/1½oz fresh tarragon, finely chopped
300g/11oz mayonnaise
15–30ml/1–2 tbsp freshly squeezed lemon juice
200g/7oz/scant 1 cup unsalted butter, melted
salt and ground black pepper

1 Preheat the oven to 180°C/350°F/Gas 4. Rinse the salmon and lay it on a large piece of foil.

2 Stuff the fish with the sliced spring onions and layer the lemon slices inside and around the fish, then sprinkle with plenty of salt and ground black pepper. Loosely fold the foil around the fish and fold the edges over to seal. Bake for about 1 hour.

3 Remove the fish from the oven. Leave to stand, wrapped in the foil, for 15 minutes, then unwrap and leave to cool. When cool, lift it on to a large plate, still covered with lemon slices. Wrap in clear film (plastic wrap) and chill for several hours.

4 Before serving, discard the lemon slices around the fish. Using a blunt knife to lift up the edge of the skin, carefully peel the skin away from the flesh, avoiding tearing the flesh, and pull out any fins at the same time. Arrange the cucumber in overlapping rows along the length of the fish, to resemble large fish scales.

5 To make the sauce, put the garlic, watercress, tarragon, mayonnaise and lemon juice in a food processor or blender or a bowl, and process or mix to combine. Add the butter, a little at a time, processing or stirring, until the sauce is thick and smooth. Cover and chill before serving. Serve the fish, garnished with dill, with the sauce and lemon wedges.

Salmon with Cucumber Sauce

Salmon is a traditional choice during the festive season and is great to serve for dinner on Christmas Day. Cucumber and fresh dill are a perfect combination in this unusual hot sauce, which really complements the baked salmon.

Serves 6–8

1.8kg/4lb salmon, cleaned and scaled
melted butter, for brushing

3 fresh parsley or thyme sprigs
½ lemon, halved
orange slices and salad leaves, to serve

For the cucumber sauce

1 large cucumber, peeled
25g/1oz/2 tbsp butter
120ml/4fl oz/½ cup dry white wine
45ml/3 tbsp finely chopped fresh dill
60ml/4 tbsp sour cream
salt and ground black pepper

1 Preheat the oven to 220°C/425°F/Gas 7. Season the salmon with salt and ground black pepper. Brush it inside and out with melted butter. Place the herb sprigs and lemon in the cavity.

2 Wrap the salmon in foil, folding the edges together securely, then bake in the preheated oven for 15 minutes.

3 Remove the fish from the oven and leave in the foil for about 1 hour, then remove the skin from the salmon.

4 Meanwhile, halve the cucumber lengthways, scoop out the seeds, then finely dice the flesh.

5 Place the cucumber in a colander, toss lightly with salt and leave for about 30 minutes to drain. Rinse well under cold running water, drain again and pat dry with kitchen paper.

6 Heat the butter in a small pan, add the diced cucumber and cook for 2 minutes until translucent.

7 Add the wine to the pan and boil briskly until the cucumber is dry. Stir in the dill and sour cream and season to taste with salt and pepper. Fillet the salmon and serve with the cucumber sauce, orange slices and salad leaves.

Baked Salmon Energy 783kcal/3242kJ; Protein 38.7g; Carbohydrate 1g, of which sugars 0.9g; Fat 69.3g, of which saturates 21.3g; Cholesterol 173mg; Calcium 102mg; Fibre 0.5g; Sodium 418mg.
Salmon and Cucumber Energy 406kcal/1686kJ; Protein 34.9g; Carbohydrate 1.5g, of which sugars 1.5g; Fat 26.7g, of which saturates 8.3g; Cholesterol 107mg; Calcium 62mg; Fibre 0.3g; Sodium 123mg.

Roasted Salmon with Honey and Mustard

Salmon is not only one of the most versatile fishes but is also one of the tastiest. This quick and easy way with salmon is sure to be popular with the whole family over the festive season. Serve with seasonal green vegetables for a delicious dinner dish.

Serves 4
30ml/2 tbsp olive oil
15ml/1 tbsp honey
30ml/2 tbsp wholegrain
   French mustard
grated rind ½ lemon
4 salmon fillets, each
   about 150g/5oz
salt and ground black pepper

1 To make the marinade, put the olive oil, honey, wholegrain mustard and lemon rind in a small bowl and mix together until well combined. Season the marinade with salt and ground black pepper to taste.

2 Put the salmon fillets in a shallow ovenproof dish or on a baking sheet lined with a sheet of baking parchment and spread the marinade over each fillet, rubbing it in with your fingers. Leave to marinate for 30 minutes.

3 Preheat the oven to 200°C/400°F/Gas 6. Roast the fish in the oven for 10–12 minutes, until the flesh flakes easily when tested with the tip of a knife. Serve immediately.

Cook's Tip
Choose the best salmon you can find to really elevate this dish. Look for wild salmon rather than the farmed variety.

Variation
This dish also tastes great using trout fillets, which come from the same family of fish as salmon. Rainbow trout is best but brown trout could also be used.

Salmon with Mixed Herb and Peppercorn Sauce

This wonderful sauce relies on absolutely fresh herbs (any combination will do) and good-quality olive oil for its fabulous flavour. The sauce is a perfect accompaniment to the rich fish. Cook the salmon simply to make the most of this sauce, which also works well with grilled beef or lamb steaks.

Serves 4–6
10ml/2 tsp cumin seeds
15ml/1 tbsp pink or green
   peppercorns in brine, drained
   and rinsed
25g/1oz/1 cup fresh mixed herbs,
   such as parsley, mint, chives
   and coriander (cilantro)
45ml/3 tbsp lemon-infused
   olive oil
4–6 salmon steaks

1 Crush the cumin seeds using a mortar and pestle. Alternatively, put the seeds in a small bowl and pound them with the end of a rolling pin. Add the pink or green peppercorns and pound a little to break them up slightly.

2 Remove any tough stalks from the herbs. Put the herbs in a food processor with the cumin seeds, peppercorns, oil and salt and process until the herbs are finely chopped, scraping the sauce down from the sides of the bowl if necessary.

3 Turn the sauce into a small serving dish, cover with clear film (plastic wrap) and chill until ready to serve.

4 Preheat the oven to 200°C/400°F/Gas 6. Roast the salmon steaks in the oven for 10–12 minutes, until the flesh flakes easily when tested with the tip of a knife.

5 Serve the salmon with the sauce drizzled over the top.

Cook's Tip
It is best to make the sauce a day in advance, to allow the flavours to mingle.

Roasted Salmon Energy 296kcal/1231kJ; Protein 25.9g; Carbohydrate 3.2g, of which sugars 3.2g; Fat 20g, of which saturates 3.2g; Cholesterol 63mg; Calcium 36mg; Fibre 0.4g; Sodium 178mg.
Salmon with Sauce nergy 526kcal/2180kJ; Protein 36.3g; Carbohydrate 2.9g, of which sugars 2.3g; Fat 40g, of which saturates 13.5g; Cholesterol 127mg; Calcium 63mg; Fibre 0.4g; Sodium 110mg.

Salmon with Herb and Lemon Butter

Fresh dill and lemon make a slightly piquant butter to serve with salmon.

Serves 4

50g/2oz/¼ cup butter, softened, plus extra for greasing
finely grated rind of 1 lemon
15ml/1 tbsp lemon juice
15ml/1 tbsp chopped fresh dill
4 salmon steaks
2 lemon slices, halved
4 sprigs of fresh dill
salt and ground black pepper

1 Place the butter, lemon rind, lemon juice and chopped fresh dill in a small bowl and mix together with a fork until blended. Season to taste with salt and ground black pepper.

2 Spoon the butter on to a piece of baking parchment and roll up, smoothing with your hands into a sausage shape. Twist the ends tightly, wrap in clear film (plastic wrap) and put in the freezer for 20 minutes until firm.

3 Meanwhile, preheat the oven to 190°C/375°F/Gas 5. Cut out four squares of foil to encase the salmon steaks and grease with butter. Place a salmon steak into the centre of each.

4 Remove the herb butter from the freezer and slice into eight rounds. Place two rounds on top of each salmon steak with a halved lemon slice in the centre and a sprig of dill on top. Lift up the edges of the foil and crinkle them together until well sealed. Place on a baking tray.

5 Bake in the oven for 20 minutes. Place the unopened parcels on warmed plates. Open the parcels and slide the contents on to the plates with the juices.

> **Variation**
> This method can also be used to cook fillets of brown trout or rainbow trout, if you prefer.

Moroccan Fish Tagine

This spicy, aromatic dish proves just how exciting fish can be. Serve with couscous and chopped fresh mint for a festive gathering.

Serves 8

1.3kg/3lb firm fish fillets, skinned and cut into 5cm/2in chunks
30ml/2 tbsp olive oil
4 onions, chopped
1 large aubergine (eggplant), cut into 1cm/½ in cubes
2 courgettes (zucchini), cut into 1cm/½ in cubes
400g/14oz can chopped tomatoes
400ml/14fl oz/1⅔ cups passata (bottled strained tomatoes)
200ml/7fl oz/scant 1 cup fish stock
1 preserved lemon, chopped
90g/3½ oz pitted olives
60ml/4 tbsp chopped fresh coriander (cilantro)
salt and ground black pepper
fresh coriander (cilantro) sprigs, to garnish
minted couscous, to serve

For the harissa
3 large fresh red chillies, seeded and chopped
3 garlic cloves, peeled
15ml/1 tbsp ground coriander
30ml/2 tbsp ground cumin
5ml/1 tsp ground cinnamon
grated rind of 1 lemon
30ml/2 tbsp sunflower oil

1 Make the harissa. Whizz everything together in a blender or food processor to form a smooth paste. Set aside. Put the chunks of fish in a wide bowl and add 30ml/2 tbsp of the harissa. Toss to coat, then cover and chill for at least 1 hour.

2 Heat 15ml/1 tbsp of the oil in a shallow, heavy pan. Cook the onions gently for 10 minutes, or until golden brown. Stir in the remaining harissa, and cook, stirring occasionally, for 5 minutes.

3 Heat the remaining oil in another pan. Add the aubergine cubes and cook for 10 minutes, or until they are golden brown. Add the cubed courgettes and cook for a further 2 minutes.

4 Add the aubergines and courgettes to the onions, with the tomatoes, passata and stock. Simmer for 20 minutes.

5 Stir the fish, lemon and olives into the pan. Cover and simmer for 15–20 minutes, until the fish is just cooked through. Stir in the coriander. Season to taste, and serve with couscous.

Salmon with Butter Energy 409kcal/1700kJ; Protein 35.6g; Carbohydrate 0.2g, of which sugars 0.2g; Fat 29.6g, of which saturates 9.8g; Cholesterol 114mg; Calcium 47mg; Fibre 0.2g; Sodium 156mg.
Moroccan Tagine Energy 221kcal/925kJ; Protein 31.6g; Carbohydrate 5g, of which sugars 4.3g; Fat 8.4g, of which saturates 1.2g; Cholesterol 75mg; Calcium 46mg; Fibre 2.1g; Sodium 357mg.

Salmon Fishcakes

The secret of a good fishcake is to make it with freshly prepared fish and mashed potatoes, as well as home-made breadcrumbs and plenty of interesting seasoning ingredients.

Serves 4

450g/1lb cooked salmon fillet
450g/1lb freshly cooked
   potatoes, mashed
25g/1oz/2 tbsp butter, melted
10ml/2 tsp wholegrain mustard
15ml/1 tbsp each chopped
   fresh dill and chopped
   fresh flat leaf parsley
grated rind and juice of ½ lemon
15g/½oz/1 tbsp plain
   (all-purpose) flour
1 egg, lightly beaten
150g/5oz/generous 1 cup
   dried breadcrumbs
60ml/4 tbsp sunflower oil
salt and ground white pepper
rocket (arugula) leaves and fresh
   chives, to garnish
lemon wedges, to serve

1 Flake the cooked salmon, discarding any skin and bones. Place the fish in a bowl with the mashed potato, melted butter and wholegrain mustard. Mix well, then stir in the chopped fresh dill and parsley, lemon rind and juice. Season to taste.

2 Divide the mixture into eight portions and shape each into a ball, then flatten into a thick disc. Dip the fishcakes first in the flour, then in the egg and finally in the breadcrumbs, making sure they are evenly coated.

3 Heat the oil in a frying pan until very hot. Fry the fishcakes in batches until golden brown and crisp all over. As each batch is ready, drain on kitchen paper and keep hot.

4 Warm some plates and then place two fishcakes on to each warmed plate, one slightly on top of the other. Garnish with rocket leaves and chives, and serve with lemon wedges.

> **Cook's Tip**
> *Almost any fresh white or hot-smoked fish is suitable; smoked cod and haddock are particularly good. A mixture of smoked and unsmoked fish also works well.*

Cod and Salmon Fishcakes

Fishcakes are a steadfast favourite throughout the world, and this baked version is a hassle-free method for making them during the busy festive period. Serve with remoulade, buttered potatoes and pickled cucumber salad to make a complete supper for the whole family.

Serves 4

450g/1lb cod or plaice fillet
225g/8oz salmon fillet
175g/6oz smoked salmon
30ml/2 tbsp finely chopped onion
40g/1½oz/3 tbsp melted butter
3 eggs
25g/1oz/¼ cup plain
   (all-purpose) flour
salt and white pepper

1 Place the cod and salmon fillets in a shallow dish, and sprinkle with 15ml/1 tbsp salt to draw some of the moisture out. Leave the fish to rest for 10 minutes, then pat dry with kitchen paper.

2 Place the cod and salmon, with the smoked salmon, in a food processor. Add the onion, butter, eggs and flour and pulse until smooth; season with salt and pepper and spoon into a bowl.

3 Preheat the oven to 190°C/375°F/Gas 5. Lightly grease a 23 × 33cm/9 × 13in baking tray. With damp hands, form the fish mixture into 16 slightly flattened, round patties, and place them on the prepared tray.

4 Bake the fishcakes in the preheated oven for about 30–35 minutes, until they are cooked through and lightly browned. Serve immediately.

> **Cook's Tip**
> *Instead of baking, the fishcakes can be shallow-fried or cooked under a hot grill (broiler), if you prefer.*

> **Variation**
> *Serve the fishcakes with mustard sauce instead of remoulade.*

Salmon Fishcakes Energy 586kcal/2453kJ; Protein 29.8g; Carbohydrate 49.9g, of which sugars 3.2g; Fat 31g, of which saturates 7.2g; Cholesterol 117mg; Calcium 79mg; Fibre 1.3g; Sodium 266mg.
Cod Fishcakes Energy 407kcal/1700kJ; Protein 48.5g; Carbohydrate 5.5g, of which sugars 0.6g; Fat 21.4g, of which saturates 7.9g; Cholesterol 259mg; Calcium 64mg; Fibre 0.3g; Sodium 1029mg.

Classic Fish Pie

Originally a fish pie was based on the 'catch of the day'. Now we can choose either the fish we like best, or the variety that offers best value for money.

Serves 4
butter, for greasing
450g/1lb mixed fish, such as
   cod or salmon fillets and
   peeled prawns (shrimp)

finely grated rind of 1 lemon
450g/1lb floury potatoes
25g/1oz/2 tbsp butter
salt and ground black pepper
1 egg, beaten

For the sauce
15g/½oz/1 tbsp butter
15ml/1 tbsp plain
  (all-purpose) flour
150ml/¼ pint/⅔ cup milk
45ml/3 tbsp chopped fresh parsley

1 Preheat the oven to 220°C/425°F/Gas 7. Grease an ovenproof dish and set aside. Cut the fish into bitesize pieces. Season the fish, sprinkle over the lemon rind and place in the base of the dish. Set aside while you make the topping.

2 Cook the potatoes in a pan of boiling salted water for about 10–15 minutes until tender.

3 Meanwhile, make the sauce. Melt the butter in a pan, add the flour and cook, stirring, for a few minutes. Remove from the heat and gradually whisk in the milk. Return to the heat and bring to the boil, then reduce the heat and simmer, whisking all the time, until the sauce has thickened and achieved a smooth consistency. Add the parsley and season to taste. Pour over the fish mixture.

4 Drain the potatoes well, and then mash with the butter. Pipe or spoon the potatoes on top of the fish mixture. Brush the beaten egg over the potatoes. Bake for 45 minutes until the top is golden brown. Serve hot.

Cook's Tip
If using frozen fish defrost it thoroughly first, as lots of water from the fish will ruin your pie.

Salmon Kulebyaka

This is an excellent festive dish in which a layer of moist salmon and eggs sits on a bed of buttery dill-flavoured rice, all encased in crisp puff pastry.

Serves 4
50g/2oz/4 tbsp butter
1 small onion, finely chopped
175g/6oz/1 cup cooked long
  grain rice

15ml/1 tbsp chopped fresh dill
15ml/1 tbsp lemon juice
450g/1lb puff pastry, defrosted
  if frozen
450g/1lb salmon fillet, skinned
  and cut into 5cm/2in pieces
3 eggs, hard-boiled and
  roughly chopped
beaten egg, for sealing and
  glazing the pastry
salt and ground black pepper
watercress, to garnish

1 Preheat the oven to 200°C/400°F/Gas 6. Melt the butter in a pan, add the finely chopped onion and cook gently for 10 minutes, or until soft. Stir in the cooked rice, fresh dill, lemon juice, salt and ground black pepper.

2 Roll out the puff pastry on a lightly floured surface to a 30cm/12in square. Spoon the rice mixture over half the pastry, leaving a 1cm/½in border around the edges.

3 Arrange the salmon on top, then sprinkle the eggs in between. Brush the pastry edges with egg, then fold it over the filling to make a rectangle, pressing the edges together firmly to seal.

4 Carefully lift the pastry on to a lightly oiled baking sheet. Glaze with beaten egg, then pierce the pastry a few times with a skewer to make holes for the steam to escape.

5 Bake on the middle shelf of the oven for 40 minutes, covering with foil after 30 minutes. Leave to cool on the baking sheet, before cutting into slices. Garnish with watercress.

Cook's Tip
To really impress your festive diners, make the pastry case into a fish shape and create a scaly pattern across the top.

Classic Fish Pie Energy 573kcal/2401kJ; Protein 36.8g; Carbohydrate 41g, of which sugars 7.3g; Fat 31.2g, of which saturates 4.7g; Cholesterol 92mg; Calcium 270mg; Fibre 1.2g; Sodium 1084mg.
Salmon Kulebyaka Energy 933kcal/3888kJ; Protein 37.3g; Carbohydrate 77.8g, of which sugars 2.4g; Fat 54.6g, of which saturates 9.8g; Cholesterol 226mg; Calcium 125mg; Fibre 0.2g; Sodium 528mg.

Chicken with Herb Stuffing

There is nothing to beat a traditional roast chicken with all the trimmings at Christmas time. Try to use a free-range bird if you can.

Serves 6
1 large chicken, about 1.8kg/4lb, with giblets and neck if possible
1 small onion, sliced
1 small carrot, sliced
small bunch of parsley and thyme
15g/¹⁄₂oz/1 tbsp butter
30ml/2 tbsp oil
6 rashers (strips) bacon

salt and ground black pepper
15ml/1 tbsp plain (all-purpose) flour

For the stuffing
1 onion, finely chopped
50g/2oz/¹⁄₄ cup butter
150g/5oz/2¹⁄₂ cups fresh white breadcrumbs
15ml/1 tbsp fresh chopped parsley
15ml/1 tbsp fresh chopped mixed herbs, such as thyme, marjoram and chives
grated rind and juice of ¹⁄₂ lemon
1 small (US medium) egg, beaten

1 Remove the giblets from the chicken and set the liver aside to use in the gravy. Put the giblets and neck into a pan with the onion, carrot, parsley, thyme and seasoning. Add cold water to cover, bring to the boil and simmer for 1 hour. Strain the stock and discard the giblets. Preheat the oven to 200°C/400°F/Gas 6.

2 For the stuffing, cook the onion in butter in a pan over low heat until soft. Remove from the heat and add the breadcrumbs, herbs and lemon rind. Mix in the lemon juice and egg and season.

3 Loosely pack the stuffing into the neck cavity and secure. Spread the breast with butter, pour the oil into a roasting pan and lay in the bird. Place the bacon over the top of the bird.

4 Weigh the stuffed chicken and allow 20 minutes per 450g/1lb and 20 minutes over. After 20 minutes in the oven, reduce to 180°C/350°F/Gas 4. Place on a serving dish and rest for 10 minutes.

5 For the gravy, pour off the excess fat from the pan, chop and add the liver and cook for 1 minute. Sprinkle in enough flour to absorb the fat and add a little giblet stock. Bring to the boil, adding more stock until the consistency is right. Season to taste. Carve the chicken and serve with the herb stuffing and gravy.

Roast Chicken with Sweet Potatoes

This delicately flavoured chicken is a delicious twist on the traditional roast bird.

Serves 4
4 garlic cloves, 2 finely chopped and 2 bruised but left whole
small bunch coriander (cilantro), with roots, coarsely chopped
10ml/2 tsp salt
5ml/1 tsp ground turmeric

5cm/2in piece fresh turmeric
1 roasting chicken, about 1.5kg/3¹⁄₄lb, preferably free-range
1 lime, cut in half
4 medium/large sweet potatoes, peeled and cut into wedges
300ml/¹⁄₂ pint/1¹⁄₄ cups chicken or vegetable stock
30ml/2 tbsp soy sauce
salt and ground black pepper

1 Preheat the oven to 190°C/375°F/Gas 5. Calculate the cooking time for the chicken: allow 20 minutes per 450g/1lb, plus 20 minutes. Using a mortar and pestle or food processor, grind the chopped garlic, coriander, salt and turmeric to a paste.

2 Place the chicken in a roasting pan and smear it with the herb paste. Squeeze the lime juice over and place the lime halves and garlic cloves in the cavity. Cover with foil and place in the oven.

3 Meanwhile, bring a pan of water to the boil and par-boil the sweet potatoes for 10–15 minutes, until just tender. Drain well and place them around the chicken in the pan. Baste with the cooking juices and season. Replace the foil and return to the oven. About 20 minutes before the end of cooking, remove the foil and baste the chicken. Turn the sweet potatoes over.

4 When the chicken is cooked, lift it out of the pan and drain out the juices collected inside the bird into the pan. Place on a chopping board, cover with foil and leave to rest before carving. Transfer the sweet potatoes to a serving dish and keep them hot in the oven while you make the gravy.

5 Pour away the oil from the roasting pan but keep the juices. Place on the stove and heat until bubbling. Pour in the stock and bring to the boil, stirring constantly. Stir in the soy sauce and check the seasoning before straining the gravy into a sauce boat. Serve with the carved meat and the sweet potatoes.

Chicken with Stuffing Energy 562kcal/2342kJ; Protein 40.9g; Carbohydrate 23.2g, of which sugars 2.7g; Fat 34.5g, of which saturates 11.9g; Cholesterol 216mg; Calcium 72mg; Fibre 1.5g; Sodium 381mg.
Roast Chicken Energy 529kcal/2201kJ; Protein 47.3g; Carbohydrate 8.7g, of which sugars 2.7g; Fat 34g, of which saturates 9.4g; Cholesterol 248mg; Calcium 26mg; Fibre 0.9g; Sodium 840mg.

Chicken with Madeira Gravy

This simple, traditional dish makes a perfect festive meal.

Serves 4
1.5kg/3¼lb oven-ready chicken
175g/6oz rindless streaky (fatty) bacon rashers (strips)
salt and ground black pepper

For the stuffing
50g/2oz/¼ cup butter
1 onion, chopped

75g/3oz/1½ cups fresh white breadcrumbs
grated rind of 1 lemon
30ml/2 tbsp chopped fresh parsley
30ml/2 tbsp chopped tarragon
1 egg yolk

For the gravy
10ml/2 tsp plain (all-purpose) flour
300ml/½ pint/1¼ cups chicken stock
dash of Madeira or sherry

1 Preheat the oven to 200°C/400°F/Gas 6. First make the stuffing. Melt half the butter in a pan and cook the onion for about 5 minutes, or until softened but not coloured. Remove the pan from the heat and add the breadcrumbs, lemon rind, parsley and half the tarragon. Season, then mix in the egg yolk to bind the ingredients into a moist stuffing.

2 Fill the neck end of the chicken with stuffing, then truss the chicken neatly and weigh it. To calculate the cooking time, allow 20 minutes per 450g/1lb, plus an extra 20 minutes. Put the chicken in a roasting pan and season well. Beat the remaining butter and tarragon together, then smear over the bird.

3 Lay the bacon rashers over the top of the chicken and roast for the calculated time. Baste every 30 minutes during cooking and cover with buttered foil if the bacon begins to overbrown.

4 Transfer the chicken to a warmed dish, cover with foil and stand for 10 minutes

5 For the gravy, pour off all but 15ml/1 tbsp fat from the pan. Place the pan on the stove and add the flour. Cook for 1 minute, until golden brown, then gradually stir in the stock and Madeira or sherry. Bring to the boil, stirring, then simmer for 3 minutes, until thickened. Season and strain into a warm sauce boat. Carve the chicken and serve it, with the stuffing and gravy.

Chicken with Forty Cloves of Garlic

The number of cloves does not have to be exact – as long as there is lots. The smell that emanates from the oven as this dish cooks is captivating.

Serves 4–5
5–6 whole garlic bulbs
15g/½oz/1 tbsp butter

45ml/3 tbsp olive oil
1.8–2kg/4–4½lb chicken
150g/5oz/1¼ cups plain (all-purpose) flour, plus 5ml/1 tsp
75ml/5 tbsp white port or other white, fortified wine
3 fresh tarragon or rosemary sprigs
30ml/2 tbsp crème fraîche
few drops of lemon juice (optional)
salt and ground black pepper

1 Separate three of the bulbs of garlic into cloves and peel them. Remove the first layer of papery skin from the remaining bulbs of garlic and cut off the tops to expose the cloves, if you like, or leave them whole. Preheat the oven to 180°C/350°F/Gas 4.

2 Heat the butter and 15ml/1 tbsp of the olive oil in a flameproof casserole that is just large enough to take the chicken and garlic. Add the chicken and cook over medium heat, turning it frequently with two large spoons, for 10–15 minutes, until it is a golden brown colour all over.

3 Sprinkle in 5ml/1 tsp flour and cook for 1 minute. Add the port or wine. Tuck in the heads of garlic and the peeled cloves with the herb sprigs. Pour over the remaining oil and season.

4 Mix the main batch of flour with sufficient water to make a firm dough. Roll it out into a long sausage and press it around the rim of the casserole, then press on the lid, folding the dough up and over it to create a tight seal. Cook in the preheated oven for 1½ hours.

5 To serve, lift off the lid to break the seal and remove the chicken and whole garlic to a serving platter and keep warm. Remove and discard the herb sprigs, then place the casserole on the stove and whisk to combine the garlic cloves with the juices. Add the crème fraîche and a little lemon juice to taste. Process the sauce in a food processor or blender. Serve the sauce alongside the chicken.

Chicken with Garlic Energy 787kcal/3275kJ; Protein 51.3g; Carbohydrate 33.2g, of which sugars 1g; Fat 50.6g, of which saturates 14.5g; Cholesterol 248mg; Calcium 77mg; Fibre 2.2g; Sodium 212mg.
Chicken with Gravy Energy 673kcal/2814kJ; Protein 41.8g; Carbohydrate 46.3g, of which sugars 7.9g; Fat 35.4g, of which saturates 13.3g; Cholesterol 246mg; Calcium 215mg; Fibre 1.7g; Sodium 537mg.

Granny's Chicken

This traditional recipe for a roast chicken is ideal for the festive season because it is easy to prepare.

800g/1¾lb waxy potatoes, sliced
100g/3¾oz/scant ⅔ cup diced
   lean smoked bacon
salt and ground black pepper

Serves 4
butter, for greasing
1.2kg/2½lb free-range chicken
2 onions
a large bunch of lemon balm, plus
   extra leaves to garnish

To serve
1kg/2¼lb red cooking pears
½ vanilla pod (bean)
45ml/3 tbsp sugar
dash of red wine
45ml/3 tbsp potato flour

1 First, make the accompaniments. Peel the pears, but leave them whole. Remove the calyx from the base, but leave the stalks. Place them in a heavy pan with the vanilla pod and sugar, add water almost to cover and bring to the boil. Lower the heat, cover and simmer for 1 hour. Add the wine, re-cover the pan and simmer for a further 2 hours.

2 Transfer the pears to a wide dish, standing them upright. Measure 500ml/17fl oz/generous 2 cups of the cooking liquid, pour into a clean pan and bring to the boil. Mix the potato flour with 90ml/6 tbsp cold water to a paste in a cup and stir into the liquid. Cook, stirring, until the liquid thickens, then remove from the heat. Pour the sauce over the pears and cool.

3 To cook the chicken, soak an unglazed clay pot in cold water for 15 minutes. Dry the inside and grease with butter. Stuff the chicken with the peeled, whole onion and the lemon balm. Rub with seasoning. Place the chicken in the pot, cover and place in a cold oven set to 240°C/475°F/Gas 9 for 30 minutes.

4 Chop the remaining onion and season the potato slices. Remove the pot from the oven and arrange the potato around the chicken. Sprinkle the bacon and chopped onion on top.

5 Bake for a further 45 minutes. Remove the lid and cook the chicken for 5–10 minutes more, until browned. Garnish with lemon balm leaves and serve immediately with the pears.

Coq au Vin

This rustic, one-pot casserole of chicken, slowly simmered in a rich red wine sauce, makes a delicious festive meal for the family.

1 bottle red wine
salt and ground black pepper
45ml/3 tbsp chopped fresh
   parsley, to garnish
boiled potatoes, to serve

Serves 6
45ml/3 tbsp light olive oil
12 shallots
225g/8oz rindless streaky (fatty)
   bacon rashers (strips), chopped
3 garlic cloves, finely chopped
225g/8oz button (white)
   mushrooms, halved
6 boneless chicken thighs
3 chicken breast fillets, halved

For the bouquet garni
3 sprigs each parsley, thyme
   and sage
1 bay leaf
4 peppercorns

For the beurre manié
25g/1oz/2 tbsp butter, softened
25g/1oz/¼ cup plain
   (all-purpose) flour

1 Heat the oil in a flameproof casserole and cook the shallots for 5 minutes until golden. Increase the heat, then add the bacon, garlic and mushrooms and cook, stirring, for 10 minutes.

2 Transfer the cooked ingredients to a plate, then brown the chicken pieces in the oil remaining in the pan, turning them until golden brown all over. Return the shallots, garlic, mushrooms and bacon to the casserole and pour in the red wine.

3 Tie the ingredients for the bouquet garni in a bundle in a piece of muslin (cheesecloth) and add to the casserole. Bring to the boil. Reduce the heat, cover and simmer for 30–40 minutes.

4 To make the beurre manié, cream the butter and flour together in a bowl using your fingers to make a smooth paste. Add small lumps of the paste to the casserole, stirring well until each piece has melted. When all the paste has been added, bring the casserole back to the boil and simmer for 5 minutes.

5 Season the casserole to taste with salt and pepper. Serve immediately, garnished with chopped fresh parsley and accompanied by boiled potatoes.

Granny's Chicken Energy 829kcal/3466kJ; Protein 47.4g; Carbohydrate 79.2g, of which sugars 40.2g; Fat 37.3g, of which saturates 11.1g; Cholesterol 213mg; Calcium 69mg; Fibre 7.9g; Sodium 573mg.
Coq au Vin Energy 630kcal/2618kJ; Protein 42.8g; Carbohydrate 19.3g, of which sugars 7.4g; Fat 41g, of which saturates 17.3g; Cholesterol 209mg; Calcium 67mg; Fibre 2.6g; Sodium 480mg.

Chicken Casserole with Spiced Figs

This is a delicious dish that is perfect for an informal festive gathering or as a tasty alternative to the usual roast bird on Christmas Day itself. Joints of chicken are cooked with bacon in a beautifully spiced sauce, which goes perfectly with a glass or two of red wine.

Serves 4

50g/2oz bacon lardons or
    pancetta, diced
15ml/1 tbsp olive oil
1.3–1.6kg/3–3¹⁄₂lb free-range
    or corn-fed chicken, jointed
    into eight pieces
120ml/4fl oz/¹⁄₂ cup dry
    white wine
finely pared rind of ¹⁄₂ lemon
50ml/2fl oz/¹⁄₄ cup chicken or
    vegetable stock
salt and ground black pepper
green salad, to serve

For the figs

150g/5oz/³⁄₄ cup sugar
120ml/4fl oz/¹⁄₂ cup white
    wine vinegar
1 lemon slice
1 cinnamon stick
120ml/4fl oz/¹⁄₂ cup water
450g/1lb fresh figs

1 Prepare the figs. In a heavy pan, simmer the sugar, vinegar, lemon and cinnamon with the water for about 5 minutes. Add the figs and cook for a further 10 minutes. Remove the pan from the heat and leave to stand for 3 hours.

2 Heat a large frying pan without any oil. Fry the bacon or pancetta, stirring frequently, for 6–8 minutes until golden. Transfer to an ovenproof dish.

3 Add the olive oil to the pan. Season the chicken, then add to the pan and quickly brown on both sides. Transfer the joints to the ovenproof dish.

4 Preheat the oven to 180°C/350°F/Gas 4. Drain the figs. Add the wine and lemon rind to the pan and boil until the wine has reduced and is syrupy. Pour over the chicken.

5 Cook the chicken in the oven, uncovered, for 20 minutes, then add the figs and chicken stock. Cover and return to the oven for a further 10 minutes. Serve with a green salad.

Chicken Fricassée

This creamy mix of tender chicken and fresh vegetables is a sophisticated dish for festive entertaining. Served with rice it is irresistible, and is a popular meal with diners of all ages. Try different herbs such as lemon thyme, chives or chervil; you can also substitute different seasonal vegetables.

Serves 4

1 chicken (approximately
    1.6kg/3¹⁄₂lb)
2 bay leaves
3 allspice berries
30ml/2 tbsp oil
200g/7oz mushrooms, quartered
2 small onions, sliced
400g/14oz white asparagus,
    peeled and cut into
    small pieces
200g/7oz frozen peas
200ml/7fl oz/scant 1 cup single
    (light) cream
juice of 1 lemon
25g/1oz/2 tbsp butter, mixed with
    25g/1oz/¹⁄₄ cup flour to make
    a beurre manié
oil, for frying
salt, ground white pepper
    and sugar
chopped parsley, to garnish
steamed or boiled rice, to serve

1 Put the chicken in a large pot and cover with water. Bring to the boil and skim. Add the spices and a pinch of salt and simmer for 60–90 minutes, until the chicken is tender.

2 Lift out the chicken and leave to cool. Strain and reserve the stock. When the chicken is cold, pick the meat off the bones and cut it into bitesize pieces.

3 Heat the oil in a large pan and fry the mushrooms for 2–3 minutes over medium heat. Add the onions, asparagus and peas and fry gently for 2 minutes until softened.

4 Pour in 500ml/17fl oz/generous 2 cups of the reserved stock and bring it to the boil. Stir in the cream and lemon juice and season to taste with salt, pepper and sugar. Whisk knobs of the beurre manié into the bubbling sauce to thicken it.

5 Finally, return the chicken to the sauce and cook gently until heated through. Garnish with the chopped parsley and serve with steamed or boiled rice.

Chicken Casserole Energy 811kcal/3396kJ; Protein 44g; Carbohydrate 69.8g, of which sugars 69.8g; Fat 39.2g, of which saturates 10.9g; Cholesterol 215mg; Calcium 183mg; Fibre 4.3g; Sodium 394mg.
Chicken Fricassée Energy 926kcal/3832kJ; Protein 55.1g; Carbohydrate 16g, of which sugars 6.1g; Fat 71.5g, of which saturates 22.6g; Cholesterol 282mg; Calcium 118mg; Fibre 5g; Sodium 264mg.

Chicken, Pea and Aubergine Koresh

This is a light chicken and vegetable version of the traditional koresh, a thick, saucy stew served with rice, which is usually made with lamb meat. It is best served with rice and garnished with mint leaves.

Serves 4–6
50g/2oz/¼ cup green split peas
45–60ml/3–4 tbsp olive oil
1 large or 2 small onions,
   finely chopped
500g/1¼lb boneless
   chicken thighs
500ml/17fl oz/2¼ cups
   chicken stock
5ml/1 tsp ground turmeric
2.5ml/½ tsp ground cinnamon
1.5ml/¼ tsp grated nutmeg
2 aubergines (eggplants), diced
8–10 ripe tomatoes, diced
2 garlic cloves, crushed
30ml/2 tbsp dried mint
salt and ground black pepper
fresh mint, to garnish
boiled rice, to serve

1 Put the split peas in a bowl, pour over cold water to cover, then leave to soak for about 4 hours. Drain well.

2 Heat a little of the oil in a pan, add two-thirds of the onions and cook for about 5 minutes. Add the chicken and cook until golden brown on all sides.

3 Add the soaked split peas to the chicken mixture, then the stock, turmeric, cinnamon and nutmeg. Cook over medium-low heat for about 40 minutes, until the split peas are tender.

4 Heat the remaining oil in a pan, add the aubergines and remaining onions and cook until lightly browned. Add the tomatoes, garlic and mint. Season.

5 Just before serving, stir the aubergine mixture into the stew. Garnish with fresh mint leaves and serve with boiled rice.

> **Variation**
> To make a lamb koresh, use 675g/1½lb lamb stew chunks in place of the chicken. Add to the onions, pour over water to cover and cook for 1½ hours, then proceed as above.

Chicken with Tarragon Cream

The aniseed-like flavour of tarragon has a particular affinity with chicken, especially in creamy sauces such as the one in this tempting alternative to the usual Christmas roast. Serve with vegetables such as Brussels sprouts, roast parsnips and cabbage.

Serves 4
30ml/2 tbsp light olive oil
4 chicken supremes, each
   weighing about 250g/9oz
3 shallots, finely chopped
2 garlic cloves, finely chopped
115g/4oz/1½ cups
   wild mushrooms or shiitake
   mushrooms, halved
150ml/¼ pint/⅔ cup dry
   white wine
300ml/½ pint/1¼ cups double
   (heavy) cream
15g/½oz mixed fresh tarragon
   and flat leaf parsley, chopped
salt and ground black pepper
fresh tarragon and flat leaf
   parsley sprigs, to garnish

1 Heat the light olive oil in a large frying pan and add the chicken, skin side down. Cook for 10 minutes, turning the chicken twice, or until it is a golden brown colour on both sides.

2 Reduce the heat and cook the chicken portions for 10 minutes more, turning occasionally. Use a slotted spoon to remove the chicken from the pan and set aside.

3 Add the shallots and garlic to the pan and cook gently, stirring, until the shallots are softened but not browned. Increase the heat, add the mushrooms and stir-fry for about 2 minutes, or until the mushrooms just start to colour.

4 Replace the chicken, nestling the pieces down into the other ingredients, and then pour in the wine. Simmer for about 5–10 minutes, or until most of the wine has evaporated.

5 Add the cream and gently move the ingredients around in the pan to mix in the cream. Simmer for 10 minutes, or until the sauce has thickened. Stir the chopped herbs into the sauce with seasoning to taste. Arrange the chicken on warm plates and spoon the sauce over. Garnish with sprigs of tarragon and flat leaf parsley and serve immediately.

Chicken Koresh Energy 316kcal/1326kJ; Protein 31.9g; Carbohydrate 19.3g, of which sugars 10.9g; Fat 12.9g, of which saturates 2.5g; Cholesterol 131mg; Calcium 52mg; Fibre 5.2g; Sodium 136mg.
Chicken with Tarragon Energy 715kcal/2976kJ; Protein 61.8g; Carbohydrate 1.6g, of which sugars 1.6g; Fat 48.7g, of which saturates 26.6g; Cholesterol 278mg; Calcium 54mg; Fibre 0.3g; Sodium 170mg.

Stuffed Chicken Rolls

These delicious chicken rolls are simple to make, but sophisticated enough to serve for a festive meal.

Serves 4

25g/1oz/2 tbsp butter
1 garlic clove, chopped
150g/5oz/1¼ cups cooked white
    long grain rice
45ml/3 tbsp ricotta cheese
10ml/2 tsp chopped fresh flat
    leaf parsley
5ml/1 tsp chopped fresh tarragon
4 skinless chicken breast fillets
3–4 slices prosciutto
15ml/1 tbsp olive oil
120ml/4fl oz/½ cup white wine
salt and ground black pepper
fresh parsley sprigs, to garnish
cooked tagliatelle and sautéed
    mushrooms, to serve (optional)

1 Preheat the oven to 180°C/350°F/Gas 4. Melt about 10g/¼oz/2 tsp of the butter in a small pan and cook the garlic for a few seconds without browning. Spoon into a bowl.

2 Add the rice, ricotta, parsley and tarragon to the bowl, and season with salt and pepper. Stir until combined.

3 Place each chicken breast fillet in turn between two sheets of clear film (plastic wrap) and flatten by beating lightly, but firmly, with a rolling pin. Divide the slices of prosciutto among the chicken fillets, trimming the ham to fit, if necessary.

4 Place a spoonful of the rice stuffing at the wider end of each ham-topped chicken portion. Roll up carefully and tie in place with cooking string or secure with a cocktail stick (toothpick).

5 Heat the oil and the remaining butter in a frying pan and lightly cook the chicken rolls until browned on all sides. Place side by side in a shallow ovenproof dish and pour in the wine.

6 Cover the dish with baking parchment and cook in the oven for 30–35 minutes until the chicken is tender.

7 Using a carving or other sharp knife, cut the rolls into neat slices and serve on a bed of cooked tagliatelle with sautéed mushrooms and a generous grinding of black pepper, if you like. Garnish with sprigs of parsley and serve immediately.

Chicken with Shallots and Fennel

This is a very simple and delicious way to cook chicken. If you have time during the busy festivities, leave the chicken to marinate for a few hours for the best flavour.

Serves 4

1.6–1.8kg/3½–4lb chicken,
    cut into 8 pieces, or 8
    chicken portions
250g/9oz shallots, peeled
1 garlic bulb, separated into cloves
    and peeled
60ml/4 tbsp extra virgin olive oil
45ml/3 tbsp tarragon vinegar
45ml/3 tbsp white wine or
    vermouth (optional)
5ml/1 tsp fennel seeds, crushed
2 bulbs fennel, cut into wedges,
    feathery tops reserved
150ml/¼ pint/⅔ cup double
    (heavy) cream
5ml/1 tsp redcurrant jelly
15ml/1 tbsp tarragon mustard
caster (superfine) sugar (optional)
30ml/2 tbsp chopped
    fresh parsley
salt and ground black pepper

1 Place the chicken pieces, shallots and all but one of the garlic cloves in a flameproof dish or roasting pan. Add the oil, vinegar, wine or vermouth, if using, and fennel seeds. Season with pepper and marinate for 2–3 hours.

2 Preheat the oven to 190°C/375°F/Gas 5. Add the fennel to the chicken, season with salt and stir to mix.

3 Cook the chicken in the oven for 50–60 minutes, stirring once or twice. The chicken juices should run clear, not pink, when the thick thigh meat is pierced with a skewer.

4 Transfer the chicken and vegetables to a serving dish and keep them warm in a low oven. Skim off some of the fat and bring the cooking juices to the boil, then pour in the cream. Stir, scraping up all the delicious juices. Whisk in the redcurrant jelly followed by the mustard. Check the seasoning, adding a little sugar to taste.

5 Chop the remaining garlic clove with the feathery fennel tops and mix with the chopped parsley. Pour the sauce over the chicken and sprinkle the chopped garlic and herb mixture over the top. Serve immediately.

Chicken Rolls Energy 364kcal/1532kJ; Protein 46.6g; Carbohydrate 12.5g, of which sugars 0.9g; Fat 12.5g, of which saturates 5.5g; Cholesterol 148mg; Calcium 35mg; Fibre 0.4g; Sodium 297mg.
Chicken with Shallots Energy 482kcal/1999kJ; Protein 32.4g; Carbohydrate 4.8g, of which sugars 4.7g; Fat 37.1g, of which saturates 9.1g; Cholesterol 160mg; Calcium 54mg; Fibre 3.4g; Sodium 143mg.

Chicken and Asparagus Risotto

If you have any left-over chicken or turkey from the Christmas Day roast, you can use it to make this delicious risotto.

Serves 4
50g/2oz/¼ cup butter
15ml/1 tbsp olive oil
1 leek, finely chopped
115g/4oz/1½ cups oyster
  mushrooms, sliced
3 skinless chicken breast
  fillets, cubed
350g/12oz asparagus
250g/9oz/1¼ cups risotto rice
900ml/1½ pints/3¾ cups boiling
  chicken stock
salt and ground black pepper
Parmesan cheese curls, to serve

1 Heat the butter with the olive oil in a heavy pan until the mixture is foaming. Add the leek and cook gently, stirring occasionally, until softened, but not coloured.

2 Add the mushrooms to the pan and cook for 5 minutes. Remove the vegetables from the pan and set aside.

3 Increase the heat and cook the cubes of chicken until golden on all sides. Do this in batches, if necessary, and then replace them all in the pan to heat through.

4 Meanwhile, discard the woody ends from the asparagus and cut the spears in half. Set the fine tips aside. Cut the thick ends in half and add them to the pan. Return the leek and mushroom mixture and stir in the rice.

5 Pour in a ladleful of boiling stock and cook gently, stirring occasionally, until the stock is absorbed. Continue adding the stock a ladleful at a time, simmering until it is absorbed, the rice is tender and the chicken is cooked.

6 Add the fine asparagus tips with the last ladleful of boiling stock for the final 5 minutes, and continue cooking the risotto gently until the asparagus is tender. The whole process should take about 25–30 minutes.

7 Season the risotto to taste with salt and pepper and spoon it into individual bowls. Garnish with Parmesan curls and serve.

Chicken with Red Wine Vinegar

These chicken breasts with their slightly tart taste make a light and tasty Christmas meal. You could substitute tarragon vinegar, if you like.

Serves 4
4 skinless chicken breast fillets,
  200g/7oz each
50g/2oz/4 tbsp unsalted butter
ground black pepper
8–12 shallots, trimmed
  and halved
60ml/4 tbsp red
  wine vinegar
2 garlic cloves, finely chopped
60ml/4 tbsp dry white wine
120ml/4fl oz/½ cup chicken or
  vegetable stock
15ml–30ml/1–2 tbsp chopped
  fresh parsley
mixed green salad, to serve

1 Using a sharp kitchen knife cut each chicken breast in half crossways to make eight pieces.

2 Melf half the butter in a heavy frying pan over medium heat. Add the chicken and cook for 3–5 minutes until golden brown, turning once, then season with pepper.

3 Add the shallots to the pan, cover and cook over low heat for 5–7 minutes, shaking the pan and stirring occasionally.

4 Transfer the chicken pieces to a plate. Add the vinegar and cook, stirring frequently, for about 1 minute until the liquid is almost evaporated. Add the garlic, wine and stock and stir.

5 Return the chicken to the pan with any accumulated liquid. Cover the pan and simmer for about 2–3 minutes until the chicken is tender and the juices run clear when the meat is pierced with a knife or skewer.

6 Transfer the chicken and the shallots to a serving dish and cover to keep warm. Increase the heat and rapidly boil the cooking liquid until it has reduced by half.

7 Off the heat, gradually add the remaining butter, whisking until the sauce is slightly thickened and glossy. Stir in the parsley and pour the sauce over the chicken pieces and shallots. Serve immediately with a green salad.

Chicken Risotto Energy 496kcal/2072kJ; Protein 36.1g; Carbohydrate 50g, of which sugars 2.7g; Fat 16.1g, of which saturates 7.4g; Cholesterol 105mg; Calcium 53mg; Fibre 2.7g; Sodium 148mg.
Chicken with Wine Energy 358kcal/1499kJ; Protein 39.3g; Carbohydrate 8.1g, of which sugars 4g; Fat 13.5g, of which saturates 3.8g; Cholesterol 139mg; Calcium 54mg; Fibre 1.4g; Sodium 453mg.

Jamaican Jerk Chicken

Try this spicy slow-cooker dish as a delicious alternative to the usual Christmas roast.

Serves 4
8 chicken pieces, such as thighs and legs
15ml/1 tbsp sunflower oil
15g/½oz/1 tbsp unsalted butter

For the sauce
1 bunch of spring onions (scallions), trimmed and finely chopped
2 garlic cloves, crushed
1 red chilli pepper, halved, seeded and finely chopped
5ml/1 tsp ground allspice
2.5ml/½ tsp ground cinnamon
5ml/1 tsp dried thyme
1.5ml/¼ tsp freshly grated nutmeg
10ml/2 tsp demerara (raw) sugar
15ml/1 tbsp plain (all-purpose) flour
300ml/½ pint/1¼ cups chicken stock
15ml/1 tbsp red or white wine vinegar
15ml/1 tbsp lime juice
10ml/2 tsp tomato purée (paste)
salt and ground black pepper
salad leaves or rice, to serve

1 Wipe the chicken pieces, then pat dry on kitchen paper. Heat the oil and butter in a frying pan until melted, then add the chicken, in batches if necessary, and cook until browned on all sides. Remove with a slotted spoon, leaving the fat in the pan, and transfer to the ceramic cooking pot. Switch the slow cooker to high.

2 Add the spring onions, garlic and chilli to the frying pan and cook gently for 4–5 minutes, or until softened, stirring frequently. Stir in the allspice, cinnamon, thyme, nutmeg and sugar. Sprinkle in the flour and stir to mix, then gradually add the chicken stock, stirring until the mixture bubbles and thickens. Remove the pan from the heat.

3 Stir the vinegar, lime juice, tomato purée and some salt and ground black pepper into the sauce. Pour over the chicken pieces, cover with a lid and cook on high for 3–4 hours, or until the chicken is cooked and very tender.

4 Remove the chicken from the sauce and place on a serving dish. Taste the sauce and adjust the seasoning, then serve separately, with salad leaves or rice as an accompaniment.

Chicken with Morels

Morels and champagne lift this dish to levels that make it ideal for festive dining.

Serves 4
40g/1½oz dried morel mushrooms
250ml/8fl oz/1 cup chicken stock
50g/2oz/4 tbsp butter
5 or 6 shallots, thinly sliced
100g/3½oz mushrooms, sliced
1.5ml/¼ tsp dried thyme
175ml/6fl oz/¾ cup double (heavy) cream
175ml/6fl oz/¾ cup brandy
4 skinless chicken breast fillets
15ml/1 tbsp vegetable oil
175ml/6fl oz/¾ cup champagne
salt and ground black pepper

1 Put the morels in a sieve (strainer) and rinse well under cold running water. Put them in a large heavy pan with the stock and bring to the boil. Remove from the heat and leave for 1 hour.

2 Remove the morels from the cooking liquid and strain the liquid through a very fine sieve, reserving it to use in the sauce. Reserve a few whole morels and slice the rest.

3 Melt half the butter in a frying pan. Cook the shallots for 2 minutes, then add the morels and mushrooms and cook for 2–3 minutes. Season and add the thyme, 100ml/3½fl oz/scant ½ cup of cream and the brandy. Simmer for 10–12 minutes. Remove the morel mixture from the frying pan and set aside.

4 Pull off the little fillets from the chicken breast fillets and reserve for another use. Make a pocket in each breast fillet by cutting a slit along the thicker edge, taking care not to cut all the way through. Fill each pocket with one-quarter of the mushroom mixture, then secure with a cocktail stick (toothpick).

5 Melt the remaining butter with the oil in a frying pan over medium heat and cook the chicken for 6–8 minutes. Transfer to a plate. Add the champagne to the pan and boil to reduce by half. Add the strained morel liquid and reduce by half.

6 Add the remaining cream and cook over medium heat for 2–3 minutes until the sauce thickens. Season. Return the chicken to the pan with any juices and the reserved whole morels, and simmer for 3–5 minutes until tender. Serve immediately.

Jamaican Chicken Energy 189kcal/794kJ; Protein 21g; Carbohydrate 7g, of which sugars 3.1g; Fat 8.8g, of which saturates 3.1g; Cholesterol 107mg; Calcium 24mg; Fibre 0.5g; Sodium 238mg.
Chicken with Morels Energy 456kcal/1902kJ; Protein 47.3g; Carbohydrate 2.5g, of which sugars 2.1g; Fat 26.9g, of which saturates 7.8g; Cholesterol 154mg; Calcium 74mg; Fibre 1.8g; Sodium 608mg.

Classic Roast Turkey

It is hard to imagine the festive season without eating this classic roast and stuffing at least once.

Serves 8
4.5kg/10lb oven-ready turkey, with giblets
1 large onion, peeled and studded with 6 whole cloves
50g/2oz/4 tbsp butter, softened
10 chipolata sausages
salt and ground black pepper

For the stuffing
225g/8oz rindless streaky (fatty) bacon rashers (strips), chopped
1 large onion, finely chopped
450g/1lb pork sausage meat (bulk sausage)
25g/1oz/⅓ cup rolled oats
30ml/2 tbsp chopped fresh parsley
10ml/2 tsp dried mixed herbs
1 large (US extra large) egg, beaten
115g/4oz ready-to-eat dried apricots, finely chopped

For the gravy
25g/1oz/2 tbsp plain (all-purpose) flour
450ml/¾ pint/scant 2 cups giblet stock

1 Preheat the oven to 200°C/400°F/ Gas 6. For the stuffing, cook the bacon and onion in a frying pan until done. Mix with the other ingredients and season well.

2 Stuff the neck-end of the turkey and secure with a small skewer. Shape the remaining stuffing into balls. Put the onion in the body cavity. Weigh the stuffed bird and calculate the cooking time; allow 15 minutes per 450g/1lb plus 15 minutes.

3 Place the bird in a large roasting pan. Spread with butter and season well. Cover with foil and cook for 30 minutes. Lower the oven to 180°C/350°F/Gas 4. Baste every 30 minutes. Remove the foil for the last hour. Put the stuffing balls and sausages into ovenproof dishes in the oven and bake for the last 20 minutes.

4 Transfer the turkey to a serving plate, cover with foil and leave to stand for 15 minutes. To make the gravy, spoon off the fat from the roasting pan, leaving the meat juices. Blend in the flour and cook for 2 minutes. Stir in the stock, bring to the boil and transfer to a gravy jug (pitcher). To serve, carve the turkey and surround with sausages and stuffing balls.

Roast Turkey with Fruit Stuffing

The sausage meat inside this bird is black morcilla, and prunes and raisins make it even more sweet and fruity. The sauce is flavoured with sweet grape juice and an intriguing splash of anis. It is the ideal way to spruce up a traditional festive roast.

Serves 8
3kg/6½lb bronze or black turkey, weighed without the giblets
60ml/4 tbsp oil
200g/7oz rashers (strips) streaky (fatty) bacon

For the stuffing
45ml/3 tbsp olive oil
1 onion, chopped
2 garlic cloves, finely chopped
115g/4oz fatty bacon lardons
150g/5oz morcilla or black pudding (blood sausage), diced
1 turkey liver, diced

50g/2oz/½ cup Muscatel raisins, soaked in 45ml/3 tbsp anis spirit, and chopped
115g/4oz ready-to-eat pitted prunes, chopped
50g/2oz/½ cup almonds, chopped
1.5ml/¼ tsp dried thyme
finely grated rind of 1 lemon
freshly grated nutmeg
60ml/4 tbsp chopped fresh parsley
1 large (US extra large) egg, beaten
60ml/4 tbsp cooked rice or stale breadcrumbs
salt and ground black pepper

For the sauce
45ml/3 tbsp plain (all-purpose) flour
350ml/12fl oz/1½ cups turkey giblet stock, warmed
350ml/12fl oz/1½ cups red grape juice
30ml/2 tbsp anis spirit
salt and ground black pepper

1 Make the stuffing. Heat 30ml/2 tbsp oil in a pan and fry the onion, garlic and bacon for 6–8 minutes. Transfer to a large bowl. Fry the morcilla or black pudding in the remaining oil for about 3–4 minutes and the liver for 2–3 minutes.

2 Add the soaked raisins, prunes, almonds, thyme, lemon rind, nutmeg, seasoning and parsley to the pan. Stir in the beaten egg and rice or breadcrumbs.

3 About 3 hours before serving, preheat the oven, with a low shelf, to 200°C/400°F/Gas 6. Remove the turkey's wishbone, running fingernails up the two sides of the neck to find it, then pull it out. Season the turkey inside with salt and pepper, then fill the cavity with the stuffing mixture and retruss the bird. Season the skin. Keep at room temperature.

4 Heat a roasting pan in the oven with 60ml/4 tbsp oil. Put in the turkey and baste the outside. Lay the bacon over the breast and legs. Reduce the temperature to 180°C/350°F/Gas 4 and roast for 2¼–2½ hours, basting once or twice. To test, insert a skewer into the thickest part of the inside leg. The juices should run clear. Remove the trussing thread and transfer the turkey to a heated serving plate. Keep warm.

5 Make the sauce. Skim as much fat as possible from the roasting pan. Sprinkle in the flour and cook gently for a few minutes, stirring constantly.

6 Stir the warm turkey stock into the pan and bring to simmering point. Add the grape juice and anis, and bring back to simmering point. Taste for seasoning and pour into a jug (pitcher). Carve the turkey and serve with the sauce.

Classic Roast Energy 828kcal/3452kJ; Protein 73.1g; Carbohydrate 19.4g, of which sugars 7g; Fat 51.3g, of which saturates 18.1g; Cholesterol 292mg; Calcium 77mg; Fibre 1.8g; Sodium 1267mg.
Roast Turkey Energy 662kcal/2772kJ; Protein 66.3g; Carbohydrate 27.9g, of which sugars 15.5g; Fat 31.5g, of which saturates 8.1g; Cholesterol 274mg; Calcium 104mg; Fibre 2.2g; Sodium 658mg.

Roast Turkey with Mushrooms

One sure way to boost the flavour and succulence of the festive turkey is to stuff it with the season's wild mushrooms. The gravy, too, can be flavoured with all kinds of mushrooms.

Serves 6–8
4.5kg/10lb fresh turkey
butter, for basting
watercress, to garnish

For the mushroom stuffing
60ml/4 tbsp unsalted butter
1 medium onion, chopped
225g/8oz/3 cups wild mushrooms

75g/3oz/1½ cups fresh white, brown, or mixed breadcrumbs
115g/4oz pork sausages, skinned
1 small fresh truffle, sliced (optional)
5 drops truffle oil (optional)
salt and ground black pepper

For the gravy
75ml/5 tbsp medium sherry
400ml/14fl oz/1⅔ cups chicken stock
15g/½oz/¼ cup dried ceps, soaked
20ml/4 tsp cornflour (cornstarch)
5ml/1 tsp Dijon mustard
2.5ml/½ tsp wine vinegar
salt and ground black pepper
butter pat

1 Preheat the oven to 220°C/425°F/Gas 7. For the stuffing, melt the butter in a pan and cook the onion for 4–6 minutes. Add the mushrooms and cook for 5 minutes. Remove from the heat, add the breadcrumbs, skinned sausages, and the truffle and truffle oil if using, season and stir well to combine. Spoon the stuffing into the neck cavity of the turkey and enclose.

2 Rub the skin of the turkey with butter, place in a large roasting pan and roast uncovered in the oven for 50 minutes. Lower the temperature to 180°C/350°F/Gas 4, cover with foil and cook for another 2 hours and 30 minutes.

3 To make the gravy, transfer the turkey to a board, and keep warm. Spoon off the fat from the roasting pan and discard. Heat the remaining liquid until reduced to half. Add the sherry and stir to loosen the residue. Stir in the stock and drained ceps.

4 Blend the cornflour and mustard with 10ml/2 tsp water and the wine vinegar. Stir this into the juices in the pan and simmer to thicken. Season and then stir in a pat of butter. Garnish the turkey with watercress. Serve the gravy separately.

Stuffed Roast Turkey

In this festive recipe the roast turkey is packed with a rich herb and liver stuffing. Serve with all the usual Christmas trimmings.

Serves 6
1 turkey, about 4.5–5.5kg/10–12lb, washed and patted dry
25g/1oz/2 tbsp butter, melted
salt and ground black pepper
cranberry jelly, to serve

For the stuffing
200g/7oz/3½ cups fresh white breadcrumbs
175ml/6fl oz/¾ cup milk
25g/1oz/2 tbsp butter
1 egg, separated
1 calf's liver, about 600g/1lb 6oz, finely chopped
2 onions, finely chopped
90ml/6 tbsp chopped fresh dill
10ml/2 tsp clear honey
salt and ground black pepper

1 For the stuffing, soak the breadcrumbs in the milk until soft. Melt the butter and mix 5ml/1 tsp with the egg yolk.

2 Heat the remaining butter in a frying pan and add the liver and onions. Fry gently for 5 minutes, until the onions are golden brown. Remove from the heat and leave to cool.

3 Preheat the oven to 180°C/350°F/Gas 4. Add the cooled liver mixture to the soaked breadcrumbs and add the butter and egg yolk mixture, with the dill, honey and seasoning.

4 Whisk the egg white to soft peaks, then fold into the mixture, stirring gently to combine thoroughly.

5 Season the turkey and fill the cavity with the stuffing, then weigh to calculate the cooking time. Allow 20 minutes per 500g/1¼lb, plus an extra 20 minutes. Tuck the legs inside the cavity and tie the end shut with string. Brush with melted butter and transfer to a roasting pan. Roast for the calculated time.

6 Baste the turkey regularly, and cover with foil for the final 30 minutes. To test whether it is cooked, pierce the thickest part of the thigh with a knife; the juices should run clear.

7 Leave to rest for 15 minutes. Carve into slices, spoon over the juices and serve with the stuffing and cranberry jelly.

Roast Turkey Energy 828kcal/3452kJ; Protein 73.1g; Carbohydrate 19.4g, of which sugars 7g; Fat 51.3g, of which saturates 18.1g; Cholesterol 292mg; Calcium 77mg; Fibre 1.8g; Sodium 1267mg.
Stuffed Turkey Energy 740kcal/3126kJ; Protein 112.3g; Carbohydrate 35.9g, of which sugars 7.3g; Fat 13.5g, of which saturates 6.6g; Cholesterol 507mg; Calcium 122mg; Fibre 1.7g; Sodium 517mg.

Roasted Stuffed Turkey with Thyme

This version of the traditional festive turkey is stuffed with a spiced lamb, nut and fruit mix. It is an ideal recipe for a stunning centrepiece on Christmas Day, or serve for dinner on New Year's Eve.

Serves 4–6

1 medium turkey, approximately
  2.25–2.5kg/5–5¹/₂lb
115g/4oz/1¹/₂ cup butter, softened
6–8 sprigs of fresh thyme
sea salt and ground black pepper

For the stuffing

30ml/2 tbsp olive oil plus a
  knob of butter
2 onions, finely chopped
30ml/2 tbsp pine nuts
30ml/2 tbsp blanched
  almonds, chopped
30ml/2 tbsp currants
225g/8oz/1 cup lean minced
  (ground) lamb
15ml/1 tbsp ground cinnamon
250g/9oz/1¹/₄ cups short grain rice
500ml/17fl oz/generous 2 cups
  chicken stock
sea salt and ground black pepper

1 Preheat the oven to 200°C/400°F/Gas 6. For the stuffing, heat the oil and butter and cook the onions until they begin to colour. Add the pine nuts, almonds and currants. Cook until the nuts brown. Add the lamb and cinnamon and stir until browned.

2 Stir in the rice, and pour in the stock. Season and bring to the boil. Reduce the heat and simmer for about 15 minutes, until the liquid has been absorbed. Remove from the heat.

3 Season the turkey. Stuff the cavity with the rice mixture and secure the opening with a skewer. Rub the turkey with butter and place it breast side up in a roasting pan. Arrange half the sprigs of thyme around it and roast for 30 minutes.

4 Reduce the heat to 180°C/350°F/Gas 4. Baste the turkey with the cooking juices and pour about 250ml/8fl oz/1 cup water into the dish. Roast for a further 1¹/₂–2 hours, or until the juices run clear when the thigh is pierced with a skewer.

5 Transfer the turkey to a serving platter and garnish with fresh sprigs of thyme. Rest for 10–15 minutes before carving. Reduce the cooking juices over medium heat, skimming off the fat. Serve the juices with the turkey.

Turkey with Marsala Cream Sauce

Marsala makes a very rich and tasty sauce for this turkey dish, which is ideal for a Christmas dinner with a difference. The lemon juice gives it a sharp edge, which helps to offset the richness.

Serves 6

6 turkey breast steaks
45ml/3 tbsp plain
  (all-purpose) flour

30ml/2 tbsp olive oil
25g/1oz/2 tbsp butter
175ml/6fl oz/³/₄ cup dry Marsala
60ml/4 tbsp lemon juice
175ml/6fl oz/³/₄ cup double
  (heavy) cream
salt and ground black pepper
lemon wedges, and chopped fresh
  parsley, to garnish
mangetouts (snow peas) and
  green beans, to serve

1 Put each turkey steak between two sheets of clear film (plastic wrap) and pound with a rolling pin to flatten and stretch them. Cut each steak in half or into quarters, cutting away and discarding any sinew. Spread out the flour in a shallow bowl. Season with salt and pepper, and use to coat the meat.

2 Heat the oil and butter in a wide heavy pan or frying pan until sizzling. Add as many pieces of turkey as the pan will hold and sauté over medium heat for about 3 minutes on each side until crispy and tender. Transfer to a warmed serving dish with tongs and keep hot. Repeat with the remaining turkey.

3 Lower the heat. Mix the Marsala and lemon juice in a jug (pitcher), add to the pan and raise the heat. Bring to the boil, stirring in the sediment, then add the cream. Simmer, stirring constantly, until the sauce is reduced and glossy. Taste for seasoning. Spoon the sauce over the turkey, garnish with the lemon wedges and fresh parsley, and serve immediately with the mangetouts and green beans.

> **Variation**
> Veal or pork escalopes or chicken breast fillets can be used instead of the turkey, and 50g/2oz/¹/₄ cup mascarpone instead of the double (heavy) cream.

Roasted Turkey Energy 761kcal/3174kJ; Protein 63.9g; Carbohydrate 43.4g, of which sugars 7.6g; Fat 36.9g, of which saturates 12.5g; Cholesterol 235mg; Calcium 68mg; Fibre 1.5g; Sodium 272mg.
Turkey with Marsala Energy 385kcal/1602kJ; Protein 25.6g; Carbohydrate 9.9g, of which sugars 4.1g; Fat 23.7g, of which saturates 12.8g; Cholesterol 106mg; Calcium 31mg; Fibre 0.2g; Sodium 83mg.

Turkey and Cranberry Pie

The cranberries add a tart layer to this delicious festive pie. Cranberry sauce can be used if fresh cranberries are not available.

Serves 8
450g/1lb pork sausage meat (bulk sausage)
450g/1lb lean minced (ground) pork
15ml/1 tbsp ground coriander
15ml/1 tbsp dried mixed herbs
finely grated rind of 2 large oranges
10ml/2 tsp grated fresh root ginger or 2.5ml/½ tsp ground ginger

10ml/2 tsp salt
450g/1lb turkey breast fillets
115g/4oz/1 cup fresh cranberries
ground black pepper
1 egg, beaten
300ml/½ pint/1¼ cups aspic jelly, made according to the instructions on the packet

For the hot water crust pastry
450g/1lb/4 cups plain (all-purpose) flour
5ml/1 tsp salt
150g/5oz/⅔ cup lard
150ml/¼ pint/⅔ cup mixed milk and water

1 Preheat the oven to 180°C/350°F/Gas 4. Place a baking sheet in the oven to preheat. In a bowl, mix together the sausage meat, pork, coriander, herbs, orange rind, ginger and salt. Season with black pepper to taste.

2 To make the pastry, sift the flour into a large bowl with the salt. Heat the lard in a small pan with the milk and water until just beginning to boil. Remove the pan from the heat and allow the mixture to cool slightly.

3 Quickly stir the liquid into the flour until a very stiff dough is formed. Place on a clean work surface and knead until smooth. Cut one-third off the dough for the lid, wrap in clear film (plastic wrap) and keep in a warm place.

4 Roll out the large piece of dough on a floured surface and use to line the base and sides of a greased 20cm/8in loose-based, springform cake tin (pan). Work with the dough while it is still warm, as it will break if it becomes too cold.

5 Thinly slice the turkey breast fillets. Put the slices between two pieces of clear film and flatten with a rolling pin to a thickness of about 3mm/⅛in.

6 Spoon half the pork mixture into the cake tin, pressing it well into the edges. Cover it with half the turkey slices and then the cranberries, followed by the remaining turkey and finally the rest of the pork mixture.

7 Roll out the remaining dough and use to cover the filling, trimming off any excess and sealing the edges with a little beaten egg. Make a steam hole in the centre of the lid and decorate the top by cutting pastry trimmings into leaf shapes. Brush with some beaten egg and bake for 2 hours. Cover the pie with foil if the top gets too brown.

8 Place the pie on a wire rack to cool. When it is cold, use a funnel to fill the pie with liquid aspic jelly. Leave the jelly to set for a few hours or overnight, before carefully unmoulding the pie and serving it in thick slices.

Turkey and Cranberry Bundles

After the traditional Christmas or Thanksgiving meal, it is easy to end up with lots of turkey left-overs. These delicious filo pastry parcels are a marvellous way of using up the small pieces of cooked turkey.

Serves 6
450g/1lb cooked turkey, cut into chunks

115g/4oz/1 cup Brie, diced
30ml/2 tbsp cranberry sauce
30ml/2 tbsp chopped fresh parsley
9 sheets filo pastry, 45 × 28cm/ 18 × 11in each, thawed if frozen
50g/2oz/¼ cup butter, melted
salt and ground black pepper
green salad, to serve

1 Preheat the oven to 200°C/400°F/Gas 6. Mix the turkey, diced Brie, cranberry sauce and chopped parsley. Season with salt and ground black pepper.

2 Cut the filo sheets in half widthways and trim to make 18 squares. Layer three pieces of pastry together, brushing them with a little melted butter so that they stick together. Repeat with the remaining filo squares to give six pieces.

3 Divide the turkey mixture among the pastry, making neat piles on each piece. Gather up the pastry to enclose the filling in neat bundles. Place on a baking sheet, brush with a little melted butter and bake for 20 minutes, or until the pastry is crisp and golden. Serve hot or warm with a green salad.

Variation
These little parcels can be made with a variety of fillings and are great for using up left-over cooked meats. To make Ham and Cheddar Bundles, replace the turkey with ham and use Cheddar in place of the Brie. A fruit-flavoured chutney would make a good alternative to the cranberry sauce. Alternatively, to make Chicken and Stilton Bundles, use cooked chicken in place of the turkey and white Stilton instead of Brie. Replace the cranberry sauce with mango chutney.

Turkey Pie Energy 670kcal/2801kJ; Protein 38.1g; Carbohydrate 50.8g, of which sugars 4.1g; Fat 36.2g, of which saturates 13.9g; Cholesterol 119mg; Calcium 155mg; Fibre 2.5g; Sodium 558mg.
Turkey Bundles Energy 285kcal/1192kJ; Protein 25.5g; Carbohydrate 15.5g, of which sugars 3.6g; Fat 13.4g, of which saturates 8g; Cholesterol 89mg; Calcium 85mg; Fibre 0.7g; Sodium 190mg.

Turkey and Tomato Hot-pot

Turkey is very versatile and is suitable more than just roasting for traditional Christmas meals. It also makes a great choice for any festive occasion. This slow-cooker dish is great for an informal Christmas gathering. The minced turkey is shaped into balls and simmered with rice in a rich tomato sauce.

Serves 4
white bread loaf, unsliced
30ml/2 tbsp milk

1 garlic clove, crushed
2.5ml/½ tsp caraway seeds
225g/8oz minced (ground) turkey
1 egg white
350ml/12fl oz/1½ cups hot
 chicken stock
400g/14oz can chopped
 tomatoes
15ml/1 tbsp tomato purée (paste)
90g/3½oz/½ cup easy-cook
 (converted) rice
salt and ground black pepper
15ml/1 tbsp chopped fresh basil,
 to garnish
courgette (zucchini) ribbons, lightly
 cooked, to serve

1 Using a serrated knife, remove the crusts from the bread loaf and cut the bread into cubes.

2 Place the bread in a mixing bowl and sprinkle with the milk, then leave to soak for about 5 minutes.

3 Add the garlic clove, caraway seeds and turkey to the bread. Season with salt and pepper and mix together well.

4 Whisk the egg white until stiff, then fold, half at a time, into the turkey mixture. Chill in the refrigerator.

5 Pour the stock into the ceramic cooking pot. Add the tomatoes and tomato purée, then switch the slow-cooker to high, cover with the lid and cook for 1 hour.

6 Meanwhile, shape the turkey mixture into 16 small balls with your hands. Stir the rice into the tomato mixture, then add the turkey balls, ensuring they are covered by the sauce.

7 Cook on high for a further hour, or until the turkey balls and rice are cooked. Serve with the courgette ribbons.

Turkey Rice Salad

This delicious, crunchy salad is an ideal way to use up left-over turkey during the holiday festivities.

Serves 8
225g/8oz/1¼ cups brown rice
50g/2oz/⅔ cup wild rice
2 red dessert apples, quartered,
 cored and chopped

2 celery sticks, coarsely sliced
115g/4oz/1 cup seedless grapes
45ml/3 tbsp lemon or
 orange juice
150ml/¼ pint/⅔ cup thick
 mayonnaise
350g/12oz cooked turkey,
 chopped into bitesize pieces
salt and ground black pepper
frilly lettuce leaves, to serve

1 Cook the brown and wild rice in boiling salted water for about 25 minutes or until tender. Rinse the rice under cold running water and drain thoroughly.

2 Turn the well-drained rice into a large mixing bowl and add the apples, celery and grapes.

3 Beat the lemon or orange juice into the mayonnaise, season with salt and pepper to taste and pour over the rice mixture.

4 Add the chopped turkey pieces to the rice and mix well to coat with the lemon or orange mayonnaise.

5 Arrange the frilly lettuce leaves over the base and around the sides of a warmed serving dish, spoon the rice salad over the top and serve immediately.

> **Cook's Tip**
> This festive salad will be even tastier if you have the time and inclination to make your own home-made mayonnaise.

> **Variation**
> You can use white rice for this recipe, if you prefer, but it will only need about half the cooking time of the brown and wild rices.

Turkey Hot-pot Energy 187kcal/797kJ; Protein 18.2g; Carbohydrate 26.6g, of which sugars 3.9g; Fat 1.7g, of which saturates 0.5g; Cholesterol 32mg; Calcium 44mg; Fibre 1g; Sodium 212mg.
Turkey Rice Salad Energy 293kcal/1222kJ; Protein 12g; Carbohydrate 26.7g, of which sugars 4.2g; Fat 15.3g, of which saturates 2.4g; Cholesterol 41mg; Calcium 16mg; Fibre 0.5g; Sodium 113mg.

Turkey Croquettes

Enjoy these festive patties of smoked turkey mixed with potato and spring onions and rolled in breadcrumbs.

115g/4oz/2 cups fresh white
   breadcrumbs
vegetable oil, for deep-frying
salt and ground black pepper

Serves 4
450g/1lb potatoes, diced
3 eggs
30ml/2 tbsp milk
175g/6oz smoked turkey rashers
   (strips), finely chopped
2 spring onions (scallions),
   finely sliced

For the sauce
15ml/1 tbsp olive oil
1 onion, finely chopped
400g/14oz can tomatoes, drained
30ml/2 tbsp tomato
   purée (paste)
15ml/1 tbsp chopped
   fresh parsley

1 Boil the potatoes for 20 minutes or until tender. Drain and return the pan to low heat to evaporate the excess water.

2 Mash the potatoes with two eggs and the milk. Season well with salt and ground black pepper. Stir in the turkey and spring onions. Chill for about 1 hour.

3 Meanwhile, to make the sauce, heat the oil in a frying pan and fry the onion for 5 minutes until soft. Add the tomatoes and purée, stir and simmer for 10 minutes. Stir in the parsley, season with salt and pepper and keep warm until needed.

4 Remove the potato mixture from the refrigerator and divide into eight pieces. Shape each piece into a sausage shape and dip in the remaining beaten egg, and then the breadcrumbs.

5 Heat the oil in a pan or deep-fat fryer to 175°C/330°F and deep-fry the croquettes for 5 minutes, or until golden and crisp. Serve immediately with the sauce.

> **Cook's Tip**
> Test the oil temperature by dropping a cube of bread into it. If it sinks, rises and sizzles in 10 seconds, the oil is ready to use.

Turkey Schnitzel

Schnitzel is a pounded-flat, crisp-coated, fried steak of turkey, chicken or veal. It is traditionally made from veal, but it is given a Christmassy twist in this recipe, which uses turkey or chicken meat and will prove to be very popular. Serve with any seasonal vegetables.

Serves 4
4 skinless turkey or chicken breast
   fillets, each weighing about
   175g/6oz

juice of 1 lemon
2 garlic cloves, chopped
plain (all-purpose) flour,
   for dusting
1–2 eggs
15ml/1 tbsp water
50g/2oz/1/2 cup matzo meal
paprika
a mixture of vegetable and olive
   oil, for shallow-frying
salt and ground black pepper
lemon wedges and a selection
   of raw or cooked seasonal
   vegetables, to serve

1 Lay each piece of meat between two sheets of baking parchment and pound with a mallet or the end of a rolling pin until it is about half its original thickness and fairly even.

2 In a bowl, combine the lemon juice, garlic, salt and pepper. Coat the meat in it, then leave to marinate.

3 Meanwhile, arrange three wide plates or shallow dishes in a row. Fill one plate or dish with flour, beat the egg and water together in another and mix the matzo meal, salt, pepper and paprika together on the third.

4 Working quickly, dip each fillet into the flour, then the egg, then the matzo meal. Pat everything in well, then arrange the crumbed fillets on a plate and chill in the refrigerator for at least 30 minutes, and up to 2 hours.

5 In a large, heavy frying pan, heat the oil until it will turn a cube of bread dropped into the oil golden brown in 30–60 seconds. Carefully add the crumbed fillets (in batches if necessary) and fry until golden brown, turning once. Remove and drain on kitchen paper. Serve immediately with lemon wedges and a selection of vegetables.

Turkey Croquettes Energy 404kcal/1698kJ; Protein 19.4g; Carbohydrate 47g, of which sugars 7.7g; Fat 16.7g, of which saturates 2.4g; Cholesterol 73mg; Calcium 93mg; Fibre 3.3g; Sodium 315mg.
Turkey Schnitzel Energy 368kcal/1546kJ; Protein 45.4g; Carbohydrate 14.7g, of which sugars 0.6g; Fat 14.6g, of which saturates 2.3g; Cholesterol 170mg; Calcium 27mg; Fibre 0.5g; Sodium 125mg.

Stuffed Guinea Fowl with Mushrooms

Guinea fowl meat is as white as chicken but tastes more like pheasant, although with a less gamey flavour.

Serves 8
25g/1oz/2 tbsp butter, plus
  15g/½oz/1 tbsp for the gravy
250g/9oz mixed wild
  mushrooms, chopped
30ml/2 tbsp chopped fresh parsley
5ml/1 tsp soy sauce
8 guinea fowl breast fillets,
  skins removed
about 750ml/1¼ pints/3 cups
  chicken stock for poaching

15ml/1 tbsp plain
  (all-purpose) flour
salt and ground black pepper

For the pearl barley risotto
200g/7oz pearl barley
15ml/1 tbsp olive oil
100g/4oz mixed wild mushrooms
2 garlic cloves, crushed
100g/4oz fresh parsley, chopped

For the roasted vegetables
200g/7oz parsnips and carrots,
  or seasonal vegetables, cut
  into cubes
120ml/4fl oz/½ cup olive oil

1 Cook the pearl barley in a pan of lightly salted water for 1–2 hours until tender. Melt 25g/1oz/2 tbsp of the butter in a pan, add the mushrooms and sauté until the juices have evaporated. Add the parsley and soy sauce and leave to cool.

2 Flatten the guinea fowl fillets between clear film (plastic wrap). Spread with the mushroom stuffing, then roll them up. Wrap each in clear film. Preheat the oven to 180°C/350°F/Gas 4.

3 Place the vegetables in a roasting pan with the oil and salt and roast for 20–25 minutes. Put the fillets in a pan with the stock. Simmer for 30 minutes.

4 For the risotto, heat the oil in a pan, and cook the mushrooms. Add the pearl barley, the garlic and parsley. Stir together and keep warm. Remove the fillets from the stock and keep warm.

5 Melt the remaining butter, add the flour and cook, stirring over low heat, for 1 minute. Remove from the heat and add the stock to form a gravy. Stir over the heat for 2–3 minutes until the gravy thickens. Season to taste. Slice the fillets and serve with the gravy, roasted vegetables and risotto.

Guinea Fowl with Cream Sauce

Accompanied by creamy sweet potato mash and whole baby leeks, guinea fowl is very festive served with a creamy whisky sauce.

Serves 4
2 guinea fowl, each weighing
  about 1kg/2¼lb

90ml/6 tbsp whisky
150ml/¼ pint/⅔ cup well-
  flavoured chicken stock
150ml/¼ pint/⅔ cup double
  (heavy) cream
20 baby leeks
salt and ground black pepper
fresh thyme sprigs, to garnish
mashed sweet potatoes, to serve

1 Preheat the oven to 200°C/400°F/Gas 6. Brown the guinea fowl on all sides in a roasting pan on the stove, then turn it breast uppermost and transfer the pan to the oven. Roast for about 1 hour, until the guinea fowl are golden and cooked through. Transfer the guinea fowl to a warmed serving dish, cover with foil and keep warm.

2 Pour off the excess fat from the pan, then heat the juices on the stove and stir in the whisky. Bring to the boil and cook until reduced. Add the stock and cream and simmer again until reduced slightly. Strain and season to taste.

3 Meanwhile, trim the leeks so that they are roughly the same length as the guinea fowl breasts, then cook them whole in boiling salted water for about 3 minutes, or until tender but not too soft. Drain the leeks in a colander.

4 Carve the guinea fowl. To serve, arrange portions of mashed sweet potato on warmed serving plates, then add the carved guinea fowl and the leeks. Garnish with sprigs of fresh thyme, and season with plenty of ground black pepper. Spoon a little of the sauce over each portion and serve the rest separately.

> **Variation**
> *If you dislike the flavour of whisky, then substitute brandy, Madeira or Marsala. Or, to make a non-alcoholic version, use freshly squeezed orange juice instead.*

Stuffed Guinea Fowl Energy 348kcal/1462kJ; Protein 27.7g; Carbohydrate 26g, of which sugars 2.4g; Fat 15.6g, ofwhich saturates 3.6g; Cholesterol 77mg; Calcium 49mg; Fibre 1.8g; Sodium 226mg.
Guinea Fowl Energy 854kcal/3568kJ; Protein 110.6g; Carbohydrate 0.6g, of which sugars 0.6g; Fat 41.7g, of which saturates 18g; Cholesterol 51mg; Calcium 159mg; Fibre 0g; Sodium 308mg.

Braised Guinea Fowl with Cabbage

The slightly gamey flavour of guinea fowl is complemented perfectly by the festive flavours of red cabbage, braised in apple juice and scented with juniper berries.

Serves 4

15ml/1 tbsp unsalted butter
1/2 red cabbage, weighing about 450g/1lb
1.3kg/3lb oven-ready guinea fowl, jointed
15ml/1 tbsp sunflower oil
3 shallots, very finely chopped
15ml/1 tbsp plain (all-purpose) flour
120ml/4fl oz/1/2 cup chicken stock
150ml/1/4 pint/2/3 cup apple juice
15ml/1 tbsp soft light brown sugar
15ml/1 tbsp red wine vinegar
4 juniper berries, lightly crushed
salt and ground black pepper

1 Use half the butter to grease the ceramic cooking pot. Cut the cabbage into wedges, removing any tough outer leaves and the central core. Shred the cabbage finely, then place in the ceramic cooking pot, packing it down tightly.

2 Rinse the guinea fowl portions and pat dry with kitchen paper. Heat the remaining butter and the oil in a pan and brown the guinea fowl on all sides. Lift from the pan, leaving the fat behind, and place on top of the red cabbage.

3 Add the shallots to the frying pan and cook gently for 5 minutes. Sprinkle with the flour, cook for a few seconds, then gradually stir in the stock followed by the apple juice. Bring to the boil, stirring, until thickened. Remove from the heat, stir in the sugar, vinegar and juniper berries, and season.

4 Pour the sauce over the guinea fowl, cover and cook on high for 4 hours, or until the meat and cabbage are tender. Check the seasoning, adding more if necessary, and serve.

Variations
• Other mild-tasting poultry or game such as chicken or pheasant can be used in place of the guinea fowl, if preferred.
• Increase the fruity flavour of the cabbage by adding 15ml/1 tbsp sultanas (golden raisins) to the pot before cooking.

Guinea Fowl with Saffron Sauce

This delicious sauce, of saffron, toasted almonds ground with parsley and several spices, adds a touch of festive luxury to this guinea fowl dish.

Serves 4

25g/1oz/1/4 cup blanched almonds
pinch of saffron threads
120ml/8 tbsp chicken stock
1.2–1.3kg/2½–3lb guinea fowl
60ml/4fl oz/½ cup olive oil
1 thick slice of bread, without crusts
2 garlic cloves, finely chopped
120ml/4fl oz/½ cup fino sherry
1 bay leaf, crumbled
4 thyme sprigs
15ml/1 tbsp finely chopped fresh parsley
pinch of freshly grated nutmeg
pinch of ground cloves
juice of ½ lemon
5ml/1 tsp paprika
salt and ground black pepper

1 Preheat the oven to 150°C/300°F/Gas 2. Spread the almonds on a baking sheet and roast in the oven for about 20 minutes, or until golden brown.

2 Crumble the saffron with your fingers into a small bowl, pour over 30ml/2 tbsp hot chicken stock and leave to soak.

3 Cut the bird into eight serving pieces, discarding the wing tips, backbone, breastbone and leg tips. This will give you two legs (split them at the joint), two wings with one-third of the breast attached, and two short breast pieces.

4 Heat the olive oil in a wide shallow flameproof casserole and fry the bread slice on both sides. Fry the garlic quickly, then remove both to a blender.

5 Season the pieces well and fry them, turning until golden on all sides. Add the remaining stock and the sherry to the pan, stirring to deglaze the pan. Add the bay leaf and thyme and cover. Cook gently for 10 minutes.

6 Grind together the bread, garlic and almonds. Add the fresh parsley, saffron liquid, nutmeg and cloves, and purée the mixture. Stir into the poultry juices, add the lemon juice and paprika, season with salt and pepper and serve immediately.

Braised Guinea Fowl Energy 456kcal/1907kJ; Protein 44.5g; Carbohydrate 20g, of which sugars 15g; Fat 22.5g, of which saturates 6.7g; Cholesterol 225mg; Calcium 96mg; Fibre 3.1g; Sodium 15mg.
Guinea Fowl Energy 589kcal/2442kJ; Protein 38.6g; Carbohydrate 4.2g, of which sugars 0.9g; Fat 42.8g, of which saturates 10.5g; Cholesterol 192mg; Calcium 40mg; Fibre 0.6g; Sodium 189mg.

Roast Goose with Black Pudding

Goose is popular at Christmas, but it should be enjoyed at any time of year.

Serves 8
1 oven-ready goose weighing about 5.5kg/12lb, with giblets
1 small onion, sliced
2 small carrots, sliced
2 celery sticks, sliced
small bunch of parsley and thyme
450/1lb black pudding (blood sausage), crumbled or chopped
1 large garlic clove, crushed
2 large cooking apples, peeled, cored and finely chopped
250ml/8fl oz/1 cup dry (hard) cider
about 15ml/1 tbsp flour
salt and ground black pepper
roast potatoes and freshly cooked seasonal vegetables, to serve

1 Remove the goose liver from the giblets and put the rest of the giblets into a pan with the onion, carrots, celery and herbs. Cover with water, season and simmer for 30–45 minutes. Chop the liver finely and mix it with the black pudding, garlic and apples. Season, then sprinkle in 75ml/2½fl oz/⅓ cup cider.

2 Preheat the oven to 200°C/400°F/Gas 6. Wipe the inside of the goose and pack with the stuffing. Season and prick the skin all over. Weigh the stuffed goose and calculate the cooking time at 15 minutes per 450g/1lb plus 15 minutes. Put the goose on a rack in a roasting pan, cover with foil and roast for 1 hour.

3 Remove the goose from the oven and pour off the hot fat. Pour the remaining cider over the goose, replace the foil, and return to the oven. Half an hour before the end of the cooking time, remove the foil and baste with the juices. Return to the oven, uncovered, and allow the skin to brown and crisp. Transfer to a serving plate and rest for 20 minutes before carving.

4 Meanwhile, make the gravy. Pour off any excess fat from the roasting pan, leaving 30ml/2 tbsp, then sprinkle in enough flour to absorb it. Stir for 1 minute, then strain in enough giblet stock for a gravy. Bring to the boil and simmer for 4 minutes, stirring. Season to taste and pour the gravy into a sauce sboat.

5 Carve the goose into slices at the table and serve with the gravy, roast potatoes and some seasonal vegetables.

Goose with Caramelized Apples

For this festive dish, choose a young goose with a pliable breastbone for the best possible flavour.

Serves 8
5kg/11lb goose, with giblets (thawed overnight, if frozen)
salt and ground black pepper

For the apple and nut stuffing
225g/8oz/2 cups prunes
150ml/1¼ pint/⅔ cup port or red wine
675g/1½lb cooking apples, peeled, cored and cubed
1 large onion, chopped
4 celery sticks, sliced
15ml/1 tbsp mixed dried herbs
finely grated rind of 1 orange
goose liver, chopped
450g/1lb pork sausage meat (bulk sausage)
115g/4oz/1 cup chopped pecans
2 eggs

For the caramelized apples
50g/2oz/4 tbsp butter
60ml/4 tbsp redcurrant jelly
30ml/2 tbsp red wine vinegar
8 small dessert apples, peeled and cored

For the gravy
30ml/2 tbsp plain (all-purpose) flour
600ml/1 pint/2½ cups giblet stock
juice of 1 orange

1 The day before you want to cook the goose, soak the prunes in the port or red wine. After the soaking time, remove each prune from the marinade, pit each one and cut it into four pieces. Reserve the port or red wine and set aside until required.

2 The next day, mix the prunes with all the remaining stuffing ingredients and season well. Moisten with half the reserved port.

3 Preheat the oven to 200°C/400°F/Gas 6. Stuff the neck-end of the goose, tucking the flap of the skin under and securing it with a small skewer. Remove the excess fat from the cavity and pack it with the stuffing. Tie the legs together to hold in place.

4 Weigh the stuffed goose to calculate the cooking time: allow 15 minutes for each 450g/1lb, plus 15 minutes. Put the bird on a rack in a roasting pan and rub the skin with salt. Prick the skin all over to help the fat run out. Roast for 30 minutes, then reduce the heat to 180°C/350°F/Gas 4 and roast for the remaining cooking time. Pour off any fat produced during cooking into a bowl. The goose is cooked if the juices run clear when the thickest part of the thigh is pierced with a skewer. Pour a little cold water over the breast to crisp the skin.

5 Meanwhile, prepare the apples. Melt the butter, redcurrant jelly and vinegar in a small roasting pan or a shallow ovenproof dish. Put in the apples, baste them well and cook in the oven for 15–20 minutes. Baste the apples halfway through the cooking time. Do not cover them or they will collapse.

6 Lift the goose on to the serving dish and let it stand for 15 minutes before carving. Pour off the excess fat from the roasting pan, leaving any sediment in the bottom. Stir in the flour, cook gently until brown, and then blend in the stock. Bring to the boil, add the remaining reserved port, orange juice and seasoning. Simmer for 2–3 minutes. Strain into a gravy boat. Surround the goose with the caramelized apples and spoon over the redcurrant glaze.

Roast Goose Energy 770kcal/3206kJ; Protein 59.3g; Carbohydrate 14.6g, of which sugars 4.5g; Fat 52.2g, of which saturates 17.2g; Cholesterol 209mg; Calcium 52mg; Fibre 0.9g; Sodium 840mg.
Goose with Apples Energy 822kcal/3437kJ; Protein 54.8g; Carbohydrate 44.1g, of which sugars 21.8g; Fat 48.7g, of which saturates 0.9g; Cholesterol 0mg; Calcium 87mg; Fibre 3.1g; Sodium 486mg.

Goose Legs with Brandy Sauce

Try goose on Christmas Day instead of the usual turkey.

Serves 4

4 goose legs, halved
75ml/5 tbsp brandy
30ml/2 tbsp lemon juice
5ml/1 tsp grated lemon rind
salt and ground black pepper

For the sauce

30ml/2 tbsp plain (all-purpose) flour
200ml/7fl oz/scant 1 cup hot chicken stock

To serve

12 pitted prunes
45ml/3 tbsp brandy
450g/1lb can chestnuts purée
15–30ml/1–2 tbsp whipping cream
400g/14oz Brussels sprouts, trimmed
12 shelled walnuts
salt

1 Place the goose legs in a non-metallic dish. Mix the brandy, lemon juice and rind in a bowl, season with pepper and pour over the legs, turning to coat. Cover and marinate in the refrigerator for 12 hours. Meanwhile, place the prunes for the accompaniments in a bowl, add the brandy and leave to soak.

2 Pat the goose legs dry. Reserve the marinade. Rub the legs with salt, and dry-fry over medium heat for 10 minutes, until browned. Lower the heat, partially cover the pan and cook for 2 hours, until the juices run clear when pierced with a sharp knife. Transfer to a plate, cover and keep warm. Reserve the fat.

3 To make the garnish, mix the chestnut purée with 15ml/1 tbsp of goose fat and the cream in a pan and season with salt. Cook over low heat, stirring, until warmed through.

4 Meanwhile, cook the Brussels sprouts for 3–5 minutes, until tender crisp. Drain well and keep warm. Drain the prunes, reserving the brandy, and stuff them with the walnuts.

5 For the sauce, heat 60ml/4 tbsp of the goose fat, add the flour and cook until browned. Add the stock and reserved marinade and simmer for 10 minutes. Add the reserved brandy.

6 Serve with the chestnut purée, prunes and the Brussels sprouts. Spoon over the sauce.

Marmalade-glazed Goose

Red cabbage with leeks and braised fennel are good with roast goose.

Serves 8

4.5kg/10lb oven-ready goose
1 cooking apple, peeled, cored and cut into eighths
1 large onion, cut into eighths
bunch of fresh sage, plus extra sprigs to garnish
30ml/2 tbsp marmalade, melted
salt and ground black pepper

For the stuffing

25g/1oz/2 tbsp butter
1 onion, finely chopped
15ml/1 tbsp marmalade
450g/1lb/2 cups ready-to-eat prunes, chopped
45ml/3 tbsp Madeira
225g/8oz/4 cups fresh white breadcrumbs
30ml/2 tbsp chopped fresh sage

For the gravy

1 onion, chopped
15ml/1 tbsp plain (all-purpose) flour
150ml/¼ pint/⅔ cup Madeira
600ml/1 pint/2½ cups chicken stock

1 Preheat the oven to 200°C/400°F/Gas 6. Prick the skin of the goose and season inside and out. Mix the apple, onion and sage and spoon the mixture into the parson's nose end of the goose.

2 For the stuffing, melt the butter and cook the onion for 5 minutes. Remove the pan from the heat and add the prunes, marmalade, Madeira, breadcrumbs and sage. Use some to stuff the neck end; secure with skewers. Put the goose in a roasting pan. Cover loosely with buttered foil, then roast for 2 hours.

3 Baste during cooking. Remove excess fat. Remove the foil and brush with melted marmalade. Roast for 30–40 minutes more, or until the juices run clear. Remove from the oven and cover, then leave to stand for 15 minutes before carving.

4 With the remaining stuffing, make balls. Put them in an ovenproof dish, add a little goose fat and bake for 15 minutes. For the gravy, heat 15ml/1 tbsp of fat, add the onion and cook for 5 minutes. Sprinkle in the flour, then stir in the Madeira and stock. Bring to the boil, then simmer until thick. Strain and serve it with the goose and stuffing. Garnish with sage leaves.

Goose Legs Energy 1033kcal/4312kJ; Protein 57.7g; Carbohydrate 62.1g, of which sugars 21.9g; Fat 55.8g, of which saturates 2.9g; Cholesterol 4mg; Calcium 135mg; Fibre 11.3g; Sodium 268mg.
Glazed Goose Energy 823kcal/3443kJ; Protein 57.6g; Carbohydrate 47.1g, of which sugars 23.8g; Fat 43.3g, of which saturates 14g; Cholesterol 177mg; Calcium 106mg; Fibre 4.5g; Sodium 395mg.

Duck with Orange Sauce

The classic partnering of duck with orange sauce makes for a tasty festive dish.

Serves 2–3

2kg/4½lb duck 2 oranges
90g/3½oz/½ cup caster
  (superfine) sugar

90ml/6 tbsp white wine vinegar
  or cider vinegar
120ml/4fl oz/½ cup Grand
  Marnier or other orange
  flavoured liqueur
salt and ground black pepper
watercress and orange slices,
  to garnish

1 Preheat the oven to 150°C/300°F/Gas 2. Trim off all the excess fat and skin from the duck and prick the skin all over with a fork. Generously season the duck inside and out, and tie the legs together with string to hold them in place.

2 Place the duck on a rack in a large roasting pan. Cover tightly with foil and cook in the preheated oven for 1½ hours. Remove the rind in wide strips from the oranges, then stack up two or three strips at a time and slice into very thin julienne strips. Squeeze the juice from the oranges and set it aside.

3 Place the sugar and vinegar in a pan and stir to dissolve the sugar. Boil over high heat, without stirring, until the mixture is a rich caramel colour. Remove the pan from the heat and carefully add the orange juice, pouring it down the side of the pan. Swirl the pan to blend, then bring back to the boil and add the orange rind and liqueur. Simmer for 2–3 minutes.

4 Remove the duck from the oven and pour off all the fat from the pan. Raise the oven temperature to 200°C/400°F/Gas 6. Roast the duck, uncovered, for 25–30 minutes, basting three or four times with the caramel mixture, until the duck is golden brown and the juices run clear when the thigh is pierced.

5 Pour the juices from the cavity into the casserole and transfer the duck to a carving board. Cover loosely with foil and leave to stand for 10–15 minutes. Pour the roasting juices into the pan with the rest of the caramel mixture, skim off the fat and simmer gently. Serve the duck with the orange sauce, garnished with sprigs of watercress and orange slices.

Duck Legs with Red Cabbage

This Christmas dish is traditionally served with red cabbage. If duck is not available, goose legs have the same rich flavour.

Serves 4

8 duck legs or 4 goose legs
15ml/1 tbsp oil
10ml/2 tsp tomato purée (paste)
200l/7fl oz/scant 1 cup red wine
salt and ground white pepper
chopped parsley, to garnish
mashed potato, to serve, optional

For the red cabbage

3 onions
60g/2½oz lard
1 red cabbage, finely sliced
100ml/3½fl oz/scant ½ cup red
  wine vinegar
15ml/1 tbsp sugar
2 bay leaves
3 pieces star anise
1 cinnamon stick
250ml/8fl oz/ 1 cup apple juice
2 apples, chopped
30ml/2 tbsp redcurrant jelly
5ml/1 tsp cornflour (cornstarch)

1 For the cabbage, chop two of the onions, melt the lard in a large pan and fry the onion for 2 minutes. Add the cabbage, vinegar, sugar, spices and apple juice, bring to the boil, cover and simmer for 30 minutes.

2 Stir the apples and redcurrant jelly into the pan and cook for a further 45 minutes, adding more apple juice if necessary. Towards the end of the cooking time, blend the cornflour with water in a cup and stir into the cabbage. Preheat the oven to 200°C/400°F/Gas 6.

3 While the cabbage is cooking, place the duck legs in a roasting pan, season, add a cup of water and roast in the oven for 20 minutes, then reduce the oven to 160°C/325°F/Gas 3 and cook for a further 40 minutes, basting from time to time.

4 When the legs are cooked, lift them out and keep them warm. Add the remaining onion, chopped, and the tomato purée to the pan and fry over high heat for 3–4 minutes. Deglaze the pan with the wine and cook for another 2 minutes.

5 Serve the duck legs with the sauce poured over, garnished with fresh parsley and accompanied by the red cabbage. Serve with mashed potato, if you like.

Duck with Orange Energy 280kcal/1181kJ; Protein 30.8g; Carbohydrate 23.8g, of which sugars 23.8g; Fat 10g, of which saturates 1.9g; Cholesterol 165mg; Calcium 48mg; Fibre 0.4g; Sodium 195mg.
Duck Legs Energy 958kcal/3961kJ; Protein 20.7g; Carbohydrate 32.7g, of which sugars 28.5g; Fat 79.8g, of which saturates 22.8g; Cholesterol 12mg; Calcium 122mg; Fibre 5.1g; Sodium 146mg.

Duck with Damson and Ginger Sauce

This is a variation of salt duck, a traditional Welsh recipe that would be well suited to serving at the festive table. Simple pan-fried duck breast fillets go well with a fruit sauce too, as in this recipe with damsons and ground ginger.

Serves 4

250g/9oz fresh damsons
5ml/1 tsp ground ginger
45ml/3 tbsp sugar
10ml/2 tsp wine vinegar or
  sherry vinegar
4 duck breast fillets
15ml/1 tbsp oil
salt and ground black pepper

1 Put the damsons in a pan with the ginger and 45ml/3 tbsp water. Bring to the boil, cover and simmer gently for 5 minutes, or until the fruit is soft. Stir frequently and add a little extra water if the fruit looks as if it is drying out or sticking to the bottom of the pan.

2 Stir in the sugar and vinegar. Press the mixture through a sieve (strainer) to remove stones (pits) and skin. Taste the sauce and add more sugar, if necessary, and seasoning to taste.

3 Meanwhile, with a sharp knife, score the fat on the duck breast portions in several places without cutting into the meat. Brush the oil over both sides of the duck. Sprinkle a little salt and pepper on the fat side only.

4 Preheat a griddle pan or heavy frying pan. When hot, add the duck breast fillets, skin side down, and cook over medium heat for about 5 minutes or until the fat is evenly browned and crisp. Turn over and cook the meat side for 4–5 minutes. Lift out and leave to rest for 5–10 minutes.

5 Cut the duck fillets into slices on the diagonal and serve immediately, accompanied by the sauce.

> **Cook's Tip**
> Both the duck and the sauce are also good when served cold. Serve with simple steamed winter vegetables.

Duck Stew with Olives

This method of cooking duck is ideal for a festive dinner. The sweetness from slow-cooking the onions balances the saltiness of the olives.

Serves 4

4 duck quarters or breast portions
225g/8oz baby (pearl) onions

2.5ml/½ tsp caster (superfine) sugar
30ml/2 tbsp plain (all-purpose) flour
250ml/8fl oz/1 cup dry red wine
250ml/8fl oz/1 cup duck or
  chicken stock
1 bouquet garni
115g/4oz/1 cup pitted green or
  black olives, or a combination
salt and ground black pepper

1 Put the duck skin side down in a large frying pan and cook for 10–12 minutes, turning to colour evenly, until browned on both sides. Lift out with a slotted spoon and place skin side up in the ceramic cooking pot. Switch the slow cooker to high.

2 Pour off most of the fat from the pan, leaving about 15ml/1 tbsp behind. Add the onions and cook over a medium-low heat until beginning to colour. Sprinkle over the sugar and cook for 5 minutes until golden, stirring frequently. Sprinkle with the flour and cook, uncovered, for 2 minutes, stirring frequently.

3 Gradually stir the red wine into the onions, followed by the stock. Bring to the boil, then pour the liquid over the duck. Add the bouquet garni to the pot, cover with the lid and cook on the high setting for 1 hour.

4 Turn the slow cooker to low and cook for a further 4–5 hours, or until the duck and onions are very tender.

5 Put the olives in a heatproof bowl and pour over very hot water to cover. Leave to stand for about 1 minute, then drain thoroughly. Add the olives to the casserole, re-cover with the lid and cook for a further 30 minutes.

6 Transfer the duck, onions and olives to a warm serving dish or individual plates. Skim all the fat from the cooking liquid and discard the bouquet garni. Season the sauce to taste with ground black pepper and a little salt, if needed, then spoon over the duck and serve immediately.

Duck with Damson Energy 275kcal/1157kJ; Protein 29.9g; Carbohydrate 17.5g, of which sugars 17.5g; Fat 12.5g, of which saturates 2.4g; Cholesterol 165mg; Calcium 39mg; Fibre 1.1g; Sodium 167mg.
Duck Stew Energy 414kcal/1736kJ; Protein 47.3g; Carbohydrate 8.2g, of which sugars 2.3g; Fat 18.5g, of which saturates 5.2g; Cholesterol 257mg; Calcium 67mg; Fibre 1.6g; Sodium 917mg.

Roast Pheasant with Sherry and Mustard Sauce

Roast pheasant makes a pleasant change from the traditional turkey, chicken or goose at Christmas time. Look out for them hanging in the window of butchers' stores in the run-up to the festive season.

Serves 4
2 young oven-ready pheasants
50g/2oz/¼ cup softened butter
200ml/7fl oz/scant 1 cup sherry
15ml/1 tbsp Dijon mustard
salt and ground black pepper

1 Preheat the oven to 200°C/400°F/Gas 6. Put the pheasants in a roasting pan and spread the butter all over both birds. Season with salt and pepper.

2 Roast the pheasants in the preheated oven for 50 minutes, basting often to stop the birds from drying out.

3 When the pheasants are cooked, take them out of the pan and leave to rest on a chopping board, loosely covered with a sheet of foil, for about 10–15 minutes.

4 Meanwhile, place the roasting pan over medium heat. Add the sherry and season with salt and pepper.

5 Simmer for 5 minutes, until the sherry has slightly reduced, then stir in the mustard. Carve the pheasants and serve with the sherry and mustard sauce.

Cook's Tips
• *Serve with potatoes braised in wine with garlic and onions, Brussels sprouts and bread sauce.*
• *Use only young pheasants for roasting in this recipe – older birds are too tough for roasting and are only suitable for long, slow cooking in a casserole.*
• *Like many gamebirds – including grouse, guinea fowl and partridge – pheasants are at their best over the festive season.*

Marinated Pheasant with Port

This warming dish is delicious served with mashed root vegetables and shredded cabbage or leeks. Marinating the pheasant in port is a good way of moistening and tenderizing pheasant, especially the legs, which can be a little tough.

Red wine can be substituted for the port, if you prefer.

Serves 4
2 pheasants, cut into portions
300ml/½ pint/1¼ cups port
50g/2oz/¼ cup butter
300g/11oz brown cap (cremini) mushrooms, halved if large

1 Place the pheasant portions in a large bowl and pour over the port. Cover and marinate for at least 3–4 hours or overnight, turning occasionally.

2 Drain the meat portions thoroughly, reserving the marinade. Pat the portions dry on kitchen paper and season lightly with salt and ground black pepper.

3 Melt three-quarters of the butter in a frying pan and cook the pheasant portions on all sides for about 5 minutes, until deep golden. Drain well, transfer to a plate, then cook the mushrooms in the fat remaining in the pan for 3 minutes.

4 Return the pheasant to the pan and pour in the reserved marinade with 200ml/7fl oz/scant 1 cup water. Bring to the boil, reduce the heat and cover, then simmer gently for about 45 minutes, until the pheasant is tender.

5 Using a slotted spoon, carefully remove the pheasant portions and mushrooms from the frying pan and set aside to keep warm. Bring the cooking juices to the boil and boil vigorously for about 5 minutes, until they are reduced and have thickened slightly.

6 Strain the juices through a fine sieve (strainer) and return them to the pan. Whisk in the remaining butter over gentle heat until it has melted. Season to taste with salt and ground black pepper, then pour the juices over the pheasant and mushrooms and serve immediately.

Roast Pheasant Energy 692kcal/2897kJ; Protein 81.7g; Carbohydrate 1.2g, of which sugars 1.1g; Fat 34.2g, of which saturates 14.5g; Cholesterol 27mg; Calcium 132mg; Fibre 0g; Sodium 456mg.
Marinated Pheasant Energy 457kcal/1910kJ; Protein 46.2g; Carbohydrate 6.4g, of which sugars 4.5g; Fat 23.1g, of which saturates 6.1g; Cholesterol 9mg; Calcium 102mg; Fibre 2g; Sodium 483mg.

Pheasant and Mushroom Ragoût

Pheasants make especially good eating at Christmas when combined with smoky, aromatic wild mushrooms and a glass of rich port.

Serves 4
4 pheasant breast fillets, skinned
15ml/1 tbsp olive oil
12 shallots, halved
2 garlic cloves, crushed

75g/3oz wild mushrooms, sliced
75ml/2½fl oz/⅓ cup port
150ml/¼ pint/⅔ cup
  chicken stock
sprigs of fresh parsley
  and thyme
1 bay leaf
grated rind of 1 lemon
200ml/7fl oz/scant 1 cup
  double (heavy) cream
salt and ground black pepper

1 Dice and season the pheasant breast fillets. Heat the olive oil in a heavy frying pan and cook the pheasant meat for about 5–6 minutes, stirring frequently until evenly browned. Remove from the pan and set aside.

2 Add the shallots to the pan, fry quickly to colour them a little, then add the garlic and sliced mushrooms. Reduce the heat and cook gently for 5 minutes.

3 Pour the port and stock into the pan and add the herbs and lemon rind. Bring to the boil, then simmer, uncovered, until the sauce has reduced and thickened a little.

4 When the shallots are nearly cooked, add the cream, reduce to thicken, then return the meat to the pan. Allow to cook for a few minutes before serving.

Cook's Tip
Serve with pilaff rice, if you like: fry a chopped onion, stir in 2.5cm/1in cinnamon stick, 2.5ml/½ tsp crushed cumin seeds, 2 crushed cardamom pods, a bay leaf and 5ml/1 tsp turmeric. Add 225g/8oz/generous 1 cup long grain rice. Stir until well coated. Pour in 600ml/1 pint/2½ cups boiling water, cover, then simmer gently for 15 minutes. Transfer to a serving dish, cover with a dish towel and leave for 5 minutes.

Pheasant with Oatmeal Stuffing

Fresh pheasant tastes bland, like chicken – in cold weather it may need a week hanging in a cool place to acquire a gamey flavour. Suitable vegetable sides include puréed chestnuts, or whole chestnuts mixed with Brussels sprouts.

Serves 4–6
2 oven-ready pheasants
6 unsmoked streaky (fatty) bacon
  rashers (strips)

50g/2oz/¼ cup softened butter
15g/½oz/2 tbsp seasoned plain
  (all-purpose) flour
450ml/¾ pint/scant 2 cups hot
  chicken stock
salt and ground black pepper
watercress or rocket (arugula),
  to garnish

For the stuffing
1 small onion, finely chopped
pheasant livers, finely chopped
115g/4oz/1 cup pinhead oatmeal
50g/2oz/¼ cup butter, melted

1 To prepare the stuffing, put the onion and the pheasant livers into a bowl with the oatmeal and butter. Mix thoroughly and season well. Add a little cold water to moisten slightly.

2 Preheat the oven to 200°C/400°F/Gas 6. Wipe the birds inside and out and divide the stuffing between the two birds, spooning it in loosely to allow the stuffing to expand during cooking.

3 Use cotton string to truss the birds for cooking, and lay the bacon rashers over the breasts. Spread half the butter over them and lay them in a roasting pan with the remaining butter.

4 Roast for 50 minutes, basting often. Ten minutes before the end of cooking, remove the rashers, baste the birds and dredge with the flour. Baste again and return to the oven to brown. When cooked, remove the strings and put the birds on to a heated serving dish. Keep warm, uncovered.

5 Reserve 30ml/2 tbsp of the fat from the roasting pan and sprinkle in the remaining flour, stirring well. Blend in the stock, season and bring to the boil. Simmer for a few minutes.

6 To serve, garnish the pheasant breasts with the bacon pieces and watercress or rocket. Hand the gravy round separately.

Pheasant Ragoût Energy 530kcal/2200kJ; Protein 34.1g; Carbohydrate 7.4g, of which sugars 5.9g; Fat 33g, of which saturates 20.2g; Cholesterol 69mg; Calcium 91mg; Fibre 1.1g; Sodium 114mg.
Pheasant with Oatmeal Energy 847Kcal/3529kJ; Protein 69.7g; Carbohydrate 25.2g, of which sugars 1.1g; Fat 52.5g, of which saturates 23.1g; Cholesterol 598mg; Calcium 92mg; Fibre 2.3g; Sodium 697mg.

Quail Hot-pot with Merlot and Winter Vegetables

Sweet, slightly tangy grapes are a classic ingredient for accompanying quail, and here they bring a fresh, fruity flavour to this festive dish. Creamy mashed potatoes are an excellent accompaniment.

Serves 4
4 quails
150g/5oz seedless red grapes
50g/2oz/¼ cup butter

4 shallots, halved
175g/6oz baby carrots, scrubbed
not peeled
175g/6oz baby turnips
450ml/¾ pint/scant 2 cups
Merlot or other red wine
salt and ground
black pepper

For the croûtes
4 slices white bread,
crusts removed
60ml/4 tbsp olive oil

1 Preheat the oven to 220°C/425°F/Gas 7. Season the birds and stuff with grapes. Melt the butter in a flameproof casserole and brown the birds. Lift out and set aside.

2 Add the shallots, carrots and turnips to the fat remaining in the casserole and cook until they are just beginning to colour. Replace the quails, breast side down, and pour in the Merlot or other red wine. Cover the casserole and transfer it to the oven. Cook for about 30 minutes, or until the quails are tender.

3 Meanwhile, make the croûtes. Use a 10cm/4in plain cutter to stamp out rounds from the bread. Heat the oil in a frying pan and cook the bread until golden on both sides. Drain on kitchen paper and keep warm.

4 Place the croûtes on plates. Use a draining spoon to set a quail on each croûte. Arrange the vegetables around the quails, cover and keep hot.

5 Boil the cooking juices hard until reduced to syrupy consistency. Skim off as much butter as possible, then season the sauce to taste. Drizzle the sauce over the quails and serve immediately with the vegetables.

Grilled Spiced Quail with Salad

This is a perfect supper dish for festive entertaining. Quail is at its best when the breast meat is removed from the carcass.

Serves 4
8 quail breast fillets
50g/2oz/¼ cup butter
5ml/1 tsp paprika

For the salad
60ml/4 tbsp walnut oil
30ml/2 tbsp olive oil
45ml/3 tbsp balsamic vinegar
25g/1oz/2 tbsp butter
75g/3oz/generous 1 cup
chanterelle mushrooms,
sliced if large
25g/1oz/3 tbsp walnut
halves, toasted
115g/4oz mixed salad leaves
salt and ground black pepper

1 Preheat the grill (broiler). Arrange the quail breasts on the grill rack, skin sides up. Dot with half the butter and sprinkle with half the paprika and a little salt.

2 Grill (broil) the quail breast fillets for 3 minutes, turn them over and dot with the remaining butter, then sprinkle with the remaining paprika and a little salt. Grill the quail breasts for a further 3 minutes, or until they are cooked through and tender.

3 Transfer the quail breasts to a warmed dish, cover and leave to stand while preparing the salad.

4 Make the salad dressing. Whisk the walnut and olive oils with the balsamic vinegar, then season well with plenty of salt and black pepper and set aside.

5 Heat the butter in a heavy pan until foaming and cook the chanterelles, stirring occasionally, for about 3 minutes, or until the mushrooms are just beginning to soften. Add the walnut halves and heat through, then remove the pan from the heat.

6 Thinly slice the cooked quail fillets and arrange them on four individual serving plates with the warmed chanterelle mushrooms and walnuts and mixed salad leaves. Drizzle the oil and vinegar dressing over the salad and serve warm.

Quail Hot-pot Energy 506kcal/2118kJ; Protein 44.6g; Carbohydrate 19.7g, of which sugars 6.8g; Fat 19.9g, of which saturates 3.7g; Cholesterol 0mg; Calcium 127mg; Fibre 2.8g; Sodium 280mg.
Grilled Quail Energy 443kcal/1837kJ; Protein 25.6g; Carbohydrate 0.9g, of which sugars 0.8g; Fat 37.5g, of which saturates 12.3g; Cholesterol 110mg; Calcium 24mg; Fibre 0.7g; Sodium 176mg.

Marinated Pigeon in Red Wine

The time taken to marinate the pigeons and cook this casserole is well rewarded by the fabulous rich flavour of the finished dish. Stir-fried green cabbage and celeriac purée are suitably festive accompaniments.

Serves 4
4 pigeons, each weighing about 225g/8oz
30ml/2 tbsp olive oil
1 onion, coarsely chopped
225g/8oz/3¼ cups brown cap (cremini) mushrooms, sliced
15ml/1 tbsp plain (all-purpose) flour
300ml/½ pint/1¼ cups hot game stock
30ml/2 tbsp chopped fresh parsley
salt and ground black pepper
flat leaf parsley, to garnish

For the marinade
15ml/1 tbsp light olive oil
1 onion, chopped
1 carrot, peeled and chopped
1 celery stick, chopped
3 garlic cloves, sliced
6 allspice berries, bruised
2 bay leaves
8 black peppercorns, bruised
150ml/¼ pint/⅔ cup red wine vinegar
150ml/¼ pint/⅔ cup red wine or Madeira
45ml/3 tbsp redcurrant jelly

1 Mix all the ingredients for the marinade in a large dish. Add the pigeons and turn them in the marinade, then cover and chill for 12 hours, turning the pigeons frequently.

2 Preheat the oven to 150°C/300°F/Gas 2. Heat the oil in a large, flameproof casserole and cook the onion and mushrooms for about 5 minutes, or until the onion has softened.

3 Meanwhile, drain the pigeons and strain the marinade into a jug (pitcher), then set both aside separately.

4 Sprinkle the flour over the pigeons and add them to the casserole, breast sides down. Pour in the marinade and stock, and add the chopped parsley and seasoning. Cover the pan and cook in the oven for 2½ hours.

5 Check the seasoning, adding more salt and black pepper if necessary. Serve the pigeons on warmed plates and ladle the sauce over them. Garnish with fresh parsley.

Grouse with Orchard Fruit Stuffing

Tart apples, plums and pears, with a hint of spice, make a festive-tasting fruit stuffing that goes perfectly with the rich gamey flavour of grouse.

Serves 2
juice of ½ lemon
2 young grouse
50g/2oz/¼ cup butter
4 Swiss chard leaves

50ml/2fl oz/¼ cup Marsala
salt and ground black pepper

For the stuffing
2 shallots, finely chopped
1 cooking apple, peeled, cored and chopped
1 pear, peeled, cored and chopped
2 plums, halved, stoned (pitted) and chopped
large pinch of mixed (apple pie) spice

1 Sprinkle the lemon juice over the grouse and season it with salt and pepper. Melt half the butter in a large flameproof casserole, add the grouse and cook for 10 minutes, or until browned, turning occasionally. Remove the grouse and set aside.

2 Add the shallots to the fat remaining in the casserole and cook until softened. Add the apple, pear, plums and mixed spice and cook for about 5 minutes, or until the fruits are just beginning to soften. Remove the casserole from the heat and spoon the hot fruit mixture into the body cavities of the birds.

3 Truss the birds neatly with string. Smear the remaining butter over the birds and wrap them in the chard leaves, then replace them in the casserole.

4 Pour in the Marsala and heat until simmering. Cover tightly and simmer for 20 minutes, or until the birds are tender. Leave to rest in a warm place for about 10 minutes before serving.

Cook's Tip
There isn't a lot of liquid in the casserole for cooking the birds – they are steamed rather than boiled, so it is very important that the casserole is heavy with a tight-fitting lid, otherwise the liquid may evaporate.

Grouse with Stuffing Energy 521kcal/2191kJ; Protein 76.5g; Carbohydrate 17.5g, of which sugars 17.3g; Fat 13.5g, of which saturates 2.9g; Cholesterol 0mg; Calcium 302mg; Fibre 5.8g; Sodium 404mg.
Marinated Pigeon Energy 286kcal/1189kJ; Protein 25.6g; Carbohydrate 1.5g, of which sugars 1g; Fat 17.4g, of which saturates 0.9g; Cholesterol 0mg; Calcium 23mg; Fibre 0.8g; Sodium 98mg.

Gammon with Cumberland Sauce

A gammon joint is a traditional addition to the kitchen at Christmas time. Serve this dish and sauce either hot as a festive main course or cold in a buffet.

Serves 8–10
2.25kg/5lb smoked or unsmoked gammon (smoked or cured ham) joint
1 onion
1 carrot
1 celery stick
bouquet garni sachet
6 peppercorns

For the glaze
whole cloves
50g/2oz/4 tbsp soft light brown or demerara (raw) sugar
30ml/2 tbsp golden (light corn) syrup
5ml/1 tsp English (hot) mustard powder

For the cumberland sauce
juice and shredded rind of 1 orange
30ml/2 tbsp lemon juice
120ml/4fl oz/½ cup port or red wine
60ml/4 tbsp redcurrant jelly

1 Soak the gammon overnight in a cool place in enough cold water to cover. Discard this water. Put the joint into a large pan and cover it with more cold water. Bring the water to the boil slowly and skim off any scum that rises to the surface. Add the vegetables and seasonings, cover and simmer gently for 2 hours.

2 Leave the meat to cool in the liquid for 30 minutes. Remove it from the liquid and strip off the skin neatly. Score the fat in diamonds with a sharp knife and stick a clove in the centre of each diamond.

3 Preheat the oven to 180°C/350°F/Gas 4. Put the sugar, golden syrup and mustard powder in a small pan and heat gently to melt them. Place the gammon in a roasting pan and spoon over the glaze. Bake until golden brown, about 20 minutes. Put it under a hot grill (broiler), if necessary, to get a good colour. Stand in a warm place for 15 minutes before carving.

4 For the sauce, put the orange and lemon juice into a pan with the port or red wine and jelly, and heat to melt the jelly. Pour boiling water on to the orange rind, drain, and add to the sauce. Cook for 2 minutes. Serve in a sauce boat.

Cider-glazed Ham

This wonderful ham glazed with cider is traditionally served with cranberry sauce and is ideal for Christmas.

1.3 litres/2¼ pints/5⅔ cups medium-dry cider
45ml/3 tbsp soft light brown sugar
flat leaf parsley, to garnish

Serves 8–10
2kg/4½lb middle gammon (smoked or cured ham) joint
1 large or 2 small onions
about 30 whole cloves
3 bay leaves
10 black peppercorns

For the cranberry sauce
350g/12oz/3 cups cranberries
175g/6oz/¾ cup soft light brown sugar
grated rind and juice of 2 clementines
30ml/2 tbsp port

1 Weigh the ham and calculate the cooking time at 20 minutes per 450g/1lb, then place it in a large casserole or pan. Stud the onion or onions with 5–10 of the cloves and add to the casserole or pan with the bay leaves and peppercorns.

2 Add 1.2 litres/2 pints/5 cups of the cider and enough water just to cover the ham. Heat until simmering, and then skim off the scum that rises to the surface. Start timing the cooking from the moment the stock simmers. Cover with a lid or foil and simmer gently for the calculated time. Towards the end of the cooking time, preheat the oven to 220°C/425°F/Gas 7.

3 Heat the sugar and remaining cider in a pan until the sugar has dissolved. Simmer for 5 minutes to make a dark, sticky glaze. Leave to cool for 5 minutes.

4 Lift the ham out of the casserole or pan. Carefully and evenly, cut the rind off, then score the fat into a neat diamond pattern. Place the ham in a roasting pan or ovenproof dish. Press a clove into the centre of each diamond, then carefully spoon over the glaze. Bake for about 20–25 minutes, or until the fat is brown, glistening and crisp.

5 Simmer all the cranberry sauce ingredients in a heavy pan for 15–20 minutes, stirring often. Transfer to a sauce boat. Serve the ham hot or cold, garnished with parsley and with the sauce.

Gammon Energy 524kcal/2212kJ; Protein 66.5g; Carbohydrate 34.7g, of which sugars 32.9g; Fat 12.4g, of which saturates 4.7g; Cholesterol 45mg; Calcium 29mg; Fibre 0g; Sodium 2512mg.
Cider-glazed Ham Energy 368kcal/1541kJ; Protein 39.6g; Carbohydrate 15.2g, of which sugars 15.2g; Fat 16.9g, of which saturates 5.6g; Cholesterol 52mg; Calcium 25mg; Fibre 0.6g; Sodium 1982mg.

Porchetta

This is a simplified version of a traditional Italian festive dish. Make sure the piece of belly pork has a good amount of crackling – because this is the best part, which guests will just love. Serve with plenty of creamy mashed potatoes and a seasonal green vegetable.

Serves 8
2kg/4½lb boned belly pork
45ml/3 tbsp fresh rosemary
    leaves, roughly chopped
50g/2oz/⅔ cup freshly grated
    Parmesan cheese
15ml/1 tbsp olive oil
salt and ground black pepper

1 Preheat the oven to 180°C/350°F/Gas 4. Lay the belly pork skin side down on a chopping board.

2 Spread the chopped rosemary leaves over the meat, pushing it in a little with your hand, and sprinkle with the grated Parmesan cheese. Season with salt and plenty of ground black pepper and drizzle over the olive oil.

3 Starting from one end, roll the pork up firmly and tie string around it at 2.5cm/1in intervals, to secure. Transfer the rolled pork to a roasting pan and cook for about 3 hours, or until cooked through and tender.

4 Transfer the pork to a chopping board and leave it to rest for about 10 minutes, this will improve the texture and flavour of the meat after the heating process. Carve the pork into thick slices and serve immediately.

> **Cook's Tip**
> *To help ensure that you have crisp crackling on the pork you should dry and score the skin. Pat the outside of the pork with kitchen paper or a clean dish towel to dry it. The skin will already have a few cuts in it but it does not hurt to add a few more. Use a very sharp paring knife or use a craft knife with a sharp, clean blade and score the skin in a few places, ensuring that you have cut just through to the fat beneath the skin.*

Tenderloin of Pork with Bacon

This easy-to-carve 'joint' is ideal for Christmas, served with a fruity onion gravy.

Serves 8
3 large pork fillets (tenderloins),
    about 1.2kg/2½lb in total,
    trimmed of fat
225g/8oz rindless streaky
    (fatty) bacon
25g/1oz/2 tbsp butter
150ml/¼ pint/⅔ cup red wine

For the prune stuffing
25g/1oz/2 tbsp butter
1 onion, very finely chopped
115g/4oz mushrooms, chopped
4 ready-to-eat prunes, pitted
    and chopped
10ml/2 tsp mixed dried herbs
115g/4oz/2 cups fresh
    white breadcrumbs
1 egg
salt and ground black pepper

To finish
16 ready-to-eat prunes
150ml/¼ pint/⅔ cup red wine
16 pickling (pearl) onions
30ml/2 tbsp plain (all-purpose) flour
300ml/½ pint/1¼ cups
    chicken stock

1 Preheat the oven to 180°C/350°F/Gas 4. Cut each fillet lengthways, three-quarters through, open them out and flatten. For the stuffing, melt the butter and cook the onion until tender, add the mushrooms and cook for 5 minutes. Transfer to a bowl and mix in the remaining stuffing ingredients. Spread the stuffing over two of the fillets and sandwich with the third fillet.

2 Overlap the rashers across the meat. Lay lengths of string at intervals over the bacon. Cover with foil, hold in place, and flip the 'joint' over. Fold the rashers over the meat and tie the string. Roll the 'joint' back on to the join and remove the foil.

3 Place in a roasting pan and spread with butter. Pour the wine around the meat and cook for 1¼ hours, basting occasionally. Simmer the remaining prunes in the wine until tender. Boil the onions in water for 10 minutes. Drain and add to the prunes.

4 Transfer the pork to a board, remove the string, cover with foil and rest for 10 minutes, before carving. Remove any fat from the pan, add the flour and cook for 2 minutes. Blend in the stock and simmer for 5 minutes. Strain the gravy on to the prunes and onions, reheat and serve.

Porchetta Energy 773kcal/3216kJ; Protein 65.2g; Carbohydrate 0g, of which sugars 0g; Fat 56.9g, of which saturates 20g; Cholesterol 219mg; Calcium 98mg; Fibre 0g; Sodium 293mg.
Pork with Bacon Energy 688kcal/2870kJ; Protein 40.6g; Carbohydrate 25.3g, of which sugars 17.1g; Fat 43.3g, of which saturates 15.5g; Cholesterol 123mg; Calcium 57mg; Fibre 1.3g; Sodium 179mg.

Roast Pork with Sage Stuffing

Sage and onion make a
festive stuffing for roast pork.

salt and ground black pepper
sprigs of thyme, to garnish

Serves 6–8
1.6kg/3½lb boneless loin of pork
60ml/4 tbsp fine, dry breadcrumbs
10ml/2 tsp chopped fresh sage
25ml/1½ tbsp plain
    (all-purpose) flour
300ml/½ pint/1¼ cups cider
150ml/¼ pint/⅔ cup water
5–10ml/1–2 tsp crab apple or
    redcurrant jelly

For the stuffing
25g/1oz/2 tbsp butter
50g/2oz bacon, finely chopped
2 large onions, finely chopped
75g/3oz/1½ cups fresh
    white breadcrumbs
30ml/2 tbsp chopped fresh sage
5ml/1 tsp chopped fresh thyme
10ml/2 tsp grated lemon rind
1 small egg, beaten

1 Preheat the oven to 220°C/425°F/Gas 7. For the stuffing,
melt the butter in a frying pan. Cook the bacon until it browns,
then add the onions and cook until they soften. Mix with the
breadcrumbs, sage, thyme, lemon rind, egg and salt and pepper.

2 Cut the rind off the joint of pork in one piece and score it
well. Place the pork fat side down and season. Add a layer of
stuffing, then roll up and tie. Lay the rind over the pork and rub
in 5ml/1 tsp salt. Roast for 2–2½ hours, basting once or twice.
Reduce the temperature to 190°C/375°F/Gas 5 after 20 minutes.

3 Shape the remaining stuffing into balls and add to the pan for
the last 30 minutes. When the pork is done, remove the rind,
increase the oven to 220°C/425°F/Gas 7 and roast the rind for
about 20–25 minutes, until crisp.

4 Mix the dry breadcrumbs and sage and press them into the
fat on the pork. Cook the pork for 10 minutes, then cover and
set aside in a warm place for 15–20 minutes.

5 For the gravy, remove all but 30–45ml/2–3 tbsp of the fat
from the roasting pan and place it on the stove. Stir in the flour,
followed by the cider and water. Simmer for 10 minutes. Strain
into a pan and add the jelly. Season and cook for 5 minutes.
Serve with slices of pork and crackling, garnished with thyme.

Pork Fillet with Crispy Onion Rings

Here, tender roast pork is
garnished with remoulade,
and delicious crispy onion
rings to make this open
sandwich – perfect for an
informal festive gathering.

Serves 4
1 pork fillet (tenderloin), about
    400g–600g/14oz–1lb 6oz
25g/1oz/2 tbsp salted butter,
    softened
2 slices rye bread
2 leaves round (butterhead) lettuce

20ml/4 tsp ready-made remoulade
4 tomato slices
4 parsley sprigs

For the crispy onion rings
250ml/8fl oz/1 cup buttermilk
1 small onion, thinly sliced,
    rings separated
175g/6oz/1½ cups plain
    (all-purpose) flour
250ml/8fl oz/1 cup vegetable oil,
    for frying
salt and white pepper

1 Preheat the oven to 190°C/375°F/Gas 5. Place the pork fillet
on to a rack in a roasting pan. Season with salt and pepper.
Place the pork in the preheated oven and cook until the meat
is no longer pink and juices are clear, or the internal
temperature reaches 70°C/160°F, which will take about 1 hour.
Allow the pork to rest for 15 minutes before cutting into 16
slices about 5mm/¼in thick.

2 Meanwhile, make the crispy onion rings. Pour the buttermilk
into a bowl and season with salt and pepper. Add the onion
rings, tossing to coat evenly, and leave to soak for about
10 minutes, then drain, discarding the buttermilk.

3 Place the flour in a shallow bowl. Dip the onion rings in the
flour to coat them on all sides. Shake off any excess flour. Heat
the oil in a heavy frying pan. Fry the onion rings, in batches,
over a medium-high heat until golden brown all over. Drain on
kitchen paper and keep warm.

4 Butter the slices of bread to the edges, top with the lettuce
leaves and cut each slice in half. Arrange four pork slices on
each sandwich. Arrange five or six crispy onion rings over the
pork on each sandwich, and garnish with 5ml/1 tsp remoulade,
a slice of tomato and a parsley sprig.

Roast Pork Energy 390kcal/1637kJ; Protein 47.9g; Carbohydrate 21.6g, of which sugars 4.8g; Fat 12.9g, of which saturates 5.2g; Cholesterol 164mg; Calcium 62mg; Fibre 1.3g; Sodium 434mg.
Pork Fillet Energy 460kcal/1911kJ; Protein 24.5g; Carbohydrate 20.1g, of which sugars 3.9g; Fat 31.8g, of which saturates 7.5g; Cholesterol 82mg; Calcium 50mg; Fibre 1.8g; Sodium 218mg.

Pork Schnitzel

This traditional recipe can be found on festive tables across Europe.

Serves 4

4 pork leg steaks or escalopes, about 200g/7oz each
60ml/4 tbsp olive oil
115g/4oz chicken livers, chopped
1 garlic clove, crushed
plain (all-purpose) flour, seasoned
salt and ground black pepper
15ml/1 tbsp chopped fresh parsley to garnish

For the sauce

1 onion, thinly sliced
115g/4oz streaky (fatty) bacon, thinly sliced
175g/6oz/2 cups mixed wild mushrooms, sliced
120ml/4fl oz/½ cup olive oil
5ml/1 tsp ready-made mustard
150ml/¼ pint/⅔ cup white wine
120ml/4fl oz/½ cup sour cream
250ml/8fl oz/1 cup double (heavy) cream
salt and ground black pepper

1 Place the pork between two sheets of clear film (plastic wrap) or baking parchment and flatten with a meat mallet or rolling pin until about 15 × 10cm/6 × 4in. Season well.

2 Heat half the oil in a frying pan and cook the chicken livers and garlic for 1–2 minutes. Remove, drain on kitchen paper and leave to cool.

3 Divide the livers evenly between the four prepared pork steaks and roll up into neat parcels. Secure with cocktail sticks (toothpicks) or string before rolling lightly in the seasoned flour.

4 Heat the remaining oil and gently fry the schnitzels for about 6–8 minutes on each side, or until golden brown. Drain on kitchen paper and keep warm.

5 Meanwhile, to make the sauce, fry the onion, bacon and mushrooms in the oil for 2–3 minutes, then add the mustard, white wine and sour cream. Stir to simmering point, then add the double cream and season.

6 Arrange the schnitzels on plates with a little of the sauce spooned around and the rest poured into a serving jug (pitcher). Garnish with the fresh parsley and serve.

Grilled Pork with Turnip Tops

The light, bitter taste of the turnip tops makes a delicious contrast to the succulent meat. Buy the best-quality pork you can for the finest flavour and texture if you plan on serving this dish to guests over the festive season. If you want to save time over the busy Christmas period, then use ready-cooked beans from a can – they are very useful to have to hand in the kitchen.

Serves 4

150g/5oz/scant 1 cup uncooked black-eyed beans (peas), or 250g/9oz/scant 1½ cups canned black-eyed beans (peas)
500g/1¼lb turnip tops
4 pork fillets (tenderloins), preferably from black pork, weighing about 175g/6oz each
105ml/7 tbsp olive oil
2 garlic cloves, chopped
100g/3¾oz/generous 1¾ cups breadcrumbs, made from cornbread
sea salt

1 If using uncooked beans, soak them overnight. Boil in a pan with plenty of water for 10 minutes, skimming any foam from the surface, Reduce the heat and simmer for about an hour, or until tender. Drain and set aside.

2 Preheat the grill (broiler) to high. Cook the turnip tops in salted boiling water for a few minutes, being careful not to overcook them. Drain well, refresh in iced water, drain again and squeeze as dry as possible. Slice thinly with a sharp knife.

3 Season the pork on both sides with salt and place on the grill rack. Cook for 2 minutes on each side, then lower the heat and cook, turning once, for a further 8 minutes, until the pork is cooked through and tender. Leave to rest for another 5 minutes in a warm place to allow the inside temperature to stabilize.

4 Heat the olive oil in a large heavy pan. Add the turnip tops, black-eyed beans and chopped garlic. Cook over low heat for about 5 minutes, stirring frequently.

5 Stir the breadcrumbs into the pan and cook for a few minutes more. Transfer the pork fillets to warm plates and serve immediately with the vegetables.

Pork Schnitzel Energy 1025kcal/4242kJ; Protein 55.3g; Carbohydrate 3.8g, of which sugars 3.4g; Fat 85g, of which saturates 34.3g; Cholesterol 358mg; Calcium 87mg; Fibre 0.7g; Sodium 554mg.
Grilled Pork Energy 604kcal/2532kJ; Protein 49.8g; Carbohydrate 41.8g, of which sugars 7.2g; Fat 27.6g, of which saturates 5.3g; Cholesterol 110mg; Calcium 142mg; Fibre 9.5g; Sodium 338mg.

Fried Pork and Apples

This is a very simple dish that turns an inexpensive cut of meat into a most enjoyable meal. It is ideal for a quick supper dish over the festive period.

Serves 4
600g/1¼lb lightly salted or
 fresh belly of pork, cut into
 thin slices
500g/1¼lb crisp eating apples
30ml/2 tbsp soft light brown sugar
salt and ground black pepper
chopped fresh parsley or chives,
 to garnish

To serve
boiled potatoes
a seasonal green vegetable,
 such as cabbage, Brussels
 sprouts or kale

1 Heat a large frying pan, without any oil or fat, until hot. Add the salted or fresh belly pork slices and fry over low heat for about 3–4 minutes each side, until golden brown. Season the pork slices with salt and pepper. Transfer to a warmed serving dish and keep warm.

2 Core the apples but do not peel, then cut the apples into rings. Add the apple rings to the frying pan and fry gently in the pork fat for about 3–4 minutes each side, until just beginning to turn golden and translucent.

3 Sprinkle the slices with the sugar and turn once more for a couple of minutes until the sugar side starts to caramelize.

4 Serve the pork slices with the apple rings. Accompany the pork with plain boiled potatoes and a green seasonal vegetable, garnished with fresh parsley.

Cook's Tips
• This is a great dish to make the most of seasonal apples, which are at their best in the run-up to Christmas. Cut the rings to a depth of 5mm/¼in across the apple. Most apples will make about four rings for this dish.
• Other seasonal vegetables that would go well with this dish include beetroot (beets), carrots, cauliflower or leeks.

Braised Pork and Chickpea Stew

Slow cooking allows the meat to become tender and juicy on the inside and crisp on the outside, and is the secret of many flavourful dishes. It also allows the fat in the meat to dry a little and release flavour. The chickpea stew, which can be a meal in itself, combines well with the pork, and with other meat, such as game – making it suitable for many festive favourites.

Serves 4
1kg/2¼lb pork loin, preferably
 from black pork
15ml/1 tbsp sweet paprika
15ml/1 tbsp chopped fresh thyme
3 garlic cloves, finely chopped
105ml/7 tbsp white wine
105ml/7 tbsp olive oil
sea salt and ground black pepper

For the stew
50ml/2fl oz/¼ cup olive oil
1 onion, finely chopped
50g/2oz/⅓ cup bacon,
 finely diced
100g/3¾oz wild mushrooms,
 such as ceps and horn of
 plenty, chopped
300g/11oz/scant 2 cups cooked
 chickpeas, plus 100ml/3½fl oz/
 scant ½ cup cooking liquid
100g/3¾oz day-old white bread,
 crust removed, cut into cubes
1 small bunch of fresh parsley,
 finely chopped

1 Trim off any excess fat from the pork and cut the meat into pieces weighing 125g/4¼oz. Place them in a shallow, ovenproof dish. Mix together the paprika, thyme, garlic, wine and olive oil in a jug (pitcher), and season with salt and pepper. Pour the mixture over the meat, cover and leave to marinate for 4 hours.

2 Preheat the oven to 140°C/275°F/Gas 1. Place the dish in the oven with the marinade and braise for 2 hours.

3 Towards the end of the cooking time, prepare the chickpea stew. Heat the oil in a pan. Add the onion and bacon and cook over low heat, stirring occasionally, for 5–8 minutes, until the onion has softened and the bacon is lightly coloured.

4 Add the mushrooms and cook for 5 minutes. Add the chickpeas, the reserved cooking liquid and the bread. Cook, stirring, until the bread has disintegrated, then add the parsley. Serve the pork immediately, with the chickpea stew.

Fried Pork and Apples Energy 645kcal/2676kJ; Protein 23.4g; Carbohydrate 19g, of which sugars 19g; Fat 53.4g, of which saturates 19.7g; Cholesterol 108mg; Calcium 21mg; Fibre 2g; Sodium 113mg.
Braised Pork Energy 756kcal/3155kJ; Protein 64.1g; Carbohydrate 26g, of which sugars 1.2g; Fat 42.8g, of which saturates 8.5g; Cholesterol 164mg; Calcium 89mg; Fibre 3.7g; Sodium 666mg.

Pork Chops in Mustard Sauce

These tasty pork loin chops with a creamy mustard dressing are great for a quick and easy meal for the whole family at Christmas time – especially when they are eaten with festive vegetables such as Brussels sprouts.

Serves 4

4 pork loin chops, about
  2.5cm/1in thick
25g/1oz/2 tbsp unsalted butter
5ml/1 tsp vegetable oil or olive oil
4 shallots, chopped
200ml/7fl oz/scant 1 cup white
  wine or blond beer
200ml/7fl oz/scant 1 cup double
  (heavy) cream
30ml/2 tbsp good-quality mustard
salt and ground
  black pepper
green beans, Brussels sprouts
  and plain boiled potatoes,
  to serve

1 Season the pork chops generously with salt and pepper. Heat a heavy frying pan over medium–high heat. Add the butter and oil and swirl to coat. Add the chops and fry them for 4 minutes on each side or until they are cooked to your taste. Using tongs, transfer the chops to a platter, cover and keep warm.

2 Reheat the fat remaining in the frying pan and sauté the shallots for 3–5 minutes, stirring frequently, until softened.

3 Add the wine or beer. Cook, stirring well to incorporate the sediment on the base of the pan, for about 2 minutes, then whisk in the cream and mustard and bring to the boil. Reduce the heat and simmer the sauce for about 3 minutes, until it is slightly thickened. Season to taste.

4 Pour the sauce over the pork chops. Serve with the beans, Brussels sprouts and potatoes.

> **Cook's Tip**
> *Pork chops can easily be overcooked and become dry. Thinner cuts will take less time and can be cooked at a higher heat. For thicker cuts, reduce the heat and increase the cooking time.*

Braised Pork Chops with Onion

The piquant sauce adds punch and flavour to this simple and tasty dish.

Serves 4

4 pork loin chops, 2cm/3/4in thick
30ml/2 tbsp plain (all-purpose) flour
45ml/3 tbsp olive oil
2 onions, thinly sliced
2 garlic cloves, finely chopped
250ml/8fl oz/1 cup dry
  (hard) cider
150ml/1/4 pint/2/3 cup vegetable,
  chicken or pork stock
generous pinch of brown sugar
2 fresh bay leaves
6 fresh thyme sprigs
2 strips lemon rind
120ml/4fl oz/1/2 cup double
  (heavy) cream
30–45ml/2–3 tbsp wholegrain
  mustard
30ml/2 tbsp chopped fresh parsley
salt and ground black pepper

1 Preheat the oven to 200°C/400°F/Gas 6. Trim the chops of excess fat. Season the flour and use to coat the chops. Heat 30ml/2 tbsp of the oil in a frying pan and brown the chops on both sides, then transfer them to an ovenproof dish.

2 Add the remaining oil to the pan and cook the onions over a fairly gentle heat until they soften and begin to brown at the edges. Add the garlic and cook for 2 minutes more.

3 Stir in any left-over flour, then gradually stir in the cider and stock. Season well and add the sugar, bay leaves, thyme and lemon rind. Bring to the boil, then pour over the chops.

4 Cover and cook in the oven for 20 minutes. Reduce the heat to 180°C/350°F/Gas 4 and cook for another 30–40 minutes. Take off the foil for the last 10 minutes of the cooking time. Remove the chops from the dish and keep warm.

5 Transfer the remaining contents of the dish into a pan or, if the dish is flameproof, place it over a direct heat. Discard the herbs and lemon rind, then bring to the boil. Add the cream and continue to boil, stirring constantly. Taste for seasoning, adding a pinch more sugar if necessary. Finally, stir in the mustard to taste and pour the sauce over the braised chops. Sprinkle with the parsley and serve immediately.

Pork Chops Energy 551kcal/2285kJ; Protein 33.7g; Carbohydrate 3.1g, of which sugars 2.6g; Fat 41.4g, of which saturates 22.4g; Cholesterol 176mg; Calcium 50mg; Fibre 0.2g; Sodium 378mg.
Braised Pork Chops Energy 541kcal/2253kJ; Protein 39g; Carbohydrate 19.4g, of which sugars 9g; Fat 32.9g, of which saturates 14.1g; Cholesterol 135mg; Calcium 78mg; Fibre 2g; Sodium 88mg.

Roast Lamb with Potatoes and Garlic

The meat and vegetables for this dish are cooked together, making a festive meal that is moist and flavourful.

Serves 6–8
1 whole leg of lamb, about 2kg/4¹⁄₂lb
3 garlic cloves, quartered lengthways, plus 6–8 whole, unpeeled garlic cloves, or 1 or 2 heads of garlic, halved

900g/2lb potatoes, peeled and quartered lengthways
juice of 1 lemon
45ml/3 tbsp extra virgin olive oil
450ml/³⁄₄ pint/scant 2 cups hot water
5ml/1 tsp dried oregano
2.5ml/¹⁄₂ tsp dried thyme or 5ml/1 tsp chopped fresh thyme
salt and ground black pepper
a few sprigs of fresh thyme, to garnish

1 Preheat the oven to 220°C/425°F/Gas 7. Place the lamb in a large roasting pan. Make several incisions in the meat, pressing the point of a sharp knife deep into the flesh, and insert one or two quartered pieces of peeled garlic into each one.

2 Arrange the quartered potatoes and whole garlic cloves or halved heads of garlic around the meat. Pour over the lemon juice and extra virgin olive oil. Add half the water to the dish, pouring it around the lamb rather than over it. Sprinkle over half the dried oregano and thyme. Season with salt and pepper.

3 Roast the lamb for 15 minutes on the high heat, then reduce the oven temperature to 190°C/375°F/Gas 5. Roast for 1 hour, basting the meat occasionally.

4 After an hour, turn the meat over so that the other side browns as well, sprinkle over the rest of the herbs and season with salt and pepper. Turn the potatoes over gently. Add the remaining hot water to the pan and continue to cook for another 25–30 minutes, basting occasionally with the pan juices.

5 Cover the meat with a clean dish towel or piece of foil and set it aside to rest for 10–15 minutes before carving and serving. The cloves of garlic can be popped out of their skins and eaten with the meat; they make a deliciously creamy accompaniment to the taste of the lamb.

Roast Stuffed Lamb

This lamb roast is stuffed with a tempting blend of kidneys, spinach and rice. It makes a great centrepiece to serve on Christmas Day instead of the more traditional roasts.

Serves 6–8
1.8–2kg/4–4¹⁄₂lb boneless leg or shoulder of lamb (not tied)
25g/1oz/2 tbsp butter, softened
15–30ml/1–2 tbsp plain (all-purpose) flour
120ml/4fl oz/¹⁄₂ cup white wine
250ml/8fl oz/1 cup chicken or

beef stock
salt and ground black pepper
watercress, to garnish
sautéed potatoes, to serve

For the stuffing
65g/2¹⁄₂oz/5 tbsp butter
1 small onion, finely chopped
1 garlic clove, finely chopped
50g/2oz/¹⁄₃ cup long grain rice
150ml/¹⁄₄ pint/²⁄₃ cup chicken stock
2.5ml/¹⁄₂ tsp dried thyme
4 lamb kidneys, halved and cored
275g/10oz young spinach leaves, well washed

1 To make the stuffing, melt 25g/1oz/2 tbsp of the butter in a pan over medium heat. Add the onion and cook for about 2–3 minutes until just softened, then add the garlic and rice and cook for 1–2 minutes, stirring constantly. Add the stock, salt and pepper and thyme, and bring to the boil, stirring occasionally, then reduce the heat and cook for 18 minutes, covered, until the rice is tender and the liquid is absorbed. Transfer the rice into a bowl and fluff with a fork.

2 In a frying pan, melt 25g/1oz/2 tbsp of the remaining butter over a medium-high heat. Add the kidneys and cook for about 2–3 minutes, turning once, until lightly browned but still pink inside, then transfer to a board and leave to cool. Cut the kidneys into pieces and add to the rice, season with salt and black pepper and toss to combine.

3 In a frying pan, heat the remaining butter over medium heat until foaming. Add the spinach leaves and cook for 1–2 minutes until wilted, drain off excess liquid, then transfer the leaves to a plate and leave to cool.

4 Preheat the oven to 190°C/375°F/Gas 5. Lay the meat skin side down on a work surface and season. Spread the spinach leaves in an even layer over the surface, then spread the stuffing in an even layer over the spinach. Roll up the meat like a Swiss roll (jelly roll) and use a skewer to close the seam. Tie the meat at 2.5cm/1in intervals to hold its shape, then place in a roasting pan, spread with the butter and season.

5 Roast for 1¹⁄₂–2 hours until the juices run slightly pink when pierced with a skewer, or until a meat thermometer inserted into the thickest part of the meat registers 57–60°C/135–140°F (for medium-rare to medium). Transfer the meat to a carving board, cover with foil and leave for about 20 minutes.

6 Skim off the fat from the roasting pan. Place the pan over a medium heat and bring to the boil. Sprinkle over the flour and cook for 3 minutes until browned, stirring and scraping the base of the pan. Whisk in the wine and stock and bring to the boil. Cook for 5 minutes until the sauce thickens. Season and strain. Garnish with watercress and serve with the gravy and potatoes.

Roast Lamb Energy 750kcal/3,132kJ; Protein 73.4g; Carbohydrate 24.3g, of which sugars 2.1g; Fat 40.4g, of which saturates 17.3g; Cholesterol 273mg; Calcium 37mg; Fibre 1.8g; Sodium 175mg.
Stuffed Lamb Energy 632kcal/2625kJ; Protein 51.9g; Carbohydrate 1g, of which sugars 0.7g; Fat 46.7g, of which saturates 15.1g; Cholesterol 202mg; Calcium 29mg; Fibre 1g; Sodium 173mg.

Shoulder of Lamb with Mint Sauce

Lamb is one of the popular meat choices that are traditionally roasted and served at Easter. It is also suited to serving at Christmas time.

Serves 6–8
boned shoulder of lamb, weighing
  1.5–2kg/3¼–4½lb
30ml/2 tbsp fresh thyme leaves
30ml/2 tbsp clear honey
150ml/¼ pint/⅔ cup dry (hard)
  cider or white wine
30–45ml/2–3 tbsp double
  (heavy) cream (optional)
salt and ground black pepper

For the mint sauce
large handful of fresh mint leaves
15ml/1 tbsp caster (superfine) sugar
45–60ml/3–4 tbsp cider vinegar
  or wine vinegar

1 Preheat the oven to 220°C/425°F/Gas 7. To make the mint sauce, finely chop the fresh mint leaves with the sugar and put the mixture into a heatproof bowl.

2 Add 30ml/2 tbsp boiling water to the mint and sugar, and stir well until the sugar has dissolved. Add the vinegar to taste and leave the sauce to stand for at least 1 hour.

3 Open out the lamb with skin side down. Season with salt and pepper, sprinkle with the thyme leaves and drizzle the honey over the top. Roll up and tie securely with string in several places. Place the meat in a roasting pan and put into the hot oven. Cook for 30 minutes until browned all over.

4 Pour the cider or wine and 150ml/¼ pint/⅔ cup water into the pan. Lower the oven to 160°C/325°F/Gas 3 and cook for about 45 minutes for medium (pink) or 1 hour for well done.

5 Remove the lamb from the oven, cover loosely with a sheet of foil and leave to stand for 20–30 minutes.

6 Lift the lamb on to a warmed serving plate. Skim any excess fat from the surface of the pan juices before reheating and seasoning to taste. Stir in the cream, if using, bring to the boil and remove from the heat. Carve the lamb and serve it with the pan juices spooned over, accompanied by the mint sauce.

Roast Leg of Lamb with Pesto

This would be a wonderful choice for a celebratory festive lunch, as it looks, tastes and smells fabulous and a whole leg of lamb will serve quite a large gathering.

Serves 6–8
2.25–2.75kg/5–6lb leg of lamb
cooked baby vegetables and
  miniature roast potatoes,
  to serve

For the pesto
50g/2oz/2 cups fresh
  basil leaves
4 garlic cloves, coarsely chopped
45ml/3 tbsp pine nuts
150ml/¼ pint/⅔ cup
  olive oil
50g/2oz/⅔ cup freshly grated
  Parmesan cheese
5ml/1 tsp salt

1 To make the pesto, combine the basil, garlic and pine nuts in a food processor, and process until finely chopped. With the motor running, gradually add the olive oil in a steady stream. Scrape the mixture into a mixing bowl. Stir in the Parmesan cheese and the salt.

2 Place the leg of lamb in a roasting pan. Make several slits in the meat with a sharp knife and spoon some of the pesto into each slit. Rub more pesto evenly over the surface of the lamb.

3 Continue patting on the pesto in a thick, even layer. Cover the lamb with a piece of clear film (plastic wrap) and leave to stand for at least 2 hours at room temperature or in the refrigerator overnight.

4 Bring the lamb back to room temperature 30 minutes before roasting. Preheat the oven to 180°C/350°F/Gas 4. Roast the lamb, allowing about 20 minutes per 450g/1lb for rare meat or 25 minutes per 450g/1lb for medium-rare. Turn the lamb over during roasting.

5 Remove the leg of lamb from the oven and transfer to a warmed serving platter. Cover it loosely with foil and leave to rest for about 10–15 minutes before carving into fairly thick slices. Serve the lamb immediately after carving with a selection of baby vegetables and miniature roast potatoes.

Shoulder of Lamb Energy 351kcal/1468kJ; Protein 36.9g; Carbohydrate 2.5g, of which sugars 2.5g; Fat 21g, of which saturates 9.8g; Cholesterol 143mg; Calcium 23mg; Fibre 0g; Sodium 202mg.
Roast Leg of Lamb Energy 924kcal/3865kJ; Protein 103.7g; Carbohydrate 0.6g, of which sugars 0.5g; Fat 56.5g, of which saturates 17.1g; Cholesterol 342mg; Calcium 141mg; Fibre 0.6g; Sodium 631mg.

Lamb Shank with Chickpeas

Lamb stews are a delicious meal to serve on a cold Christmas evening when you have family and friends round for a celebratory feast. The trick is to keep it simple. Slow cooking is one of the secrets and it is also important to use a lot of sliced onions, as well as black pepper, paprika, bay leaves and garlic for flavour.

Serves 4
50ml/2fl oz/¼ cup olive oil
4 lamb shanks, about 275g/10oz each

4 onions, thinly sliced
2 garlic cloves, chopped
50ml/2fl oz/¼ cup white wine
1 bay leaf
1 chorizo sausage
125g/4¼oz bacon, cut into four pieces
2 carrots, sliced
125g/4¼oz green beans, cut into short lengths
2 turnips, diced
400g/14oz/2⅓ cups cooked chickpeas
salt
1 small bunch of mint, chopped, to garnish

1 Heat half the olive oil in a pan big enough to hold the lamb shanks. Add the lamb shanks and cook over medium heat, turning occasionally, for 5–8 minutes, until lightly coloured. Remove them from the pan and reserve.

2 Discard the oil and wipe out the pan with kitchen paper. Place the remaining olive oil, the onions and garlic in the pan. Return the lamb shanks to the pan.

3 Add the white wine, bay leaf, sausage and bacon, then cover with a tight-fitting lid and cook over low heat, stirring occasionally, for 2 hours, until tender. Season with salt to taste.

4 Cook the carrots, green beans and turnips in salted boiling water until tender. Drain well.

5 Remove the sausage from the pan and cut into 2cm/¾in slices. Return the sausage to the pan, add the vegetables and chickpeas, and cook for a further 5 minutes so that all the flavours blend together. Transfer to a warm serving dish and garnish with the fresh mint.

Rack of Lamb with Herb Crust

This dish is very popular for special occasions so is ideal for an elegant Christmas dinner party. Serve with creamy potato gratin, baby carrots and vegetables such as mangetouts or green beans. Offer mint jelly separately.

Serves 6–8
2 racks of lamb (fair end), chined and trimmed by the butcher

salt, ground black pepper and a pinch of cayenne pepper

For the herb crust
115g/4oz/½ cup butter
10ml/2 tsp mustard powder
175g/6oz/3 cups fresh white breadcrumbs
2 garlic cloves, finely chopped
30ml/2 tbsp chopped fresh parsley
5ml/1 tsp very finely chopped fresh rosemary

1 Preheat the oven to 200°C/400°F/Gas 6. Remove any meat and fat from the top 4–5cm/1½–2in of the bones and scrape the bones clean, then wrap the bones in foil to prevent burning. Remove almost all the fat from the lamb and score the thin layer remaining to make a lattice pattern.

2 Season the lamb with salt, pepper and cayenne pepper, and cook the racks in the preheated oven for 20 minutes. Remove from the oven and cool to room temperature.

3 Next make the herb crust: when the lamb is cold, blend 75g/3oz/6 tbsp of the butter with the mustard to make a smooth paste, and spread it over the fatty sides of the lamb.

4 Mix the breadcrumbs, garlic, parsley and rosemary together in a bowl. Melt the remaining butter, and stir it into the bowl. Divide the herb mixture between the two racks, laying it on top of the butter paste and pressing it well on to the lamb. Set aside and keep at room temperature until ready to finish cooking.

5 When ready to cook the meat, preheat the oven to 200°C/400°F/Gas 6, and roast for a final 20 minutes. To serve, remove the foil from the bones; finish them with paper cutlet frills, if you wish. Carve into cutlets, allowing two or three per person, and replace any of the crust that falls off.

Lamb Shank Energy 688kcal/2868kJ; Protein 39.3g; Carbohydrate 34.9g, of which sugars 11.8g; Fat 43.7g, of which saturates 14.6g; Cholesterol 115mg; Calcium 134mg; Fibre 7.9g; Sodium 1143mg.
Rack of Lamb Energy 455kcal/1899kJ; Protein 26.4g; Carbohydrate 22.7g, of which sugars 0.9g; Fat 29.4g, of which saturates 16.1g; Cholesterol 130mg; Calcium 51mg; Fibre 0.7g; Sodium 438mg.

Barbecue Lamb Steaks with Salsa

Vibrant red pepper salsa brings out the best in succulent lamb steaks to make a dish that looks as good as it tastes. Serve a selection of salads and crusty bread with the lamb.

Serves 6
6 lamb steaks
about 15g/1/2oz/1/2 cup fresh
   rosemary leaves
2 garlic cloves, sliced
60ml/4 tbsp olive oil
30ml/2 tbsp maple syrup
salt and ground black pepper

For the salsa
200g/7oz red (bell) peppers,
   roasted, peeled, seeded
   and chopped
1 plump garlic clove,
   finely chopped
15ml/1 tbsp chopped fresh chives
30ml/2 tbsp extra virgin olive oil
fresh flat leaf parsley, to garnish

1 Place the lamb steaks in a dish and season with salt and pepper. Pull the leaves off the rosemary and sprinkle them over the meat. Add the slices of garlic, then drizzle the oil and maple syrup over the top. Cover with clear film (plastic wrap) and chill until ready to cook. The lamb can be left to marinate in the refrigerator for up to 24 hours.

2 Make sure the steaks are liberally coated with the marinating ingredients, then cook them over a hot barbecue for 2–5 minutes on each side. The cooking time depends on the heat of the barbecue coals and the thickness of the steaks as well as the result required – rare, medium or well cooked.

3 While the lamb steaks are cooking, mix together all the ingredients for the salsa. Serve the barbecue lamb steaks freshly cooked, and offer the salsa separately or spoon it on to the plates with the meat. Garnish with sprigs of flat leaf parsley.

> **Cook's Tip**
> *Christmas may not be the best time to be out in the garden cooking over a barbecue. This dish, however, is just as successful when cooked under a medium-hot grill (broiler) or on a ridged griddle pan on top of the stove.*

Lamb in Dill Sauce

In this slow-cooker recipe, the lamb is cooked with vegetables to make a clear well-flavoured broth, which is then thickened to make a smooth delicate sauce.

Serves 6
1.3kg/3lb lean boneless lamb
1 small onion, quartered
1 carrot, thickly sliced
1 bay leaf
4 sprigs of fresh dill, plus
   45ml/3 tbsp chopped
1 thinly pared strip of lemon rind
750ml/1 1/4 pints/3 cups near-
   boiling lamb or vegetable stock
15ml/1 tbsp olive oil
15g/1/2oz/1 tbsp unsalted butter
225g/8oz small shallots, peeled
15ml/1 tbsp plain (all-purpose) flour
115g/4oz frozen petits pois
   (baby peas), defrosted
1 egg yolk
75ml/2 1/2fl oz/1/3 cup single (light)
   cream, at room temperature
salt and ground
   black pepper
new potatoes and carrots,
   to serve

1 Trim the lamb and cut into 2.5cm/1in pieces. Place in the ceramic cooking pot with the onion, carrot, bay leaf, sprigs of dill and lemon rind. Pour over the stock, cover and cook on high for 1 hour. Skim off any scum, then re-cover and cook for a further 2 hours on high or 4 hours on low.

2 Remove the meat from the pot. Strain the stock, discarding the vegetables and herbs. Clean the pot. Return the meat and half the stock (reserving the rest), cover and switch to high.

3 Heat the oil and butter in a pan, add the shallots and cook gently, stirring, for 10–15 minutes, or until browned and tender. Transfer the shallots to the cooking pot, using a slotted spoon.

4 Sprinkle the flour over the fat remaining in the pan, then stir in the reserved stock. Bring to the boil, stirring all the time until thickened, then stir into the lamb and shallot mixture. Stir in the peas and season. Cook on high for 30 minutes until piping hot.

5 Blend the egg yolk and the cream together, then stir in a few spoonfuls of the hot stock. Add to the casserole in a thin stream, stirring until slightly thickened. Stir in the chopped dill and serve immediately, with steamed new potatoes and carrots.

Barbecue Lamb Steaks Energy 363kcal/1513kJ; Protein 33.2g; Carbohydrate 3g, of which sugars 2.9g; Fat 24.4g, of which saturates 9.5g; Cholesterol 127mg; Calcium 26mg; Fibre 0.8g; Sodium 146mg.
Lamb in Dill Sauce Energy 631kcal/2629kJ; Protein 60.9g; Carbohydrate 7g, of which sugars 3.5g; Fat 40g, of which saturates 17.5g; Cholesterol 249mg; Calcium 123mg; Fibre 1.9g; Sodium 566mg.

Spiced Lamb with Honey and Prunes

This classic dish is eaten at Rosh Hashanah – the Jewish New Year – when sweet foods are served in hope of a sweet new year to come.

Serves 6
130g/4^1/2oz/generous ^{1}/2 cup pitted prunes
350ml/12fl oz/1^1/2 cups hot tea
1kg/2^1/4lb stewing or braising lamb, such as shoulder
30ml/2 tbsp olive oil
1 onion, chopped
2.5ml/^{1}/2 tsp ground ginger
2.5ml/^{1}/2 tsp curry powder
pinch of freshly grated nutmeg
10ml/2 tsp ground cinnamon
1.5ml/^{1}/4 tsp saffron threads
30ml/2 tbsp hot water
75ml/5 tbsp clear honey
200ml/7fl oz/scant 1 cup near-boiling lamb or beef stock
salt and ground black pepper
115g/4oz/1 cup blanched almonds, toasted
30ml/2 tbsp chopped fresh coriander (cilantro) and 3 hard-boiled eggs, cut into wedges, to garnish

1 Put the prunes in a heatproof bowl, then pour over the tea and leave to soak. Meanwhile, trim the lamb and cut into chunky pieces, no larger than 2.5cm/1in. Heat the oil in a frying pan and sauté the lamb in batches for 5 minutes, stirring frequently, until well browned. Remove with a slotted spoon and transfer to the ceramic cooking pot.

2 Add the onion to the frying pan and cook for 5 minutes, until starting to soften. Stir in the ginger, curry powder, nutmeg, cinnamon, salt and black pepper, and cook for 1 minute. Add to the ceramic cooking pot with the meat and its juices.

3 Drain the prunes, adding the soaking liquid to the lamb. Cover the prunes. Soak the saffron in the hot water for 1 minute, then add to the cooking pot with the honey and stock. Cover with the lid and cook on high or auto for 1 hour. Reduce the temperature to low and cook for a further 5–7 hours, or until the lamb is very tender.

4 Add the prunes to the cooking pot and stir to mix. Cook for 30 minutes, or until warmed through. Serve sprinkled with the toasted almonds and chopped fresh coriander, and topped with the wedges of hard-boiled egg.

Lamb Pie with Mustard Thatch

Here, a slow-cooker shepherd's pie is given a contemporary twist with a tangy topping of mashed potato flavoured with peppery mustard, helping to make it a good dish for informal festive entertaining. Serve with lots of seasonal vegetables.

Serves 4
450g/1lb lean minced (ground) lamb
1 onion, very finely chopped
2 celery sticks, thinly sliced
2 carrots, finely diced
15ml/1 tbsp cornflour (cornstarch) blended into 150ml/^{1}/4 pint/^{2}/3 cup lamb stock
15ml/1 tbsp Worcestershire sauce
30ml/2 tbsp chopped fresh rosemary, or 10ml/2 tsp dried
800g/1^3/4lb floury potatoes, diced
60ml/4 tbsp milk
15ml/1 tbsp wholegrain mustard
25g/1oz/2 tbsp butter
salt and ground black pepper

1 Heat a non-stick frying pan, then add the lamb, breaking it up with a wooden spoon, and cook until lightly browned all over. Add the onion, celery and carrots to the pan and cook for 2–3 minutes, stirring frequently.

2 Stir the stock and cornflour mixture into the pan. Bring to the boil, stirring constantly, then remove from the heat. Add the Worcestershire sauce and rosemary, and season well with salt and ground black pepper.

3 Transfer the mixture to the ceramic cooking pot and switch the slow cooker to the high setting. Cover the pot with the cooker lid and cook for 3 hours.

4 Towards the end of the cooking time, cook the potatoes in a large pan of boiling salted water until tender. Drain well, mash, and stir in the milk, mustard and butter. Season to taste with salt and ground black pepper.

5 Spoon the mashed potatoes on top of the lamb, spreading the mixture out evenly. Cook for a further 45 minutes. Brown the topping under a pre-heated grill (broiler) for a few minutes, if you like, then serve immediately.

Spiced Lamb Energy 490kcal/2051kJ; Protein 43.6g; Carbohydrate 23.8g, of which sugars 23.4g; Fat 25.2g, of which saturates 10.3g; Cholesterol 279mg; Calcium 41mg; Fibre 1.4g; Sodium 197mg.
Lamb Pie Energy 458kcal/1920kJ; Protein 26.5g; Carbohydrate 42.2g, of which sugars 8.1g; Fat 21.5g, of which saturates 10.6g; Cholesterol 101mg; Calcium 84mg; Fibre 3.5g; Sodium 264mg.

Lancashire Hot-pot

This dish is traditionally made without browning the lamb or vegetables, and relies on long, slow cooking to develop the flavour. It will be much appreciated by your guests – especially if they arrive on a cold winter night.

Serves 4

8 middle neck or loin lamb chops, about 900g/2lb in total weight

900g/2lb potatoes, thinly sliced
2 onions, peeled and sliced
2 carrots, peeled and sliced
1 stick celery, trimmed and sliced
1 leek, peeled and sliced
225g/8oz/generous 3 cups button (white) mushrooms, sliced
5ml/1 tsp dried mixed herbs
small sprig of rosemary
475ml/16fl oz/2 cups lamb or beef stock
15g/½oz/1 tbsp butter, melted
salt and ground black pepper

1 Trim the lamb chops of excess fat. Place a layer of sliced potatoes in the base of the ceramic cooking pot, and top with some sliced vegetables and a sprinkling of dried herbs, salt and black pepper. Place four of the chops on top.

2 Repeat the layers of sliced potatoes and vegetables, dried herbs and meat, tucking the rosemary sprig down the side of the pot. Continue layering up the remaining vegetables, finishing with a neat layer of potatoes on the top.

3 Pour the meat stock into the ceramic cooking pot, then cover the pot with the lid and switch the slow cooker to high or auto. Cook for 1 hour.

4 Reduce the temperature to low or leave on auto and cook for 6–8 hours or until tender.

5 Brush the top layer of potatoes with melted butter. Place under a preheated grill (broiler) and cook for 5 minutes, or until the potatoes are lightly browned. Serve immediately.

Cook's Tip
You can dispense with browning under the grill (broiler), if you like.

Lamb Fricassée

When combined with the sauce and vegetables, this fricassée retains the freshness of the individual ingredients, creating a dish that will go down a treat for a festive family meal.

Serves 4–6

1.2kg/2½lb boneless piece of shoulder or breast of lamb
5ml/1 heaped tsp salt per 1 litre/ 1¾ pint/4 cups of water

For the vegetables
2 carrots, peeled and sliced obliquely

115g/4oz green beans, trimmed and cut in half
115g/4oz peas
small cauliflower, trimmed and cut into medium florets

For the sauce
40g/1½oz/3 tbsp butter
50g/2oz/½ cup plain (all-purpose) flour
750ml/1¼ pints/3 cups stock
salt and ground black pepper

To serve
15ml/1 tbsp chopped parsley
boiled potatoes or rice

1 Place the meat in a pan and cover it with water. Remove the meat and add salt according to the amount of water. Bring the water to the boil, then add the meat. Bring the liquid back to the boil, then skim off any froth that has risen to the surface and lower the heat until the water does no more than gently quiver. Cook for 2½ hours or until tender.

2 Cook the vegetables individually in salted water, leaving them slightly underdone. Drain and refresh in cold water. Once the meat is cooked, leave it in the stock.

3 Melt the butter, stir in the flour and cook gently for about 2 minutes. Skim fat from the stock, then gradually add to the butter and flour, stirring until the sauce is smooth and thickened. Season to taste. Simmer gently for 2–3 minutes.

4 Pour boiling water over the vegetables to reheat and cut the meat into bitesize pieces. Place the lamb in a warmed serving dish, add the drained vegetables, pour over the sauce, garnish with the chopped fresh parsley and serve immediately, accompanied by plain boiled potatoes or rice.

Lancashire Hot-pot Energy 850Kcal/3544kJ; Protein 44.7g; Carbohydrate 45.3g, of which sugars 10.1g; Fat 55.8g, of which saturates 26.5g; Cholesterol 186mg; Calcium 72mg; Fibre 4.3g; Sodium 274mg.
Lamb Fricassée Energy 496kcal/2072kJ; Protein 44.9g; Carbohydrate 14.4g, of which sugars 5.6g; Fat 29.2g, of which saturates 14.2g; Cholesterol 166mg; Calcium 66mg; Fibre 3.9g; Sodium 229mg.

Braised Shoulder of Lamb with Barley

This one-pot dish is great for warming up your guests on a cold Christmas evening. The lamb becomes beautifully tender and the pearl barley absorbs all the glorious flavours.

Serves 4
60ml/4 tbsp olive oil
1 large onion, chopped
2 garlic cloves, chopped
2 celery sticks, sliced
a little plain (all-purpose) flour
675g/1½lb boned shoulder of
  lamb, cut into cubes
900ml–1 litre/1½–1¾ pints/
  3¾–4 cups lamb stock
115g/4oz pearl barley
225g/8oz baby carrots
225g/8oz baby turnips
salt and ground black pepper
30ml/2 tbsp chopped fresh
  marjoram, to garnish

1 Heat 45ml/3 tbsp of the oil in a flameproof casserole. Cook the onion and garlic until softened, add the celery, then cook until the vegetables brown.

2 Season the flour with salt and pepper and place in a plastic bag. Toss the lamb in the bag until evenly coated in the flour.

3 Use a slotted spoon to remove the vegetables from the casserole. Add and heat the remaining oil with the juices in the casserole. Brown the lamb, in batches, until golden.

4 When all the meat is browned, return it to the casserole with the vegetables. Stir in 900ml/1½ pints/3¾ cups of the stock and the pearl barley. Cover the pan, then bring to the boil, reduce the heat and simmer for 1 hour, or until the pearl barley and the lamb are tender.

5 Add the baby carrots and baby turnips to the casserole for the final 15 minutes of cooking.

6 Stir the meat occasionally during cooking and add the remaining stock, if necessary. Stir in seasoning to taste and serve piping hot, garnished with marjoram. Warm, crusty bread would make a good accompaniment.

Spicy Tagine of Lamb with Herby Couscous

A tagine is an easy way to provide a tasty dish for a festive gathering of guests.

Serves 6
1kg/2¼lb lean boneless lamb,
  such as shoulder or neck fillet
25g/1oz/2 tbsp butter
15ml/1 tbsp sunflower oil
1 large onion, chopped
2 garlic cloves, chopped
2.5cm/1in piece fresh root ginger,
  peeled and finely chopped
1 red (bell) pepper, chopped
900ml/1½ pints/3¾ cups lamb
  stock or water
250g/9oz ready-to-eat
  pitted prunes
juice of 1 lemon
15ml/1 tbsp clear honey
1.5ml/¼ tsp saffron strands
1 cinnamon stick, broken in half
50g/2oz/½ cup flaked (sliced)
  almonds, toasted
salt and ground black pepper

To serve
450g/1lb/2½ cups couscous
25g/1oz/2 tbsp butter
30ml/2 tbsp chopped fresh
  coriander (cilantro)

1 Trim the lamb and cut it into 2.5cm/1in cubes. Heat the butter and oil in a large flameproof casserole. Add the onion, garlic and ginger and cook until softened but not coloured.

2 Add the lamb and red pepper to the pan and mix well until the ingredients are well combined. Pour in the stock or water. Add the prunes, lemon juice, honey, saffron strands and cinnamon. Season and stir well. Bring to the boil, then reduce the heat and cover the casserole. Simmer for 1½–2 hours, stirring occasionally, or until the meat is tender.

3 Meanwhile, cook the couscous according to packet instructions. Stir in the butter and chopped fresh coriander, and season to taste with salt and pepper.

4 Taste the stew for seasoning and add more salt and black pepper if necessary. Pile the couscous into a large, warmed serving dish or on to individual warmed bowls or plates. Ladle the stew on to the couscous and sprinkle the toasted flaked almonds over the top. Serve immediately.

Shoulder of Lamb Energy 560kcal/2342kJ; Protein 37g; Carbohydrate 36g, of which sugars 10.2g; Fat 30.9g, of which saturates 10.4g; Cholesterol 128mg; Calcium 82mg; Fibre 3.7g; Sodium 179mg.
Tagine of Lamb Energy 652kcal/2716kJ; Protein 35.2g; Carbohydrate 30.9g, of which sugars 26g; Fat 44.2g, of which saturates 16.4g; Cholesterol 141mg; Calcium 97mg; Fibre 5.4g; Sodium 223mg.

Lamb Stew with Chilli Sauce

The chillies in this stew add depth and richness to the sauce, while the potato slices make sure that it is substantial enough to serve on its own as a handy one-pot Christmas meal.

Serves 6

6 dried red chillies, seeded
2 dried black chillies, seeded
250ml/8fl oz/1 cup hot water
3 garlic cloves, peeled
5ml/1 tsp ground cinnamon
2.5ml/½ tsp ground cloves
2.5ml/½ tsp ground black pepper
15ml/1 tbsp vegetable oil
1kg/2¼lb lean boneless
   lamb shoulder, cut into
   2cm/¾in cubes
400g/14oz potatoes, scrubbed
   and cut into 1cm/½in
   thick slices
salt
strips of red (bell) pepper and
   fresh oregano, to garnish

1 Snap or tear the dried chillies into large pieces, put them in a heatproof bowl and pour over the hot water to cover the chillies. Leave to soak for 30 minutes.

2 Transfer the contents of the bowl into a food processor or blender. Add the garlic and spices and process until smooth.

3 Heat the vegetable oil in a large pan. Add the lamb cubes, in batches, and stir-fry over high heat until the cubes are evenly browned on all sides.

4 Return all the lamb cubes to the pan, spread them out, then cover them with a layer of potato slices. Add salt to taste. Put a lid on the pan and cook over medium heat for 10 minutes.

5 Pour over the chilli mixture and mix well. Replace the lid and simmer over low heat for about 1 hour or until the meat and the potatoes are tender. Serve with a rice dish, and garnish with strips of red pepper and fresh oregano.

> **Cook's Tip**
> When stir-frying the lamb, don't be tempted to cook too many cubes at once, as the meat will steam rather than fry.

Lamb Meatballs with Tomato Sauce

Serve these piquant Italian-style meatballs with pasta and a leafy salad. Sprinkle with a little grated Parmesan cheese for that extra touch.

Serves 4

450g/1lb lean minced
   (ground) lamb
50g/2oz/1 cup fresh white
   breadcrumbs
1 large onion, grated
1 garlic clove, crushed
15ml/1 tbsp chopped fresh parsley
1 small egg, lightly beaten
30ml/2 tbsp olive oil
salt and ground black pepper
60ml/4 tbsp finely grated
   Parmesan cheese and rocket
   (arugula) leaves, to serve

For the sauce
1 onion, finely chopped
400g/14oz can chopped tomatoes
200ml/7fl oz/scant 1 cup passata
   (bottled strained tomatoes)
5ml/1 tsp sugar
2 green chillies, seeded and
   finely chopped
30ml/2 tbsp chopped
   fresh oregano
salt and ground black pepper

1 Soak a small clay pot in cold water for 15 minutes, then drain. Alternatively, the meatballs may be cooked in a lidded ovenproof dish or flameproof casserole.

2 Place the minced lamb, breadcrumbs, onion, garlic, parsley and seasoning in a bowl and mix well. Add the beaten egg and mix by hand to bind the meatball mixture together thoroughly.

3 Shape the mixture into 20 small, even balls. Heat the olive oil in a frying pan, add the meatballs and cook over high heat, stirring occasionally, until they are browned all over.

4 Meanwhile, to make the tomato sauce, mix together the chopped onion, tomatoes, passata, sugar, seeded and chopped chillies and oregano. Season well with salt and black pepper and pour the sauce into the clay pot.

5 Place the meatballs in the sauce, then cover and place in an unheated oven. Set the oven to 200°C/400°F/Gas 6 and cook for 1 hour, stirring after 30 minutes. Serve with Parmesan cheese and a few rocket leaves.

Lamb Stew Energy 364kcal/1524kJ; Protein 34.2g; Carbohydrate 10.8g, of which sugars 1g; Fat 20.8g, of which saturates 9g; Cholesterol 127mg; Calcium 21mg; Fibre 0.7g; Sodium 152mg.
Lamb Meatballs Energy 389kcal/1626kJ; Protein 26.9g; Carbohydrate 21.9g, of which sugars 10.1g; Fat 22.3g, of which saturates 8.1g; Cholesterol 129mg; Calcium 83mg; Fibre 2.7g; Sodium 345mg.

Rib of Beef with Yorkshire Puddings

Roast beef has always been traditional fare at Christmas.

Serves 6–8
rib of beef joint, weighing
   about 3kg/6½lb
oil, for brushing
salt and ground black pepper

For the Yorkshire puddings
115g/4oz/1 cup plain
   (all-purpose) flour
1.5ml/¼ tsp salt
1 egg
200ml/7fl oz/scant 1 cup milk
olive oil or beef dripping, to grease

For the gravy
600ml/1 pint/2½ cups beef stock

1 Preheat the oven to 220°C/425°F/Gas 7. Weigh the joint and calculate the cooking time required as follows: 10–15 minutes per 500g/1¼lb for rare beef, 15–20 minutes for medium and 20–25 minutes for well done.

2 Put the joint into a large roasting pan. Brush with oil and season with salt and pepper. Put into the hot oven and cook for 30 minutes, until the beef is browned. Lower the oven temperature to 160°C/325°F/Gas 3 and cook for the calculated time, basting the meat occasionally during cooking.

3 For the Yorkshire puddings, sift the flour and salt into a bowl and add the egg. Make the milk up to 300ml/½ pint/1¼ cups with water. Blend into the flour to make a batter. Set aside while the beef cooks. Grease eight Yorkshire pudding tins (muffin pans).

4 At the end of its cooking time, remove the beef from the oven, cover with foil and leave to stand for 30–40 minutes.

5 Increase the oven temperature to 220°C/425°F/Gas 7 and put the prepared tins on the top shelf for 5 minutes until very hot. Pour in the batter and cook for about 15 minutes until well risen, crisp and golden brown.

6 For the gravy, transfer the beef to a serving plate. Pour off the fat, leaving the meat juices. Add the stock, bring to the boil and reduce by half. Season. Carve the beef and serve with the gravy, Yorkshire puddings and roast potatoes.

Roast Sirloin with Sweet Peppers

This substantial and warming dish makes an ideal dinner for cold winter nights during the Christmas period. It is also good enough to serve as the main course on Christmas Day.

Serves 8
1.3–1.6kg/3–3½lb piece of sirloin
15ml/1 tbsp olive oil
450g/1lb small red (bell) peppers

115g/4oz/¾ cup mushrooms
175g/6oz thick-sliced
   pancetta, cubed
50g/2oz/2 tbsp plain
   (all-purpose) flour
150ml/¼ pint/⅔ cup full-bodied
   red wine
300ml/½ pint/1¼ cups
   beef stock
30ml/2 tbsp Marsala
10ml/2 tsp mixed dried herbs
salt and ground black pepper

1 Preheat the oven to 190°C/375°F/Gas 5. Season the meat. Heat the oil in a pan, then brown the meat. Place in a roasting pan and cook for 1¼ hours.

2 Put the red peppers in the oven to roast for 20 minutes (or roast for 45 minutes if using larger peppers).

3 Near the end of the meat's cooking time, prepare the gravy. Roughly chop the mushroom caps and stems.

4 Heat the pan again and add the pancetta. Cook until the fat runs from the meat. Add the flour to the pan and cook for a few minutes until browned.

5 Stir in the red wine and stock and bring to the boil. Lower the heat and add the Marsala, herbs and seasoning.

6 Add the mushrooms and heat through. Remove the sirloin from the oven and leave to stand for 10 minutes. Serve with the roasted peppers and hot gravy.

> **Cook's Tip**
> To serve this beef joint on Christmas Day, simply accompany it with all the usual festive trimmings.

Rib of Beef Energy 1037kcal/4338kJ; Protein 129g; Carbohydrate 15.1g, of which sugars 4.1g; Fat 51.5g, of which saturates 24.3g; Cholesterol 352mg; Calcium 123mg; Fibre 0.5g; Sodium 249mg.
Roast Sirloin Energy 490kcal/2043kJ; Protein 35.7g; Carbohydrate 19.5g, of which sugars 5.2g; Fat 30.4g, of which saturates 7.5g; Cholesterol 99mg; Calcium 29mg; Fibre 2.2g; Sodium 109mg.

Collops of Beef with Shallots

In this recipe, the beef is paired with the sweetness of onions – a combination you will find time and again in traditional cooking. Here, shallots are being used, left whole to impart a wonderful texture and flavour to the meal.

Serves 4
4 fillet steaks (beef tenderloin)
15ml/1 tbsp olive oil
50g/2oz/¼ cup butter
20 shallots, peeled
5ml/1 tsp caster (superfine) sugar
150ml/¼ pint/⅔ cup beef stock
salt and ground black pepper

1 Take the steaks out of the refrigerator well before you need them and dry with kitchen paper. Heat the oil and butter in a large frying pan, then cook the steaks as you like them.

2 Once cooked, remove the steaks from the pan and keep warm. Put the shallots in the pan and brown lightly in the meat juices, stirring occasionally.

3 Add the sugar and then the stock. Reduce the heat to low and allow the liquid to evaporate, shaking the pan from time to time. The shallots will end up slightly soft, browned and caramelized with a shiny glaze. Season with salt and pepper.

4 Serve the steaks on warmed plates and spoon over the caramelized shallots and juices from the pan.

Cook's Tip
Experienced cooks can tell if the steak is ready by pressing it down with their fingers and feeling how springy the meat inside is. If you are unsure of this technique, then simply cut into the steak to ensure it is cooked to your liking.

Variation
This recipe can be used for other cuts of beef such as sirloin or rump (round) steak, or even with slices of roasted beef joint.

Steak with Mustard Sauce

This steak recipe is quite delicious, with plenty of sauce in which the potatoes can be submerged. The mustard used should not be overly spicy, but rather slightly sweet.

Serves 4
25g/1oz/2 tbsp butter
30ml/2 tbsp olive oil

4 fillet steaks (beef tenderloin),
    weighing about 175g/6oz each
30ml/2 tbsp mild mustard
    (preferably Savora)
105ml/7 tbsp single (light) cream
105ml/7 tbsp milk
juice of ½ lemon
sea salt and ground black pepper
chips (French fries) or fried
    potatoes, to serve

1 Melt the butter with the oil in a large frying pan. Season the steaks with salt and black pepper, add to the pan and cook until done to your liking: about 2 minutes each side for rare and 3 minutes each side for medium.

2 Remove the steaks from the pan and set aside to keep warm. Spoon off and discard the fat from the pan, reserving any juices left over from cooking the steaks.

3 Put the mustard, cream, milk and lemon juice in the pan. Return the steaks to the pan and heat gently, shaking the pan to blend everything together. Serve hot with chips.

Cook's Tip
Savora is the kind of mustard traditionally used for this dish. It is slightly sweet and a little spicy.

Variation
A fillet steak (beef tenderloin) is a fine cut of meat and is special enough to serve for a festive meal. If doing this, serve with roast potatoes rather than chips (French fries) and the traditional vegetables such as Brussels sprouts, roasted parsnips and carrots. Let diners help themselves to horseradish cream.

Collops of Beef Energy 424kcal/1767kJ; Protein 43.2g; Carbohydrate 6.1g, of which sugars 4.6g; Fat 25.4g, of which saturates 12.5g; Cholesterol 149mg; Calcium 27mg; Fibre 0.9g; Sodium 166mg.
Steak with Mustard Energy 475kcal/1976kJ; Protein 42.1g; Carbohydrate 2.6g, of which sugars 2.4g; Fat 33g, of which saturates 14.2g; Cholesterol 131mg; Calcium 70mg; Fibre 0g; Sodium 390mg.

Rib-eye Steak with Ham and Garlic

This is a classic steak recipe, traditionally prepared in a terracotta dish. If you have some beef stock available, add it to the sauce to make it richer. Rib-eye is a fantastic cut as its fat melts during cooking, flavouring the meat. Salt the meat immediately before frying, using sea salt instead of the refined variety, as it improves the taste.

Serves 4
50ml/2fl oz/¼ cup olive oil
4 rib-eye steaks, each weighing about 240g/8½oz
4 garlic cloves, lightly crushed
4 small bay leaves
120ml/4fl oz/½ cup white wine
8 slices of cured ham
sea salt
deep-fried potato slices or baked potatoes, to serve

1 Heat half the oil in a large pan. Lightly season the steaks with sea salt, add them to the pan and cook until done to your liking (use about 3 minutes each side for rare and 4 minutes each side for medium). Remove the cooked steaks from the pan and keep them warm.

2 Add the remaining oil, the garlic and bay leaves, then pour in the white wine and cook for a few minutes more.

3 Place the steaks on warm plates, top each with two slices of ham and spoon the sauce over them. Serve immediately, with the potatoes of your choice.

Cook's Tip
This is an excellent way of eating up the Christmas ham if you have cooked or bought one for the festive period.

Variation
Not only is this dish suitable for other cuts of beef such as sirloin or rump (round) steak, but it can also be used for chicken or turkey breast fillets.

Sirloin Steak with Whiskey Sauce

A good steak is always popular and Christmas time is no exception. Top quality raw materials plus timing are the keys to success. Choose small, thick steaks rather than large, thin ones if you can. Traditional accompaniments include potato chips, fried onions, mushrooms and peas.

Serves 4
4 × 225–350g/8–12oz sirloin steaks, at room temperature
5ml/1 tsp oil
15g/½oz/1 tbsp butter
50ml/2fl oz/¼ cup Irish whiskey
300ml/½ pint/1¼ cups double (heavy) cream
salt and ground black pepper

1 Dry the steaks with kitchen paper and season with pepper. Heat a cast-iron frying pan, or other heavy pan, over high heat. When it is very hot, add the oil and butter.

2 Add the steaks to the foaming butter, one at a time, to seal the meat quickly. Lower the heat to moderate. Allowing about 3–4 minutes for rare, 4–5 minutes for medium or 5–6 minutes for well-done steaks, leave undisturbed for half of the specified cooking time; very thick steaks will take longer than thin ones. Turn the steaks only once during cooking.

3 To test if the timing is right, press down gently in the middle of the steak with your fingertips: soft meat will be rare; when there is some resistance but the meat underneath the outside crust feels soft, it will be medium; if it is firm to the touch, the steak will be well done.

4 When the steaks are cooked to your liking, transfer them to warmed plates and keep warm. Pour off the fat from the pan and discard. Add the whiskey and stir around to scrape off all the sediment from the base of the pan.

5 Allow the liquid to reduce a little, then add the cream and simmer over low heat for a few minutes, until the cream has thickened slightly. Season to taste with salt and pepper, pour the sauce around or over the steaks, as preferred, and serve immediately with accompaniments.

Rib-eye Steak Energy 539kcal/2246kJ; Protein 57.7g; Carbohydrate 4.5g, of which sugars 0.8g; Fat 30.2g, of which saturates 10g; Cholesterol 145mg; Calcium 21mg; Fibre 1g; Sodium 446mg.
Sirloin Steaks Energy 738kcal/3062kJ; Protein 54.1g; Carbohydrate 1.3g, of which sugars 1.3g; Fat 54.2g, of which saturates 31.6g; Cholesterol 226mg; Calcium 49mg; Fibre 0g; Sodium 197mg.

Filet Mignon with Mushrooms

This luxurious dish is excellent for a special festive occasion. It was originally made with truffle slices but large mushroom caps are less expensive and look just as attractive, especially when they are fluted.

Serves 4

4 thin slices white bread
120g/4oz pâté de foie gras or
   mousse de foie gras
4 white (button) mushroom caps
70g/2½oz/5 tbsp butter
10ml/2 tsp vegetable oil or
   olive oil
4 fillet steaks (beef tenderloin),
   about 2.5cm/1in thick
45–60ml/3–4 tbsp Madeira
   or port
125ml/4fl oz/½ cup beef or
   vegetable stock
watercress or rocket (arugula),
   to garnish

1 Cut the bread into rounds about the same diameter as the steaks, using a large round cutter or by cutting it into squares, then cutting off the corners.

2 Toast the bread and spread with the foie gras, dividing it evenly. Place the bread on warmed plates.

3 Flute the mushroom caps using the edge of a knife blade. Melt about 25g/1oz/1 tbsp of the butter in a pan and sauté the mushrooms until golden and tender. Transfer the mushrooms to a plate and keep warm.

4 In the same pan, melt another 25g/1oz/1 tbsp of the butter with the oil, swirling to combine. When the butter just begins to brown, add the steaks and cook for 6–8 minutes, turning once, until cooked as preferred (medium-rare meat will still be slightly soft when pressed, medium will be springy, and well-done firm). Place the steaks on the toasted bread with the foie gras and top with the cooked mushroom caps.

5 Add the Madeira or port to the pan and boil for about 20–30 seconds. Add the beef or vegetable stock and boil until reduced by about three-quarters. Swirl in the remaining butter. Pour a little of the sauce over each steak, then garnish with sprigs of watercress or rocket and serve immediately.

Chateaubriand with Béarnaise Sauce

Chateaubriand is a lean and tender cut of beef from the thick centre of the fillet that is pounded to give it its characteristic shape. It is perfect for a romantic Christmas meal for two.

Serves 2

150g/5oz/⅔ cup butter, cut
   into pieces
25ml/1½ tbsp tarragon vinegar
25ml/1½ tbsp dry white wine
1 shallot, finely chopped
2 egg yolks
450g/1lb beef fillet, about
   12.5–15cm/5–6in long, cut
   from the thickest part
   of the fillet
15ml/1 tbsp vegetable oil
salt and ground black pepper
sautéed potatoes, to serve

1 Clarify the butter by melting in a pan over low heat; do not boil. Skim off any foam and set aside.

2 Put the vinegar, wine and shallot in a heavy pan over high heat and boil to reduce until the liquid has almost evaporated. Remove from the heat and cool slightly. Add the egg yolks and whisk for 1 minute. Over a very low heat, whisk constantly until the yolk mixture begins to thicken and the whisk begins to leave tracks on the base of the pan, then remove the pan from the heat.

3 Whisk in the butter, slowly at first, then more quickly, until the sauce thickens. Season and keep warm.

4 Place the meat between two sheets of baking parchment or clear film (plastic wrap) and pound with the flat side of a meat pounder or roll with a rolling pin to flatten to about 4cm/1½in thick. Season with plenty of salt and pepper.

5 Heat the vegetable oil in a heavy frying pan over a medium-high heat. Add the meat and cook for about 10–12 minutes, turning once, until cooked as preferred (medium-rare will be slightly soft, medium will be springy and well-done will be firm).

6 Transfer the steak to a board and carve in thin, diagonal slices. If you prefer a smooth sauce, strain it through a fine sieve (strainer) then serve with the steak and sautéed potatoes.

Filet Mignon Energy 452kcal/1878kJ; Protein 28.3g; Carbohydrate 8.5g, of which sugars 1.9g; Fat 32.7g, of which saturates 15.9g; Cholesterol 149mg; Calcium 29mg; Fibre 0.5g; Sodium 504mg.
Chateaubriand Energy 1065kcal/4406kJ; Protein 54.4g; Carbohydrate 0.1g, of which sugars 0.1g; Fat 93.2g, of which saturates 51.2g; Cholesterol 505mg; Calcium 47mg; Fibre 0g; Sodium 716mg.

Individual Beef Wellingtons

The sauce can be made the day before and reheated just before serving. The Wellingtons can be made several hours before cooking, as long as the meat is quite cold before you wrap it in pastry.

Serves 8
30ml/2 tbsp olive oil
8 fillet steaks (beef tenderloins),
    cut 2.5 cm/1 in thick, weighing
    about 115g/4oz each
900g/2lb puff pastry
225g/8oz smooth garlic liver
    sausage or pâté
30ml/2 tbsp chopped fresh parsley
30ml/2 tbsp chopped fresh chives
1 egg, beaten with
    15ml/1 tbsp water

For the sauce
25g/1oz/2 tbsp butter
1 onion, finely chopped
115g/4oz mushrooms, chopped
30ml/2 tbsp plain (all-purpose) flour
2.5ml/½ tsp tomato purée (paste)
2.5ml/½ tsp caster
    (superfine) sugar
150ml/¼ pint/⅔ cup red wine
300ml/½ pint/1¼ cups hot
    beef stock
salt and ground black pepper

1 Heat the oil in a large frying pan and quickly brown the steaks on both sides. Transfer to a plate and leave to cool. Preheat the oven to 200°C/400°F/Gas 6.

2 Divide the pastry in two equal halves. On a lightly floured work surface, roll each piece out thinly and trim to a 40cm/16in square. Cut into four 20 cm/8 in squares. (Save the trimmings for the decoration.)

3 Mix the liver sausage or pâté with the herbs. Place a cold fillet steak on each piece of pastry and divide the sausage or pâté between each. Spread evenly over the top and sides.

4 Brush the pastry with beaten egg and fold the sides over like a parcel. Pinch the edges to seal. Bake for 25 minutes.

5 For the sauce, cook the onion in the butter until tender. Add the mushrooms and cook for 5 minutes, then stir in the flour, tomato paste and sugar. Blend in the red wine and stock. Bring to the boil and simmer for 10 minutes. Season to taste, strain and serve separately.

Fillet of Beef with Ratatouille

This succulent rare beef is served cold with a colourful garlicky ratatouille.

Serves 8
675–900g/1½–2lb fillet of beef
45ml/3 tbsp olive oil
300ml/½ pint/1¼ cups aspic jelly,
    made up as packet instructions

For the marinade
30ml/2 tbsp sherry
30ml/2 tbsp olive oil
30ml/2 tbsp soy sauce
10ml/2 tsp grated fresh root ginger
2 garlic cloves, crushed

For the ratatouille
60ml/4 tbsp olive oil
1 onion, sliced
2–3 garlic cloves, crushed
1 large aubergine (eggplant), cubed
1 small red (bell) pepper, sliced
1 small green (bell) pepper, sliced
1 small yellow (bell) pepper, sliced
225g/8oz courgettes
    (zucchini), sliced
450g/1lb tomatoes, skinned
    and quartered
15ml/1 tbsp chopped mixed herbs
30ml/2 tbsp French dressing
salt and ground black pepper

1 Mix all the marinade ingredients together in a shallow dish, put the beef in and turn it over to coat it. Cover with clear film (plastic wrap) and leave for 30 minutes.

2 Preheat the oven to 220°C/425°F/Gas 7. Lift the fillet out of the marinade and pat it dry. Heat the oil in a frying pan until smoking hot and then brown the beef all over to seal it. Transfer to a roasting pan and roast for 10–15 minutes, basting it with the marinade. Transfer to a plate and leave to cool.

3 Meanwhile, for the ratatouille, heat the oil in a large pan and cook the onion and garlic over low heat until tender. Add the aubergine and cook for 5 minutes, until soft. Add the peppers and courgettes, cook for 2 minutes. Then add the tomatoes, herbs and seasoning and cook for a few minutes longer.

4 Transfer the ratatouille to a dish and cool. Drizzle with a little French dressing. Slice the beef and arrange on a serving platter. Brush with aspic jelly that is on the point of setting.

5 Leave the jelly to set completely, then brush with a second coat. Spoon the ratatouille on to the dish and serve.

Beef Wellingtons Energy 511kcal/2131kJ; Protein 41.7g; Carbohydrate 19.3g, of which sugars 1.2g; Fat 30.6g, of which saturates 7.2g; Cholesterol 128mg; Calcium 41mg; Fibre 0.4g; Sodium 320mg.
Fillet of Beef Energy 250kcal/1043kJ; Protein 21.9g; Carbohydrate 7.7g, of which sugars 7.2g; Fat 14.8g, of which saturates 4.4g; Cholesterol 51mg; Calcium 28mg; Fibre 2.7g; Sodium 66mg.

Smoked Beef with Potato Pancakes

Chargrilled beef fillet is a delicious alternative to the usual Christmas Day fare.

Serves 4
500g/1¼lb trimmed beef fillet
oil, for chargrilling
salt and ground black pepper
herb sprigs, to garnish
broccoli florets, white turnip and
 courgettes (zucchini), to serve

For the potato pancakes
250g/9oz potatoes, cooked
50g/2oz/½ cup plain
 (all-purpose) flour

1 egg
freshly grated nutmeg
oil, for frying

For the sauce
4 shallots, finely diced
200ml/7fl oz/scant 1 cup
 chicken stock
120ml/4fl oz/½ cup white wine
200ml/7fl oz/scant 1 cup double
 (heavy) cream
15ml/1 tbsp chopped fresh
 herbs, such as flat leaf parsley,
 tarragon, chervil and basil
lemon juice, to taste

1 To make the potato pancakes, blend the potatoes with the flour and egg to make a thick batter. Add nutmeg and seasoning.

2 Lightly oil and heat a heavy pan, then use the batter to make eight pancakes, cooking them on both sides until golden brown.

3 To make the sauce, put the shallots, stock, wine and half the cream into a pan and cook over medium heat until they are reduced by two-thirds. Purée the mixture and strain it, then mix in enough herbs to turn the sauce green.

4 Season the beef with salt and pepper. In a heavy, preheated pan, seal the meat on all sides over a medium heat. Place the meat in a smoker for about 10 minutes until medium-rare. Alternatively, to chargrill the meat, preheat a dry cast-iron ridged pan until very hot. Brush the meat with a little oil and cook for 3–5 minutes, turning once. Keep warm.

5 To serve, whip the remaining cream and fold it into the sauce, adjusting the seasoning and lemon juice to taste. Divide the sauce and beef between four warm plates. Add the pancakes, garnish with herbs and serve with the vegetables.

Cantonese Beefsteak

This is a typical Hong Kong restaurant dish, in which steak is cooked by the traditional Cantonese stir-fried method. The unusual ingredient here is Worcestershire sauce, very likely a British colonial touch. This imparts a subtle vinegar and pepper flavour to the dish. Serve with fried rice or noodles for a more substantial meal to serve to unexpected guests.

Serves 4
600g/1lb 6oz sirloin or rump
 (round) steak
15ml/1 tbsp cornflour
 (cornstarch)
30ml/2 tbsp Chinese Mui Kwai Lo
 wine or sweet sherry
15ml/1 tbsp Worcestershire sauce
30ml/2 tbsp oyster sauce
45ml/3 tbsp oil
15ml/1 tbsp grated fresh
 root ginger
2.5ml/½ tsp sugar
lettuce leaves, to serve

1 Slice the sirloin or rump steak thinly into medallions. Put the cornflour in a large bowl or strong plastic bag. Add the steak medallions and toss to coat in the cornflour.

2 In a small bowl, mix the Chinese wine or sweet sherry, Worcestershire sauce and oyster sauce. Stir, then set aside.

3 Heat the oil in a wok or large, heavy frying pan. Add the grated ginger and fry, stirring constantly, for 30 seconds.

4 Add the beef to the wok or pan. Stir-fry over high heat for about 1 minute until sealed.

5 Pour the wine and sauce mixture into the pan. Stir-fry the mixture for 1 minute more, then sprinkle over the sugar.

6 Continue to stir for 2 minutes more for medium-rare, or 3 minutes for well-done beef. Serve on a bed of lettuce leaves.

> **Cook's Tip**
> This stir-fry is a good choice for a quick and easy supper for friends or family over the Christmas period.

Smoked Beef Energy 683kcal/2834kJ; Protein 32.9g; Carbohydrate 23g, of which sugars 3g; Fat 49.5g, of which saturates 27.5g; Cholesterol 219mg; Calcium 82mg; Fibre 1.9g; Sodium 166mg.
Cantonese Beefsteak Energy 365kcal/1518kJ; Protein 34.2g; Carbohydrate 5g, of which sugars 1.5g; Fat 22.2g, of which saturates 6.7g; Cholesterol 87mg; Calcium 17mg; Fibre 0g; Sodium 322mg.

Meatballs

These tasty meatballs will be very popular with children and adults alike over the festive period.

Serves 4
2 eggs
225g/8oz minced (ground) veal
225g/8oz minced (ground) pork
25g/1oz/¹/₂ cup fine
    white breadcrumbs
40g/1¹/₂oz/¹/₂ cup finely
    chopped onion
250ml/8fl oz/1 cup milk
75ml/3oz/6 tbsp butter
salt and ground black pepper

1 In a small bowl, beat the eggs well. In a separate, larger bowl, mix the minced meats, breadcrumbs and onion together until well blended. Mix in the beaten egg. Use your hands rather than a spoon to blend the ingredients properly.

2 Add the milk, salt and pepper to the bowl and continue mixing until all the ingredients are thoroughly blended to make a soft, moist mixture. Chill the mixture for 15–30 minutes, or until you are ready to cook the meatballs.

3 Melt the butter in a large frying pan over medium heat. Use two spoons to form 16–20 oval patties about 4cm/1¹/₂in across: scoop the meat mixture with one spoon and use the second to slide the patty into the pan.

4 Cook the meatballs for 8–10 minutes, in batches of four or five if necessary, turning once, until the patties are golden brown. Cut one to check that the meat is not pink in the centre. Remove the cooked meatballs from the pan and drain on kitchen paper. Keep warm until all the remaining meatballs are cooked. Serve immediately.

Cook's Tip
Make a double batch of meatballs and freeze them, uncooked, for up to three months. You can also freeze them after they are fried, and then reheat them in the oven. When rolled into much smaller balls, the meatballs can be served at Christmas parties as finger food, with pickles.

Beef Stew with Beer

This tasty stew is a great way to feed a lot of people at a Christmas gathering. The quantities can be easily increased to feed any number of guests.

Serves 4–6
500g/1¹/₄lb stewing beef or
    chuck steak, cubed
20g/³/₄oz/3 tbsp plain (all-purpose)
    flour, for dusting
25g/1oz/2 tbsp butter
30ml/2 tbsp vegetable oil
1 large onion, chopped
2 garlic cloves, crushed
330ml/11¹/₂fl oz bottle of dark
    beer, such as Chimay
bouquet garni
30ml/2 tbsp red wine vinegar
30ml/2 tbsp soft light
    brown sugar
2 slices of rustic bread
30ml/2 tbsp Dijon mustard
handful of fresh parsley, chopped
salt and ground black pepper

To serve
fries, potato purée or breads
pickles

1 Generously season the beef cubes with salt and pepper, then coat them in the flour. Heat a large, heavy frying pan that has a tight-fitting lid. Melt the butter and the oil over medium to high heat. Add the cubed beef in batches and brown over fairly high heat for about 4 minutes to seal. As each batch browns, remove the cubes from the pan and place them on a plate.

2 Add the onion to the fat remaining in the pan and cook for 6–8 minutes, until translucent. Add the garlic and fry for 3 minutes.

3 Return the meat to the frying pan and stir well to combine with the onions. Pour in the beer and bring the mixture to just below boiling point. Add the bouquet garni, vinegar and brown sugar. Cover, reduce the heat and simmer for 1¹/₂ hours.

4 Spread the bread thickly with mustard and place it on top of the stew, mustard-side down. Replace the lid and simmer the stew for 20–30 minutes more, stirring occasionally. The bread will absorb the pan juices and dissolve to thicken the stew.

5 Taste and adjust the seasoning if necessary. Remove the bouquet garni and stir in the parsley. Serve with potato purée, fries or rustic bread, with pickles on the side.

Meatballs Energy 404kcal/1683kJ; Protein 28.4g; Carbohydrate 8.7g, of which sugars 3.8g; Fat 28.8g, of which saturates 14.9g; Cholesterol 211mg; Calcium 112mg; Fibre 0.3g; Sodium 307mg.
Beef Stew Energy 317kcal/1324kJ; Protein 21.6g; Carbohydrate 19.8g, of which sugars 8.9g; Fat 15.7g, of which saturates 5.9g; Cholesterol 57mg; Calcium 47mg; Fibre 1.1g; Sodium 314mg.

Fillet of Beef Stroganoff

Tender strips of beef with mushrooms in a creamy sauce with brandy is a luxurious dish, well suited to serving at Christmas time. It is quick and easy to prepare as none of the ingredients needs long cooking, so it is very useful over the busy festive season.

Serves 8

1.2kg/2½lb fillet of beef
30ml/2 tbsp plain
   (all-purpose) flour
large pinch each of cayenne
   pepper and paprika
75ml/5 tbsp sunflower oil
1 large onion, chopped
3 garlic cloves, finely chopped
450g/1lb/6½ cups brown cap
   (cremini) mushrooms, sliced
75ml/5 tbsp brandy
300ml/½ pint/1¼ cups beef
   stock or consommé
300ml/½ pint/1¼ cups
   sour cream
45ml/3 tbsp chopped fresh flat
   leaf parsley
salt and ground black pepper

1 Thinly slice the fillet of beef across the grain, then cut it into fine strips. Season the flour with the cayenne pepper and paprika.

2 Heat half the oil in a large frying pan, add the onion and garlic, and cook gently until the onion has softened.

3 Add the mushrooms and stir-fry over high heat. Transfer the vegetables and their juices to a dish and set aside.

4 Wipe the pan, then add and heat the remaining oil. Coat a batch of meat with flour, then fry over high heat until browned. Remove from the pan, then coat and stir-fry another batch.

5 When the last batch of steak is cooked, place all the meat and vegetables back into the pan. Add the brandy and simmer until it has almost evaporated.

6 Stir in the stock or consommé and seasoning and cook for 10–15 minutes, stirring frequently, or until the meat is tender and the sauce is thick and glossy.

7 Add the sour cream and sprinkle with chopped parsley. Serve immediately with rice and a simple salad.

Spicy Shredded Beef

The essence of this quick and easy recipe is that the beef is cut into very fine strips. Stir-fry food is great during the busy festive holidays because it takes very little time to cook.

Serves 2

225g/8oz rump (round) or fillet
   (tenderloin) of beef
15ml/1 tbsp light soy sauce
15ml/1 tbsp dark soy sauce
15ml/1 tbsp rice wine or
   medium-dry sherry
5ml/1 tsp soft dark brown sugar
90ml/6 tbsp vegetable oil
1 large onion, thinly sliced
2.5cm/1in piece fresh root ginger,
   peeled and grated
1–2 carrots, cut into thin batons
2–3 fresh or dried chillies,
   halved, seeded (optional)
   and chopped
salt and ground black pepper
fresh chives, to garnish

1 With a sharp knife, slice the beef very thinly, then cut each slice into fine strips or shreds.

2 Mix together the light and dark soy sauces with the rice wine or sherry and sugar in a bowl. Add the strips of beef to the bowl and stir well to make sure that they are evenly coated with the marinade.

3 Heat a wok or large frying pan and add half the oil. When it is hot, stir-fry the onion and ginger for about 3–4 minutes, then transfer to a plate using a slotted spoon.

4 Add the carrot, stir-fry for 3–4 minutes until slightly softened, then transfer to a plate and keep warm.

5 Heat the remaining oil in the wok, then quickly add the beef with the marinade, followed by the chillies. Cook over a high heat for 2 minutes, stirring all the time.

6 Return the onion and ginger to the wok and stir-fry for 1 minute more. Season with salt and ground black pepper to taste, cover and cook for 30 seconds.

7 Spoon the meat into two warmed bowls and add the strips of carrot. Garnish with fresh chives and serve.

Beef Stroganoff Energy 399kcal/1659kJ; Protein 34.6g; Carbohydrate 6.5g, of which sugars 3g; Fat 23.9g, of which saturates 9.8g; Cholesterol 114mg; Calcium 56mg; Fibre 1.1g; Sodium 85mg.
Spicy Beef Energy 524kcal/2170kJ; Protein 26.7g; Carbohydrate 15.8g, of which sugars 12.7g; Fat 39.8g, of which saturates 6.6g; Cholesterol 71mg; Calcium 49mg; Fibre 2.6g; Sodium 1153mg.

Chilli Con Carne

Make a large pan of this tasty chilli con carne and you will be sure to keep festive diners happy.

Serves 8
1.2kg/2½lb lean braising steak
30ml/2 tbsp sunflower oil
1 large onion, chopped
2 garlic cloves, finely chopped
15ml/1 tbsp plain
   (all-purpose) flour
300ml/½ pint/1¼ cups red wine
300ml/½ pint/1¼ cups beef stock
30ml/2 tbsp tomato purée
fresh coriander (cilantro) leaves,
   to garnish
salt and ground black pepper

For the beans
30ml/2 tbsp olive oil
1 onion, chopped
1 fresh red chilli, seeded
   and chopped
2 × 400g/14oz cans red kidney
   beans, drained and rinsed
400g/14oz can chopped tomatoes

For the topping
6 tomatoes, peeled, seeded
   and chopped
1 fresh green chilli, seeded
   and chopped
30ml/2 tbsp chopped fresh chives
30ml/2 tbsp chopped fresh
   coriander (cilantro)
150ml/¼ pint/⅔ cup sour cream

1 Cut the meat into thick strips and then cut it crossways into small cubes. Heat the oil in a flameproof casserole. Add the onion and garlic, and cook until softened. Meanwhile, season the flour and place on a plate, then toss a batch of meat in it.

2 Use a slotted spoon to remove the onion from the pan, then add the floured beef and cook over high heat until browned. Remove and set aside, then flour and brown another batch.

3 When the last batch of meat is browned, return all the meat and onion to the pan. Stir in the wine, stock and tomato purée. Bring to the boil, reduce the heat and simmer for 45 minutes.

4 Meanwhile, for the beans, heat the olive oil in a frying pan and cook the onion and chilli until softened. Add the kidney beans and tomatoes and simmer gently for 20–25 minutes.

5 Mix the tomatoes, chilli, chives and coriander for the topping. Ladle the meat mixture on to plates. Add the bean mixture and topping. Finish with sour cream and garnish with coriander.

Boeuf Bourguignon

The is a classic French dish of beef cooked in Burgundy style, with red wine, pieces of bacon, shallots and mushrooms. It is baked in a low oven for hours, giving you the chance to spend more time with your guests at Christmas.

Serves 6
175g/6oz rindless streaky (fatty)
   bacon rashers (strips), chopped
900g/2lb lean braising steak, such
   as top rump (round) steak

30ml/2 tbsp plain
   (all-purpose) flour
45ml/3 tbsp sunflower oil
25g/1oz/2 tbsp butter
12 shallots
2 garlic cloves, crushed
175g/6oz/2½ cups
   mushrooms, sliced
450ml/¾ pint/scant 2 cups
   robust red wine
150ml/¼ pint/⅔ cup beef stock
1 bay leaf
2 sprigs each of fresh thyme,
   parsley and marjoram
salt and ground black pepper

1 Preheat the oven to 160°C/325°F/Gas 3. Heat a large flameproof casserole, then add the chopped bacon and cook, stirring occasionally, until the pieces are crisp and golden brown.

2 Meanwhile, cut the beef into 2.5cm/1in cubes. Season the flour with salt and pepper and use to coat the meat. Use a slotted spoon to remove the bacon from the casserole and set aside. Add the oil, and then fry the beef in batches until lightly browned all over. Set aside with the bacon.

3 Add the butter to the fat remaining in the casserole. Cook the shallots and garlic until they are just beginning to colour, then add the mushrooms and cook for a further 5 minutes.

4 Return the bacon and beef to the casserole, and stir in the red wine and the beef stock or consommé. Tie the herbs together to create a bouquet garni and add to the casserole.

5 Cover with a tight-fitting lid and cook in the oven for about 1½–2 hours, or until the meat is tender, stirring once or twice during the cooking time. Season to taste with salt and black pepper and serve with creamy mashed root vegetables, such as celeriac and potatoes.

Chilli Con Carne Energy 470kcal/1969kJ; Protein 42g; Carbohydrate 28.4g, of which sugars 11.2g; Fat 18.9g, of which saturates 6.9g; Cholesterol 106mg; Calcium 124mg; Fibre 8.2g; Sodium 517mg
Boeuf Bourguignon Energy 749kcal/3117kJ; Protein 63.3g; Carbohydrate 15.2g, of which sugars 8.8g; Fat 40.3g, of which saturates 14g; Cholesterol 167mg; Calcium 69mg; Fibre 2.8g; Sodium 868mg.

Stir-fried Beef and Mushrooms

The combination of garlic and salted black beans is a classic seasoning for beef.

Serves 4
30ml/2 tbsp soy sauce
30ml/2 tbsp Chinese rice wine or sherry
10ml/2 tsp cornflour (cornstarch)
10ml/2 tsp sesame oil
450g/1lb fillet (tenderloin) or rump (round) steak, trimmed of fat
12 dried shiitake mushrooms
25ml/1½ tbsp salted black beans
5ml/1 tsp caster (superfine) sugar
120ml/4fl oz/½ cup groundnut (peanut) oil
4 garlic cloves, thinly sliced
2.5cm/1in piece fresh root ginger, cut into fine strips
200g/7oz mushrooms, sliced
1 bunch spring onions (scallions), sliced diagonally
1 fresh red chilli, seeded and finely shredded
salt and ground black pepper

1 In a large bowl, mix half the soy sauce, half the rice wine or sherry, half the cornflour and all the sesame oil with 15ml/1 tbsp cold water until smooth. Add a good pinch of salt and pepper. Cut the beef into very thin slices, no more than 5mm/¼in thick. Coat the slices in the cornflour mixture. Set aside.

2 Soak the dried mushrooms in boiling water for 25 minutes. Drain, reserving 45ml/3 tbsp of the soaking water. Remove and discard the hard stalks and cut the caps in half.

3 Using a fork, mash the black beans with the sugar in a small bowl. Stir the remaining cornflour, soy sauce and rice wine or sherry together in another small bowl.

4 Heat the oil in a wok until very hot, then stir-fry the beef for 30–45 seconds, until just brown. Transfer it to a plate. Pour off some oil to leave about 45ml/3 tbsp in the wok. Add the garlic and ginger, stir-fry for 1 minute, then add the shiitake and fresh mushrooms and stir-fry for 2 minutes. Set aside a handful of the green part of the spring onions, then add the rest to the wok. Add the mashed black beans and stir-fry for 1–2 minutes.

5 Stir the beef back into the wok, then add 45ml/3 tbsp of the shiitake water. Pour in the cornflour mixture, stir and simmer for 4–5 minutes. Add the chilli and green spring onions and serve.

Veal and Prune Stew

This hearty, rich stew is a delicious mixture of veal, prunes, lemon and cream. It would make a satisfying meal for friends and family over the festive season.

Serves 8
20 ready-to-eat pitted prunes
100ml/3½fl oz/scant ½ cup brandy
2.5ml/½ tsp grated lemon rind
65g/2½oz/5 tbsp butter
600g/1lb 6oz braising veal, diced
200ml/7fl oz/scant 1 cup veal stock or water
30ml/2 tbsp lemon juice
1 thyme sprig
1 bay leaf
200ml/7fl oz/scant 1 cup whipping cream
5ml/1 tsp potato flour or cornflour (cornstarch)
salt and ground black pepper
chopped fresh parsley, to garnish
young peas, carrots and small new potatoes, to serve

1 Put the prunes in a bowl, add the brandy and lemon rind, cover and soak overnight.

2 Melt the butter in a pan, add the veal and cook over a medium heat, stirring frequently, for about 10 minutes, until evenly browned. Season and add the stock or water, lemon juice, thyme and bay leaf. Lower the heat, cover and simmer for 1 hour, or until tender.

3 Arrange the vegetables in a ring on a warm serving plate. Using a slotted spoon, transfer the veal to the centre of the plate and keep warm.

4 Bring the cooking liquid to the boil and reduce slightly, then stir in the cream. Remove and discard the thyme and bay leaf. Season the sauce with salt and pepper.

5 Mix the potato flour or cornflour with 15ml/1 tbsp cold water to a paste in a small bowl and stir into the sauce until thickened and smooth. Add the prunes with their soaking liquid and warm through.

6 Pour the sauce over the veal, sprinkle the vegetables with parsley and serve immediately.

Stir-fried Beef Energy 370kcal/1536kJ; Protein 25.5g; Carbohydrate 2.6g, of which sugars 2.4g; Fat 28.7g, of which saturates 7.2g; Cholesterol 69mg; Calcium 19mg; Fibre 0.9g; Sodium 588mg.
Veal Stew Energy 610kcal/2536kJ; Protein 34.4g; Carbohydrate 19.9g, of which sugars 18.7g; Fat 37.9g, of which saturates 22.4g; Cholesterol 213mg; Calcium 86mg; Fibre 3.5g; Sodium 286mg

Veal Escalopes

Try these quick and easy veal escalopes for a little variety during Christmas.

Serves 4

4 veal escalopes, about 175g/6oz each
75g/3oz/2/3 cup plain (all-purpose) flour, seasoned
2 eggs, beaten
115g/4oz/2 cups dried white breadcrumbs
30ml/2 tbsp oil
50g/2oz/4 tbsp butter
coarsely ground white pepper
vegetable oil, for brushing
chives and paprika, to garnish
lemon wedges, buttered tagliatelle and green salad, to serve

1 Place the veal escalopes in between two sheets of clear film (plastic wrap) or baking parchment and flatten with a meat mallet or rolling pin until half as large again. Press a little ground white pepper into both sides of the escalopes.

2 Place the flour, eggs and breadcrumbs on to separate plates. Brush the meat with a little oil, then dip into the flour. Shake off any extra flour, then dip the escalopes into the egg and then finally the breadcrumbs, ensuring they are evenly coated. Set aside, loosely covered, for 30 minutes.

3 Heat the oil and half of the butter together in a large frying pan and gently fry the escalopes, one at a time, over a low–medium heat for 3–4 minutes on each side. Be aware that too much heat will cause the veal to toughen. Keep the escalopes warm while you cook the remainder.

4 Top each escalope with one-quarter of the remaining butter. Garnish with chives and a sprinkling of paprika. Serve with lemon wedges and buttered tagliatelle, with a green salad or seasonal vegetables, if you like.

> **Cook's Tip**
> To prevent the breadcrumb coating on the veal escalopes from cracking during cooking, use the back of a knife and lightly form a criss-cross pattern.

Veal in a Wheat Beer Sauce

The bitterness of the beer in this stew is matched by the sweet onions and carrots.

Serves 4

900g/2lb boned shoulder or leg of veal, cut into 5cm/2in cubes
45ml/3 tbsp plain (all-purpose) flour, seasoned
65g/2½oz/5 tbsp butter
3 shallots, finely chopped
1 celery stick
fresh parsley sprig
2 fresh bay leaves
5ml/1 tsp caster (superfine) sugar, plus a good pinch
250ml/8fl oz/1 cup wheat beer
475ml/16fl oz/2 cups veal stock
20–25 large silverskin onions or small pickling (pearl) onions
450g/1lb carrots, thickly sliced
2 large egg yolks
105ml/7 tbsp double (heavy) cream
a little lemon juice (optional)
30ml/2 tbsp chopped fresh parsley
salt and ground black pepper

1 Dust the veal with the flour. Heat 25g/1oz/2 tbsp of the butter in a frying pan, add the veal and quickly cook until just golden. Remove the veal and set aside. Add 15g/½oz/1 tbsp butter to the pan and gently cook the shallots for 5–6 minutes.

2 Replace the veal. Tie the celery, parsley and 1 bay leaf together, then add to the pan with a pinch of sugar. Pour in the beer and allow to bubble briefly, then add the stock. Season, cover and simmer for 40–50 minutes, or until the veal is tender.

3 Meanwhile, melt the remaining butter in another frying pan. Cook the onions until golden all over. Remove from the pan and set aside. Add the carrots, 5ml/1 tsp sugar, a pinch of salt, the second bay leaf and water to cover. Bring to the boil and cook for 10–12 minutes. Add the onions and continue to cook until the onions and carrots are tender and slightly caramelized.

4 Transfer the veal to a bowl and discard the celery and herb bundle. Mix the egg yolks and cream in another bowl, then add a ladleful of carrot liquid. Return this mixture to the pan and cook over very low heat, stirring, until the sauce has thickened.

5 Add the veal to the sauce, add the onions and carrots and reheat until warmed through. Season to taste, adding lemon juice, if necessary, then serve, sprinkled with the parsley.

Veal Escalopes Energy 398kcal/1666kJ; Protein 39.7g; Carbohydrate 9.4g, of which sugars 1.4g; Fat 19.6g, of which saturates 3.4g; Cholesterol 88mg; Calcium 44mg; Fibre 0.9g; Sodium 105mg.
Veal in Beer Sauce Energy 672kcal/2801kJ; Protein 53.4g; Carbohydrate 32.4g, of which sugars 17.4g; Fat 36.2g, of which saturates 19.5g; Cholesterol 358mg; Calcium 147mg; Fibre 5.4g; Sodium 389mg.

Roast Leg of Venison

The marinade for this recipe forms the base for a deliciously tangy, slightly sweet sauce which complements perfectly the richness of roasted venison. This is a great dish for the table on Christmas Day.

Serves 6–8
1 onion, chopped
1 carrot, chopped
1 celery stick, chopped
3 or 4 garlic cloves, crushed
4–6 fresh parsley sprigs
4–6 fresh thyme sprigs
2 bay leaves
15ml/1 tbsp peppercorns, crushed
750ml/1¼ pints/3 cups red wine
60ml/4 tbsp vegetable oil, plus more for brushing
1 young venison haunch, about 2.75kg/6lb, trimmed
30ml/2 tbsp plain (all-purpose) flour
250ml/8fl oz/1 cup beef stock
1 unwaxed orange
1 unwaxed lemon
60ml/4 tbsp redcurrant or raspberry jelly
60ml/4 tbsp ruby port or Madeira
15ml/1 tbsp cornflour (cornstarch), blended with 30ml/2 tbsp water
15ml/1 tbsp red wine vinegar
fresh herbs, to garnish

1 Place the onion, carrot, celery, garlic, parsley, thyme, bay leaves, peppercorns, wine and oil in a dish large enough to hold the venison, then add the venison and turn to coat. Cover the dish with clear film (plastic wrap) and leave to marinate in the refrigerator for 2–3 days, turning occasionally.

2 Preheat the oven to 180°C/350°F/Gas 4. Remove the meat from its marinade and pour the marinade into a pan. Pat the meat dry, then brush with a little oil and wrap in foil.

3 Roast the venison for 15–20 minutes per 450g/1lb for rare to medium meat. About 25 minutes before the end of the cooking time, remove the foil, sprinkle the venison with the flour and baste with the juices.

4 Add the stock to the marinade and bring to the boil. Continue to boil until reduced by half, then strain and set aside.

5 Using a vegetable peeler, remove the rind from the orange and half the lemon. Cut the pieces of rind into thin julienne strips. Bring a large pan of water to the boil and add the orange and lemon strips. Simmer them for 5 minutes, then drain and rinse under cold water.

6 Squeeze the juice of the orange into a medium pan. Add the redcurrant or raspberry jelly and cook over low heat, stirring constantly, until it has fully melted. Stir the port or Madeira into the pan, and add the reduced marinade. Simmer gently for about 10 minutes, stirring occasionally.

7 Stir the blended cornflour mixture into the marinade and cook, stirring frequently, until the sauce is slightly thickened. Add the vinegar and the orange and lemon strips and simmer for a further 2–3 minutes. Keep warm, stirring occasionally, to keep the fruit strips separated.

8 Transfer the venison to a board and allow to stand, loosely covered with foil, for 10 minutes before carving. Garnish with your chosen fresh herbs and serve with the sauce.

Osso Bucco with Risotto Milanese

Osso bucco is a luxurious stew of veal, onions and leeks in wine. It is a glorious dish, worthy of serving to guests for festive feasting.

Serves 4
50g/2oz/¼ cup butter
15ml/1 tbsp olive oil
1 large onion, chopped
1 leek, finely chopped
45ml/3 tbsp plain (all-purpose) flour
4 portions of veal shin, hind cut
600ml/1 pint/2½ cups dry white wine
salt and ground black pepper

For the risotto
25g/1oz/2 tbsp butter
1 onion, finely chopped
350g/12oz/1⅔ cups risotto rice
1 litre/1¾ pints/4 cups boiling chicken stock
2.5ml/½ tsp saffron strands
60ml/4 tbsp white wine
50g/2oz/⅔ cup Parmesan cheese, coarsely grated

For the gremolata
grated rind of 1 lemon
30ml/2 tbsp chopped fresh parsley
1 garlic clove, finely chopped

1 Heat the butter and oil in a frying pan. Add the onion and leek, and cook for 5 minutes without browning. Season the flour and dust the veal, then cook over high heat until browned.

2 Gradually stir in the wine and heat until simmering. Cover the pan and simmer for 1½ hours, stirring occasionally, until the meat is tender. Use a draining spoon to transfer the veal to a warmed dish, then boil the sauce until reduced a little.

3 Make the risotto about 30 minutes before the stew is ready. Melt the butter in a large pan and cook the onion until softened. Stir in the rice to coat all the grains in butter. Add a ladleful of stock and mix well. Add the stock a ladleful at a time, as it is absorbed by the rice.

4 Pound the saffron strands in a mortar, then stir in the wine. Pour into the risotto and cook for a final 5 minutes. Remove the pan from the heat and stir in the Parmesan.

5 Make the gremolata by mixing the lemon rind, parsley and garlic. Serve the risotto and veal, sprinkled with the gremolata.

Leg of Venison Energy 493kcal/2083kJ; Protein 84.2g; Carbohydrate 5.6g, of which sugars 3.7g; Fat 12.7g, of which saturates 4.4g; Cholesterol 193mg; Calcium 26mg; Fibre 0.1g; Sodium 223mg.
Osso Bucco Energy 901kcal/3764kJ; Protein 49.1g; Carbohydrate 92g, of which sugars 8g; Fat 25.9g, of which saturates 13.7g; Cholesterol 130mg; Calcium 248mg; Fibre 2.9g; Sodium 349mg.

Venison Stew

Once the preserve of nobility, venison is now a popular meat, lean and full of flavour. This simple yet deeply flavoured stew combines the dark, rich meat of venison with red wine, sweet redcurrant jelly and bacon. Serve it with mashed potato and green vegetables, or with all the usual Christmas trimmings.

Serves 4

1.3kg/3lb stewing venison
  (shoulder or topside), trimmed
  and cut into chunks
50g/2oz/4 tbsp butter
225g/8oz piece of streaky (fatty)
  bacon, cut into 2cm/³⁄₄in cubes
2 large onions, chopped
1 large carrot, chopped
1 large garlic clove, crushed
30ml/2 tbsp plain
  (all-purpose) flour
¹⁄₂ bottle red wine, about
  350ml/12fl oz/1 ¹⁄₂ cups
300ml/¹⁄₂ pint/1 ¹⁄₄ cups dark
  beef or venison stock
1 bay leaf
sprig of fresh thyme
200g/7oz button (white)
  mushrooms, sliced
30ml/2 tbsp redcurrant jelly
salt and ground black pepper

1 Pat dry the venison thoroughly using kitchen paper and set aside while preparing the other ingredients.

2 Melt the butter in a large, heavy pan, then cook the bacon pieces over a medium-high heat, stirring occasionally, until starting to brown.

3 Reduce the heat to medium, add the onions and carrot to the pan and cook until the vegetables are lightly browned, stirring occasionally.

4 Add the pieces of venison to the pan together with the garlic and stir into the mixture. Sprinkle on the flour and mix well until it has been absorbed by the fat in the pan.

5 Pour in the wine and sufficient dark stock to cover. Add the bay leaf, thyme, mushrooms and redcurrant jelly.

6 Cover the pan and simmer over low heat for 1¹⁄₂–2 hours until the meat is cooked. Check the seasoning before serving.

Venison with Cranberry Sauce

Venison steaks are now readily available. Lean and low in fat, they make a healthy choice for a special occasion. Served with a sauce of fresh seasonal cranberries, port and ginger, they make a dish with a wonderful combination of festive flavours.

Serves 4

1 orange
1 lemon
75g/3oz/1 cup fresh or
  frozen cranberries
5ml/1 tsp grated fresh root ginger
1 thyme sprig
5ml/1 tsp Dijon mustard
60ml/4 tbsp redcurrant jelly
150ml/¹⁄₄ pint/²⁄₃ cup ruby port
30ml/2 tbsp sunflower oil
4 venison steaks
2 shallots, finely chopped
salt and black pepper
thyme sprigs, to garnish
creamy mashed potatoes
  and broccoli, to serve

bungil Pare the rind from half the orange and half the lemon using a vegetable peeler, then cut into very fine strips. Blanch the strips in a small pan of boiling water for about 5 minutes until tender. Drain the strips and refresh under cold water.

2 Squeeze the juice from the orange and lemon and then pour into a pan. Add the cranberries, ginger, thyme sprig, mustard, redcurrant jelly and port. Cook over low heat until the jelly melts.

3 Bring the sauce to the boil, stirring occasionally, then cover the pan and reduce the heat. Cook gently, for about 15 minutes, until the cranberries are just tender.

4 Heat the oil in a heavy frying pan, add the venison steaks and cook over high heat for 2–3 minutes. Turn over the steaks and add the shallots to the pan. Cook the steaks on the other side for 2–3 minutes, depending on how you like your meat.

5 Just before the end of cooking, pour in the sauce and add the strips of rind. Leave the sauce to bubble for a few seconds to thicken slightly. Remove the thyme and adjust the seasoning.

6 Transfer the steaks to plates and spoon over the sauce. Garnish with thyme and serve with mashed potatoes and broccoli.

Venison Stew Energy 727kcal/3045kJ; Protein 83.8g; Carbohydrate 17.5g, of which sugars 14.4g; Fat 31.3g, of which saturates 13.8g; Cholesterol 226mg; Calcium 70mg; Fibre 2.9g; Sodium 985mg.
Venison with Cranberry Energy 315kcal/1328kJ; Protein 33.7g; Carbohydrate 17.8g, of which sugars 17.8g; Fat 8.9g, of which saturates 1.9g; Cholesterol 75mg; Calcium 16mg; Fibre 0.4g; Sodium 106mg.

Venison Medallions with Dumplings

Venison is lean and full of flavour. This recipe makes a spectacular festive dinner party dish – it gives the appearance of being difficult to make but is actually very easy.

Serves 4
600ml/1 pint/2½ cups
    venison stock
120ml/4fl oz/½ cup port
15ml/1 tbsp sunflower oil
4 × 175g/6oz medallions
    of venison

chopped parsley, to garnish
steamed baby vegetables, such as
    carrots, courgettes (zucchini)
    and turnips, to serve

For the dumplings
75g/3oz/⅔ cup self-raising
    (self-rising) flour
40g/1½oz beef suet (US chilled,
    grated shortening)
15ml/1 tbsp chopped fresh
    mixed herbs
5ml/1 tsp creamed horseradish
45–60ml/3–4 tbsp water

1 First make the dumplings: mix the flour, suet and herbs and make a well in the middle. Add the horseradish and water, then mix to make a soft but not sticky dough. Shape the dough into walnut-sized balls and chill in the refrigerator for up to 1 hour.

2 Place the venison stock in a large pan. Bring to the boil and simmer vigorously until the stock has reduced by half.

3 Add the port to the stock and continue boiling the mixture until reduced again by about half, then pour the reduced stock into a large, heavy frying pan.

4 Heat the stock until it is simmering and add the dumplings. Poach gently for 5–10 minutes, until risen and cooked through. Use a slotted spoon to remove the dumplings from the pan.

5 Smear the sunflower oil over a non-stick griddle, and heat until very hot. Add the venison medallions and cook for 2–3 minutes on each side.

6 Place the venison medallions on warm serving plates and pour the sauce over. Serve with the dumplings and the vegetables, garnished with parsley.

Venison Casserole

Low in fat but high in flavour, venison is an excellent choice for healthy, yet rich, casseroles that make warming winter suppers. Cranberries and orange bring a festive fruitiness to this recipe, and the addition of allspice gives the sauce a complex, spicy depth of flavour. It is delicious served with small baked potatoes and steamed green vegetables.

Serves 4
30ml/2 tbsp olive oil
1 onion, chopped
2 celery sticks, sliced
10ml/2 tsp ground allspice
15ml/1 tbsp plain
    (all-purpose) flour
675g/1½lb stewing
    venison, cubed
225g/8oz cranberries
grated rind and juice of 1 orange
900ml/1½ pints/3¾ cups beef
    or venison stock
salt and ground black pepper

1 Heat the olive oil in a flameproof casserole. Add the onion and celery and cook for 5 minutes until softened.

2 Meanwhile, mix the ground allspice with the flour and either spread the mixture out on a large plate or place in a large plastic bag. Toss the venison in the flour mixture a few pieces at a time (to prevent them from becoming soggy) until all the meat is lightly coated.

3 When the onion and celery are softened, remove from the casserole using a slotted spoon and set aside. Add the venison pieces to the casserole in batches and cook until evenly browned and sealed on all sides.

4 Add the cranberries, orange rind and juice to the casserole, pour in the beef or venison stock, and stir well.

5 Return the vegetables and all the venison to the casserole and heat until simmering, then cover tightly and reduce the heat. Simmer, stirring occasionally, for about 45 minutes, or until the meat is cooked and tender.

6 Season the venison casserole to taste with salt and ground black pepper before serving.

Venison Medallions Energy 393kcal/1651kJ; Protein 29.1g; Carbohydrate 33.4g, of which sugars 6.4g; Fat 16.3g, of which saturates 7.5g; Cholesterol 67mg; Calcium 136mg; Fibre 2.3g; Sodium 189mg.
Venison Casserole Energy 242kcal/1025kJ; Protein 38.3g; Carbohydrate 10.4g, of which sugars 7.2g; Fat 6.6g, of which saturates 1.8g; Cholesterol 84mg; Calcium 27mg; Fibre 1.4g; Sodium 105mg.

Classic Mixed Mushroom Risotto

A classic risotto of mixed mushrooms, herbs and fresh Parmesan cheese, this is best simply served with a mixed leaf salad tossed in a light vinaigrette dressing. It can be a delicious festive main course for a dinner party or serve as a tasty appetizer for your guests.

Serves 4
15ml/1 tbsp olive oil
4 shallots, finely chopped
2 garlic cloves, crushed

10g/¼oz dried porcini mushrooms, soaked in 150ml/¼ pint/⅔ cup hot water for 20 minutes
450g/1lb mixed mushrooms, such as brown cap (cremini) and field (portabello) mushrooms, sliced
250g/9oz/1¼ cups long grain rice
900ml/1½ pints/3¾ cups hot, well-flavoured vegetable stock
30–45ml/2–3 tbsp chopped fresh flat leaf parsley
50g/2oz/⅔ cup freshly grated Parmesan cheese
salt and ground black pepper

1 Heat the oil in a large pan, then add the shallots and garlic and cook gently for 5 minutes, stirring constantly.

2 Drain the porcini, reserving their liquid, and chop roughly. Add all the mushrooms to the pan with the porcini soaking liquid, the rice and 300ml/½ pint/1¼ cups of the stock.

3 Bring the mixture to the boil, then reduce the heat and simmer uncovered, stirring almost constantly, until all the liquid has been absorbed by the rice.

4 Add a ladleful of the hot stock and stir the risotto frequently until all the stock has again been absorbed by the rice.

5 Continue cooking and adding the hot stock, a ladleful at a time, stirring frequently, until the rice is cooked and creamy but al dente. This should take about 35 minutes and it may not be necessary to add all the stock.

6 Season to taste with salt and black pepper, then stir in the chopped fresh parsley and grated Parmesan cheese and serve immediately. Alternatively, sprinkle the Parmesan over the risotto just before serving.

Vegetable Couscous

A North African favourite that is perfect for a festive buffet table, this spicy dish makes an excellent low-fat meal for vegetarians.

Serves 4
15ml/1 tbsp olive oil
1 onion, chopped
2 garlic cloves, crushed
5ml/1 tsp ground cumin
5ml/1 tsp paprika
400g/14oz can chopped tomatoes
300ml/½ pint/1¼ cups vegetable stock
1 cinnamon stick

generous pinch of saffron threads
4 baby aubergines (eggplants), quartered
8 baby courgettes (zucchini), trimmed
8 baby carrots
225g/8oz/1⅓ cups couscous
425g/15oz can chickpeas, rinsed and drained
175g/6oz/¾ cup pitted prunes
45ml/3 tbsp chopped fresh parsley
45ml/3 tbsp chopped fresh coriander (cilantro)
10–15ml/2–3 tsp harissa
salt

1 Heat the oil in a large non-stick pan. Add the onion and garlic and cook gently for 5 minutes, or until soft. Add the cumin and paprika and cook, stirring, for 1 minute.

2 Add the tomatoes, stock, cinnamon stick, saffron threads, aubergines, courgettes and carrots. Season with salt. Bring to the boil, then reduce the heat, cover and cook for 20 minutes until the vegetables are just tender.

3 Line a steamer, metal sieve (strainer) or colander with a double thickness of muslin (cheesecloth) and set aside. Soak the couscous according to the instructions on the packet. Add the chickpeas and prunes to the vegetables and cook for 5 minutes. Fork the couscous to break up any lumps and spread it in the prepared steamer. Place on top of the vegetables, cover, and cook for 5 minutes, or until hot.

4 Stir the chopped parsley and coriander into the vegetables. Heap the couscous on to a warmed serving plate. Using a slotted spoon, arrange the vegetables on top. Spoon over a little sauce and toss gently to combine. Stir the harissa into the remaining sauce and serve separately.

Mushroom Risotto Energy 328kcal/1386kJ; Protein 11.7g; Carbohydrate 52.8g, of which sugars 2.1g; Fat 9.3g, of which saturates 3.5g; Cholesterol 13mg; Calcium 189mg; Fibre 3.2g; Sodium 148mg.
Vegetable Couscous Energy 397kcal/1671kJ; Protein 14.8g; Carbohydrate 71.5g, of which sugars 26g; Fat 7.6g, of which saturates 1g; Cholesterol 0mg; Calcium 137mg; Fibre 12g; Sodium 253mg.

Red Pepper Risotto

This delicious Italian risotto creates a flavourful and low-fat supper or lunch dish, ideal served with a mixed leaf salad and fresh Italian bread for an informal Christmas gathering.

Serves 4
3 large red (bell) peppers
10ml/2 tsp olive oil
3 large garlic cloves, thinly sliced
400g/14oz can chopped tomatoes
225g/8oz can chopped tomatoes
2 bay leaves
1.2–1.5 litres/2–2½ pints/5–6¼
    cups vegetable stock
450g/1lb/2¼ cups arborio rice or
    long grain brown rice
6 fresh basil leaves,
    finely shredded
salt and ground black pepper

1 Preheat the grill (broiler) to high. Place the red peppers in a grill pan and grill (broil) until the skins have blackened in places and blistered all over.

2 Transfer the peppers to a bowl, cover with a damp dish towel and leave for 10 minutes. Peel off and discard the skins, then slice the peppers, discarding the cores and seeds. Set aside.

3 Heat the oil in a large, non-stick pan. Add the garlic and tomatoes and cook gently, stirring occasionally, for about 5 minutes, then add the prepared pepper slices and the bay leaves. Stir well, then cook gently over low heat, stirring occasionally, for 15 minutes.

4 Pour the vegetable stock into a separate large, heavy pan and heat it to simmering point. Stir the rice into the vegetable mixture and cook for about 2 minutes, then add two or three ladlefuls of the hot stock. Cook, stirring occasionally, until all the stock has been absorbed into the rice.

5 Continue to add stock, making sure each addition has been absorbed before adding the next. When the rice is tender, season to taste with salt and pepper.

6 Remove the pan from the heat, cover and leave to stand for 10 minutes. Remove and discard the bay leaves, then stir in the shredded basil. Serve immediately.

Spicy Chickpea Stew

This is a popular spicy dish. It makes the most of the wonderful combination of vegetables, tomatoes and exotic spices.

Serves 4
3 large aubergines (eggplants),
    cut into cubes
200g/7oz/1 cup chickpeas,
    soaked for 8 hours or overnight
60ml/4 tbsp olive oil
3 garlic cloves, chopped
2 large onions, chopped
2.5ml/½ tsp ground cumin
2.5ml/½ tsp ground cinnamon
2.5ml/½ tsp ground coriander
3 × 400g/14oz cans chopped
    tomatoes
200g/7oz fresh tomatoes,
    chopped
salt and ground black pepper
cooked rice, to serve

For the garnish
30ml/2 tbsp olive oil
1 onion, sliced
1 garlic clove, sliced
fresh coriander (cilantro) sprigs

1 Place the aubergines in a colander and sprinkle with salt. Leave for 30 minutes, to allow any bitter juices to escape. Rinse with cold water and dry on kitchen paper. Drain the chickpeas and put in a pan with enough water to cover. Bring to the boil and simmer for about 1 hour, or until tender. Drain.

2 Heat the oil in a large pan. Add the garlic and onions and cook gently, until soft. Add the spices and cook, stirring, for a few seconds. Stir in the aubergines and stir to coat with the spices and onions. Cook for 5 minutes. Add the tomatoes and chickpeas and season. Cover and simmer for 20 minutes.

3 To make the garnish, heat the oil in a frying pan and, when very hot, add the sliced onion and garlic. Cook until golden and crisp. Serve the stew with rice, topped with the onion and garlic, and garnished with coriander.

> **Cook's Tip**
> If you are in a hurry during the festivities, substitute two cans of chickpeas for the dried variety. Rinse and drain before adding to the tomato mixture, and cook for about 15 minutes.

Red Pepper Risotto Energy 490kcal/2052kJ; Protein 10.9g; Carbohydrate 103.8g, of which sugars 13.6g; Fat 3.1g, of which saturates 0.5g; Cholesterol 0mg; Calcium 44mg; Fibre 3.9g; Sodium 20mg.
Spicy Stew Energy 334kcal/1410kJ; Protein 16.9g; Carbohydrate 48.7g, of which sugars 21.1g; Fat 9.5g, of which saturates 1.2g; Cholesterol 0mg; Calcium 169mg; Fibre 12.9g; Sodium 144mg.

Lentil Frittata

Throughout the Mediterranean a variety of thick, vegetable omelettes are cooked. This tasty supper dish combines green lentils, red onions, broccoli and cherry tomatoes. Serve as a tasty brunch for the whole family on a chilly Christmas morning.

Serves 6

75g/3oz/scant ½ cup
   green lentils
225g/8oz small broccoli florets
2 red onions, halved and
   thickly sliced
15ml/1 tbsp olive oil
8 eggs
45ml/3 tbsp water
45ml/3 tbsp chopped fresh mixed
   herbs, such as oregano, parsley,
   tarragon and chives, plus extra
   sprigs to garnish
175g/6oz cherry tomatoes,
   cut in half
salt and ground black pepper

1 Place the lentils in a pan, cover with cold water and bring to the boil, then reduce the heat and simmer for 25 minutes until tender. Add the broccoli, return to the boil and cook for 1 minute.

2 Meanwhile, place the onion slices and olive oil in a shallow earthenware dish or cazuela about 23–25cm/9–10in in diameter, and place in a cold oven. Set the oven to 200°C/400°F/Gas 6 and cook for 25 minutes.

3 In a bowl, whisk together the eggs, water, a pinch of salt and plenty of black pepper. Stir in the chopped herbs and set aside.

4 Drain the lentils and broccoli and stir into the onions. Add the cherry tomatoes and sir gently to combine.

5 Pour the egg mixture evenly over the vegetables. Reduce the oven temperature to 190°C/375°F/Gas 5. Return the dish to the oven and cook for 10 minutes, then push the mixture from the sides into the centre of the dish using a spatula, allowing the raw egg mixture in the centre to flow to the edges.

6 Return the dish to the oven and cook the frittata for a further 15 minutes, or until it is just set. Garnish with sprigs of fresh herbs and serve warm, cut into thick wedges.

Tomato and Vegetable Hot-pot

Here's a one-dish Mediterranean meal that's suitable for feeding large numbers of people for a festive feast. It's low in fat, lightly spiced and has plenty of garlic.

Serves 4

30ml/2 tbsp extra virgin olive oil
   or sunflower oil
1 large onion, chopped
2 small–medium aubergines
   (eggplants), cut into small cubes
4 courgettes (zucchini), cut into
   small chunks
2 red, yellow or green (bell)
   peppers, seeded and chopped
115g/4oz/1 cup frozen peas
115g/4oz green beans
200g/7oz can flageolet or
   small cannellini beans, rinsed
   and drained
450g/1lb new or salad potatoes,
   peeled and cubed
2.5ml/½ tsp ground cinnamon
2.5ml/½ tsp ground cumin
5ml/1 tsp paprika
4–5 tomatoes, skinned
400g/14oz can chopped tomatoes
30ml/2 tbsp chopped fresh parsley
3–4 garlic cloves, crushed
350ml/12fl oz/1½ cups stock
salt and ground black pepper
black olives, to garnish
fresh parsley, to garnish

1 Preheat the oven to 190°C/375°F/Gas 5. Heat about 15ml/1 tbsp of the oil in a heavy non-stick pan, and sauté the onion until golden and softened.

2 Add the aubergines, sauté for 3 minutes, then add the courgettes, peppers, peas, beans and potatoes, and stir in the spices and seasoning. Cook, stirring constantly, for 3 minutes.

3 Cut the fresh tomatoes in half and scoop out and discard the seeds. Chop the tomatoes finely and place them in a bowl. Stir in the canned tomatoes with the chopped parsley, garlic and the remaining olive oil. Spoon the aubergine mixture into a shallow ovenproof dish and level the surface.

4 Pour the stock over the aubergine mixture and then spoon the prepared tomato mixture over the top.

5 Cover the dish with foil and bake in the preheated oven for 30–45 minutes, or until the vegetables are tender. Serve hot, garnished with black olives and parsley.

Lentil Frittata Energy 182kcal/761kJ; Protein 14.2g; Carbohydrate 14.1g, of which sugars 5.7g; Fat 8.2g, of which saturates 2.2g; Cholesterol 254mg; Calcium 99mg; Fibre 3.2g; Sodium 108mg.
Tomato Hot-pot Energy 320kcal/1346kJ; Protein 13.4g; Carbohydrate 50.3g, of which sugars 22.8g; Fat 8.7g, of which saturates 1.6g; Cholesterol 0mg; Calcium 105mg; Fibre 13.2g; Sodium 251mg.

Provençal Stuffed Peppers

This colourful Mediterranean recipe makes a tasty low-fat dish for vegetarian guests.

Serves 4

10ml/1 tsp olive oil
1 red onion, sliced
1 courgette (zucchini), diced
115g/4oz mushrooms, sliced
1 garlic clove, crushed
400g/14oz can chopped tomatoes
15ml/1 tbsp tomato purée (paste)
40g/1½oz/scant ⅓ cup pine nuts
30ml/2 tbsp chopped fresh basil
4 (bell) peppers, halved
  and seeded
50g/2oz/½ cup finely grated
  fresh Parmesan or half-fat Red
  Leicester cheese
salt and ground black pepper
fresh basil leaves, to garnish

1 Preheat the oven to 180°C/350°F/Gas 4. Heat the oil and add the onion, courgette, mushrooms and garlic. Cook gently, stirring occasionally, for 3 minutes.

2 Stir in the tomatoes and tomato purée, bring to the boil and simmer for 10–15 minutes, or until thickened. Remove from the heat and stir in the pine nuts, chopped basil and seasoning.

3 Blanch the peppers for 3 minutes. Drain. Place them, cut side up, in an ovenproof dish and fill with the vegetable mixture. Cover with foil and bake for 20 minutes. Remove the foil, sprinkle with a little grated cheese and bake for 5–10 minutes, or until the cheese is melted. Garnish with basil and serve.

Roasted Squash

Gem squash has a sweet, subtle flavour that is a perfect partner for the olives and sun-dried tomatoes in this recipe. The rice adds enough substance to make this dish suitable for serving as a festive main course, and it's sure to please all your guests, whether they are vegetarian or not.

Serves 2

4 whole gem squashes
225g/8oz/2 cups cooked white
  long grain rice
75g/3oz/1½ cups sun-dried
  tomatoes, chopped
40g/1½ oz/⅓ cup pitted black
  olives, chopped
50g/2oz/¼ cup soft goat's cheese
10ml/2 tsp olive oil
15ml/1 tbsp chopped fresh basil
  leaves, plus basil sprigs, to serve
green salad, to serve

1 Preheat the oven to 180°C/350°F/Gas 4. Trim away the base of each squash, slice off the top and scoop out and discard the seeds from inside.

2 Mix together the rice, tomatoes, olives, goat's cheese, olive oil and chopped basil in a large bowl.

3 Divide the rice mixture evenly between the squashes and place them in a shallow non-stick baking tin (pan) or ovenproof dish, just large enough to hold the squashes side by side.

4 Cover with foil and bake in the oven for 45–50 minutes, or until the squashes are tender when pierced with a skewer. Garnish with basil sprigs and serve with a green salad.

Onions Stuffed with Goat's Cheese

Roasted onions and tangy cheese are a winning combination. These stuffed onions make an excellent main course when served with a rice or cracked wheat pilaff.

Serves 4

4 large onions
150g/5oz goat's cheese, crumbled
  or cut into cubes
50g/2oz/1 cup fresh breadcrumbs
8 sun-dried tomatoes in olive oil,
  drained and chopped
1–2 garlic cloves, finely chopped
2.5ml/½ tsp chopped
  fresh thyme
30ml/2 tbsp chopped fresh parsley
1 small (US medium) egg, beaten
45ml/3 tbsp pine nuts, toasted
30ml/2 tbsp olive oil (use oil from
  the tomatoes)
salt and ground black pepper

1 Bring a large pan of lightly salted water to the boil. Add the whole onions in their skins and boil for 10 minutes. Drain and cool, then cut each onion in half horizontally and peel.

2 Using a teaspoon, remove the centre of each onion, leaving a thick shell. Reserve the flesh and place the shells in an oiled ovenproof dish. Preheat the oven to 190°C/375°F/Gas 5.

3 Chop the scooped-out onion flesh and place in a bowl. Add the goat's cheese, breadcrumbs, sun-dried tomatoes, garlic, thyme, parsley and egg. Mix well, then season with salt and pepper and add the toasted pine nuts.

4 Divide the stuffing among the onions and cover with foil. Bake for about 25 minutes. Uncover, drizzle with the oil and cook for another 30–40 minutes, until bubbling and well cooked. Baste occasionally during cooking.

> **Variation**
> If you prefer, you can substitute 175g/6oz Roquefort or Stilton for the goat's cheese, omit the sun-dried tomatoes and pine nuts, and add 75g/3oz chopped walnuts and 115g/4oz chopped celery, cooked until soft with the chopped onion in 25ml/1½ tbsp olive oil.

Stuffed Peppers Energy 223kcal/930kJ; Protein 10.4g; Carbohydrate 16.9g, of which sugars 15.9g; Fat 13.1g, of which saturates 3.5g, Cholesterol 13mg; Calcium 190mg; Fibre 5g; Sodium 155mg.
Roasted Squash Energy 419kcal/1766kJ; Protein 15.7g; Carbohydrate 58.2g, of which sugars 18.4g; Fat 15g, of which saturates 6.6g, Cholesterol 23mg; Calcium 359mg; Fibre 11.1g; Sodium 605mg.
Onions with Goat's Cheese Energy 430kcal/1785kJ; Protein 15.9g; Carbohydrate 31g, of which sugars 15.8g; Fat 27.9g, of which saturates 8.8g; Cholesterol 82mg; Calcium 153mg; Fibre 4.5g; Sodium 350mg.

Baked Polenta with Tomato Sauce

Polenta, or cornmeal, is a tasty and healthy choice for festive entertaining. It is cooked like a sort of porridge, and eaten soft, or set, cut into shapes then baked or grilled.

Serves 4
5ml/1 tsp salt
250g/9oz/2¼ cups quick cook polenta
5ml/1 tsp paprika
2.5ml/½ tsp freshly grated nutmeg
10ml/2 tsp olive oil
1 large onion, finely chopped
2 garlic cloves, crushed
2 × 400g/14oz cans chopped tomatoes
15ml/1 tbsp tomato purée (paste)
5ml/1 tsp sugar
salt and ground black pepper

1 Lightly grease an ovenproof dish and set aside. Line a 28 x 18cm/11 x 7in baking tin (pan) with clear film (plastic wrap). In a large, heavy pan, bring 1 litre/1¾ pints/4 cups water to the boil with the salt.

2 Pour in the polenta in a steady stream and cook, stirring constantly, for 5 minutes.

3 Beat the paprika and nutmeg into the polenta, then pour the mixture into the prepared baking tin and smooth the surface with a knife. Leave to cool.

4 Heat the oil in a non-stick pan and cook the onion and garlic until soft. Add the tomatoes, tomato purée and sugar. Season with salt and pepper. Bring to the boil, then reduce the heat and simmer for 20 minutes.

5 Meanwhile, preheat the oven to 200°C/400°F/Gas 6. Turn out the cooled polenta on to a clean chopping board, and cut into 5cm/2in squares.

6 Place half the polenta squares in the prepared dish. Spoon over half the tomato sauce, and sprinkle with half the cheese. Repeat the layers. Bake in the oven for about 25 minutes, or until golden. Serve immediately.

Festive Lentil and Nut Roast

An excellent celebration mould which can be served with all the trimmings, including vegetarian gravy. Garnish it with fresh cranberries and parsley for a really festive effect.

Serves 6–8
115g/4oz/½ cup red lentils
115g/4oz/1 cup hazelnuts
115g/4oz/1 cup walnuts
1 large carrot
2 celery sticks
1 large onion
115g/4oz mushrooms
50g/2oz/4 tbsp butter
10ml/2 tsp mild curry powder
30ml/2 tbsp tomato ketchup
30ml/2 tbsp vegetarian Worcestershire sauce
1 egg, beaten
10ml/2 tsp salt
60ml/4 tbsp fresh flat leaf parsley, chopped
150ml/¼ pint/⅔ cup water

1 Soak the lentils for 1 hour in cold water, then drain well. Grind the nuts in a food processor until quite fine but not too smooth. Set the nuts aside.

2 Chop the carrot, celery, onion and mushrooms into small chunks, then process them in a food processor or blender until they are quite finely chopped.

3 Fry the vegetables gently in the butter for 5 minutes, then stir in the curry powder and cook for a minute. Cool.

4 Mix the soaked lentils with the nuts, vegetables, ketchup, Worcestershire sauce, egg, salt, parsley and water.

5 Grease and line the base and sides of a long 1kg/2lb loaf tin (pan) with baking parchment or a sheet of foil. Press the mixture into the tin. Preheat the oven to 190°C/375°F/Gas 5.

6 Bake in the preheated oven for about 1–1¼ hours until just firm, covering the top with baking parchment or foil if it starts to brown too quickly.

7 Allow the roast to stand for about 15 minutes before you turn it out and peel off the paper or foil. It will be fairly soft when cut as it is a moist loaf.

Baked Polenta Energy 380kcal/1590kJ; Protein 15.2g; Carbohydrate 55.8g, of which sugars 9.5g; Fat 10.4g, of which saturates 4.3g; Cholesterol 19mg; Calcium 250mg; Fibre 3.9g; Sodium 724mg.
Nut Roast Energy 386kcal/1604kJ; Protein 11.7g; Carbohydrate 23.1g, of which sugars 5.4g; Fat 28.1g, of which saturates 6.4g; Cholesterol 44mg; Calcium 205mg; Fibre 3.2g; Sodium 281mg.

Spicy Potato Strudel

Wrap up a tasty mixture of vegetables in a spicy, creamy sauce with crisp filo pastry for a festive centrepiece. Serve with a good selection of chutneys or a yogurt sauce, or as a side dish with the Christmas Day meal.

Serves 4
1 onion, chopped
2 carrots, coarsely grated
1 courgette (zucchini), chopped

350g/12oz firm potatoes, diced
65g/2½ oz/5 tbsp butter
10ml/2 tsp mild curry paste
2.5ml/½ tsp dried thyme
150ml/¼ pint/⅔ cup water
1 egg, beaten
30ml/2 tbsp single (light) cream
50g/2oz/½ cup grated
   Cheddar cheese
8 sheets filo pastry, thawed
   if frozen
sesame seeds, for sprinkling
salt and ground black pepper

1 In a large frying pan, cook the onion, carrots, courgette and potatoes in 25g/1oz/2 tbsp of the butter for 5 minutes, tossing frequently so they cook evenly. Add the curry paste and stir in. Continue to cook the vegetables for a further minute or so.

2 Add the thyme and water to the pan, and season with salt and pepper. Bring to the boil, then reduce the heat and simmer for 10 minutes, until tender, stirring occasionally.

3 Remove from the heat and leave to cool. Transfer the mixture into a large bowl and then mix in the egg, cream and cheese. Chill until ready to fill the filo pastry.

4 Melt the remaining butter in a pan and lay out four sheets of filo pastry on a chopping board, slightly overlapping them to form a fairly large rectangle. Brush with some melted butter and fit the other sheets on top. Brush again.

5 Preheat the oven to 190°C/375°F/Gas 5. Spoon the filling along one long side, then roll up the pastry. Form it into a circle and set on a baking sheet. Brush again with the last of the butter and sprinkle over the sesame seeds.

6 Bake the strudel in the oven for about 25 minutes until golden and crisp. Stand for 5 minutes before cutting.

Mushroom, Nut and Prune Jalousie

The pie has a rich, nutty filling and, served with crisp roast potatoes and steamed vegetables, makes a great alternative to a festive roast.

Serves 6
75g/3oz/⅓ cup green lentils, rinsed
5ml/1 tsp vegetable
   bouillon powder
15ml/1 tbsp sunflower oil
2 large leeks, sliced
2 garlic cloves, chopped

200g/7oz/3 cups field (portabello)
   mushrooms, finely chopped
10ml/2 tsp dried mixed herbs
75g/3oz/¾ cup chopped
   mixed nuts
15ml/1 tbsp pine nuts (optional)
75g/3oz/⅓ cup pitted prunes
25g/1oz/½ cup fresh breadcrumbs
2 eggs, beaten
2 sheets ready-rolled puff pastry,
   total weight about 425g/15oz
flour, for dusting
salt and ground black pepper

1 Put the lentils in a pan and cover with water. Bring to the boil, then reduce the heat and add the bouillon powder. Partly cover and simmer for 20 minutes until the lentils are tender. Set aside.

2 Heat the oil in a frying pan, and cook the leeks and garlic for 5 minutes or until softened. Add the mushrooms and herbs and cook for 5 minutes. Transfer the mixture to a bowl. Stir in the nuts, pine nuts, if using, prunes, breadcrumbs and lentils.

3 Preheat the oven to 220°C/425°F/Gas 7. Add two-thirds of the beaten egg to the mixture and season. Set aside to cool.

4 Meanwhile, unroll one of the pastry sheets. Cut off 2.5cm/1in from its width and length, then lay it on a dampened baking sheet. Unroll the second pastry sheet, dust with flour, then fold in half lengthways. Make a series of cuts across the fold, 1cm/½in apart, leaving a 2.5cm/1in border around the edge of the pastry.

5 Spoon the filling over the pastry base, leaving a 2.5cm/1in border. Dampen the edges with water. Open out the folded piece and carefully lay it over the top. Trim the edges, then press the edges of the pastry together to seal and crimp.

6 Brush the top of the pastry with the remaining beaten egg and bake for 25–30 minutes until golden. Serve hot.

Potato Strudel Energy 362kcal/1512kJ; Protein 9.8g; Carbohydrate 34.8g, of which sugars 6.5g; Fat 21.1g, of which saturates 12.7g; Cholesterol 98mg; Calcium 169mg; Fibre 3g; Sodium 227mg.
Mushroom Jalousie Energy 480kcal/2004kJ; Protein 13.5g; Carbohydrate 42.3g, of which sugars 7.3g; Fat 30.5g, of which saturates 1.6g; Cholesterol 63mg; Calcium 99mg; Fibre 4.2g; Sodium 281mg.

Red Onion Tart

Red onions are wonderfully mild and sweet when cooked and they go well with fontina cheese and thyme in this wintery tart.

Serves 5–6
60ml/4 tbsp olive oil
1kg/2¼lb red onions, thinly sliced
2–3 garlic cloves, thinly sliced
5ml/1 tsp chopped fresh thyme, plus a few whole sprigs
5ml/1 tsp soft dark brown sugar

10ml/2 tsp sherry vinegar
225g/8oz fontina cheese, sliced
salt and ground black pepper

For the pastry
115g/4oz/1 cup plain (all-purpose) flour
75g/3oz/¾ cup fine yellow cornmeal
5ml/1 tsp soft dark brown sugar
5ml/1 tsp chopped fresh thyme
90g/3½oz/7 tbsp butter
1 egg yolk

1 For the pastry, sift the flour and cornmeal into a bowl with 5ml/1 tsp salt. Add black pepper and stir in the sugar and thyme. Rub in the butter until it looks like breadcrumbs. Beat the egg yolk with 30ml/2 tbsp iced water and use to bind the pastry. Gather the dough into a ball, wrap and chill for 40 minutes.

2 Heat 45ml/3 tbsp of the oil in a large, deep frying pan and add the onions. Cover and cook slowly, stirring occasionally, for 20–30 minutes. They should collapse but not brown.

3 Add the garlic and thyme, then cook for another 10 minutes. Increase the heat slightly, then add the sugar and sherry vinegar. Cook, uncovered, for 5–6 minutes, until the onions start to caramelize slightly. Season to taste with salt and pepper. Cool.

4 Preheat the oven to 190°C/375°F/Gas 5. Roll out the pastry thinly and use to line a 25cm/10in loose-based metal flan tin (quiche pan). Prick the pastry all over with a fork and support the sides with foil. Bake for 12–15 minutes, until lightly coloured.

5 Remove the foil and spread the onions evenly over the base of the pastry. Add the fontina and pepper. Drizzle over the remaining oil, then bake for 15–20 minutes, until the filling is piping hot and the cheese is beginning to bubble. Garnish the tart with thyme and serve immediately.

Vegetable Tarte Tatin

This is a vegetable version of the classic upside-down pie, combining rice, garlic, onions and olives.

Serves 6
30ml/2 tbsp sunflower oil
25ml/1½ tbsp olive oil
1 aubergine (eggplant), sliced lengthways
1 large red (bell) pepper, seeded and cut into long strips

10 tomatoes
2 red shallots, finely chopped
1–2 garlic cloves, crushed
150ml/¼ pint/⅔ cup white wine
10ml/2 tsp chopped fresh basil
225g/8oz/2 cups cooked brown long grain rice
40g/1½oz/⅓ cup pitted black olives, chopped
350g/12oz vegan puff pastry
ground black pepper
salad leaves, to serve

1 Preheat the oven to 190°C/375°F/Gas 5. Heat the sunflower oil with 15ml/1 tbsp of the olive oil in a frying pan and fry the aubergine slices, in batches if necessary, for 4–5 minutes on each side until golden brown. As each aubergine slice softens and browns, lift it out and drain on several sheets of kitchen paper to remove as much oil as possible.

2 Add the pepper strips to the oil remaining in the pan, turning them to coat. Cover the pan with a lid or foil and sweat the peppers over a medium-high heat for 5–6 minutes, stirring occasionally, until the pepper strips are soft and flecked with brown. Slice two of the tomatoes and set aside.

3 Plunge the remaining tomatoes into boiling water for 30 seconds, then drain. Peel off the skins, cut them into quarters and remove the core and seeds. Chop them roughly.

4 Heat the remaining oil in the frying pan and fry the shallots and garlic for 3–4 minutes until softened. Add the chopped tomatoes and cook for a few minutes until softened.

5 Stir in the white wine and fresh basil, with black pepper to taste. Bring the mixture to the boil, then remove from the heat and stir in the cooked rice and pitted black olives, making sure they are well distributed.

6 Arrange the tomato slices, cooked aubergine slices and peppers in a single layer over the base of a heavy, 30cm/12in shallow ovenproof dish. Spread the rice mixture on top.

7 Roll out the puff pastry to a circle slightly larger than the diameter of the dish and place it on top of the rice. Tuck the edges of the pastry circle down inside the dish.

8 Bake the tatin for 25–30 minutes, or until the pastry is golden and risen. Leave to cool slightly, then invert the tart on to a large, warmed serving plate. Serve in slices, accompanied by a leafy green salad or simply dressed lamb's lettuce or mâche.

> **Cook's Tip**
> *This tart would make a lovely festive lunch or supper dish. Serve it hot with roast potatoes and a fresh green vegetable, such as broccoli, Brussels sprouts or green beans.*

Red Onion Tart Energy 621kcal/2581kJ; Protein 18.1g; Carbohydrate 45.6g, of which sugars 12.5g; Fat 40.6g, of which saturates 20.7g; Cholesterol 122mg; Calcium 424mg; Fibre 3.8g; Sodium 443mg.
Tarte Tatin Energy 535kcal/2241kJ; Protein 8.2g; Carbohydrate 59.1g, of which sugars 8.8g; Fat 29.5g, of which saturates 1.2g; Cholesterol 0mg; Calcium 89mg; Fibre 2.6g; Sodium 521mg.

Spinach and Goat's Cheese Roulade

This vegetarian soufflé roll is rich and flavoursome. It is delicious either served alone, with a side salad or with seasonal vegetables.

Serves 4
300ml/½ pint/1¼ cups milk
50g/2oz/½ cup plain
   (all-purpose) flour
150g/5oz/⅔ cup butter
100g/3¾oz goat's cheese, chopped
40g/1½oz/½ cup freshly grated
   Parmesan cheese, plus extra
   for dusting
4 eggs, separated
250g/9oz/2¼ cups fresh shiitake
   mushrooms, sliced
275g/10oz baby spinach leaves
45ml/3 tbsp crème fraîche
salt and ground black pepper

1 Preheat the oven to 190°C/375°F/Gas 5. Line a 30 × 20cm/12 × 8in Swiss roll tin (jelly roll pan) with baking parchment. Grease the parchment lightly.

2 Put the milk, flour and 50g/2oz/¼ cup of the butter in a large pan. Bring to the boil, whisking until thick and creamy. Lower the heat and simmer for 2 minutes. Mix in the goat's cheese and half the Parmesan. Cool slightly, then beat in the egg yolks. Season.

3 Whisk the egg whites in a grease-free bowl until soft peaks form. Carefully fold the whites into the cheese mixture, using a large metal spoon. Spoon the mixture into the prepared tin, spread gently to level, then bake for about 15 minutes, until the top feels just firm. Leave to cool slightly.

4 Dust a sheet of baking parchment with a little Parmesan and invert the roulade on top. Remove the lining paper from the roulade. Roll up in the baking parchment and cool completely.

5 For the filling, melt the rest of the butter in a pan, reserving 30ml/2 tbsp. Add the mushrooms and stir-fry for 3 minutes. In a separate pan, cook the spinach until it wilts. Drain, add to the mushrooms and stir in the crème fraîche. Season, then cool.

6 Unroll the roulade and spread over the filling. Roll it up, brush with the butter and sprinkle with the remaining Parmesan. Bake for 15 minutes, until risen and golden. Serve immediately.

Herb Crêpes with Tomato Sauce

Turn light herb crêpes into something special for a festive feast.

Serves 4
25g/1oz/1 cup chopped fresh herbs
15ml/1 tbsp sunflower oil, plus
   extra for frying and greasing
120ml/4fl oz/½ cup milk
3 eggs
25g/1oz/¼ cup plain
   (all-purpose) flour
pinch of salt

For the sauce
30ml/2 tbsp olive oil

1 small onion, chopped
2 garlic cloves, crushed
400g/14oz can chopped tomatoes
pinch of soft light brown sugar

For the filling
450g/1lb fresh spinach, cooked
   and drained
175g/6oz/¾ cup ricotta cheese
25g/1oz/¼ cup pine nuts, toasted
5 sun-dried tomato halves in olive
   oil, drained and chopped
30ml/2 tbsp shredded fresh basil
4 egg whites
salt, freshly grated nutmeg and
   ground black pepper

1 To make the crêpes, place the herbs and oil in a food processor and process until smooth. Add the milk, eggs, flour and salt and process again until smooth. Leave for 30 minutes.

2 Heat a small non-stick frying pan and add a very small amount of oil. Add a ladleful of the batter. Swirl around until the batter covers the base evenly. Cook for 2 minutes, turn over and cook for a further 1–2 minutes. Make seven more crêpes.

3 To make the sauce, heat the oil in a small pan, add the onion and garlic, and cook for 5 minutes. Stir in the tomatoes and sugar, and cook for 10 minutes. Process in a blender, then strain.

4 For the filling, put the spinach in a bowl with the ricotta, pine nuts, tomatoes and basil. Season with salt, nutmeg and pepper. Whisk the egg whites until they form stiff peaks. Stir one-third into the spinach mixture, then gently fold in the rest.

5 Preheat the oven to 190°C/375°F/Gas 5. Place one crêpe at a time on a lightly oiled baking sheet, add a spoonful of filling and fold into quarters. Bake for 12 minutes until set. Serve immediately with the tomato sauce.

Spinach Roulade Energy 625kcal/2589kJ; Protein 22.7g; Carbohydrate 15.3g, of which sugars 5.6g; Fat 52.9g, of which saturates 31.7g; Cholesterol 321mg; Calcium 423mg; Fibre 2.5g; Sodium 691mg.
Herb Crêpes Energy 409kcal/1698kJ; Protein 18.4g; Carbohydrate 12.9g, of which sugars 7.4g; Fat 32g, of which saturates 11.6g; Cholesterol 184mg; Calcium 333mg; Fibre 3.6g; Sodium 471mg.

Goat's Cheese and Garlic Soufflé

The mellow flavour of roasted garlic pervades this simple soufflé. Balance the rich soufflé with a crisp green salad, including peppery leaves, such as mizuna and watercress. It can also be served as a sophisticated appetizer for a festive dinner party.

Serves 3–4
2 large heads of garlic (choose heads with plump cloves)
3 fresh thyme sprigs
15ml/1 tbsp olive oil
250ml/8fl oz/1 cup milk
1 fresh bay leaf
2 × 1cm/½ in thick onion slices
2 cloves
50g/2oz/¼ cup butter
40g/1½oz/⅓ cup plain (all-purpose) flour, sifted
3 eggs, separated, plus 1 egg white
150g/5oz goat's cheese, crumbled
50g/2oz/⅔ cup freshly grated Parmesan cheese
5ml/1 tsp chopped fresh thyme
2.5ml/½ tsp cream of tartar
salt and ground black pepper
cayenne pepper

1 Preheat the oven to 180°C/350°F/Gas 4. Place the garlic and thyme sprigs on a piece of foil. Sprinkle with the oil and close the foil around the garlic, then bake for about 1 hour, until the garlic is soft. Leave to cool.

2 Squeeze the cooked garlic out of its skin into a bowl. Discard the thyme sprigs and the garlic skins, then purée the garlic flesh with the olive oil.

3 Meanwhile, put the milk, bay leaf, onion slices and cloves in a small pan. Bring to the boil, then remove from the heat. Cover and leave to infuse (steep) for 30 minutes.

4 Melt 40g/1½oz/3 tbsp of the butter in another pan. Stir in the flour and cook gently for 2 minutes, stirring. Reheat and strain the milk, then gradually stir it into the flour and butter.

5 Cook the sauce very gently for 10 minutes, stirring frequently. Season with salt, pepper and a pinch of cayenne. Cool slightly. Preheat the oven to 200°C/400°F/Gas 6.

6 Beat in the egg yolks one at a time. Then beat in the goat's cheese, all but 15ml/1 tbsp of the Parmesan cheese and the chopped fresh thyme. Use the remaining butter to lightly grease 1 large soufflé dish (1 litre/1¾ pints/4 cups) or 4 large ramekins (about 250ml/8fl oz/1 cup).

7 Whisk the egg whites and cream of tartar in a scrupulously clean, grease-free bowl until firm, but not dry. Stir 45ml/3 tbsp of the whites into the sauce, then gently, but thoroughly, fold in the remainder of the whites.

8 Pour the mixture into the prepared dish or dishes. Run a knife around the edge of each dish, pushing the mixture away from the rim. Sprinkle with the reserved grated Parmesan.

9 Place the dish or dishes on a baking sheet and cook for 25–30 minutes for a large soufflé or 20 minutes for four small soufflés. The mixture should be risen and firm to a light touch in the centre; it should not wobble excessively when given a light push. Serve immediately.

Potato, Mozzarella and Garlic Pizza

New potatoes, smoked mozzarella and garlic make this pizza unique. Serve it for lunch with a mixed salad, or make it for part of a festive buffet spread.

Serves 2–3
350g/12oz small new or salad potatoes
45ml/3 tbsp olive oil
2 garlic cloves, crushed
1 pizza base, about 25–30cm/10–12in diameter
1 red onion, thinly sliced
150g/5oz/1¼ cups smoked mozzarella cheese, grated
10ml/2 tsp chopped fresh rosemary or sage
salt and ground black pepper
30ml/2 tbsp freshly grated Parmesan cheese, to garnish

1 Preheat the oven to 220°C/425°F/Gas 7. Put the potatoes in a large pan. Add water to cover and bring to the boil. Add salt, then simmer for about 5 minutes, or until the potatoes are just becoming tender. Drain thoroughly and leave to cool.

2 When the potatoes are cool enough to handle, peel them and cut into thin slices.

3 Heat 30ml/2 tbsp of the oil in a large frying pan. Add the sliced potatoes and the garlic and fry for about 5–8 minutes, turning frequently until tender.

4 Brush the pizza base with the remaining oil. Sprinkle the onion over, then arrange the sliced potatoes on top.

5 Sprinkle over the grated mozzarella and rosemary or sage, and season with plenty of black pepper. Bake for 15–20 minutes until the cheese is melted and golden. Remove the pizza from the oven, and sprinkle with the Parmesan cheese and more ground black pepper. Serve immediately.

> **Variation**
> If serving the pizza for non-vegetarians, you could add sliced smoked pork sausage or slices of pastrami to the pizza to make it into an even more substantial meal.

Potato Pizza Energy 413kcal/1727kJ; Protein 14.1g; Carbohydrate 39.5g, of which sugars 3.7g; Fat 23.1g, of which saturates 8.5g; Cholesterol 29mg; Calcium 222mg; Fibre 2.1g; Sodium 302mg.
Cheese Soufflé Energy 563kcal/2339kJ; Protein 28.8g; Carbohydrate 16.5g, of which sugars 5.8g; Fat 42.9g, of which saturates 24.1g; Cholesterol 294mg; Calcium 422mg; Fibre 0.7g; Sodium 710mg.

Vegetable Korma

The careful blending of spices is warming and stimulating in traditional Indian cooking. This korma dish is rich, creamy and subtly flavoured.

Serves 4
50g/2oz/¼ cup butter
2 onions, sliced
2 garlic cloves, crushed
2.5cm/1in piece fresh root
  ginger, grated
5ml/1 tsp ground cumin
15ml/1 tbsp ground coriander
6 cardamom pods
5cm/2in piece of cinnamon stick
5ml/1 tsp ground turmeric
1 fresh red chilli, seeded and
  finely chopped

1 potato, peeled and cut into
  2.5cm/1in cubes
1 small aubergine
  (eggplant), chopped
115g/4oz/1½ cups mushrooms,
  thickly sliced
175ml/6fl oz/¾ cup water
115g/4oz/1 cup green beans,
  cut into 2.5cm/1in lengths
60ml/4 tbsp natural
  (plain) yogurt
150ml/¼ pint/⅔ cup double
  (heavy) cream
5ml/1 tsp garam masala
salt and ground black pepper
fresh coriander (cilantro) sprigs,
  to garnish
boiled rice and poppadums,
  to serve

1 Melt the butter in a heavy pan. Add the onions and cook over medium heat for 5 minutes until soft. Add the garlic and ginger and cook for 2 minutes, then stir in the cumin, coriander, cardamom pods, cinnamon stick, turmeric and finely chopped chilli. Cook, stirring constantly, for 30 seconds.

2 Add the potato cubes, aubergine and mushrooms to the pan, and pour in the water. Cover the pan, bring the mixture to the boil, then lower the heat and simmer for 15 minutes. Add the beans to the pan and cook, uncovered, for about 5 minutes. With a slotted spoon, remove the vegetables to a warmed serving dish and keep hot.

3 Increase the heat and allow the cooking liquid to bubble up until it has reduced a little. Season with salt and pepper, then stir in the yogurt, cream and garam masala. Pour the sauce over the vegetables and garnish with fresh coriander. Serve with boiled rice and crisp poppadums.

Pasta with Pesto, Potatoes and Beans

The combination of pasta and potatoes may seem odd, but is delicious with pesto.

Serves 4
50g/2oz/½ cup pine nuts
2 large garlic cloves, chopped
90g/3½oz fresh basil leaves, plus
  a few extra leaves
90ml/6 tbsp extra virgin olive oil
50g/2oz/⅔ cup freshly grated
  Parmesan cheese
40g/1½oz/½ cup freshly grated
  Pecorino cheese

For the pasta mixture
275g/10oz waxy potatoes,
  thickly sliced or cut into
  1cm/½in cubes
200g/7oz fine green beans
350g/12oz dried trenette,
  linguine, tagliatelle or tagliarini
salt and ground black pepper

To serve
extra virgin olive oil
pine nuts, toasted
Parmesan cheese, grated

1 Toast the pine nuts in a dry frying pan until golden. (Watch them carefully to make sure they don't burn.) Place in a mortar with the garlic and a pinch of salt, and crush with a pestle. Add the basil and continue pounding the mixture. Gradually add a little oil as you work the mixture to form a paste. Then work in the Parmesan and Pecorino with the remaining oil. (Alternatively, blend the pine nuts, garlic, basil and oil in a food processor, then stir in the cheeses.)

2 Bring a pan of lightly salted water to the boil and add the potatoes. Cook for 10–12 minutes, until tender. Add the green beans to the pan for the last 5–6 minutes of cooking.

3 Meanwhile, cook the pasta in salted, boiling water for 8–12 minutes, or according to the packet instructions, until just tender. Try to time the cooking so that both pasta and potatoes are ready at the same time.

4 Drain the pasta and potatoes and beans. Place in a large, warmed bowl and toss with two-thirds of the pesto. Season with black pepper and sprinkle extra basil leaves over the top.

5 Serve immediately with the rest of the pesto, extra olive oil, pine nuts and grated Parmesan cheese.

Vegetable Korma Energy 363kcal/1499kJ; Protein 4.8g; Carbohydrate 16.6g, of which sugars 8.2g; Fat 31.3g, of which saturates 19.2g; Cholesterol 78mg; Calcium 88mg; Fibre 3.7g; Sodium 104mg.
Pasta with Pesto Energy 658kcal/2760kJ; Protein 20g; Carbohydrate 78.6g, of which sugars 5.9g; Fat 31.5g, of which saturates 5.8g; Cholesterol 13mg; Calcium 241mg; Fibre 5.7g; Sodium 154mg.

Spaghetti with Fresh Tomato Sauce

This is a simple recipe, great for a light supper after a big Christmas lunch. It is important to use really ripe, well-flavoured tomatoes.

Serves 4

675g/1½lb ripe plum tomatoes
   or sweet cherry tomatoes

20ml/4 tsp extra virgin olive oil
   or sunflower oil
1 onion, finely chopped
350g/12oz fresh or
   dried spaghetti
a small handful fresh
   basil leaves
salt and ground black pepper
coarsely shaved Parmesan
   cheese, to serve (optional)

1 With a sharp knife, cut a cross in the base end of each tomato. Plunge the tomatoes, a few at a time, into a bowl of boiling water. Leave for 30 seconds or so, then lift them out with a slotted spoon and drop them into a bowl of cold water. Drain well. The skin will have begun to peel back from the crosses. Remove it entirely.

2 Place the tomatoes on a chopping board and cut into quarters, then eighths, and chop as finely as possible.

3 Heat the oil in a large non-stick pan, add the onion and cook over low heat, stirring frequently, for about 5 minutes, or until softened and lightly coloured.

4 Add the tomatoes, season with salt and pepper to taste, bring to a simmer, then reduce the heat to low and cover the pan with a lid. Cook, stirring occasionally, for 30–40 minutes, or until the mixture is thick.

5 Meanwhile, cook the pasta in a separate pan, according to the instructions on the packet. Shred the basil leaves finely, or tear them into small pieces.

6 Remove the sauce from the heat, stir in the shredded basil and adjust the seasoning to taste. Drain the pasta, then transfer the spaghetti into a warmed bowl, pour the sauce over and toss to mix well. Serve immediately, sprinkled with shaved fresh Parmesan, if you like.

Baked Vegetable Lasagne

Vegetable lasagne is made extra special by using fresh pasta and tasty wild mushrooms, and is great for serving to friends for an informal Christmas meal.

Serves 8

30ml/2 tbsp olive oil
1 medium onion, finely chopped
500g/1¼lb tomatoes, chopped
75g/3oz/6 tbsp butter
675g/1½lb/8 cups wild
   mushrooms, sliced

2 garlic cloves, finely chopped
juice of ½ lemon
12–16 fresh lasagne sheets,
   precooked if necessary
175g/6oz/2 cups freshly grated
   Parmesan cheese
salt and ground black pepper

For the white sauce
50g/2oz/¼ cup butter
50g/2oz/½ cup plain
   (all-purpose) flour
900ml/1½ pints/3¾ cups
   hot milk

1 Preheat the oven to 200°C/400°F/Gas 6. Heat the oil in a pan and sauté the onion until translucent. Add the tomatoes and cook for 6–8 minutes, stirring often. Season and set aside.

2 Heat half the butter in a frying pan and cook the mushrooms until the juices run. Add the garlic, lemon juice and seasoning. Cook until the liquid has almost completely evaporated and the mushrooms are starting to brown. Set aside.

3 Make the white sauce. Melt the butter in a pan, add the flour and cook, stirring, for 1–2 minutes. Gradually add the hot milk, stirring until the sauce boils and thickens.

4 Spread a spoonful of the white sauce over the base of an ovenproof dish and cover it with 3–4 sheets of lasagne. Add a thin layer of mushrooms, then one of white sauce. Sprinkle with a little Parmesan. Make another layer of pasta, spread with a thin layer of the tomato mixture, then add a layer of white sauce. Sprinkle with cheese. Repeat the layers, ending with a layer of pasta coated with white sauce, saving some cheese.

5 Sprinkle with the remaining Parmesan cheese, dot with the remaining butter and bake in the oven for 20 minutes, until the cheese is bubbling and golden. Serve immediately.

Spaghetti with Tomato Sauce Energy 360kcal/1531kJ; Protein 11.9g; Carbohydrate 71.3g, of which sugars 9g; Fat 5.1g, of which saturates 0.8g; Cholesterol 0mg; Calcium 38mg; Fibre 4.4g; Sodium 18mg.
Vegetable Lasagne Energy 466kcal/1943kJ; Protein 19.2g; Carbohydrate 34.8g, of which sugars 9.8g; Fat 28.7g, of which saturates 13g; Cholesterol 50mg; Calcium 456mg; Fibre 2.6g; Sodium 787mg.

Stuffed Pasta Shells

This tasty baked gratin makes a perfect light lunch or supper. Serve with a green or mixed salad on the side.

Serves 4
20 large pasta shells for stuffing
25g/1oz/2 tbsp butter
1 small onion, finely chopped
275g/10oz fresh spinach leaves, trimmed, washed and shredded
1 garlic clove, crushed

1 sachet of saffron powder
nutmeg
250g/9oz ricotta cheese
1 egg
600ml/1 pint/2½ cups passata (bottled strained tomatoes)
about 150ml/¼ pint/⅔ cup dry white wine or vegetable stock
100ml/3½fl oz/scant ½ cup double (heavy) cream
50g/2oz/⅔ cup freshly grated Parmesan cheese
salt and ground black pepper

1 Preheat the oven to 190°C/375°F/Gas 5. Bring a pan of salted water to the boil. Cook the pasta for 10 minutes. Drain the shells, half fill the pan with cold water and add the shells.

2 Melt the butter in a pan, add the onion and cook gently, stirring, for 5 minutes until softened. Add the spinach, garlic and saffron, then grate in plenty of nutmeg and season to taste. Stir well, increase the heat to medium and cook for 5–8 minutes, stirring frequently, until the spinach is wilted and tender.

3 Increase the heat and stir until the water evaporates. Place the spinach in a bowl, add the ricotta and beat well to mix. Taste for seasoning, then add the egg and beat well again.

4 Pour the passata into a measuring jug and make it up to 750ml/1¼ pints/3 cups with wine, stock or water. Add the double cream, stir well to mix and taste for seasoning.

5 Spread about half the sauce over the bottom of four individual gratin dishes. Drain the pasta shells and fill with the spinach and ricotta mixture using a teaspoon. Arrange five shells in the centre of each dish, spoon the remaining sauce over them, then cover with the grated Parmesan. Bake for 10–12 minutes or until heated through. Leave to stand for about 5 minutes before serving.

Cheesy Baked Eggs and Leeks

This delicious dish of potatoes, leeks, eggs and cheese sauce is a traditional favourite. A nice variation is to add a little freshly grated nutmeg to the cheese sauce.

Serves 4
500g/1lb 2oz potatoes, peeled
3 leeks, sliced

6 eggs
600ml/1 pint/2½ cups milk
50g/2oz/3 tbsp butter, cut into small pieces
50g/2oz/½ cup plain (all-purpose) flour
100g/3½oz/1 cup Caerphilly cheese, grated
salt and ground black pepper

1 Cook the potatoes in boiling, lightly salted water for about 15 minutes or until soft. Meanwhile, cook the leeks in a little water for about 10 minutes until soft. Boil the eggs for 10 minutes, drain and put under cold running water to cool them.

2 Preheat the oven to 200°C/400°F/Gas 6. Drain the potatoes thoroughly and mash them with a potato masher. Drain the leeks and stir into the potatoes with plenty of black pepper to taste. Remove the shells from the hard-boiled eggs and cut each in half or into quarters lengthways.

3 Pour the milk into a pan and add the butter and flour. Stirring constantly, bring slowly to the boil and bubble gently for 2 minutes, until thickened and smooth. Remove from the heat, stir in half the cheese and season to taste.

4 Arrange the eggs in four shallow ovenproof dishes (or use one large one). Spoon the potato and leek mixture around the edge of the dishes. Pour the cheese sauce over and top with the remaining cheese. Place into the hot oven and cook for about 15–20 minutes, until bubbling and golden brown.

Cook's Tip
To save time, the leeks could just as easily be cooked in the microwave in a covered dish: there is no need to add water. Stir once or twice during cooking.

Stuffed Pasta Shells Energy 358kcal/1505kJ; Protein 11.6g; Carbohydrate 43.3g, of which sugars 7.7g; Fat 16.7g, of which saturates 5.6g; Cholesterol 20mg; Calcium 56mg; Fibre 2.9g; Sodium 542mg.
Baked Eggs Energy 540kcal/2259kJ; Protein 26.6g; Carbohydrate 41.3g, of which sugars 12.3g; Fat 30.6g, of which saturates 16.2g; Cholesterol 345mg; Calcium 471mg; Fibre 5g; Sodium 443mg.

Vegetarian Christmas Pie

This flan is a lovely addition to the Christmas feast.

Serves 8
225g/8oz/2 cups plain
  (all-purpose) flour
175g/6oz/³⁄₄ cup butter
115g/4oz Parmesan cheese, grated
1 egg
15ml/1 tbsp Dijon mustard

For the filling
25g/1oz/2 tbsp butter
1 onion, finely chopped
1–2 garlic cloves, crushed

350g/12oz/5 cups
  mushrooms, chopped
10ml/2 tsp mixed dried herbs
15ml/1 tbsp chopped fresh parsley
50g/2oz/1 cup fresh
  white breadcrumbs
salt and ground black pepper

For the cheese topping
25g/1oz/2 tbsp butter
25g/1oz/2 tbsp plain
  (all-purpose) flour
300ml/½ pint/1¼ cups milk
25g/1oz Parmesan cheese, grated
75g/3oz mature (sharp) Cheddar
  cheese, grated

1 For the pastry, rub the butter into the flour. Add the Parmesan cheese. Bind to a dough with the egg and 15ml/ 1 tbsp water. Knead, wrap in clear film (plastic wrap) and chill.

2 For the filling, melt the butter and cook the onion until tender. Add the garlic and mushrooms and cook, uncovered, for 5 minutes until there is no liquid left. Remove from the heat and add the dried herbs, parsley, breadcrumbs and seasoning.

3 Preheat the oven to 190°C/375°F/Gas 5. Put a baking tray in the oven. On a floured surface, roll out the pastry and use it to line a 23cm/9in loose-based flan tin (pan). Chill for 20 minutes.

4 For the topping, melt the butter, add the flour and cook for 2 minutes. Blend in the milk. Bring to the boil and simmer for 2–3 minutes. Remove from the heat and add the cheeses and egg yolk, and season. Beat until smooth. Whisk the egg white until softly peaking, then fold into the topping.

5 Spread the Dijon mustard over the flan base. Spoon in the mushroom filling. Add the cheese topping and bake the pie for about 35–45 minutes until set and golden. Serve immediately.

Vegetable Gougère

This makes a light vegetarian supper or a main meal served with baked potatoes.

Serves 4
50g/2oz/4 tbsp butter
150ml/¼ pint/²⁄₃ cup water
65g/2½oz/²⁄₃ cup plain
  (all-purpose) flour
2 eggs, beaten
1.5ml/¼ tsp English (hot)
  mustard powder
50g/2oz Gruyère or Cheddar
  cheese, cubed
salt and ground black pepper
10ml/2 tsp chopped fresh parsley,
  to garnish

For the filling
25g/1oz/2 tbsp butter
1 onion, sliced
1 garlic clove, crushed
225g/8oz/3 cups sliced mushrooms
15ml/1 tbsp plain
  (all-purpose) flour
400g/14oz can tomatoes plus
  their juice
5ml/1 tsp caster (superfine) sugar
225g/8oz courgettes (zucchini),
  thickly sliced

For the topping
15ml/1 tbsp grated
  Parmesan cheese
15ml/1 tbsp breadcrumbs, toasted

1 Preheat the oven to 200°C/400°F/Gas 6. To make the choux pastry, melt the butter in a large pan, add the water and bring to the boil. As soon as the liquid is boiling, remove from the heat and beat in the flour all at once, and continue beating until a smooth, glossy paste is formed. Turn the paste into a large mixing bowl and set aside to allow to cool slightly.

2 Beat the eggs into the paste. Season, add the mustard powder and fold in the cheese. Set aside.

3 For the filling, melt the butter in a large pan and cook the onion until soft. Add the garlic and mushrooms and cook for 3 minutes. Stir in the flour and tomatoes. Bring to the boil, stirring. Season with salt, pepper and sugar. Add the courgettes.

4 Butter a 1.2 litre/2 pint/5 cup ovenproof dish. Spoon the choux pastry in rough mounds around the sides of the dish and turn the filling into the centre. Sprinkle the Parmesan cheese and breadcrumbs on top of the filling. Bake for 35–40 minutes, until the pastry is well risen and golden brown. Sprinkle with chopped parsley and serve hot.

Christmas Pie Energy 513kcal/2135kJ; Protein 17.4g; Carbohydrate 31.9g, of which sugars 3.1g; Fat 35.8g, of which saturates 22.7g; Cholesterol 123mg; Calcium 437mg; Fibre 2g; Sodium 586mg.
Vegetable Gougère Energy 364kcal/1513kJ; Protein 14.7g; Carbohydrate 17.4g, of which sugars 4.5g; Fat 26.1g, of which saturates 14.1g; Cholesterol 150mg; Calcium 283mg; Fibre 2.4g; Sodium 327mg.

Cheese, Rice and Vegetable Strudel

This dish makes a perfect vegetarian main course or, for meat-eaters, a welcome side dish to cold left-over turkey or sliced ham.

Serves 8
175g/6oz/⅞ cup long grain rice
25g/1oz/2 tbsp butter
1–2 leeks, thinly sliced
350g/12oz mushrooms, sliced

225g/8oz Gruyère or Cheddar
  cheese, grated
225g/8oz feta cheese, cubed
30ml/2 tbsp currants
50g/2oz/½ cup chopped
  almonds or hazelnuts, toasted
30ml/2 tbsp chopped fresh parsley
275g/10oz packet frozen filo
  pastry, thawed
30ml/2 tbsp olive oil
salt and ground black pepper

1 Cook the rice in boiling, salted water for 10–12 minutes, until tender but still with a little 'bite'. Drain, rinse under cold running water and set aside. Melt the butter and cook the leeks and mushrooms for 5 minutes. Transfer to a bowl and leave to cool. Add the well-drained rice, the cheeses, currants, toasted almonds or hazelnuts, chopped fresh parsley and seasoning.

2 Preheat the oven to 190°C/375°F/Gas 5. Unwrap the filo pastry. Cover it with a piece of clear film (plastic wrap) and a clean damp cloth. Lay a sheet of pastry on a large piece of baking parchment and brush with oil. Lay a second sheet on top, overlapping the first by 2.5cm/1in. Put another sheet with its long side running at right angles to the first two. Lay a fourth sheet in the same way, overlapping by 2.5cm/1in. Continue in this way, alternating the layers of two sheets so that the join between the two runs in the opposite direction for each layer.

3 Place the filling mixture along the centre of the pastry sheet and shape it into a rectangle, measuring 10 × 30cm/4 × 12in. Fold the layers of filo pastry over the filling and carefully roll it over, with the help of the baking parchment, so that the join ends up being hidden on the underside of the strudel.

4 Lift the strudel on to a greased baking tray and tuck the edges under, so that the filling does not escape. Brush with oil and bake for 30–40 minutes, until golden and crisp. Leave to stand for 5 minutes before cutting into thick slices and serving.

Vegetable Crumble

This tasty, warming dish will be enjoyed by vegetarians and non-vegetarians alike, especially when the latter are feeling sated with a lot of rich, meaty meals. For non-vegetarians, you could add a 40g/1½oz can anchovies, drained and chopped, to the vegetables.

Serves 8
450g/1lb potatoes
225g/8oz leeks
25g/1oz/2 tbsp butter

450g/1lb carrots, chopped
2 garlic cloves, crushed
225g/8oz/3 cups mushrooms, sliced
450g/1lb Brussels sprouts, sliced
salt and ground black pepper

For the cheese crumble
50g/2oz/4 tbsp plain
  (all-purpose) flour
50g/2oz/4 tbsp butter
50g/2oz/1 cup fresh breadcrumbs
50g/2oz Cheddar cheese, grated
30ml/2 tbsp chopped fresh parsley
5ml/1 tsp English (hot)
  mustard powder

1 Peel and halve the potatoes and parboil them in salted water until just tender. Drain and cool. Cut the leeks in half lengthways and wash them thoroughly to remove any small pieces of grit or soil. Drain on kitchen paper and slice in 1cm/½in pieces.

2 Melt the butter and cook the leeks and carrots for about 2–3 minutes. Add the garlic and sliced mushrooms and cook for a further 3 minutes. Add the Brussels sprouts. Season with salt and pepper to taste. Transfer to a 2.5 litre/4 pint/10 cup ovenproof dish.

3 Preheat the oven to 200°C/400°F/Gas 6. Slice the cooked potatoes and arrange them on top of the vegetables.

4 To make the crumble, sift the flour into a bowl and rub in the butter until the mixture resembles fine breadcrumbs, or process in a food processor.

5 Add the breadcrumbs and fold in the grated cheese. Add the chopped parsley and the mustard powder. Mix together well. Spoon evenly over the vegetables to cover them, and bake for about 20–30 minutes until the crumble topping is golden and crispy.

Cheese Strudel Energy 487kcal/2031kJ; Protein 19.4g; Carbohydrate 43.7g, of which sugars 4.7g; Fat 26g, of which saturates 12.7g; Cholesterol 77mg; Calcium 387mg; Fibre 2.8g; Sodium 646mg.
Vegetable Crumble Energy 256kcal/1068kJ; Protein 9.97g; Carbohydrate 18.3g, of which sugars 6.6g; Fat 16g, of which saturates 3.9g; Cholesterol 14mg; Calcium 209mg; Fibre 5.8g; Sodium 277mg.

Filo Vegetable Pie

This stunning pie makes a delicious main course for vegetarians, or serve as part of a festive party buffet with left-over turkey or ham.

Serves 6–8
225g/8oz leeks
165g/5½oz/11 tbsp butter
225g/8oz carrots, cubed
225g/8oz/3 cups sliced mushrooms
225g/8oz Brussels sprouts, cut
    into quarters

2 garlic cloves, crushed
115g/4oz/½ cup cream cheese
115g/4oz/½ cup Roquefort or
    Stilton cheese
150ml/¼ pint/⅔ cup double
    (heavy) cream
2 eggs, beaten
225g/8oz cooking apples
225g/8oz/1 cup cashew nuts or
    pine nuts, toasted
350g/12oz frozen filo
    pastry, defrosted
salt and ground black pepper

1 Preheat the oven to 180°C/350°F/Gas 4. Cut the leeks in half through the root and wash them, separating the layers slightly to check they are clean. Slice into 1cm/½in pieces, drain and dry.

2 Heat 40g/1½oz/3 tbsp of the butter in a large pan and cook the leeks and carrots, covered, over medium heat for 5 minutes. Add the mushrooms, sprouts and garlic and cook for another 2 minutes. Turn the vegetables into a bowl and let them cool.

3 Whisk the cream cheese and blue cheese, cream, eggs and seasoning together in a bowl. Pour them over the vegetables. Peel and core the apples and cut into 1cm/½in cubes. Stir them into the vegetables. Lastly, add the toasted cashew or pine nuts.

4 Melt the remaining butter. Brush all over the inside of a 23cm/9in loose-based springform cake tin (pan) with melted butter. Brush two-thirds of the filo pastry sheets with butter, one sheet at a time, and use them to line the base and sides of the tin, overlapping the layers so that there are no gaps.

5 Spoon in the filling and fold over the excess pastry to cover. Brush the remaining sheets with butter and cut into 2.5cm/1in strips. Cover the top of the pie with the strips, in a rough mound. Bake for 40 minutes until golden brown. Leave to stand for 5 minutes, and then gently remove the tin and serve.

Cheese and Spinach Flan

This flan freezes well and can be reheated. It makes an excellent addition to a festive buffet party.

Serves 8
115g/4oz/½ cup butter
225g/8oz/2 cups plain
    (all-purpose) flour
2.5ml/½ tsp English (hot)
    mustard powder
2.5ml/½ tsp paprika
large pinch of salt
115g/4oz/1 cup grated
    Cheddar cheese

45–60ml/3–4 tbsp cold water
1 egg, beaten, to glaze

For the filling
450g/1lb frozen spinach
1 onion, chopped
pinch of grated nutmeg
225g/8oz/1 cup cottage cheese
2 large (US extra large)
    eggs, beaten
50g/2oz/½ cup Parmesan
    cheese, grated
150ml/¼ pint/⅔ cup single
    (light) cream
salt and ground black pepper

1 Using your fingertips, rub the butter into the flour until it resembles fine breadcrumbs. Mix in the next four ingredients. Alternatively, process in a food processor. Bind to a dough with the cold water. Knead until smooth and pliable, wrap in clear film (plastic wrap) and chill for about 30 minutes.

2 Put the spinach and onion in a pan, cover, and cook slowly. Increase the heat to drive off any water. Season with salt, pepper and nutmeg. Turn the spinach into a bowl, and leave to cool slightly. Add the remaining filling ingredients.

3 Preheat the oven to 200°C/400°F/Gas 6. Put a baking tray in the oven to preheat. Cut one-third off the pastry for the lid. Roll out the remaining pastry and line a 23cm/9in loose-based flan tin (pan). Press the pastry into the edges and make a lip around the top edge. Remove any excess pastry. Carefully pour the filling into the flan case.

4 Roll out the remaining pastry, cut it with a lattice pastry cutter and open it out. Using a rolling pin, lay it over the flan. Brush the joins with egg glaze. Press the edges together and trim off any excess. Brush the lattice with egg glaze and bake for 40 minutes, until golden brown. Serve hot or cold.

Filo Pie Energy 748kcal/3102kJ; Protein 16.1g; Carbohydrate 34.8g, of which sugars 7.4g; Fat 62.4g, of which saturates 26.5g; Cholesterol 178mg; Calcium 160mg; Fibre 4.7g; Sodium 379mg.
Cheese Flan Energy 401kcal/1674kJ; Protein 17.5g; Carbohydrate 24.1g, of which sugars 2.4g; Fat 26.4g, of which saturates 15.6g; Cholesterol 147mg; Calcium 374mg; Fibre 2.2g; Sodium 389mg.

Chestnut and Mushroom Loaf

You can prepare this festive dish ahead, freezing it unbaked. Thaw overnight before baking.

Serves 8
45ml/3 tbsp olive oil, plus extra
  for brushing
2 medium onions, chopped
2 cloves garlic, chopped
75g/3oz/1¼ cups chopped
  button (white) mushrooms
100ml/4fl oz/½ cup red wine
225g/8oz can unsweetened
  chestnut purée
50g/2oz/1 cup fresh wholemeal
  (whole-wheat) breadcrumbs
75g/3oz/¾ cup fresh cranberries,
  plus extra to decorate
450g/1lb pastry
flour, for dusting
1 small egg, beaten, to glaze
salt and ground black pepper

1 Preheat the oven to 190°C/375°F/Gas 5. Heat the oil in a pan and fry the onions over medium heat until translucent. Add the garlic and mushrooms and fry for 3 minutes. Pour in the wine, stir well and simmer until it has evaporated, stirring occasionally. Remove from the heat, stir in the chestnut purée and breadcrumbs and season with salt and pepper. Set aside.

2 Simmer the cranberries in a little water for 5 minutes until they start to pop, then drain and leave to cool. Lightly brush a 600ml/1 pint/2½ cup loaf tin (pan) with oil.

3 On a lightly floured surface, roll out the pastry to a thickness of 3mm/⅛in. Cut rectangles to fit the base and sides of the tin and press them in place. Press the edges together to seal them. Cut a piece of pastry to fit the top of the tin and set it aside.

4 Spoon half the chestnut mixture into the tin and level the surface. Sprinkle on a layer of the cranberries and cover with the remaining chestnut mixture. Cover with the pastry lid and pinch the edges to the sides. Cut festive shapes from the pastry trimmings to use as decorations.

5 Brush the pastry top and the decorative shapes with the beaten egg glaze and arrange the shapes in a pattern on top. Bake in the oven for 35 minutes, or until golden brown. Decorate the top with fresh cranberries. Serve hot.

Pumpkin Gnocchi

A chanterelle sauce provides both richness and flavour to this tasty, wintery dish.

Serves 4
50g/1lb floury potatoes, peeled
450g/1lb peeled pumpkin, chopped
2 egg yolks
200g/7oz/1¾ cups plain
  (all-purpose) flour
pinch of ground allspice
1.5ml/¼ tsp ground cinnamon
pinch of grated nutmeg
finely grated rind of ½ orange
salt and ground black pepper

For the sauce
30ml/2 tbsp olive oil
1 shallot
175g/6oz chanterelles, sliced
10ml/2 tsp almond butter
150ml/¼ pint/⅔ cup crème fraîche
a little milk or water
75ml/5 tbsp chopped fresh parsley
50g/2oz/½ cup grated
  Parmesan cheese

1 Cover the potatoes with cold salted water, bring to the boil and cook for 20 minutes. Drain and set aside. Wrap the pumpkin in foil and bake at 180°C/350°F/Gas 4 for 30 minutes. Drain well, then add to the potato and process briefly in a food processor or blender. Transfer to a bowl, add the egg yolks, flour, spices, rind and seasoning and mix well to make a soft dough.

2 Bring a large pan of salted water to the boil, then dredge a work surface with flour. Spoon the gnocchi mixture into a piping (pastry) bag fitted with a 1cm/½in nozzle. Pipe on to the floured surface to make a 15cm/6in sausage shape. Roll in flour and cut into 2.5cm/1in pieces. Repeat the process, making more sausage shapes, until the dough is used up. Mark each gnocchi lightly with a fork and cook for 3–4 minutes in the boiling water.

3 Meanwhile, make the sauce. Heat the oil in a non-stick frying pan. Add the shallot and fry until soft without colouring. Add the chanterelles and cook briefly, then add the almond butter. Stir to melt, and stir in the crème fraîche. Simmer briefly and adjust the consistency with milk or water. Add the parsley and season to taste with salt and pepper.

4 Lift the gnocchi out of the water with a slotted spoon, turn into warmed bowls and spoon the sauce over the top. Sprinkle with the grated Parmesan cheese and serve immediately.

Chestnut Loaf Energy 428kcal/1785kJ; Protein 5.3g; Carbohydrate 46.3g, of which sugars 6.3g; Fat 25g, of which saturates 7g; Cholesterol 21mg; Calcium 83mg; Fibre 3.3g; Sodium 285mg.
Pumpkin Gnocchi Energy 576kcal/2411kJ; Protein 16g; Carbohydrate 62.1g, of which sugars 6.2g; Fat 31g, of which saturates 16g; Cholesterol 161mg; Calcium 325mg; Fibre 5.1g; Sodium 185mg.

Carrot and Parsnip Purée

One of the most widely used root vegetables, carrots mix well with all the other root vegetables, which are at their best over the festive season. Carrots and parsnips work especially well together and are often found in a soup, or in this popular side dish. Serve this purée as one of the many accompaniments to a typical Christmas Day feast.

Serves 6–8
350g/12oz carrots
450g/1lb parsnips
pinch of freshly grated nutmeg
    or ground mace
15g/½oz/1 tbsp butter
about 15ml/1 tbsp single (light)
    cream, or top of the milk
    (optional)
1 small bunch parsley leaves,
    chopped (optional), plus extra
    to garnish
salt and ground black pepper

1 Peel the carrots and slice fairly thinly. Peel the parsnips and cut into bitesize chunks (they are softer and will cook more quickly than the carrots). Boil the two vegetables, separately, in salted water, until tender.

2 Drain them well and purée them together in a food processor or blender with the grated nutmeg or mace, a good seasoning of salt and ground black pepper and the butter. Taste for seasoning.

3 If you like, blend in some cream or the top of the milk to taste, and add chopped parsley for extra flavour.

4 Transfer the carrot and parsnip purée to a warmed serving bowl, sprinkle with chopped parsley to garnish and serve hot.

Cook's Tips
• Any left-over purée can be thinned to taste with a little good quality chicken stock and gently heated to make a quick and tasty home-made soup.
• Carrots are equally good roasted in chunks, either alone or as a mixed side dish with roasted swede (rutabaga) and parsnip, or with a meaty pot-roast.

Glazed Carrots with Cider

This recipe is simple to make. The carrots are cooked in the minimum of liquid, and the cider adds a pleasant sharpness.

Serves 4
450g/1lb young carrots, trimmed
25g/1oz/2 tbsp butter

15ml/1 tbsp soft light
    brown sugar
120ml/4fl oz/½ cup cider
60ml/4 tbsp vegetable stock
    or water
5ml/1 tsp Dijon mustard
15ml/1 tbsp finely chopped
    fresh parsley

1 Peel the carrots, then cut them into julienne strips. Sauté the carrots in butter for 4–5 minutes, stirring often. Sprinkle with the sugar and cook, stirring, for 1 minute or until the sugar has dissolved.

2 Add the cider and stock or water to the pan. Bring to the boil and add the Dijon mustard. Partially cover the pan and simmer for 10–12 minutes, until the carrots are just tender. Remove the lid and cook until the liquid has reduced to a thick sauce. Remove from the heat and stir in the parsley. Spoon the carrots into a serving dish and serve with grilled (broiled) meat or fish or alongside the Christmas roast.

Braised Leeks with Carrots

Sweet carrots and leeks are good finished with chopped mint, chervil or parsley.

Serves 4
70g/2½ oz/5 tbsp butter
675g/1½lb carrots, thickly sliced
2 fresh bay leaves

675g/1½lb leeks, cut into
    5cm/2in lengths
125ml/4fl oz/½ cup white wine
30ml/2 tbsp chopped fresh mint,
    chervil or parsley
sugar
salt and ground black pepper

1 Melt 25g/1oz/2 tbsp of the butter in a pan and cook the carrots, without allowing them to brown, for about 5 minutes. Add the bay leaves, seasoning, a pinch of sugar and 75ml/5 tbsp water. Bring to the boil, cover and cook for 10 minutes.

2 Uncover the pan and boil until the juices are reduced and the carrots are moist and glazed. Remove from the pan and set aside.

3 Melt 25g/1oz/2 tbsp of the remaining butter in the pan. Add the leeks and cook over low heat for 4–5 minutes.

4 Add seasoning, a pinch of sugar, the wine and half the chopped herbs. Heat until simmering, then cover and cook gently for 5–8 minutes, until the leeks are tender but still holding together. Uncover and turn the leeks in the buttery juices, then increase the heat and boil the liquid rapidly until reduced to a few tablespoonfuls.

5 Add the carrots to the leeks and reheat gently, stirring occasionally, then add the remaining butter. Taste and adjust the seasoning. Transfer to a warmed serving dish and serve sprinkled with the remaining chopped herbs.

Carrot and Parsnip Purée Energy 92kcal/385kJ; Protein 1.8g; Carbohydrate 14.1g, of which sugars 8.7g; Fat 3.5g, of which saturates 1.8g; Cholesterol 7mg; Calcium 48mg; Fibre 4.9g; Sodium 38mg.
Carrots with Cider Energy 122kcal/507kJ; Protein 1g; Carbohydrate 11.1g, of which sugars 10.4g; Fat 8.6g, of which saturates 2.8g; Cholesterol 1mg; Calcium 32mg; Fibre 2.7g; Sodium 85mg.
Leeks with Carrots Energy 163kcal/677kJ; Protein 3.8g; Carbohydrate 18.5g, of which sugars 16.4g; Fat 6.5g, of which saturates 3.6g; Cholesterol 13mg; Calcium 87mg; Fibre 7.8g; Sodium 85mg.

Stir-fried Brussels Sprouts

This recipe makes the most of the sprouts' flavour and has an Asian twist.

Serves 4
450g/1lb Brussels sprouts
15ml/1 tbsp sunflower oil
6–8 spring onions (scallions), cut into 2.5cm/1in lengths
2 slices fresh root ginger
40g/1½oz/⅓ cup slivered almonds
150–175ml/4–6fl oz/⅔–¾ cup vegetable or chicken stock

1 Remove any large outer leaves and trim the bases of the Brussels sprouts. Cut into slices about 1cm/½in thick.

2 Heat the oil in a wok or heavy frying pan, and fry the spring onions and ginger for 2–3 minutes, stirring often. Add the almonds and stir-fry until the onions and almonds brown.

3 Discard the ginger, reduce the heat and stir in the sprouts. Stir-fry for a few minutes and then add the stock and gently cook for 5–6 minutes, or until the sprouts are nearly tender. Increase the heat to boil off the excess liquid. Spoon the sprouts into a warmed serving dish and serve.

Festive Brussels Sprouts

Peeling chestnuts can be fiddly but is worth the effort.

Serves 8
450g/1lb fresh chestnuts
450ml/¾ pint/1⅞ cups stock
450g/1lb Brussels sprouts, trimmed
450g/1lb carrots, sliced
25g/1oz/2 tbsp butter
salt and ground black pepper

1 Drop the chestnuts into boiling water for a few minutes, and remove with a slotted spoon. The skins should slip off easily. Put them in a pan with the stock. Simmer for 10 minutes, then drain. Boil the sprouts in salted water for 5 minutes. Drain.

2 Cook the carrots for 6 minutes. Drain. Melt the butter in a pan, add the chestnuts, sprouts and carrots and season. Serve.

Creamed Leeks

This dish is a real festive favourite, delicious with the full roast meal, or even on its own. It is very important to have good firm leeks without a core in the middle. Christmas is one time of year when leeks are at their best.

Serves 4
2 leeks, tops trimmed and roots removed
50g/2oz/¼ cup butter
200ml/7fl oz/scant 1 cup double (heavy) cream
salt and ground black pepper

1 Split the leeks down the middle, then cut across so you make pieces approximately 2cm/¾in square. Wash thoroughly and drain in a colander.

2 Melt the butter in a large pan and when quite hot throw in the leeks, stirring to coat them in the butter, and heat through. They will wilt but should not exude water. Keep the heat high but don't allow them to colour. You need to create a balance between keeping the temperature high so the water steams out of the vegetable, keeping it bright green, while taking care not to burn or brown the leeks too much.

3 Keeping the heat high, pour in the cream, mix in thoroughly and allow to bubble and reduce. Season with salt and ground black pepper. When the texture is smooth, thick and creamy the leeks are ready to serve.

> **Cook's Tip**
> When buying leeks, choose smaller and less bendy ones as they are more tender than the larger specimens.

> **Variation**
> Although these leeks have a wonderful taste themselves, you may like to add extra flavourings, such as a little chopped garlic or some chopped fresh tarragon or thyme.

Stir-fried Sprouts Energy 341kcal/1426kJ; Protein 11.1g; Carbohydrate 34.7g, of which sugars 10.2g; Fat 18.5g, of which saturates 8.8g; Cholesterol 40mg; Calcium 78mg; Fibre 9.3g; Sodium 485mg.
Festive Sprouts Energy 341kcal/1426kJ; Protein 11.1g; Carbohydrate 34.7g, of which sugars 10.2g; Fat 18.5g, of which saturates 8.8g; Cholesterol 40mg; Calcium 78mg; Fibre 9.3g; Sodium 485mg.
Creamed Leeks Energy 363kcal/1496kJ; Protein 2.5g; Carbohydrate 3.8g, of which sugars 3.1g; Fat 37.6g, of which saturates 23.3g; Cholesterol 95mg; Calcium 51mg; Fibre 2.2g; Sodium 89mg.

Peas with Baby Onions and Cream

This classic side dish is perfect to serve with a festive feast.

Serves 4
175g/6oz baby (pearl) onions
15g/½oz/1 tbsp butter
350g/12oz/3 cups
  frozen peas
150ml/¼ pint/⅔ cup double
  (heavy) cream
15g/½oz/1 tbsp plain
  (all-purpose) flour
10ml/2 tsp chopped fresh parsley
15–30ml/1–2 tbsp lemon juice
  (optional)
salt and ground black pepper

1 Remove the outer layer of skin from the onions and then halve them, if necessary. Melt the butter in a flameproof casserole and fry the onions for 5–6 minutes over medium heat, until they are just begining to brown and are tender.

2 Add the peas to the pan and cook for a 5–6 minutes, stirring constantly, until softened.

3 Add 120ml/4fl oz/½ cup water and bring to the boil. Simmer for about 10 minutes until both are tender. There should be a thin layer of water on the base of the pan.

4 Blend the cream with the flour. Remove the frying pan from the heat and stir in the cream, flour and fresh parsley and season to taste with salt and pepper.

5 Cook the mixture over a gentle heat for about 3–4 minutes, until the sauce has reduced and thickened slightly. Add a little lemon juice, if using, before serving.

Cook's Tip
Frozen peas can be used in this recipe, since fresh ones are unlikely to be available at Christmas, but frozen onions tend to be insipid and are not worth using. As an alternative you could use the white part of spring onions.

Stir-fried Brussels Sprouts with Caraway

This is a great way of cooking Brussels sprouts at Christmas, helping to retain their sweet flavour and crunchy texture. Stir-frying guarantees that there will not be a single soggy sprout in sight, which is what puts people off these vegetables.

Serves 4
450g/1lb Brussels sprouts,
  trimmed and washed
30ml/2 tbsp sunflower oil
2 streaky (fatty) bacon rashers
  (strips), finely chopped
10ml/2 tsp caraway seeds,
  lightly crushed
salt and ground black pepper

1 Using a sharp knife, cut the Brussels sprouts into fine shreds and set aside. Heat the oil in a wok or large frying pan and add the bacon. Cook for 1–2 minutes, or until the bacon is beginning to turn golden.

2 Add the shredded sprouts to the wok or pan and stir-fry for 1–2 minutes, or until lightly cooked.

3 Season the sprouts with salt and ground black pepper to taste and stir in the caraway seeds. Cook for a further 30 seconds, then serve immediately.

Green Beans with Bacon and Cream

This baked vegetable accompaniment is rich and full of flavour. It is particularly good with many chicken dishes, and would be equally tasty made without the bacon for vegetarians. Serve as an accompaniment with the roast turkey on Christmas Day.

Serves 4
350g/12oz green beans
50–75g/2–3oz bacon, chopped
25g/1oz/2 tbsp butter
  or margarine
15ml/1 tbsp plain
  (all-purpose) flour
350ml/12fl oz/1½ cups milk and
  single (light) cream, mixed
salt and ground black pepper

1 Preheat the oven to 190°C/375°F/Gas 5. Trim the beans and cook in lightly salted boiling water for about 5 minutes until just tender. Drain and place them in an ovenproof dish.

2 Dry fry the bacon until crisp, stirring it constantly to make sure that it doesn't stick to the frying pan. Crumble the bacon into very small pieces. Stir into the ovenproof dish with the beans and set aside.

3 Melt the butter or margarine in a large pan, stir in the flour and then add the milk and cream to make a smooth sauce, stirring constanty until well blended. Season well with plenty of salt and ground black pepper.

4 Pour the sauce over the beans and bacon in the dish and carefully mix it in. Cover the dish with a piece of foil and bake in the oven for 15–20 minutes until hot. Serve immediately.

Peas with Onions Energy 161kcal/670kJ; Protein 9.1g; Carbohydrate 15.9g, of which sugars 6.8g; Fat 7.4g, of which saturates 3.7g; Cholesterol 13mg; Calcium 73mg; Fibre 6.5g; Sodium 47mg.
Stir-fried Brussels Sprouts Energy 131kcal/545kJ; Protein 5.9g; Carbohydrate 4.6g, of which sugars 3.5g; Fat 10g, of which saturates 2g; Cholesterol 8mg; Calcium 30mg; Fibre 4.6g; Sodium 164mg.
Green Beans with Bacon Energy 312kcal/1292kJ; Protein 9.1g; Carbohydrate 11.8g, of which sugars 5.2g; Fat 25.7g, of which saturates 12.3g; Cholesterol 56mg; Calcium 118mg; Fibre 3.9g; Sodium 206mg.

Creamy Spinach Purée

This is a great way to serve this healthy vegetable. Crème fraîche usually gives this dish its creamy richness, but try this quick, light alternative, which uses soft cheese and a little milk in place of the crème fraîche.

Serves 4

675g/1½lb leaf spinach, stems
  removed, rinsed
115g/4oz/1 cup full- or medium-
  fat soft cheese
milk (if needed)
freshly grated nutmeg
salt and ground black pepper

1 Place the spinach in a deep frying pan or wok with just the water clinging to the leaves. Cook, uncovered, over medium heat for 3–4 minutes until wilted. Drain in a colander, pressing out excess moisture with the back of a spoon.

2 In a food processor fitted with a metal blade, purée the spinach and soft cheese until well blended, then transfer it to a large bowl. If the purée is too thick to fall easily from a spoon, add a little of the milk, spoonful by spoonful. Season with salt, pepper and nutmeg. Reheat and serve hot.

Braised Swiss Chard

Swiss chard makes two tasty meals: on the first day, cook the leaves only; the next day cook the stalks in the same way as asparagus and serve with cream or a white sauce.

Serves 4

900g/2lb Swiss chard
15g/½oz/1 tbsp butter
a little freshly grated nutmeg
salt and ground black pepper

1 Remove the stalks from the Swiss chard. Wash the leaves well and transfer to a pan with the water clinging to the leaves.

2 Cover and cook over medium heat for about 3–5 minutes, or until just tender, shaking the pan occasionally.

3 Drain, add the butter and nutmeg, and season. When the butter has melted, toss it into the Swiss chard and serve.

Cauliflower Cheese

This traditional side dish is a firm favourite at Christmas time. Serve as part of a festive feast for the whole family, or it is just as enjoyable eaten on its own for supper with some fresh crusty bread and maybe a mixed green salad.

Serves 4

1 medium cauliflower
25g/1oz/2 tbsp butter
25g/1oz/4 tbsp plain
  (all-purpose) flour
300ml/½ pint/1¼ cups milk
115g/4oz mature (sharp) Cheddar
  or Cheshire cheese, grated
salt and ground black pepper

1 Trim the cauliflower and cut it into florets. Bring a pan of lightly salted water to the boil, drop in the cauliflower and cook for 5–8 minutes or until just tender. Drain and transfer the florets to an ovenproof dish.

2 To make the sauce, melt the butter in a heavy pan, stir in the flour and cook gently, stirring constantly, for about 1 minute (do not allow the flour to brown).

3 Remove from the heat and gradually stir in the milk. Return the pan to the heat and cook, stirring, until the mixture thickens and comes to the boil. Simmer the sauce gently for about 1–2 minutes.

4 Stir three-quarters of the cheese into the sauce and stir until melted and combined. Season to taste with salt and pepper. Preheat the grill (broiler) to medium-high.

5 Spoon the cheese sauce over the cooked cauliflower florets and sprinkle the remaining cheese on top.

6 Place the dish under a hot grill until the cheese is bubbling and golden brown. Serve immediately.

> **Cook's Tip**
> You can boost the cheese flavour by adding a little English (hot) mustard to the cheese sauce.

Spinach Purée Energy 94kcal/388kJ; Protein 7.4g; Carbohydrate 3.6g, of which sugars 3.4g; Fat 5.5g, of which saturates 2.8g; Cholesterol 12mg; Calcium 287mg; Fibre 3.6g; Sodium 236mg.
Braised Swiss Chard Energy 84kcal/347kJ; Protein 6.3g; Carbohydrate 3.6g, of which sugars 3.4g; Fat 4.9g, of which saturates 2.2g; Cholesterol 8mg; Calcium 383mg; Fibre 4.7g; Sodium 338mg.
Cauliflower Cheese Energy 318kcal/1318kJ; Protein 17.4g; Carbohydrate 4.4g, of which sugars 3.9g; Fat 25.8g, of which saturates 16.3g; Cholesterol 71mg; Calcium 371mg; Fibre 1.8g; Sodium 453mg.

Creamy Potato and Cabbage

This accompaniment will enhance any meat dish.

Serves 4
450g/1lb potatoes, peeled and chopped
50g/2oz/¼ cup butter
50ml/2fl oz/¼ cup milk
450g/1lb cabbage, washed and finely shredded
30ml/2 tbsp olive oil
50ml/2fl oz/¼ cup double (heavy) cream
salt and ground black pepper

1 Place the potatoes in boiling water and boil for 15–20 minutes. Drain, replace on the heat for a few minutes, then mash. Heat the butter and milk in a small pan and then mix into the mashed potatoes. Season to taste.

2 Heat the olive oil in a large frying pan, add the shredded cabbage and fry for a few minutes. Season to taste with salt and ground black pepper. Add the mashed potato, mix well, then stir in the cream. Serve immediately.

Sweet and Sour Red Cabbage

Serve with goose, pork or strong-flavoured game dishes.

Serves 8
900g/2lb red cabbage
30ml/2 tbsp olive oil
2 large onions, sliced
2 large cooking apples, peeled, cored and sliced
30ml/2 tbsp cider vinegar
30ml/2 tbsp soft light brown sugar
225g/8oz rindless streaky (fatty) bacon, chopped (optional)
salt and ground black pepper

1 Preheat the oven to 180°C/350°F/Gas 4. Cut the cabbage into quarters and shred it finely with a sharp knife. Heat the oil in a large flameproof casserole. Cook the onion over a gentle heat for 2 minutes.

2 Stir the cabbage, apples, vinegar, sugar and seasoning into the casserole. Cover and cook in the oven for 1 hour, until tender. Stir halfway through cooking. Fry the bacon, if using, until crisp. Stir it into the cabbage before serving.

Parsnip and Chestnut Croquettes

This is a tasty way to serve Christmas vegetables.

Serves 10–12
450g/1lb parsnips, cut roughly into small pieces
115g/4oz frozen chestnuts
25g/1oz/2 tbsp butter
1 garlic clove, crushed
15ml/1 tbsp chopped fresh coriander (cilantro)
1 egg, beaten
40–50g/1½–2oz/½ cup fresh white breadcrumbs
vegetable oil, for frying
salt and ground black pepper
sprig of coriander (cilantro), to garnish

1 Cook the parsnips in simmering water for about 15–20 minutes, until tender. Drain. Cook the chestnuts in the same way for 8–10 minutes, until tender. Drain, then mash roughly.

2 Cook the garlic in the butter for 30 seconds. Mash the parsnips with the garlic butter. Add the chestnuts, coriander and seasoning.

3 Form into croquettes, 7.5cm/3in long. Dip into the beaten egg, then roll in breadcrumbs. Fry for 3–4 minutes until golden. Drain and serve, garnished with coriander.

Thyme-roasted Onions

These slow-roasted onions are ideal served with festive roast meats.

Serves 4
75ml/5 tbsp olive oil
50g/2oz/4 tbsp unsalted butter
900g/2lb small onions, skinned
30ml/2 tbsp chopped fresh thyme
salt and ground black pepper

1 Preheat the oven to 220°C/425°F/ Gas 7. Heat the oil and butter in a roasting pan. Add the onions and toss them over medium heat until they are very lightly sautéed.

2 Add the thyme and seasoning to the pan and roast for about 45 minutes, basting regularly.

Creamy Potato Energy 183kcal/766kJ; Protein 3.9g; Carbohydrate 24g, of which sugars 7.3g; Fat 8.5g, of which saturates 2.4g; Cholesterol 7mg; Calcium 73mg; Fibre 3.5g; Sodium 24mg.
Sweet and Sour Cabbage Energy 148kcal/620kJ; Protein 2.2g; Carbohydrate 23.8g, of which sugars 22.2g; Fat 4g, of which saturates 0.4g; Cholesterol 0mg; Calcium 60mg; Fibre 2.9g; Sodium 19mg.
Parsnip Croquettes Energy 107kcal/445kJ; Protein 1.8g; Carbohydrate 10.8g, of which sugars 2.9g; Fat 6.6g, of which saturates 1.8g; Cholesterol 21mg; Calcium 27mg; Fibre 2.2g; Sodium 52mg.
Thyme-roasted Onions Energy 297kcal/1225kJ; Protein 2.8g; Carbohydrate 17.8g, of which sugars 12.6g; Fat 24.4g, of which saturates 8.7g; Cholesterol 29mg; Calcium 58mg; Fibre 3.2g; Sodium 101mg.

Griddle Potatoes

This crispy side dish makes an easy and tasty accompaniment to grilled meat or fish. It can be made with any leftover boiled potatoes you may have from other festive meals.

Serves 4–6
2 onions, peeled and chopped
450–675g/1lb–1½lb potatoes, boiled in their skins
a mixture of butter and oil, for shallow-frying
salt and ground black pepper

1 Put the onions in a large pan and scald them briefly in boiling water. Refresh under cold water and drain. Peel and slice them. Slice the boiled potatoes.

2 Heat a mixture of butter and oil in a heavy frying pan, and fry the onions until tender. Add the potato slices and brown them, turning them to brown on both sides. Transfer to a serving dish and season with salt and pepper. Serve very hot.

Hasselback Potatoes

This is an attractive way to cook potatoes. They will look stunning as part of the Christmas Day banquet instead of the traditional plain roast potatoes. Use the juices from a festive roast to baste them.

Serves 4
4 large potatoes
75g/3oz/6 tbsp butter
45ml/3 tbsp olive oil
50g/2oz/1 cup fresh breadcrumbs
50g/2oz/⅔ cup grated Parmesan cheese
salt and ground black pepper

1 Preheat the oven to 200°C/400°F/Gas 6. Peel the potatoes, then cut them widthways, not lengthways, to three-quarters of their depth at 3mm/⅛in intervals, preferably at a slight angle.

2 Place the potatoes, cut sides up, in an ovenproof dish. Melt the butter, and mix with the oil. Brush the mixture over the potatoes, then season well. Sprinkle over the breadcrumbs and cheese. Roast for about 1 hour, depending on their size, until golden brown and fanned apart along the cut lines. Serve hot.

Mashed Potatoes

Fluffy mashed potatoes are the traditional partner to sausages – or 'bangers'.

Serves 4
1kg/2¼lb floury potatoes, such as Maris Piper, peeled
about 150ml/¼ pint/⅔ cup milk
115g/4oz/½ cup butter
salt and ground black pepper
freshly grated nutmeg (optional)

1 Cook the potatoes for about 20 minutes or until soft throughout. Drain. Warm the milk and butter in a large pan.

2 Push the warm potatoes through a ricer, pass them through a mouli (food mill), or mash with a potato masher or fork.

3 Add the potato to the warm milk and beat until well combined, adding extra milk if necessary to achieve the desired consistency. Season to taste with salt, ground black pepper and a little nutmeg, if using.

Savoury Potato Cakes

Make these crisp cakes of grated potato any size.

Serves 4
50g/1lb potatoes, grated, rinsed, drained and dried
1 small onion, grated
3 rashers (slices) streaky (fatty) bacon, finely chopped
30ml/2 tbsp self-raising (self-rising) flour
2 eggs, beaten
vegetable oil, for frying
salt and ground black pepper

1 Mix the potatoes with the onion, bacon, flour, eggs and seasoning. Heat 1cm/½in oil in a frying pan, add about 15ml/1 tbsp of the mixture and spread it with the back of the spoon.

2 Add a few more spoonfuls, leaving space between them, and cook for 4–5 minutes, until golden underneath. Turn the cakes over and cook for 3–4 minutes until golden brown and cooked through. Keep warm while you cook the remaining mixture.

Griddle Potatoes Energy 163kcal/681kJ; Protein 3.4g; Carbohydrate 26.4g, of which sugars 5g; Fat 5.5g, of which saturates 3.3g; Cholesterol 13mg; Calcium 26mg; Fibre 2.6g; Sodium 49mg.
Hasselback Potatoes Energy 380kcal/1593kJ; Protein 9.9g; Carbohydrate 42g, of which sugars 3.1g; Fat 20.4g, of which saturates 12.5g; Cholesterol 52mg; Calcium 182mg; Fibre 2.3g; Sodium 367mg.
Mashed Potatoes Energy 338kcal/1424kJ; Protein 5.9g; Carbohydrate 50.4g, of which sugars 3.3g; Fat 14g, of which saturates 9.1g; Cholesterol 39mg; Calcium 42mg; Fibre 3.6g; Sodium 140mg.
Savoury Potato Cakes Energy 186kcal/776kJ; Protein 6g; Carbohydrate 12.3g, of which sugars 1.2g; Fat 12.6g, of which saturates 4.2g; Cholesterol 38mg; Calcium 126mg; Fibre 1g; Sodium 246mg.

Pan Haggerty

This traditional dish of pan-fried potatoes works best with firm-fleshed, waxy potatoes such as Cara, Charlotte or Maris Peer. Serve it cut into wedges or spoon it from the pan.

Serves 4
60ml/4 tbsp vegetable oil
450g/1lb firm potatoes,
    thinly sliced
1 large onion, thinly sliced
115g/4oz/1 cup grated mature
    (sharp) Cheddar cheese
salt and ground black pepper

1 Heat the oil in a large frying pan. Remove the pan from the heat and add alternate layers of potato, onion slices and cheese, starting and ending with potatoes, and seasoning each layer as you go. Replace the pan over low heat.

2 Cook for 30 minutes, until the potatoes are soft and the underside has browned. Meanwhile, preheat the grill (broiler).

3 Place the pan under the grill for 5–10 minutes to brown the top. Serve immediately.

Roast Potatoes

Roast potatoes can be cooked around a festive joint of meat, to absorb the juices. For crisp potatoes with soft fluffy insides, roast them in a separate dish in one layer.

Serves 4
1.3kg/3lb floury potatoes
90ml/6 tbsp vegetable oil,
    lard or goose fat
salt

1 Preheat the oven to 200°C/400°F/Gas 6. Peel the potatoes and cut them into chunks. Boil in salted water for 5 minutes, drain, return to the pan, and shake them to roughen the edges.

2 Put the fat into a large roasting pan and heat in the oven. Add the potatoes, coating them in the fat. Cook for about 40–50 minutes, turning once or twice, until the potatoes are crisp and cooked through.

Potato and Root Vegetable Mash

This winter root vegetable dish is excellent with any Christmas roast, or serve with haggis or on top of shepherd's pie in place of just potato. Turnips give an earthy flavour, and swede introduces a sweet accent. It is also slightly less heavy than mashed potato.

Serves 4
450g/1lb potatoes
450g/1lb turnips or swede
    (rutabaga)
50g/2oz/¼ cup butter
50ml/2fl oz/¼ cup milk
5ml/1 tsp freshly grated nutmeg
30ml/2 tbsp chopped
    fresh parsley
salt and ground black pepper

1 Peel the potatoes and turnips or swede, then cut them into small chunks of roughly equal size. You will need a large sharp knife for the turnips.

2 Place the chopped vegetables in a pan and cover with cold water. Bring to the boil over medium heat, then reduce the heat and simmer until both vegetables are cooked, which will take about 15–20 minutes. Test the vegetables by pushing the point of a sharp knife into one of the cubes; if it goes in easily and the cube begins to break apart, then it is cooked.

3 Drain the vegetables through a colander. Return to the pan and allow them to dry out for a few minutes over low heat, stirring occasionally to prevent any from sticking and burning on to the base of the pan.

4 Melt the butter with the milk in a small pan over low heat. Mash the dry potato and turnip or swede mixture, then add the milk mixture. Grate in the nutmeg, add the parsley, mix thoroughly and season to taste with salt and pepper. Serve immediately with roast meat or game.

> **Cook's Tip**
> This is an excellent dish to serve during the festive season because it is the time of year when maincrop potatoes, turnips and swedes (rutabagas) are at their best.

Pan Haggerty Energy 271kcal/1128kJ; Protein 9.8g; Carbohydrate 21.1g, of which sugars 3.6g; Fat 16.9g, of which saturates 7.5g; Cholesterol 30mg; Calcium 215mg; Fibre 1.7g; Sodium 206mg.
Roast Potatoes Energy 484kcal/2048kJ; Protein 9.4g; Carbohydrate 84.2g, of which sugars 2g; Fat 14.6g, of which saturates 5.9g; Cholesterol 13mg; Calcium 26mg; Fibre 5.9g; Sodium 29mg.
Potato and Root Mash Energy 204kcal/852kJ; Protein 3.4g; Carbohydrate 24.1g, of which sugars 7.2g; Fat 11.2g, of which saturates 6.8g; Cholesterol 27mg; Calcium 78mg; Fibre 3.8g; Sodium 111mg.

Roast Parsnips with Honey and Nutmeg

Parsnips are at their best in winter, so they are always popular at Christmas. They are delicious when roasted around a festive joint of beef or a roast turkey. Their sweetness mingles well with the spice and honey.

Serves 4–6
4 medium parsnips
30ml/2 tbsp plain (all-purpose) flour seasoned with salt and pepper
60ml/4 tbsp vegetable oil
15–30ml/1–2 tbsp clear honey
freshly grated nutmeg

1 Preheat the oven to 200°C/400°F/Gas 6. Peel the parsnips and cut each one lengthways into rough quarters, removing and discarding any tough woody cores.

2 Place the parsnips into a pan of boiling water and cook for 5 minutes until slightly softened.

3 Drain the parsnips thoroughly, then toss in the seasoned flour, shaking off any excess.

4 Pour the oil into a roasting pan and put into the oven until hot. Add the parsnips, tossing them in the oil and arranging them in a single layer.

5 Return the pan to the oven and cook the parsnips for about 30 minutes, turning occasionally, until crisp, golden brown and tender.

6 Drizzle with the honey and sprinkle with a little grated nutmeg. Return the parsnips to the oven for 5 minutes to warm through before serving.

Cook's Tip
The Romans considered parsnips to be a culinary luxury, at which time they were credited with a variety of medicinal and aphrodisiac qualities.

Celeriac Purée

Celeriac is a versatile vegetable that is good grated raw or cooked.

Serves 4
1 celeriac bulb, cut into chunks
1 lemon, halved
2 potatoes, cut into chunks
300ml/½ pint/1¼ cups double (heavy) cream
salt and ground black pepper
chopped fresh chives, to garnish

1 Place the celeriac in a pan. Add the lemon halves. Add the potatoes to the pan and just cover with cold water. Cover the pan, boil, then simmer until tender, about 20 minutes.

2 Remove the lemon and drain the vegetables. Return to the pan and steam dry for a few minutes over low heat.

3 Purée in a food processor. Bring the cream to the boil. Add the celeriac mixture and mix. Season, top with chives and serve.

Parsnip Chips

These chips are particularly good served with game meats at Christmas time.

Serves 4
vegetable oil, for deep-frying
2 large parsnips, peeled
30ml/2 tbsp plain (all-purpose) flour
salt
good pinch of mild curry powder (optional)

1 Heat the oil to about 180°C/350°F. Season the flour with salt and curry powder, if using.

2 Using a potato peeler, cut lengthways strips from the parsnips. Put them into a pan, cover with water and bring to the boil. Drain and dry, then toss the strips in the flour.

3 Fry the strips, in batches, in the oil until crisp and golden outside and soft inside. Drain on kitchen paper. Sprinkle with a little salt and curry powder (if using) to serve.

Roast Parsnips Energy 144kcal/600kJ; Protein 2g; Carbohydrate 16.2g, of which sugars 6.7g; Fat 8.3g, of which saturates 1g; Cholesterol 0mg; Calcium 41mg; Fibre 4g; Sodium 9mg.
Celeriac Purée Energy 403kcal/1661kJ; Protein 2.2g; Carbohydrate 7.9g, of which sugars 2.3g; Fat 40.5g, of which saturates 25.1g; Cholesterol 103mg; Calcium 65mg; Fibre 1.1g; Sodium 58mg.
Parsnip Chips Energy 230kcal/956kJ; Protein 2.3g; Carbohydrate 16.8g, of which sugars 5.1g; Fat 17.6g, of which saturates 2.1g; Cholesterol 0mg; Calcium 47mg; Fibre 4.3g; Sodium 9mg.

Young Vegetables with Tarragon

The vegetables here are just lightly cooked to bring out their flavours. It is a great addition to the festive feast.

Serves 4
5 spring onions (scallions)
50g/2oz/¼ cup butter

1 garlic clove, crushed
115g/4oz asparagus tips
115g/4oz mangetouts
  (snowpeas), trimmed
115g/4oz broad (fava) beans
2 Little Gem (Bibb) lettuces
5ml/1 tsp chopped fresh tarragon
salt and ground black pepper

1 Cut the spring onions into quarters lengthways and fry gently over medium-low heat in half the butter with the garlic.

2 Add the asparagus tips, mangetouts and broad beans. Mix in, covering all the pieces with oil. Just cover the base of the pan with water, season, and allow to simmer for a few minutes.

3 Cut the lettuces into quarters and add to the pan. Cook for 3 minutes then, off the heat, swirl in the remaining butter and the tarragon, and serve immediately.

Crispy Cabbage

This quick side dish makes a crunchy base for slices of ham or left-over turkey. Savoy cabbage is especially pretty cooked this way.

Serves 4–6
1 medium green or small
  white cabbage
30ml/2 tbsp vegetable oil
salt and ground black pepper

1 Remove any coarse outside leaves from the cabbage and also the central rib from the larger remaining leaves. Shred the leaves finely. Wash well under cold running water, shake well and blot on kitchen paper to dry.

2 Heat a wok or wide-based flameproof casserole over a fairly high heat. Heat the oil and add the cabbage. Stir-fry for about 2–3 minutes, or until it is just cooked but still crunchy. Season with salt and pepper and serve.

Cabbage with Bacon

Bacon, especially if smoked, makes all the difference to the flavour of the cabbage, turning it into a delicious vegetable accompaniment to serve with a festive turkey or even with roast beef or grilled chicken.

Serves 4
30ml/2 tbsp vegetable oil
1 onion, finely chopped
115g/4oz smoked bacon,
  finely chopped
500g/1¼lb cabbage (red, white
  or Savoy)
salt and ground black pepper

1 Heat the oil in a large pan over medium heat, add the chopped onion and the smoked bacon and cook for about 7 minutes, stirring occasionally.

2 Remove and discard any tough outer leaves from the cabbage and wash the leaves. Shred the leaves quite finely, discarding the core and any tough spines.

3 Add the cabbage to the pan and season with salt and ground black pepper. Stir for a few minutes until the cabbage begins to lose volume.

4 Continue to cook the cabbage, stirring frequently, for about 8–10 minutes until it is tender but still crisp. Serve immediately.

> **Cook's Tip**
> If you prefer softer cabbage, then cover the pan for part of the cooking time in step 4.

> **Variations**
> • This dish is equally delicious if you use spring greens (collards) instead of cabbage. You could also use curly kale, which is in season over the Christmas period.
> • To make a more substantial dish to serve for lunch or supper, add more bacon, some chopped button (white) mushrooms and skinned, seeded and chopped tomatoes.

Celery, Avocado and Walnut Salad

The crunchiness of the celery and walnuts contrasts perfectly with the smooth avocado. Serve it with a sour cream dressing as suggested or simply dressed with a little extra virgin olive oil and freshly squeezed lemon juice.

Serves 4
3 streaky (fatty) bacon rashers (strips) optional

8 tender white or green celery sticks, very thinly sliced
3 spring onions (scallions), finely chopped
50g/2oz/½ cup chopped walnuts
1 ripe avocado
lemon juice

For the dressing
120ml/4fl oz/½ cup sour cream
15ml/1 tbsp extra virgin olive oil
pinch of cayenne pepper

1 Dry fry the bacon, if using, in a heavy frying pan until golden and then chop into small pieces and place in a salad bowl with the celery, spring onions and walnuts.

2 Halve the avocado and remove the stone (pit). Using a very sharp knife, cut the avocado halves into thin slices. Peel away the skin from each slice, sprinkle generously with lemon juice and add to the celery mixture.

3 Lightly beat the sour cream, olive oil and cayenne pepper together in a jug (pitcher) or small bowl. Either fold carefully into the salad or serve separately.

> **Cook's Tip**
> *Whenever you need to prepare avocado for a salad dish, sprinkle it liberally with lemon juice to prevent the flesh from discolouring before the dish is served.*

> **Variation**
> *This salad is equally delicious served without the bacon if you have any vegetarian guests for dinner during Christmas.*

Roast Beetroot with Horseradish

Beetroot is enhanced by horseradish and vinegar. Serve with a festive roast.

Serves 4–6
10–12 small whole beetroot (beets)

30ml/2 tbsp vegetable oil
45ml/3 tbsp grated fresh horseradish
15ml/1 tbsp white wine vinegar
10ml/2 tsp caster (superfine) sugar
150ml/¼ pint/⅔ cup double (heavy) cream

1 Preheat the oven to 180°C/350°F/Gas 4. Wash the beetroot without breaking their skins. Trim the stalks short but do not remove them completely. Toss the beetroot in the oil and season with salt. Spread them in a roasting pan and cover with foil and roast for 1½ hours. Leave to cool, covered, for 10 minutes.

2 Meanwhile, make the horseradish sauce. Mix the horseradish, vinegar and sugar in a bowl. Whip the cream and fold into the horseradish mixture. Cover and chill until required.

3 When the beetroot are cool enough to handle, slip off the skins and serve with the sauce.

Kale with Mustard Dressing

This is a classic winter side dish – ideal for Christmas. Use curly kale if you can't get sea kale. You will need to boil it for a few minutes before chilling and serving.

Serves 4
250g/9oz sea kale or curly kale
45ml/3 tbsp light olive oil
5ml/1 tsp wholegrain mustard
15ml/1 tbsp white wine vinegar
pinch of caster (superfine) sugar
salt and ground black pepper

1 Wash the sea kale, drain thoroughly, then trim it and cut in two. Whisk the oil and mustard in a bowl. Whisk in the white wine vinegar. It should begin to thicken.

2 Season the mustard dressing to taste with sugar, salt and pepper. Toss the sea kale in the dressing and serve immediately.

Celery Salad Energy 318kcal/1318kJ; Protein 17.4g; Carbohydrate 4.4g, of which sugars 3.9g; Fat 25.8g, of which saturates 16.3g; Cholesterol 71mg; Calcium 371mg; Fibre 1.8g; Sodium 453mg.
Roast Beetroot Energy 254kcal/1052kJ; Protein 2.1g; Carbohydrate 10g, of which sugars 9.1g; Fat 22.2g, of which saturates 3.2g; Cholesterol 1mg; Calcium 26mg; Fibre 2.3g; Sodium 143mg.
Kale with Mustard Dressing Energy 99kcal/409kJ; Protein 2.1g; Carbohydrate 1.9g, of which sugars 1.9g; Fat 9.3g, of which saturates 1.3g; Cholesterol 0mg; Calcium 82mg; Fibre 2g; Sodium 27mg.

Christmas Beetroot, Apple and Potato Salad

This salad is delicious and great for serving at a festive get-together. It is ideal served with a meal on Christmas Eve, just as the excitement mounts.

Serves 4

1 apple
3 cooked potatoes, finely diced
2 large gherkins, finely diced
3 cooked beetroot (beets), finely diced
3 cooked carrots, finely diced
1 onion, finely chopped
500ml/17fl oz/generous 2 cups double (heavy) cream
3 hard-boiled eggs, roughly chopped
15ml/1 tbsp chopped fresh parsley
salt and ground white pepper

1 Cut the apple into small dice. Put in a bowl and add the potatoes, gherkins, beetroot, carrots and onion and season with salt and pepper. Carefully mix together and spoon into individual serving glasses or bowls.

2 Mix any beetroot juice into the cream to flavour and give it a pinkish colour, then spoon over the vegetables and apple. Sprinkle the chopped eggs and chopped fresh parsley over the top before serving.

Cook's Tip
Take care when preparing beetroot. They should be cleaned carefully so as not to penetrate the skin, otherwise the colour and nutrients will leach out into the boiling water. Also, only trim the tops of the stalks – if too much is taken off, you may damage the skin. Peel the beetroot once cooled after cooking.

Variation
Stir in ½ finely chopped salted herring fillet or 2 finely chopped anchovy fillets to the mixture with the parsley to add an extra dimension to the dish. Omit the added salt.

Herby Carrot, Apple and Orange Salad

This dish is as delicious as it is easy to make. The garlic and herb dressing adds a necessary contrast to the sweetness of the salad.

Serves 4

350g/12oz young carrots, finely grated
2 eating apples
15ml/1 tbsp lemon juice
1 large orange

For the dressing
45ml/3 tbsp olive oil
60ml/4 tbsp sunflower oil
45ml/3 tbsp lemon juice
1 garlic clove, crushed
60ml/4 tbsp natural (plain) yogurt
15ml/1 tbsp chopped mixed fresh herbs such as tarragon, parsley or chives
salt and ground black pepper

1 Place the carrots in a large serving bowl. Quarter the apples, remove the core and then slice thinly. Sprinkle the slices with the lemon juice, to prevent them from discolouring, and then add them to the carrots.

2 Using a sharp knife, remove the peel and pith from the orange and then separate the flesh into segments. Add these to the carrots and apples.

3 To make the dressing, place both the oils with the lemon juice, crushed garlic, natural yogurt, mixed fresh herbs and seasoning in a jar with a lid and shake to blend.

4 Just before serving, pour the dressing over the salad and toss well together to mix thoroughly.

Cook's Tip
This is a great salad for having in the refrigerator over the busy festive season in case unexpected hungry guests arrive. You can prepare the dressing in advance and keep it in the refrigerator for up to a week, meaning you can prepare the rest of the ingredients at very short notice.

Christmas Salad Energy 717kcal/2959kJ; Protein 8.5g; Carbohydrate 11g, of which sugars 10.2g; Fat 71.5g, of which saturates 42.9g; Cholesterol 314mg; Calcium 114mg; Fibre 2.3g; Sodium 132mg.
Coleslaw Energy 183kcal/766kJ; Protein 3.9g; Carbohydrate 24g, of which sugars 7.3g; Fat 8.5g, of which saturates 2.4g; Cholesterol 7mg; Calcium 73mg; Fibre 3.5g; Sodium 24mg.

Classic Tomato Salad

This tasty tomato salad is quick to prepare and will be ideal as part of a festive buffet or quick lunch.

Serves 4
4 ripe but firm tomatoes
 on the vine

2–3 shallots, finely chopped
45ml/3 tbsp chopped fresh
 parsley or dill
30ml/2 tbsp red wine vinegar
90ml/6 tbsp vegetable oil,
 olive oil or a mixture
salt and ground black pepper

1 Remove the stem and core from each tomato, then slice them evenly and arrange them on a serving platter.

2 Sprinkle the shallots over the sliced tomatoes. Season with salt and ground black pepper and sprinkle with the chopped fresh parsley or dill.

3 Make a simple salad dressing by putting the red wine vinegar in a bowl and whisking in the oil until well combined. Drizzle the dressing over the tomatoes.

4 Cover the tomato salad with clear film (plastic wrap) and marinate for 30 minutes at room temperature before serving. If chilled for any time, return the salad to room temperature.

> **Cook's Tip**
> The fresher the tomatoes, the better this salad will be. They should be full-flavoured and firm enough to slice neatly with a serrated knife. If you like, you can peel the tomatoes before slicing them, but this is not strictly necessary.

> **Variation**
> The herbs can be varied, depending on what is available. Tarragon is a good addition, especially if the salad is to be served with fish. Strip the leaves from a sprig of tarragon and chop them finely before sprinkling them over the salad.

Potato Salad

This is a classic salad which should be part of every festive buffet spread. It is a great salad to prepare in advance and keep chilled in the refrigerator – giving you more time to spend entertaining your Christmas guests rather than cooking in the kitchen.

Serves 6–8
1.8kg/4lb waxy potatoes
45ml/3 tbsp finely chopped onion
2 celery stalks, finely chopped
250ml/8fl oz/1 cup sour cream
250ml/8fl oz/1 cup mayonnaise
5ml/1 tsp mustard powder
4ml/¾ tsp celery seed
75ml/5 tbsp chopped fresh dill
salt and ground white pepper

1 Boil the potatoes in lightly salted water for 20–25 minutes, until tender, then drain and allow to cool. Peel and coarsely chop the potatoes and place them in a large mixing bowl. Add the onion and celery to the bowl.

2 Meanwhile, make the dressing: in a separate bowl, stir together the sour cream, mayonnaise, mustard, celery seed, dill, salt and ground white pepper.

3 Add the dressing to the potatoes and toss gently to coat evenly with the dressing. Adjust the seasoning, cover the bowl and chill until ready to serve.

> **Cook's Tips**
> • It is best to add the dressing to the potatoes while they are still slightly warm rather than completely cold. They will soak up more of the delicious dressing.
> • Use waxy potatoes for this salad as they will hold their shape better than the floury variety, which tend to break apart when they have been cooked.

> **Variation**
> Add chopped cucumber, crumbled crisp bacon, or chopped hard-boiled eggs to the potato salad.

Potato Salad Energy 440kcal/1834kJ; Protein 5.2g; Carbohydrate 38.5g, of which sugars 4.9g; Fat 30.5g, of which saturates 7.7g; Cholesterol 42mg; Calcium 50mg; Fibre 2.4g; Sodium 183mg.
Classic Tomato Salad Energy 171kcal/705kJ; Protein 1.1g; Carbohydrate 3.9g, of which sugars 3.5g; Fat 16.9g, of which saturates 2g; Cholesterol 0mg; Calcium 34mg; Fibre 1.6g; Sodium 11mg.

Raw Vegetable Salad

This colourful array of vegetables, served with a creamy and flavourful dip, makes an enticing and unusual side dish to accompany a selection of cold meats. Or, it will look great on a buffet table.

Serves 6–8
225g/8oz fresh baby corn cobs
175–225g/6–8oz thin
  asparagus, trimmed
2 red and 2 yellow (bell) peppers,
  seeded and sliced lengthwise
1 chicory (Belgian endive)
  head, trimmed and leaves
  separated
1 small bunch radishes
  with small leaves
175g/6oz cherry tomatoes
12 quail's eggs, boiled for
  3 minutes, drained,
  refreshed and peeled
aioli or tapenade, to serve

1 Bring a large pan of water to the boil, add the baby corn cobs and trimmed asparagus and bring back to the boil. Blanch for 1–2 minutes, then drain and cool quickly under cold running water or dip in a bowl of iced water. Drain well.

2 Arrange the corn cobs, asparagus, chicory leaves, radishes and tomatoes on a serving plate together with the quail's eggs.

3 Cover with a damp dish towel until ready to serve. Serve with aioli or tapenade for dipping.

> **Cook's Tips**
> • *To make tapenade, place 175g/6oz/1 ½ cups pitted black olives, 50g/2oz drained anchovy fillets and 30ml/2 tbsp capers in a food processor with 120ml/4fl oz/½ cup olive oil and the finely grated rind of 1 lemon. Lightly process to blend, then season with black pepper and add a little more oil if very dry.*
> • *To make a herby aioli, beat together 2 egg yolks, 5ml/1 tsp Dijon mustard and 10ml/2 tsp white wine vinegar. Gradually blend in 250m/8fl oz/1 cup olive oil, a trickle at a time, whisking well after each addition, until thick and smooth. Season with salt and pepper to taste, then stir in 45ml/3 tbsp chopped mixed fresh herbs and 4–5 crushed garlic cloves.*

Pumpkin Salad

Pumpkins are at their best over the autumn and winter months so are ideal for serving at Christmas. Red wine vinegar brings out the sweet flavour of the pumpkin. No salad leaves are used in this salad, just plenty of fresh flat leaf parsley. This is a great dish for serving at a cold festive buffet.

Serves 4
1 large red onion, peeled and very
  thinly sliced
200ml/7fl oz/scant 1 cup olive oil
60ml/4 tbsp red wine vinegar
675g/1½lb pumpkin, peeled and
  cut into 4cm/1½in pieces
40g/1½oz/¾ cup fresh flat leaf
  parsley leaves, chopped
salt and ground black pepper
fresh flat leaf parsley sprigs, to
  garnish (optional)

1 Mix the onion, olive oil and vinegar in a large bowl. Season with salt and pepper, then stir well to combine.

2 Put the pumpkin pieces in a large pan of cold salted water. Bring to the boil, then lower the heat and simmer gently for 15–20 minutes. Drain.

3 Immediately add the drained pumpkin pieces to the bowl containing the dressing and toss lightly with your hands to coat the pumpkin evenly. Leave to cool.

4 Add the chopped parsley to the pumpkin and toss gently. Cover the bowl with clear film (plastic wrap) and chill in the refrigerator until needed.

5 Allow the salad to come back to room temperature before serving. Garnish with fresh parsley sprigs, if you like.

> **Cook's Tips**
> • *Other fresh herbs will also work in this salad, depending on what is available. Try coriander (cilantro), mint or basil – or a combination of them with the flat leaf parsley.*
> • *If the salad isn't at room temperature when served, the delicious flavours will be subdued.*

Grilled Leek and Fennel Salad

This is an excellent salad for the festive season, when leeks are at their best. It has a pleasant kick from the chilli flakes.

Serves 6
675g/1½lb leeks
2 large fennel bulbs
120ml/4fl oz/½ cup olive oil
2 shallots, chopped
150ml/¼ pint/⅔ cup dry white
   wine or white vermouth
5ml/1 tsp fennel seeds, crushed
6 fresh thyme sprigs
2–3 bay leaves
pinch of dried red chilli flakes
350g/12oz tomatoes, peeled,
   seeded and diced
5ml/1 tsp sun-dried tomato
   paste (optional)
good pinch of sugar (optional)
75g/3oz/¾ cup small black
   pitted olives
salt and ground black pepper

1 Cook the leeks in boiling salted water for 4–5 minutes. Using a slotted spoon, place them in a colander to drain and cool. Then cut into 7.5cm/3in lengths. Reserve the cooking water.

2 Trim and slice the fennel. Keep the tops for a garnish. Cook the fennel in the reserved water for about 5 minutes, drain, then toss with 30ml/2 tbsp of olive oil. Season to taste with salt and ground black pepper.

3 Heat a ridged cast iron griddle on the stove until hot, and cook the vegetables until tinged deep brown, then place them in a large shallow dish.

4 Heat the remaining oil, the shallots, white wine or vermouth, crushed fennel seeds, thyme, bay leaves and chilli flakes in a large pan and bring to the boil over medium heat. Lower the heat and simmer for 10 minutes.

5 Add the diced tomatoes and cook briskly until the consistency of the dressing has thickened. Add the tomato paste, adjust the seasoning, and add a pinch of sugar, if you like.

6 Toss the fennel and leeks in the dressing and leave to cool. Garnish the salad with the fennel fronds and olives before serving at room temperature.

Vegetable Rice

Serve this tasty dish with roast chicken or steamed fish. The vegetables are added near the end of cooking so that they remain crisp and flavoursome.

Serves 4
350g/12oz/1¾ cups basmati rice
45ml/3 tbsp vegetable oil
1 onion, chopped
2 garlic cloves, crushed
750ml/1¼ pints/3 cups vegetable
   stock or water
115g/4oz/⅔ cup fresh or drained
   canned corn kernels
½ red or green (bell) pepper,
   seeded and chopped
1 large carrot, grated
salt
fresh chervil sprigs, to garnish
salt and ground black pepper
frilly lettuce leaves, to serve

1 Rinse the rice in a sieve (strainer) under cold water, then leave to drain thoroughly for about 15 minutes.

2 Heat the oil in a large, heavy pan and fry the onion for a few minutes over a medium heat until it starts to soften.

3 Add the rice and fry for 10 minutes, stirring constantly to prevent the rice sticking to the pan. Stir in the crushed garlic.

4 Pour in the stock or water, season with salt if necessary, and stir well. Bring to the boil, then lower the heat, cover and simmer for 10 minutes.

5 Sprinkle the corn kernels, chopped pepper and grated carrot over the rice, then cover the pan tightly. Steam over a low heat for a few minutes, until the rice is tender, then mix together with a fork, pile on to a platter and garnish with chervil. Serve the vegetable rice immediately.

> **Variation**
> Other vegetables can be used in this dish instead of corn, peppers and carrot. You could make it with green vegetables such as broccoli, courgettes (zucchini), leeks and peas. Garnish with parsley or fresh coriander (cilantro) in place of the chervil.

Grilled Salad Energy 193kcal/800kJ; Protein 2.8g; Carbohydrate 6.7g, of which sugars 5.9g; Fat 14.7g, of which saturates 2.2g; Cholesterol 0mg; Calcium 53mg; Fibre 4.6g; Sodium 297mg.
Vegetable Rice Energy 455kcal/1902kJ; Protein 8.3g; Carbohydrate 84.2g, of which sugars 8.5g; Fat 9.3g, of which saturates 1.1g; Cholesterol 0mg; Calcium 34mg; Fibre 1.9g; Sodium 84mg.

Mushroom Pilau

This dish is simplicity itself. Serve with ham or gammon as part of a hot buffet at Christmas. It is also delicious with any Indian dish or with roast lamb or chicken.

Serves 4
30ml/2 tbsp vegetable oil
2 shallots, finely chopped
1 garlic clove, crushed
3 green cardamom pods

25g/1oz/2 tbsp ghee or butter
175g/6oz/2½ cups button
  (white) mushrooms, sliced
225g/8oz/generous 1 cup
  basmati rice, soaked
5ml/1 tsp grated fresh
  root ginger
good pinch of garam masala
450ml/¾ pint/scant 2 cups water
15ml/1 tbsp chopped fresh
  coriander (cilantro)
salt

1 Heat the oil in a flameproof casserole or large, heavy frying pan and fry the shallots, garlic and cardamom pods over medium heat for 3–4 minutes until the shallots have softened and are beginning to brown.

2 Add the ghee or butter to the pan. When it has melted, add the mushrooms and fry for 2–3 minutes more.

3 Add the rice, ginger and garam masala to the pan. Stir-fry over low heat for 2–3 minutes, then stir in the water and a little salt.

4 Bring to the boil, then cover tightly and simmer over very low heat for 10 minutes.

5 Remove the casserole from the heat. Leave to stand, covered, for 5 minutes. Add the chopped coriander and fork it through the rice. Spoon the pilau into a warmed serving bowl and serve immediately.

> **Variation**
> Instead of the button (white) mushrooms, try making a mixed wild mushroom pilau. Choose from ceps, chanterelle, field (portabello) or morel mushrooms.

Ham and Bulgur Wheat Salad

This flavoursome, nutty salad is ideal for using up left-over cooked ham for a quick and simple addition to a Christmas buffet menu.

Serves 8
225g/8oz/1⅓ cup bulgur wheat
45ml/3 tbsp olive oil

30ml/2 tbsp lemon juice
1 red (bell) pepper
225g/8oz cooked ham, diced
30ml/2 tbsp chopped fresh mint
30ml/2 tbsp currants
salt and ground black pepper
sprigs of fresh mint and lemon
  slices, to garnish

1 Put the bulgur wheat into a large heatproof bowl, pour over enough boiling water to cover and leave to stand until all the water has been absorbed by the bulgur wheat and the grains look as if they have swelled up.

2 Add the olive oil and lemon juice to the bulgur wheat. Season to taste with salt and black pepper. Toss to separate the grains using two forks.

3 Quarter the pepper, removing the stalk and seeds. Rinse under running water. Using a sharp knife, cut the pepper quarters into wide strips and then into diamonds.

4 Add the pepper, ham, chopped fresh mint and currants to the wheat in the bowl. Mix with a spoon to ensure the ingredients are well distributed.

5 Transfer the salad to a serving dish, garnish with the fresh mint sprigs and lemon slices and serve.

> **Variations**
> • This dish can also be made with 225g/8oz/1⅓ cup couscous instead of the bulgur wheat. To prepare, cover the couscous with boiling water as in Step 1.
> • This is a versatile salad, letting you improvise depending on what meat you have been cooking for Christmas. You can use left-over turkey or chicken in place of the ham, if you prefer.

Mushroom Pilau Energy 309kcal/1286kJ; Protein 5.2g; Carbohydrate 46.3g, of which sugars 1g; Fat 11.2g, of which saturates 4g; Cholesterol 13mg; Calcium 18mg; Fibre 0.7g; Sodium 41mg.
Ham and Bulgur Salad Energy 148kcal/619kJ; Protein 7.1g; Carbohydrate 18.7g, of which sugars 4.2g; Fat 5.4g, of which saturates 0.9g; Cholesterol 16mg; Calcium 13mg; Fibre 0.4g; Sodium 339mg.

Wild Rice Pilaff

Wild rice isn't a rice at all, but is actually a type of wild grass. Call it what you will, it has a wonderful nutty flavour and combines well with long grain rice in this fruity mixture. Serve as a side dish.

Serves 6
200g/7oz/1 cup wild rice
40g/1½oz/3 tbsp butter
½ onion, finely chopped
200g/7oz/1 cup long
  grain rice
475ml/16fl oz/2 cups
  chicken stock
75g/3oz/¾ cup flaked
  (sliced) almonds
115g/4oz/⅔ cup sultanas
  (golden raisins)
30ml/2 tbsp chopped
  fresh parsley
salt and ground black pepper

1 Bring a large pan of water to the boil. Add the wild rice and 5ml/1 tsp salt. Lower the heat, cover and simmer gently for 45–60 minutes, until the rice is tender. Drain well.

2 Meanwhile, melt 15g/½oz/1 tbsp of the butter in another pan. Add the onion and cook over medium heat for about 5 minutes until it is just softened. Stir in the long grain rice and cook for 1 minute more.

3 Stir in the chicken stock and bring to the boil. Cover the pan and simmer gently for 30–40 minutes, until the rice is tender and the liquid has been absorbed. Stir in the wild rice.

4 Melt the remaining butter in a small pan. Add the almonds and cook until they are just golden.

5 Put the rice mixture in a bowl and add the almonds, sultanas and half the parsley. Stir to mix. Taste and adjust the seasoning if necessary. Transfer to a warmed serving dish, sprinkle with the remaining fresh parsley and serve.

> **Cook's Tip**
> Like all dishes made with stock, this will taste best if you use a good home-made stock.

Californian Citrus Fried Rice

As with all fried rice dishes, it is important to make sure the rice is cold. Add it when all the other ingredients are cooked, and heat it through.

Serves 4–6
4 eggs
10ml/2 tsp Japanese rice vinegar
30ml/2 tbsp light soy sauce
about 45ml/3 tbsp groundnut
  (peanut) oil
50g/2oz/½ cup cashew nuts
2 garlic cloves, crushed
6 spring onions (scallions),
  diagonally sliced
2 small carrots, cut into strips
225g/8oz asparagus, each spear
  cut diagonally into 4 pieces
175g/6oz/2¼ cups button
  (white) mushrooms, halved
30ml/2 tbsp rice wine
30ml/2 tbsp water
450g/1lb/4 cups cooked white
  long grain rice
about 10ml/2 tsp sesame oil
1 pink grapefruit or orange, cut
  into segments
thin strips of orange rind,
  to garnish

For the hot dressing
5ml/1 tsp grated orange rind
30ml/2 tbsp Japanese rice wine
45ml/3 tbsp oyster sauce
30ml/2 tbsp freshly squeezed
  pink grapefruit or orange juice
5ml/1 tsp hot chilli sauce

1 Beat the eggs with the vinegar and 10ml/2 tsp of the soy sauce. Heat 15ml/1 tbsp of the oil in a wok and cook the eggs until lightly scrambled. Transfer to a plate and set aside. Add the cashew nuts to the wok and stir-fry for 1–2 minutes. Set aside.

2 Heat the remaining oil and add the garlic and spring onions. Cook over medium heat for 1–2 minutes until the onions begin to soften, then add the carrots and stir-fry for 4 minutes.

3 Add the asparagus and cook for 2–3 minutes, then stir in the mushrooms and stir-fry for a further 1 minute. Stir in the rice wine, the remaining soy sauce and the water. Simmer for a few minutes until the vegetables are just tender but still firm.

4 Mix the dressing ingredients, then add to the wok and bring to the boil. Add the rice, scrambled eggs and cashew nuts. Toss over low heat for 3–4 minutes, until the rice is heated through. Just before serving, stir in the sesame oil and the grapefruit or orange segments. Garnish with strips of orange rind and serve.

Wild Rice Pilaff Energy 424kcal/1769kJ; Protein 8.4g; Carbohydrate 68.3g, of which sugars 14.5g; Fat 13g, of which saturates 4g; Cholesterol 14mg; Calcium 69mg; Fibre 1.7g; Sodium 48mg.
Citrus Fried Rice Energy 264kcal/1107kJ; Protein 6.5g; Carbohydrate 32.3g, of which sugars 7.7g; Fat 12.6g, of which saturates 2.1g; Cholesterol 13mg; Calcium 48mg; Fibre 2.3g; Sodium 517mg.

Rice and Peas

This is an ideal dish for a hot Christmas buffet menu featuring a selection of meat and fish. Although the recipe is called 'Rice and Peas', traditionally, the dish is nearly always made with a variety of beans.

Serves 4–6

175g/6oz/³⁄₄ cup dried red
   kidney beans
2 fresh thyme sprigs

50g/2oz piece of creamed
   coconut or 60ml/4 tbsp
   coconut cream
2 bay leaves
1 onion, finely chopped
2 garlic cloves, crushed
2.5ml/¹⁄₂ tsp ground allspice
115g/4oz/²⁄₃ cup chopped red
   (bell) pepper
600ml/1 pint/2¹⁄₂ cups water
450g/1lb/2¹⁄₃ cups white long
   grain rice
salt and ground black pepper

1 Place the red kidney beans in a large bowl. Cover with water and leave to soak overnight.

2 Drain the beans, place in a large pan and pour in enough water to cover them by about 2.5cm/1in. Bring to the boil. Boil over high heat for 10 minutes, skimming off any foam that gathers on the surface. Lower the heat and simmer for about 1¹⁄₂ hours or until tender. Drain and return to the pan.

3 Add the thyme, creamed coconut or coconut cream, bay leaves, onion, garlic, allspice and red pepper to the beans. Season well with plenty of salt and ground black pepper and stir in the measured water.

4 Bring to the boil and add the rice. Stir well, lower the heat and cover the pan. Simmer for 25–30 minutes, until all the liquid has been absorbed by the rice. Serve immediately, as an accompaniment to fish, meat or vegetarian dishes.

> **Cook's Tip**
> To save time and effort over the busy Christmas period, you can use a 400g/14oz can of red kidney beans, if you prefer. Add them along with the rice.

Sweet and Sour Rice

This popular rice dish is flavoured with fruit and spices. It is delicious served with lamb or chicken.

Serves 4

50g/2oz/¹⁄₂ cup zereshk
   (dried barberries)
45g/1¹⁄₂oz/3 tbsp butter

50g/2oz/¹⁄₃ cup raisins
50g/2oz/¹⁄₄ cup sugar
5ml/1 tsp ground cinnamon
5ml/1 tsp ground cumin
350g/12oz/1³⁄₄ cups basmati
   rice, soaked
2–3 saffron strands, soaked in
   15ml/1 tbsp boiling water
pinch of salt

1 Thoroughly wash the zereshk in cold water at least four or five times to rinse off any bits of grit. Drain well.

2 Melt 15g/¹⁄₂oz/1 tbsp of the butter in a frying pan and fry the raisins for about 1–2 minutes.

3 Add the zereshk to the pan, fry for a few seconds, and then add the sugar, with half of the cinnamon and cumin. Cook briefly and then set aside.

4 Drain the rice, then put it in a pan with plenty of boiling, lightly salted water. Bring back to the boil, reduce the heat and simmer for 4 minutes. Drain and rinse once again, if you like.

5 Melt half the remaining butter in the clean pan, add 15ml/1 tbsp water and stir in half the cooked rice. Sprinkle with half the zereshk mixture and top with all but 45ml/3 tbsp of the rice. Sprinkle over the remaining raisin and zereshk mixture.

6 Mix the remaining cinnamon and cumin with the reserved rice, and sprinkle this mixture evenly over the layered mixture. Melt the remaining butter, drizzle it over the surface, then cover the pan with a clean dish towel. Cover with a tight-fitting lid, lifting the corners of the cloth back over the lid. Steam the rice over a very low heat for about 20–30 minutes, until tender.

7 Just before serving, mix 45ml/3 tbsp of the rice with the saffron water. Spoon the sweet and sour rice on to a large, flat serving dish and sprinkle the saffron rice over the top, to garnish.

Rice and Peas Energy 289kcal/1200kJ; Protein 11.5g; Carbohydrate 40.3g, of which sugars 2.6g; Fat 9.1g, of which saturates 2.1g; Cholesterol 11mg; Calcium 42mg; Fibre 4.4g; Sodium 213mg.
Sweet and Sour Rice Energy 465kcal/1943kJ; Protein 7g; Carbohydrate 87g, of which sugars 17.2g; Fat 9.8g, of which saturates 5.9g; Cholesterol 24mg; Calcium 32mg; Fibre 0.6g; Sodium 77mg.

Rice with Dill and Broad Beans

This is a fabulous rice dish. The combination of broad beans, fresh dill and warm spices is delicious, and the saffron rice adds a splash of bright colour to a cold winter's day. It works well as part of a festive feast where guests help themselves to food.

Serves 4

275g/10oz/1½ cups basmati rice, soaked for 1 hour
750ml/1¼ pints/3 cups water
40g/1½oz/3 tbsp butter
175g/6oz/1½ cups frozen baby broad (fava) beans, thawed and peeled
90ml/6 tbsp finely chopped fresh dill, plus 1 fresh dill sprig, to garnish
5ml/1 tsp ground cinnamon
5ml/1 tsp ground cumin
2–3 saffron strands, soaked in 15ml/1 tbsp boiling water
salt and ground black pepper

1 Drain the rice, put it into a pan and pour in the water. Add a little salt. Bring to the boil, then lower the heat and simmer very gently for 5 minutes. Drain, rinse well in warm water and drain once again.

2 Melt the butter in a non-stick pan. Pour two-thirds of the melted butter into a small jug (pitcher) and set aside.

3 Spoon enough rice into the pan to cover the bottom. Add a quarter of the beans and a little dill. Spread over another layer of rice, then a layer of beans and dill. Repeat the layers until all the rice, beans and dill have been used up, ending with a layer of rice. Cook over low heat for 8 minutes until nearly tender.

4 Pour the reserved melted butter over the rice. Sprinkle with the ground cinnamon and cumin. Cover the pan with a clean dish towel and a tight-fitting lid, lifting the corners of the cloth back over the lid. Cook over low heat for 25–30 minutes.

5 Spoon about 45ml/3 tbsp of the cooked rice into the bowl of saffron water; mix well to coat all the rice. Mound the remaining rice mixture on a large serving plate and spoon the saffron rice on one side to decorate. Serve immediately, decorated with the sprig of dill.

Sweet and Hot Vegetable Noodles

This noodle dish has the colour of fire, but only the mildest suggestion of heat. Ginger and plum sauce give it its fruity flavour.

Serves 4

130g/4½oz dried rice noodles
30ml/2 tbsp groundnut (peanut) oil
2.5cm/1in piece fresh root ginger, sliced into thin batons
1 garlic clove, crushed
130g/4½oz drained canned bamboo shoots, sliced in batons
2 medium carrots, sliced in batons
130g/4½oz/1½ cups beansprouts
1 small white cabbage, shredded
30ml/2 tbsp Thai fish sauce
30ml/2 tbsp soy sauce
30ml/2 tbsp plum sauce
10ml/2 tsp sesame oil
15ml/1 tbsp palm sugar (jaggery) or light muscovado (brown) sugar
juice of ½ lime
90g/3½oz mooli (daikon), sliced into thin batons
small bunch fresh coriander (cilantro), chopped
60ml/4 tbsp sesame seeds, toasted

1 Cook the noodles in a large pan of boiling water, following the instructions on the packet. Meanwhile, heat the oil in a wok or large frying pan and stir-fry the ginger and garlic together for 2–3 minutes over medium heat, until golden.

2 Drain the noodles and keep warm. Add the bamboo shoots to the wok, increase the heat to high and stir-fry for 5 minutes. Add the carrots, beansprouts and cabbage and stir-fry for a further 5 minutes, until they are beginning to char at the edges.

3 Stir in the sauces, sesame oil, sugar and lime juice. Add the mooli and coriander, toss to mix, and serve with the noodles in warmed bowls, sprinkled with toasted sesame seeds.

Cook's Tip
Use a large, sharp knife for shredding cabbage. Remove any tough outer leaves, if necessary, then cut the cabbage into quarters. Cut off and discard the hard core from each quarter, place flat side down, then slice the cabbage leaves very thinly to make fine shreds.

Rice with Dill Energy 363kcal/1516kJ; Protein 9.2g; Carbohydrate 60.6g, of which sugars 1.1g; Fat 9.1g, of which saturates 5.3g; Cholesterol 21mg; Calcium 77mg; Fibre 3.8g; Sodium 70mg.
Sweet Noodles Energy 368kcal/1530kJ; Protein 8.8g; Carbohydrate 45.8g, of which sugars 17.6g; Fat 16.5g, of which saturates 2.3g; Cholesterol 0mg; Calcium 200mg; Fibre 6.2g; Sodium 650mg.

Fried Noodles with Ginger and Coriander

Here is a simple noodle dish that goes well with most oriental dishes, or serve for a festive feast that features lots of exotic dishes. It can also be served as a quick snack for 2–3 people.

Serves 2–6

a handful of fresh coriander
  (cilantro) sprigs
225g/8oz dried egg noodles
45ml/3 tbsp groundnut
  (peanut) oil
5cm/2in piece of fresh root
  ginger, peeled and cut into
  fine shreds
6–8 spring onions (scallions),
  cut into shreds
30ml/2 tbsp light soy sauce
salt and ground black pepper

1 Strip the leaves from the coriander stalks. Pile them on a chopping board and coarsely chop them using a herb chopper, cleaver or large sharp knife.

2 Bring a large pan of lightly salted water to the boil and cook the noodles until they are just tender. Drain, rinse under cold water and drain again. Return to the clean pan and toss with 15ml/1 tbsp of the groundnut oil.

3 Preheat a wok until hot, add the remaining oil and swirl it around. Add the ginger and stir-fry for a few seconds, then add the noodles and spring onions. Stir-fry over medium heat for about 3–4 minutes, until hot.

4 Sprinkle the soy sauce and chopped coriander into the wok, and season the mixture with salt and ground black pepper to taste. Toss well to combine all the ingredients, transfer to a warmed bowl and serve immediately.

Cook's Tip
Many of the dried egg noodles available are sold in skeins or bundles. As a guide, allow 1 skein of noodles per person as an average portion for a main dish.

Rice Noodles with Cucumber and Fresh Herbs

The thin, wiry noodles known as rice sticks or rice vermicelli are a feature of this delicious side dish. It is a cold salad so will work well on a festive buffet table.

Serves 4

half a small cucumber
225g/8oz dried rice sticks
  (vermicelli)
4–6 lettuce leaves, shredded
115g/4oz/½ cup beansprouts
1 bunch of mixed fresh basil,
  coriander (cilantro), mint
  and oregano, stalks removed,
  leaves shredded
juice of half a lime
nuoc mam or nuoc cham,
  to drizzle

1 Peel the cucumber, cut it in half lengthways, remove the seeds, and cut into matchsticks.

2 Add the rice sticks to a pan of boiling water, loosening them gently, and cook for 3–4 minutes, or until white and al dente.

3 Drain the cooked noodles, rinse under cold running water, and thoroughly drain again.

4 In a large mixing bowl, toss together the shredded lettuce, beansprouts, cucumber and herbs until well combined.

5 Add the noodles and lime juice to the bowl and toss together. Drizzle with a little nuoc mam or nuoc cham for seasoning, and serve immediately.

Cook's Tips
• Use whatever quantities of the fresh herbs that you prefer in this dish. If you wish, you can take out one or two of the herbs, if you or your guests don't like them. Just be sure that you still have a substantial bunch of herbs to add to the salad.
• Look for nuoc mam and nuoc cham in Asian stores or markets and large supermarkets.

Noodles with Ginger Energy 168kcal/711kJ; Protein 5g; Carbohydrate 27.7g, of which sugars 1.5g; Fat 5g, of which saturates 1.1g; Cholesterol 11mg; Calcium 17mg; Fibre 1.3g; Sodium 425mg.
Rice Noodles with Fresh Herbs Energy 221kcal/926kJ; Protein 4g; Carbohydrate 48g, of which sugars 1g; Fat 0g, of which saturates 0g; Cholesterol 0mg; Calcium 44mg; Fibre 0.8g; Sodium 0.01g.

Stir-fried Noodles with Beansprouts

Beansprouts are highly nutritious and make a valuable contribution to this low-fat dish, which combines egg noodles with peppers and soy sauce.

Serves 4

175g/6oz dried egg noodles
15ml/1 tbsp vegetable oil
1 garlic clove, finely chopped
1 small onion, halved and sliced
225g/8oz/1 cup beansprouts
1 small red (bell) pepper, seeded and cut into strips
1 small green (bell) pepper, seeded and cut into strips
2.5ml/½ tsp salt
1.5ml/¼ tsp ground white pepper
30ml/2 tbsp light soy sauce

1 Bring a pan of water to the boil. Cook the noodles for 4 minutes until just tender, or according to the instructions on the packet. Drain, refresh under cold water and drain again.

2 Heat the oil in a non-stick frying pan or wok. When the oil is very hot, add the garlic, stir briefly, then add the onion slices. Cook, stirring, for about 1 minute.

3 Add the beansprouts and strips of peppers to the pan. Stir-fry for about 2–3 minutes.

4 Stir the cooked noodles into the pan and toss over the heat, using two spatulas or wooden spoons, for about 2–3 minutes or until the ingredients are thoroughly mixed and all the noodles have heated through.

5 Season with the salt and ground white pepper. Add the soy sauce and stir thoroughly before serving the noodle mixture in heated bowls.

> **Cook's Tip**
> *Store beansprouts in the refrigerator and use within a day of purchase, as they tend to lose their crispness and become slimy and unpleasant quite quickly. The most commonly used beansprouts are sprouted mung beans, but you could use other types of beansprouts instead.*

Celebration Noodles

This traditional Filipino dish is served for all kinds of special celebrations, including weddings and birthdays, as well as Christmas. It has a rich combination of flavours, and often features as the centrepiece of a celebratory meal, rather than a side dish. It's perfect as part of a buffet spread, or you can use the quantities given to serve four people as a main course.

Serves 8

30ml/2 tbsp palm or coconut oil
1 large onion, finely chopped
2–3 garlic cloves, finely chopped
250g/9oz pork loin, cut into strips
250g/9oz fresh shelled prawns (shrimp)
2 carrots, cut into matchsticks
½ small green cabbage, finely shredded
about 250ml/8fl oz/1 cup pork or chicken stock
50ml/2fl oz/¼ cup soy sauce
15ml/1 tbsp palm sugar (jaggery)
450g/1lb fresh egg noodles
2 hard-boiled eggs, finely chopped
1 lime, quartered

1 Heat 15ml/1 tbsp oil in a wok or a large, heavy frying pan, stir in the onion and garlic and fry for 5 minutes. Add the pork and prawns, stir-fry for 2 minutes, then transfer to a plate.

2 Return the wok to the heat, add the remaining oil, then stir in the carrots and cabbage and stir-fry for 2–3 minutes. Put the vegetables on to the plate with the pork and prawns.

3 Pour the stock, soy sauce and sugar into the wok and stir until the sugar has dissolved. Add the noodles, untangling them with chopsticks, and cook for about 3 minutes, until tender but still firm to the bite. Toss in the pork, prawns, cabbage and carrots, making sure that they are thoroughly mixed.

4 Transfer the noodles to a serving dish and sprinkle with the eggs. Serve with the lime wedges to squeeze over them.

> **Cook's Tip**
> *Fresh egg noodles are available in Chinese and South-east Asian stores and supermarkets.*

Celebration Noodles Energy 364kcal/1535kJ; Protein 21.8g; Carbohydrate 49g, of which sugars 8.5g; Fat 10.4g, of which saturates 2.5g; Cholesterol 145mg; Calcium 80mg; Fibre 3.2g; Sodium 652mg.
Stir-fried Noodles Energy 244kcal/1030kJ; Protein 8g; Carbohydrate 39.9g, of which sugars 7.8g; Fat 7g, of which saturates 1.5g; Cholesterol 13mg; Calcium 34mg; Fibre 3.5g; Sodium 352mg.

Christmas Pudding

This can be made up to a month before Christmas and stored in a cool, dry place.

Serves 8
115g/4oz/½ cup butter
225g/8oz/1 cup soft dark
  brown sugar
50g/2oz/½ cup self-raising
  (self-rising) flour
5ml/1 tsp mixed (apple pie) spice
1.5ml/¼ tsp grated nutmeg
2.5ml/½ tsp ground cinnamon
2 eggs
115g/4oz/2 cups fresh white
  breadcrumbs

175g/6oz/1¼ cups sultanas
  (golden raisins)
175g/6oz/1¼ cup raisins
115g/4oz/½ cup currants
25g/1oz/3 tbsp mixed (candied)
  peel, chopped finely
25g/1oz/¼ cup chopped almonds
1 small cooking apple, peeled,
  cored and coarsely grated
finely grated rind of 1 orange
  or lemon
juice of 1 orange or lemon, made
  up to 150ml/¼ pint/⅔ cup
  with brandy, rum or sherry

1 Cut a disc of baking parchment to fit the base of a 1.2-litre /2-pint/5-cup heatproof bowl and butter the disc and bowl.

2 Whisk the butter and sugar together in a mixing bowl until soft. Beat in the flour, spices and eggs. Add the rest of the ingredients and mix well. The mixture should have a soft dropping consistency.

3 Transfer to the greased bowl and level the top. Cover with another disc of buttered baking parchment.

4 Make a pleat across the centre of a large piece of baking parchment and cover the bowl with it, tying it in place with string under the rim. Cut off the excess paper.

5 Cover with pleated foil in the same way, tucking it around the bowl, and tie with string to form a handle.

6 Steam the pudding over simmering water for 6 hours. Leave to cool, then replace the foil and paper with clean pieces. Clean the bowl and replace the pudding. To reheat for serving, steam for about 2 hours.

Rum Butter

No Christmas Dinner would be complete without the traditional Christmas pudding to round it off. This rich and luscious rum butter is the perfect accompaniment.

Serves 8
225g/8oz/1 cup unsalted butter
  at room temperature
225g/8oz/1 cup soft light
  brown sugar
90ml/6 tbsp dark rum, or to taste

1 Beat the butter and sugar until the mixture is soft, creamy and pale in colour. Gradually add the rum, almost drop by drop, beating to incorporate each addition before adding more. If you are too hasty in adding the rum, the mixture may curdle.

2 When all the rum has been added, spoon the mixture into a covered container and chill for at least 1 hour. The butter will keep well in the refrigerator for about 4 weeks.

Brandy Butter

This alcohol-spiked butter is traditionally served with Christmas pudding and mince pies, but a good spoonful over a hot oven-baked apple is equally delicious.

Serves 6
115g/4oz/½ cup butter
115g/4oz/½ cup icing
  (confectioners'), caster
  (superfine) or soft light
  brown sugar
45ml/3 tbsp brandy

1 Cream the butter in a mixing bowl until very pale and soft. Beat in the sugar gradually.

2 Add the brandy to the sugared butter, a few drops at a time, beating constantly. Add enough for a good flavour but take care it does not curdle.

3 Pile the brandy butter into a small serving dish and set aside to harden. Alternatively, spread it out on to aluminium foil and chill in the refrigerator until firm. Cut the butter into festive shapes with small fancy cutters.

Christmas Pudding Energy 448kcal/1902kJ; Protein 2.4g; Carbohydrate 99.8g, of which sugars 92.5g; Fat 7.1g, of which saturates 3.6g; Cholesterol 20mg; Calcium 67mg; Fibre 0.9g; Sodium 123mg.
Rum Butter Energy 213kcal/888kJ; Protein 4.1g; Carbohydrate 9.6g, of which sugars 9.6g; Fat 7.2g, of which saturates 4.5g; Cholesterol 20mg; Calcium 146mg; Fibre 0g; Sodium 89mg.
Brandy Butter Energy 204kcal/851kJ; Protein 0.2g; Carbohydrate 17.4g, of which sugars 17.4g; Fat 13.6g, of which saturates 9g; Cholesterol 38mg; Calcium 11mg; Fibre 0g; Sodium 126mg.

Crème Anglaise

Here is the classic English custard; it is light and creamy without the harsh flavours or gaudy colouring of its poorer package relations. Serve hot or cold with your festive dessert.

Serves 4
1 vanilla pod (bean)
450ml/¾ pint/scant 2 cups milk
40g/1½oz/⅓ cup icing (confectioners') sugar
4 egg yolks

1 Put the vanilla pod in a pan with the milk. Bring slowly to the boil. Remove from the heat and steep for 10 minutes before removing the pod.

2 In a heatproof mixing bowl, beat together the sugar and egg yolks until the mixture is thick, light and creamy.

3 Slowly pour the warm milk on to the egg mixture in the mixing bowl, stirring constantly.

4 Place the bowl over a pan of hot water. Stir the mixture frequently over low heat for 10 minutes or until it has thickened and coats the back of the spoon.

5 Strain the custard into a jug (pitcher) if serving hot or, if serving cold, strain into a bowl and cover the surface with buttered baking parchment or clear film (plastic wrap).

Cook's Tip
Crème anglaise can curdle if left to simmer too long, so once the custard has thickened in step 4, ensure that the bowl is removed from the heat immediately.

Variation
If you prefer a fruit-flavoured crème anglaise, you can steep a few strips of thinly pared lemon or orange rind with the milk, instead of the vanilla pod (bean).

Apple Pudding

This delicious pudding is a real treat on a wintry night during the festive season. It is sure to be popular with the whole family.

Serves 4
4 crisp eating apples
a little lemon juice

300ml/½ pint/1¼ cups milk
40g/1½oz/3 tbsp butter
40g/1½oz/⅓ cup plain (all-purpose) flour
25g/1oz/2 tbsp caster (superfine) sugar
2.5ml/½ tsp vanilla extract
2 eggs, separated

1 Preheat the oven to 200°C/400°F/Gas 6. Butter an ovenproof dish measuring 20–23cm/8–9in in diameter and 5cm/2in deep. Peel, core and slice the apples and put in the dish. Sprinkle with lemon juice and toss to coat.

2 Put the milk, butter and flour in a pan. Cook over medium heat, whisking constantly, until it thickens and comes to the boil.

3 Let it bubble for 1–2 minutes, stirring well to make sure it does not stick and burn on the bottom. Pour into a bowl, add the sugar and vanilla extract, and then stir in the egg yolks.

4 In a separate bowl, whisk the egg whites until stiff peaks form. With a large, metal spoon fold the egg whites into the custard. Pour the custard mixture over the apples in the dish.

5 Put into the hot oven and cook for about 40 minutes until puffed up, deep golden brown and firm to the touch.

6 Serve the pudding straight out of the oven, before the soufflé-like topping begins to fall.

Variation
Stewed fruit, such as cooking apples, plums, rhubarb or gooseberries sweetened with honey or sugar, would also make a good base for this pudding, as would fresh summer berries (blackberries, raspberries, redcurrants and blackcurrants).

Crème Anglaise Energy 152kcal/640kJ; Protein 6.7g; Carbohydrate 16.1g, of which sugars 16.1g; Fat 7.4g, of which saturates 2.7g; Cholesterol 208mg; Calcium 164mg; Fibre 0g; Sodium 72mg.
Apple Pudding Energy 240kcal/1006kJ; Protein 7g; Carbohydrate 26.8g, of which sugars 19.2g; Fat 12.5g, of which saturates 6.8g; Cholesterol 121mg; Calcium 127mg; Fibre 1.9g; Sodium 131mg.

Bread and Butter Pudding

Comfort food suits the festive season well, and desserts do not come more warming and enjoyable than this one. The whiskey sauce is heavenly, but the pudding can also be served with chilled cream or vanilla ice cream – the contrast between the hot and cold is delicious.

Serves 6
8 slices of white bread, buttered
115–150g/4–5oz/³⁄₄–1 cup
  sultanas (golden raisins), or
  mixed dried fruit
2.5ml/¹⁄₂ tsp grated nutmeg
150g/5oz/³⁄₄ cup caster
  (superfine) sugar
2 large (US extra large) eggs
300ml/¹⁄₂ pint/1¹⁄₄ cups single
  (light) cream
450ml/³⁄₄ pint/scant 2 cups milk
5ml/1 tsp vanilla extract
light muscovado (brown) sugar, for
  sprinkling (optional)

For the whiskey sauce
150g/5oz/10 tbsp butter
115g/4oz/generous ¹⁄₂ cup caster
  (superfine) sugar
1 egg
45ml/3 tbsp Irish whiskey

1 Preheat the oven to 180°C/350°F/Gas 4. Remove the crusts from the bread and put four slices, buttered side down, in the base of an ovenproof dish. Sprinkle with the fruit, some of the nutmeg and 15ml/1 tbsp sugar.

2 Place the remaining four slices of bread on top, buttered side down, and sprinkle again with nutmeg and 15ml/1 tbsp sugar.

3 Beat the eggs lightly, add the cream, milk, vanilla extract and the remaining sugar, and mix well to make a custard. Pour this mixture over the bread, and sprinkle light muscovado sugar over the top, if you like to have a crispy crust.

4 Bake in the preheated oven for 1 hour, or until all the liquid has been absorbed and the pudding is risen and brown.

5 Meanwhile, make the whiskey sauce: melt the butter in a heavy pan, add the caster sugar and dissolve over gentle heat. Remove from the heat and add the egg, whisking vigorously, and then add the whiskey. Serve the pudding on hot serving plates, with the whiskey sauce poured over the top.

Monmouth Pudding

Another dessert with bread as a main ingredient, this is layered with milk-drenched breadcrumbs, set with eggs.

Serves 4
450ml/³⁄₄ pint/scant 2 cups milk
25g/1oz/2 tbsp caster
  (superfine) sugar
finely grated rind of 1 lemon
175g/6oz/3 cups fresh white
  breadcrumbs
2 eggs, separated
60ml/4 tbsp strawberry, raspberry
  or other red jam

1 Pour the milk into a pan, add the sugar and lemon rind and bring to the boil. Pour the hot milk mixture over the breadcrumbs and leave for 15 minutes.

2 Preheat the oven to 150°C/300°F/Gas 2. Lightly butter a 23cm/9in × 15cm/6in ovenproof dish.

3 Stir the egg yolks into the breadcrumb mixture. Whisk the egg whites until stiff peaks form and, with a large metal spoon, fold them into the breadcrumb mixture.

4 Melt the jam (on the hob or in the microwave) and drizzle half of it into the bottom of the prepared dish.

5 Spoon half the breadcrumb mixture on top, gently levelling the surface, and drizzle the jam over it.

6 Spread the remaining breadcrumb mixture over the top of the pudding to make an even layer. Put into the hot oven and cook for about 30–40 minutes or until light golden brown on top and set throughout. Serve warm.

> **Cook's Tips**
> • Cooking the pudding in an ovenproof glass dish shows off the pudding's layers.
> • The jam layers in the pudding could be replaced with lightly cooked summer berries or plums.

Bread Pudding Energy 757kcal/3168kJ; Protein 11.7g; Carbohydrate 82g, of which sugars 65.2g; Fat 40.8g, of which saturates 24.3g; Cholesterol 207mg; Calcium 232mg; Fibre 0.9g; Sodium 472mg.
Monmouth Pudding Energy 309kcal/1313kJ; Protein 12g; Carbohydrate 57.1g, of which sugars 24.3g; Fat 5.4g, of which saturates 1.9g; Cholesterol 101mg; Calcium 205mg; Fibre 1g; Sodium 418mg.

Crêpes with Citrus Sauce

This is a popular favourite after a filling feast. For a festive dinner party, you can make the crêpes in advance, and then coat them in the tangy orange sauce at the last minute before serving.

Serves 6
115g/4oz/1 cup plain
  (all-purpose) flour
1.5ml/¼ tsp salt
25g/1oz/2 tbsp caster
  (superfine) sugar
2 eggs, lightly beaten
about 250ml/8fl oz/1 cup milk
about 60ml/4 tbsp water
30ml/2 tbsp orange flower water,
  Cointreau or orange liqueur
25g/1oz/2 tbsp unsalted
  butter, melted, plus extra
  for frying

For the sauce
75g/3oz/6 tbsp unsalted butter
50g/2oz/¼ cup caster
  (superfine) sugar
grated rind and juice of
  1 large orange
grated rind and juice of 1 lemon
150ml/¼ pint/⅔ cup freshly
  squeezed orange juice
60ml/4 tbsp Cointreau or
  orange liqueur, plus more
  for flaming (optional)
brandy, for flaming (optional)
orange segments, to decorate

1 Sift the flour, salt and sugar into a large bowl. Make a well in the centre and add the eggs. Beat in the eggs, gradually.

2 Whisk in the milk, water and orange flower water or liqueur to make a very smooth batter. Strain into a jug (pitcher) and set aside for 20–30 minutes.

3 Heat an 18–20cm/7–8in crêpe pan over medium heat. If the crêpe batter has thickened, add a little more water or milk to thin it. Stir the melted butter into the batter.

4 Brush the hot pan with a little extra melted butter and pour in about 30ml/2 tbsp of batter. Quickly tilt and rotate the pan to cover the base evenly with a thin layer of batter. Cook for about 1 minute, or until the top is set and the base is golden. With a metal spatula, lift the edge to check the colour, then carefully turn over the crêpe and cook for 20–30 seconds, just to set. Transfer on to a plate.

5 Continue cooking the crêpes, stirring the batter occasionally and brushing the pan with a little more melted butter as and when necessary. Place a sheet of clear film (plastic wrap) or baking parchment between each crêpe as they are stacked to prevent them from sticking.

6 To make the sauce, melt the butter in a large frying pan over a medium heat, then stir in the sugar, orange and lemon rind and juice, the additional orange juice and the orange liqueur.

7 Place a crêpe in the pan browned side down, swirling gently to coat with the sauce. Fold it in half, then in half again to form a triangle, and push to the side of the pan. Continue heating and folding the crêpes until all are warm and coated in sauce.

8 To flame the crêpes, heat 30–45ml/2–3 tbsp each of orange liqueur and brandy in a small pan over medium heat. Remove from the heat, carefully ignite the liquid, then pour over the crêpes. Sprinkle over the orange segments and serve.

Baked Apples with Mincemeat

This quintessential British fruit was once thought to have magical powers and, to this day, apples are linked with many English traditions and festivals. Here, they are baked in the oven with a filling of sweetened dried fruit, giving them a lovely festive feel.

Serves 4
25g/1oz/2 tbsp butter, plus extra
  for greasing
4 cooking apples
about 60ml/4 tbsp mincemeat
30ml/2 tbsp honey

1 Preheat the oven to 180°C/350°F/Gas 4. Butter a shallow ovenproof dish, which can hold all the apples in one layer.

2 With an apple corer or a small sharp knife, remove the cores from the apples. Run a sharp knife around the middle of each apple, cutting through the skin but not deep into the flesh. Stand the apples in the dish.

3 Fill the hollow centres of the apples with the mincemeat. Drizzle the honey over the top of each apple and dot with butter. Add 60ml/4 tbsp water to the dish. Bake in the preheated oven for about 45–50 minutes until they are soft throughout, and serve immediately.

Cook's Tips
• The apples are best served straight from the oven, while still puffed up and before they begin to crumple.
• Serve with hot custard or brandy butter cream, or enjoy the hot and cold sensations and serve it with cold double (heavy) cream or ice cream.

Variation
You can replace the mincemeat with chopped dried apricots or dates, if you prefer.

Crêpes with Citrus Energy 316kcal/1323kJ; Protein 5.6g; Carbohydrate 34.2g, of which sugars 19.6g; Fat 17.2g, of which saturates 10.1g; Cholesterol 103mg; Calcium 100mg; Fibre 0.6g; Sodium 152mg.
Baked Apples Energy 70kcal/301kJ; Protein 0.7g; Carbohydrate 17.4g, of which sugars 17.4g; Fat 0.3g, of which saturates 0g; Cholesterol 0mg; Calcium 30mg; Fibre 2.4g; Sodium 9mg.

Apple Crêpes with Butterscotch Sauce

These wonderful dessert crêpes are flavoured with sweet cider, filled with slices of caramelized apples and drizzled with a rich, smooth butterscotch sauce. Serve them after a Christmas feast.

Serves 4
115g/4oz/1 cup plain
  (all-purpose) flour
pinch of salt
2 eggs
175ml/6fl oz/³/4 cup creamy milk
120ml/4fl oz/¹/2 cup sweet
  (hard) cider
butter, for frying

For the filling and sauce
4 eating apples
90g/3¹/2oz/scant ¹/2 cup butter
225g/8oz/1 cup light muscovado
  (brown) sugar
150ml/¹/4 pint/²/3 cup double
  (heavy) cream

1 Make the crêpe batter. Sift the flour and salt into a large bowl. Add the eggs and milk and beat until smooth. Stir in the cider; set aside for 30 minutes.

2 Heat a small heavy non-stick frying pan. Add a knob of butter and ladle in enough batter to coat the pan thinly. Cook until the crêpe is golden underneath, then flip it over and cook the other side until golden. Slide the crêpe on to a plate. Repeat with the remaining mixture to make seven more.

3 Make the filling. Core the apples and cut them into thick slices. Heat 15g/¹/2oz/1 tbsp of the butter in a large frying pan. Add the apple slices to the pan. Cook until golden on both sides, then transfer the slices to a bowl with a slotted spoon and set them aside.

4 Add the rest of the butter to the pan. As soon as it has melted, add the muscovado sugar. When the sugar has dissolved and the mixture is bubbling, stir in the cream. Continue cooking until it forms a smooth sauce.

5 Fold each pancake in half, then fold in half again to form a cone; fill each with some of the fried apples. Place two filled pancakes on each dessert plate, drizzle over some of the butterscotch sauce and serve immediately.

Apple Charlottes

These tempting little fruit Charlottes are a wonderful way to use the glut of apples that appear over Christmas time.

Serves 4
175g/6oz/³/4 cup butter
450g/1lb cooking apples
225g/8oz eating apples
60ml/4 tbsp water
130g/4¹/2oz/scant ²/3 cup caster
  (superfine) sugar
2 egg yolks
pinch of grated nutmeg
9 thin slices white bread,
  crusts removed
extra-thick double (heavy) cream
  or custard, to serve

1 Preheat the oven to 190°C/375°F/Gas 5. Put a knob of the butter in a pan. Peel and core the apples, dice them finely and put them in the pan with the water. Cover and cook for 10 minutes or until the cooking apples have pulped down.

2 Stir in 115g/4oz/¹/2 cup of the sugar. Boil, uncovered, until any liquid has evaporated and what remains is a thick pulp. Remove from the heat, beat in the egg yolks and nutmeg and set aside.

3 Melt the remaining butter in a separate pan over low heat until the white curds start to separate from the clear yellow liquid. Remove from the heat. Leave to stand for a few minutes, then strain the clear clarified butter through a muslin-lined (cheesecloth-lined) sieve (strainer).

4 Brush four 150ml/¹/4 pint/²/3 cup individual Charlotte moulds or pudding tins (pans) with a little of the clarified butter; sprinkle with the remaining caster sugar. Cut the bread slices into 2.5cm/1in strips. Dip the strips into the remaining clarified butter; use to line the moulds or tins. Overlap the strips on the base to give the effect of a swirl and let the excess bread overhang the tops of the moulds or tins.

5 Fill each bread case with apple pulp. Fold the excess bread over the top of each mould or tin to make a lid; press down lightly. Bake for 45–50 minutes or until golden. Run a knife between each Charlotte and its mould or tin, then turn out on to dessert plates. Serve with double (heavy) cream or custard.

Apple Crêpes Energy 489kcal/2057kJ; Protein 8.2g; Carbohydrate 71.5g, of which sugars 49.6g; Fat 20.1g, of which saturates 11.3g; Cholesterol 139mg; Calcium 137mg; Fibre 2.1g; Sodium 69mg.
Apple Charlottes Energy 686kcal/2874kJ; Protein 7.5g; Carbohydrate 79.2g, of which sugars 50.8g; Fat 40g, of which saturates 23.6g; Cholesterol 194mg; Calcium 111mg; Fibre 3.6g; Sodium 591mg.

Apple and Kumquat Sponge Pudding

The intense flavour of kumquats makes these puddings special – ideal for a festive dinner party.

Serves 8
150g/5oz/10 tbsp butter, at room temperature, plus extra for greasing
175g/6oz cooking apples, peeled and thinly sliced
75g/3oz kumquats, thinly sliced
150g/5oz/¾ cup golden caster (superfine) sugar
2 eggs
115g/4oz/1 cup self-raising (self-rising) flour

For the sauce
75g/3oz kumquats, thinly sliced
75g/3oz/6 tbsp caster (superfine) sugar
250ml/8fl oz/1 cup water
150ml/¼ pint/⅔ cup crème fraîche
5ml/1 tsp cornflour (cornstarch) mixed with 10ml/2 tsp water
lemon juice to taste

1 Prepare a steamer. Butter eight 150ml/¼ pint/⅔ cup dariole moulds or ramekins and put a disc of buttered baking parchment on the base of each.

2 Melt 25g/1oz/2 tbsp butter in a frying pan. Add the apples, kumquats and 25g/1oz/2 tbsp sugar and cook over medium heat for 5–8 minutes, or until the apples start to soften and the sugar begins to caramelize. Leave to cool.

3 Cream the remaining butter with the remaining sugar until pale and fluffy. Add the eggs, one at a time, beating after each addition. Fold in the flour.

4 Evenly divide the apple and kumquat mixture among the prepared moulds. Top with the sponge mixture. Cover the moulds and put into the steamer. Steam for 45 minutes.

5 For the sauce, put the kumquats, sugar and water in a pan and bring to the boil, stirring to dissolve the sugar. Simmer for 5 minutes. Stir in the crème fraîche and bring back to the boil. Remove from the heat and gradually whisk in the cornflour mixture. Return the pan to the heat and simmer gently for 2 minutes, stirring constantly. Add lemon juice to taste. Turn out the puddings and serve hot, with the sauce.

Streusel Plum Cake

This kind of cake, with a shortcrust base and a crumble topping, can be made with various different fruits, depending on the time of year. This is a great way to make the most of plums. It makes a tasty festive dessert that the whole family will enjoy.

Serves 16
200g/7oz/scant 1 cup butter, softened
150g/5oz/¾ cup caster (superfine) sugar
pinch of salt
7.5ml/1½ tsp vanilla extract or 2 packs vanilla sugar (about 10g/¼oz)
2 eggs
400g/14oz/3½ cups plain (all-purpose) flour
icing (confectioners') sugar, to dust
whipped double (heavy) cream, to serve

For the filling
800g/1¾lb plums, halved and stoned (pitted)
100g/3½oz/½ cup caster (superfine) sugar

1 Preheat the oven to 180°C/350°F/Gas 4. Put the butter in a bowl with the sugar, salt, vanilla, eggs and flour. Rub the mixture with your fingertips until it is crumbly.

2 Use half the crumble dough to line a 40 × 30cm/16 × 12in baking tray, pressing it evenly over the base and up the sides.

3 Put in the halved plums and sprinkle the sugar on top. Sprinkle the rest of the crumble on top of the plums.

4 Bake the cake in the preheated oven for 45–60 minutes, until golden. Dust the top with icing sugar and cut the cake into squares to serve with whipped cream.

Variation
If plums are hard to come by over the festive season, then you can make this dessert with apples instead. Simply replace the plums with a similar quantity of apples, and cut them into thick slices before laying them on top of the crumble base. You can use cooking apples such as Bramleys or eating apples.

Apple Pudding Energy 402kcal/1680kJ; Protein 3.7g; Carbohydrate 44.4g, of which sugars 33.7g; Fat 24.5g, of which saturates 15.3g; Cholesterol 109mg; Calcium 93mg; Fibre 1g; Sodium 190mg.
Streusel Plum Cake Energy 265kcal/1115kJ; Protein 3.5g; Carbohydrate 39.9g, of which sugars 20.9g; Fat 11.3g, of which saturates 7g; Cholesterol 53mg; Calcium 55mg; Fibre 1.5g; Sodium 105mg.

Citrus Fruit Flambé with Praline

A fruit flambé makes a dramatic finale for a Christmas dinner. Topping this refreshing citrus fruit dessert with crunchy pistachio praline makes it extra special.

Serves 4
4 oranges
2 ruby grapefruit
2 limes

50g/2oz/¼ cup butter
50g/2oz/¼ cup light muscovado (brown) sugar
45ml/3 tbsp Cointreau
fresh mint sprigs, to decorate

For the praline
vegetable oil, for greasing
115g/4oz/generous ½ cup caster (superfine) sugar
50g/2oz/½ cup pistachio nuts

1 First, make the pistachio praline. Brush a baking sheet lightly with oil. Place the caster sugar and pistachio nuts in a small heavy pan and cook gently, swirling the pan occasionally until the sugar has completely melted.

2 Continue to cook over a fairly low heat until the nuts start to pop and the sugar has turned a dark golden colour. Pour on to the oiled baking sheet and set aside to cool. Using a sharp knife, chop the praline into rough chunks.

3 Cut off all the rind and pith from the citrus fruit. Holding each fruit in turn over a large bowl, cut between the membranes so that the segments fall into the bowl, with any juice.

4 Heat the butter and muscovado sugar together in a heavy frying pan until the sugar has completely melted and the mixture is golden.

5 Strain the citrus juices into the pan and continue to cook, stirring occasionally, until the juice has reduced and is syrupy.

6 Add the fruit segments and warm through without stirring. Pour over the Cointreau and carefully set it alight. As soon as the flames die down, spoon the fruit flambé into serving dishes. Sprinkle some praline over each portion and decorate with the mint sprigs. Serve immediately.

Chocolate and Orange Pancakes

These fabulous pancakes, in a rich sauce, make a delicious finale for a special meal, or serve on Christmas Day morning for brunch.

Serves 4
115g/4oz/1 cup self-raising (self-rising) flour
30ml/2 tbsp unsweetened cocoa powder
2 eggs
50g/2oz plain (semisweet) chocolate, broken into squares

200ml/7fl oz/scant 1 cup milk
finely grated rind of 1 orange
30ml/2 tbsp orange juice
butter or oil, for frying
chocolate curls, to decorate

For the sauce
2 large oranges
25g/1oz/2 tbsp unsalted butter
40g/1½oz/3 tbsp soft light brown sugar
225g/8oz/1 cup crème fraîche
30ml/2 tbsp Grand Marnier

1 Sift the flour and cocoa powder into a mixing bowl and make a well in the centre. Add the eggs and beat well, incorporating the dry ingredients as you work to make a smooth batter.

2 Put the chocolate into a heavy pan and pour in the milk. Heat gently, stirring constantly, until the chocolate has melted, then beat the mixture into the batter until smooth and bubbly. Finally, stir the grated orange rind and juice into the batter.

3 Heat a heavy frying pan and grease with butter or oil. Drop in 2 tablespoons of batter at a time. When the pancakes are lightly browned underneath and bubbly on top, flip them over to cook the other side. Slide on to a plate and keep hot.

4 Make the sauce. Pare and shred the rind of 1 orange and set aside. Peel the second orange, carefully remove all the pith from both oranges, then finely slice the oranges into sections. Heat the butter and sugar in a frying pan over low heat, stirring until the sugar dissolves. Stir in the crème fraîche and heat gently.

5 Add the pancakes and orange slices to the sauce, heat very gently for 2 minutes, then pour over the liqueur. Transfer to a large serving plate, sprinkle with the reserved orange rind and decorate with the chocolate curls. Serve immediately.

Citrus Fruit Flambé Energy 446kcal/1872kJ; Protein 4.8g; Carbohydrate 65.2g, of which sugars 64.8g; Fat 17.4g, of which saturates 7.4g; Cholesterol 27mg; Calcium 127mg; Fibre 4.4g; Sodium 155mg.
Chocolate Pancakes Energy 431kcal/1797kJ; Protein 7g; Carbohydrate 33.3g, of which sugars 20.4g; Fat 30.5g, of which saturates 15.5g; Cholesterol 106mg; Calcium 162mg; Fibre 2.2g; Sodium 174mg.

Syrupy Brioche Slices with Ice Cream

Keep a few individual brioche buns in the freezer during the festivities to make this superb quick and easy dessert.

Serves 4
butter, for greasing
finely grated rind and juice
   of 1 orange, such as Navelina
   or blood orange
50g/2oz/¼ cup caster
   (superfine) sugar
90ml/6 tbsp water
1.5ml/¼ tsp ground cinnamon
4 brioche buns
15ml/1 tbsp icing
   (confectioners') sugar
400ml/14fl oz/1⅔ cups vanilla
   ice cream

1 Lightly grease a gratin dish and set aside. Put the orange rind and juice, sugar, water and cinnamon in a heavy pan. Heat gently, stirring, until the sugar has dissolved, then boil rapidly, without stirring, for 2 minutes, until thickened and syrupy.

2 Remove the orange syrup from the heat and pour it into a shallow heatproof dish. Preheat the grill (broiler). Cut each brioche vertically into three thick slices. Dip one side of each slice in the hot syrup and arrange in the gratin dish, syrupy sides down. Reserve the remaining syrup. Grill (broil) the brioche slices until they are lightly toasted.

3 Using tongs, turn the brioche slices over and dust well with icing sugar. Grill for about 3 minutes more, or until they are just beginning to caramelize around the edges.

4 Transfer the hot brioche slices to serving plates and top with scoops of vanilla ice cream. Spoon the remaining syrup over them and serve immediately.

> **Cook's Tip**
> *You could also use slices of a larger brioche, rather than the smaller buns, or madeleines, sliced horizontally in half. These are traditionally flavoured with lemon or orange flower water, making them especially tasty.*

Apricots with Almond Paste

The traditional topping for Christmas cake, almond paste also tastes wonderful with many kinds of fruit, especially when delicately scented with orange flower water.

Serves 6
75g/3oz/6 tbsp caster
   (superfine) sugar
30ml/2 tbsp lemon juice
300ml/½ pint/1¼ cups water
115g/4oz/1 cup ground almonds
50g/2oz/½ cup icing
   (confectioners') sugar
a little orange flower water
25g/1oz/2 tbsp unsalted
   butter, melted
2.5ml/½ tsp almond extract
900g/2lb fresh apricots
fresh mint sprigs, to decorate

1 Preheat the oven to 180°C/350°F/Gas 4. Place the sugar, lemon juice and water in a small pan and bring to the boil, stirring occasionally until the sugar has all dissolved. Simmer gently for 5–10 minutes to make a thin syrup.

2 Place the ground almonds, icing sugar, orange flower water, butter and almond extract in a bowl and blend together to make a smooth paste.

3 Wash the apricots and then make a slit in the flesh and ease out the stone (pit). Take small pieces of the almond paste, roll into balls and press one into each of the apricots.

4 Arrange the stuffed apricots in a shallow ovenproof dish and carefully pour the sugar syrup around them. Cover with foil and bake in the oven for 25–30 minutes.

5 Serve the apricots with a little of the syrup, and decorated with sprigs of fresh mint.

> **Cook's Tip**
> *Always use a heavy pan when making syrup and stir constantly with a wooden spoon until the sugar has completely dissolved. Do not let the liquid come to the boil before it has dissolved, or the result will be grainy.*

Syrupy Brioche Slices Energy 399kcal/1681kJ; Protein 8.5g; Carbohydrate 65.5g, of which sugars 42.5g; Fat 12g, of which saturates 7.2g; Cholesterol 25mg; Calcium 174mg; Fibre 1.3g; Sodium 252mg.
Apricots with Almond Energy 124kcal/521kJ; Protein 1.7g; Carbohydrate 15.6g, of which sugars 15.4g; Fat 5.8g, of which saturates 2.4g; Cholesterol 9mg; Calcium 27mg; Fibre 1.7g; Sodium 29mg.

Oranges in Hot Coffee Syrup

This recipe makes a lovely dessert and also works well with most citrus fruits.

Serves 6
6 medium oranges
200g/7oz/1 cup sugar

50ml/2fl oz/¼ cup cold water
100ml/3½fl oz/scant ½ cup
   boiling water
100ml/3½fl oz/scant ½ cup
   fresh strong brewed coffee
50g/2oz/⅓ cup pistachio nuts,
   chopped (optional)

1 Finely pare the rind from one orange, shred and reserve the rind. Peel the remaining oranges.

2 Cut each orange crossways into slices, then re-form into the original spherical shape and hold in place with a cocktail stick (toothpick) through the centre.

3 Put the sugar and cold water in a pan. Heat gently, stirring constantly, until the sugar dissolves, then bring to the boil and cook until the syrup turns pale gold.

4 Remove from the heat and carefully pour the boiling water into the pan. Return to the heat until the syrup has dissolved in the water. Stir in the coffee.

5 Add the oranges and the shredded rind to the coffee syrup. Simmer for 15–20 minutes, turning the oranges once during cooking. Sprinkle with pistachio nuts, if using, and serve hot.

Cook's Tip
When making this dessert, use a pan in which the oranges will just fit in a single layer.

Variation
Try the sweet clementines or tangerines that are in abundance over the Christmas period as an alternative to the oranges in this recipe, if you prefer.

Figs and Pears in Honey

A stunningly simple dessert using fresh figs and pears scented with the warm fragrances of cinnamon and cardamom and drenched in a lemon and honey syrup. Pears are at their best around Christmas time and this dessert really makes the most of them.

Serves 4
1 lemon
90ml/6 tbsp clear honey
1 cinnamon stick
1 cardamom pod
2 pears
8 fresh figs, halved

1 Pare the rind from the lemon using a zester. Alternatively, use a vegetable peeler and then cut the peeled rind into very thin strips, no bigger than the size of a matchstick.

2 Place the lemon rind, honey, cinnamon stick, cardamom pod and 350ml/12fl oz/1½ cups water in a heavy pan and bring to the boil. Continue to boil, uncovered, for about 10 minutes until reduced by about half.

3 Cut the pears into eighths, discarding the cores. Place the pieces in the syrup, add the figs and simmer for about 5 minutes, or until the fruit is tender.

4 Transfer the fruit to a serving bowl. Continue cooking the liquid until syrupy, then discard the cinnamon stick and pour over the figs and pears. Serve.

Cook's Tips
• You can leave the peel on the pears or discard, depending on your preference.
• Figs vary in colour from pale green and yellow to dark purple. When buying them, look for firm fruit that is free from bruises or blemishes on the skin. A ripe fig will yield gently in your hand without pressing.
• It is best to use pale green or light beige cardamom pods, rather than the coarser dark brown ones.

Oranges in Coffee Syrup Energy 183kcal/782kJ; Protein 2g; Carbohydrate 46.4g, of which sugars 46.3g; Fat 0.1g, of which saturates 0g; Cholesterol 0mg; Calcium 84mg; Fibre 2.3g; Sodium 10mg.
Figs and Pears in Honey Energy 143kcal/606kJ; Protein 1.7g; Carbohydrate 34.4g, of which sugars 34.4g; Fat 0.7g, of which saturates 0g; Cholesterol 0mg; Calcium 109mg; Fibre 4.7g; Sodium 28mg.

Toffee Bananas

This can be a bit tricky to master. You need to work fast, especially when dipping the fruit in the caramel. The luscious results, however, are worth the effort and will delight your festive guests.

Serves 4
4 firm bananas
75g/3oz/²⁄₃ cup plain
  (all-purpose) flour

50g/2oz/¹⁄₂ cup cornflour
  (cornstarch)
10ml/2 tsp baking powder
175ml/6fl oz/³⁄₄ cup water
5ml/1 tsp sesame oil
groundnut (peanut), sunflower or
  corn oil, for deep-frying

For the caramel
225g/8oz/1 cup sugar
30ml/2 tbsp sesame seeds
60ml/4 tbsp water

1 Peel the bananas, then cut them diagonally into thick slices. Sift the flours and baking powder into a large bowl. Beat in the water and sesame oil. Stir in the bananas until coated.

2 Heat the groundnut, sunflower or corn oil in a deep pan until it registers 180°C/350°F or until a cube of bread, added to the oil, turns pale brown in 45 seconds. Using a fork, remove a piece of banana from the batter, allowing the excess batter to drain back into the bowl. Gently lower the piece of banana into the hot oil. Add more pieces in the same way but do not overcrowd the pan. Fry for about 2 minutes until golden.

3 As they are cooked, remove the banana fritters from the oil with a slotted spoon and place on kitchen paper to drain. Cook the rest of the battered bananas in the same way.

4 Make the caramel. Mix the sugar, sesame seeds and water in a pan. Heat gently, stirring occasionally, until the sugar has dissolved. Raise the heat and continue cooking, without stirring, until the syrup becomes a light caramel. Remove from the heat.

5 Have ready a bowl of iced water. Working quickly, drop one fritter at a time into the caramel. Flip over with a fork, remove immediately and plunge the piece into the water. Remove from the water quickly (carefully using your fingers for speed) and drain on a wire rack while coating the rest. Serve immediately.

Fresh Cherry and Hazelnut Strudel

Serve this wonderful treat as a warm dessert with custard after a festive meal, or allow it to cool and offer it as a scrumptious cake with afternoon tea or coffee to warm the soul on a cold winter's day.

Serves 6–8
75g/3oz/6 tbsp butter
90ml/6 tbsp light muscovado
  (brown) sugar
3 egg yolks

grated rind of 1 lemon
1.5ml/¹⁄₄ tsp grated nutmeg
250g/9oz/generous 1 cup
  ricotta cheese
8 large sheets filo pastry, thawed
  if frozen
75g/3oz ratafias, crushed
450g/1lb/2¹⁄₂ cups
  cherries, pitted
30ml/2 tbsp chopped hazelnuts
icing (confectioners') sugar,
  for dusting
crème fraîche, to serve

1 Preheat the oven to 190°C/375°F/Gas 5. Soften 15g/¹⁄₂oz/ 1 tbsp of the butter. Place it in a bowl and beat in the sugar and egg yolks until light and fluffy. Beat in the lemon rind, nutmeg and ricotta, then set aside.

2 Melt the remaining butter in a small pan. Working quickly, place a sheet of filo on a clean dish towel and brush it generously with melted butter. Place a second sheet on top and repeat the process. Continue until all the filo has been layered and buttered, reserving some of the melted butter.

3 Sprinkle the crushed ratafias over the top, leaving a 5cm/2in border around the outside. Spoon the ricotta mixture over the biscuits, spread it lightly to cover, then sprinkle over the cherries.

4 Fold in the filo pastry border and use the dish towel to carefully roll up the strudel, Swiss-roll (jelly-roll) style, beginning from one of the long sides of the pastry. Grease a baking sheet with the remaining melted butter.

5 Place the strudel on the baking sheet and sprinkle the hazelnuts over the surface. Bake for 35–40 minutes or until the strudel is golden and crisp. Dust with icing sugar and serve with a dollop of crème fraîche.

Toffee Bananas Energy 551kcal/2324kJ; Protein 4.7g; Carbohydrate 101.6g, of which sugars 73.5g; Fat 16.7g, of which saturates 2.2g; Cholesterol 0mg; Calcium 111mg; Fibre 2.3g; Sodium 13mg.
Fresh Cherry Strudel Energy 317kcal/1326kJ; Protein 6.5g; Carbohydrate 34.2g, of which sugars 22.9g; Fat 18.1g, of which saturates 9.1g; Cholesterol 109mg; Calcium 54mg; Fibre 1.2g; Sodium 93mg.

Bitter Chocolate Fondue

Vanilla-scented poached pears and scoops of ice cream are dipped into a rich chocolate fondue for this splendid dessert which will be stunning as part of a Christmas menu. Rosemary adds a lovely herby flavour.

Serves 4–6
200g/7oz dark (bittersweet) chocolate, broken into pieces
75ml/2½fl oz/⅓ cup strong black coffee
75g/3oz/scant ⅓ cup soft light brown sugar
120ml/4fl oz/½ cup double (heavy) cream
small, firm scoops of vanilla ice cream, to serve

For the poached pears
juice of 1 lemon
90g/3½oz/½ cup vanilla caster (superfine) sugar
1–2 fresh rosemary sprigs
12–18 small pears, or 4–6 large pears

1 To poach the pears, put the lemon juice, sugar, rosemary sprigs and 300ml/½ pint/1¼ cups water in a pan large enough to accommodate the pears all in one layer. Bring to the boil, stirring until the sugar dissolves in the water.

2 Peel the pears, and halve the large ones, if using, but leave the stalks intact. Add to the hot syrup and spoon over to cover.

3 Cook the pears for 5–10 minutes, depending on size and ripeness, spooning the syrup over them and turning frequently, until they are just tender.

4 Transfer to a serving plate, then remove the rosemary sprigs from the syrup. Stir about 15–30ml/1–2 tbsp of the rosemary leaves into the syrup and then leave to cool.

5 Put the chocolate in a heatproof bowl over a pan of barely simmering water. Add the coffee and sugar and heat, without stirring, until the chocolate is melted. Stir in the cream and heat gently. Transfer the fondue to a fondue pot and place on a burner set at low heat at the table.

6 Serve the pears and syrup together with the vanilla ice cream to dip into the hot chocolate fondue.

Caramel Rice Dessert

This traditional rice pudding is delicious served with crunchy fresh fruit.

Serves 4
15g/½oz/1 tbsp butter
50g/2oz/¼ cup short grain pudding rice
75ml/5 tbsp demerara (raw) sugar
pinch of salt
400g/14oz can evaporated milk made up to 600ml/1 pint/2½ cups with water
2 fresh baby pineapples
2 figs
1 crisp eating apple
10ml/2 tsp lemon juice

1 Preheat the oven to 150°C/300°F/Gas 2. Grease a soufflé dish (1 litre/1¾ pints/4 cups) lightly with a little of the butter. Put the rice in a sieve (strainer) and wash it thoroughly under cold water. Drain well and put into the soufflé dish.

2 Add 30ml/2 tbsp of the sugar to the dish, with the salt. Pour on the diluted evaporated milk and stir gently.

3 Dot the surface of the rice with butter. Bake for 2 hours, then leave to cool for 30 minutes.

4 Meanwhile, cut the pineapples and the figs into quarters. Cut the apple into segments and toss the pieces in the lemon juice. Preheat the grill (broiler).

5 Sprinkle the remaining sugar evenly over the rice. Grill (broil) for 5 minutes or until the sugar has caramelized. Leave the rice to stand for 5 minutes to allow the caramel to harden, then serve with the fresh fruit.

Christmas Rice Pudding

This rice pudding can be topped with some winter fruit, such as prunes. The scope for adding festive ingredients, such as almonds or spices, is endless.

Serves 4
90g/3½oz/½ cup short grain rice
1.2 litres/2 pints/5 cups milk
pinch of salt
15ml/1 tbsp ground cinnamon
200ml/7fl oz/scant 1 cup double (heavy) cream
50g/2oz/¼ cup caster (superfine) sugar
25g/1oz/¼ cup toasted flaked (sliced) almonds

To serve
100g/3¾oz/scant ½ cup prunes
50ml/2fl oz/¼ cup brandy

1 Put the rice and milk in a pan and bring to the boil. Add the salt, lower the heat, cover and simmer gently for about 1 hour, until the rice has absorbed most of the milk and is almost tender. Stir frequently to prevent the rice from sticking and burning on the bottom of the pan.

2 Add the cinnamon, cream, sugar and almonds to the rice and cook for a further 10 minutes, until the rice is tender.

3 Meanwhile, put the prunes and brandy in a pan and heat gently. Serve the rice in individual bowls with the prunes on top.

Bitter Fondue Energy 464kcal/1949kJ; Protein 2.8g; Carbohydrate 71.9g, of which sugars 71.6g; Fat 20.3g, of which saturates 12.3g; Cholesterol 29mg; Calcium 59mg; Fibre 5.6g; Sodium 15mg.
Caramel Rice Dessert Energy 313kcal/1321kJ; Protein 9.6g; Carbohydrate 54.3g, of which sugars 44.3g; Fat 7.6g, of which saturates 4.5g; Cholesterol 25mg; Calcium 312mg; Fibre 1.9g; Sodium 147mg.
Christmas Pudding Energy 617kcal/2577kJ; Protein 14.7g; Carbohydrate 54.9g, of which sugars 36.8g; Fat 35.7g, of which saturates 20.2g; Cholesterol 86mg; Calcium 419mg; Fibre 1.9g; Sodium 145mg.

Chocolate Crêpes with Plums

The crêpes, filling and sauce can be made in advance and assembled at the last minute. You can use apples instead of plums for this dessert.

Serves 6
50g/2oz plain (semisweet)
 chocolate, broken into squares
200ml/7fl oz/scant 1 cup milk
120ml/4fl oz/½ cup single
 (light) cream
30ml/2 tbsp unsweetened
 cocoa powder
115g/4oz/1 cup plain
 (all-purpose) flour
2 eggs

For the filling
500g/1¼lb red or golden plums
50g/2oz/¼ cup caster
 (superfine) sugar
30ml/2 tbsp water
30ml/2 tbsp port
vegetable oil, for frying
175g/6oz/¾ cup crème fraîche

For the sauce
150g/5oz plain (semisweet)
 chocolate, broken into squares
175ml/6fl oz/¾ cup double
 (heavy) cream
30ml/2 tbsp port

1 Place the chocolate and milk in a heavy pan. Heat gently until the chocolate melts. Pour into a blender or food processor and add the cream, cocoa, flour and eggs. Process until smooth. Turn into a jug (pitcher) and chill for 30 minutes.

2 Meanwhile, make the filling. Halve and stone (pit) the plums. Place in a pan with the sugar and water. Bring to the boil, then lower the heat, cover and simmer for about 10 minutes, or until the plums are tender. Stir in the port and simmer for a further 30 seconds. Remove from the heat and keep warm.

3 Heat a crêpe pan, grease with oil, then pour in enough batter to cover the base, swirling to coat it evenly. Cook until the crêpe is set, then flip to cook the other side. Slide on to baking parchment, then cook 11 more crêpes in the same way.

4 Make the sauce. Put the chocolate and double cream in a pan. Heat gently, stirring until the chocolate has melted and combined with the cream. Add the port and stir for 1 minute. Divide the plums between the crêpes, add a spoonful of crème fraîche to each and roll up. Serve with the sauce spooned over.

De Luxe Mincemeat Tart

Fruity home-made mincemeat is the perfect partner to the crumbly, nutty pastry in this rich and festive pie. Serve with custard or cream.

Serves 8
225g/8oz/2 cups plain
 (all-purpose) flour
10ml/2 tsp ground cinnamon
50g/2oz/½ cup finely
 ground walnuts
115g/4oz/½ cup butter
50g/2oz/¼ cup caster (superfine)
 sugar, plus extra for dusting
1 egg
2 drops vanilla extract
15ml/1 tbsp cold water

For the mincemeat
2 eating apples, peeled, cored
 and grated
225g/8oz/generous 1½ cups raisins
115g/4oz/ ½ cup ready-to-eat
 dried apricots, chopped
115g/4oz/⅔ cup ready-to-eat
 dried figs or prunes, chopped
225g/8oz/2 cups green grapes,
 halved and seeded
50g/2oz/ ½ cup chopped almonds
finely grated rind of 1 lemon
30ml/2 tbsp lemon juice
30ml/2 tbsp brandy or port
1.5ml/ ¼ tsp mixed (apple
 pie) spice
115g/4oz/½ cup soft light
 brown sugar
25g/1oz/2 tbsp butter, melted

1 Process the flour, cinnamon, ground walnuts and butter in a food processor or blender to make fine crumbs. Turn into a bowl and stir in the sugar. Beat the egg with the vanilla extract and water, and stir into the dry ingredients. Form a soft dough, knead until smooth, then wrap and chill for 30 minutes.

2 Mix the mincemeat ingredients together. Use two-thirds of the pastry to line a 23cm/9in, loose-based flan tin (pan). Trim and fill with the mincemeat.

3 Roll out the remaining pastry and cut into 1cm/½in strips. Arrange the strips in a lattice over the top of the pastry, wet the joins and press them together. Chill for 30 minutes.

4 Preheat a baking sheet in the oven at 190°C/375°F/Gas 5. Brush the pastry with a little water and dust with the caster sugar. Bake the tart on the baking sheet for 30–40 minutes. Leave to cool in the tin on a wire rack for about 15 minutes, then remove the tin and serve.

Chocolate Crêpes Energy 867kcal/3604kJ; Protein 10.6g; Carbohydrate 57.4g, of which sugars 41.7g; Fat 67g, of which saturates 36.7g; Cholesterol 184mg; Calcium 175mg; Fibre 3.4g; Sodium 115mg.
Mincemeat Tart Energy 434kcal/1822kJ; Protein 4.8g; Carbohydrate 63.6g, of which sugars 42.1g; Fat 19.6g, of which saturates 8.1g; Cholesterol 57mg; Calcium 74mg; Fibre 1.8g; Sodium 108mg.

Bakewell Tart

This is a modern version of the Bakewell pudding, which is made with puff pastry and has a custard-like almond filling. It is said to be the result of a 19th-century kitchen accident and is still baked in the original shop in Bakewell, Derbyshire, UK. This popular, tart-like version is simpler to make and is sure to become a favourite dessert. It is easy and quick to make and would be a delicious pudding to eat during the festive season as a change from spicier, richer desserts.

Serve 4

For the pastry
115g/4oz/1 cup plain
  (all-purpose) flour
pinch of salt
50g/2oz/4 tbsp
  butter, diced

For the filling
30ml/2 tbsp raspberry or
  apricot jam
2 whole eggs and 2 extra yolks
115g/4oz/generous ½ cup caster
  (superfine) sugar
115g/4oz/½ cup butter, melted
55g/2oz/⅔ cup ground almonds
few drops of almond extract
icing (confectioners') sugar,
  to dust

1 Sift the flour and salt and rub in the butter until the mixture resembles fine breadcrumbs. Stir in about 20ml/2 tbsp cold water and gather into a smooth ball of dough. Wrap the dough in clear film and chill for 30 minutes. Preheat the oven to 200°C/400°F/Gas 6.

2 Roll out the pastry and use to line an 18cm/7in loose-based flan tin (pan). Spread the jam over the pastry.

3 Whisk the eggs, egg yolks and sugar together in a large bowl until the mixture is thick and pale.

4 Gently stir in the melted butter, ground almonds and the almond extract.

5 Pour the mixture over the jam in the pastry case (pie shell). Put the tart into the hot oven and cook for 30 minutes until just set and browned. Sift a little icing sugar over the top before serving warm.

Mince Pies with Orange Pastry

Home-made mince pies are so much nicer at Christmas time than those bought from a store, especially with this flavoursome pastry.

Makes 18
225g/8oz/2 cups plain
  (all-purpose) flour
40g/1½oz/⅓ cup icing
  (confectioners') sugar

10ml/2 tsp ground cinnamon
150g/5oz/generous 1 cup cold
  butter, diced
grated rind of 1 orange
about 60ml/4 tbsp iced water
225g/8oz/⅔ cup mincemeat
1 egg, beaten, to glaze
icing (confectioners') sugar,
  for dusting

1 Sift together the flour, icing sugar and cinnamon in a large mixing bowl. Rub in the butter with your fingertips until it resembles fine breadcrumbs. Stir in the grated orange rind.

2 Mix to a firm dough with the water. Knead lightly, then roll out on a lightly floured surface to a 5mm/¼in thickness. Using a 6cm/2½in round pastry (cookie) cutter, stamp out 18 circles, then stamp out 18 smaller 5cm/2in circles.

3 Line two bun trays with the larger circles. Place a small spoonful of mincemeat into each pastry case (pie shell) and top with the smaller pastry circles, pressing the edges to seal.

4 Brush the tops with egg glaze and leave in the refrigerator for 30 minutes. Preheat the oven to 200°C/400°F/Gas 6.

5 Bake for 15–20 minutes, or until golden brown. Remove to cool on wire racks. Serve just warm, dusted with icing sugar.

Cook's Tip
This sweet and spicy pastry works for all kinds of sweet pies and tarts. This quantity will line a 23cm/9in flan tin (pan) as well as leaving enough for a lattice or cut-out pastry shapes to decorate the top. It is particularly suitable for autumn fruit pies made with apples, plums or pears.

Bakewell Tart Energy 700kcal/2919kJ; Protein 10.8g; Carbohydrate 57.1g, of which sugars 36.7g; Fat 49.9g, of which saturates 17.1g; Cholesterol 257mg; Calcium 110mg; Fibre 0.9g; Sodium 394mg.
Mince Pies with Orange Pastry Energy 145kcal/610kJ; Protein 1.3g; Carbohydrate 19.3g, of which sugars 9.7g; Fat 7.6g, of which saturates 4.4g; Cholesterol 18mg; Calcium 24mg; Fibre 0.6g; Sodium 53mg.

Christmas Stars

These pretty pastries are a delicious twist on the usual mince pies, although the prune filling is less sweet than mincemeat and does not include any alcohol.

Makes 9
200g/7oz/1¾ cups plain (all-purpose) flour
5ml/1 tsp baking powder
130g/4½oz/½ cup butter, softened
150ml/¼ pint/⅔ cup cold water, or enough to bind
200g/7oz/scant 1 cup ready-to-eat prunes
1 egg, beaten, to glaze

1 Preheat the oven to 200°C/400°F/Gas 6. Sift the flour and baking powder into a large bowl.

2 Cut the butter into small pieces, add to the flour and rub in until the mixture resembles fine breadcrumbs. Alternatively, put the flour and baking powder in a food processor, add the butter and, using a pulsating action, blend to form fine breadcrumbs. Gradually add cold water and mix until it forms a dough.

3 On a lightly floured surface, roll out the pastry to a square about 3mm/⅛in thick, then cut the square into a further nine equal squares. Make a diagonal cut from each corner of the squares towards the centre.

4 Chop the prunes into small pieces. Put a spoonful of the chopped prunes in the centre of each square of pastry, then lift each corner of the pastry and fold it over to the centre to form a rough star shape.

5 Place the stars on a baking sheet and brush with beaten egg. Bake in the preheated oven for about 15 minutes, or until golden brown. Serve warm.

> **Cook's Tip**
> *A little brandy, mixed into the prunes, adds an extra delicious dimension to these tasty treats.*

American Pumpkin Pie

This spicy sweet pie is traditionally served at Thanksgiving, or at Halloween, but it also makes a delicious dessert at Christmas time.

Serves 8
200g/7oz/1¾ cups plain (all-purpose) flour
2.5ml/½ tsp salt
90g/3½oz/7 tbsp unsalted butter
1 egg yolk

For the filling
900g/2lb piece of pumpkin
2 large (US extra large) eggs
75g/3oz/6 tbsp soft light brown sugar
60ml/4 tbsp golden (light corn) syrup
250ml/8fl oz/1 cup double (heavy) cream
15ml/1 tbsp mixed (pumpkin pie) spice
2.5ml/½ tsp salt
icing (confectioners') sugar, for dusting

1 Sift the flour and salt into a mixing bowl. Rub in the butter until the mixture resembles breadcrumbs, then mix in the egg yolk and enough iced water (about 15ml/1 tbsp) to make a dough. Roll the dough into a ball, wrap it up in clear film (plastic wrap) and chill it for at least 30 minutes.

2 Make the filling. Peel the pumpkin and remove the seeds. Cut the flesh into cubes. Place in a heavy pan, add water to cover and boil for 20 minutes or until tender. Mash until smooth, then leave in a sieve (strainer) set over a bowl to drain thoroughly.

3 Roll out the pastry on a lightly floured surface and line a 23–25cm/9–10in loose-bottomed flan tin (pan). Prick the base and line with baking parchment and baking beans. Chill for 15 minutes. Preheat the oven to 200°C/400°F/Gas 6.

4 Bake the pastry case (pie shell) for 10 minutes, remove the parchment and baking beans, return the pastry case to the oven and bake for 5 minutes more.

5 Lower the oven temperature to 190°C/375°F/Gas 5. Put the pumpkin in a bowl. Beat in the eggs, sugar, syrup, cream, mixed spice and salt. Pour into the pastry case. Bake for 40 minutes or until the filling is set. Dust with icing sugar and serve.

Christmas Stars Energy 140kcal/583kJ; Protein 1.3g; Carbohydrate 13g, of which sugars 6g; Fat 9.5g, of which saturates 5.9g; Cholesterol 24mg; Calcium 21mg; Fibre 1.3g; Sodium 70mg.
Pumpkin Pie Energy 416kcal/1736kJ; Protein 5.3g; Carbohydrate 38.2g, of which sugars 18.6g; Fat 28g, of which saturates 16.9g; Cholesterol 114mg; Calcium 98mg; Fibre 1.9g; Sodium 360mg.

Whisky Trifle

This luxuriously rich trifle is made the traditional way, with real sponge cake, fresh fruit and rich egg custard, but with whisky rather than the usual sherry. If you like, you can decorate the top with glacé (candied) cherries and angelica, to add Christmas colours. A good egg custard is essential, so don't be tempted to use a convenient alternative.

Serves 6–8
1 × 15–18cm/6–7in sponge cake
225g/8oz raspberry jam

150ml/¼ pint/⅔ cup whisky
450g/1lb ripe fruit, such as pears and bananas
300ml/½ pint/1¼ cups whipping cream
flaked (sliced) almonds, toasted to decorate (optional)

For the custard
450ml/¾ pint/scant 2 cups full cream (whole) milk
1 vanilla pod (bean) or a few drops of vanilla extract
3 eggs
25g/1oz/2 tbsp caster (superfine) sugar

1 To make the custard, put the milk into a pan with the vanilla pod, if using, and bring almost to the boil. Remove the pan from the heat. Whisk the eggs and sugar together lightly. Remove the pod. Gradually whisk the milk into the egg mixture.

2 Rinse out the pan with cold water, return the mixture to it and stir over low heat until it thickens enough to coat the back of a spoon; do not allow it to boil. Alternatively, for a very slow method of cooking, use a double boiler, or a bowl over a pan of boiling water. Turn the custard into a bowl and add the vanilla extract, if using. Cover and set aside until needed.

3 Halve the sponge cake horizontally, spread with the jam and make a sandwich. Cut it into slices and use them to line the bottom and lower sides of a large glass serving bowl.

4 Sprinkle with the whisky. Peel and slice the fruit, then spread it out over the sponge in a layer. Pour the custard on top, cover with clear film (plastic wrap), and leave to cool and set. Chill until required. Before serving, whip the cream and spread it over the custard. Decorate with the toasted flaked almonds, if using.

Chilled Fruit Pudding

This trifle-like dish is just as good made with frozen fruits so it is great for making at Christmas time.

Serves 4–6
550g/1lb 4oz mixed soft fruit, such as raspberries, blackberries, blackcurrants, redcurrants

50g/2oz/4 tbsp sugar
large thick slice of bread with crusts removed, about 125g/4¼oz without crusts
300ml/½ pint/1¼ cups double (heavy) cream
45ml/3 tbsp elderflower cordial
150ml/¼ pint/⅔ cup thick natural (plain) yogurt

1 Reserve a few raspberries, blackberries, blackcurrants or redcurrants for decoration, then put the remainder into a pan with the sugar and 30ml/2 tbsp water. Bring just to the boil, cover and simmer gently for 4–5 minutes until the fruit is soft and plenty of juice has formed.

2 Cut the slice of bread into cubes, measuring about 2.5cm/1in, and put them into one large dish or individual serving bowls or dessert glasses.

3 Spoon the fruit mixture over the bread and leave to cool.

4 Whip the cream with the elderflower cordial until stiff peaks begin to form. Gently stir in the yogurt and spoon the mixture over the top of the fruit.

5 Chill in the refrigerator until required. Just before serving, decorate the top with the reserved fruit.

> **Cook's Tip**
> Use bread from an unsliced farmhouse loaf for this recipe.

> **Variation**
> Instead of mixing yogurt into the topping, try using the same quantity of ready-made custard – it gives a richer result.

Whisky Trifle Energy 710kcal/2959kJ; Protein 12.1g; Carbohydrate 58g, of which sugars 42.6g; Fat 43.2g, of which saturates 14.4g; Cholesterol 171mg; Calcium 194mg; Fibre 2.3g; Sodium 336mg.
Fruit Pudding Energy 382kcal/1592kJ; Protein 5.2g; Carbohydrate 29.9g, of which sugars 20.2g; Fat 27.8g, of which saturates 16.9g; Cholesterol 69mg; Calcium 124mg; Fibre 2.6g; Sodium 144mg.

Syllabub

This dish can be traced back to the 17th century, when it is said to have been made by pouring fresh milk, straight from the cow, on to spiced cider or ale, creating a frothy foam. Later, cream and wine were used to make an impressive and luxurious dessert, which is perfect for a festive dinner party with friends.

Serves 6
1 orange
65g/2¹/₂oz/¹/₃ cup caster (superfine) sugar
60ml/4 tbsp medium dry sherry
300ml/¹/₂ pint/1¹/₂ cups double (heavy) cream
strips of crystallized (candied) orange, to decorate
sponge fingers or crisp biscuits (cookies), to serve

1 Finely grate about 2.5ml/¹/₂ tsp rind from the orange, then squeeze out its juice.

2 Put the orange rind and juice, sugar and sherry into a large bowl and stir until the sugar is completely dissolved. Stir in the cream. Whip the mixture until thick and soft peaks form.

3 Spoon the syllabub equally into six wine glasses. Alternatively, you can use special dessert glasses or plain bowls.

4 Chill the glasses of syllabub in the refrigerator until ready to serve, then decorate with the strips of crystallized orange. Serve with sponge fingers or crisp biscuits.

Cook's Tips
Syllabub is lovely spooned over a bowl of fresh soft fruit such as strawberries, apricots, raspberries or blackberries. Or choose festive fruits like cranberries, apples and pears.

Variation
For a festive touch, you can add a pinch of ground cinnamon to the mixture in step 2, if you like.

Christmas Cranberry Bombe

This is a light and refreshing alternative to traditional but heavy Christmas pudding. It is still very special and will look stunning in the middle of the festive table, alone or with a selection of other desserts.

Serves 6

For the sorbet centre
225g/8oz/2 cups fresh or frozen cranberries

150ml/¹/₄ pint/²/₃ cup orange juice
finely grated rind of ¹/₂ orange
2.5ml/¹/₂ tsp allspice
60ml/4 tbsp demerara (raw) sugar

For the outer layer
600ml/1 pint/2²/₃ cups vanilla ice cream
30ml/2 tbsp chopped angelica
30ml/2 tbsp chopped crystallized (candied) citrus rind
15ml/1 tbsp flaked (sliced) almonds, toasted

1 Put the cranberries, orange juice, rind and spice in a pan and cook gently until the cranberries are soft. Add the sugar, then purée in a food processor until almost smooth, but still with some texture. Leave to cool.

2 Allow the vanilla ice cream to soften slightly then stir in the chopped angelica, crystallized citrus rind and almonds.

3 Pack the mixture into a 1.2 litre/2 pint/5 cup pudding mould and, using a metal spoon, hollow out the centre. Freeze the mould until firm to the touch. This will take at least 3 hours.

4 Fill the hollowed-out centre of the bombe with the cranberry mixture, smooth over the top with a knife and place in the freezer until firm. To serve, allow to soften slightly at room temperature, turn out and slice.

Variation
If you are making this dessert outside of the festive period, you can replace the cranberries with other seasonal fruits. In summer, you could use other soft fruits such as strawberries, raspberries or blackberries.

Syllabub Energy 310kcal/1282kJ; Protein 1.1g; Carbohydrate 14.5g, of which sugars 14.5g; Fat 26.9g, of which saturates 16.7g; Cholesterol 69mg; Calcium 41mg; Fibre 0.3g; Sodium 15mg.
Christmas Bombe Energy 147kcal/622kJ; Protein 4.6g; Carbohydrate 22.7g, of which sugars 22.5g; Fat 5g, of which saturates 1.7g; Cholesterol 65mg; Calcium 91mg; Fibre 0.9g; Sodium 64mg.

Passion Fruit Crème Caramels

Christmas is a time when passion fruit are at their best. The fruit has an aromatic flavour that really permeates these crème caramels. Use some of the caramel for dipping the physalis in, to create a unique decoration for these pretty festive treats.

Serves 4
185g/6½oz/scant 1 cup caster (superfine) sugar
75ml/5 tbsp water
4 passion fruit
4 physalis
3 eggs plus 1 egg yolk
150ml/¼ pint/⅔ cup double (heavy) cream
150ml/¼ pint/⅔ cup creamy milk

1 Place 150g/5oz/⅔ cup of the caster sugar in a heavy pan. Add the water and heat the mixture gently until the sugar has dissolved. Increase the heat and boil until the syrup turns a dark golden colour.

2 Meanwhile, cut each passion fruit in half. Scoop out the seeds from the passion fruit into a sieve (strainer) set over a bowl. Press the seeds against the sieve to extract all their juice. Spoon a few of the seeds into each of four 150ml/¼ pint/⅔ cup ramekins. Set the juice aside.

3 Peel back the papery casing from each physalis and dip the orange berries into the caramel. Place on a sheet of non-stick baking parchment and set aside. Pour the remaining caramel carefully into the ramekins.

4 Preheat the oven to 150°C/300°F/Gas 2. Whisk the eggs, egg yolk and remaining sugar in a bowl. Whisk in the cream and milk, then the passion fruit juice. Strain through a sieve into each ramekin, then place the ramekins in a baking tin (pan). Pour in hot water to come halfway up the sides of the dishes; bake for 40–45 minutes or until just set.

5 Remove the custards from the tin and leave to cool, then cover and chill them for 4 hours before serving. Run a knife between the edge of each ramekin and the custard and invert each in turn on to a dessert plate. Shake the ramekins firmly to release the custards. Decorate each with a dipped physalis.

Baked Caramel Custard

Baked custards are traditionally served on their own with a sprinkling of grated nutmeg or to accompany poached fruits. This recipe is simply a dressed-up version of the more homely dish. Serve it as it is, or with cream and, perhaps, some light, crisp biscuits.

Serves 6
75g/3oz/scant ½ cup sugar
600ml/1 pint/2½ cups milk
vanilla pod (bean) or a few drops of vanilla extract
6 eggs
75g/3oz/scant ½ cup caster (superfine) sugar

1 Preheat the oven to 160°C/325°F/Gas 3. Put the sugar into a heavy pan and stir over medium heat to make a golden caramel syrup. Remove from the heat and very carefully stir in 15ml/1 tbsp water. Return to the heat.

2 Pour the caramel into an ungreased, heated 900ml/1½ pint/3¾ cup baking dish, or divide among six ramekins. Using oven gloves or a cloth, tilt the dish to coat the base evenly with the hot caramel, then place in a shallow roasting pan.

3 To make the custard, scald the milk in a small pan with the vanilla pod, if using. Lightly beat the eggs and caster sugar in a bowl. When the milk is nearly boiling, remove the vanilla pod and whisk into the egg mixture. Add the vanilla extract, if using. Pour the custard into the prepared dish.

4 Fill the roasting pan to a depth of about 2.5cm/1in with cold water, cover the dishes with buttered baking parchment and bake in the centre of the oven until the custard has set, about 1–1½ hours, if baking one large dish, or about 30 minutes for individual ones. Leave to cool, and then chill.

5 To serve, loosen around the edge with a knife and tilt the dish to ease the custard away from the sides. Select a dish for serving that is flat in the middle but with a deep enough rim to contain the caramel syrup. Invert the serving dish over the baking dish and turn upside down. If using ramekins, turn out on to small plates. Serve immediately.

Passion Fruit Caramels 318kcal/1336kJ; Protein 9.8g; Carbohydrate 36.6g, of which sugars 36.6g; Fat 16g, of which saturates 8.2g; Cholesterol 221mg; Calcium 150mg; Fibre 0g; Sodium 108mg.
Caramel Custard Energy 233kcal/983kJ; Protein 11g; Carbohydrate 30.8g, of which sugars 30.8g; Fat 8.4g, of which saturates 2.9g; Cholesterol 234mg; Calcium 168mg; Fibre 0g; Sodium 129mg.

Whisky Mac Cream

The warming tipple whisky mac is a combination of whisky and ginger wine. This recipe turns the drink into a rich, smooth, creamy dessert – very decadent and a suitable end to a festive feast.

Serves 4
4 egg yolks
15ml/1 tbsp caster (superfine) sugar, plus 50g/2oz/¼ cup
600ml/1 pint/2½ cups double (heavy) cream
15ml/1 tbsp whisky
green ginger wine, to serve

1 In a large bowl, whisk the egg yolks thoroughly with the first, smaller amount of the caster sugar. Whisk briskly until the egg yolks are light and pale.

2 Pour the double cream into a heavy pan with the whisky and the remainder of the caster sugar. Bring the mixture to scalding point but do not let it boil.

3 Pour the mixture from the pan on to the egg yolks, whisking continually. Return to the pan and, over low heat, stir until the custard has thickened slightly.

4 Pour the mixture into individual ramekin dishes, cover each with a piece of clear film (plastic wrap) and set aside for a few hours or overnight to set.

5 To serve, pour just enough green ginger wine over the top of each ramekin to cover the cream.

> **Cook's Tip**
> Green ginger wine is made by two main companies in the UK – Stone's and Crabbie's. To make a simple Whisky Mac as a drink, mix equal parts Scotch whisky (it should traditionally be this variety but not a single malt) with equal parts ginger wine – or a little more whisky to ginger wine if you like it less sweet. Whether or not you add ice to the drink is a matter of preference although it will often be decided by how cold the festive weather is outside.

Frozen Grand Marnier Soufflés

These luxurious puddings make a wonderful end to any Christmas-time meal.

Serves 8
200g/7oz/1 cup caster (superfine) sugar

6 large (US extra large) eggs, separated
250ml/8fl oz/1 cup milk
15g/½oz powdered gelatine
90ml/6 tbsp cold water
450ml/¾ pint/scant 2 cups double (heavy) cream
60ml/4 tbsp Grand Marnier

1 Fold a double collar of baking parchment around eight ramekin dishes and tie with string. Put 75g/3oz/6 tbsp of the caster sugar in a large mixing bowl with the egg yolks and whisk until the yolks are pale. This will take about 5 minutes by hand and about 3 minutes if you use an electric hand mixer.

2 Heat the milk until almost boiling and pour it on to the yolks, whisking all the time. Return to the pan and stir it over a gentle heat until it is thick enough to coat the back of the spoon. Remove the pan from the heat.

3 In a small bowl, soak the gelatine in 45ml/3 tbsp of the cold water for a few minutes, then dissolve over a pan of barely simmering water. When it is clear, remove from the pan and cool. Stir the gelatine into the custard. Pour into a bowl and leave to cool. Whisk occasionally, until the custard is almost set.

4 Put the remaining sugar in a pan with the rest of the water and dissolve it over low heat. Bring to the boil and boil rapidly until it reaches 119°C/238°F, or it forms a soft ball when a little is dropped into cold water. Remove from the heat.

5 In a clean bowl, whisk the egg whites until they are stiff. Pour the hot syrup on to the whites, whisking all the time. Cool.

6 Whisk the cream until it holds soft peaks. Add the Grand Marnier to the cold custard and fold into the cold meringue, with the cream. Pour into the prepared ramekin dishes. Freeze overnight. Remove the paper collars. Leave at room temperature for 30 minutes before serving.

Whisky Mac Cream Energy 892kcal/3682kJ; Protein 5.4g; Carbohydrate 19.7g, of which sugars 19.7g; Fat 86.1g, of which saturates 51.7g; Cholesterol 407mg; Calcium 107mg; Fibre 0g; Sodium 44mg.
Frozen Soufflés Energy 478kcal/1991kJ; Protein 6.7g; Carbohydrate 33.7g, of which sugars 33.7g; Fat 34.9g, of which saturates 20.3g; Cholesterol 222mg; Calcium 99mg; Fibre 0g; Sodium 79mg.

Tiramisù in Chocolate Cups

Give in to the temptation of tiramisù at Christmas, with its magical mocha flavour.

Serves 6
1 egg yolk
30ml/2 tbsp caster (superfine) sugar
2.5ml/½ tsp vanilla extract
250g/9oz/generous 1 cup mascarpone
120ml/4fl oz/½ cup strong black coffee

15ml/1 tbsp unsweetened cocoa powder
30ml/2 tbsp coffee liqueur
16 amaretti
unsweetened cocoa powder, for dusting

For the chocolate cups
175g/6oz good quality plain (semisweet) chocolate, broken into squares
25g/1oz/2 tbsp unsalted butter

1 Make the chocolate cups. Cut out six 15cm/6in rounds of baking parchment. Melt the chocolate and butter in a heatproof bowl over barely simmering water. Stir until smooth, then spread a spoonful over each circle, to within 2cm/¾in of the edge.

2 Carefully lift each paper round and drape it over an upturned teacup or ramekin so that the edges curve into frills. Leave until completely set, then carefully lift off and peel away the paper to reveal the chocolate cups.

3 To make the filling, beat the egg yolk and sugar in a bowl until smooth, then stir in the vanilla extract and mascarpone. Mix until smooth and creamy. In another bowl, mix the coffee, cocoa and liqueur. Break up the biscuits and stir into the mixture.

4 Divide half the biscuit mixture among the chocolate cups, then spoon over half the mascarpone mixture. Spoon over the remaining biscuit mixture, top with the rest of the mascarpone mixture and dust with cocoa. Serve as soon as possible.

> **Cook's Tip**
> When spreading the chocolate for the cups, don't aim for perfectly regular edges; uneven edges will give a prettier effect.

Mocha Velvet Cream Pots

These dainty pots of chocolate heaven are a fabulous way to round off a special festive meal.

Serves 8
15ml/1 tbsp instant coffee powder
475ml/16fl oz/2 cups milk
75g/3oz/6 tbsp caster (superfine) sugar

225g/8oz plain (semisweet) chocolate, chopped into small pieces
10ml/2 tsp vanilla extract
30ml/2 tbsp coffee-flavoured liqueur (optional)
7 egg yolks
whipped double (heavy) cream and crystallized mimosa balls, to decorate (optional)

1 Preheat the oven to 160°C/325°F/Gas 3. Place eight 120ml/4fl oz/½ cup custard cups or ramekins in a roasting pan. Set aside.

2 Put the instant coffee in a pan. Stir in the milk, then add the sugar and place the pan over medium heat. Bring to the boil, stirring constantly, until both the coffee and the sugar have dissolved completely.

3 Remove the pan from the heat and add the chocolate. Stir until it has melted and the sauce is smooth. Stir in the vanilla extract and coffee liqueur, if using.

4 In a bowl, whisk the egg yolks to blend them lightly. Slowly whisk in the chocolate mixture until well combined, then strain the mixture into a large jug (pitcher) and divide it equally among the cups or ramekins.

5 Pour enough boiling water into the roasting pan to come halfway up the sides of the cups or ramekins. Carefully place the roasting pan in the oven.

6 Bake in the oven for 30–35 minutes, until the custard is just set and a knife inserted into the custard comes out clean. Remove the cups or ramekins from the roasting pan and allow to cool completely. Place on a baking sheet, cover and chill. Decorate the pots with whipped cream and crystallized mimosa balls, if you wish.

Tiramisù Energy 351kcal/1469kJ; Protein 6.9g; Carbohydrate 34.5g, of which sugars 29.6g; Fat 20.4g, of which saturates 12.1g; Cholesterol 62mg; Calcium 33mg; Fibre 1.2g; Sodium 86mg.
Mocha Velvet Cream Pots Energy 261kcal/1095kJ; Protein 6g; Carbohydrate 30.5g, of which sugars 30.2g; Fat 13.7g, of which saturates 6.7g; Cholesterol 182mg; Calcium 106mg; Fibre 0.7g; Sodium 36mg.

Chocolate and Chestnut Pots

The chestnut purée adds substance and a festive flavour to these mousses. Crisp, delicate cookies, such as langues-de-chat, provide a good foil to the richness.

Serves 6

250g/9oz plain (semisweet)
  chocolate

60ml/4 tbsp Madeira
25g/1oz/2 tbsp butter, diced
2 eggs, separated
225g/8oz/scant 1 cup
  unsweetened chestnut purée
crème fraîche or whipped double
  (heavy) cream, to decorate

1 Make a few chocolate curls for decoration by rubbing a grater along the length of the bar of chocolate. Break the rest of the chocolate into squares and melt it in a pan with the Madeira over very low heat.

2 Remove the pan from the heat and add the butter, a few pieces at a time, stirring until melted and smooth.

3 Beat the egg yolks quickly into the mixture, then beat in the chestnut purée, mixing until smooth.

4 Whisk the egg whites in a clean, grease-free bowl until stiff. Stir about 15ml/1 tbsp of the whites into the chestnut mixture to lighten it, then fold in the rest smoothly and evenly.

5 Spoon the mixture into six small ramekin dishes and chill in the refrigerator until it is set.

6 Remove the pots from the refrigerator 30 minutes before serving. Serve the pots topped with a spoonful of crème fraîche or whipped cream and decorated with chocolate curls.

> **Cook's Tips**
> • If Madeira is not available, use brandy or rum instead.
> • These pots can be frozen successfully for up to 2 months, making them ideal for a prepare-ahead Christmas dessert.

Chocolate Amaretto Marquise

This wickedly rich chocolate dessert is truly extravagant – perfect for a festive treat.

Serves 10–12

15ml/1 tbsp flavourless vegetable
  oil, such as groundnut (peanut)
  or sunflower
75g/3oz/7–8 amaretti,
  finely crushed
25g/1oz/¼ cup unblanched
  almonds, toasted and
  finely chopped
450g/1lb plain (semisweet) or
  dark (bittersweet) chocolate,
  chopped into small pieces

75ml/5 tbsp Amaretto
  Disaronno liqueur
75ml/5 tbsp golden (light
  corn) syrup
475ml/16fl oz/2 cups
  double (heavy) cream
unsweetened cocoa powder,
  for dusting

For the amaretto cream

350ml/12fl oz/1½ cups
  whipping cream or double
  (heavy) cream
30–45ml/2–3 tbsp Amaretto
  Disaronno liqueur

1 Lightly oil a 23cm/9in heart-shaped or springform cake tin (pan). Line the bottom with baking parchment, then oil the paper. In a small bowl, combine the crushed amaretti and the chopped almonds. Sprinkle evenly on to the base of the tin.

2 Place the chocolate, Amaretto liqueur and golden syrup in a medium pan over a very low heat. Stir frequently until the chocolate has melted and the mixture is smooth. Remove from the heat and allow it to cool for about 6–8 minutes, until the mixture feels just warm to the touch.

3 Whip the cream until it just begins to hold its shape. Stir a large spoonful into the chocolate mixture, to lighten it, then quickly add the remaining cream and gently fold in. Pour into the prepared tin, on top of the amaretti mixture. Level the surface. Cover with clear film (plastic wrap) and chill overnight.

4 To unmould, run a slightly warmed, thin-bladed sharp knife around the edge of the dessert, then unmould. Carefully peel off the paper, replacing any crust that sticks to it, and dust with cocoa. In a bowl, whip the cream and Amaretto liqueur to soft peaks. Serve separately.

Chocolate Pots Energy 348kcal/1455kJ; Protein 5g; Carbohydrate 41.4g, of which sugars 29.9g; Fat 18g, of which saturates 9.9g; Cholesterol 75mg; Calcium 42mg; Fibre 2.6g; Sodium 56mg.
Chocolate Marquise Energy 589kcal/2444kJ; Protein 3.9g; Carbohydrate 38.2g, of which sugars 35.1g; Fat 46.4g, of which saturates 27.5g; Cholesterol 87mg; Calcium 63mg; Fibre 1.2g; Sodium 57mg.

Chunky Chocolate-coffee Ice Cream

This wonderful combination of dark coffee with a hint of coffee liqueur, peppered with crunchy chocolate-covered coffee beans, is sure to be a big hit at Christmas. The beans can be coated with whichever type of chocolate you desire.

Serves 6
4 egg yolks
75g/3oz/scant ½ cup caster (superfine) sugar
5ml/1 tsp cornflour (cornstarch)

300ml/½ pint/1¼ cups semi-skimmed (low-fat) milk
30ml/2 tbsp instant coffee granules or powder
300ml/½ pint/1¼ cups double (heavy) cream
120ml/4fl oz/½ cup Kahlúa or other coffee liqueur
115g/4oz assorted chocolate-covered coffee beans
a little sifted unsweetened cocoa powder, to decorate

1 Whisk the egg yolks, sugar and cornflour in a bowl until the mixture is thick and pale. Warm the milk in a pan but do not boil, then gradually whisk into the yolk mixture.

2 Return the custard to the pan and cook over low heat, stirring constantly so that it does not burn on the bottom.

3 When the custard has thickened and is smooth, pour it back into the bowl and mix in the instant coffee granules or powder, stirring constantly until all of the coffee has completely dissolved. Cover the custard with clear film (plastic wrap) to prevent a skin from forming, leave to cool, then chill well before churning.

4 Stir the cream and Kahlúa into the coffee custard, then pour into an ice cream maker. Churn until thick. Roughly chop 75g/3oz of the chocolate-covered coffee beans, add to the ice cream and churn until firm enough to scoop. Transfer to a freezer container and freeze until required.

5 Scoop the ice cream into coffee cups and decorate with the remaining chocolate-covered coffee beans and a light dusting of cocoa powder.

Iced Tiramisù

This favourite Italian combination is not usually served as a frozen dessert, but in fact it does make a marvellous ice cream.

Serves 4
150g/5oz/¾ cup caster (superfine) sugar
150ml/¼ pint/⅔ cup water
250g/9oz/generous 1 cup mascarpone

200g/7oz/scant 1 cup virtually fat-free fromage frais or low-fat cream cheese
5ml/1 tsp vanilla extract
10ml/2 tsp instant coffee, dissolved in 30ml/2 tbsp boiling water
30ml/2 tbsp coffee liqueur
75g/3oz sponge fingers
unsweetened cocoa powder and chocolate curls, to decorate

1 Put 115g/4oz/generous ½ cup of the sugar into a small pan. Add the water and bring to the boil, stirring, until the sugar has dissolved. Leave the syrup to cool, then chill.

2 Put the mascarpone into a bowl. Beat with a spoon until it is soft, then stir in the fromage frais or cream cheese. Add the chilled syrup, a little at a time, then stir in the vanilla extract.

3 Spoon the mixture into a freezer container and freeze for 4 hours, beating twice with a fork, electric whisk or in a food processor to break up the ice crystals. Alternatively, use an ice cream maker and churn the mascarpone mixture until it is thick but too soft to scoop.

4 Meanwhile, put the coffee in a bowl, sweeten with the remaining sugar, then add the liqueur. Stir well, then cool. Crumble the sponge fingers and toss in the coffee mixture.

5 Spoon a third of the ice cream into a 900ml/1½ pint/3¾ cup freezer container, spoon over half the crumbled sponge, then top with half the remaining ice cream. Sprinkle over the rest of the crumbled sponge, then cover with the remaining ice cream.

6 Freeze for about 2–3 hours until the ice cream is firm enough to scoop. Serve dusted with cocoa powder and decorated with chocolate curls.

Chunky Ice Cream Energy 504kcal/2094kJ; Protein 4.9g; Carbohydrate 32.2g, of which sugars 31.3g; Fat 38.2g, of which saturates 20.8g; Cholesterol 173mg; Calcium 112mg; Fibre 0.4g; Sodium 57mg.
Iced Tiramisù Energy 362kcal/1526kJ; Protein 11.7g; Carbohydrate 54.5g, of which sugars 50.3g; Fat 10.5g, of which saturates 6.1g; Cholesterol 69mg; Calcium 78mg; Fibre 0.2g; Sodium 35mg.

Fig, Port and Clementine Sundaes

These sundaes are an ideal finale to a fine festive meal. The figs and clementines contrast beautifully with the warm spices and port.

Serves 6

6 clementines
30ml/2 tbsp clear honey
1 cinnamon stick, halved
15ml/1 tbsp light muscovado
   (brown) sugar
60ml/4 tbsp port
6 fresh figs
about 500ml/17fl oz/2¼ cups
   orange sorbet

1 Finely grate the rind from two clementines and put it in a small, heavy pan. Cut the peel off the clementines, then slice the flesh thinly. Add the honey, cinnamon, sugar and port to the rind. Heat gently until the sugar has dissolved, to make a syrup.

2 Put the clementine slices in a heatproof bowl and pour over the syrup. Cool completely, then chill.

3 Slice the figs thinly and add to the clementines and syrup, tossing the ingredients together gently. Leave to stand for 10 minutes, then discard the cinnamon stick.

4 Arrange half the fig and clementine slices around the sides of six serving glasses. Half fill the glasses with scoops of orange sorbet. Arrange the remaining fruit slices around the sides of the glasses, then pile more sorbet into the centre. Pour over the port syrup and serve immediately.

> **Cook's Tip**
> *A variety of different types of fresh figs are available. Dark purple skinned figs have a deep red flesh; the yellowy-green figs have a pink flesh and green skinned figs have an amber coloured flesh. All types can be eaten, complete with the skin, simply as they are or baked and served with Greek (US strained plain) yogurt and honey for a quick dessert. When they are ripe, you can split them open with your fingers to reveal the soft, sweet flesh full of edible seeds.*

Fragrant Fruit Salad

A medley of colourful and exotic fruit, this fresh-tasting salad is the perfect dessert for a festive dinner party.

Serves 6

130g/4½oz/scant ¾ cup sugar
thinly pared rind and juice
   of 1 lime
150ml/¼ pint/⅔ cup water
60ml/4 tbsp brandy
5ml/1 tsp instant coffee granules
   or powder dissolved in
   30ml/2 tbsp boiling water
1 small pineapple
1 papaya
2 pomegranates
1 mango
2 passion fruit or kiwi fruit
strips of lime rind, to decorate

1 Put the sugar and lime rind in a small pan with the water. Heat gently until the sugar dissolves, then bring to the boil and simmer for 5 minutes. Leave to cool, then strain into a large serving bowl, discarding the lime rind. Stir in the lime juice, brandy and dissolved coffee.

2 Using a sharp knife, cut the plume and stalk ends from the pineapple. Cut off the peel, then remove the central core and discard. Slice the flesh into bitesize pieces and add to the bowl.

3 Halve the papaya and scoop out the seeds. Cut away the skin, then slice the papaya. Halve the pomegranates and scoop out the seeds. Add to the bowl.

4 Cut the mango lengthwise into three pieces, along each side of the stone (pit). Peel the skin off the flesh. Cut the flesh into chunks and add to the bowl.

5 Halve the passion fruit and scoop out the flesh using a teaspoon, or peel and chop the kiwi fruit. Add to the bowl and serve, decorated with lime rind.

> **Cook's Tip**
> *Allow the salad to stand at room temperature for 1 hour before serving so that the many fruit flavours have plenty of time to blend together.*

Fig Sundaes Energy 282kcal/1205kJ; Protein 3.7g; Carbohydrate 66.5g, of which sugars 66.5g; Fat 0.9g, of which saturates 0g; Cholesterol 0mg; Calcium 173mg; Fibre 5.4g; Sodium 50mg.
Fragrant Fruit Salad Energy 146kcal/620kJ; Protein 1g; Carbohydrate 33.2g, of which sugars 33.2g; Fat 0.3g, of which saturates 0g; Cholesterol 0mg; Calcium 40mg; Fibre 2.9g; Sodium 7mg.

Pomegranate Salad

Variations of this pretty, decorative salad are prepared throughout the Middle East. It can be offered to guests as a mark of hospitality, or it can be served as a refreshing dish between courses, at the end of a meal, and as an accompaniment to other sweet dishes. Pomegranate is a great seasonal fruit to serve at Christmas time.

Serves 4–6
45–60ml/3–4 tbsp pine nuts
3 ripe pomegranates
30ml/2 tbsp orange
   flower water
15–30ml/1–2 tbsp fragrant
   runny honey
handful of small mint leaves,
   to decorate

1 Place the pine nuts in a bowl, cover with water and leave to soak for 2 hours.

2 Cut the pomegranates into quarters on a plate so that you catch the juice. Extract the seeds, taking care to discard the bitter pith and membrane, and place in a bowl with the juice.

3 Drain the pine nuts and add them to the bowl. Stir gently to mix the fruit and nuts.

4 Stir in the orange flower water and honey, cover the bowl, and chill in the refrigerator. Serve chilled, or at room temperature, decorated with mint leaves.

Cook's Tip
The pomegranate is a fruit about the size of a large orange. It has a thin, smooth skin and is tightly packed with many small seeds, which are in sections separated by a pale yellow membrane. The seeds are tiny and are covered with a red clear pulp that has a sweet yet sharp flavour. While the seeds and pulp are edible, the membrane should be discarded when the pomegranate is being prepared. Pomegranates can be used in sweet or savoury dishes.

Fresh Fruit with Mango Sauce

Fruit coulis became trendy in the 1970s with nouvelle cuisine. It makes a simple fruit dish that bit special for a festive occasion.

Serves 6
1 large ripe mango, peeled, stoned
  (pitted) and chopped
rind of 1 unwaxed orange
juice of 3 oranges
caster (superfine) sugar, to taste

2 peaches
2 nectarines
1 small mango, peeled
2 plums
1 pear or ½ small melon
25–50g/1–2oz wild
   strawberries (optional)
25–50g/1–2oz raspberries
25–50g/1–2oz blueberries
juice of 1 lemon
small fresh mint sprigs,
   to decorate

1 In a food processor fitted with the metal blade, process the large mango until smooth. Add the orange rind, juice and sugar to taste and process again until very smooth. Press through a sieve (strainer) into a bowl and chill the sauce.

2 Peel the peaches, if you like, then slice and stone (pit) the peaches, nectarines, small mango and plums. Quarter and core the pear, or if using, slice the melon thinly and remove the peel.

3 Place the sliced fruits on a large plate, sprinkle the fruits with the lemon juice and chill, covered with clear film (plastic wrap), for up to 3 hours before serving.

4 To serve, arrange the sliced fruits on serving plates, spoon the berries on top, drizzle with a little of the mango sauce and decorate with the fresh mint sprigs. Serve the remaining sauce separately for diners to help themselves.

Variation
Use a raspberry coulis instead of a mango one: purée raspberries with a little lemon juice and icing (confectioners') sugar to taste, then pass through a sieve (strainer) to remove the seeds. You can use frozen raspberries for this, so it can be made during the festive season.

Pomegranate Salad Energy 82kcal/344kJ; Protein 1.3g; Carbohydrate 8.2g, of which sugars 8.1g; Fat 5.2g, of which saturates 0.4g; Cholesterol 0mg; Calcium 4mg; Fibre 1.2g; Sodium 2mg.
Fresh Fruit Energy 82kcal/351kJ; Protein 1.9g; Carbohydrate 19.2g, of which sugars 19.1g; Fat 0.3g, of which saturates 0.1g; Cholesterol 0mg; Calcium 22mg; Fibre 3.3g; Sodium 5mg.

Tropical Scented Red and Orange Fruit Salad

This fresh fruit salad, with its special colour and exotic flavour, is perfect after the rich, heavy meals that are so common over the Christmas period. It is a great dish to serve during the festivities, when the oranges are particularly good – or you could use other festive fruits such as clementines or tangerines.

Serves 4–6
350–400g/12–14oz/3–3¹/₂ cups strawberries, hulled and halved
3 oranges, peeled and segmented
3 small blood oranges, peeled and segmented
1–2 passion fruit
120ml/4fl oz/¹/₂ cup dry white wine
sugar, to taste

1 Put the halved strawberries and the two types of orange segments into a serving bowl.

2 Halve the passion fruit and spoon the flesh into the bowl.

3 Pour the wine over the fruit and add sugar to taste. Toss gently and then chill until ready to serve.

Cook's Tip
Peeling and segmenting oranges can be a time-consuming and fiddly process but the resulting salad will make the effort worthwhile because bits of pith will detract from the textures. Peel away the rind from the oranges and cut away as much of the pith as possible using a short sharp knife. Then simply pull the segments apart without breaking.

Variation
Other fruits can be used in this recipe to give it a more seasonal flavour. Try it with chopped apple, pear, kiwi fruit and banana. Add a sprinkling of cranberries for that festive touch.

Exotic Fruit Salad with Passion Fruit Dressing

Passion fruit makes a superb dressing for any fruit, but really brings out the flavour of exotic varieties. You can easily double the recipe, then serve the rest for a healthy breakfast.

Serves 6
1 mango
1 papaya
2 kiwi fruit
coconut or vanilla ice cream, to serve

For the dressing
3 passion fruit
thinly pared rind and juice of 1 lime
5ml/1 tsp hazelnut or walnut oil
15ml/1 tbsp clear honey

1 Peel the mango, cut it into three slices, then cut the flesh into chunks and place it in a large bowl. Peel the papaya and cut it in half. Scoop out the seeds, then chop the flesh.

2 Cut both ends off each kiwi fruit, then stand them on a board. Using a small sharp knife, cut off the skin from top to bottom. Cut each kiwi fruit in half lengthways, then cut into thick slices. Combine all the fruit in a large bowl.

3 Make the dressing. Cut each passion fruit in half and scoop the seeds out into a sieve (strainer) set over a small bowl. Press the seeds well to extract all their juices.

4 Lightly whisk the remaining dressing ingredients into the passion fruit juice, then pour the dressing over the fruit. Mix gently to combine the ingredients.

5 Leave to chill in the refrigerator for 1 hour before serving with scoops of coconut or vanilla ice cream.

Cook's Tip
A clear golden honey scented with orange blossom or acacia blossom would be perfect for the dressing.

Tropical Fruit Salad Energy 80kcal/339kJ; Protein 2.1g; Carbohydrate 15.3g, of which sugars 15.3g; Fat 0.2g, of which saturates 0g; Cholesterol 0mg; Calcium 74mg; Fibre 3.1g; Sodium 12mg.
Exotic Fruit Salad Energy 66kcal/278kJ; Protein 1g; Carbohydrate 14.6g, of which sugars 14.5g; Fat 0.8g, of which saturates 0.1g; Cholesterol 0mg; Calcium 26mg; Fibre 2.9g; Sodium 7mg.

Key Lime Pie

This American classic is ideal for a festive treat.

Serves 10
225g/8oz/2 cups plain
   (all-purpose) flour
115g/4oz/½ cup chilled
   butter, diced
30ml/2 tbsp caster
   (superfine) sugar
2 egg yolks
pinch of salt
30ml/2 tbsp cold water
thinly pared lime rind and mint
   leaves, to decorate

For the filling
4 eggs, separated
400g/14oz can sweetened
   condensed milk
grated rind and juice of 3 limes
a few drops of green food
   colouring (optional)
30ml/2 tbsp caster
   (superfine) sugar

For the topping
300ml/½ pint/1¼ cups double
   (heavy) cream
2–3 limes, thinly sliced

1 Sift the flour and rub in the butter until the mixture resembles breadcrumbs. Add the sugar, egg yolks, salt and water. Mix to a soft dough. Roll out the pastry and use to line a deep 21cm/8½in fluted flan tin (pan), allowing the excess pastry to hang over the edge. Prick the pastry base and chill for 30 minutes.

2 Preheat the oven to 200°C/400°F/Gas 6. Trim off the excess pastry from the edge of the pastry case (pie shell) and line the pastry case with baking parchment and baking beans. Bake the pastry case blind for 10 minutes. Remove the paper and beans and return the case to the oven for 10 minutes.

3 Meanwhile, make the filling. Beat the egg yolks in a bowl until light and creamy, then beat in the condensed milk, with the lime rind and juice. Add the food colouring, if using, and beat until the mixture is thick. In a grease-free bowl, whisk the egg whites to stiff peaks. Whisk in the caster sugar, then fold into the filling.

4 Lower the oven to 160°C/325°F/Gas 3. Pour the filling into the pastry case. Bake for 20–25 minutes or until it has set and is browned. Cool, then chill. Before serving, whip the cream and spoon around the edge. Twist the lime slices and arrange between the cream. Decorate with lime rind and mint leaves.

Meringue Layer Cake with Berries

This stunning dessert is a great centrepiece to have on the festive table after a celebratory meal. Frozen raspberries can be used if fresh ones are not available.

Serves 8–10
4 egg whites
225g/8oz/generous 1 cup
   caster (superfine) sugar

For the filling
300ml/½ pint/1¼ cups
   whipping cream
caster (superfine) sugar, to taste
3–4 drops of vanilla extract or
   2.5ml/½ tsp liqueur, such as
   Kirsch or Crème de Framboise
about 450g/1lb/2¾ cups
   raspberries
icing (confectioners') sugar,
   for dusting

1 Preheat the oven to 150°C/300°F/Gas 2. Line two baking sheets with baking parchment and draw two circles: one 23cm/9in in diameter and the other 20cm/8in. Fit a piping (icing) bag with a 1cm/½in star nozzle.

2 Whisk the egg whites until stiff peaks form. Keeping the machine running, add half of the sugar, 15ml/1 tbsp at a time; keep whisking until the mixture stands in stiff peaks. Using a metal spoon, carefully fold in the remaining sugar to mix thoroughly without the loss of volume.

3 Use most of the mixture to spread or pipe inside the circles, then put the remaining meringue into the bag and use to pipe nine mini meringues on to the surrounding baking parchment.

4 Cook in the preheated oven for 50–60 minutes, until lightly coloured and quite dry (the small ones will take less time). Peel off the parchment, cool the meringues on wire racks and, when cold, store immediately in airtight containers.

5 Whip the cream, sweeten lightly with caster sugar and flavour with a little vanilla extract or liqueur. Lay the larger meringue circle on a platter. Spread with three-quarters of the cream and three-quarters of the raspberries, reserving the best berries for the top. Add the smaller meringue circle and spread with the remaining cream. Arrange the small meringues around the edge. Decorate with the berries and dust with icing sugar.

Key Lime Pie Energy 510kcal/2126kJ; Protein 9.2g; Carbohydrate 46.6g, of which sugars 29.4g; Fat 33.2g, of which saturates 19.5g; Cholesterol 196mg; Calcium 182mg; Fibre 0.7g; Sodium 163mg.
Meringue Layer Cake Energy 298kcal/1252kJ; Protein 3.2g; Carbohydrate 39.5g, of which sugars 39.5g; Fat 15.3g, of which saturates 9.5g; Cholesterol 39mg; Calcium 55mg; Fibre 1.4g; Sodium 44mg.

Lemon Tart

This is one of the classic desserts, and it is difficult to beat. A rich lemon curd, encased in crisp pastry. Crème fraîche is an optional accompaniment.

Serves 6

For the pastry
225g/8oz/2 cups plain
  (all-purpose) flour
115g/4oz/1/2 cup butter

30ml/2 tbsp icing
  (confectioners') sugar
1 egg
5ml/1 tsp vanilla extract

For the filling
6 eggs, beaten
275g/10oz/1 1/2 cups sugar
115g/4oz/1/2 cup unsalted butter
grated rind and juice of 4 lemons
icing (confectioners') sugar,
  for dusting

1 Preheat the oven to 200°C/400°F/Gas 6. Sift the flour into a large mixing bowl and add the butter. Work the butter in with your fingertips until the mixture resembles fine breadcrumbs. Stir in the 30ml/2 tbsp icing sugar.

2 Add the egg to the flour mixture, along with the vanilla extract and about 10ml/2 tsp of cold water, then work the mixture to a dough.

3 Roll the pastry out on a lightly floured surface, and use to line a 23cm/9in flan tin (pan). Line the base of the pastry with foil or baking parchment and fill with dried beans or rice, or baking beans if you have them. Bake the pastry case (pie shell) in the preheated oven for 10 minutes.

4 Meanwhile, make the filling. Put the eggs, sugar and butter into a heavy pan, and stir over low heat until the sugar has dissolved completely. Add the lemon rind and juice to the pan, and continue cooking, stirring constantly, until the lemon curd has thickened slightly.

5 Pour the filling mixture into the pastry case. Bake in the oven for about 20 minutes, or until the filling is set and the pastry is starting to brown. Transfer the tart to a wire rack to cool. Dust with icing sugar just before serving.

Classic American Creamy Cheesecake

There are a million cheesecake recipes, including ones that are topped with fruit or scented with lemon, but this classic version is the most tempting. It makes a perfect dessert for a festive family meal, or you can keep it as a quick standby in the freezer.

Serves 6–8
130g/4 1/2oz/generous 1/2 cup
  butter, melted, plus extra
  for greasing

350g/12oz digestive biscuits
  (graham crackers),
  finely crushed
350–400g/12–14oz/1 3/4–2 cups
  caster (superfine) sugar
350g/12oz/1 1/2 cups full-fat
  soft white (farmer's) cheese
3 eggs, lightly beaten
15ml/1 tbsp vanilla extract
350g/12oz/1 1/2 cups sour cream
strawberries, blueberries,
  raspberries and icing
  (confectioners') sugar,
  to serve (optional)

1 Butter a deep 23cm/9in springform tin (pan). Put the biscuit crumbs and 60ml/4 tbsp of the sugar in a bowl and mix together, then add the melted butter and mix well. Press the mixture into the prepared tin to cover the base and sides. Chill for about 30 minutes.

2 Preheat the oven to 190°C/375°F/Gas 5. Using an electric mixer, food processor or wooden spoon, beat the cheese until soft. Beat in the eggs, then 250g/9oz/1 1/4 cups of the sugar and 10ml/2 tsp of the vanilla extract.

3 Pour the mixture over the crumb base and bake for about 45 minutes, or until a cocktail stick (toothpick), inserted in the centre, comes out clean. Leave to cool slightly for about 10 minutes. (Do not turn the oven off.)

4 Meanwhile, combine the sour cream and remaining sugar, to taste. Stir in the remaining vanilla extract. When the cheesecake has cooled, pour over the topping, spreading it out evenly. Return to the oven and bake for a further 5 minutes to glaze.

5 Leave to cool, then chill. Serve with a few fresh strawberries, blueberries and raspberries, dusted with icing sugar, if you like.

Lemon Tart Energy 268kcal/1122kJ; Protein 5.6g; Carbohydrate 27g, of which sugars 10.9g; Fat 16.1g, of which saturates 5.8g; Cholesterol 148mg; Calcium 57mg; Fibre 0.7g; Sodium 173mg.
Classic Cheesecake Energy 634kcal/2628kJ; Protein 7.8g; Carbohydrate 31.8g, of which sugars 7.7g; Fat 53.8g, of which saturates 31.5g; Cholesterol 192mg; Calcium 137mg; Fibre 1g; Sodium 536mg.

Raspberry and White Chocolate Cheesecake

This cheesecake, which is a delicious mix of flavours and textures, makes an attractive festive treat.

Serves 8
50g/2oz/4 tbsp unsalted butter
225g/8oz/2⅓ cups ginger nut
    biscuits (gingersnaps), crushed
50g/2oz/½ cup chopped pecan
    nuts or walnuts

For the filling
275g/10oz/1¼ cups mascarpone
175g/6oz/¾ cup fromage frais or
    soft white (farmer's) cheese

2 eggs, beaten
40g/1½oz/3 tbsp caster
    (superfine) sugar
250g/9oz white chocolate,
    broken into squares
225g/8oz/1⅓ cups fresh or
    frozen raspberries

For the topping
115g/4oz/½ cup mascarpone
75g/3oz/⅓ cup fromage
    frais or soft white
    (farmer's) cheese
white chocolate curls and
    raspberries, to decorate

1 Preheat the oven to 150°C/300°F/Gas 2. Melt the butter in a pan, then stir in the crushed biscuits and nuts. Press into the base of a 23cm/9in springform cake tin (pan).

2 Make the filling. Beat the mascarpone and fromage frais or white cheese in a large bowl, then beat in the eggs and caster sugar until evenly mixed.

3 Melt the white chocolate gently in a heatproof bowl over a pan of simmering water. Stir the chocolate into the cheese mixture with the raspberries.

4 Turn into the prepared tin and spread evenly, then bake for about 1 hour or until just set. Switch off the oven, but do not remove the cheesecake. Leave it until cold and completely set.

5 Remove the cheesecake from the tin. Make the topping. Mix the mascarpone with the fromage frais or soft white cheese and spread over the cheesecake. Decorate with chocolate curls and raspberries before serving.

Baked Chocolate and Raisin Cheesecake

This classic cheesecake features a chocolate pastry base with a fruit and chocolate chip filling, topped with even more chocolate. It is great for serving at a Christmas party.

Serves 8–10
75g/3oz/⅔ cup plain
    (all-purpose) flour
45ml/3 tbsp unsweetened
    cocoa powder
75g/3oz/½ cup semolina
50g/2oz/¼ cup caster
    (superfine) sugar
115g/4oz/½ cup unsalted
    butter, softened

For the filling
225g/8oz/1 cup cream cheese
120ml/4fl oz/½ cup natural
    (plain) yogurt
2 eggs, beaten
75g/3oz/6 tbsp caster
    (superfine) sugar
finely grated rind of 1 lemon
75g/3oz/½ cup raisins
45ml/3 tbsp plain (semisweet)
    chocolate chips

For the topping
75g/3oz plain (semisweet)
    chocolate, chopped into pieces
30ml/2 tbsp golden
    (light corn) syrup
40g/1½oz/3 tbsp butter

1 Preheat the oven to 150°C/300°F/Gas 2. Sift the flour and cocoa and stir in the semolina and sugar. Using your fingertips, work the butter into the flour mixture until a firm dough forms.

2 Press the dough into the base of a 22cm/8½in springform tin (pan). Prick all over with a fork and bake in the oven for 15 minutes. Remove the tin but leave the oven on.

3 Make the filling. In a large bowl, beat the cream cheese with the yogurt, eggs and sugar until evenly mixed. Stir in the lemon rind, raisins and chocolate chips. Smooth the cream cheese mixture over the chocolate base and bake for a further 35–45 minutes or until the filling is pale gold and just set. Cool in the tin on a wire rack.

4 Make the topping. Melt the chocolate, syrup and butter in a bowl over simmering water, then pour over the cheesecake. Leave until set. Remove the cheesecake from the tin and serve.

Raspberry Cheesecake Energy 551kcal/2305kJ; Protein 12.8g; Carbohydrate 53.9g, of which sugars 41.4g; Fat 33.1g, of which saturates 17g; Cholesterol 88mg; Calcium 170mg; Fibre 1.4g; Sodium 195mg.
Baked Cheesecake Energy 441kcal/1841kJ; Protein 5.8g; Carbohydrate 41.4g, of which sugars 29.3g; Fat 29.3g, of which saturates 17.7g; Cholesterol 93mg; Calcium 86mg; Fibre 1.4g; Sodium 243mg.

Boston Banoffee Pie

A great American creation, you simply press the biscuit pastry into the tin, rather than rolling it out. Add the toffee filling and sliced banana and chocolate topping and it'll prove irresistible.

Serves 6
115g/4oz/½ cup butter, diced
200g/7oz can skimmed, sweetened condensed milk
115g/4oz/½ cup soft light brown sugar
30ml/2 tbsp golden (light corn) syrup
2 small bananas, sliced
a little lemon juice
whipped cream, to decorate
5ml/1 tsp grated plain (semisweet) chocolate

For the pastry
150g/5oz/1¼ cups plain (all-purpose) flour
115g/4oz/½ cup butter, diced
50g/2oz/¼ cup caster (superfine) sugar

1 Make the pastry. Preheat the oven to 160°C/325°F/Gas 3. In a food processor, process the flour and diced butter until it resembles breadcrumbs. Stir in the caster sugar and mix to form a soft, pliable dough.

2 Press into the base and sides of a 20cm/8in loose-based flan tin (pan). Bake in the oven for 30 minutes.

3 Meanwhile, make the filling. Place the butter in a medium pan with the condensed milk, brown sugar and golden syrup. Heat gently, stirring constantly, until the butter has melted and the sugar has completely dissolved.

4 Bring the mixture to a gentle boil, then reduce the heat and simmer for 7–10 minutes, stirring constantly, until the mixture thickens and turns a light caramel colour.

5 Pour the hot caramel filling into the pastry case (pie shell) and leave until completely cold.

6 Sprinkle the banana slices with lemon juice and arrange in overlapping circles on top of the filling, leaving a gap in the centre. Pipe a generous swirl of whipped cream in the centre and sprinkle with the grated chocolate.

Marbled Chocolate Cheesecake

This attractive-looking dessert will be a big hit when served to festive guests – or take as a gift when visiting friends.

Serves 6
butter or margarine, for greasing
50g/2oz/½ cup unsweetened cocoa powder
75ml/5 tbsp hot water
900g/2lb/4 cups cream cheese, at room temperature
200g/7oz/1 cup caster (superfine) sugar
4 eggs
5ml/1 tsp vanilla extract
75g/3oz digestive biscuits (graham crackers), crushed

1 Preheat the oven to 180°C/350°F/Gas 4. Line a deep 20cm/8in cake tin (pan) with baking parchment. Grease the paper.

2 Sift the cocoa powder into a bowl. Pour over the hot water and stir to blend.

3 In another bowl, beat the cheese until smooth, then beat in the sugar, followed by the eggs, one at a time. Do not overmix.

4 Divide the mixture evenly between two bowls. Stir the chocolate mixture into one bowl, then add the vanilla extract to the remaining mixture.

5 Pour a cup or ladleful of the plain mixture into the centre of the tin; it will spread out into an even layer. Slowly pour over a cupful of chocolate mixture in the centre. Continue to alternate the cake mixtures in this way until both are used up. Draw a metal skewer through the cake mixture for a marbled effect.

6 Place the tin in a roasting pan and pour in hot water to come 4cm/1½in up the sides of the tin. Bake for about 1½ hours, until the top is golden. (The cake will rise during baking but will sink later.) Cool in the tin on a wire rack.

7 Run a knife around the inside edge of the cheesecake. Invert a flat plate over the tin and turn out the cake. Sprinkle the crushed biscuits over the cake. Invert another plate on top, and turn over again. Chill for at least 3 hours before serving.

Boston Banoffee Pie Energy 608kcal/2547kJ; Protein 6.4g; Carbohydrate 78.5g, of which sugars 58.9g; Fat 32g, of which saturates 20.1g; Cholesterol 82mg; Calcium 169mg; Fibre 1.1g; Sodium 299mg.
Marbled Cheesecake Energy 923kcal/3828kJ; Protein 11.3g; Carbohydrate 44.4g, of which sugars 36.5g; Fat 79.3g, of which saturates 47.8g; Cholesterol 274mg; Calcium 206mg; Fibre 1.3g; Sodium 653mg.

Christmas Star Cakes

Mascarpone and Marsala add a delicious nuance to these cakes, which are topped with a smooth velvety cream and decorated with festive stars and holly leaves.

Makes 8–10
150g/5oz/10 tbsp butter, softened
200g/7oz/scant 1 cup golden caster (superfine) sugar
3 eggs
175g/6oz/¾ cup mascarpone
5ml/1 tsp grated lemon rind
30ml/2 tbsp buttermilk
15ml/1 tbsp unsweetened cocoa powder, plus extra for dusting
25ml/1½ tbsp espresso coffee
15ml/1 tbsp Marsala
250g/9oz/2¼ cups self-raising (self-rising) flour

For the topping
250ml/8fl oz/1 cup double (heavy) cream
225g/8oz/1 cup mascarpone
15ml/1 tbsp golden caster (superfine) sugar
15ml/1 tbsp Marsala
seeds from ½ vanilla pod (bean)
25g/1oz milk chocolate, melted

For the stars and leaves
100g/3¾oz plain (semisweet) chocolate
100g/3¾oz milk chocolate

1 Preheat the oven to 180°C/350°F/Gas 4. Line the cups of a bun tin (pan) with paper cases.

2 Beat the butter and sugar together until light and creamy. Gradually beat in the eggs, one at a time, beating well after each addition. Stir in the mascarpone, lemon rind, buttermilk, cocoa, coffee and Marsala, then fold in the flour.

3 Fill the prepared cases. Bake for 25 minutes, or until firm to the touch. Turn out on to a wire rack to cool.

4 Meanwhile, make the topping. Beat the cream with the mascarpone, sugar, Marsala and vanilla seeds. Lightly fold in the melted milk chocolate.

5 For the decorations, melt the chocolates separately. Spread on baking parchment and chill until set. Cut out the shapes.

6 Spoon the topping on to the cakes, and press on the festive stars and leaves. Dust with cocoa powder.

Christmas Spice Cakes

Mincemeat and brandy liven up these delicious celebration cupcakes. The decorations will require a small snowflake or other Christmas themed cutter.

Makes 14
2 eggs
115g/4oz/½ cup golden caster (superfine) sugar
50ml/2fl oz/¼ cup double (heavy) cream
grated rind of 1 clementine
115g/4oz/⅓ cup mincemeat
115g/4oz/1 cup self-raising (self-rising) flour
2.5ml/½ tsp baking powder
5ml/1 tsp mixed (apple pie) spice
10ml/2 tsp brandy
50g/2oz/4 tbsp butter, melted

For the icing
350g/12oz/3 cups icing (confectioners') sugar, sifted
15ml/1 tbsp hot water
red food colouring

To decorate
175g/6oz ready-to-roll fondant
red paste food colouring (or use 115g/4oz red and 50g/2oz white ready-to-roll fondant)

1 Preheat the oven to 180°C/350°F/ Gas 4. Line the cups of a bun tin (pan) with paper cases.

2 Lightly beat the eggs with the sugar. Beat the cream into the egg mixture for about 1 minute, then add the grated clementine rind. Fold in the mincemeat. Sift in the flour, baking powder and mixed spice and fold in. Finally add the brandy and the melted butter and stir to combine.

3 Half-fill the paper cases with the batter. Place in the centre of the oven and bake for 12–15 minutes until risen and golden. Test by lightly pressing the centre of the cakes; the sponge should spring back. Leave on a wire rack to cool.

4 To make the icing, mix the sugar with hot water to make a soft icing. Tint one-third of it with the food colouring and spoon over four cakes. Ice the remaining cakes with the white icing.

5 Set aside one-third of the fondant and colour the rest red. Roll both out and stamp out 10 red and 4 white snowflakes. Stick one on each cake before the icing sets.

Christmas Star Cakes Energy 718kcal/2990kJ; Protein 8g; Carbohydrate 56.8g, of which sugars 36.7g; Fat 53.7g, of which saturates 32.1g; Cholesterol 167mg; Calcium 146mg; Fibre 1g; Sodium 297mg.
Christmas Spice Cakes Energy 272kcal/1153kJ; Protein 2g; Carbohydrate 56g, of which sugars 49.7g; Fat 6.1g, of which saturates 3.4g; Cholesterol 40mg; Calcium 43mg; Fibre 0.4g; Sodium 52mg.

Christmas Tree Cakes

These chocolate cakes have a crème fraîche icing, which can be made using either dark or white chocolate. Cut the tree decorations out of contrasting chocolate, and bake the cakes in gold cases to sparkle on the festive table.

Makes 20
150g/5oz dark (bittersweet) chocolate
175ml/6fl oz/¾ cup single (light) cream
5ml/1 tsp vanilla extract
225g/8oz/1 cup golden caster (superfine) sugar

200g/7oz/scant 1 cup butter
3 eggs
225g/8oz/2 cups plain (all-purpose) flour
20g/¾oz/2 tbsp unsweetened cocoa powder
10ml/2 tsp baking powder

For the icing and decoration
200g/7oz dark (bittersweet) or white chocolate
50g/2oz/4 tbsp butter
250ml/8fl oz/1 cup crème fraîche
75g/3oz/¾ cup icing (confectioners') sugar, sifted
225/8oz white or dark (bittersweet) chocolate, to decorate

1 Preheat the oven to 190°C/375°F/Gas 5. Line the cups of two bun tins (pans) with paper cases. Melt the chocolate with the cream over low heat, stirring. Stir in the vanilla and set aside.

2 Beat the sugar and butter together until light and fluffy, then beat in the eggs one at a time. Sift the flour, cocoa powder and baking powder over the butter mixture and fold in, alternating with the chocolate cream, until the batter is combined. Half-fill the prepared cups and lightly smooth the tops level. Bake for 20–25 minutes, until the centres are firm. Cool on a wire rack.

3 To make the icing, melt the chocolate and butter over a pan of simmering water, stirring, until smooth. Leave to cool a little, then stir in the crème fraîche followed by the sugar. Spread the icing over the cupcakes with a metal spatula.

4 Melt the chocolate for the trees over a pan of simmering water and pour on to a tray lined with baking parchment. Chill until just set, then cut out the shapes and chill again until firm. Stick the decorations on to the cakes.

Ginger Cupcakes with Lemon Icing

Lemon icing offsets the ginger flavour of these delicious cakes, which are decorated with figures cut out of spiced marzipan.

Makes 12–14
175g/6oz/¾ cup butter, softened
175g/6oz/generous ¾ cup golden caster (superfine) sugar
3 eggs, lightly beaten
25ml/1½ tbsp black treacle (molasses)
35ml/2½ tbsp syrup from a jar of preserved ginger
225g/8oz/2 cups self-raising (self-rising) flour, sifted

10ml/2 tsp ground ginger
25ml/1½ tbsp ground almonds
30ml/2 tbsp single (light) cream

For the icing
350g/12oz/3 cups icing (confectioners') sugar
60ml/4 tbsp lemon juice
10ml/2 tsp water

For the decoration
115g/4oz golden marzipan
2.5ml/½ tsp mixed (apple pie) spice
a few drops ginger-brown food colouring

1 Preheat the oven to 180°C/350°F/Gas 4. Line the cups of a large bun tin (pan) with paper cases.

2 Beat the butter and sugar together until light and creamy. Gradually beat in the eggs in batches, beating well between each addition. Fold in the black treacle and the ginger syrup. Sift in the flour with the ground ginger and fold in lightly. Add the ground almonds, then the cream, and stir until well combined.

3 Half-fill the cases and bake for 20 minutes, or until springy to the touch. Leave for a few minutes. Turn out on to a wire rack.

4 To make the icing, sift the icing sugar into a bowl and gradually mix in the lemon juice until the mixture is smooth, adding the water if necessary to get the correct consistency. When the cakes are completely cold, spoon the icing on to each one and smooth it level with a metal spatula.

5 To make the figures, knead the mixed spice and food colouring into the marzipan and roll it out thinly. Using a small figure cutter, cut out the shapes and stick on each iced cake.

Christmas Tree Cakes Energy 419kcal/1751kJ; Protein 4.2g; Carbohydrate 43.8g, of which sugars 33.6g; Fat 26.5g, of which saturates 16.4g; Cholesterol 79mg; Calcium 57mg; Fibre 0.5g; Sodium 125mg.
Ginger Cupcakes Energy 314kcal/1320kJ; Protein 3.9g; Carbohydrate 45.6g, of which sugars 33.3g; Fat 14.1g, of which saturates 7.6g; Cholesterol 71mg; Calcium 64mg; Fibre 0.8g; Sodium 115mg.

Spice Muffins with Dove Cookies

These luxurious and festive creations are ideal for a Christmas occasion.

Makes 5 jumbo muffins

90g/3½oz/½ cup golden caster (superfine) sugar
200g/7oz/scant 1 cup clear honey
grated rind of 1 large orange
150g/5oz/1¼ cups rye flour
175g/6oz/1½ cups plain (all-purpose) flour
10ml/2 tsp baking powder
pinch of mixed (apple pie) spice
pinch of ground cloves
pinch of ground cinnamon
1 egg yolk

For the dove cookies

50g/2oz/¼ cup soft light brown sugar
50g/2oz/4 tbsp butter, softened
90g/3½oz/scant 1 cup plain (all-purpose) flour
5ml/1 tsp baking powder
2.5ml/½ tsp ground cinnamon
2.5ml/½ tsp ground ginger
2.5ml/½ tsp freshly grated nutmeg
12.5ml/2½ tsp milk

For the icing

1 egg white
75g/3oz icing (confectioners') sugar, sifted
silver balls for eyes

1 Preheat the oven to 180°C/350°F/Gas 4. Line the cups of a jumbo muffin tin (pan) with paper cases. To make the muffins, heat 120ml/4fl oz/¼ cup water, the sugar, honey and orange rind in a pan until the sugar dissolves. Leave to cool slightly.

2 Sift the flours, baking powder and spices into a bowl. Make a well in the centre. Gently stir in half the honey liquid with the egg yolk. Add the remaining honey liquid and stir until just mixed. Spoon the batter into the paper cases. Bake for 30–35 minutes until risen and golden. Leave for a few minutes, then transfer to a wire rack to cool. Turn the oven to 150°C/300°F/Gas 2.

3 For the cookies, beat the sugar and butter together. Sift in the dry ingredients and mix, adding the milk. Knead the dough until smooth. Roll out to a 5mm/¼in thickness and cut out doves. Place on a greased baking sheet and bake for 17 minutes. Leave to set for a few minutes, then transfer to a wire rack until cold.

4 Mix the icing ingredients and spread most over the muffins. Fill a piping (icing) bag fitted with a plain nozzle with the remaining icing. Pipe your choice of decoration and add an eye.

Banoffee Muffins with Caramel

The addition of coffee to the icing helps to balance the sweetness of these fabulous muffins.

Makes 8–9 large muffins

75g/3oz/6 tbsp butter, softened
115g/4oz/½ cup soft light brown sugar
1 egg, lightly beaten
225g/8oz/2 cups self-raising (self-rising) flour
12.5ml/2½ tsp baking powder
2 large bananas
rind of 1 orange, finely grated
rind of ½ lemon, finely grated

30ml/2 tbsp buttermilk or sour cream
45ml/3 tbsp dulce de leche

For the icing

2.5ml/½ tsp instant coffee powder, dissolved in 5ml/1 tsp hot water
150ml/¼ pint/⅔ cup double (heavy) cream
7.5ml/1½ tsp dulce de leche
½ banana, sliced into 18 discs

For the toffee syrup

10ml/2 tsp dark muscovado (molasses) sugar
30ml/2 tbsp dulce de leche

1 Preheat the oven to 190°C/375°F/Gas 5. Lightly grease the cups of a muffin tin (pan). In a large bowl, beat the butter and sugar until creamy. Gradually add the egg. Sift the flour and baking powder into a separate bowl and set aside.

2 Mash the bananas and fold half into the butter–sugar mixture. Add the grated rinds and half of the flour. Fold in the remaining flour and bananas with the buttermilk or sour cream, until just combined.

3 Spoon the batter into the muffin cups until three-quarters full. Bake for 20 minutes until golden and springy to the touch. Let stand for 5 minutes, then turn out on to a rack and leave to cool completely. Make a cavity in the top of each muffin. Fill with dulce de leche.

4 To make the icing, beat together the coffee, cream and dulce de leche. Spread over the cakes. Top with the banana slices.

5 For the syrup, dissolve the sugar in a cup with 5ml/1 tsp boiling water. Add the dulce de leche. Drizzle over the cakes. Serve immediately or chill in the refrigerator.

Spice Muffins Energy 601kcal/2549kJ; Protein 8.8g; Carbohydrate 124.8g, of which sugars 60.6g; Fat 10.9g, of which saturates 6g; Cholesterol 63mg; Calcium 112mg; Fibre 5.2g; Sodium 86mg.
Banoffee Muffins Energy 341kcal/1432kJ; Protein 4g; Carbohydrate 45.5g, of which sugars 26g; Fat 18.1g, of which saturates 10.6g; Cholesterol 82mg; Calcium 64mg; Fibre 1g; Sodium 79mg.

Double Apricot and Amaretto Muffins

Amaretto has a special affinity with apricots, and although it is an expensive addition, the scent alone makes it worthwhile. Tie festive bows around the muffins to bring some extra Christmas cheer.

Makes 8–9
225g/8oz/2 cups plain (all-purpose) flour
12.5ml/2½ tsp baking powder
2.5ml/½ tsp ground cinnamon

115g/4oz/generous ½ cup caster (superfine) sugar
75g/3oz/6 tbsp butter, melted
1 egg, beaten
150ml/¼ pint/⅔ cup buttermilk
a handful ready-to-eat dried apricots, cut into strips
2–3 amaretti, crumbled

For the fruit and glaze
275g/10oz fresh apricots
15ml/1 tbsp apricot jam
15ml/1 tbsp clear honey
30ml/2 tbsp amaretto liqueur

1 Preheat the oven to 200°C/400°F/Gas 6. Lightly grease the cups of a muffin tin (pan) or line them with paper cases.

2 To cook the fruit, stone (pit) the apricots, cut into quarters and put on a baking tray. Add the jam and honey. Bake in the preheated oven for about 5 minutes, basting once. Drizzle the apricots with the amaretto. Leave to cool.

3 Reduce the oven temperature to 180°C/350°F/Gas 4. Sift the dry ingredients into a large bowl.

4 Mix the butter with the egg and buttermilk. Add to the dry ingredients and part blend. Add the cooked apricots, reserving the syrup. Spoon the batter into the paper cases. Bake for 25 minutes, until well risen and firm to the touch.

5 Decorate the tops with the dried apricot strips and crumbled amaretti. Return to the oven for 4–5 minutes until the tops look golden. Leave to cool slightly.

6 Heat the reserved syrup in a small pan for 30 seconds, then brush the hot glaze on top of the muffins. When the cakes are cool enough to handle, transfer them to a wire rack to go cold.

Chocolate Truffle Muffins

Not an everyday muffin, these luscious chocolate treats are perfect for Christmas time. There is a hidden truffle centre and equally sinful soft chocolate icing beneath pretty seashell chocolates. The chocolates can be bought or you could make your own using plastic moulds.

Makes 9
165g/5½oz/scant ¾ cup butter, softened
150g/5oz/⅔ cup light muscovado (brown) sugar
3 eggs, lightly beaten
150g/5oz/1¼ cups self-raising (self-rising) flour

25g/1oz/¼ cup unsweetened cocoa powder
7.5ml/1½ tsp baking powder
chocolate seashells to decorate (optional)

For the truffles
150g/5oz dark (bittersweet) chocolate, broken into pieces
20ml/4 tsp double (heavy) cream

For the icing
250ml/8fl oz/1 cup double (heavy) cream
75g/3oz/⅓ cup soft light brown sugar
5ml/1 tsp vanilla extract
150g/5oz dark (bittersweet) chocolate, grated

1 Preheat the oven to 180°C/350°F/Gas 4. Line the cups of a muffin tin (pan) with paper cases.

2 Melt the chocolate in a heatproof bowl set over a pan of simmering water. Remove from the heat and stir in the cream. Set aside to cool before scooping into nine balls.

3 For the muffins, beat the butter and sugar in a bowl. Beat in the eggs. Sift in the flour, cocoa and baking powder and mix.

4 Half fill the paper cases. Add a truffle to the centre. Spoon the remaining cake batter on top. Bake for 22–25 minutes or until risen and springy to the touch. Cool.

5 For the icing, put the cream, sugar and vanilla in a pan and heat to boiling point. Remove from the heat. Stir in the chocolate until melted. Leave to cool, then spread over the cold muffins and decorate with chocolate seashells, if you like.

Double Apricot Muffins Energy 216kcal/909kJ; Protein 3.8g; Carbohydrate 34.5g, of which sugars 15g; Fat 7.9g, of which saturates 4.8g; Cholesterol 41mg; Calcium 68mg; Fibre 0.8g; Sodium 84mg.
Chocolate Muffins Energy 331kcal/1381kJ; Protein 3.6g; Carbohydrate 28.6g, of which sugars 27.4g; Fat 23.5g, of which saturates 14.3g; Cholesterol 110mg; Calcium 32mg; Fibre 0.3g; Sodium 191mg.

Pear and Cardamom Spice Cake

Fresh pears and cardamoms – a classic combination of tastes – are used together in this moist fruit and nut cake. It is packed with warm spice flavours that are the essence of Christmas.

Makes one 20cm/8in cake
115g/4oz/½ cup butter
115g/4oz/generous ½ cup caster (superfine) sugar
2 eggs, lightly beaten
225g/8oz/2 cups plain (all-purpose) flour
15ml/1 tbsp baking powder
30ml/2 tbsp milk
crushed seeds from 2 cardamom pods
50g/2oz/½ cup walnuts, finely chopped
15ml/1 tbsp poppy seeds
500g/1¼lb dessert pears, peeled, cored and thinly sliced
3 walnut halves, to decorate
clear honey, to glaze

1 Preheat the oven to 180°C/350°F/Gas 4. Grease and base-line a 20cm/8in round, loose-based cake tin (pan).

2 Cream the butter and sugar in a large bowl until pale and light. Gradually beat in the eggs.

3 Sift the flour and baking powder into the bowl with the egg mixture, and fold in gently with the milk.

4 Stir in the cardamom seeds, chopped nuts and poppy seeds. Reserve one-third of the pear slices, and chop the remainder. Fold into the creamed mixture.

5 Transfer to the cake tin. Smooth the surface, making a small dip in the centre. Place the walnut halves in the centre of the cake and fan the reserved pear slices around the walnuts, covering the cake mixture.

6 Place the cake in the preheated oven and bake for about 1¼–1½ hours, or until a skewer inserted into the centre of the cake comes out clean.

7 Remove the cake from the oven and brush with the honey. Leave in the tin for 20 minutes, then transfer to a wire rack to cool completely before serving.

Spiced Honey Nut Cake

A combination of ground pistachio nuts and breadcrumbs replaces flour in this recipe, resulting in a light, moist sponge cake.

Makes one 20cm/8in square cake
115g/4oz/generous ½ cup caster (superfine) sugar
4 eggs, separated
grated rind and juice of 1 lemon
130g/4½oz/generous 1 cup ground pistachio nuts
50g/2oz/scant 1 cup dried breadcrumbs

For the glaze
1 lemon
90ml/6 tbsp clear honey
1 cinnamon stick, broken in pieces
15ml/1 tbsp brandy

1 Preheat the oven to 180°C/350°F/Gas 4. Grease and line the base of a 20cm/8in square cake tin (pan).

2 Beat the sugar, egg yolks, lemon rind and juice together in a large bowl until pale and creamy. Fold in 115g/4oz/1 cup of the ground pistachio nuts and the breadcrumbs.

3 Whisk the egg whites in a grease-free bowl until stiff peaks form and fold into the creamed mixture.

4 Transfer to the cake tin and bake for 15 minutes, or until risen and springy to the touch. Cool in the tin for 10 minutes, then transfer to a wire rack.

5 To make the glaze, pare thin pieces of lemon rind and then cut them into very thin strips using a sharp knife.

6 Squeeze the lemon juice into a small pan and add the honey and cinnamon pieces. Bring the mixture to the boil, add the shredded rind, and boil fast for 1 minute. Cool slightly and stir in the brandy.

7 Place the cake on a serving plate, prick all over with a skewer so that the syrupy glaze will drain into the cake, and pour over the cooled syrup, lemon shreds and cinnamon pieces. Sprinkle over the reserved pistachio nuts.

Pear Spice Cake Energy 2781kcal/11648kJ; Protein 44.8g; Carbohydrate 348.8g, of which sugars 177g; Fat 143.8g, of which saturates 66.6g; Cholesterol 628mg; Calcium 592mg; Fibre 19.7g; Sodium 882mg.
Spiced Nut Cake Energy 1965kcal/8248kJ; Protein 55g; Carbohydrate 238.3g, of which sugars 197.6g; Fat 95.2g, of which saturates 15.8g; Cholesterol 761mg; Calcium 387mg; Fibre 9g; Sodium 366mg.

Spice Cake with Ginger Frosting

Preserved stem ginger makes the frosting for this cake particularly delicious, and the spices add a warming festive flavour.

Makes one 20cm/8in round cake

300ml/½ pint/1¼ cups milk
30ml/2 tbsp golden (light corn) syrup
10ml/2 tsp vanilla extract
75g/3oz/¾ cup chopped walnuts
175g/6oz/¾ cup butter, at room temperature
285g/10½oz/generous 1½ cups caster (superfine) sugar
1 whole egg, plus 3 egg yolks
275g/10oz/2½ cups plain (all-purpose) flour

15ml/1 tbsp baking powder
5ml/1 tsp freshly grated nutmeg
5ml/1 tsp ground cinnamon
2.5ml/½ tsp ground cloves
1.5ml/¼ tsp ground ginger
1.5ml/¼ tsp mixed (apple pie) spice
preserved stem ginger pieces, to decorate

For the frosting

175g/6oz/¾ cup cream cheese
25g/1oz/2 tbsp unsalted butter
200g/7oz/1¾ cups icing (confectioners') sugar
30ml/2 tbsp finely chopped preserved stem ginger
30ml/2 tbsp syrup from stem ginger jar

1 Preheat the oven to 180°C/350°F/Gas 4. Line and grease three 20cm/8in shallow round cake tins (pans) with baking parchment. In a bowl, combine the milk, golden syrup, vanilla extract and chopped walnuts.

2 Cream the butter and caster sugar until light and fluffy. Beat in the egg and egg yolks.

3 Add the milk and syrup mixture, and stir well. Sift together the flour, baking powder and spices three times. Add to the butter mixture in four batches, folding in carefully.

4 Divide the mixture between the tins. Bake for 25 minutes. Leave in the tins for 5 minutes, then cool on a wire rack.

5 For the frosting, combine the cream cheese with the butter, icing sugar, stem ginger and ginger syrup, beating with a wooden spoon until smooth. Spread the frosting between the layers and over the top. Decorate with pieces of stem ginger.

Carrot and Almond Cake

Made with grated carrots and ground almonds, this unusual fat-free sponge makes a delicious afternoon treat on a winter's day.

Makes one 20cm/8in round cake

5 eggs, separated
finely grated rind of 1 lemon

300g/11oz/1½ cups caster (superfine) sugar
350g/12oz carrots, peeled and finely grated
225g/8oz/1¼ cups ground almonds
115g/4oz/1 cup self-raising (self-rising) flour, sifted
sifted icing (confectioners') sugar, to decorate
marzipan carrots, to decorate

1 Preheat the oven to 190°C/375°F/Gas 5. Grease a deep 20cm/8in round cake tin (pan), line the base with baking parchment and grease the paper.

2 Place the egg yolks, lemon rind and sugar in a bowl. Beat with an electric mixer for about 5 minutes, until the mixture is thick and pale. Mix in the grated carrots, ground almonds and flour and stir until evenly combined.

3 In a clean, dry bowl, whisk the egg whites until stiff. Using a large metal spoon or rubber spatula, mix a little of the whisked egg whites into the carrot mixture, then fold in the rest.

4 Spoon the mixture into the prepared cake tin and bake in the centre of the oven for about 1¼ hours, or until a skewer inserted into the centre of the cake comes out clean.

5 Leave for 5 minutes, then turn out on to a wire rack, peel off the paper and leave to cool. Decorate with the sugar and carrots.

> **Cook's Tip**
> For the marzipan carrots, knead a little orange food colouring into 115g/4oz marzipan. Divide the marzipan into even pieces, about the size of small walnuts. Mould into carrot shapes and press lines across. Press pieces of angelica into the ends.

Spice Cake with Frosting Energy 263kcal/1099kJ; Protein 2.3g; Carbohydrate 28.6g, of which sugars 28.6g; Fat 16.3g, of which saturates 8.5g; Cholesterol 70mg; Calcium 50mg; Fibre 0.1g; Sodium 108mg.
Carrot and Almond Cake Energy 4720kcal/19680kJ; Protein 49g; Carbohydrate 461g, of which sugars 354g; Fat 310g, of which saturates 85g; Cholesterol 648mg; Calcium 728mg; Fibre 12g; Sodium 792mg.

Passion Cake

Although traditionally eaten at Easter, this cake is suitable for any occasion and looks great on the Christmas table.

**Makes one 20cm/8in
   round cake**
200g/7oz/1¾ cups self-raising
   (self-rising) flour
10ml/2 tsp baking powder
5ml/1 tsp cinnamon
2.5ml/½ tsp freshly grated nutmeg
150g/5oz/10 tbsp butter, softened,
   or sunflower margarine
150g/5oz/generous 1 cup soft light
   brown sugar
grated rind of 1 lemon

2 eggs, beaten
2 carrots, coarsely grated
1 ripe banana, mashed
115g/4oz/¾ cup raisins
50g/2oz/½ cup chopped walnuts
   or pecan nuts
30ml/2 tbsp milk
6–8 walnuts, halved, to decorate
coffee crystal sugar, to decorate

For the icing
200g/7oz/scant 1 cup cream
   cheese, softened
30g/1½oz/scant ⅓ cup icing
   (confectioners') sugar
juice of 1 lemon
grated rind of 1 orange

1 Line and grease a deep 20cm/8in round cake tin (pan). Preheat the oven to 180°C/350°F/Gas 4. Sift the flour, baking powder and spices into a bowl.

2 In another bowl, cream the butter or margarine and sugar with the lemon rind until it is light and fluffy, then beat in the eggs. Fold in the flour mixture, then the carrots, banana, raisins, chopped nuts and the milk.

3 Spoon the mixture into the prepared cake tin, level the top and bake in the oven for about 1 hour, or until risen and the top is springy to the touch. Turn the tin upside down and allow the cake to cool in the tin for 30 minutes. Then turn out on to a wire rack and leave to cool completely. When cold, split the cake in half.

4 To make the icing, cream the cheese with the icing sugar, lemon juice and orange rind, then sandwich the two halves of the cake together with half of the icing. Spread the rest of the icing on top and decorate with walnut halves and the coffee crystal sugar before serving.

Festive Victoria Sandwich

A light sponge cake is given a Christmas theme with a pattern of festive stars. This recipe can be used as the base for other cakes.

**Makes one 18cm/7in
   round cake**
175g/6oz/1½ cups self-raising
   (self-rising) flour

a pinch of salt
175g/6oz/¾ cup butter, softened
175g/6oz/scant 1 cup caster
   (superfine) sugar
3 eggs

To finish
60–90ml/4–6 tbsp raspberry jam
caster (superfine) sugar or icing
   (confectioners') sugar

1 Preheat the oven to 180°C/350°F/Gas 4. Grease two 18cm/7in shallow round cake tins (pans), line the bases with baking parchment and grease the paper.

2 Put the flour, salt, butter, caster sugar and eggs into a large bowl. Whisk the ingredients together until smooth and creamy.

3 Divide the mixture between the prepared cake tins and smooth the surfaces. Bake for 25–30 minutes, or until a skewer inserted into the centre of the cakes comes out clean.

4 Turn out on to a wire rack, peel off the lining paper and leave to cool. Place one of the cakes on a serving plate and spread with the raspberry jam. Place the other cake on top.

5 Cut out paper star shapes, place on the cake and dredge with sugar. Remove the paper to reveal the pattern.

> **Variation**
> *Outside of the festive season, this sponge cake is delicious with strawberries and cream. Whip 300ml/½ pint/1¼ cups double (heavy) cream with 5ml/1 tsp icing (confectioners') sugar until stiff. Wash and hull 450g/1lb/4 cups strawberries, then cut in half. Spread one of the cakes with half of the cream and sprinkle over half of the strawberries. Top with the other cake, spread with the remaining cream and arrange the remaining strawberries.*

Passion Cake Energy 4318kcal/18033kJ; Protein 50.9g; Carbohydrate 456.2g, of which sugars 300.8g; Fat 267.4g, of which saturates 144.1g; Cholesterol 890mg; Calcium 798mg; Fibre 14.7g; Sodium 1777mg.
Victoria Sandwich Energy 2965kcal/12419kJ; Protein 37.5g; Carbohydrate 361.3g, of which sugars 227.9g; Fat 162.8g, of which saturates 96.2g; Cholesterol 944mg; Calcium 462mg; Fibre 5.4g; Sodium 304mg.

Apricot Brandy-snap Roulade

A magnificent combination of soft and crisp textures, this cake looks impressive after a Christmas meal and is easy to prepare.

Makes one 33cm/13in roll
4 eggs, separated
7.5ml/1½ tsp fresh orange juice
115g/4oz/generous ½ cup caster
  (superfine) sugar

175g/6oz/1½ cups
  ground almonds
4 brandy snaps, crushed,
  to decorate

For the filling
150g/5oz canned apricots, drained
300ml/½ pint/1¼ cups double
  (heavy) cream
25g/1oz/¼ cup icing
  (confectioners') sugar

1 Preheat the oven to 190°C/375°F/Gas 5. Base-line and grease a 33 × 23cm/13 × 9in Swiss roll tin (jelly roll pan).

2 Beat together the egg yolks, orange juice and sugar until thick and pale, about 10 minutes. Fold in the ground almonds.

3 Whisk the egg whites until they hold stiff peaks. Fold them into the almond mixture, then transfer to the Swiss roll tin and smooth the surface with a knife.

4 Bake in the preheated oven for 20 minutes, or until a skewer inserted into the centre comes out clean. Leave to cool in the tin, covered with a just-damp dish towel.

5 To make the filling, process the apricots in a blender or food processor until smooth. Whip the cream and icing sugar until it holds soft peaks. Fold in the apricot purée.

6 Spread the crushed brandy snaps over a sheet of baking parchment. Spread about one-third of the cream mixture over the cake, then carefully invert it on to the brandy snaps. Peel off the lining paper.

7 Use the remaining cream mixture to cover the whole cake, then gently roll up the roulade from a short end, being careful not to disturb the brandy snap coating. Transfer the roulade to a serving platter.

Chocolate Chestnut Roulade

A traditional version of Bûche de Noël, the delicious French Christmas gateau.

**Makes one 33cm/13in
  long roll**
225g/8oz plain
  (semisweet) chocolate
50g/2oz white chocolate
4 eggs, separated

115g/4oz/generous ½ cup caster
  (superfine) sugar, plus extra
  for dusting

For the chestnut filling
150ml/¼ pint/⅔ cup double
  (heavy) cream
225g/8oz can chestnut purée
50–65g/2–2½oz/4–5 tbsp icing
  (confectioners') sugar, plus
  extra for dusting

1 Preheat the oven to 180°C/350°F/Gas 4. Line and grease a 33 × 23cm/13 × 9in Swiss roll tin (jelly roll pan).

2 For the chocolate curls, melt 50g/2oz of the plain and all of the white chocolate in separate bowls set over pans of simmering water. Spread on a non-porous surface and leave to set.

3 Hold a long sharp knife at a 45-degree angle to the chocolate and push it along the chocolate, using a sawing motion. Put the curls on baking parchment.

4 Melt the remaining plain chocolate. Beat the egg yolks and caster sugar until thick and pale. Stir in the chocolate.

5 Whisk the egg whites until they form stiff peaks, then fold into the chocolate mixture. Turn into the prepared tin and bake for 15–20 minutes. Leave to cool, covered with a just-damp dish towel, on a wire rack.

6 Sprinkle a sheet of baking parchment with caster sugar. Turn the roulade out on to it. Peel off the lining paper and trim the edges of the roulade. Cover with the dish towel.

7 To make the filling, whip the cream until softly peaking. Beat together the chestnut purée, icing sugar and brandy until smooth, then fold in the cream. Spread over the roulade and roll it up. Top with chocolate curls and dust with icing sugar.

Apricot Roulade Energy 3674Kcal/15272kJ; Protein 69.4g; Carbohydrate 208.1g, of which sugars 193.9g; Fat 291.3g, of which saturates 114.1g; Cholesterol 1172mg; Calcium 809mg; Fibre 14.7g; Sodium 511mg.
Chocolate Roulade Energy 3752kcal/15688kJ; Protein 49g; Carbohydrate 428g, of which sugars 359g; Fat 217g, of which saturates 121g; Cholesterol 1304mg; Calcium 544mg; Fibre 13.6g; Sodium 456mg.

Fresh Fruit Genoese

This Italian classic cake can be made with any selection of seasonal fruits so make the most of the delicious fruits at Christmas time.

Makes one 20cm/8in round cake
175g/6oz/1½ cups plain (all-purpose) flour
a pinch of salt
4 eggs
115g/4oz/generous ½ cup caster (superfine) sugar
90ml/6 tbsp orange-flavoured liqueur, such as Cointreau

For the filling and topping
60ml/4 tbsp vanilla sugar
600ml/1 pint/2½ cups double (heavy) cream
450g/1lb mixed fresh fruits
150g/5oz/1¼ cups chopped pistachio nuts
60ml/4 tbsp apricot jam, warmed

1 Preheat the oven to 180°C/350°F/Gas 4. Grease and base-line a 20cm/8in springform cake tin (pan) with baking parchment.

2 Sift the flour and salt together three times, then set aside. Using an electric mixer, beat the eggs and sugar together for 10 minutes until thick and pale.

3 Fold the flour mixture into the egg mixture. Transfer the cake mixture to the prepared tin and bake for 30–35 minutes.

4 Leave the cake in the tin for about 5 minutes, and then transfer to a wire rack, remove the paper and cool completely.

5 Cut the cake horizontally into two layers, and place one layer on a plate. Sprinkle both layers with liqueur.

6 To make the filling and topping, add the vanilla sugar to the cream and whisk until the cream holds soft peaks. Spread about two-thirds of the cream over the cake base layer and top with half the mixed fresh fruit.

7 Top with the second layer of cake and spread the top and sides with the remaining cream. Press the nuts around the sides, and arrange the remaining fresh fruit on top. Brush the fruit with the warmed apricot jam and leave to cool.

Coconut Lime Gateau

Fresh lime and coconut give this gateau a fabulous flavour, and it looks suitably festive sat on the Christmas table.

Makes one 23cm/9in round cake
225g/8oz/2 cups plain (all-purpose) flour
12.5ml/2½ tsp baking powder
1.5ml/¼ tsp salt
225g/8oz/1 cup butter, softened
225g/8oz/generous 1 cup caster (superfine) sugar
grated rind of 2 limes
4 eggs
60ml/4 tbsp fresh lime juice
75g/3oz/1 cup desiccated (dry unsweetened shredded) coconut

For the icing
450g/1lb/generous 2 cups sugar
60ml/4 tbsp water
a pinch of cream of tartar
1 egg white, whisked until stiff peaks form

1 Preheat the oven to 180°C/350°F/Gas 4. Grease and base-line two 23cm/9in shallow round cake tins (pans). Sift together the flour, baking powder and salt.

2 Beat the butter until soft. Add the sugar and lime rind, and beat until pale and fluffy. Beat in the eggs, one at a time.

3 Gradually fold in the dry ingredients, alternating with the lime juice, then stir in two-thirds of the coconut.

4 Divide the mixture between the cake tins, level the tops and bake for 30–35 minutes. Cool in the tins on a wire rack for 10 minutes, then turn out and peel off the lining paper.

5 Bake the remaining coconut on a baking sheet until golden brown, stirring occasionally.

6 To make the icing, heat the sugar, water and cream of tartar until dissolved, stirring. Boil to reach 120°C/250°F on a sugar thermometer. Remove from the heat and, when the bubbles subside, whisk in the egg white until thick.

7 Sandwich and cover the cake with the icing. Sprinkle over the toasted coconut. Leave to set before serving.

Fruit Genoese Energy 815kcal/3411kJ; Protein 8.5g; Carbohydrate 99.6g, of which sugars 85.9g; Fat 43g, of which saturates 21.8g; Cholesterol 158mg; Calcium 128mg; Fibre 2g; Sodium 132mg.
Coconut Gateau Energy 5859kcal/24634kJ; Protein 58g; Carbohydrate 886.4g, of which sugars 714.9g; Fat 256.6g, of which saturates 163.9g; Cholesterol 1241mg; Calcium 846mg; Fibre 17.3g; Sodium 1773mg.

Hazelnut and Chocolate Cake

These crunchy, nutty squares are made in a single bowl. They are ideal to keep the children busy at Christmas.

Makes one 23cm/9in square cake

50g/2oz plain (semisweet) chocolate
65g/2½oz/5 tbsp butter
225g/8oz/generous I cup caster (superfine) sugar
50g/2oz/½ cup plain (all-purpose) flour
2.5ml/½ tsp baking powder
2 eggs, beaten
2.5ml/½ tsp vanilla extract
115g/4oz/I cup skinned hazelnuts, roughly chopped

1 Preheat the oven to 180°C/350°F/Gas 4. Lightly grease a 20cm/8in square baking tin (pan).

2 In a heatproof bowl set over a pan of barely simmering water, melt the plain chocolate and the butter. Remove the bowl from the heat.

3 Add the sugar, flour, baking powder, eggs, vanilla extract and half of the hazelnuts to the melted mixture and stir well with a wooden spoon.

4 Pour the mixture into the prepared tin. Bake in the oven for 10 minutes, then sprinkle the reserved hazelnuts over the top. Return to the oven and continue baking until firm to the touch, about 25 minutes.

5 Cool in the tin set on a wire rack for 10 minutes, then unmould on to the rack and cool completely. Cut the cake into even squares before serving.

> **Cook's Tip**
> To remove the skins from the hazelnuts, put them on a foil-covered grill (broiling) pan and lightly toast them under the grill (broiler) on a high heat until the skins loosen. Make sure that the hazelnuts do not brown too much or they will overcook when the cake is baked in the oven.

Walnut Coffee Gateau

The mix of walnuts, coffee and chocolate with rum makes a heavenly festive treat.

Makes one 23cm/9in round cake

150g/5oz/scant I cup walnuts
150g/5oz/¾ cup caster (superfine) sugar
5 eggs, separated
50g/2oz/I cup dry breadcrumbs
15ml/I tbsp unsweetened cocoa powder
15ml/I tbsp instant coffee
30ml/2 tbsp rum or lemon juice
1.5ml/¼ tsp salt
90ml/6 tbsp redcurrant jelly, warmed
chopped walnuts, to decorate

For the icing
225g/8oz plain (semisweet) chocolate
750ml/1¼ pint/3 cups whipping cream

1 To make the icing, combine the chocolate and cream in the top of a double boiler until the chocolate melts. Cool, then cover and chill overnight, or until the mixture is firm.

2 Preheat the oven to 180°C/350°F/Gas 4. Line and grease a 23cm/9in cake tin (pan). Grind the nuts with 45ml/3 tbsp of the sugar in a food processor, blender or coffee grinder.

3 With an electric mixer, beat the egg yolks and remaining sugar until thick and pale. Fold in the walnuts. Stir in the breadcrumbs, cocoa, coffee and rum or lemon juice.

4 In another bowl, beat the egg whites with the salt until they hold stiff peaks. Fold into the walnut mixture. Pour the meringue batter into the prepared tin and bake until the top springs back when touched, about 45 minutes. Leave for 5 minutes, then turn out and cool, before slicing the cake in half horizontally.

5 With an electric mixer, beat the icing mixture on low speed for about 30 seconds. Brush redcurrant jelly over the cut cake layer. Spread with some of the icing, then top with the remaining cake layer. Brush the top of the cake with more jelly, then cover the side and top with the remaining icing. Make a starburst pattern with a knife and sprinkle chopped walnuts around the edge.

Hazelnut Cake Energy 4410kcal/18360kJ; Protein 65g; Carbohydrate 343g, of which sugars 304g; Fat 319g, of which saturates 136g; Cholesterol 1017mg; Calcium 558mg; Fibre 18g; Sodium 1548mg.
Walnut Gateau Energy 5208kcal/21656kJ; Protein 76g; Carbohydrate 348g, of which sugars 308g; Fat 400g, of which saturates 199g; Cholesterol 1400mg; Calcium 808mg; Fibre 14g; Sodium 1192mg.

Sour Cherry Panforte

Panforte is a dense and spicy festive fruit cake, made by stirring a range of ingredients into a fudge sugar syrup.

**Makes 2 18cm/7in
round cakes**

4 sheets of rice paper
*500g/1¼lb whole almonds,
   skins on*
100g/3¾oz candied citron peel
100g/3¾oz candied lemon peel
*200g/7oz candied orange
   or clementine peel*
200g/7oz dried sour cherries
*250g/9oz/2¼ cups plain
   (all-purpose) flour*
2.5ml/½ tsp salt
5ml/1 tsp ground cinnamon
*2.5ml/½ tsp freshly
   grated nutmeg*
2.5ml/½ tsp ground black pepper
2.5ml/½ tsp ground cloves
pinch ground cayenne pepper
350g/12oz honey
300g/11oz/1½ cups sugar
175g/6oz golden (light corn) syrup
*icing (confectioners') sugar,
   for dusting*

1 Preheat the oven to 170°C/340°F/Gas 3½. Spread the whole almonds out on a baking sheet lined with baking parchment and bake for 12 minutes. Transfer the almonds to a large bowl and set aside. Reduce the oven to 150°C/300°F/Gas 2.

2 Butter and flour two 18cm/7in cake tins (pans). Cut circles and strips of rice paper to line the bottoms and sides of the tins.

3 Chop all of the candied peel and the dried cherries into small, even pieces. Add the fruit to the toasted nuts in the bowl.

4 Sift together the flour, salt, cinnamon, nutmeg, black pepper, cloves and cayenne and add to the fruit and nuts.

5 Combine the honey, sugar and golden syrup in a pan. Heat to (119°C/238°F), or until the mixture forms a soft ball when a little is dropped in cold water.

6 Add all of the prepared ingredients in the bowl to the pan and stir quickly to combine. Transfer to the prepared tins. Place in the oven to bake for 35 minutes exactly. Remove from the oven and leave to cool in the tins. When cool, carefully turn out on to a serving plate. Sift over icing sugar and serve.

Chocolate Layer Cake

The surprise ingredient – beetroot – makes a beautifully moist cake.

Makes one 23cm/9in cake

*unsweetened cocoa powder,
   for dusting*
*225g/8oz can cooked whole beetroot
   (beets), drained and juice reserved*
*115g/4oz/½ cup unsalted
   butter, softened*
*550g/1lb 6oz/2¾ cups soft light
   brown sugar*
3 eggs
15ml/1 tbsp vanilla extract
*75g/3oz unsweetened
   chocolate, melted*
*275g/10oz/2½ cups plain
   (all-purpose) flour*
10ml/2 tsp baking powder
2.5ml/½ tsp salt
120ml/4fl oz/½ cup buttermilk
chocolate curls, to decorate (optional)

For the icing
*450ml/16fl oz/2 cups double
   (heavy) cream*
*500g/1¼lb plain (semisweet)
   chocolate, chopped*
15ml/1 tbsp vanilla extract

1 Preheat the oven to 180°C/350°F/Gas 4. Grease two 23cm/9in cake tins (pans) and dust with cocoa powder. Grate the beetroot and add it to its juice. Beat the butter, brown sugar, eggs and vanilla until pale and fluffy. Beat in the chocolate.

2 Sift together the flour, baking powder and salt. With an electric mixer on low speed and beginning and ending with flour mixture, alternately beat in flour and buttermilk. Add the beetroot and juice and beat for 1 minute. Transfer the mixture to the prepared cake tins and bake for 30–35 minutes, until a skewer inserted in the centre comes out clean. Cool in the tins for about 10 minutes, then unmould and transfer to a wire rack to cool.

3 To make the icing, heat the cream in a pan until it just begins to boil, stirring occasionally to prevent scorching. Remove from the heat and stir in the chocolate, until melted and smooth. Stir in the vanilla extract. Strain into a bowl and chill, stirring every 10 minutes, for 1 hour.

4 Sandwich and cover the cake layers with the icing, and top with chocolate curls, if you like. Allow to set for 20–30 minutes, then chill in the refrigerator before serving.

Cherry Panforte Energy 2601kcal/10964kJ; Protein 45.3g; Carbohydrate 424.2g, of which sugars 356.9g; Fat 92.3g, of which saturates 7.8g; Cholesterol 0mg; Calcium 783mg; Fibre 21.7g; Sodium 565mg.
Layer Cake Energy 9521kcal/39888kJ; Protein 94.2g; Carbohydrate 1196.3g, of which sugars 972.4g; Fat 518.1g, of which saturates 312.1g; Cholesterol 1472mg; Calcium 1419mg; Fibre 27.5g; Sodium 1382mg.

Stollen

Stollen is a fruity yeast bread traditionally served at Christmas time.

Makes one loaf

150ml/¼ pint/²⁄₃ cup
 lukewarm milk
40g/1½oz/3 tbsp caster
 (superfine) sugar
10ml/2 tsp easy-blend (rapid-rise)
 dried yeast
350g/12oz/3 cups plain
 (all-purpose) flour, plus extra
 for dusting

1.5ml/¼ tsp salt
115g/4oz/½ cup butter, softened
1 egg, beaten
50g/2oz seedless raisins
25g/1oz cup sultanas
 (golden raisins)
40g/1½oz/⅓ cup candied
 orange peel, chopped
25g/1oz/¼ cup blanched
 almonds, chopped
5ml/1 tbsp rum
40g/1½oz/3 tbsp butter, melted
50g/2oz/½ cup icing
 (confectioners') sugar

1 Mix together the warm milk, sugar and yeast and leave it in a warm place until it is frothy.

2 Sift together the flour and salt, make a well in the centre and pour on the yeast mixture. Add the softened butter and egg and mix to form a soft dough. Mix in the raisins, sultanas, peel and almonds and sprinkle on the rum. Knead the dough on a lightly floured board until it is pliable.

3 Place the dough in a large, greased mixing bowl, cover it with baking parchment and set it aside in a warm place for about 2 hours, until it has doubled in size.

4 Turn the dough out on to a floured board and knead it lightly until it is smooth and elastic again. Shape the dough to a rectangle about 25 × 20cm/10 × 8in. Fold the dough over along one of the long sides and press the two layers together. Cover the loaf and leave it to stand for 20 minutes.

5 Heat the oven to 200°C/400°F/Gas 6. Bake the loaf in the oven for 25–30 minutes, until it is well risen. Allow it to cool slightly on the baking sheet, then brush it with melted butter. Sift the sugar over the top and transfer the loaf to a wire rack to cool. Serve the stollen in thin slices.

Panettone

This popular Italian cake is perfect for the festivities.

Makes one cake

150ml/¼ pint/²⁄₃ cup
 lukewarm milk
1 packet easy-blend (rapid-rise)
 dried yeast
about 400g/14oz/3½ cups plain
 (all-purpose) flour

60g/2½oz/⅓ cup sugar
10ml/2 tsp salt
2 eggs
5 egg yolks
175g/6oz/¾ cup unsalted butter,
 at room temperature
115g/4oz/¾ cup raisins
grated rind of 1 lemon
75g/3oz/½ cup candied citrus
 peel, chopped

1 Combine the milk and yeast in a large, warmed mixing bowl and leave for 10 minutes to dissolve the yeast. Sift in 115g/4oz/1 cup of the flour, stir in and cover loosely, and leave in a warm place for 30 minutes.

2 Sift over the remaining flour. Make a well in the centre and add the sugar, salt, eggs and egg yolks. Stir the dough mixture with a wooden spoon until it becomes too stiff, then continue to stir the mixture with your hands to obtain a very elastic and sticky dough. Add a little more flour, if necessary, blending it in well, to keep the dough as soft as possible.

3 Smear the butter into the dough, then work it in with your hands. When evenly distributed, cover and leave to rise in a warm place until doubled in volume, 3–4 hours.

4 Line the bottom of a 2 litre/3½ pint/8 cup Charlotte mould with baking parchment, then grease the bottom and sides.

5 Knock back the dough and transfer to a floured surface. Knead in the raisins, lemon rind and citrus peel.

6 Transfer the dough to the mould. Cover and leave to rise until the dough is above the top of the mould, about 2 hours.

7 Preheat the oven to 200°C/400°F/Gas 6. Bake for 15 minutes, cover with foil, and lower the heat to 180°C/350°F/Gas 4. Bake for 30 minutes. Cool in the mould, then transfer to a rack.

Panettone Energy 2453kcal/10412kJ; Protein 62.2g; Carbohydrate 515.1g, of which sugars 210.3g; Fat 30.7g, of which saturates 8.2g; Cholesterol 791mg; Calcium 1032mg; Fibre 19.4g; Sodium 1590mg.
Stollen Energy 3828kcal/16064kJ; Protein 55.8g; Carbohydrate 511.7g, of which sugars 256.5g; Fat 178.8g, of which saturates 95.2g; Cholesterol 393mg; Calcium 1064mg; Fibre 21.5g; Sodium 1590mg.

Mini Dundee Cakes

These cakes look festive topped with glacé fruits.

Makes 3 x 15cm/6in round cakes
225g/8oz/1½ cups raisins
225g/8oz/1 cup currants
225g/8oz/1½ cups sultanas
(golden raisins)
50g/2oz/¼ cup sliced glacé
(candied) cherries
115g/4oz/¾ cup mixed
(candied) peel
grated rind of 1 orange
300g/11oz/2¾ cups plain
(all-purpose) flour

2.5ml/½ tsp baking powder
5ml/1 tsp mixed (apple pie) spice
225g/8oz/1 cup unsalted
butter, softened
225g/8oz/generous 1 cup caster
(superfine) sugar
5 eggs

For the topping
50g/2oz/½ cup whole
blanched almonds
50g/2oz/¼ cup halved glacé
(candied) cherries
50g/2oz/½ cup sliced glacé
(candied) fruits
45ml/3 tbsp apricot jam, warmed

1 Preheat the oven to 150°C/300°F/Gas 2. Grease and line 3 x 15cm/6in round cake tins (pans). Mix all the fruit, peel and orange rind together in a bowl. In another bowl, sift the flour, baking powder and mixed spice. Add the butter, sugar and eggs. Mix together and beat for 2–3 minutes until smooth and glossy. Or, use a food processor or blender for 1 minute.

2 Add the mixed fruit to the cake mixture and fold in until blended. Divide the cake mixture between the tins and level the tops. Arrange the almonds in circles over the top of one cake, the glacé cherries over the second cake and the mixed glacé fruits over the last one. Bake in the oven for 2–2½ hours or until a skewer inserted into the centre comes out clean.

3 Leave in their tins until cold. Turn out, remove the paper and brush the tops with sieved (strained) apricot jam. Leave to set.

> **Cook's Tip**
> These mini cakes would be perfect to offer as gifts to friends when visiting at Christmas.

Yule Log

This rich seasonal treat will be welcome to anyone who is not keen on the traditional iced fruit cake at Christmas.

Makes one 28cm/11in roll
4 eggs, separated
150g/5oz/¾ cup caster
(superfine) sugar, plus extra
for dusting

5ml/1 tsp vanilla extract
a pinch of cream of tartar
115g/4oz/1 cup plain
(all-purpose) flour, sifted
250ml/8fl oz/1 cup
whipping cream
300g/11oz plain (semisweet)
chocolate, chopped
30ml/2 tbsp rum or Cognac

1 Preheat the oven to 190°C/375°F/Gas 5. Grease, line and flour a 40 × 28cm/16 × 11in Swiss roll tin (jelly roll pan).

2 Whisk the egg yolks with all but 25g/1oz/2 tbsp of the sugar until pale and thick. Add the vanilla extract.

3 Whisk the egg whites with the cream of tartar until they form soft peaks. Add the reserved sugar and continue whisking until the mixture is stiff and glossy.

4 Fold half the flour into the yolk mixture. Add a quarter of the egg whites and fold in to lighten the mixture. Fold in the remaining flour, then the remaining egg whites.

5 Spread the mixture in the tin. Bake for 15 minutes. Turn on to paper sprinkled with caster sugar. Roll up and leave to cool.

6 Put the cream into a small pan and bring it to the boil. Put the chocolate in a bowl and add the cream. Stir until the chocolate has melted, then beat until it is fluffy and has thickened to a spreading consistency. Mix one-third of the chocolate cream with the rum or Cognac.

7 Unroll the cake and spread with the rum mixture. Re-roll and cut off about a quarter, at an angle. Arrange to form a branch. Spread the chocolate cream over the cake. Mark with a fork and add Christmas decorations.

Dundee Cakes Energy 1952kcal/8199kJ; Protein 29.1g; Carbohydrate 277.2g, of which sugars 218.6g; Fat 86g, of which saturates 34.5g; Cholesterol 315mg; Calcium 464mg; Fibre 11.4g; Sodium 609mg.
Yule Log Energy 3826kcal/16020kJ; Protein 56.6g; Carbohydrate 443.4g, of which sugars 353g; Fat 208.4g, of which saturates 119.9g; Cholesterol 1042mg; Calcium 599mg; Fibre 11.1g; Sodium 373mg.

Chocolate Coconut Roulade

A delicious coconut version of the traditional chocolate roll. Use a vegetable peeler to create the coconut curls for the topping.

Makes one 23cm/9in roll
115g/4oz/generous ½ cup caster (superfine) sugar
5 eggs, separated
50g/2oz/½ cup unsweetened cocoa powder

For the filling
300ml/½ pint/1¼ cups double (heavy) cream
45ml/3 tbsp whisky or brandy
50g/2oz creamed coconut, grated, or desiccated (dry unsweetened shredded) coconut
30ml/2 tbsp caster (superfine) sugar

For the topping
fresh coconut curls
dark (bittersweet) chocolate curls

1 Preheat the oven to 180°C/350°F/Gas 4. Grease and line a 33 × 23cm/13 × 9in Swiss roll tin (jelly roll pan). Dust a large sheet of baking parchment with 30ml/2 tbsp of the caster sugar.

2 Place the egg yolks in a heatproof bowl. Add the remaining caster sugar and whisk with a hand-held electric mixer until the mixture leaves a trail. Sift the cocoa over, then carefully fold in.

3 Whisk the egg whites in a clean, grease-free bowl until they form soft peaks. Fold about 15ml/1 tbsp of the whites into the chocolate mixture to lighten it, then fold in the rest evenly.

4 Scrape the mixture into the prepared tin and smooth the surface. Bake for 20–25 minutes or until well risen and springy. Turn the cooked roulade out on to the sugar-dusted baking parchment and carefully peel off the lining paper. Cover with a damp, clean dish towel and leave to cool completely.

5 Make the filling. Whisk the cream with the whisky or brandy until the mixture holds its shape. Stir in the coconut and sugar.

6 Spread about three-quarters of the cream mixture on the sponge. Roll up carefully and transfer to a plate. Spoon the remaining cream mixture on top. Decorate with the coconut and chocolate curls.

Creole Christmas Cake

This rich cake can be stored for a year, wrapped in foil, before decorating.

Makes one 23cm/9in cake
450g/1lb/3 cups raisins
225g/8oz/1 cup currants
115g/4oz/¾ cup sultanas (golden raisins)
115g/4oz/½ cup prunes, chopped
115g/4oz/⅔ cup candied orange peel, chopped
115g/4oz/1 cup chopped walnuts
60ml/4 tbsp soft dark brown sugar
5ml/1 tsp vanilla extract
5ml/1 tsp ground cinnamon
1.5ml/¼ tsp freshly grated nutmeg
1.5ml/¼ tsp ground cloves
5ml/1 tsp salt
60ml/4 tbsp each rum, brandy and whisky

For the second stage
225g/8oz/2 cups plain (all-purpose) flour
5ml/1 tsp baking powder
225g/8oz/1 cup demerara (raw) sugar
225g/8oz/1 cup butter
4 eggs, beaten

For the topping
225g/8oz/scant ¾ cup apricot jam, sieved (strained)
pecan halves, crystallized kumquat slices, glacé (candied) cherries and bay leaves, to decorate

1 Put the fruit, nuts, sugar, spices, salt and alcohol into a pan, mix well and heat gently. Simmer over low heat for 15 minutes. Set aside to cool. Transfer to a lidded jar and leave in the refrigerator for 7 days, stirring at least once a day.

2 Preheat the oven to 140°C/275°F/Gas 1. Line a 23cm/9in round cake tin (pan) with a double thickness of baking parchment and grease it well. Beat the flour, baking powder, sugar and butter together until smooth, then gradually beat in the eggs until the mixture is well blended and smooth.

3 Fold in the fruit mixture and stir well to mix. Spoon the mixture into the tin, level the surface and bake for 3 hours. Cover with foil and continue baking for 1 hour, or until the cake feels springy. Cool on a wire rack, then remove from the tin.

4 To decorate, heat the jam with 30ml/2 tbsp water, and brush half over the cake. Arrange the nuts, fruit and bay leaves over the cake and brush with the remaining apricot glaze.

Coconut Roulade Energy 414kcal/1724kJ; Protein 6.2g; Carbohydrate 30.5g, of which sugars 29.8g; Fat 29.3g, of which saturates 18g; Cholesterol 170mg; Calcium 60mg; Fibre 0.8g; Sodium 115mg.
Creole Cake Energy 8205kcal/34536kJ; Protein 87.7g; Carbohydrate 1285g, of which sugars 1112.7g; Fat 293.5g, of which saturates 130.3g; Cholesterol 1241mg; Calcium 1430mg; Fibre 38.6g; Sodium 2437mg.

Light Fruit Cake

If you cover this fruit cake with marzipan and icing, omit the decoration.

Makes one 20cm/8in round cake

115g/4oz/½ cup currants
115g/4oz/⅔ cup sultanas
    (golden raisins)
225g/8oz/1 cup mixed glacé
    (candied) cherries, quartered
50g/2oz/⅓ cup mixed (candied)
    peel, finely chopped
30ml/2 tbsp rum, brandy or sherry
225g/8oz/1 cup butter

225g/8oz/generous 1 cup caster
    (superfine) sugar
grated rind of 1 orange
grated rind of 1 lemon
4 eggs
50g/2oz/½ cup chopped almonds
50g/2oz/5 tbsp ground almonds
225g/8oz/2 cups plain
    (all-purpose) flour

For the decoration

50g/2oz/⅓ cup whole blanched
    almonds, pecan halves and
    glacé fruits (optional)
15ml/1 tbsp apricot jam

1 A day in advance of baking, soak the currants, sultanas, glacé cherries and mixed peel in the rum, brandy or sherry, cover and leave to soak overnight.

2 Grease and line a 20cm/8in round cake tin (pan) with a double thickness of baking parchment. Preheat the oven to 160°C/325°F/Gas 3. Beat the butter, sugar, and orange and lemon rinds together until light and fluffy. Beat in the eggs, one at a time.

3 Mix in the chopped almonds, ground almonds, soaked fruits (with the liquid) and the flour. Spoon into the cake tin and level the top. Bake for 30 minutes.

4 To decorate, arrange the almonds, pecans and fruits, if using, on top of the cake (do not press them into the cake or they will sink during cooking). Return the cake to the oven and cook for 1½–2 hours, or until the centre is firm to the touch.

5 Let the cake cool in the tin for 30 minutes, then turn it out in its paper on to a wire rack. When cold, wrap foil over the paper and store in a cool place. To finish, warm the jam, then strain it and use to glaze the cake.

Christmas Stocking Cake

A bright and happy cake that is sure to delight children at Christmas time. The stocking, packed with toys, is simple to make.

Makes one 20cm/8in square cake

20cm/8in square rich fruit cake
    (see page 222)
45ml/3 tbsp apricot jam, warmed
    and sieved (strained)
900g/2lb ready-made marzipan

1.2kg/2½lb/7½ cups ready-to-roll
    fondant icing
15ml/1 tbsp ready-made
    royal icing
red and green food colouring

Materials/equipment

25cm/10in square silver
    cake board
1.5m/1½ yd red ribbon,
    2cm/¾in wide
1m/1yd green ribbon,
    2cm/¾in wide

1 Brush the fruit cake with the apricot jam and place on the cake board. Roll out the marzipan and use to cover the cake.

2 Set aside 225g/8oz/1½ cups of the fondant icing. Cover the cake with the remainder. Leave to dry.

3 Secure the red ribbon around the board and the green ribbon around the cake with royal icing.

4 Divide the reserved fondant icing in half and roll out one half on a lightly floured surface. Using a template, cut out two fondant stockings, one about 5mm/¼in larger all round. Put the smaller one on top of the larger one.

5 Divide the other half of the fondant into two and tint one red and the other green. Roll out and cut each colour into seven 1cm/½in strips. Alternate the strips on top of the stocking. Roll lightly to fuse and press the edges together. Leave to dry.

6 Shape the remaining white fondant into four parcels. Trim each with red and green fondant ribbons. Use the remaining red and green fondant to make thin strips to decorate the cake sides. Secure the strips in place with royal icing and stick small fondant balls to cover the joins in the strips. Arrange the stocking and parcels on the cake top.

Fruit Cake Energy 5298kcal/22248kJ; Protein 66g; Carbohydrate 751.5g, of which sugars 578.7g; Fat 239.3g, of which saturates 126.1g; Cholesterol 1241mg; Calcium 1080mg; Fibre 19.6g; Sodium 1909mg.
Stocking Cake Energy 11915kcal/50432kJ; Protein 110.5g; Carbohydrate 2373.9g, of which sugars 2205.9g; Fat 237.3g, of which saturates 45.3g; Cholesterol 692mg; Calcium 2208mg; Fibre 39.6g; Sodium 2566mg.

Marbled Cracker Cake

This stunning Christmas cake is decorated in an original way. Fondant is easy to make yourself but you can also use ready-to-roll icing.

Makes one 20cm/8in round cake
20cm/8in round rich fruit cake (see page 223)
45ml/3 tbsp apricot jam, warmed and sieved (strained)

675g/1½lb marzipan
750g/1¾ lb/5¼ cups ready-to-roll fondant icing
red and green food colouring
edible gold balls

Materials/equipment
wooden cocktail sticks (toothpicks)
25cm/10in round cake board
red, green and gold thin gift-wrapping ribbon
3 red and 3 green ribbon bows

1 Brush the top of the cake with the jam. Roll out the marzipan and use it to cover the cake. Leave to dry overnight.

2 Form a roll with 500g/1¼lb/3¾ cups of the fondant icing. With a cocktail stick, dab a few drops of red colouring on to the icing. Repeat with the green. Knead lightly.

3 Roll out the fondant icing until it has marbled. Brush the marzipan with water and cover with the icing. Position the cake on the cake board.

4 Colour half of the remaining fondant icing red and the remainder green. Use half of each colour to make five crackers, about 6cm/2½in long. Decorate each with a gold ball. Leave to dry on a piece of baking parchment.

5 Roll out the remaining red and green icings, and cut into 1cm/½in wide strips. Cut the strips into 12 red and 12 green diamonds. Attach the diamonds alternately around the top and base of the cake with water.

6 Cut the ribbons into 10cm/4in lengths. Arrange them with the crackers on top of the cake. Attach the bows with softened fondant icing, positioning them between the coloured diamonds at the top cake edge.

Spiced Christmas Cake

This light cake mixture is flavoured with spices and fruit. It can be served with a dusting of icing sugar and decorated with holly leaves for a festive look.

Makes one 20cm/8in ring cake
225g/8oz/1 cup butter, plus extra for greasing
15g/½oz/1 tbsp fresh white breadcrumbs
225g/8oz/generous 1 cup caster (superfine) sugar

50ml/2fl oz/¼ cup water
3 eggs, separated
225g/8oz/2 cups self-raising (self-rising) flour
7.5g/1½ tsp mixed (apple pie) spice
25g/1oz/2 tbsp chopped angelica
25g/1oz/2 tbsp mixed chopped (candied) peel
50g/2oz/¼ cup chopped glacé (candied) cherries
50g/2oz/½ cup chopped walnuts
icing (confectioners') sugar, for dusting

1 Preheat the oven to 180°C/350°F/Gas 4. Brush a 20cm/8in, 1.5 litre/2½ pint fluted ring mould with melted butter and coat with breadcrumbs, shaking out any excess.

2 Place the butter, sugar and water into a pan. Heat gently, stirring occasionally, until the sugar has dissolved. Boil for 3 minutes until syrupy, then allow to cool.

3 In a clean bowl, whisk until the egg whites until stiff. Sift the flour and spice into another bowl, add the angelica, mixed peel, cherries and walnuts and stir well to mix. Add the egg yolks.

4 Pour the cooled syrup mixture into the bowl and beat to form a soft batter. Gradually fold in the egg whites, until the mixture is evenly blended.

5 Pour the mixture into the prepared mould and bake in the preheated oven for about 50–60 minutes or until the cake springs back when pressed in the centre.

6 Leave the cake in the mould for a few minutes, then turn out and allow to cool on a wire rack. Dust with the icing sugar and decorate with holly leaves to serve.

Cracker Cake Energy 9858kcal/41695kJ; Protein 97g; Carbohydrate 1908.3g, of which sugars 1740.3g; Fat 208.7g, of which saturates 43g; Cholesterol 692mg; Calcium 1901mg; Fibre 35.3g; Sodium 2503mg.
Spiced Cake Energy 4813kcal/20022kJ; Protein 88.5g; Carbohydrate 322.9g, of which sugars 277.4g; Fat 355.2g, of which saturates 51.2g; Cholesterol 13mg; Calcium 800mg; Fibre 28.2g; Sodium 497mg.

Vegan Christmas Cake

As it contains neither eggs nor dairy products, this cake is suitable for vegans and will prove to be a real treat at Christmas.

Makes one 20cm/8in square cake

350g/12oz/3 cups plain (all-purpose) wholemeal (whole-wheat) flour
5ml/1 tsp mixed (apple pie) spice
175g/6oz/³⁄₄ cup soya margarine
175g/6oz/³⁄₄ cup muscovado (molasses) sugar, plus 30ml/2 tbsp
175g/6oz/generous 1 cup sultanas (golden raisins)
175g/6oz/³⁄₄ cup currants
175g/6oz/generous 1 cup raisins

75g/3oz/¹⁄₂ cup mixed chopped (candied) peel
150g/5oz/generous ¹⁄₂ cup glacé (candied) cherries, halved
finely grated rind of 1 orange
30ml/2 tbsp ground almonds
25g/1oz/¹⁄₄ cup chopped blanched almonds
5ml/1 tsp bicarbonate of soda (baking soda)
120ml/4fl oz/¹⁄₂ cup soya milk
75ml/2¹⁄₂fl oz/¹⁄₃ cup sunflower oil
30ml/2 tbsp malt vinegar

To decorate
mixed nuts
glacé (candied) cherries
angelica
60ml/4 tbsp clear honey, warmed

1 Preheat the oven to 150°C/300°F/Gas 2. Grease a deep 20cm/8in square loose-based cake tin (pan) and double-line with baking parchment.

2 Sift together the flour and mixed spice in a large mixing bowl. Rub in the soya margarine. Stir in the sugar, sultanas, currants and raisins, mixed peel, cherries, orange rind, ground almonds and blanched almonds.

3 Dissolve the bicarbonate of soda in a little of the milk. Warm the remaining milk with the oil and vinegar, and add the bicarbonate of soda mixture. Stir into the flour mixture.

4 Spoon into the tin and smooth the surface. Bake for about 2¹⁄₂ hours, until a skewer inserted in the centre comes out clean. Leave in the tin for 5 minutes, then turn out and cool on a wire rack. Decorate with the nuts, cherries and angelica, and brush with the warmed honey to glaze the cake.

Noel Cake

If you like a traditional royal-iced Christmas fruit cake, this is a simple design that uses only one icing and easy-to-pipe decorations yet it will make a stunning centrepiece for your cake.

Makes one 20cm/8in round cake

20cm/8in round rich fruit cake (see page 223)
30ml/2 tbsp apricot jam, warmed and sieved (strained)
750g/1lb 10oz marzipan

900g/2lb/6 cups ready-made royal icing
green and red food colouring

Materials/equipment
23cm/9in round silver cake board
3 baking parchment piping (icing) bags
44 large gold dragées
fine writing nozzle
2 very fine writing nozzles
2.5m/2¹⁄₂ yd gold ribbon, 2cm/³⁄₄ in wide
2.5m/2¹⁄₂ yd red ribbon, 5mm/¹⁄₄in wide

1 Brush the fruit cake with the apricot jam, cover with the marzipan and place on the cake board.

2 Using a metal spatula, flat-ice the top of the cake with two layers of royal icing and leave to dry. Ice the sides of the cake and then peak the royal icing using the metal spatula, leaving a space around the centre for the ribbon. Leave to dry. Reserve the remaining royal icing.

3 Pipe tiny beads of icing around the top edge of the cake and place a gold dragée on alternate beads.

4 Using the fine writing nozzle, write 'NOEL' across the cake and pipe holly leaves, stems and berries around the top.

5 Secure the ribbons around the side of the cake. Tie a red bow and attach to the front of the cake. Use the remaining ribbon for the board. Leave to dry overnight.

6 Tint 30ml/2 tbsp of the royal icing bright green and 15ml/1 tbsp bright red. Using a very fine writing nozzle, overpipe the word 'NOEL' in red. Add the edging beads and berries. Overpipe the holly in green with the other very fine nozzle. Leave to dry.

Vegan Cake Energy 6098kcal/25669kJ; Protein 74.3g; Carbohydrate 977.4g, of which sugars 759.6g; Fat 236.7g, of which saturates 38.2g; Cholesterol 12mg; Calcium 1047mg; Fibre 55.6g; Sodium 2160mg.
Noel Cake Energy 10111kcal/42759kJ; Protein 100.9g; Carbohydrate 1948.7g, of which sugars 1780.7g; Fat 218.3g, of which saturates 43.7g; Cholesterol 692mg; Calcium 1949mg; Fibre 36.8g; Sodium 2514mg.

Christmas Tree Cake

No piping is involved in this bright and colourful cake, making it an easy choice.

Makes one 20cm/8in round cake

45ml/3 tbsp apricot jam
20cm/8in round rich fruit cake
(see next recipe)

900g/2lb marzipan
green, red, yellow and purple
food colouring
225g/8oz/1½ cups royal icing
edible silver balls

Materials/equipment
25cm/10in round cake board

1 Warm, then sieve (strain) the apricot jam and brush the cake with it. Colour 675g/1½lb/4½ cups of the marzipan green. Use to cover the cake. Leave to dry overnight.

2 Secure the cake to the cake board by using a thin layer of royal icing. Spread the icing halfway up the cake side. Press the flat side of a metal spatula into the icing, then pull it away sharply to create the peaks.

3 Make three different-sized Christmas tree templates. Tint half the remaining marzipan a deeper green than the marzipan used for the cake. Using the templates, cut out three tree shapes and arrange them on the cake.

4 Divide the remaining marzipan into three portions and then colour them red, yellow and purple. Use a little of each marzipan to make five 9cm/3in rolls. Loop them alternately around the top edge of the cake. Make small red balls and press on to the loop ends.

5 Use the remaining marzipan to make the tree decorations. Stick them on the cake with water, then add the silver balls.

> **Cook's Tip**
> A rich fruit cake suitable for a Christmas cake improves with storage so remember to make yours at least 3 weeks before you begin decorating and icing.

Moist and Rich Christmas Cake

This festive cake can be made 4–6 weeks ahead.

Makes one 20cm/8in cake
225g/8oz/1⅓ cups sultanas
(golden raisins)
225g/8oz/1 cup currants
225g/8oz/1⅓ cups raisins
115g/4oz/1 cup pitted and
chopped prunes
50g/2oz/¼ cup halved glacé
(candied) cherries
50g/2oz/⅓ cup mixed chopped
(candied) peel
45ml/3 tbsp brandy or sherry
225g/8oz/2 cups plain
(all-purpose) flour
pinch of salt

2.5ml/½ tsp ground cinnamon
2.5ml/½ tsp grated nutmeg
15ml/1 tbsp unsweetened
cocoa powder
225g/8oz/1 cup butter
225g/8oz/1 cup brown sugar
4 large (US extra large) eggs
finely grated rind of 1 orange
50g/2oz/⅔ cup ground almonds
50g/2oz/½ cup chopped almonds

To decorate
60ml/4 tbsp apricot jam, warmed
450g/1lb ready-made
almond paste
450g/1lb ready-to-roll
fondant icing
225g/8oz ready-made royal icing

1 Put the dried fruits, cherries and peel in a bowl with the brandy or sherry, covered, overnight. The next day, grease a 20cm/8in round cake tin (pan) and line it with baking parchment.

2 Preheat the oven to 160°C/325°F/Gas 3. Sift together the flour, salt, spices and cocoa powder. Whisk the butter and sugar until fluffy and beat in the eggs, then mix in the orange rind, all the almonds, soaked fruits and liquid, and the flour mixture. Spoon into the cake tin and level the top. Bake for 3 hours. Cool in the tin on a wire rack for an hour, then turn out, leaving the paper on. When cold, wrap in foil and store.

3 Strain the apricot jam. Remove the paper from the cake, place on a cake board and brush it with apricot glaze. Cover with almond paste, then fondant icing. Pipe a border around the base of the cake with royal icing. Tie a ribbon around the sides.

4 From the trimmings, make a bell motif, leaves and holly berries. Dry for 24 hours. Attach all to the cake with a dab of royal icing.

Tree Cake Energy 9354kcal/39507kJ; Protein 107.1g; Carbohydrate 1694.8g, of which sugars 1526.8g; Fat 237.3g, of which saturates 45.3g; Cholesterol 692mg; Calcium 1863mg; Fibre 39.6g; Sodium 2535mg.
Moist Rich Cake Energy 8145kcal/34415kJ; Protein 74.4g; Carbohydrate 1528.9g, of which sugars 1385.8g; Fat 204.6g, of which saturates 105.4g; Cholesterol 1154mg; Calcium 1859mg; Fibre 38.1g; Sodium 2326mg.

Chocolate Amaretti

Enjoy these delightful cookies over the festive season with a glass of chilled champagne.

Makes 24

150g/5oz/scant 1 cup blanched, toasted whole almonds
115g/4oz/generous ½ cup caster (superfine) sugar
15ml/1 tbsp unsweetened cocoa powder
30ml/2 tbsp icing (confectioners') sugar
2 egg whites
a pinch of cream of tartar
5ml/1 tsp almond extract
flaked (sliced) almonds, to decorate

1 Preheat the oven to 160°C/325°F/Gas 3. Line a large baking sheet with baking parchment or foil. In a food processor fitted with a metal blade, process the toasted almonds with half the sugar until they are finely ground but not oily. Transfer to a large bowl and sift in the cocoa and icing sugar; stir to blend evenly. Set aside.

2 Beat the egg whites and cream of tartar until stiff peaks form. Sprinkle in the remaining sugar 15ml/1 tbsp at a time, beating well after each addition, and continue beating until the whites are glossy and stiff. Beat in the almond extract.

3 Sprinkle over the almond mixture and gently fold into the egg whites until just blended. Spoon the mixture into a large piping (pastry) bag fitted with a plain 1cm/½in nozzle. Pipe 4cm/1½in rounds, 2.5cm/1in apart, on the baking sheet. Press a flaked almond into the centre of each.

4 Bake the cookies for 12–15 minutes, or until they appear crisp. Remove the baking sheet to a wire rack to cool for 10 minutes. With a metal spatula, remove the cookies to the wire rack to cool completely.

Variation
As an alternative decoration, lightly press a few coffee sugar crystals on top of each cookie before baking.

Christmas Tree Cookies

These simple cookies are not too rich, and are always popular with children, to make as well as to eat.

Makes 30

175g/6oz/¾ cup unsalted butter, at room temperature
275g/10oz/1½ cups caster (superfine) sugar
1 egg
1 egg yolk
5ml/1 tsp vanilla extract
grated rind of 1 lemon
1.5ml/¼ tsp salt
275g/10oz/2½ cups plain (all-purpose) flour

For decorating (optional)

175g/6oz/1½ cups icing (confectioners') sugar
small decorations

1 Preheat the oven to 180°C/350°F/Gas 4. With an electric mixer, cream the butter until soft. Add the sugar gradually and continue beating until the mixture is light and fluffy.

2 Using a wooden spoon, gradually beat in the whole egg and the egg yolk. Add the vanilla extract, lemon rind and salt. Stir to mix well. Gradually add the flour, stirring between each addition, until blended.

3 Gather the mixture into a ball, wrap in baking parchment and chill for 30 minutes.

4 On a floured surface, carefully roll out the mixture until it is about 3mm/⅛in thick. Stamp out shapes with a Christmas tree cutter.

5 Bake the cookies for about 8 minutes, or until they are lightly coloured. Using a spatula, transfer them to a wire rack and leave to cool completely. The cookies can be left plain, or iced and decorated.

6 To ice the cookies, mix the icing sugar with enough water to make a thick icing consistency.

7 Fill a piping (icing) bag fitted with a fine nozzle with the icing and pipe dots, lines and patterns on to the cookies. Finish with small decorations such as edible silver balls.

Amaretti Energy 65kcal/270kJ; Protein 1.8g; Carbohydrate 5.8g, of which sugars 5.5g; Fat 4g, of which saturates 0.4g; Cholesterol 0mg; Calcium 20mg; Fibre 0.6g; Sodium 12mg.
Christmas Cookies Energy 118kcal/495kJ; Protein 1.3g; Carbohydrate 17.3g, of which sugars 10.1g; Fat 5.3g, of which saturates 3.2g; Cholesterol 26mg; Calcium 21mg; Fibre 0.3g; Sodium 39mg.

Apple and Elderflower Stars

These delicious, crumbly apple cookies are topped with a sweet yet very sharp icing. Packaged in a pretty box, they would make a delightful festive gift for someone special.

Makes 18
115g/4oz/½ cup unsalted butter, at room temperature, diced
75g/3oz/scant ½ cup caster (superfine) sugar
2.5ml/½ tsp mixed (apple pie) spice

1 large (US extra large) egg yolk
25g/1oz dried apple rings, finely chopped
200g/7oz/1¾ cups self-raising (self-rising) flour
5–10ml/1–2 tsp milk, if necessary

For the topping
200g/7oz/1¾ cups icing (confectioners') sugar, sifted
60–90ml/4–6 tbsp elderflower cordial
sugar, for sprinkling

1 Preheat the oven to 190°C/375°F/Gas 5. Cream together the butter and sugar until light and fluffy.

2 Beat the mixed spice and egg yolk into the butter and sugar. Add the chopped apple and flour and stir together. The mixture should form a stiff dough but if it is too dry, add some milk.

3 Roll the dough out on a lightly floured surface to a 5mm/¼in thickness. Draw a five-pointed star on cardboard. Cut out and use as a template for the cookies. Alternatively, use a star biscuit (cookie) cutter.

4 Place the cookies on non-stick baking sheets and bake for about 10–15 minutes, or until just beginning to brown around the edges. Carefully transfer the cookies to a wire rack to cool.

5 Meanwhile, make the topping. Sift the icing sugar into a bowl and add just enough elderflower cordial to mix the icing to a thick but pourable consistency.

6 When the cookies are cold, trickle the icing over them in a random crisscross pattern. Sprinkle them with a little sugar and leave to set.

Glazed Lemon Rings

These delicately flavoured, pretty cookies look almost too good to eat. The icing contains Italian liqueur, so they are strictly for adult parties at Christmas time.

Makes 16
200g/7oz/1¾ cups self-raising (self-rising) flour
50g/2oz/¼ cup unsalted butter, at room temperature, diced

25ml/1½ tbsp milk
50g/2oz/¼ cup caster (superfine) sugar
finely grated rind of ½ lemon
1 egg, beaten

For the topping
150g/5oz/1¼ cups icing (confectioners') sugar, sifted
30ml/2 tbsp Limoncello liqueur
15ml/1 tbsp chopped candied angelica

1 Preheat the oven to 180°C/350°F/Gas 4. Line two large baking sheets with baking parchment.

2 Sift the self-raising flour into a large mixing bowl and rub in the butter with your fingertips.

3 Put the milk, caster sugar and lemon rind in a small pan and stir over low heat until the sugar has dissolved.

4 Add the milk mixture to the flour mixture, together with the egg, and mix well. Knead lightly until smooth.

5 Roll walnut-size pieces of the dough into strands about 15cm/6in long. Twist two strands together and join the ends to make a circular shape.

6 Place the circles on the prepared baking sheets and bake in the oven for 15–20 minutes, or until golden. Transfer the cookies to a wire rack to cool.

7 To make the topping, stir the icing sugar and liqueur together in a small bowl to make a pouring consistency.

8 Dip the top of each cookie into the topping and sprinkle with some chopped angelica. Leave to set.

Apple Stars Energy 157kcal/659kJ; Protein 1.4g; Carbohydrate 26.6g, of which sugars 18.1g; Fat 5.7g, of which saturates 3.4g; Cholesterol 25mg; Calcium 27mg; Fibre 0.4g; Sodium 42mg.
Glazed Lemon Rings Energy 125kcal/530kJ; Protein 1.7g; Carbohydrate 23.5g, of which sugars 14g; Fat 3.1g, of which saturates 1.8g; Cholesterol 19mg; Calcium 28mg; Fibre 0.4g; Sodium 25mg.

Orange Shortbread Fingers

These are a real tea-time treat at Christmas. The fingers will keep in an airtight container for up to two weeks, meaning you will have some to offer your guests throughout the festive period – as long as you make plenty of them in the first place.

Makes 18
115g/4oz/½ cup unsalted
   butter, softened
50g/2oz/4 tbsp caster (superfine)
   sugar, plus a little extra
   for sprinkling
finely grated rind of 2 oranges
175g/6oz/1½ cups plain
   (all-purpose) flour

1 Preheat the oven to 190°C/375°F/Gas 5. In a bowl, beat the butter and sugar together until they are soft and creamy.

2 Beat the orange rind into the butter and sugar mixture. Gradually sift in the flour and gently pull the dough together with your hands to form a soft ball.

3 Transfer the dough on to a lightly floured surface and roll it out to about 1cm/½in thick.

4 Cut the dough into 18 fingers with a sharp knife. Sprinkle over a little extra sugar, prick with a fork and bake for 20 minutes, or until the fingers are a light golden colour.

> **Cook's Tip**
> This recipe is the ideal life-saver for busy cooks at Christmas time. It is a good idea to make extra dough and store it, well wrapped in clear film (plastic wrap), in the refrigerator. When guests arrive unexpectedly over the festive period, you will be able to make up freshly baked fingers in minutes.

> **Variation**
> You can cut the dough into whatever shapes you choose. There are also moulds available in attractive designs.

Christmas Star Cookies

These spiced biscuits may be used as edible festive decorations: thread them with coloured ribbon and hang on the branches of the Christmas tree.

Makes 30
50g/2oz/¼ cup butter
15ml/1 tbsp golden (light corn)
   syrup or clear honey
50g/2oz/¼ cup soft light
   brown sugar

225g/8oz/2 cups plain
   (all-purpose) flour
10ml/2 tsp ground cinnamon
5ml/1 tsp ground ginger
1.5ml/¼ tsp grated nutmeg
2.5ml/½ tsp bicarbonate of soda
   (baking soda)
45ml/3 tbsp milk
1 egg yolk
30ml/2 tbsp sugar crystals

1 Preheat the oven to 180°C/350°F/Gas 4. Line two baking sheets with baking parchment. Melt the butter, syrup or honey and brown sugar in a pan. Leave to cool for 5 minutes.

2 Sift the flour, cinnamon, ginger, nutmeg and bicarbonate of soda into a bowl. Make a well in the centre. Pour in the melted butter mixture, milk and egg yolk. Mix to a soft dough.

3 Knead the dough until smooth, then roll out between two sheets of baking parchment until 5mm/¼in thick. Stamp out stars using biscuit (cookie) cutters.

4 Place the cookies on the baking sheets. Make a hole in each with a skewer if you wish to hang them up later. Sprinkle with coloured sugar crystals.

5 Bake in the preheated oven for 10 minutes, until a slightly darker shade. Cool slightly on the baking sheets, then transfer to a wire rack and leave to cool completely.

> **Cook's Tip**
> Roll out the dough while it is still warm, since it becomes hard and quite brittle as it cools.

Orange Shortbread Fingers Energy 92kcal/383kJ; Protein 1g; Carbohydrate 10.5g, of which sugars 3.1g; Fat 5.4g, of which saturates 3.4g; Cholesterol 14mg; Calcium 16mg; Fibre 0.3g; Sodium 39mg.
Star Cookies Energy 118kcal/495kJ; Protein 1.3g; Carbohydrate 17.3g, of which sugars 10.1g; Fat 5.3g, of which saturates 3.2g; Cholesterol 26mg; Calcium 21mg; Fibre 0.3g; Sodium 39mg.

Festive Holly Cookies

Dainty, hand-painted cookies look delightful served at Christmas. These are great fun for children to make as presents, and any shape of cookie cutter can be used.

Makes about 12
75g/3oz/6 tbsp butter
50g/2oz/½ cup icing (confectioners') sugar
finely grated rind of 1 small lemon
1 egg yolk
175g/6oz/1½ cups plain (all-purpose) flour
a pinch of salt

To decorate
2 egg yolks
red and green food colouring

1 Beat the butter, icing sugar and lemon rind together until pale and fluffy. Beat in the egg yolk, and then sift in the flour and salt. Knead together to form a smooth dough. Wrap and chill in the refrigerator for 30 minutes.

2 Preheat the oven to 190°C/375°F/Gas 5 and lightly grease two large baking sheets.

3 On a lightly floured surface, roll out the dough to 3mm/⅛in thick. Using a 6cm/2½in fluted cutter, stamp out as many cookies as you can, with the cutter dipped in flour to prevent it from sticking to the dough.

4 Transfer the cookies to the prepared baking sheets. Mark the tops lightly with a 2.5cm/1in holly leaf cutter and use a 5mm/¼in plain piping (icing) nozzle for the berries. Chill for 10 minutes, until firm.

5 Meanwhile, to make the decoration, put each egg yolk into a small cup. Mix red food colouring into one and green food colouring into the other. Using a small, clean paintbrush, carefully paint the colours on to the cookies.

6 Bake the cookies in the preheated oven for 10–12 minutes, or until they begin to colour around the edges. Let them cool slightly on the baking sheets, then carefully transfer them to a wire rack to cool completely.

Christmas Tree Angels

Why not make these charming edible decorations to brighten your Yuletide?

Makes 20–30
90g/3½oz/scant ½ cup demerara (raw) sugar
200g/7oz/scant 1 cup golden (light corn) syrup
5ml/1 tsp ground ginger
5ml/1 tsp ground cinnamon
1.5ml/¼ tsp ground cloves
115g/4oz/½ cup unsalted butter, cut into pieces
10ml/2 tsp bicarbonate of soda (baking soda)
1 egg, beaten
500g/1¼lb/4½ cups plain (all-purpose) flour, sifted

For the decoration
1 egg white
175–225g/6–8oz/1½–2 cups icing (confectioners') sugar, sifted
silver and gold balls
fine ribbon

1 Preheat the oven to 160°C/325°F/Gas 3. Line two baking sheets with baking parchment. Bring the demerara sugar, syrup, ginger, cinnamon and cloves to the boil over low heat, stirring constantly. Remove from the heat.

2 Put the butter in a bowl and add the sugar mixture. Add the bicarbonate of soda and stir until the butter has melted. Beat in the egg, then stir in the flour. Mix, then knead to form a dough.

3 Divide the dough into four and roll out between sheets of baking parchment, to a thickness of 3mm/⅛in. To make angels, stamp out rounds using a plain cutter. Cut off two segments from either side of the round to give a body and wings. Place the wings, rounded side down, behind the body and press.

4 Roll a small piece of dough for the head, place at the top of the body and flatten. Make a wide hole in the cookies for threading ribbon. Place on the sheets. Bake for 10–15 minutes until golden brown. Transfer to a wire rack to cool.

5 For the decoration, beat the egg white with a fork. Whisk in the sugar until it forms soft peaks. Put the icing in a piping (icing) bag fitted with a small nozzle and decorate the cookies. Add silver and gold balls. Finally, thread the ribbon.

Festive Holly Cookies Energy 118kcal/494kJ; Protein 1.7g; Carbohydrate 15.7g, of which sugars 4.6g; Fat 5.8g, of which saturates 3.4g; Cholesterol 30mg; Calcium 26mg; Fibre 0.5g; Sodium 39mg.
Christmas Tree Angels Energy 147kcal/622kJ; Protein 1.9g; Carbohydrate 28.7g, of which sugars 16g; Fat 3.6g, of which saturates 2.1g; Cholesterol 15mg; Calcium 31mg; Fibre 0.5g; Sodium 45mg.

Chocolate Kisses

These rich little biscuits look very Christmassy when mixed together on a plate and dusted with icing sugar – especially when decorated with a festive holly leaf. Serve them with ice cream for dessert or simply as a sweet accompaniment to a cup of coffee after a festive feast or on a cold winter's afternoon as a tasty pick-me-up.

Makes about 24

75g/3oz plain (semisweet) chocolate, broken into squares
75g/3oz white chocolate, broken into squares
115g/4oz/½ cup butter
115g/4oz/generous ½ cup caster (superfine) sugar
2 eggs
225g/8oz/2 cups plain (all-purpose) flour
icing (confectioners') sugar, to decorate

1 Put each pile of chocolate squares into a small heatproof bowl and, stirring occasionally, melt it over a pan of hot, but not boiling, water. Set aside to cool.

2 Whisk together the butter and caster sugar in a bowl until they are pale and fluffy.

3 Gradually beat the eggs into the butter and sugar, one at a time. Then sift in the flour and mix together well.

4 Halve the mixture and divide it between the two bowls of melted chocolate. Mix the chocolate with the two dough mixtures until thoroughly combined.

5 Knead the doughs until smooth and pliable, wrap them in clear film (plastic wrap) and set aside to chill them for about 1 hour. Preheat the oven to 190°C/375°F/Gas 5.

6 Shape slightly rounded teaspoonfuls of both doughs roughly into balls. Roll the balls in the palms of your hands to make neater ball shapes.

7 Arrange the balls on greased baking trays and bake them for 10–12 minutes. Dust with sifted icing sugar and then transfer them to a wire rack to cool.

Loop Biscuits

These are traditional favourites for enjoying at Christmas with a coffee after a dinner. They are unusual in that cooked egg yolk is used in addition to raw eggs, and the mixture produces a very appealing texture.

Makes about 48

2 hard-boiled eggs, yolks only
2 eggs, separated
225g/8oz/1 generous cup sugar
475g/1lb/4½ cups plain (all-purpose) flour
350g/12oz/1½ cups butter, softened
coarse sugar, for coating

1 Put the hard-boiled egg yolks and fresh egg yolks in a bowl and mash together. Beat in the sugar, a little at a time.

2 Add the flour alternately with the softened butter, mixing well to make a stiff dough. Wrap the dough in clear film (plastic wrap) and put in the refrigerator for 2–3 hours.

3 Line a baking tray with baking parchment. On a lightly floured surface, using your hands, roll out pieces of the dough into strips the thickness of a pencil. Cut into 10–13cm/4–5in lengths, then form into small wreaths by making a round loop and placing one end over the other. Place on the prepared baking tray and chill in the refrigerator for 30 minutes.

4 Preheat the oven to 190°C/375°F/Gas 5. Lightly beat the egg white, brush it over each wreath, then dip into coarse sugar.

5 Return to the baking tray and bake in the oven for about 10–12 minutes until very light brown. Leave on the baking tray for 2–3 minutes, then transfer to a wire rack and leave to cool. Store the biscuits (cookies) in an airtight tin.

> **Cook's Tip**
> The wreaths spread during cooking so make sure that the loops are large enough not to close up during baking. Chilling the wreaths in the refrigerator before cooking helps to stop the dough spreading too much.

Chocolate Kisses Energy 125kcal/524kJ; Protein 1.9g; Carbohydrate 16.1g, of which sugars 9g; Fat 6.4g, of which saturates 3.7g; Cholesterol 26mg; Calcium 28mg; Fibre 0.4g; Sodium 39mg.
Loop Biscuits Energy 107kcal/447kJ; Protein 1.1g; Carbohydrate 12.1g, of which sugars 4.5g; Fat 6.4g, of which saturates 3.9g; Cholesterol 24mg; Calcium 18mg; Fibre 0.3g; Sodium 45mg.

Vanilla Christmas Biscuits

These heart-shaped treats are a traditional Christmas favourite in Norway. They are not only ideal with a cup of tea or coffee but are delicious when served to accompany a dessert such as fruit salad. A little box of them wrapped with a big red bow also makes a delightful present.

Makes about 24
225g/8oz/2 cups plain (all-purpose) flour
5ml/1 tsp baking powder
150g/5oz/10 tbsp butter, at room temperature
90g/3½oz/½ cup caster (superfine) sugar
1 egg, lightly beaten
7.5ml/1½ tsp vanilla extract
120ml/4fl oz/½ cup milk

1 Sift the flour and baking powder together in a large mixing bowl. Put the butter and sugar in a separate large bowl and beat together until light and fluffy.

2 Add the egg and vanilla extract, then add the milk, alternating it with the sifted flour mixture. Mix together, then knead the dough lightly. Chill in the refrigerator for 30 minutes.

3 Preheat the oven to 180°C/350°F/Gas 4. Butter a large baking tray. Transfer the dough to a lightly floured surface and roll it out to 1cm/½in thickness.

4 Using a heart-shaped cutter, cut out hearts from the dough and place on the prepared baking tray. Bring the trimmings together, knead the dough lightly, roll out again and cut out more hearts.

5 Bake the biscuits (cookies) for about 10 minutes until lightly golden brown. Leave on the tray for 2–3 minutes, then transfer to a wire rack and leave to cool.

Cook's Tip
A pretty finish to the biscuits (cookies) could be provided by brushing the hearts with lightly beaten egg white and sprinkling with caster (superfine) sugar before baking.

Lebkuchen

These sweet and spicy cakes are traditionally baked at Christmas, and are packed with festive flavours.

Makes about 20
115g/4oz/1 cup blanched almonds, finely chopped
50g/2oz/⅓ cup candied orange peel, finely chopped
finely grated rind of ½ lemon
3 cardamom pods
5ml/1 tsp ground cinnamon
1.5ml/¼ tsp grated nutmeg
1.5ml/¼ tsp ground cloves
2 eggs
115g/4oz/generous ½ cup caster (superfine) sugar
150g/5oz/1¼ cups plain (all-purpose) flour
2.5ml/½ tsp baking powder
rice paper (optional)

For the icing
½ egg white
75g/3oz/⅔ cup icing (confectioners') sugar, sifted
5ml/1 tsp white rum

1 Preheat the oven to 180°C/350°F/Gas 4. Set aside some of the almonds for sprinkling and put the remainder in a bowl with the candied orange peel and lemon rind.

2 Remove the black seeds from the cardamom pods and crush using a mortar and pestle. Add to the bowl with the cinnamon, nutmeg and cloves and mix well.

3 Whisk the eggs and sugar in a mixing bowl until thick and foamy. Sift in the flour and baking powder, then gently fold into the eggs before adding to the nut and spice mixture.

4 Spoon dessertspoons of the mixture on to sheets of rice paper, if using, or baking parchment placed on baking sheets, allowing room for spreading. Sprinkle over the reserved almonds.

5 Bake for 20 minutes, until golden. Allow to cool for a few minutes, then break off the surplus rice paper or remove the biscuits from the baking parchment and cool on a wire rack.

6 Put the egg white for the icing in a bowl and lightly whisk with a fork. Stir in a little of the icing sugar at a time, then add the rum. Drizzle over the lebkuchen and leave to set. Keep in an airtight container for up to 2 weeks before serving.

Vanilla Biscuits Energy 100kcal/420kJ; Protein 1.4g; Carbohydrate 11.9g, of which sugars 4.8g; Fat 5.6g, of which saturates 3.4g; Cholesterol 22mg; Calcium 24mg; Fibre 0.3g; Sodium 43mg.
Lebkuchen Energy 105kcal/444kJ; Protein 2.4g; Carbohydrate 16.3g, of which sugars 11.7g; Fat 3.9g, of which saturates 0.4g; Cholesterol 19mg; Calcium 33mg; Fibre 0.7g; Sodium 16mg.

Chocolate Marzipan Cookies

The soft marzipan filling is a delicious contrast to the crunchy outside of these rich chocolate cookies. They look delightful along with other cakes served after a festive feast.

Makes about 36
200g/7oz/scant 1 cup unsalted butter, softened

200g/7oz/scant 1 cup light muscovado (brown) sugar
1 egg, beaten
300g/11oz/2¾ cups plain (all-purpose) flour
60ml/4 tbsp unsweetened cocoa powder
200g/7oz ready-made white almond paste
115g/4oz white chocolate, chopped into small pieces

1 Preheat the oven to 190°C/375°F/Gas 5. Grease two baking sheets. Using a hand-held electric mixer, cream the butter with the sugar in a bowl until pale and fluffy. Add the egg and beat well.

2 Sift the flour and cocoa over the mixture. Stir in with a wooden spoon until all the flour mixture has been smoothly incorporated, then use clean hands to press the mixture together to make a fairly soft dough.

3 Using a rolling pin and keeping your touch light, roll out about half the dough on a lightly floured surface to a thickness of about 5mm/¼in. Using a 5cm/2in plain or fluted cookie cutter, cut out 36 rounds, re-rolling the dough as required. Wrap the remaining dough in clear film (plastic wrap) and set it aside.

4 Cut the almond paste into 36 equal pieces. Roll into balls, flatten slightly and place one on each round of dough. Roll out the remaining dough, cut out more rounds, then place on top of the almond paste. Press the dough edges to seal.

5 Bake for 10–12 minutes, or until the cookies have risen well and are beginning to crack on the surface. Cool on the baking sheet for about 2–3 minutes, then finish cooling on a wire rack.

6 Melt the white chocolate, then either drizzle it over the cookies to decorate, or spoon into a paper piping (icing) bag and quickly pipe a design on to the cookies.

Gingerbread Family

You can have great fun with these cookies at Christmas by creating characters with different features. To add variation, use plain or milk chocolate for decorating.

Makes about 12
350g/12oz/3 cups plain (all-purpose) flour
5ml/1 tsp bicarbonate of soda (baking soda)

5ml/1 tsp ground ginger
115g/4oz/½ cup unsalted butter, chilled and diced
175g/6oz/scant 1 cup light muscovado (brown) sugar
1 egg
30ml/2 tbsp black treacle (molasses) or golden (light corn) syrup
150g/5oz white chocolate, to decorate

1 Preheat the oven to 180°C/350°F/Gas 4. Grease two large baking sheets. Put the flour, bicarbonate of soda, ginger and diced butter into a food processor. Process until the mixture begins to resemble fine breadcrumbs. If necessary, scrape down the sides of the food processor bowl with a wooden spoon or spatula to remove any crumbs that have become stuck to the sides and process a little more.

2 Add the sugar, egg and black treacle or golden syrup to the food processor and process the mixture until it begins to form into a ball. Turn the dough out on to a lightly floured surface, and knead until smooth and pliable.

3 Roll out the dough on a lightly floured surface (you might find it easier to roll half of the dough out at a time). Cut out figures using people-shaped cutters, then transfer to the baking sheets. Re-roll any trimmings and cut out more figures.

4 Bake in the oven for 15 minutes until slightly risen and starting to colour around the edges. Leave for 5 minutes, then transfer to a wire rack to cool.

5 To decorate, put the chocolate into a bowl over a pan of simmering water and heat, stirring, until melted. Spoon the melted chocolate into a paper piping (icing) bag, snip off the tip, then pipe faces and clothes on to the cookies. Leave to set.

Chocolate Cookies Energy 137kcal/576kJ; Protein 1.9g; Carbohydrate 18.1g, of which sugars 11.6g; Fat 6.9g, of which saturates 3.8g; Cholesterol 17mg; Calcium 31mg; Fibre 0.6g; Sodium 57mg.
Gingerbread Family Energy 305kcal/1281kJ; Protein 4.1g; Carbohydrate 47.6g, of which sugars 25.2g; Fat 12.2g, of which saturates 7.3g; Cholesterol 37mg; Calcium 71mg; Fibre 1.2g; Sodium 71mg.

Ginger Florentines

These colourful, chewy biscuits are delicious with ice cream at Christmas and are certain to disappear as soon as they are served. Store in an airtight container.

Makes 30

50g/2oz/¼ cup butter
115g/4oz/generous ½ cup caster (superfine) sugar
50g/2oz/¼ cup chopped mixed glacé (candied) cherries
25g/1oz/2 tbsp mixed chopped (candied) peel
50g/2oz/½ cup flaked (sliced) almonds
50g/2oz/½ cup chopped walnuts
25g/1oz/1 tbsp chopped glacé (candied) ginger
30ml/2 tbsp plain (all-purpose) flour
2.5ml/½ tsp ground ginger

To finish

50g/2oz plain (semisweet) chocolate
50g/2oz white chocolate

1 Preheat the oven to 180°C/350°F/Gas 4. Whisk together the butter and sugar in a large mixing bowl until they are light and fluffy. Thoroughly mix in all the remaining ingredients, except for the plain and white chocolates.

2 Line several large baking trays with baking parchment. Put four small spoonfuls of the mixture on to each tray, spacing them well apart to allow for spreading. Gently flatten the biscuits (cookies) with the palm of your hand and bake them for about 5 minutes.

3 Remove the biscuits from the oven and flatten them with a wet fork, shaping them into neat rounds. Return to the oven for 3–4 minutes, until they are golden brown.

4 Allow the biscuits to cool on the baking trays for about 2 minutes, to firm up, and then, using a metal spatula, carefully transfer them to a wire rack.

5 When the biscuits are cold and firm, melt the plain and the white chocolates in bowls over pans of simmering water. Spread dark chocolate on the undersides of half the biscuits and spread white chocolate on the undersides of the rest.

Ginger Cookies

These are a supreme Christmas treat for ginger lovers – richly spiced cookies packed with chunks of succulent preserved stem ginger. Serve small cookies as an after-dinner treat or give them as a festive gift.

Makes 30 small or 20 large cookies

350g/12oz/3 cups self-raising (self-rising) flour
pinch of salt
200g/7oz/1 cup golden caster (superfine) sugar
15ml/1 tbsp ground ginger
5ml/1 tsp bicarbonate of soda (baking soda)
115g/4oz/½ cup unsalted butter
90g/3½oz/generous ¼ cup golden (light corn) syrup
1 large (US extra large) egg, beaten
150g/5oz preserved stem ginger in syrup, drained and coarsely chopped

1 Preheat the oven to 160°C/325°F/Gas 3. Line three baking sheets with baking parchment.

2 Sift the flour into a large bowl, add the salt, caster sugar, ground ginger and bicarbonate of soda and stir to combine.

3 Dice the butter and put it in a small pan with the golden syrup. Heat gently, stirring, until the butter has melted. Set aside to cool until it is just warm.

4 Pour the butter mixture over the dry ingredients, then add the egg and two-thirds of the ginger. Mix well, then use your hands to bring the dough together.

5 Shape the dough into 20 large or 30 small balls, depending on the size you require. Place them, spaced well apart, on the baking sheets. Gently flatten the balls with your hand, then press a few pieces of the remaining preserved stem ginger into the top of each of the cookies.

6 Bake for 12–15 minutes, depending on the size of your cookies, until light golden in colour. Leave to cool for 1 minute on the baking sheets to firm up. Using a metal spatula, transfer to a wire rack to cool completely.

Florentines Energy 71kcal/298kJ; Protein 0.9g; Carbohydrate 8.6g, of which sugars 7.8g; Fat 3.9g, of which saturates 1.3g; Cholesterol 2mg; Calcium 16mg; Fibre 0.3g; Sodium 11mg.
Ginger Cookies Energy 114kcal/479kJ; Protein 1.4g; Carbohydrate 20.4g, of which sugars 11.5g; Fat 3.5g, of which saturates 2.1g; Cholesterol 15mg; Calcium 23mg; Fibre 0.4g; Sodium 42mg.

Brandysnap Cookies

As thin, delicate and elegant as fine glass, these ginger cookies are ideal served with creamy desserts, syllabubs, sorbets and ice creams.

Makes 18

50g/2oz/¼ cup unsalted
   butter, diced
40g/1½oz/3 tbsp liquid glucose
   (clear corn syrup)
90g/3½oz/½ cup caster
   (superfine) sugar
40g/1½oz/⅓ cup plain
   (all-purpose) flour
5ml/1 tsp ground ginger

1 Put the butter and liquid glucose in a heatproof bowl set over a pan of gently simmering water. Stir together until melted. Set aside to cool slightly.

2 Put the sugar in a large bowl and sift over the flour and ginger. Stir into the butter mixture, then beat well until combined. Cover with clear film (plastic wrap) and chill for about 25 minutes, until firm.

3 Meanwhile, preheat the oven to 180°C/350°F/Gas 4 and line three large baking sheets with baking parchment.

4 Roll teaspoonfuls of the mixture into about 18 balls and place them, spaced well apart to allow room for spreading, on the prepared baking sheets.

5 Place a second piece of baking parchment on top and roll the cookies thinly. Peel off the top sheet. Stamp each cookie with a 7.5cm/3in plain round cutter to make a neat circle.

6 Bake for 5–6 minutes, or until golden. Leave for a few seconds on the baking sheets, then either leave flat or curl over in half. Allow to cool completely.

Cook's Tip
These cookies also make lovely Christmas gifts when presented in an attractive box tied with coloured ribbons.

Chocolate Treacle Snaps

These elegantly thin, treacle-flavoured snap cookies have a delicate hint of spice and a decorative lick of chocolate on top. They are particularly good with a steaming cup of hot coffee.

Makes about 35

90g/3½oz/7 tbsp unsalted
   butter, diced
175ml/6fl oz/¾ cup golden
   (light corn) syrup
50ml/2fl oz/¼ cup black
   treacle (molasses)
250g/9oz/2¼ cups plain
   (all-purpose) flour
150g/5oz/¾ cup golden
   caster (superfine) sugar
5ml/1 tsp bicarbonate of
   soda (baking soda)
1.5ml/¼ tsp mixed
   (apple pie) spice
100g/3¾oz milk chocolate
100g/3¾oz white chocolate

1 Preheat the oven to 180°C/350°F/Gas 4. Line two or three baking sheets with baking parchment.

2 Put the butter, syrup and treacle in a small pan. Heat gently, stirring constantly, until the butter has melted. Remove from the heat and set aside until required.

3 Sift the flour into a large mixing bowl. Add the sugar, bicarbonate of soda and mixed spice, and mix well using a wooden spoon. Slowly pour in the butter and treacle mixture and stir to combine well.

4 Place large teaspoonfuls of the mixture well apart on the prepared baking sheets. Bake the cookies for 10–12 minutes, until just beginning to brown around the edges.

5 Leave them to cool for a few minutes on the baking sheets. When firm enough to handle, transfer the cookies to a wire rack to cool completely.

6 Melt the milk chocolate and white chocolate separately in the microwave or in heatproof bowls set over pans of simmering water. Swirl a little of each into the centre of each cookie and leave to set.

Brandysnap Cookies Energy 55kcal/231kJ; Protein 0.3g; Carbohydrate 8.9g, of which sugars 6.2g; Fat 2.3g, of which saturates 1.5g; Cholesterol 6mg; Calcium 6mg; Fibre 0.1g; Sodium 21mg.
Treacle Snaps Energy 109kcal/459kJ; Protein 1.2g; Carbohydrate 18.2g, of which sugars 12.8g; Fat 4g, of which saturates 2.4g; Cholesterol 6mg; Calcium 35mg; Fibre 0.2g; Sodium 38mg.

Tiramisù Biscuits

These sophisticated biscuits taste like the famed Italian dessert, with its flavours of coffee, chocolate and rum. A perfect luxurious accompaniment to ices, fools or other light dishes.

Makes 14
50g/2oz/¼ cup butter, at room
   temperature, diced
90g/3½oz/½ cup caster
   (superfine) sugar
1 egg, beaten
50g/2oz/½ cup plain
   (all-purpose) flour

For the filling
150g/5oz/⅔ cup mascarpone
15ml/1 tbsp dark rum
2.5ml/½ tsp instant
   coffee powder
15ml/1 tbsp light muscovado
   (brown) sugar

For the topping
75g/3oz white chocolate
15ml/1 tbsp milk
30ml/2 tbsp crushed
   chocolate flake

1 Make the filling. Put the mascarpone in a bowl. Mix together the rum and coffee powder until the coffee has dissolved. Add to the cheese, with the sugar, and mix together well. Cover with clear film (plastic wrap) and chill until required.

2 Preheat the oven to 200°C/400°F/Gas 6. Line two or three baking sheets with baking parchment. Make the biscuits (cookies). Cream together the butter and sugar in a bowl until light and fluffy. Add the egg and mix well. Stir in the flour and mix thoroughly.

3 Put the mixture into a piping (pastry) bag fitted with a 1.5cm/½in plain nozzle and pipe 28 small blobs on to the baking sheets, spaced slightly apart. Cook for 6–8 minutes, until firm in the centre and just beginning to brown on the edges. Remove from the oven and set aside to cool.

4 To assemble, spread a little of the filling on to half the biscuits and place the other halves on top. Put the chocolate and milk in a heatproof bowl and melt over a pan of hot water. When melted, stir vigorously until spreadable. Spread the chocolate evenly over the biscuits, then top with crushed chocolate flake.

Peanut Butter and Raspberry Jelly Cookies

These cookies are a twist on the original American peanut butter cookie and are a real festive hit with kids and adults alike.

Makes 20–22
227g/8oz jar crunchy peanut
   butter (with no added sugar)
75g/3oz/6 tbsp unsalted
   butter, at room
   temperature, diced

90g/3½oz/½ cup golden caster
   (superfine) sugar
50g/2oz/¼ cup light muscovado
   (brown) sugar
1 large (US extra large)
   egg, beaten
150g/5oz/1¼ cups self-raising
   (self-rising) flour
250g/9oz/scant 1 cup seedless
   raspberry jam

1 Preheat the oven to 180°C/350°F/Gas 4. Line three or four baking sheets with baking parchment.

2 Put the peanut butter and unsalted butter in a large bowl and beat together until well combined and creamy.

3 Add the caster and muscovado sugars to the bowl and beat well. Add the beaten egg to the mixture and blend well. Sift in the flour and mix to a stiff dough.

4 Roll the dough into 40–44 walnut-size balls between the palms of your hands (make an even number of balls). Place the balls on the prepared baking sheets, spaced well apart to allow for spreading, and gently flatten each one with a fork to make a rough-textured cookie with a lightly ridged surface. (Don't worry if the dough cracks slightly.)

5 Bake in the oven for 10–12 minutes, or until cooked but not browned. Using a metal spatula, carefully transfer the cookies to a wire rack to cool completely.

6 Spoon a little raspberry jam on to the flat side of one cookie and place a second cookie on top. Continue to sandwich the remaining cookies in this way.

Tiramisù Biscuits Energy 178kcal/742kJ; Protein 2.4g; Carbohydrate 15.5g, of which sugars 12.8g; Fat 7.2g, of which saturates 4.3g; Cholesterol 26mg; Calcium 28mg; Fibre 0.2g; Sodium 34mg.
Peanut Butter Cookies Energy 169kcal/709kJ; Protein 3.4g; Carbohydrate 21g, of which sugars 15.3g; Fat 8.5g, of which saturates 3.2g; Cholesterol 18mg; Calcium 35mg; Fibre 0.8g; Sodium 89mg.

Marzipan Fruits

These eye-catching and realistic fruits will make a perfect gift for lovers of marzipan during the festive season.

Makes 450g/1lb

450g/1lb white marzipan
yellow, green, red, orange and
*   burgundy food colouring dusts*
30g/1½oz/2 tbsp whole cloves

1 Cover a baking sheet with baking parchment. Quarter the marzipan. Cut one piece into ten even pieces. Place a little of each of the food colouring dusts on a plate. Cut two-thirds of the cloves into two pieces, making a stem and core end.

2 Shape the ten pieces into neat balls. Dip one ball into the yellow food colouring and roll to colour. Re-dip into the green colouring and re-roll to tint. Roll one end to make a pear shape. Press a clove stem into the top and a core end into the base. Repeat with the remaining balls. Place on the baking sheet.

3 Cut another piece of the marzipan into ten pieces and shape into neat balls. Dip each piece of marzipan into the green food colouring dust and roll in the palms to colour evenly. Add a spot of red colouring dust and roll gently to blend the colour. Using the end of a fine paint-brush, indent the top and base to make an apple shape. Make a stem and core, using cloves.

4 Repeat as above, using another piece of the marzipan to make ten orange-coloured balls. Roll each over a fine grater to give the texture of an orange. Press a clove core into the base.

5 Take the remaining piece of marzipan, reserve a small piece, and mould the rest into lots of tiny marzipan beads. Colour them burgundy with the food colouring. Place a whole clove on the baking sheet. Arrange a cluster of beads in the shape of a bunch of grapes. Repeat with the remaining burgundy beads of marzipan to make another three bunches of grapes.

6 Roll out the remaining piece of marzipan thinly and brush with green food colouring. Using a vine leaf cutter, cut out eight leaves, mark the veins with a knife and place two on each grape bunch. Leave the fruits to dry, then pack into gift boxes.

Peppermint Chocolate Sticks

These delicious bitesize chocolate sticks will prove irresistible when served with coffee after a special Christmas meal.

Makes about 80
115g/4oz/½ cup sugar

150ml/¼ pint/⅔ cup water
2.5ml/½ tsp peppermint extract
200g/7oz dark (bittersweet)
*   chocolate, broken into squares*
60ml/4 tbsp toasted desiccated
*   (dry unsweetened*
*   shredded) coconut*

1 Lightly grease a large baking sheet. Place the sugar and water in a small heavy pan over medium-low heat. Heat gently, until the sugar has dissolved. Stir occasionally.

2 Bring the mixture to the boil and boil rapidly until the syrup registers 138°C/280°F on a sugar thermometer. Remove from the heat. Add the peppermint extract and pour on to the greased baking sheet. Leave to set.

3 Break up the peppermint mixture into a small bowl and use the end of a rolling pin to crush it into small pieces.

4 Melt the chocolate in a large heatproof bowl set over a pan of gently simmering water, stirring occasionally. Remove the chocolate from the heat and stir in the broken mint pieces and the toasted desiccated coconut.

5 Spread the chocolate mixture over a 30 × 25cm/12 × 10in sheet of baking parchment, to make a rectangle measuring about 25 × 20cm/10 × 8in. Leave to set.

6 When the chocolate is firm, use a sharp knife to cut it into thin sticks, each about 6cm/2½in long.

> **Variation**
> *Other flavours can be added to these chocolate sticks. Try adding a little grated orange rind to the chocolate to create delicious minty chocolate-orange treats.*

Marzipan Fruits Energy 2100kcal/8798kJ; Protein 48.9g; Carbohydrate 228g, of which sugars 222.6g; Fat 116.8g, of which saturates 10.3g; Cholesterol 170mg; Calcium 615mg; Fibre 14.8g; Sodium 103mg.
Peppermint Sticks Energy 23kcal/96kJ; Protein 0.2g; Carbohydrate 3.1g, of which sugars 3.1g; Fat 1.2g, of which saturates 0.8g; Cholesterol 0mg; Calcium 2mg; Fibre 0.2g; Sodium 0mg.

Champagne Truffles

Real gold dust has been used for an opulent and festive look to these truffles.

Makes 50
250g/9oz dark (bittersweet) chocolate (70% cocoa solids), chopped or broken
200g/7oz milk chocolate (40% cocoa solids), chopped
150ml/¼ pint/⅔ cup double (heavy) cream

50g/2oz unsalted butter
100ml/3½fl oz/scant ½ cup champagne or other sparkling wine
15ml/1 tbsp brandy
700g/1lb 10oz dark chocolate (70% cocoa solids)
icing (confectioners') sugar for rolling
edible gold dust (optional)

1 Butter a 20cm/8in square baking tin (pan) and line with clear film (plastic wrap). Line a baking sheet with baking parchment. Put the dark and milk chocolate in a heatproof bowl. Set aside.

2 Put the cream and butter in a heavy pan and heat to just under a boil over medium heat. Pour over the chocolate and leave for a minute before adding the champagne and brandy. Whisk by hand until all the chocolate is melted and you have a smooth ganache. Pour into the tin. Leave to firm up.

3 To form the truffles, scrape the ganache up into a piping (icing) bag fitted with a 1cm/½in plain nozzle. Pipe out even little blobs on to the lined baking sheet. Place in the refrigerator for about 20 minutes or until firm. Dust your hands with icing sugar and roll the blobs into balls. Chill for 10 minutes, until firm.

4 Line another baking sheet with parchment paper. Using a dipping fork, dunk each ball of ganache into the dark chocolate and place it on a cooling rack to set.

5 Dip a clean, dry pastry brush into the pot of gold dust. Hold it over the truffles and tap the handle to release the dust and allow it to fall evenly over the truffles. Serve immediately or store the truffles in the refrigerator in an airtight container. Remove from the refrigerator at least 30 minutes before serving, as chocolate should be eaten at room temperature.

Chocolate Christmas Cups

These festive treats are a perfect way of using up any Christmas pudding left-overs.

Makes 30–35
275g/10oz/2½ cups plain (semisweet) chocolate, broken into pieces

70–80 foil or paper sweet (candy) cases
175g/6oz cooked, cold Christmas pudding
75ml/2½fl oz/⅓ cup brandy or whisky
chocolate holly leaves and crystallized cranberries, to decorate

1 Place the chocolate in a bowl over a pan of barely simmering water until it melts, stirring until smooth. Using a pastry brush, coat melted chocolate on to the inside of about 35 sweet (candy) cases. Allow to set, then apply a second coat, reheating the chocolate if necessary. Leave for 4–5 hours to set. Reserve the remaining chocolate.

2 Crumble the cooked Christmas pudding into a small bowl. Sprinkle with brandy or whisky and leave to stand for about 30–40 minutes, until the brandy or whisky has been absorbed by the pudding crumbs.

3 Spoon a little of the pudding mixture into each chocolate cup, smoothing the top. Reheat the remaining chocolate and spoon over the top of each cup to cover the surface right to the edge. Leave to set.

4 When the chocolate cups are completely set, carefully peel off the sweet cases and replace them with clean ones. Decorate the tops of the cups with chocolate holly leaves and crystallized cranberries.

> **Cook's Tip**
> To crystallize cranberries, beat an egg white until frothy; dip each cranberry in the egg white, then in caster (superfine) sugar. Place the coated cranberries on sheets of baking parchment and leave until dry.

Champagne Truffles Energy 144kcal/601kJ; Protein 1.3g; Carbohydrate 14.8g, of which sugars 13.7g; Fat 9.2g, of which saturates 5.4g; Cholesterol 9mg; Calcium 18mg; Fibre 0g; Sodium 16mg.
Chocolate Christmas Cups Energy 59kcal/249kJ; Protein 0.6g; Carbohydrate 7.5g, of which sugars 6.6g; Fat 2.7g, of which saturates 1.3g; Cholesterol 0mg; Calcium 7mg; Fibre 0.3g; Sodium 10mg.

Truffle Christmas Puddings

Truffles disguised as
Christmas puddings are
great fun both to make and
receive. Make any flavour
truffles, and decorate them
as you like.

Makes 20
15ml/1 tbsp unsweetened
  cocoa powder

15ml/1 tbsp icing
  (confectioners') sugar
20 plain (semisweet)
  chocolate truffles
225g/8oz/1 cup white
  chocolate chips, melted
50g/2oz/¼ cup white marzipan
green and red food colourings
yellow food colouring dust

1 Sift the cocoa powder and icing sugar together in a bowl and use it to coat the chocolate truffles.

2 Spread two-thirds of the white chocolate over a piece of non-stick baking paper. Using a small daisy cutter, stamp out 20 rounds. Place a truffle on the centre of each daisy shape, secured with a little of the reserved melted chocolate.

3 Colour two-thirds of the marzipan green and one-third red using the food colourings. Roll out the green marzipan thinly and stamp out 40 leaves, using a tiny holly leaf cutter. Mark the veins with a sharp knife.

4 Mould lots of tiny red beads. Colour the remaining white chocolate with yellow food colouring dust and place in a paper piping (icing) bag. Fold down the top, cut off the tip and pipe the marzipan over the top of each truffle to resemble custard.

5 Arrange the holly leaves and berries on the top of the puddings. When the truffle puddings have set, arrange them in gift boxes, label and tie with ribbon.

Cook's Tip
These little truffles are fun to make at home and children will love to help. They may be able to coat the truffles, do some stamping, or pack the finished puddings in a box as a present.

Creamy Fudge

A good selection of fudge always makes a welcome change from chocolates at Christmas. Mix and match the flavours to make a gift-wrapped assortment.

Makes 900g/2lb
50g/2oz/4 tbsp unsalted butter,
  plus extra for greasing
450g/1lb/2 cups sugar
300ml/½ pint/1¼ cups double
  (heavy) cream
150ml/¼ pint/⅔ cup milk

45ml/3 tbsp water (this can be
  replaced with orange, apricot or
  cherry brandy, or strong coffee)

For the flavourings
225g/8oz/1 cup plain (semisweet)
  or milk chocolate chips
115g/4oz/1 cup chopped
  almonds, hazelnuts, walnuts
  or brazil nuts
115g/4oz/½ cup chopped glacé
  (candied) cherries, dates or
  dried apricots

1 Grease a 20cm/8in shallow square tin (pan). Place the butter, sugar, cream, milk and water or other flavourings into a large heavy pan. Heat very gently, until all the sugar has dissolved.

2 Bring the mixture to a rolling boil, until the fudge reaches the soft ball stage.

3 If you are making chocolate-flavoured fudge, add the chocolate chips to the mixture at this stage. Remove the pan from the heat and beat thoroughly until the mixture starts to thicken and become opaque.

4 Just before this consistency has been reached, add chopped nuts for a nutty fudge, or glacé cherries or dried fruit for a fruit-flavoured fudge. Beat well until evenly blended.

5 Pour the fudge into the prepared tin, taking care as the mixture is very hot. Leave the mixture until cool and almost set. Using a sharp knife, mark the fudge into small squares and leave in the tin until quite firm.

6 Turn the fudge out on to a board and invert. Using a long-bladed knife, cut into neat squares. You can dust some with icing sugar and drizzle others with melted chocolate, if desired.

Truffle Christmas Puddings Energy 148kcal/616kJ; Protein 1.3g; Carbohydrate 11.9g, of which sugars 10.3g; Fat 10.5g, of which saturates 6.2g; Cholesterol 22mg; Calcium 19mg; Fibre 0.5g; Sodium 31mg.
Creamy Fudge Energy 5886kcal/24635kJ; Protein 40.4g; Carbohydrate 708.8g, of which sugars 704.5g; Fat 340.8g, of which saturates 171g; Cholesterol 540mg; Calcium 874mg; Fibre 14.1g; Sodium 512mg.

Marshmallows

These light and fragrant mouthfuls of pale pink mousse are flavoured with rose water.

Makes 500g/1¼lb
oil, for greasing
45ml/3 tbsp icing
  (confectioners') sugar
45ml/3 tbsp cornflour (cornstarch)

50ml/2fl oz/¼ cup cold water
45ml/3 tbsp rose water
25g/1oz/1 tbsp powdered
  gelatine
pink food colouring
450g/1lb/2 cups sugar
30ml/2 level tbsp liquid glucose
  (clear corn syrup)
250ml/8fl oz/1 cup boiling water
2 egg whites

1 Lightly oil a 28 × 18cm/11 × 7in Swiss roll tin (jelly roll pan). Sift together the icing sugar and cornflour and use some to coat the inside of the tin.

2 Mix the cold water, rose water, gelatine and a drop of food colouring in a heatproof bowl. Place over a pan of hot water. Stir until the gelatine has dissolved.

3 Place the sugar, liquid glucose and boiling water in a heavy pan. Stir until the sugar is dissolved.

4 Bring to the boil and boil steadily without stirring until the temperature reaches 127°C/260°F on a sugar thermometer. Remove from the heat and stir in the gelatine mixture.

5 While the syrup is boiling, whisk the egg whites stiffly in a large bowl using an electric hand whisk. Pour a steady stream of syrup on to the egg whites while whisking constantly for about 3 minutes, until the mixture is thick and foamy. At this stage add more food colouring, if the mixture looks too pale.

6 Pour the mixture into the prepared tin and allow to set for about 4 hours or overnight. Sift some of the remaining icing sugar mixture over the surface of the marshmallow and the rest over a board or baking sheet. Ease the mixture away from the tin using an oiled metal spatula and invert on to the board. Cut into 2.5cm/1in squares, coating the cut sides with the icing sugar mixture. Pack into glass containers or tins and seal well.

Turkish Delight

Turkish Delight is a favourite at Christmas, and this recipe can be made in minutes. Try different flavours, such as lemon, crème de menthe and orange.

Makes 450g/1lb
450g/1lb/2 cups sugar
300ml/½ pint/1¼ cups water

25g/1oz/2 tbsp powdered
  gelatine
2.5ml/½ tsp cream of tartar
30ml/2 tbsp rose water
pink food colouring
25g/1oz/3 tbsp icing
  (confectioners') sugar, sifted
15ml/1 tbsp cornflour
  (cornstarch)

1 Wet the insides of 2 × 18cm/7in shallow square tins (pans) with water. Place the sugar and all but 60ml/4 tbsp of water into a heavy pan. Heat gently, stirring occasionally, until the sugar has completely dissolved.

2 Blend the gelatine and remaining water in a small bowl and place over a pan of hot water. Stir occasionally until dissolved.

3 Bring the sugar syrup to the boil and boil steadily for about 8 minutes, or until the syrup registers 127°C/260°F on a sugar thermometer. Stir the cream of tartar into the gelatine, then pour it into the boiling syrup and stir until well blended. Remove the pan from the heat.

4 Add the rose water and a few drops of pink food colouring to the syrup mixture and stir, adding a few more drops, as necessary, to tint the mixture pale pink.

5 Pour the mixture into the prepared tins and allow to set for several hours or overnight.

6 Dust a sheet of baking parchment with some of the icing sugar and cornflour. Dip the base of the tins in hot water and invert on to the prepared parchment.

7 Cut the Turkish delight into 2.5cm/1in squares, using an oiled knife. Toss the squares in the icing sugar to coat evenly before storing in an airtight container.

Turkish Delight Energy 1335kcal/5696kJ; Protein 5.1g; Carbohydrate 350.1g, of which sugars 317.3g; Fat 0.2g, of which saturates 0g; Cholesterol 0mg; Calcium 165mg; Fibre 0g; Sodium 132mg.
Marshmallows Energy 258kcal/1088kJ; Protein 6.5g; Carbohydrate 42.3g, of which sugars 38.7g; Fat 7.4g, of which saturates 5.1g; Cholesterol 22mg; Calcium 208mg; Fibre 0g; Sodium 98mg.

Crab-apple and Lavender Jelly

This fragrant, clear jelly can be made in the months before Christmas and stored until needed. It also makes an attractive gift.

Makes about 900g/2lb

900g/2lb/5 cups crab-apples
1.75 litres/3 pints/7½ cups water
lavender stems
900g/2lb/4 cups sugar

1 Cut the crab-apples into chunks and place in a large pan with the water and two stems of lavender. Bring to the boil, then cover the pan and simmer very gently for 1 hour, stirring occasionally until the fruit is pulpy.

2 Suspend a jelly bag and place a large bowl underneath. Sterilize the jelly bag by pouring through some boiling water. When the bowl is full of water, discard the water and replace the bowl to sit underneath the bag.

3 Pour the pulped fruit mixture from the pan slowly into the jelly bag. Allow the juice from the mixture to drip slowly through for several hours. Do not try to speed up the straining process by squeezing the bag or the jelly will become cloudy.

4 Discard the pulp and measure the quantity of juice gathered in the bowl. To each 600ml/1 pint/2½ cups of juice add 450g/1lb/2 cups of sugar and pour into a clean pan. Sterilize the glass jars and lids required in a very hot oven.

5 Heat the juice gently, stirring occasionally, until the sugar has dissolved. Bring to the boil and boil rapidly for about 8–10 minutes until setting point has been reached. When tested, the temperature should be 105°C/221°F. If you don't have a sugar thermometer, put a small amount of jelly on a cold plate and allow to cool. The surface should wrinkle when you push the jelly. If not yet set, continue to boil and then re-test.

6 Remove from the heat and remove any froth from the surface. Pour the jelly into the warm sterilized jars. Dip the lavender into boiling water and insert a stem into each jar. Cover the jar with a disc of baking parchment and then with cellophane paper and a rubber band.

Macaroons

These little macaroons can be served as petits fours with coffee after a special festive feast of other meal. Dust with icing sugar or unsweetened cocoa powder before serving.

Makes 30
50g/2oz/⅔ cup ground almonds
50g/2oz/¼ cup caster (superfine) sugar

15ml/1 tbsp cornflour (cornstarch)
1.5–2.5ml/¼–½ tsp almond extract
1 egg white, whisked
15 flaked (sliced) almonds
4 glacé (candied) cherries, cut into quarters
icing (confectioners') sugar or unsweetened cocoa powder, to dust

1 Preheat the oven to 160°C/325°F/ Gas 3. Line two baking sheets with baking parchment.

2 Place the ground almonds, sugar, cornflour and almond extract into a large mixing bowl and mix together well to combine, using a wooden spoon.

3 Stir just enough egg white into the bowl with the other ingredients to form a soft piping consistency.

4 Place the mixture into a nylon piping (icing) bag fitted with a 1cm/½in plain piping nozzle.

5 Pipe about 15 rounds of the mixture on to each prepared baking sheet, spaced well apart to allow for any spreading while they are cooking in the oven.

6 Press a flaked almond on to half the macaroons and glacé cherries on to the remainder. Bake for 10–15 minutes.

Variation
You can make chocolate-flavoured macaroons, if you prefer. Simply replace the cornflour (cornstarch) with the same amount of unsweetened cocoa powder.

Crab-apple Jelly Energy 48kcal/205kJ; Protein 0.1g; Carbohydrate 12.7g, of which sugars 12.7g; Fat 0g, of which saturates 0g; Cholesterol 0mg; Calcium 6mg; Fibre 0.1g; Sodium 1mg.
Macaroons Energy 102kcal/426kJ; Protein 2.8g; Carbohydrate 7.8g, of which sugars 7.5g; Fat 6.9g, of which saturates 0.6g; Cholesterol 13mg; Calcium 33mg; Fibre 0.9g; Sodium 5mg.

Orange, Mint and Coffee Meringues

These tiny, crisp meringues are flavoured with orange, coffee and mint chocolate sticks and liqueurs. Pile them into dry, airtight glass jars or decorative tins for a festive gift.

Makes 90
25g/1oz/8 chocolate mint sticks
25g/1oz/8 chocolate orange sticks
25g/1oz/8 chocolate coffee sticks
2.5ml/½ tsp crème de menthe
2.5ml/½ tsp orange curaçao or Cointreau
2.5ml/½ tsp Tia Maria
3 egg whites
175g/6oz/¾ cup caster (superfine) sugar
5ml/1 tsp unsweetened cocoa powder

1 Preheat the oven to 110°C/225°F/Gas ¼. Line two or three baking sheets with baking parchment.

2 Chop each flavour of chocolate stick separately and place each into separate bowls, retaining a teaspoonful of each flavour of stick. Stir in the liquid flavourings to match the flavour of the chocolate sticks in the bowls.

3 Place the egg whites in a clean bowl and whisk until stiff. Gradually add the sugar, whisking well until thick.

4 Add one-third of the meringue to each bowl and fold in gently, using a clean spatula, until evenly blended.

5 Place about 30 teaspoons of each mixture on to the baking sheets, spaced apart. Sprinkle the top of each meringue with the reserved chopped chocolate sticks.

6 Bake in the preheated oven for 1 hour or until crisp. Leave to cool, then dust with the cocoa powder.

Cook's Tip
These little meringues are ideal served with coffee after a festive dinner party. Alternatively, they make an original topping to serve with ice-cream sundaes.

Sugar Mice

Sugar mice are traditionally found in the Christmas stockings of British children, and will still prove very popular as a festive gift. Get creative with the decoration. Small candies instead of the coffee beans could be used to decorate and embellish the mice.

Makes 1
50g/2oz fondant per mouse
a few drops of pink or brown food colouring (optional)
coffee beans
silver balls or other decorations, for eyes
string
inexpensive new pastry brush, to use for whiskers (optional)

1 Wearing latex gloves, colour the fondant. Use either pink or brown food colouring, depending what colour you want the mouse to be. You could also leave the fondant white.

2 Shape the fondant into a rough pear shape with a flat bottom. Carefully mould the mice ears, using a sugar shaping tool or a wooden skewer to form indentations in which the coffee beans can be securely placed.

3 Push the coffee beans into the shaped ears, then add silver balls or other decorations for the eyes. You could add an extra ball for a nose, if you like.

4 Cut a length of string for the tail and pieces of the pastry brush for the whiskers, if you like. Using sugar-working tools or a wooden skewer, push the decorations into place.

5 Place the mouse in a safe place and leave it to dry completely for at least 4 hours or overnight.

Variations
These mice can be made from sugar set with egg whites or egg white powder, or they can be formed from soft sugar fondant. The former is made much like a sugar egg, using a mould. The latter can be made by hand and make a great project to do at home with the children.

Orange Meringues Energy 13kcal/54kJ; Protein 0.2g; Carbohydrate 2.6g, of which sugars 2.6g; Fat 0.3g, of which saturates 0.1g; Cholesterol 0mg; Calcium 1mg; Fibre 0g; Sodium 3mg.
Sugar Mice Energy 194kcal/826kJ; Protein 0.9g; Carbohydrate 45.3g, of which sugars 43.2g; Fat 2.3g, of which saturates 1.4g; Cholesterol 0mg; Calcium 31mg; Fibre 0.1g; Sodium 18mg.

Chocolate Citrus Candies

Home-candied peel makes a superb sweetmeat, especially when dipped in chocolate. You can also use bought candied peel for this recipe, but make sure it is the very best quality.

Makes about 100g/4oz petits fours
1 orange or 2 lemons
25g/1oz/2 tbsp sugar
about 50g/2oz good quality plain (semisweet) chocolate

1 Using a vegetable knife, peel the rind from the fruit, without taking too much of the pith. Slice into matchsticks.

2 Blanch in boiling water for 4–5 minutes, until beginning to soften, then refresh under cold water and drain thoroughly.

3 In a small pan, heat the sugar and 30ml/2 tbsp water gently together until the sugar has dissolved.

4 Add the strips of rind and simmer for about 8–10 minutes, or until the water has evaporated and the peel is transparent.

5 Lift out the peel with a slotted spoon and spread out on baking parchment to cool. When cold the peel can be stored in an airtight container for up to 2 days before using, if required.

6 To coat, melt the chocolate carefully in a double boiler or in a bowl over a pan of hot water. Spear each piece of peel on to a cocktail stick (toothpick) and dip one end into the chocolate.

7 To dry the candies, stick the cocktail sticks into a large potato. When the chocolate is completely dry, remove the sticks and then arrange the citrus candies attractively on a dish to serve after dinner or with drinks.

Variation
A mixture of the three types – chocolate- and sugar-coated peel, and ginger – makes an attractive selection of sweet nibbles for a special occasion such as Christmas.

Glacé Fruits

These sweetmeats are very popular at Christmas. Choose one type or select a variety of fruits.

Makes 24 pieces
450g/1lb fruit
1kg/2¼lb/4½ cups sugar
115g/4oz/1 cup powdered glucose

1 Remove any stones (pits) from stone fruit. Peel and core pineapple and cut into cubes or rings. Peel, core and quarter apples and thinly slice citrus fruits.

2 Place enough fruit in a pan to cover the base. Add water to cover and simmer until almost tender. Repeat, then transfer the fruit to a dish, reserving the liquid and removing any skins.

3 Measure 300ml/½ pint/1¼ cups of the liquid, or make up this quantity with water if necessary. Pour into the pan and add 50g/2oz/4 tbsp sugar and the glucose. Heat gently, stirring occasionally, until dissolved. Bring to the boil and pour over the fruit in the dish, completely immersing it, and leave overnight.

4 DAY 2. Drain the syrup into the pan and add 50g/2oz/4 tbsp sugar. Dissolve the sugar and bring to the boil. Pour over the fruit and leave overnight. Repeat this process each day, draining off the syrup, dissolving 50g/2oz/4 tbsp sugar, boiling the syrup and immersing the fruit. Leave overnight on Days 3, 4, 5, 6 and 7.

5 DAY 8. Drain the fruit, dissolve 75g/3oz/½ cup sugar in the syrup and bring to the boil. Add the fruit and cook gently for 3 minutes. Return to the dish and leave for 2 days. DAY 10. Repeat as for Day 8. The syrup should now look like honey. Leave in the dish for at least 10 days, or up to 3 weeks.

6 Arrange the fruits on a wire rack. Dry the fruit in a warm, dry place until they no longer feel sticky. To coat in sugar, spear each piece of fruit and plunge into boiling water, then roll in sugar. To dip into syrup, place the remaining sugar and 175ml/6fl oz/ ¾ cup of water in a pan. Heat until the sugar has dissolved, then boil for 1 minute. Dip each piece of fruit into boiling water, then quickly into the syrup. Place on the rack and leave in a warm place until dry. Place in small paper cases and pack into boxes.

Chocolate Candies Energy 438kcal/1845kJ; Protein 4.4g; Carbohydrate 74g, of which sugars 72.6g; Fat 15.8g, of which saturates 8.9g; Cholesterol 15mg; Calcium 208mg; Fibre 3.6g; Sodium 270mg.
Glacé Fruits Energy 18kcal/78kJ; Protein 0g; Carbohydrate 4.8g, of which sugars 4.8g; Fat 0g, of which saturates 0g; Cholesterol 0mg; Calcium 2mg; Fibre 0g; Sodium 0mg.

Christmas Spirit

This colourful festive drink has a sharp but sweet taste. It is excellent served as a winter warmer or after a Christmas meal, but it also makes a good summer drink served with crushed ice.

Makes 750g/1¼ pints/3 cups

450g/1lb/2 cups cranberries
2 clementines
450g/1lb/2 cups sugar
1 cinnamon stick
475ml/16fl oz/2 cups vodka

1 Crush the cranberries in a food processor or blender and spoon the purée into a large sterilized jar. Pare the rind from the clementines and add to jar.

2 Squeeze the juice from the clementines and add to the cranberries and pared rind in the jar.

3 Add the sugar, cinnamon stick and vodka to the jar and seal with the lid or a double thickness of plastic, and tie down securely. Shake the jar well to combine all the ingredients.

4 Store the jar in a cool place for 1 month, shaking the jar on a daily basis for 2 weeks, then occasionally.

5 When the drink has matured, sterilize some small decorative bottles and, using a funnel with a filter paper inside, strain the liquid into the bottles and cork immediately. Label the bottles clearly and tie a gift tag around the neck.

Cook's Tip
Sterilize the bottles you are using with a campden tablet, available from wine making suppliers, dissolved in boiling water.

Variation
Other fruits can be used in this recipe. Try other berries such as raspberries, blackcurrants or blackberries in place of the cranberries, and a lemon or a lime in place of the clementines.

Festive Liqueurs

These may be made with a variety of flavours and spirits. Allow to mature for 3 months.

Makes 900ml/1½ pints/ 3¾ cups of each liqueur

For the plum brandy
450g/1lb plums
225g/8oz/1 cup demerara (raw) sugar
600ml/1 pint/2½ cups brandy

For the fruit gin
450g/1lb/3 cups raspberries, blackcurrants or sloes
350g/12oz/1½ cups sugar
750ml/1¼ pints/3 cups gin

For the citrus whisky
1 large orange
1 small lemon
1 lime
225g/8oz/1 cup sugar
600ml/1 pint/2½ cups whisky

1 Sterilize three jars and lids. Wash and halve the plums, remove the stones (pits) and slice. Place the plums in the sterilized jar with the sugar and brandy. Crack three of the plum stones, remove the kernels and chop. Add to the jar and stir in.

2 Place the raspberries, blackcurrants or sloes into the prepared jar. If using sloes, prick the surface of the berries to extract the flavour. Add the sugar and gin and stir until well blended.

3 To make the citrus whisky, first scrub the fruit. Using a sharp knife or vegetable peeler, pare the rind from the fruit, taking care not to include the white pith. Squeeze out all of the juice and place in the jar with the fruit rinds. Add the sugar and whisky, and stir until well blended.

4 Cover the three jars with lids or double-thickness pieces of plastic tied down. Store in a cool, dark place for 3 months.

5 Shake the Fruit Gin daily for 1 month, and then occasionally. Shake the Plum Brandy and Citrus Whisky daily for 2 weeks, then occasionally. Sterilize the bottles and corks or stoppers.

6 When each liqueur is ready to be bottled, strain the liquid, then pour it into sterilized bottles through a funnel fitted with a filter paper. Fit the corks or stoppers and label the bottles.

Christmas Spirit Energy 2968kcal/12544kJ; Protein 4.1g; Carbohydrate 519.1g, of which sugars 519.1g; Fat 0.6g, of which saturates 0g; Cholesterol 0mg; Calcium 267mg; Fibre 7.3g; Sodium 46mg.
Festive Liqueurs Energy 2288kcal/9601kJ; Protein 3.1g; Carbohydrate 268.3g, of which sugars 268.3g; Fat 0.4g, of which saturates 0g; Cholesterol 0mg; Calcium 167mg; Fibre 6g; Sodium 22mg.

Bread Sauce

Smooth and surprisingly delicate, this old-fashioned sauce is traditionally served with roast chicken, turkey and game birds.

Serves 6
1 small onion
4 cloves
bay leaf
300ml/½ pint/1¼ cup milk
115g/4oz/2 cups fresh
   white breadcrumbs
15ml/1 tbsp butter
15ml/1 tbsp single (light) cream
salt and ground black pepper

1 Peel the onion and stick the cloves into it. Put it into a pan with the bay leaf and pour in the milk. Bring to the boil, then remove from the heat and steep for 15–20 minutes. Remove the bay leaf and onion.

2 Return to the heat and stir in the crumbs. Simmer for 4–5 minutes or until thick and creamy. Stir in the butter and cream. Season with salt and pepper and serve.

Cranberry Sauce

This is the sauce for roast turkey, but don't just keep it for festive occasions. The vibrant colour and tart taste are perfect partners for any white roast meat.

Serves 6
1 orange
225g/8oz/2 cups cranberries
250g/9oz/1¼ cups sugar

1 Pare the rind thinly from the orange, taking care not to remove any white pith. Squeeze the juice.

2 Place the orange rind in a heavy pan with the cranberries, sugar and 150ml/¼ pint/⅔ cup water.

3 Bring to the boil, stirring until the sugar has dissolved, then simmer for 10–15 minutes or until the berries burst. Remove the rind. Leave to cool before serving.

Apricot and Raisin Stuffing

Stuffing is an essential part of the Christmas Day meal. Not only is it a tasty accompaniment but it also helps to keep the roast turkey moist while it is cooking. This meat-free stuffing is full of fruit flavours.

Makes about 400g/14oz
40g/1½oz/3 tbsp butter
1 large onion, sliced
100g/3¾oz/1 cup ready-to-eat
   dried apricot pieces, soaked
   and drained
115g/4oz/⅔ cup seedless raisins
juice and grated rind of 1 orange
1 cooking apple, peeled, cored
   and chopped
100g/3¾oz/2 cups fresh
   white breadcrumbs
1.5ml/¼ tsp ground ginger
salt and ground black pepper

1 Heat the butter in a small pan and add the sliced onion. Fry the onion over medium heat for 4–6 minutes, stirring occasionally, until it has turned translucent.

2 Turn the onion into a large mixing bowl and stir in the dried apricots, raisins, orange juice and rind, chopped apple, breadcrumbs and ground ginger.

3 Season with salt and ground black pepper. Mix well with a wooden spoon, then set aside to cool. Use the stuffing to pack the neck end of the bird.

Cook's Tip
If you are cooking a joint of meat rather than a full roast turkey or chicken, you can still enjoy this stuffing. Simply roll the stuffing into walnut-size balls and cook in a roasting pan alongside the meat or other vegetables until browned.

Variation
Other fruits can be used for this stuffing. Try sultanas (golden raisins) or currants instead of raisins, pear instead of apple, and lemon rind instead of the orange rind.

Bread Sauce Energy 100kcal/419kJ; Protein 3.4g; Carbohydrate 11.6g, of which sugars 3.2g; Fat 4.8g, of which saturates 2.9g; Cholesterol 13mg; Calcium 88mg; Fibre 0.3g; Sodium 123mg.
Cranberry Sauce Energy 178kcal/759kJ; Protein 0.6g; Carbohydrate 46.8g, of which sugars 46.8g; Fat 0g, of which saturates 0g; Cholesterol 0mg; Calcium 46mg; Fibre 1.4g; Sodium 5mg.
Apricot Stuffing Energy 1246kcal/5255kJ; Protein 22.9g; Carbohydrate 220.9g, of which sugars 136.8g; Fat 36.4g, of which saturates 21.6g; Cholesterol 92mg; Calcium 358mg; Fibre 17.2g; Sodium 1147mg.

Chestnut Stuffing

This stuffing is packed with the flavours of Christmas. Chestnuts, nutmeg and orange give this stuffing a delicious festive quality.

Makes about 400g/14oz
40g/1½oz/3 tbsp butter
1 large onion, chopped
450g/1lb can unsweetened chestnut purée
50g/2oz/1 cup fresh white breadcrumbs
45ml/3 tbsp orange juice
5ml/1 tsp grated nutmeg
2.5ml/½ tsp caster (superfine) sugar
salt and ground black pepper

1 Heat the butter in a small pan and add the sliced onion. Fry the onion over medium heat for 3–4 minutes, stirring occasionally, until it has turned translucent.

2 Remove the pan from the heat and transfer the softened onion to a large mixing bowl.

3 Add the chestnut purée, breadcrumbs, orange juice, grated nutmeg and sugar to the bowl with the onion. Mix well until all the ingredients are thoroughly combined.

4 Season with plenty of salt and ground black pepper. Set aside the stuffing to cool. Use the stuffing to pack the neck end of the turkey ready for roasting.

> **Cook's Tip**
> *To make home-made chestnut purée, cook 1 sliced onion and 2 crushed garlic cloves in a pan with 50g/2oz butter. Cook until soft and transparent, then add 200ml/7fl oz/scant 1 cup chicken stock, a bouquet garni, 400ml/14fl oz/1½ cups water, 450g/1lb frozen or pre-cooked chestnuts (you can roast and peel your own if you prefer but this is much easier) and a bag of peppercorns. Bring to the boil, then simmer and cook for 10–15 minutes. When cooked, leave to cool before straining the liquid into a bowl, leaving the mixture in the colander. Remove the bouquet garni and bag of peppercorns. Blend the mixture to a fine purée in a blender or food processor.*

Cranberry and Rice Stuffing

This healthy and delicious stuffing has a wonderful tang from the cranberries and citrus juice. The rice is cooked in stock to give the stuffing plenty of flavour.

Makes about 450g/1lb
225g/8oz/1¼ cups long grain rice
600ml/1 pint/2½ cups meat or poultry stock
50g/2oz/4 tbsp butter
1 large onion, chopped
150g/6oz/1 cup cranberries
60ml/4 tbsp orange juice
15ml/1 tbsp chopped fresh parsley
10ml/2 tsp chopped fresh thyme
5ml/1 tsp grated nutmeg
salt and ground black pepper

1 Wash the rice in plenty of cold water and drain thoroughly. Place the meat or poultry stock in a heavy pan and bring to the boil. Add the rice and bring the stock back to the boil.

2 Cover the pan with a tight-fitting lid and reduce the heat to low-medium. Simmer the rice for about 12–15 minutes, or according to the packet instructions, until tender.

3 When cooked, drain the rice thoroughly and transfer into a large mixing bowl. Set aside.

4 Heat the butter in a small pan and add the sliced onion. Fry the onion over medium heat for 4–6 minutes, stirring occasionally, until it has turned translucent. Add the cooked onion to the rice in the bowl.

5 Put the cranberries and orange juice in the cleaned pan and simmer over low heat until the fruit is tender. Transfer the fruit and any remaining juice into the rice and mix well.

6 Stir the chopped parsley and thyme into the rice, and mix in the nutmeg. Mix thoroughly to ensure all the ingredients in the bowl are well combined.

7 Season the stuffing with plenty of salt and ground black pepper. Set aside the stuffing to cool. Use to pack the turkey neck ready for roasting.

Chestnut Stuffing Energy 2450kcal/10236kJ; Protein 62.7g; Carbohydrate 210.8g, of which sugars 46.2g; Fat 156.8g, of which saturates 71.7g; Cholesterol 287mg; Calcium 548mg; Fibre 15.8g; Sodium 4950mg.
Cranberry Stuffing Energy 1339kcal/5584kJ; Protein 21.5g; Carbohydrate 215.3g, of which sugars 31g; Fat 43.2g, of which saturates 27g; Cholesterol 115mg; Calcium 212mg; Fibre 7.8g; Sodium 407mg.

Piccalilli

The piquancy of this relish partners well with sausages, as well as with most bacon or ham dishes.

Makes 3 × 450g/1lb jars
675g/1½lb cauliflower
450g/1lb baby (pearl) onions

350g/12oz/2 cups French
 (green) beans
5ml/1 tsp ground turmeric
5ml/1 tsp dry mustard powder
10ml/2 tsp cornflour (cornstarch)
600ml/1 pint/2½ cups
 cider vinegar

1 Cut the cauliflower into tiny florets. Peel the onions and top and tail the French beans.

2 In a small pan, measure in the turmeric, mustard powder and cornflour. Pour the vinegar into the pan. Stir well and simmer for 10 minutes over low heat.

3 Pour the vinegar mixture over the vegetables in a large pan, mix well and simmer for 45 minutes.

4 Carefully pour the piccalilli into sterilized jars. Seal each jar with a wax disc and a tightly fitting cellophane top. Store the jars in a cool, dark place. The piccalilli will keep well, in unopened jars, for up to a year.

Cook's Tips
• Piccalilli is perfect for serving with slices of Christmas ham or left-over turkey for a quick festive lunch.
• Once opened, store the piccalilli in the refrigerator and consume within one week.

Variation
Other vegetables can be used in this relish. Try adding some chopped courgettes (zucchini). Fruit such as chopped pears also goes well in this condiment. Simply cook any extra ingredients with the other vegetables in the vinegar as above.

Christmas Chutney

This savoury mixture of spices and dried fruit takes its inspiration from mincemeat, and makes a delicious addition to the Boxing Day buffet.

Makes 900g–1.5 kg/2–3½lb
450g/1lb cooking apples, peeled, cored and chopped

500g/1¼lb/3 cups luxury mixed
 dried fruit
grated rind of 1 orange
30ml/2 tbsp mixed
 (apple pie) spice
150ml/¼ pint/⅔ cup
 cider vinegar
350g/12oz/1½ cups soft light
 brown sugar

1 Place the chopped apples, dried fruit and grated orange rind in a large, heavy pan.

2 Stir in the mixed spice, vinegar and sugar. Heat gently, stirring until all the sugar has dissolved.

3 Bring the mixture to the boil, then lower the heat and simmer for about 40–45 minutes, stirring occasionally, until the mixture has thickened.

4 Ladle the chutney into warm sterilized jars, cover and seal. Keep for 1 month before using.

Cook's Tip
Watch the chutney carefully towards the end of the cooking time, as it has a tendency to catch on the bottom of the pan. Stir frequently at this stage.

Variation
If you like, you can use a combination of apples and pears in this recipe. There is a glut of both these fruits over the festive season when they are at their best, so it is an ideal time to make this recipe. Simply replace half the quantity of the apples in the recipe with pears.

Piccalilli Energy 453kcal/1919kJ; Protein 11.4g; Carbohydrate 100.3g, of which sugars 88.7g; Fat 4g, of which saturates 0.4g; Cholesterol 0mg; Calcium 185mg; Fibre 6.9g; Sodium 1337mg.
Chutney Energy 1299kcal/5525kJ; Protein 10.9g; Carbohydrate 299.5g, of which sugars 297.7g; Fat 14.9g, of which saturates 1.1g; Cholesterol 0mg; Calcium 254mg; Fibre 10.4g; Sodium 3974mg.

Cranberry and Red Onion Relish

This wine-enriched relish is perfect for serving with hot roast game at a celebratory meal. It is also good served with cold meats or stirred into a beef or game casserole for a touch of sweetness. It can be made several months in advance.

Makes about 900g/2lb
450g/1lb small red onions
30ml/2 tbsp olive oil

225g/8oz/generous 1 cup soft
   light brown sugar
450g/1lb/4 cups cranberries
120ml/4fl oz/½ cup red
   wine vinegar
120ml/4fl oz/½ cup red wine
15ml/1 tbsp yellow
   mustard seeds
2.5ml/½ tsp ground ginger
30ml/2 tbsp orange liqueur
   or port
salt and ground black pepper

1 Halve the red onions and slice them very thinly. Heat the oil in a large pan, add the onions and cook over a very low heat for about 15 minutes, stirring occasionally, until softened.

2 Add 30ml/2 tbsp of the sugar and cook for a further 5 minutes, or until the onions are brown and caramelized.

3 Meanwhile, put the cranberries in another pan with the remaining sugar, and add the vinegar, red wine, mustard seeds and ginger. Stir in well and heat gently, stirring constantly, until the sugar has dissolved, then cover and bring to the boil.

4 Simmer the relish for about 12–15 minutes, then add in the caramelized onions. Stir them into the mixture. Increase the heat slightly and cook the relish uncovered for a further 10 minutes, stirring the mixture frequently, until it is well reduced and nicely thickened.

5 Remove the pan from the heat, then season to taste with salt and pepper. Allow to cool completely before pouring.

6 Transfer the relish to warmed sterilized jars. Spoon a little of the orange liqueur or port over the top of each, then cover and seal. This relish can be stored for up to 6 months. Store in the refrigerator once opened and use within 1 month.

Caramelized Onion Relish

The slow, gentle cooking reduces the onions to a soft, caramelized relish to serve with everything from baked cheese to left-over turkey or ham.

Serves 4
3 large onions
50g/2oz/4 tbsp butter

30ml/2 tbsp olive oil
30ml/2 tbsp light muscovado
   (brown) sugar
30ml/2 tbsp pickled capers
30ml/2 tbsp chopped
   fresh parsley
salt and ground black pepper

1 Peel the onions and halve them vertically, through the core, then slice them thinly.

2 Heat the butter and oil together in a large pan. Add the onions and the sugar and cover the pan with a tight-fitting lid. Cook gently for about 30–40 minutes over very low heat, stirring occasionally, until the onions and sugar have reduced to a soft rich brown caramelized mixture.

3 Roughly chop the capers and stir them into the onions. Allow the mixture to cool completely.

4 Stir in the chopped fresh parsley and season with salt and ground black pepper to taste. Cover and chill in the refrigerator until ready to serve.

> **Cook's Tip**
> *When cooking the onions, the heat should be very low to prevent the onions from catching and burning on the bottom of the pan. Using a good-quality heavy pan will also deter this.*

> **Variation**
> *Try making this recipe with red onions or shallots for a subtle variation in the flavours.*

Cranberry Relish Energy 1532kcal/6486kJ; Protein 8g; Carbohydrate 314.6g, of which sugars 304.2g; Fat 23.3g, of which saturates 3.1g; Cholesterol 0mg; Calcium 259mg; Fibre 13.5g; Sodium 46mg.
Caramelized Onion Relish Energy 225kcal/933kJ; Protein 1.9g; Carbohydrate 19.7g, of which sugars 16.3g; Fat 16g, of which saturates 7.5g; Cholesterol 29mg; Calcium 43mg; Fibre 2.1g; Sodium 99mg.

Tomato Chutney

This spicy, dark, sweet-sour chutney is delicious served with a selection of well-flavoured cheeses after a festive feast. It is also popular in sandwiches and chunky rolls packed with cold roast meats such as ham or turkey.

Makes about 1.8kg/4lb
900g/2lb tomatoes, skinned
225g/8oz/1½ cups raisins
225g/8oz onions, chopped
225g/8oz/generous 1 cup caster (superfine) sugar
600ml/1 pint/2½ cups malt vinegar or red wine vinegar or sherry vinegar

1 Chop the tomatoes roughly and place in a preserving pan. Add the raisins, onions and caster sugar.

2 Pour the vinegar into the pan and bring the mixture to the boil over a medium heat. Reduce the heat and simmer for 2 hours, uncovered, until soft and thickened.

3 Transfer the chutney to warmed sterilized jars. Top each jar with waxed discs to prevent moulds from growing. Use good airtight lids, especially if you mean to store them for a long period. Store the jars in a cool, dark place and leave to mature for at least 1 month before use.

Cook's Tip
The chutney will keep unopened for up to 1 year if properly airtight and stored in a cool place. Once the jars have been opened, store in the refrigerator and use within 1 month.

Variations
• Dried dates may be used in place of the raisins. Stone (pit) and chop them into small pieces. You can also buy stoned cooking dates that have been compressed in a block and these will need chopping finely.
• Red wine vinegar or sherry vinegar may be used in place of the malt vinegar, making a more delicate flavour.

Apple and Sultana Chutney

Use wine or cider vinegar for this chutney to give it a subtle and mellow flavour. For a mild chutney, add only a little cayenne, for a spicier one increase the quantity to taste. The chutney is perfect served with farmhouse cheese and freshly made rustic bread.

Makes about 900g/2lb
350g/12oz cooking apples
115g/4oz/⅔ cup sultanas (golden raisins)
50g/2oz onion
25g/1oz/¼ cup almonds, blanched
5ml/1 tsp white peppercorns
2.5ml/½ tsp coriander seeds
175g/6oz/scant 1 cup sugar
10ml/2 tsp salt
5ml/1 tsp ground ginger
450ml/¾ pint/scant 2 cups cider vinegar
1.5ml/¼ tsp cayenne pepper red chillies (optional)

1 Peel, core and chop the apples. Chop the sultanas, onion and the blanched almonds.

2 Tie the peppercorns and coriander seeds in muslin (cheesecloth), using a long piece of string, and then tie to the handle of a preserving pan or stainless-steel pan.

3 Put the sugar, salt, ground ginger and vinegar into the pan, with the cayenne pepper to taste. Heat gently, stirring, until the sugar has completely dissolved.

4 Add the chopped fruit. Bring to the boil and simmer for 1½–2 hours, or until most of the liquid has evaporated.

5 Spoon into warmed, sterilized jars and place one chilli in each jar, if using. Leave until cold, then cover, seal and label.

Cook's Tip
Store in a cool dark place. The chutney is best left for a month to mature before use and will keep for at least 6 months, if it is correctly stored.

Tomato Chutney Energy 1733kcal/7385kJ; Protein 14.9g; Carbohydrate 436.7g, of which sugars 431.6g; Fat 4.1g, of which saturates 0.9g; Cholesterol 0mg; Calcium 342mg; Fibre 16.6g; Sodium 236mg.
Apple Chutney Energy 1299kcal/5525kJ; Protein 10.9g; Carbohydrate 299.5g, of which sugars 297.7g; Fat 14.9g, of which saturates 1.1g; Cholesterol 0mg; Calcium 254mg; Fibre 10.4g; Sodium 3970mg.

Chunky Pear and Walnut Chutney

This chutney recipe is ideal for using up hard windfall pears. Its mellow flavour is well suited to being brought out after a festive dinner with a lovely selection of strong cheeses served with freshly made oatcakes or warm crusty bread.

Makes about 1.8kg/4lb
1.2kg/2¹/₂lb firm pears
225g/8oz cooking apples
225g/8oz onions
450ml/³/₄ pint/scant 2 cups cider vinegar
175g/6oz/ generous 1 cup sultanas (golden raisins)
finely grated rind and juice of 1 orange
400g/14oz/2 cups granulated (white) sugar
115g/4oz/1 cup walnuts, roughly chopped
2.5ml/¹/₂ tsp ground cinnamon

1 Peel and core the fruit, then chop into 2.5cm/1in chunks. Peel and quarter the onions, then chop into pieces the same size as the fruit chunks. Place in a large preserving pan with the vinegar.

2 Slowly bring to the boil, then reduce the heat and simmer for 40 minutes, until the apples, pears and onions are tender, stirring the mixture occasionally.

3 Meanwhile, put the sultanas in a small bowl, pour over the orange juice and leave to soak.

4 Add the orange rind, sultanas and orange juice, and the sugar to the pan. Heat gently, stirring constantly, until the sugar has completely dissolved, then leave to simmer for 30–40 minutes, or until the chutney is thick and no excess liquid remains. Stir frequently towards the end of cooking to prevent the chutney from sticking to the base of the pan.

5 Gently toast the walnuts in a non-stick pan over low heat for 5 minutes, stirring frequently, until lightly coloured. Stir the nuts into the chutney with the ground cinnamon.

6 Spoon the chutney into warmed sterilized jars, cover and seal. Store in a cool, dark place and leave to mature for at least 1 month. Use within 1 year.

Cranberry and Claret Jelly

The slight sharpness of cranberries makes this a superb jelly for serving with rich meats such as lamb or game. Together with claret, the cranberries give the jelly a beautifully festive deep red colour.

Makes about 1.2kg/2¹/₂lb
900g/2lb/8 cups fresh or frozen cranberries, thawed
350ml/12fl oz/1¹/₂ cups water
about 900g/2lb/4¹/₂ cups preserving or granulated (white) sugar
250ml/8fl oz/1 cup claret

1 Wash the cranberries, if fresh, and put them in a large heavy pan with the water. Cover the pan and bring to the boil.

2 Reduce the heat under the pan and simmer for about 20 minutes, or until the cranberries are soft.

3 Pour the fruit and juices into a sterilized jelly bag suspended over a large bowl. Leave to drain for at least 3 hours or overnight, until the juices stop dripping.

4 Measure the juice and wine into the cleaned preserving pan, adding 400g/14oz/2 cups preserving or granulated sugar for every 600ml/1 pint/2¹/₂ cups liquid.

5 Heat the mixture gently, stirring occasionally, until the sugar has dissolved, then bring to the boil and boil rapidly for about 10 minutes until the jelly reaches setting point (105°C/220°F). Remove the pan from the heat.

6 Skim any scum from the surface using a slotted spoon and pour the jelly into warmed sterilized jars. Cover and seal. Store in a cool, dark place and use within 2 years. Once opened, keep in the refrigerator and eat within 3 months.

> **Cook's Tip**
> *When simmering the cranberries, keep the pan covered until they stop 'popping', as they can occasionally explode and jump out of the pan.*

Chunky Chutney Energy 3506kcal/14818kJ; Protein 30.9g; Carbohydrate 705.4g, of which sugars 699.5g; Fat 81.4g, of which saturates 6.4g; Cholesterol 0mg; Calcium 634mg; Fibre 40.7g; Sodium 118mg.
Cranberry Jelly Energy 3821kcal/16,290kJ; Protein 5.7g; Carbohydrate 967.7g, of which sugars 967.7g; Fat 0.3g, of which saturates 0g; Cholesterol 0mg; Calcium 506mg; Fibre 4.8g; Sodium 78mg.

Whisky Marmalade

Real home-made marmalade tastes delicious, and flavouring it with whisky makes it a special treat at Christmas time – great for spreading on fresh muffins for breakfast.

Makes 3.6–4.5kg/8–10lb

1.3kg/3lb Seville (Temple) oranges
juice of 2 large lemons
2.75kg/6lb/13½ cups
   sugar, warmed
about 300ml/½ pint/1¼ cups
   Scotch whisky

1 Scrub the oranges thoroughly using a nylon brush and pick off the disc at the stalk end. Cut the oranges in half widthways and squeeze the juice, retaining the pips (seeds). Quarter the peel, cut away and reserve any thick white pith, and shred the peel – thickly or thinly depending on your prefererence.

2 Cut up the reserved pith roughly and tie it up with the pips in a square of muslin (cheesecloth) using a long piece of string. Tie the bag loosely, so that water can circulate during cooking and will extract the pectin from the pith and pips. Hang the bag from the handle of the preserving pan.

3 Add the cut peel, strained juices and 3.5 litres/6 pints/15 cups water to the pan. Bring to the boil and simmer for 1½–2 hours, or until the peel is very tender.

4 Lift up the bag of pith and pips and squeeze it out well between two plates over the pan to extract as much of the juices as possible. Add the sugar to the pan and stir over a low heat until it has completely dissolved.

5 Bring to the boil and boil hard for 15–20 minutes or until setting point is reached. To test, allow a spoonful to cool slightly, and then see if a skin has formed. If not, boil a little longer.

6 Skim, if necessary, and leave to cool for 15 minutes, then stir. Divide the whisky among 8–10 warmed, sterilized jars and swill it around. Using a heatproof jug (pitcher), pour in the marmalade.

7 Cover and seal while still hot. Label when cold, and store in a cool, dark place for up to 6 months.

Mulled Claret

This mull is a blend of claret, cider and orange juice. It can be varied to suit the occasion by increasing or decreasing the proportion of fruit juice or, to give the mull more pep, by adding up to 150ml/ ¼ pint/⅔ cup brandy.

Makes 16 × 150ml/ ¼ pints/⅔ cup glasses

1 orange
75ml/5 tbsp clear honey
30ml/2 tbsp seedless raisins
2 clementines
a few cloves
whole nutmeg
60ml/4 tbsp demerara
   (raw) sugar
2 cinnamon sticks
1½ litres/2½ pints/6¼ cups
   inexpensive claret
600ml/1 pint/2½ cups medium
   (hard) cider
300ml/½ pint/1¼ cups
   orange juice

1 With a sharp knife or a vegetable peeler, pare off a long strip of the orange rind.

2 Place the orange rind, honey and raisins in a large heavy pan. Stud the clementines all over with the cloves and add them to the pan with the fruit and honey.

3 Grate a little nutmeg into the sugar and then add it to the pan along with the cinnamon sticks. Pour on the wine and heat over low heat, stirring until the sugar has completely dissolved and the honey has melted.

4 Pour the cider and the orange juice into the pan and continue to heat the mull over low heat. Do not allow it to boil or all the alcohol will evaporate.

5 Warm a punch bowl or other large serving bowl. Remove the clementines and cinnamon sticks from the pan and strain the mull into the bowl to remove the raisins.

6 Add the clementines studded with cloves, and serve the mull hot, in warmed glasses or in glasses containing a silver spoon (to prevent the glass breaking). Using a nutmeg grater, add a little nutmeg over each serving, if you wish.

Whisky Marmalade Energy 10,736kcal/45,734kJ; Protein 22.8g; Carbohydrate 2657.8g, of which sugars 2657.8g; Fat 1.3g, of which saturates 0g; Cholesterol 0mg; Calcium 1.74g; Fibre 15.6g; Sodium 187mg.
Mulled Claret Energy 174kcal/728kJ; Protein 0.2g; Carbohydrate 16.3g, of which sugars 16.3g; Fat 0g, of which saturates 0g; Cholesterol 0mg; Calcium 16mg; Fibre 0g; Sodium 11mg.

Brandied Eggnog

This frothy blend of eggs, milk and spirits definitely comes into the nightcap category of drinks during the festivities.

Serves 4
4 eggs, separated

30ml/2 tbsp caster (superfine) sugar
60ml/4 tbsp dark rum
60ml/4 tbsp brandy
300ml/½ pint/1¼ cups milk (or according to the volume of the glasses), hot
whole nutmeg

1 Beat the egg yolks with the sugar in a bowl. Beat the whites to soft peaks. Mix and pour into four heatproof glasses.

2 Add the rum and brandy to the glasses. You will need about 15ml/1 tbsp of each in each glass.

3 Top up the glass with hot milk. Grate the nutmeg over the top and serve immediately.

Mulled Cider

This hot cider cup is easy to make and traditional at Halloween, but it makes a good and inexpensive warming brew for any winter gathering, particularly for a festive drinks party with lots of finger food.

Makes about 20 glasses
2 lemons
1 litre/1¾ pints/4 cups apple juice
2 litres/3½ pints/9 cups medium sweet cider
3 small cinnamon sticks
4–6 whole cloves
slices of lemon, to serve (optional)

1 Wash the lemons and pare the rinds with a vegetable peeler. Blend all the ingredients together in a large stainless-steel pan.

2 Set the pan over low heat and heat the mixture through to infuse (steep) for 15 minutes; do not allow it to boil.

3 Strain the liquid through a sieve (strainer) and serve with extra slices of lemon, if you like.

Whiskey Punch

Also known as a 'hot toddy', this traditional 'cure' for colds is more often drunk for pleasure as a nightcap, particularly to round off a day's winter sporting activities or a hectic Christmas Day, and it is a great drink to hold and sip on cold winter evenings.

Serves 1
4–6 whole cloves
60ml/4 tbsp Irish whiskey
1 thick slice of lemon, halved
5–10ml/1–2 tsp demerara (raw) sugar, to taste

1 Stick the cloves into the lemon slice, and put it into a large stemmed glass (or one with a handle).

2 Pour the whiskey into the glass and add the sugar. Give the sugar a quick swirl with the whiskey.

3 Put a metal teaspoon inside the glass – this is to prevent the hot water from cracking it – then top it up with boiling water. Stir well to dissolve the sugar and serve immediately.

> **Cook's Tips**
> • All three types of Irish whiskey (single malt, pure pot-stilled and a column-and-pot still blend of grain and malt) work well in this recipe.
> • The word 'toddy' comes from tari, the Hindu word used for the sap or juice of a palm tree. In Asia, this sap was often fermented to create an alcoholic beverage. British sailors picked up on the idea, which eventually evolved into the toddy.

> **Variation**
> You can, of course, use other types of whisky (or whiskey, with an 'e', if Irish or American) in this drink. Scotch, Bourbon and Canadian rye whiskies will all make just as good a drink – it all depends on what you have in the drinks cabinet.

Brandied Eggnog Energy 375kcal/1566kJ; Protein 9.1g; Carbohydrate 29.6g, of which sugars 29.6g; Fat 19.9g, of which saturates 10.7g; Cholesterol 232mg; Calcium 112mg; Fibre 0.1g; Sodium 98mg.
Mulled Cider Energy 61kcal/258kJ; Protein 0.1g; Carbohydrate 9.3g, of which sugars 9.3g; Fat 0.1g, of which saturates 0g; Cholesterol 0mg; Calcium 12mg; Fibre 0g; Sodium 8mg.
Whiskey Punch Energy 149kcal/619kJ; Protein 0g; Carbohydrate 4.2g, of which sugars 4.2g; Fat 0g, of which saturates 0g; Cholesterol 0mg; Calcium 2mg; Fibre 0g; Sodium 0mg.

Grand Marnier, Papaya and Fruit Punch

The term 'punch' comes from the Hindi word *panch* (five), relating to the five ingredients traditionally contained in the drink – alcohol, lemon or lime, tea, sugar and water. The ingredients may have altered somewhat over the years, but the best punches still combine a mixture of spirits, flavourings and an innocent top-up of fizz or juice. Make a bowl of this drink for a festive gathering of friends and family.

Serves 15

2 large papayas
4 passion fruit
300g/11oz lychees, peeled and stoned (pitted)
300ml/½ pint/1¼ cups freshly squeezed orange juice
200ml/7fl oz/scant 1 cup Grand Marnier or other orange-flavoured liqueur
8 whole star anise
2 small oranges
ice cubes
1.5 litres/2½ pints/6¼ cups soda water (club soda)

1 Halve the papayas and discard the seeds. Halve the passion fruit and press the pulp through a sieve (strainer) into a small punch bowl or a pretty serving bowl.

2 Push the papayas through a juicer, adding 100ml/3½fl oz/scant ½ cup water to help the pulp through. Juice the lychees.

3 Add the juices to the bowl with the orange juice, liqueur and star anise. Thinly slice the oranges and add to the bowl. Chill for at least 1 hour or until ready to serve.

4 Add plenty of ice cubes to the bowl and top up with soda water. Ladle into punch cups or small glasses to serve.

Cook's Tip
Cointreau is one of the most famous orange liqueurs but there are others to choose from. Look out for bottles labelled 'curaçao' or 'triple sec'.

Pineapple and Rum Crush with Coconut

This thick and slushy tropical cooler is unbelievably rich thanks to the combination of coconut milk and thick cream. The addition of sweet, juicy, slightly tart pineapple, and finely crushed ice, offers a refreshing foil, making it all too easy to sip your way through several glasses at a Christmas party.

Serves 4–5

1 pineapple
30ml/2 tbsp lemon juice
200ml/7fl oz/scant 1 cup coconut milk
150ml/¼ pint/⅔ cup double (heavy) cream
200ml/7fl oz/scant 1 cup white rum
30–60ml/2–4 tbsp caster (superfine) sugar
500g/1¼lb finely crushed ice

1 Trim off the ends from the pineapple, then cut off the skin. Cut away the core and chop the flesh. Put the chopped flesh in a blender or food processor with the lemon juice and whizz until very smooth.

2 Add the coconut milk, cream, rum and 30ml/2 tbsp of the sugar. Blend until thoroughly combined, then taste and add more sugar if necessary.

3 Pack the crushed ice into serving glasses and pour the drink over. Serve immediately.

Cook's Tip
This is a great cocktail for making ahead of time. Blend the drink in advance and chill in a jug (pitcher). Store the crushed ice in the freezer ready for serving as soon as it's required.

Variation
If you prefer, you can use a dark rum or even a spiced rum, such as that made by Morgans, instead of the white rum.

Grand Marnier Punch Energy 65kcal/274kJ; Protein 0.5g; Carbohydrate 11.6g, of which sugars 11.6g; Fat 0.1g, of which saturates 0g; Cholesterol 0mg; Calcium 10mg; Fibre 0.9g; Sodium 6mg.
Pineapple Rum Crush Energy 336kcal/1400kJ; Protein 1.3g; Carbohydrate 24.9g, of which sugars 24.9g; Fat 16.5g, of which saturates 10.1g; Cholesterol 41mg; Calcium 58mg; Fibre 1.9g; Sodium 54mg.

Irish Chocolate Velvet

This smooth, sophisticated drink will always be appreciated on cold Christmas evenings.

Serves 4

120ml/4fl oz/½ cup double (heavy) cream
400ml/14fl oz/1⅔ cups milk
30ml/2 tbsp unsweetened cocoa powder
115g/4oz milk chocolate, broken into squares
60ml/4 tbsp Irish whiskey
whipped double (heavy) cream, for topping
plain (semisweet) chocolate curls, to decorate

1 Whip the double cream in a mixing bowl until it is thick enough to hold its shape.

2 Put the milk into a pan and whisk in the cocoa powder. Add the chocolate squares and heat gently, stirring, until the chocolate has melted. Bring the chocolate milk to the boil.

3 Remove the pan from the heat and add the whipped double cream and Irish whiskey. Stir the mixture gently for about 1 minute to blend well.

4 Pour the drink quickly into four heatproof mugs or serving glasses and add to each one a generous spoonful of the whipped cream for topping. Decorate the tops with chocolate curls and serve the drinks immediately.

Cook's Tip
Make chocolate curls for decorating the drinks by running a vegetable peeler down the side of a chilled bar of chocolate. You can also use a grater to create them.

Variation
If Irish whiskey is not available, you can use brandy instead for this drink. Any liqueur that uses Irish whiskey, Scotch whisky or brandy as its base will also work.

Cranberry Frost

A non-alcoholic cocktail with the colour of holly berries will delight younger and older guests alike at Christmas time. It is the perfect 'one-for-the-road' drink to serve at the end of a festive gathering.

Serves 10

115g/4oz/generous ½ cup caster (superfine) sugar
juice of 2 oranges
still water, enough to dissolve the sugar
120ml/4fl oz/½ cup fresh cranberry juice
1 litre/1¾ pints/4 cups sparkling mineral water
45ml/3 tbsp fresh cranberries, to decorate
handful fresh mint sprigs, to decorate

1 Put the caster sugar, orange juice and still water into a small pan and stir the mixture over a low heat until the sugar has completely dissolved.

2 Bring the mixture to the boil and boil vigorously for about 3 minutes. Set aside to cool.

3 Pour the syrup into a chilled serving bowl, pour on the cranberry juice and mix well to combine.

4 To serve, pour on the mineral water and decorate with cranberries and mint leaves.

Cook's Tip
This is a great drink to make during the festivities because the syrup can be made in advance and stored in a covered container in the refrigerator.

Variation
To make this fabulous non-alcoholic drink the very essence of festive colour, chill with ice cubes made by freezing fresh red cranberries and tiny mint leaves in the water.

Irish Velvet Energy 390kcal/1623kJ; Protein 7.5g; Carbohydrate 22.4g, of which sugars 21.6g; Fat 28.3g, of which saturates 17.3g; Cholesterol 54mg; Calcium 208mg; Fibre 1.1g; Sodium 145mg.
Cranberry Frost Energy 56kcal/237kJ; Protein 0.1g; Carbohydrate 14.6g, of which sugars 14.6g; Fat 0g, of which saturates 0g; Cholesterol 0mg; Calcium 8mg; Fibre 0.1g; Sodium 2mg.